ISBN: 978-1-78139-252-2.

Front cover: *Joan of Arc* by Dante Gabriel Rossetti.

Back Cover: *Joan of Arc* by John Everett Millais.

© 2012 Benediction Classics, Oxford.

Joan of Arc
(from a painting by Deruet)

THE LIFE
OF
JOAN OF ARC

BY

ANATOLE FRANCE

TRANSLATED BY
WINIFRED STEPHENS

VOLUMES I AND II

Contents

JOAN OF ARC Volume II 421

List of Illustrations

PREFACE
TO THE ENGLISH EDITION

SCHOLARS have been good enough to notice this book; and the majority have treated it very kindly, doubtless because they have perceived that the author has observed all the established rules of historical research and accuracy. Their kindness has touched me. I am especially grateful to MM. Gabriel Monod, Solomon Reinach and Germain Lefèvre-Pontalis, who have discovered in this work certain errors, which will not be found in the present edition.

My English critics have a special claim to my gratitude. To the memory of Joan of Arc they consecrate a pious zeal which is almost an expiatory worship. Mr. Andrew Lang's praiseworthy scruples with regard to my references have caused me to correct some and to add several.

The hagiographers alone are openly hostile. They reproach me, not with my manner of explaining the facts, but with having explained them at all. And the more my explanations are clear, natural, rational and derived from the most authoritative sources, the more these explanations displease them. They would wish the history of Joan of Arc to remain mysterious and entirely supernatural. I have restored the Maid to life and to humanity. That is my crime. And these zealous inquisitors, so intent on condemning my work, have failed to discover therein any grave fault, any flagrant inexactness. Their severity has had to content itself with a few inadvertences and with a few printer's errors. What flatterers could better have gratified "the proud weakness of my heart?"[1]

Paris, January, 1909.

INTRODUCTION

Y first duty should be to make known the authorities for this history. But L'Averdy, Buchon, J. Quicherat, Vallet de Viriville, Siméon Luce, Boucher de Molandon, MM. Robillard de Beaurepaire, Lanéry d'Arc, Henri Jadart, Alexandre Sorel, Germain Lefèvre-Pontalis, L. Jarry, and many other scholars have published and expounded various documents for the life of Joan of Arc. I refer my readers to their works which in themselves constitute a voluminous literature,[2] and without entering on any new examination of these documents, I will merely indicate rapidly and generally the reasons for the use I have chosen to make of them. They are: first, the trial which resulted in her condemnation; second, the chronicles; third, the trial for her rehabilitation; fourth, letters, deeds, and other papers.

First, in the trial[3] which resulted in her condemnation the historian has a mine of rich treasure. Her cross-examination cannot be too minutely studied. It is based on information, not preserved elsewhere, gathered from Domremy and the various parts of France through which she passed. It is hardly necessary to say that all the judges of 1431 sought to discover in Jeanne was idolatry, heresy, sorcery and other crimes against the Church. Inclined as they were, however, to discern evil in every one of the acts and in each of the words of one whom they desired to ruin, so that they might dishonour her king, they examined all available information concerning her life. The high value to be set upon the Maid's replies is well known; they are heroically sincere, and for the most part perfectly lucid. Nevertheless they must not all be interpreted literally. Jeanne, who never regarded either the bishop or the promoter as her judge, was not so simple as to tell them the whole truth. It was very frank of her to warn them that they would not know all.[4] That her memory was curiously defective must also be admitted. I am aware that the clerk of the court was astonished that after a fortnight she should remember exactly the answers she had given in her cross-examination.[5] That may be possible, although she did not always say the same thing. It is none the less certain that after the lapse of a year she retained but an indistinct recollection of some of the important acts of her life. Finally, her constant hallucinations generally rendered her incapable of distinguishing between the true and the false.

The record of the trial is followed by an examination of Jeanne's sayings in *articulo mortis*.[6] This examination is not signed by the clerks of the court. Hence from a legal point of view the record is out of order; nevertheless, regarded as a historical document, its authenticity cannot be doubted. In my opinion the actual occurrences cannot have widely differed from what is related in this unofficial report. It tells of Jeanne's second recantation, and of this recantation there can be no question, for Jeanne received the communion before her death. The veracity of this document was never assailed,[7] even by those who during the rehabilitation trial pointed out its irregularity.[8]

Secondly, the chroniclers of the period, both French and Burgundian, were paid chroniclers, one of whom was attached to every great baron. Tringant says that his master did not expend any money in order to obtain mention in the chronicles,[9] and that therefore he is omitted from them. The earliest chronicle in which the Maid occurs is that of Perceval de Cagny, who was in the service of the house of Alençon and Duke John's master of the house.[10] It was drawn up in the year 1436, that is, only six years after Jeanne's death. But it was not written by him. According to his own confession he had "not half the sense, memory, or ability necessary for putting this, or even a matter of less than half its importance, down in writing."[11] This chronicle is the work of a painstaking clerk. One is not surprised to find a chronicler in the pay of the house of Alençon representing the differences concerning the Maid, which arose between the Sire de la Trémouille and the Duke of Alençon, in a light most unfavourable to the King. But from a scribe, supposed to be writing at the dictation of a retainer of Duke John, one would have expected a less inaccurate and a less vague account of the feats of arms accomplished by the Maid in company with him whom she called her fair duke. Although this chronicle was written at a time when no one dreamed that the sentence of 1431 would ever be revoked, the Maid is regarded as employing supernatural means, and her acts are stripped of all verisimilitude by being recorded in the manner of a hagiography. Further, that portion of the chronicle attributed to Perceval de Cagny, which deals with the Maid, is brief, consisting of twenty-seven chapters of a few lines each. Quicherat is of opinion that it is the best chronicle of Jeanne d'Arc[12] existing, and the others may indeed be even more worthless.

Gilles le Bouvier,[13] king at arms of the province of Berry, who was forty-three in 1429, is somewhat more judicious than Perceval de Cagny; and, in spite of some confusion of dates, he is better informed of military proceedings. But his story is of too summary a nature to tell us much.

Jean Chartier,[14] precentor of Saint-Denys, held the office of chronicler of France in 1449. Two hundred years later he would have been described as historiographer royal. His office may be divined from the manner in which he relates Jeanne's death. After having said that she had been long imprisoned by the order of John of Luxembourg, he adds: "The said Luxembourg sold her to the English, who took her to Rouen, where she was harshly treated; in so much that after long delay, they had her publicly burnt in that town of Rouen, without a trial, of their own tyrannical will, which was cruelly done, seeing the life and the rule she lived, for every week she confessed and received the body of Our Lord, as beseemeth a good catholic."[15] When Jean Chartier says that the English burned her without trial, he means apparently that the Bailie of Rouen did not pronounce sentence. Concerning the ecclesiastical trial and the two accusations of lapse and relapse he says not a word; and it is the English whom he accuses of having burnt a good Catholic without a trial. This example proves how seriously the condemnation of 1431 embarrassed the government of King Charles. But what can be thought of a historian who suppresses Jeanne's trial because he finds it inconvenient? Jean Chartier was extremely weak-minded and trivial; he seems to believe in the magic of Catherine's sword and in Jeanne's loss of power when she broke it;[16] he records the most puerile of fables. Nevertheless it is interesting to note that the official chronicler of the Kings of France, writing about 1450, ascribes to the Maid an important share in the delivery of Orléans, in the conquest of fortresses on the Loire and in the victory of Patay, that he relates how the King formed the army at Gien "by the counsel of the said maid,"[17] and that he expressly states that Jeanne caused[18] the coronation and consecration. Such was certainly the opinion which prevailed at the Court of Charles VII. All that we have to discover is whether that opinion was sincere and reasonable or whether the King of France may not have deemed it to his advantage to owe his kingdom to the Maid. She was held a heretic by the heads of the Church Universal, but in France her memory was honoured, rather, however, by the lower orders than by the princes of the blood and the leaders of the army. The services of the latter the King was not desirous to extol after the revolt of 1440. During this *Praguerie*,[19] the Duke of Bourbon, the Count of Vendôme, the Duke of Alençon, whom the Maid called her fair duke, and even the cautious Count Dunois had been seen joining hands with the plunderers and making war on the sovereign with an ardour they had never shown in fighting against the English.

"Le Journal du Siège"[20] was doubtless kept in 1428 and 1429; but the edition that has come down to us dates from 1467.[21] What relates to Jeanne before her coming to Orléans is interpolated; and the interpolator was so unskilful as to date Jeanne's arrival at Chinon in the month of February, while it took place on March 6, and to assign Thursday, March 10, as the date of the departure from Blois, which did not occur until the end of April. The diary from April 28 to May 7 is less inaccurate in its chronology, and the errors in dates which do occur may be attributed to the copyist. But the facts to which these dates are assigned, occasionally in disagreement with financial records and often tinged with the miraculous, testify to an advanced stage of Jeanne's legend. For example, one cannot possibly attribute to a witness of the siege the error made by the scribe concerning the fall of the Bridge of Les Tourelles.[22] What is said on page 97 of P. Charpentier's and C. Cuissart's edition concerning the relations of the inhabitants and the men-at-arms seems out of place, and may very likely have been inserted there to efface the memory of the grave dissensions which had occurred during the last week. From the 8th of May the diary ceases to be a diary; it becomes a series of extracts borrowed from Chartier, from Berry, and from the rehabilitation trial. The episode of the big fat Englishman slain by Messire Jean de Montesclère at the Siege of Jargeau is obviously taken from the evidence of Jean d'Aulon in 1446; and even this plagiarism is inaccurate, since Jean d'Aulon expressly says he was slain at the Battle of Les Augustins.[23]

The chronicle entitled *La Chronique de la Pucelle*,[24] as if it were the chief chronicle of the heroine, is taken from a history entitled *Geste des nobles François*, going back as far as Priam of Troy. But the extract was not made until the original had been changed and added to. This was done after 1467. Even if it were proved that *La Chronique de la Pucelle* is the work of Cousinot, shut up in Orléans during the siege, or even of two Cousinots, uncle and nephew according to some, father and son according to others, it would remain none the less true that this chronicle is largely copied from Jean Chartier, the *Journal du Siège* and the rehabilitation trial. Whoever the author may have been, this work reflects no great credit upon him: no very high praise can be given to a fabricator of tales, who, without appearing in the slightest degree aware of the fact, tells the same stories twice over, introducing each time different and contradictory circumstances. *La Chronique de la Pucelle* ends abruptly with the King's return to Berry after his defeat before Paris.

Le Mystère du siège[25] must be classed with the chronicles. It is in fact a rhymed chronicle in dialogue, and it would be extremely interesting for its antiquity alone were it possible to do what some have attempted and to assign to it the date 1435. The editors, and following them several scholars, have believed it possible to identify this poem of 20,529 lines with a *certain mistaire*[26] played on the sixth anniversary of the delivery of the city. They have drawn their conclusions from the following circumstances: the Maréchal de Rais, who delighted to organise magnificent farces and mysteries, was in Duke Charles's city expending vast sums[27] there from September, 1434, till August, 1435; in 1439 the city purchased out of its municipal funds "a standard and a banner, which had belonged to Monseigneur de Reys and had been used by him to represent the manner of the storming of Les Tourelles and their capture from the English."[28] From such a statement it is impossible to prove that in 1435 or in 1439, on May 8, there was acted a play having the Siege for its subject and the Maid for its heroine. If, however, we take "the manner of the storming of Les Tourelles" to mean a mystery rather than a pageant or some other form of entertainment, and if we consider the *certain mistaire* of 1435 as indicating a representation of that siege which had been laid and raised by the English, we shall thus arrive at a mystery of the siege. But even then we must examine whether it be that mystery the text of which has come down to us.

Among the one hundred and forty speaking personages in this work is the Maréchal de Rais. Hence it has been concluded that the mystery was written and acted before the lawsuit ended by that sentence to which effect was given above the Nantes Bridge, on

October 20, 1440. How, indeed, it has been asked, after so ignominious a death could the vampire of Machecoul have been represented to the people of Orléans as fighting for their deliverance? How could the Maid and Blue Beard be associated in a heroic action? It is hard to answer such a question, because we cannot possibly tell how much of that kind of thing could be tolerated by the barbarism of those rude old times. Perhaps our text itself, if properly examined, will be found to contain internal evidence as to whether it is of an earlier or later date than 1440.

The bastard of Orléans was created Count of Dunois on July 14, 1439.[29] The lines of the mystery, in which he is called by this title, cannot therefore be anterior to that date. They are numerous, and, by a singularity which has never been explained, are all in the first third of the book. When Dunois reappears later he is the Bastard again. From this fact the editors of 1862 concluded that five thousand lines were prefixed to the primitive text subsequently, although they in no way differ from the rest, either in language, style, or prosody. But may the rest of the poem be assigned to 1435 or 1439?

That is not my opinion. In the lines 12093 and 12094 the Maid tells Talbot he will die by the hand of the King's men. This prophecy must have been made after the event: it is an obvious allusion to the noble captain's end, and these lines must have been written after 1453.

Six years after the siege no clerk of Orléans would have thought of travestying Jeanne as a lady of noble birth.

In line 10199 and the following of the *"Mistère du Siège"* the Maid replies to the first President of the Parlement of Poitiers when he questions her concerning her family:

"As for my father's mansion, it is in the Bar country; and he is of gentle birth and rank right noble, a good Frenchman and a loyal."[30]

Before a clerk would write thus, Jeanne's family must have been long ennobled and the first generation must have died out, which happened in 1469; there must have come into existence that numerous family of the Du Lys, whose ridiculous pretensions had to be humoured. Not content with deriving their descent from their aunt, the Du Lys insisted on connecting the good peasant Jacquot d'Arc with the old nobility of Bar.

Notwithstanding that Jeanne's reference to "her father's mansion" conflicts with other scenes in the same mystery, this lengthy work would appear to be all of a piece.

It was apparently compiled during the reign of Louis XI, by a citizen of Orléans who was a fair master of his subject. It would be interesting to make a more detailed study of his authorities than has been done hitherto. This poet seems to have known a *Journal du siège* very different from the one we possess.

Was his mystery acted during the last thirty years of the century at the festival instituted to commemorate the taking of Les Tourelles? The subject, the style, and the spirit are all in harmony with such an occasion. But it is curious that a poem composed to celebrate the deliverance of Orléans on May 8 should assign that deliverance to May 9. And yet this is what the author of the mystery does when he puts the following lines into the mouth of the Maid:

"Remember how Orléans was delivered in the year one thousand four hundred and twenty-nine, and forget not also that of May it was the ninth day."[31]

Such are the chief chroniclers on the French side who have written of the Maid. Others who came later or who have only dealt with certain episodes in her life, need not be quoted here; their testimony will be best examined when we come to that of the facts in detail. Placing on one side any information to be obtained from *La Chronique de l'établissement de la fête*,[32] from *La Relation*[33] of the Clerk of La Rochelle and other contemporary documents, we are now in a position to realise that if we depended on the French chroniclers for our knowledge of Jeanne d'Arc we should know just as much about her as we know of Sakya Muni.

We shall certainly not find her explained by the Burgundian chroniclers. They, however, furnish certain useful information. The earliest of these Burgundian chroniclers is a clerk of Picardy, the author of an anonymous chronicle, called *La Chronique des Cordeliers*,[34] because the only copy of it comes from a house of the Cordeliers at Paris. It is a history of the world from the creation to the year 1431. M. Pierre Champion[35] has proved that Monstrelet made use of it. This clerk of Picardy knew divers matters, and was acquainted with sundry state documents. But facts and dates he curiously confuses. His knowledge of the Maid's military career is derived from a French and a popular source. A certain credence has been attached to his story of the leap from Beaurevoir; but his account if accurate destroys the idea that Jeanne threw herself from the top of the keep in

9

a fit of frenzy or despair.[36] And it does not agree with what Jeanne said herself.

Monstrelet,[37] "more drivelling at the mouth than a mustard-pot,"[38] is a fountain of wisdom in comparison with Jean Chartier. When he makes use of *La Chronique des Cordeliers* he rearranges it and presents its facts in order. What he knew of Jeanne amounts to very little. He believed that she was an inn servant. He has but a word to say of her indecision at Montépilloy, but that word, to be found nowhere else, is extremely significant. He saw her in the camp at Compiègne; but unfortunately he either did not realise or did not wish to say what impression she made upon him.

Wavrin du Forestel,[39] who edited additions to Froissart, Monstrelet, and Mathieu d'Escouchy, was at Patay; he never saw Jeanne there. He knows her only by hearsay and that but vaguely. We do not therefore attach great importance to what he relates concerning Robert de Baudricourt, who, according to him, indoctrinated the Maid and taught her how to appear "inspired by Divine Providence."[40] On the other hand, he gives valuable information concerning the war immediately after the deliverance of Orléans.

Le Fèvre de Saint-Rémy, Counsellor to the Duke of Burgundy and King-at-arms of the Golden Fleece,[41] was possibly at Compiègne when Jeanne was taken; and he speaks of her as a brave girl.

Georges Chastellain copies Le Fèvre de Saint Remy.[42]

The author of *Le Journal* ascribed to *un Bourgeois de Paris*,[43] whom we identify as a Cabochien clerk, had only heard Jeanne spoken of by the doctors and masters of the University of Paris. Moreover he was very ill-informed, which is regrettable. For the man stands alone in his day for energy of feeling and language, for passion of wrath and of pity, and for intense sympathy with the people.

I must mention a document which is neither French nor Burgundian, but Italian. I refer to the *Chronique d'Antonio Morosini*, published and annotated with admirable erudition by M. Germain Lefèvre-Pontalis. This chronicle, or to be more precise, the letters it contains, are very valuable to the historian, but not on account of the veracity of the deeds here attributed to the Maid, which on the contrary are all imaginary and fabulous. In the *Chronique de Morosini*,[44] every single fact concerning Jeanne is presented in a wrong character and in a false light. And yet Morosini's correspondents are men of business, thoughtful, subtle Venetians. These letters reveal how there were being circulated throughout Christendom a whole multitude of fictitious stories, imitated some from the Romances of Chivalry, others from the Golden Legend, concerning that *Demoiselle* as she is called, at once famous and unknown.

Another document, the diary of a German merchant, one Eberhard de Windecke,[45] a conscientious and clever edition of which has also been published by M. Germain Lefèvre-Pontalis, presents the same phenomenon. Nothing here related of the Maid is even probable. As soon as she appears a whole cycle of popular stories grow up round her name. Eberhard obviously delights to relate them. Thus we learn from these good foreign merchants that at no period of her existence was Jeanne known otherwise than by fables, and that if she moved multitudes it was by the spreading abroad of countless legends which sprang up wherever she passed and made way before her. And indeed, there is much food for thought in that dazzling obscurity, which from the very first enwrapped the Maid, in those radiant clouds of myth, which, while concealing her, rendered her all the more imposing.

Thirdly, with its memoranda, its consultations, and its one hundred and forty depositions, furnished by one hundred and twenty-three deponents, the rehabilitation trial forms a very valuable collection of documents.[46] M. Lanéry d'Arc has done well to publish in their entirety the memoranda of the doctors as well as the treatise of the Archbishop of Embrun, the propositions of Master Heinrich von Gorcum and the *Sibylla Francica*.[47] From the trial of 1431 we learn what theologians on the English side thought of the Maid. But were it not for the consultations of Théodore de Leliis and of Paul Pontanus and the opinions included in the later trial we should not know how she was regarded by the doctors of Italy and France. It is important to ascertain what were the views held by the whole Church concerning a damsel condemned during her lifetime, when the English were in power, and rehabilitated after her death when the French were victorious.

Doubtless many matters were elucidated by the one hundred and twenty-three witnesses heard at Domremy, at Vaucouleurs, at Toul, at Orléans, at Paris, at Rouen, at Lyon, witnesses drawn from all ranks of life – churchmen, princes, captains, burghers, peasants, artisans. But we are bound to admit that they come far short of satisfying our curiosity, and for several reasons. First, because they replied to a list of questions drawn up with the object of establishing a certain number of facts within the scope of ecclesiastical jurisdiction. The Holy Inquisitor who conducted the trial was curious, but his curiosity was not ours. This is the first reason for the insufficiency of the evidence from our point of view.[48]

But there are other reasons. Most of the witnesses appear excessively simple and lacking in discernment. In so large a number of men of all ages and of all ranks it is sad to find how few were equipped with lucid and judicial minds. It would seem as if the human intellect of those days was enwrapped in twilight and incapable of seeing anything distinctly. Thought as well as speech was curiously puerile. Only a slight acquaintance with this dark age is enough to make one feel as if among children. Want and ignorance and wars interminable had impoverished the mind of man and starved his moral nature. The scanty, slashed, ridiculous garments of the nobles and the wealthy betray an absurd poverty of taste and weakness of intellect.[49] One of the most striking characteristics of these small minds is their triviality; they are incapable of attention; they retain nothing. No one who reads the writings of the period can fail to be struck by this almost universal weakness.

By no means all the evidence given in these one hundred and forty depositions can be treated seriously. The daughter of Jacques Boucher, steward to the Duke of Orléans, depones in the following terms: "At night I slept alone with Jeanne. Neither in her words or her acts did I ever observe anything wrong. She was perfectly simple, humble, and chaste."[50]

This young lady was nine years old when she perceived with a discernment somewhat precocious that her sleeping companion was simple, humble, and chaste.

That is unimportant. But to show how one may sometimes be deceived by the witnesses whom one would expect to be the most reliable, I will quote Brother Pasquerel.[51] Brother Pasquerel is Jeanne's chaplain. He may be expected to speak as one who has seen and as one who knows. Brother Pasquerel places the examination at Poitiers before the audience granted by the King to the Maid in the château of Chinon.[52]

Forgetting that the whole relieving army had been in Orléans since May 4, he supposes that, on the evening of Friday the 6th, it was still expected.[53] From such blunders we may judge of the muddled condition of this poor priest's brain. His most serious shortcoming,

12

however, is the invention of miracles. He tries to make out that when the convoy of victuals reached Orléans, there occurred, by the Maid's special intervention, and in order to carry the barges up the river, a sudden flood of the Loire which no one but himself saw.[54]

The evidence of Dunois[55] is also somewhat deceptive. We know that Dunois was one of the most intelligent and prudent men of his day, and that he was considered a good speaker. In the defence of Orléans and in the coronation campaign he had displayed considerable ability. Either his evidence must have seriously suffered at the hands of the translator and the scribes, or he must have caused it to be given by his chaplain. He speaks of the "great number of the enemy" in terms more appropriate to a canon of a cathedral or a woollen draper than to a captain entrusted with the defence of a city and expected to know the actual force of the besiegers. All his evidence dealing with the transport of victuals on April 28 is well-nigh unintelligible. And Dunois is unable to state that Troyes was the first stage in the army's march from Gien.[56] Relating a conversation he held with the Maid after the coronation, he makes her speak as if her brothers were awaiting her at Domremy, whereas they were with her in France.[57] Curiously blundering, he attempts to prove that Jeanne had visions by relating a story much more calculated to give the impression that the young peasant girl was an apt feigner and that at the request of the nobles she reproduced one of her ecstasies, like the Esther of the lamented Doctor Luys.[58]

In that portion of this work which deals with the rehabilitation trial I have given my opinion of the evidence of the clerks of the court, of the usher Massieu, of the Brothers Isambard de la Pierre and Martin Ladvenu.[59] All these burners of witches and avengers of God worked as heartily at Jeanne's rehabilitation as they had at her condemnation.

In many cases and often on events of importance, the evidence of witnesses is in direct conflict with the truth. A woollen draper of Orléans, one Jean Luillier, comes before the commissioners and as bold as brass maintains that the garrison could not hold out against so great a besieging force.[60] Now this statement is proved to be false by the most authentic documents, which show that the English round Orléans were very weak and that their resources were greatly reduced.[61]

When the evidence given at the second trial has obviously been dressed up to suit the occasion, or even when it is absolutely contrary to the truth, we must blame not only those who gave it, but those who received it. In its elicitation the latter were too artful. This evidence has about as much value as the evidence in a trial by the Inquisition. In certain matters it may represent the ideas of the judges as much as those of the witnesses.

What the judges in this instance were most desirous to establish was that Jeanne had not understood when she was spoken to of the Church and the Pope, that she had refused to obey the Church Militant because she believed the Church Militant to be Messire Cauchon and his assessors. In short, it was necessary to represent her as almost an imbecile. In ecclesiastical procedure this expedient was frequently adopted. And there was yet another reason, a very strong one, for passing her off as an innocent, a damsel devoid of intelligence. This second trial, like the first, had been instituted with a political motive; its object was to make known that Jeanne had come to the aid of the King of France not by devilish incitement, but by celestial inspiration. Consequently in order that divine wisdom might be made manifest in her she must be shown to have had no wisdom of her own. On this string the examiners were constantly harping. On every occasion they drew from the witnesses the statement that she was simple, very simple. *Una simplex bergereta,*[62] says one. *Erat multum simplex et ignorans,*[63] says another.

But since, despite her ignorance, this innocent damsel had been sent of God to deliver or to capture towns and to lead men at arms, there must needs be innate in her a knowledge of the art of war, and in battle she must needs manifest the strength and the counsel she had received from above. Wherefore it was necessary to obtain evidence to establish that she was more skilled in warfare than any man.

Damoiselle Marguerite la Touroulde makes this affirmation.[64] The Duke of Alençon declares that the Maid was apt alike at wielding the lance, ranging an army, ordering a battle, preparing artillery, and that old captains marvelled at her skill in placing cannon.[65] The Duke quite understands that all these gifts were miraculous and that to God alone was the glory. For if the merit of the victories had been Jeanne's he would not have said so much about them.

And if God had chosen the Maid to perform so great a task, it must have been because in her he beheld the virtue which he preferred above all others in his virgins. Henceforth it sufficed not for her to have been chaste; her chastity must become miraculous, her chastity and her moderation in eating and drinking must be exalted into sanctity. Wherefore the witnesses are never tired of stating: *Erat casta, erat castissima. Ille loquens non credit aliquam mulierem plus esse castam quam ista Puella erat. Erat sobria in potu et cibo. Erat sobria in cibo et potu.*[66]

The heavenly source of such purity must needs have been made manifest by Jeanne's possessing singular immunities. And on this point there is a mass of evidence. Rough men at arms, Jean de Novelompont, Bertrand de Poulengy, Jean d'Aulon; great nobles, the Count of Dunois and the Duke of Alençon, come forward and affirm on oath that in them Jeanne never provoked any carnal desires. Such a circumstance fills these old captains with astonishment; they boast of their past vigour and wonder that for once their youthful ardour should have been damped by a maid. It seems to them most unnatural and humanly impossible. Their description of the effect Jeanne produced upon them recalls Saint Martha's binding of the Tarascon beast. Dunois in his evidence is very much occupied with miracles. He points to this one as, to human reason, the most incomprehensible of all. If he neither desired nor solicited this damsel, of this unique fact he can find but one explanation, it is that Jeanne was holy, *res divina.* When Jean de Novelompont and Bertrand de Poulengy describe their sudden continence, they employ identical forms of speech, affected and involved. And then there comes a king's equerry, Gobert Thibaut, who declares that in the army there was much talk of this divine grace, vouchsafed to the Armagnacs[67] and denied to English and Burgundians, at least, so the behaviour of a certain knight of Picardy, and of one Jeannotin, a tailor of Rouen, would lead us to believe.[68]

Such evidence obviously answers to the ideas of the judges, and turns, so to speak, on theological rather than on natural facts.

In inquisitorial inquiries there abound such depositions as those of Jean de Novelompont and of Bertrand de Poulengy, containing passages drawn up in identical terms. But I must admit that in the rehabilitation trial they are rare, partly because the witnesses were heard at long intervals of time and in different countries, and partly because in the Maid's case no elaborate proceedings were necessary owing to her adversaries not being represented.

It is to be regretted that all the evidence given at this trial, with the exception of that of Jean d'Aulon, should have been translated into

Latin. This process has obscured fine shades of thought and deprived the evidence of its original flavour.

Sometimes the clerk contents himself with saying that the depositions of a witness were like those of his predecessor. Thus on the raising of the siege of Orléans all the burgesses depone like the woollen draper, who himself was not thoroughly conversant with the circumstances in which his town had been delivered. Thus the Sire de Gaucourt, after a brief declaration, gives the same evidence as Dunois, although the Count had related matters so strikingly individual that it seems strange they should have been common to two witnesses.[69]

Certain evidence would appear to have been cut short. Brother Pasquerel's abruptly comes to an end at Paris. This circumstance, if we did not possess his signature at the conclusion of the Latin letter to the Hussites, would lead us to believe that the good Brother left the Maid immediately after the attack on La Porte Saint-Honoré. It surely cannot have chanced that in so long a series of questions and answers not one word was said of the departure from Sully or of the campaign which began at Lagny and ended at Compiègne.[70]

We conclude, therefore, that in the study of this voluminous evidence we must exercise great judgment and that we must not expect it to enlighten us on all the circumstances of Jeanne's life.

Fourthly. On certain points of the Maid's history the only exact information is to be obtained from account-books, letters, deeds, and other authentic documents of the period. The records published by Siméon Luce and the lease of the Château de l'Île inform us of the circumstances among which Jeanne grew up.[71] Neither the two trials nor the chronicles had revealed the terrible conditions prevailing in the village of Domremy from 1412 to 1425.

The fortress accounts kept at Orléans[72] and the documents of the English administration[73] enable us to estimate approximately the respective forces of defenders and besiegers of the city. On this point also they enable us to correct the statements of chroniclers and witnesses in the rehabilitation trial.

From the letters in the archives at Reims, copied by Rogier in the seventeenth century, we learn how Troyes, Châlons, and Reims surrendered to the King. From these letters also we see how very far from accurate is Jean Chartier's account of the capitulation of the city and how insufficient, especially considering the character of the witness, is the evidence of Dunois on this subject.[74]

16

Four or five records throw a faint light here and there on the obscurity which shrouds the unfortunate campaign on the Aisne and the Oise.

The registers of the chapter of Rouen, the wills of canons and sundry other documents, discovered by M. Robillard de Beaurepaire in the archives of Seine-Inférieure, serve to correct certain errors in the two trials.[75]

How many other detached papers, all valuable to the historian, might I not enumerate! Surely this is another reason for mistrusting records false or falsified, as, for example, the patent of nobility of Guy de Cailly.[76]

Rapid as this examination of authorities has been, I think nothing essential has been omitted. To sum up, even in her lifetime the Maid was scarce known save by fables. Her oldest chroniclers were devoid of any critical sense, for the early legends concerning her they relate as facts.

The Rouen trial, certain accounts, a few letters, sundry deeds, public and private, are the most trustworthy documents. The rehabilitation trial is also useful to the historian, provided always that we remember how and why that trial was conducted.

By means of such records we may attain to a pretty accurate knowledge of Jeanne d'Arc's life and character.

The salient fact which results from a study of all these authorities is that she was a saint. She was a saint with all the attributes of fifteenth-century sanctity. She had visions, and these visions were neither feigned nor counterfeited. She really believed that she heard the voices which spoke to her and came from no human lips. These voices generally addressed her clearly and in words she could understand. She heard them best in the woods and when the bells were ringing. She saw forms, she said, like myriads of tiny shapes, like sparks on a dazzling background. There is no doubt she had visions of another nature, since she tells us how she beheld Saint Michael in the guise of a *prud'homme*, that is as a good knight, and Saint Catherine and Saint Margaret, wearing crowns. She saw them saluting her; she kissed their feet and inhaled their sweet perfume.

What does this mean if not that she was subject to hallucinations of hearing, sight, touch, and smell? But the most strongly affected of her senses was her hearing. She says that her voices appear to her; she sometimes calls them her council. She hears them very plainly unless there is a noise around her. Generally she obeys them; but sometimes she resists. We may doubt whether her visions were really so distinct as she makes out. Because she either could not, or would not, she never gave her judges at Rouen any very clear or precise description of them. The angel she described most in detail was the one which brought the crown, and which she afterwards confessed to have seen only in imagination.

At what age did she become subject to these trances? We cannot say exactly. But it was probably towards the end of her childhood, notwithstanding that according to Jean d'Aulon, childhood was a state out of which she never completely developed.[77]

Although it is always hazardous to found a medical diagnosis on documents purely historical, several men of science have attempted to define the pathological conditions which rendered the young girl subject to false perceptions of sight and hearing.[78] Owing to the rapid strides made by psychiatry during recent years, I have consulted an eminent man of science, who is thoroughly conversant with the present stage attained by this branch of pathology, to which he has himself rendered important service. I asked Doctor Georges Dumas, Professor at the Sorbonne, whether sufficient material exists for science to make a retrospective diagnosis of Jeanne's case. He replied to my inquiry in a letter which appears as the first Appendix to this work.[79]

With such a subject I am not qualified to deal. But it does lie within my province to make an observation concerning the hallucinations of Jeanne d'Arc, which has been suggested to me by a study of the documents. This observation is of infinite significance. I shall be careful to restrict it to the limits prescribed by the object and the nature of this work.

Those visionaries, who believe they are entrusted with a divine mission, are distinguished by certain characteristics from other inspired persons. When mystics of this class are studied and compared with one another, resemblances are found to exist which may extend to very slight details: certain of their words and acts are identical. Indeed as we come to recognise how vigorous is the determinism controlling the actions of these visionaries, we are astonished to find the human machine, when impelled by the same mysterious agent, performing its functions with inevitable uniformity. To this group of the religious Jeanne belongs. In this connection it is interesting to compare her with Saint Catherine of Sienna,[80] Saint Colette of Corbie,[81] Yves Nicolazic, the peasant of Kernanna,[82] Suzette Labrousse, the inspired woman of the Revolution Church,[83] and with many other seers and seeresses of this order, who all bear a family likeness to one another.

Three visionaries especially are closely related to Jeanne. The earliest in date is a vavasour of Champagne, who had a mission to speak to King John; of this holy man I have written sufficiently in the present work. The second is a farrier of Salon, who had a mission to speak to Louis XIV; the third, a peasant of Gallardon, named Martin, who had a mission to speak to Louis XVIII. Articles on the farrier and the farmer, who both saw apparitions and showed signs to their respective kings, will be found in the appendices at the end of this work.[84] In spite of difference in sex, the points of similarity between Jeanne d'Arc and these three men are very close and very significant; they are inherent in the very nature of Jeanne and her fellow visionaries; and the variations, which at a first glance might seem to separate widely the latter from Jeanne, are æsthetic, social, historical, and consequently external and contingent. Between them and her there are of course striking contrasts in appearance and in fortune. They were entirely wanting in that charm which she never failed to exercise; and it is a fact that while they failed miserably she grew in strength and flowered in legend. But it is the duty of the scientific mind to recognise common characteristics, proving identity of origin alike in the noblest individual and in the most wretched abortion of the same species.

The free-thinkers of our day, imbued as they are, for the most part, with transcendentalism, refuse to recognise in Jeanne not merely that automatism which determines the acts of such a seeress, not only the influence of constant hallucination, but even the suggestions of the religious spirit. What she achieved through saintliness and devoutness, they make her out to have accomplished by intelligent enthusiasm. Such a disposition is manifest in the excellent and erudite Quicherat, who all unconsciously introduces into the piety of the Maid a great deal of eclectic philosophy. This point was not without its drawbacks. It led free-thinking historians to a ridiculous exaggeration of Jeanne's intellectual faculties, to the absurdity of attributing military talent to her and to the substitution of a kind of polytechnic phenomenon for the fifteenth century's artless marvel. The Catholic historians of the present day when they make a saint of the Maid are much nearer to nature and to truth. Unfortunately the Church's idea of saintliness has grown insipid since the Council of Trent, and orthodox historians are disinclined to study the variations of the Catholic Church down the ages. In their hands therefore she becomes sanctimonious and bigoted. So much so that in a search for the most curiously travestied of all the Jeannes d'Arc we should have been driven to choose between their miraculous protectress of Christian France, the patroness of officers, the inimitable model of the pupils of Saint-Cyr, and the romantic Druidess, the inspired woman-soldier of the national guard, the patriot gunneress of the Republicans, had there not arisen a Jesuit Father to create an ultramontane Jeanne d'Arc.[85]

On the subject of Jeanne's sincerity I have raised no doubts. It is impossible to suspect her of lying; she firmly believed that she received her mission from her voices. But whether she were not unconsciously directed is more difficult to ascertain. What we know of her before her arrival at Chinon comes to very little. One is inclined to believe that she had been subject to certain influences; it is so with all visionaries: some unseen director leads them. Thus it must have been with Jeanne. At Vaucouleurs she was heard to say that the Dauphin held the kingdom in fief (*en commende*).[86] Such a term she had not learnt from the folk of her village. She uttered a prophecy which she had not invented and which had obviously been fabricated for her.

She must have associated with priests who were faithful to the cause of the Dauphin Charles, and who desired above all things the end of the war. Abbeys were being burned, churches pillaged, divine service discontinued.[87] Those pious persons who sighed for peace, now that they saw the Treaty of Troyes failing to establish it, looked for the realisation of their hopes to the expulsion of the English. And the wonderful, the unique point about this young peasant girl – a point suggesting the ecclesiastic and the monk – is not that she felt herself called to ride forth and fight, but that in "her great pity" she announced the approaching end of the war, by the victory and coronation of the King, at a time when the nobles of the two countries, and the men-at-arms of the two parties, neither expected nor desired the war ever to come to an end.

The mission, with which she believed the angel had entrusted her and to which she consecrated her life, was doubtless extraordinary, marvellous; and yet it was not unprecedented: it was no more than saints, both men and women, had already endeavoured to accomplish in human affairs. Jeanne d'Arc arose in the decline of the great Catholic age, when sainthood, usually accompanied by all manner of oddities, manias, and illusions, still wielded sovereign power over the minds of men. And of what miracles was she not capable when acting according to the impulses of her own heart, and the grace of her own mind? From the thirteenth to the fifteenth centuries God's servants perform wondrous works. Saint Dominic, possessed by holy wrath, exterminates heresy with fire and sword; Saint Francis of Assisi for the nonce founds poverty as an institution of society; Saint Antony of Padua defends merchants and artisans against the avarice and cruelty of nobles and bishops; Saint Catherine brings the Pope back to Rome. Was it impossible, therefore, for a saintly damsel, with God's aid, to re-establish within the hapless realm of France that royal power instituted by our Lord Himself and to bring to his coronation a new Joash snatched from death for the salvation of the holy people?

Thus did pious French folk, in the year 1428, regard the mission of the Maid. She represented herself as a devout damsel inspired by God. There was nothing incredible in that. When she announced that she had received revelations touching the war from my Lord Saint Michael, she inspired the men-at-arms of the Armagnac party and the burghers of the city of Orléans with a confidence as great as could have been communicated to the troops, marching along the Loire in the winter of 1871, by a republican engineer who had invented a smokeless powder or an improved form of cannon. What was expected from science in 1871 was expected from religion in 1428, so that the Bastard of Orléans would as naturally employ Jeanne as Gambetta would resort to the technical knowledge of M. de Freycinet.

What has not been sufficiently remarked upon is that the French party made a very adroit use of her. The clerks at Poitiers, while inquiring at great length into her religion and her morals, brought her into evidence. These Poitiers clerks were no monks ignorant of the world; they constituted the Parliament of the lawful King; they were the banished members of the University, men deeply involved in political affairs, compromised by revolutions, despoiled and ruined, and very impatient to regain possession of their property. They were directed by the cleverest man in the King's Council, the Duke Archbishop of Reims, the Chancellor of the kingdom. By the ceremoniousness and the deliberation of their inquiries, they drew upon Jeanne the curiosity, the interest, and the hopes of minds lost in amazement.[88]

The defences of the city of Orléans consisted in its walls, its trenches, its cannon, its men-at-arms, and its money. The English had failed both to surround it and to take it by assault. Convoys and companies passed between their bastions. Jeanne was introduced into the town with a strong relieving army. She brought flocks of oxen, sheep, and pigs. The townsfolk believed her to be an angel of the Lord. Meanwhile the men and the money of the besiegers were waxing scant. They had lost all their horses. Far from being in a position to attempt a new attack, they were not likely to be able to hold out long in their bastions. At the end of April there were four thousand English before Orléans and perhaps less, for, as it was said, soldiers were deserting every day; and companies of these deserters went plundering through the villages. At the same time the city was defended by six thousand men-at-arms and archers, and by more than three thousand men of the town bands. At Saint Loup, there were fifteen hundred French against four hundred English; at Les Tourelles, there were five thousand French against four or five hundred English. By their retreat from Orléans the *Godons* abandoned to their fate the small garrisons of Jargeau, Meung, and Beaugency.[89] The Battle of Patay gives us some idea of the condition of the English army. It was no battle but a massacre, and one which Jeanne only reached in time to mourn over the cruelty of the conquerors. And yet the King, in his letters to his good towns, attributed to her a share in the victory. Evidently the Royal Council made a point of glorifying its Holy Maid.

But at heart what did they really think, those who employed her, those Regnaults de Chartres, those Roberts le Maçon, those Gérards Machet? They were certainly in no position to discuss the origin of the illusions which enveloped her. And, albeit there were atheists even among churchmen, to the majority there would be nothing to cause astonishment in the appearance of Saint Michael, the Archangel. In those days nothing appeared more natural than a miracle. But a miracle vanishes when closely observed. And they had the damsel before their very eyes. They perceived that good and saintly as she was, she wielded no supernatural power.

While the men-at-arms and all the common folk welcomed her as the maid of God and an angel sent from heaven for the salvation of the realm, these good lords thought only of profiting from the sentiments of confidence which she inspired and in which they had little share. Finding her as ignorant as possible, and doubtless deeming her less intelligent than she really was, they intended to do as they liked with her. They must soon have discovered that it was not always easy. She was a saint, saints are intractable. What were the true relations between the Royal Council and the Maid? We do not know; and it is a mystery which will never be solved. The judges at Rouen thought they knew that she received letters from Saint Michael.[90] It is possible that her simplicity was sometimes taken advantage of. We have reason for believing that the march to Reims was not suggested to her in France; but there is no doubt that the Chancellor of the kingdom, Messire Regnault de Chartres, Archbishop of Reims, eagerly desired his restoration to the see of the Blessed Saint Remi and the enjoyment of his benefices.

The coronation campaign was really nothing but a series of negotiations, backed by an army. Its object was to show the good towns a king saintly and pacific. Had there been any idea of fighting, the campaign would have been directed against Paris or against Normandy.

At the inquiry of 1456, five or six witnesses, captains, magistrates, ecclesiastics, and an honest widow, gave evidence that Jeanne was well versed in the art of war. They agreed in saying that she rode a horse and wielded a lance better than any one. A master of requests stated that she amazed the army by the length of time she could remain in the saddle. Such qualities we are not entitled to deny her, neither can we dispute the diligence and the ardour which Dunois praised in her, on the occasion of a demonstration by night before Troyes.[91] As to the opinion that this damsel was clever in arraying and leading an army and especially skilled in the management of artillery, that is more difficult to credit and would require to be vouched for by some one more trustworthy than the poor Duke of Alençon, who was never considered a very rational person.[92] What we have said about the rehabilitation trial sufficiently explains this curious glorification of the Maid. It was understood that Jeanne's military inspiration came from God. Henceforth there was no danger of its being too much admired and it came to be praised somewhat at random.

After all the Duke of Alençon was quite moderate when he represented her as a distinguished artillery-woman. As early as 1429, a humanist on the side of Charles VII asserted in Ciceronian language that in military glory she equalled and surpassed Hector, Alexander, Hannibal and Cæsar: "Non Hectore reminiscat et gaudeat Troja, exultet Græcia Alexandro, Annibale Africa, Italia Cæsare et Romanis

23

ducibus omnibus glorietur, Gallia etsi ex pristinis multos habeat, hac tamen una Puella contenta, audebit se gloriari et laude bellica caeteris nationibus se comparare, verum quoque, si expediet, se anteponere."[93]

For ever praying and for ever wrapped in ecstasy, Jeanne never observed the enemy; she did not know the roads; she paid no heed to the number of troops engaged; she did not take into account either the height of walls or the breadth of trenches. Even to-day officers are to be heard discussing the Maid's military tactics.[94] Those tactics were simple; they consisted in preventing men from blaspheming against God and consorting with light women. She believed that for their sins they would be destroyed, but that if they fought in a state of grace they would win the victory. Therein lay all her military science, save that she never feared danger.[95] She displayed a courage which was at once proud and gentle; she was more valiant, more constant, more noble than the men and in that worthy to lead them. And is it not admirable and rare to find such heroism united to such innocence?

Certain of the leaders indeed, and notably the princes of the blood royal, knew no more than she. The art of war in those days resolved itself into the art of riding. Any idea of marching along converging lines, of concentrated movements, of a campaign methodically planned, of a prolonged effort with a view to some great result was unknown. Military tactics were nothing more than a collection of peasants' stratagems and a few rules of chivalry. The freebooters, captains, and soldiers of fortune were all acquainted with the tricks of the trade, but they recognised neither friend nor foe; and their one desire was pillage. The nobles affected great concern for honour and praise; in reality they thought of nothing but gain. Alain Chartier said of them: "They cry 'to arms,' but they fight for money."[96]

Seeing that war was to last as long as life, it was waged with deliberation. Men-at-arms, horse-soldiers and foot, archers, cross-bowmen, Armagnacs as well as English and Burgundians, fought with no great ardour. Of course they were brave: but they were cautious too and were not ashamed to confess it. Jean Chartier, precentor of Saint-Denys, chronicler of the Kings of France, relating how on a day the French met the English near Lagny, adds: "And there the battle was hard and fierce, for the French were barely more than the English."[97] These simple folk, seeing that one man is as good as another, admitted the risk of fighting one to one. Their minds had not fed on Plutarch as had those of the Revolution and the Empire. And for their encouragement they had neither the *carmagnoles* of Barrère, nor the songs of Marie-Joseph Chénier, nor the bulletins of *la grande armée*. Why did these captains, these men-at-arms go and fight in one place rather than in another seems to be a natural question.... Because they wanted goods.

This perpetual warfare was not sanguinary. During what was described as Jeanne d'Arc's mission, that is from Orléans to Compiègne, the French lost barely a few hundred men. The English suffered much more heavily, because they were the fugitives, and in a rout it was the custom for the conquerors to kill all those who were not worth holding to ransom. But battles were rare, and so consequently were defeats, and the number of the combatants was small. There were but a handful of English in France. And they may be said to have fought only for plunder. Those who suffered from the war were those who did not fight, burghers, priests, and peasants. The peasants endured terrible hardships, and it is quite conceivable that a peasant girl should have displayed a firmness in war, a persistence and an ardour unknown throughout the whole of chivalry.

It was not Jeanne who drove the English from France. If she contributed to the deliverance of Orléans, she retarded the ultimate salvation of France by causing the opportunity of conquering Normandy to be lost through the coronation campaign. The misfortunes of the English after 1428 are easily explained. While in peaceful Guyenne they engaged in agriculture, in commerce, in navigation, and set the finances in good order, the country which they had rendered prosperous was strongly attached to them. On the banks of the Seine and the Loire it was very different; there they had never taken root; in numbers they were always too few, and they had never obtained any hold on the country. Shut up in fortresses and châteaux, they did not cultivate the country enough to conquer it, for one must work on the land if one would take possession of it. They left it waste and abandoned it to the soldiers of fortune by whom it was ravaged and exhausted. Their garrisons, absurdly small, were prisoners in the country they had conquered. The English had long teeth, but a pike cannot swallow an ox. That they were too few and that France was too big had been plainly seen after Crécy and after Poitiers. Then, after Verneuil, during the troubled reign of a child, weakened by civil discord, lacking men and money, and bound to keep in subjection the countries of Wales, Ireland, and Scotland, were they likely to succeed better? In 1428, they were but a handful in France, and to maintain themselves there they depended on the help of the Duke of Burgundy, who henceforth deserted them and wished them every possible harm.

They lacked means alike for the capture of new provinces and the pacification of those they had already conquered. The very character of the sovereignty their princes claimed, the nature of the rights they asserted, which were founded on institutions common to the two countries, rendered the organisation of their conquest difficult without the consent and even, one may say, without the loyal concurrence and friendship of the conquered. The Treaty of Troyes did not subject France to England, it united one country to the other. Such a union occasioned much anxiety in London. The Commons did not conceal their fear that Old England might become a mere isolated province of the new kingdom.[98] France for her part did not concur in the union. It was too late. During all the time that they had been making war on these *Coués*[99] they had grown to hate them. And possibly there already existed an English character and a French character which were irreconcilable. Even in Paris, where the Armagnacs were as much feared as the Saracens, the *Godons*[100] met with very unwilling support. What surprises us is not that the English should have been driven from France, but that it should have happened so slowly. Does this amount to saying that the young saint had no part whatever in the work of deliverance? By no means. Hers was the nobler, the better part; the part of sacrifice; she set the example of the highest courage and displayed heroism in a form unexpected and charming. The King's cause, which was indeed the national cause, she served in two ways: by giving confidence to the men-at-arms of her party, who believed her to be a bringer of good fortune, and by striking fear into the English, who imagined her to be the devil.

Our best historians cannot forgive the ministers and captains of 1428 for not having blindly obeyed the Maid. But that was not at all the advice given at the time by the Archbishop of Embrun to King Charles; he, on the contrary, recommended him not to abandon the means inspired by human reason.[101]

It has frequently been repeated that the lords and captains were jealous of her, especially old Gaucourt.[102] But such a statement shows an absolute ignorance of human nature. They were envious one of another; this and no other sentiment was the jealousy that made them tolerate the Maid's assuming the title of commander in war.[103]

Those secret intrigues on the part of the King and his captains, who are said to have plotted together the destruction of the saint, I admit having found it impossible to discover. To certain historians they appear very obvious: for my part, do what I may, I cannot discern them. The Chamberlain, the Sire de la Trémouille, had no pretensions to nobility of character; and the Chancellor Regnault de Chartres was hard-hearted, but what strikes me is that the Sire de la Trémouille refused to give up this valuable damsel to the Duke of Alençon when he asked for her, and that the Chancellor retained her in order to make use of her.[104] I am not of the opinion that Jeanne was a prisoner at Sully. I believe that when she went to join the Chancellor, who employed her until her capture by the Burgundians, she quitted the castle in estate, with trumpeters, and banners flying. After the girl saint he employed a boy saint, a shepherd who had stigmata; which proves that he did not regret having made use of a devout person to fight against the King's enemies and to recover his own archbishopric.

The excellent Quicherat and the magnanimous Henri Martin are very hard on the Government of 1428. According to them it was a treacherous Government. Yet the only reproach they bring against Charles VII and his councillors is that they did not understand the Maid as they themselves understood her. But such an understanding has required the lapse of four hundred years. To arrive at the illuminated ideas of a Quicherat and a Henri Martin concerning Jeanne d'Arc, three centuries of absolute monarchy, the Reformation, the Revolution, the wars of the Republic and of the Empire, and the sentimental Neo-Catholicism of '48, have all been necessary. Through all these brilliant prisms, through all these succeeding lights do romantic historians and broad-minded palaeographers view the figure of Jeanne d'Arc; and we ask too much from the poor Dauphin Charles, from La Trémouille, from Regnault de Chartres, from the Lord of Trèves, from old Gaucourt, when we require them to have seen Jeanne as centuries have made and moulded her.[105]

This, however, remains: after having made so much use of her, the Royal Council did nothing to save her.

Must the disgrace of such neglect fall upon the whole Council and upon the Council alone? Who ought really to have interfered? And how? What ought King Charles to have done? Should he have offered to ransom the Maid? She would not have been surrendered to him at any price. As for capturing her by force, that is a mere child's dream.

Had they entered Rouen, the French would not have found her there; Warwick would always have had time to put her in a place of safety, or to drown her in the river. Neither money nor arms would have availed to recapture her.

But this was no reason for standing with folded arms. Influence could have been brought to bear on those who were conducting the trial. Doubtless they were all on the side of the *Godons*; that old *Cabochien* of a Pierre Cauchon was very much committed to them; he detested the French; the clerks, who owed allegiance to Henry VI, were naturally inclined to please the Great Council of England which disposed of patronage; the doctors and masters of the University of France greatly hated and feared the Armagnacs. And yet the judges of the trial were not all infamous prevaricators; the chapter of Rouen lacked neither courage nor independence.[106] Among those members of the University who were so bitter against Jeanne, there were men highly esteemed for doctrine and character. They for the most part believed this trial to be a purely religious one. By dint of seeking for witches, they had come to find them everywhere. These females, as they called them, they were sending to the stake every day, and receiving nothing but thanks for it. They believed as firmly as Jeanne in the possibility of the apparitions which she said had been vouchsafed to her, only they were persuaded either that she lied or that she saw devils. The Bishop, the Vice-Inquisitor and the assessors, to the number of forty and upwards, were unanimous in declaring her heretical and devilish. There were doubtless many who imagined that by passing sentence against her they were maintaining Catholic orthodoxy and unity of obedience against the abettors of schism and heresy; they wished to judge wisely. And even the boldest and the most unscrupulous, the Bishop and the Promoter, would not have dared too openly to infringe the rules of ecclesiastical justice in order to please the English. They were priests, and they preserved priestly pride and respect for formality. Here was their weak point; in this respect for formality they might have been struck. Had the other side instituted vigorous legal proceedings, theirs might possibly have been thwarted, arrested, and the fatal sentence prevented. If the metropolitan of the Bishop of Beauvais, the Archbishop of Reims, had intervened in the trial, if he had suspended his suffragan for abuse of authority, or some other reason, Pierre Cauchon would have been greatly embarrassed; if, as he decided to do later, King Charles VII had brought about the intervention of the mother and brothers of the

28

Maid; if Jacques d'Arc and la Romée had protested in due form against an action so manifestly one-sided; if the register of Poitiers[107] had been sent for inclusion among the documents of the trial; if the high prelates subject to King Charles VII had asked for a safe conduct in order to come and give evidence in Jeanne's favour at Rouen; finally, if the King, his Council, and the whole Church of France had demanded an appeal to the Pope, as they were legally entitled to do, then the trial might have had a different issue.

But they were afraid of the University of Paris. They feared lest Jeanne might be after all what so many learned doctors maintained her to be, a heretic, a miscreant seduced by the prince of darkness. Satan transforms himself into an angel of light, and it is difficult to distinguish the true prophets from the false. The hapless Maid was deserted by the very clergy whose crosiers had so recently been carried before her; of all the Poitiers masters not one was found to testify in the château of Rouen to that innocence which they had officially recognised eighteen months before.

It would be very interesting to trace the reputation of the Maid down the ages. But to do so would require a whole book. I shall merely indicate the most striking revolutions of public opinion concerning her. The humanists of the Renaissance display no great interest in her: she was too Gothic for them. The Reformers, for whom she was tainted with idolatry, could not tolerate her picture.[108] It seems strange to us to-day, but it is none the less certain, and in conformity with all we know of French feeling for royalty, that whilst the monarchy endured it was the memory of Charles VII that kept alive the memory of Jeanne d'Arc and saved her from oblivion.[109] Respect due to the Prince generally hindered his faithful subjects from too closely inquiring into the legends of Jeanne as well as into those of the Holy Ampulla, the cures for King's evil, the *oriflamme* and all other popular traditions relating to the antiquity and celebrity of the royal throne of France. In 1609, when in a college of Paris, the Maid was the subject of sundry literary themes in which she was unfavourably treated,[110] a certain lawyer, Jean Hordal, who boasted that he came of the same race as the heroine, complained of these academic disputes as being derogatory to royal majesty – "I am greatly astonished," he said, "that ... public declamations against the honour of France, of King Charles VII and his Council,[111] should be suffered in France." Had Jeanne not been so closely associated with royalty, her memory would have been very much neglected by the wits of the seventeenth century.

In the minds of scholars, Catholics and Protestants alike, who considered the life of St. Margaret as mere superstition,[112] her apparitions did her harm. In those days even the *Sorbonagres* themselves were expurgating the martyrology and the legends of saints. One of them, Edmond Richer, like Jeanne a native of Champagne, the censor of the university in 1600, and a zealous Gallican, wrote an apology for the Maid who had defended the Crown of Charles VII.[113] with her sword. Albeit a firm upholder of the liberties of the French Church, Edmond Richer was a good Catholic. He was pious and of sound doctrine; he firmly believed in angels, but he did not believe either in Saint Catherine or Saint Margaret, and their appearing to the Maid greatly embarrassed him. He solved the difficulty by supposing that the angels had represented themselves to the Maid as the two saints, whom in her ignorance she devoutly worshipped. The hypothesis seemed to him satisfactory, "all the more so," he said, "because the Spirit of God, which governs the Church, accommodates himself to our infirmity." Thirty or forty years later, another doctor of the Sorbonne, Jean de Launoy, who was always ferreting after saints, completed the discrediting of Saint Catherine's legend.[114] The voices of Domremy were falling into disrepute.

Take Chapelain, for example, whose poem was first published in 1656. Chapelain is unconsciously burlesque; he is a Scarron without knowing it. It is none the less interesting to learn from him that he merely treated his subject as an occasion for glorifying the Bastard of Orléans. He expressly says in his preface: "I did not so much regard her (the Maid) as the chief character of the poem, who, strictly speaking, is the Comte de Dunois." Chapelain was in the pay of the Duc de Longueville, a descendant of Dunois.[115] It is of Dunois that he sings; "the illustrious shepherdess" contributes the marvellous element to his poem, and, according to the good man's own expression, furnishes *les machines nécessaires* for an epic. Saint Catherine and Saint Margaret are too commonplace to be included among *ces machines*. Chapelain tells us that he took particular care so to arrange his poem that "everything which happens in it by divine favour might be believed to have taken place through human agency carried to the highest degree to which nature is capable of ascending." Herein we discern the dawn of the modern spirit.

Bossuet also is careful not to mention Saint Catherine and Saint Margaret. The four or five quarto pages which he devotes to Jeanne d'Arc in his "Abrégé de l'Histoire de France pour l'instruction du

Dauphin"[116] are very interesting, not for his statement of facts, which is confused and inexact,[117] but for the care the author takes to represent the miraculous deeds attributed to Jeanne in an incidental and dubious manner. In Bossuet's opinion, as in Gerson's, these things are matters of edification, not of faith. Writing for the instruction of a prince, Bossuet was bound to abridge; but his abridgment goes too far when, representing Jeanne's condemnation to be the work of the Bishop of Beauvais, he omits to say that the Bishop of Beauvais pronounced this sentence with the unanimous concurrence of the University of Paris, and in conjunction with the Vice-Inquisitor.[118]

The eighteenth-century philosophers did not descend on France like a cloud of locusts; they were the result of two centuries of the critical spirit. If the story of Jeanne d'Arc contained too much monkish superstition for their taste, it was because they had learned their ecclesiastical history from the Baillets and the Tillemonts, who were pious indeed, but very critical of legends. Voltaire, writing of Jeanne, jeered at the rascally monks and their dupes. But if we quote the lines of *La Pucelle*, why not also the article[119] in the *Dictionnaire Philosophique*, which contains three pages of profounder truth and nobler thought than certain voluminous modern works in which Voltaire is insulted in clerical jargon?

It was precisely at the end of the eighteenth century that Jeanne began to be better known and more justly appreciated, first through a little book, which the Abbé Lenglet du Fresnoy derived almost wholly from the unpublished history of old Richer,[120] then by l'Averdy's erudite researches into the two trials.[121]

Nevertheless humanism, and after humanism the Reformation, and after the Reformation Cartesianism, and after Cartesianism experimental philosophy had banished the old credulity from thoughtful minds. When the Revolution came, the bloom had already long faded from the flower of Gothic legend. It seemed as if the glory of Jeanne d'Arc, so intimately related to the traditions of the royal house of France, could not survive the monarchy, and as if the tempest which scattered the royal ashes of Saint Denys and the treasure of Reims, would also bear away the frail relics and the venerated images of the saint of the Valois. The new *régime* did indeed refuse to honour a memory so inseparable from royalty and from religion. The festival of Jeanne d'Arc at Orléans, shorn of ecclesiastical pomp in 1791, was discontinued in 1793. Later the Maid's history appeared somewhat too

Gothic even to the *emigrés*; Chateaubriand did not dare to introduce her into his "Génie du Christianisme."[122]

But in the year XI the First Consul, who had just concluded the Concordat and was meditating the restoration of all the pageantry of the coronation, reinstituted the festival of the Maid with its incense and its crosses. Glorified of old in Charles VII's letters to his good towns, Jeanne was now exalted in *Le Moniteur* by Bonaparte.[123]

Only by constant transformation do the figures of poetry and history live in the minds of nations. Humanity cannot be interested in a personage of old time unless it clothe it in its own sentiments and in its own passions. After having been associated with the monarchy of divine right, the memory of Jeanne d'Arc came to be connected with the national unity which that monarchy had rendered possible; in Imperial and Republican France she became the symbol of *la patrie*. Certainly the daughter of Isabelle Romée had no more idea of *la patrie* as it is conceived to-day than she had of the idea of landed property which lies at its base. She never imagined anything like what we call the nation. That is something quite modern; but she did conceive of the heritage of kings and of the domain of the House of France. And it was there, in that domain and in that heritage, that the French gathered together before forming themselves into *la patrie*.

Under influences which it is impossible for us exactly to discover, the idea came to her of re-establishing the Dauphin in his inheritance; and this idea appeared to her so grand and so beautiful that in the fullness of her very ingenuous pride, she believed it to have been suggested to her by angels and saints from Paradise. For this idea she gave her life. That is why she has survived the cause for which she suffered. The very highest enterprises perish in their defeat and even more surely in their victory. The devotion, which inspired them, remains as an immortal example. And if the illusion, under which her senses laboured, helped her to this act of self-consecration, was not that illusion the unconscious outcome of her own heart? Her foolishness was wiser than wisdom, for it was that foolishness of martyrdom, without which men have never yet founded anything great or useful. Cities, empires, republics rest on sacrifice. It is not without reason therefore, not without justice that, transformed by enthusiastic imagination, she became the symbol of *la patrie* in arms.

In 1817, Le Brun de Charmettes,[124] a royalist jealous of imperial glory, wrote the first patriotic history of Jeanne d'Arc. The history is an able work. It has been followed by many others, conceived in the same spirit, composed on the same plan, written in the same style. From 1841 to 1849, Jules Quicherat, by his publication of the two trials and the evidence, worthily opened an incomparable period of research and discovery. At the same time, Michelet in the fifth volume of his "Histoire de France," wrote pages of high colour and rapid movement, which will doubtless remain the highest expression of the romantic art as applied to the Maid.[125]

But of all the histories written between 1817 and 1870, or at least of all those with which I have made acquaintance, for I have not attempted to read them all, the most discerning in my opinion is the fourth book of Vallet de Viriville's "Histoire de Charles VII" in which his chief preoccupation is to place the Maid in that group of visionaries to which she really belongs.[126]

Wallon's book has been widely circulated if not widely read. A monotonous, conscientious work moderately enthusiastic, it owes its success to its unimpeachable exactitude.[127] If there must be an orthodox Jeanne d'Arc to suit fashionable persons, then for such a purpose, M. Marius Sepet's representation of the Maid would be equally exact and more graceful.[128]

After the war of 1871, the twofold influence of the patriotic spirit, exalted by defeat, and the revival of Catholicism among the middle class gave a new impetus to admiration of the Maid. Arts and letters completed the transfiguration of Jeanne.

Catholics, like the learned Canon Dunand,[129] vie in zeal and enthusiasm with free-thinking idealists like M. Joseph Fabre.[130] By reproducing the two trials in a very artistic manner, in modern French and in a direct form of speech, M. Fabre has popularised the most ancient and the most touching impression of the Maid.[131]

From this period date almost innumerable works of erudition, among which must be noted those of Siméon Luce, which henceforth no one who would treat of Jeanne's early years can afford to neglect.[132]

We are equally indebted to M. Germain Lefèvre-Pontalis for his fine editions and his discerning studies so eruditely graceful and exact.

Throughout this period of romantic and Neo-Catholic enthusiasm the arts of painting and sculpture produced numerous representations of Jeanne, which had hitherto been very rare. Now everywhere were to be found Jeanne in armour and on horseback, Jeanne in prayer, Jeanne in captivity, Jeanne suffering martyrdom. Of all these images expressing in different manners and with varying merit the taste and the sentiment of the period, one work only appears great and true, and of striking beauty: Rude's Jeanne d'Arc beholding a vision.[133]

The word *patrie* did not exist in the days of the Maid. People spoke of the kingdom of France.[134] No one, not even jurists, knew exactly what were its limits, which were constantly changing. The diversity of laws and customs was infinite, and quarrels between nobles were constantly arising. Nevertheless, men felt in their hearts that they loved their native land and hated the foreigner. If the Hundred Years' War did not create the sentiment of nationality in France, it fostered it. In his "Quadrilogue Invectif" Alain Chartier represents France, indicated by her robe sumptuously adorned with the emblems of the nobility, of the clergy and of the *tiers état*, but lamentably soiled and torn, adjuring the three orders not to permit her to perish. "After the bond of the Catholic faith," she says to them, "Nature has called you before all things to unite for the salvation of your native land, and for the defence of that lordship under which God has caused you to be born and to live."[135] And these are not the mere maxims of a humourist versed in the virtues of antiquity. On the hearts of humble Frenchmen it was laid to serve the country of their birth. "Must the King be driven from his kingdom, and must we become English?" cried a man-at-arms of Lorraine in 1428.[136] The subjects of the Lilies, as well as those of the Leopard, felt it incumbent upon them to be loyal to their liege lord. But if any change for the worse occurred in the lordships to which they belonged, they were quite ready to make the best of it, because a lordship must increase or decrease, according to power and fortune, according to the good right or the good pleasure of the holder; it may be dismembered by marriages, or gifts, or inheritance, or alienated by various contracts. On the occasion of the Treaty of Bretigny, which seriously narrowed the dominions of King John, the folk of Paris strewed the streets with grass and flowers as a sign of rejoicing.[137] As a matter of fact, nobles changed their allegiance as often as it was necessary. Juvénal des Ursins relates in his Journal[138] how at the time of the English conquest of Normandy, a young widow was known to quit her domain with her three children in order to escape doing homage to the King from beyond the seas. But how many Norman nobles were like her in refusing to swear fealty to the former enemies of the kingdom? The example of fidelity to the king was not always set by those of his own family. The Duke of Bourbon, in the name of all the princes of the blood royal, prisoners with him in the hands of the English, proposed to Henry V that they should go and negotiate in France for the cession of Harfleur, promising that if the Royal Council met them with refusal they would acknowledge Henry V to be King of France.[139]

Every one thought first of himself. Whoever possessed land owed himself to his land; his neighbour was his enemy. The burgher thought only of his town. The peasant changed his master without knowing it. The three orders were not yet united closely enough to form, in the modern sense of the word, a state.

Little by little the royal power united the French. This union became stronger in proportion as royalty grew more powerful. In the sixteenth and seventeenth centuries, that desire to think and act in common, which creates great nations, became very strong among us – at least in those families which furnished officers to the Crown – and it even spread among the lower orders of society. Rabelais introduces François Villon and the King of England into a tale so inflamed with military bravado that it might have been told over the camp fire in an almost identical manner by one of Napoleon's grenadiers.[140] In his preface to the poem we have just quoted, Chapelain writes of the occasions when "*la patrie* who is our common mother, has need of all her children." Already the old poet expresses himself like the author of the *Marseillaise*.[141]

It cannot be denied that the feeling for *la patrie* did exist under the old *régime*. The impulse imparted to this sentiment by the Revolution was none the less immense. It added to it the idea of national unity and national territorial integrity. It extended to all the right of property hitherto reserved to a small number, and thus, so to speak, divided *la patrie* among the citizens. While rendering the peasant capable of possessing, the new *régime* imposed upon him the obligations of defending his actual or potential possessions. Recourse to arms is a necessity alike for whomsoever acquires or wishes to acquire territory. Hardly had the Frenchman come to enjoy the rights of a man and of a citizen, hardly had he entered into possession or thought he might enter into possession of a home and lands of his own, when the armies of the Coalition arrived "to drive him back to ancient slavery." Then the patriot became a soldier. Twenty-three years of warfare, with the inevitable alternations of victories and defeats, built up our fathers in their love of *la patrie* and their hatred of the foreigner.

35

Since then, as the result of industrial progress, there have arisen in one country and another, rivalries which are every day growing more bitter. The present methods of production by multiplying antagonism among nations, have given rise to imperialism, to colonial expansion and to armed peace.

But how many contrary forces are at work in this formidable creation of a new order of things! In all countries the great development of trade and manufactures has given birth to a new class. This class, possessing nothing, having no hope of ever possessing anything, enjoying none of the good things of life, not even the light of day, does not share the fear which haunted the peasant and burgher of the Revolution, of being despoiled by an enemy coming from abroad; the members of this new class, having no wealth to defend, regard foreign nations with neither terror nor hatred. At the same time over all the markets of the world there have arisen financial powers, which, although they often affect respect for old traditions, are by their very functions essentially destructive of the national and patriotic spirit. The universal capitalist system has created in France, as everywhere else, the internationalism of the workers and the cosmopolitanism of the financiers.

To-day, just as two thousand years ago, in order to discern the future, we must regard not the enterprises of the great but the confused movements of the working classes. The nations will not indefinitely endure this armed peace which weighs so heavily upon them. Every day we behold the organising of an universal community of workers.

I believe in the future union of nations, and I long for it with that ardent charity for the human race, which, formed in the Latin conscience in the days of Epictetus and Seneca, and through so many centuries extinguished by European barbarism, has been revived in the noblest breasts of modern times. And in vain will it be argued against me that these are the mere dream-illusions of desire: it is desire that creates life and the future is careful to realise the dreams of philosophers. Nevertheless, that we to-day are assured of a peace that nothing will disturb, none but a madman would maintain. On the contrary, the terrible industrial and commercial rivalries growing up around us indicate future conflicts, and there is nothing to assure us that France will not one day find herself involved in a great European or world conflagration. Her obligation to provide for her defence increases not a little those difficulties which arise from a social order profoundly agitated by competition in production and antagonism between classes.

An absolute empire obtains its defenders by inspiring fear; democracy only by bestowing benefits. Fear or interest lies at the root of all devotion. If the French proletariat is to defend the Republic heroically in the hour of peril, then it must either be happy or have the hope of becoming so. And what use is it to deceive ourselves? The lot of the workman to-day is no better in France than in Germany, and not so good as in England or America.

On these important subjects I have not been able to forbear expressing the truth as it appears to me; there is a great satisfaction in saying what one believes useful and just.

It now only remains for me to submit to my readers a few reflections on the difficult art of writing history, and to explain certain peculiarities of form and language which will be found in this work.

To enter into the spirit of a period that has passed away, to make oneself the contemporary of men of former days, deliberate study and loving care are necessary. The difficulty lies not so much in what one must know as in what one must not know. If we would really live in the fifteenth century, how many things we must forget: knowledge, methods, all those acquisitions which make moderns of us. We must forget that the earth is round, and that the stars are suns, and not lamps suspended from a crystal vault; we must forget the cosmogony of Laplace, and believe in the science of Saint Thomas, of Dante, and of those cosmographers of the Middle Age who teach the Creation in seven days and the foundation of kingdoms by the sons of Priam, after the destruction of Great Troy. Such and such a historian or palaeographer is powerless to make us understand the contemporaries of the Maid. It is not knowledge he lacks, but ignorance – ignorance of modern warfare, of modern politics, of modern religion.

But when we have forgotten, as far as possible, all that has happened since the youth of Charles VII, in order to think like a clerk in exile at Poitiers, or a burgher at Orléans serving on the ramparts of his city, we must recover all our intellectual resources in order to embrace the entirety of events, and discover that sequence between cause and effect which escape the clerk or the burgher. "I have contracted my horizon," says the Chatterton of Alfred de Vigny, when he explains how he is conscious of nothing that has happened since the days of the old Saxons. But Chatterton wrote poems, pseudo chronicles, and not history. The historian must alternately contract his horizon and widen it. If he undertake to tell an old story, he must needs successively – or sometimes at one and the same moment – assume the credulity of the folk he restores to life, and the discernment of the most accomplished critic. By a strange process, he must divide his personality. He must be at once the ancient man and the modern man; he must live on two different planes, like that curious character in a story by Mr. H.G. Wells, who lives and moves in a little English town, and all the time sees herself at the bottom of the ocean.

I have carefully visited cities and countries in which the events I propose to relate took place. I have seen the valley of the Meuse amidst the flowers and perfumes of spring, and I have seen it again beneath a mass of mist and cloud. I have travelled along the smiling banks of the Loire, so full of renown; through La Beauce, with its vast horizons bordered with snow-topped mountains; through l'Île-de-France, where the sky is serene; through La Champagne, with its stony hills covered with those low vines which, trampled upon by the coronation army, bloomed again into leaves and fruit, says the legend, and by St. Martin's Day yielded a late but rich vintage.[142] I have lingered in barren Picardy, along the Bay of the Somme so sad and bare beneath the flight of its birds of passage. I have wandered through the fat meadows of Normandy to Rouen with its steeples and towers, its ancient charnel houses, its damp streets, its last remaining timbered houses with high gables. I have imagined these rivers, these lands, these châteaux and these towns as they were five hundred years ago.

I have accustomed my gaze to the forms assumed by the beings and the objects of those days. I have examined all that remains of stone, of iron, or of wood worked by the hands of those old artisans, who were freer and consequently more ingenious than ours, and whose handicraft reveals a desire to animate and adorn everything. To the best of my ability I have studied figures carved and painted, not exactly in France – for there, in those days of misery and death, art was little practised – but in Flanders, in Burgundy, in Provence, where the workmanship is often in a style at once affected and *naïf*, and frequently beautiful. As I gazed at the old miniatures, they seemed to live before me, and I saw the nobles in the absurd magnificence of their *étoffes à tripes*,[143] the dames and the damoiselles somewhat devilish with their horned caps and their pointed shoes; clerks seated at the desk, men-at-arms riding their chargers and merchants their mules, husbandmen performing from April till March all the tasks of the rural

38

calendar; peasant women, whose broad coifs are still worn by nuns. I drew near to these folk, who were our fellows, and who yet differed from us by a thousand shades of sentiment and of thought; I lived their lives; I read their hearts.

It is hardly necessary to say that there exists no authentic representation of Jeanne. In the art of the fifteenth century all that relates to her amounts to very little: hardly anything remains – a small piece of *bestion* tapestry, a slight pen-and-ink figure on a register, a few illuminations in manuscripts of the reigns of Charles VII, Louis XI, and Charles VIII, that is all. I have found it necessary to contribute to this very meagre iconography of Jeanne d'Arc, not because I had anything to add to it, but in order to expunge the contributions of the forgers of that period. In Appendix IV, at the end of this work, will be found the short article in which I point out the forgeries which, for the most part, are already old, but had not been previously denounced. I have limited my researches to the fifteenth century, leaving to others the task of studying those pictures of the Renaissance in which the Maid appears decked out in the German fashion, with the plumed hat and slashed doublet of a Saxon ritter or a Swiss mercenary.[144] I cannot say who served as a prototype for these portraits, but they closely resemble the woman accompanying the mercenaries in *La Danse des morts*, which Nicholas Manuel painted at Berne, on the wall of the Dominican Monastery, between 1515 and 1521.[145] In *le Grand Siècle* Jeanne d'Arc becomes Clorinda, Minerva, Bellona in ballet costume.[146]

To my mind a continuous story is more likely than any controversy or discussion to make my subject live, and bring home its verities to my readers. It is true that the documents relating to the Maid do not lend themselves very easily to this kind of treatment. As I have just shown, they may nearly all be regarded as doubtful from several points of view, and objections to them arise at every moment. Nevertheless, I think that by making a cautious and judicious use of these documents one may obtain material sufficient for a truthful history of considerable extent. Besides, I have always indicated the sources of my facts, so that every one may judge for himself of the trustworthiness of my authorities.

In the course of my story I have related many incidents which, without having a direct relation to Jeanne, reveal the spirit, the morals, and the beliefs of her time. These incidents are usually of a religious order. They must necessarily be so, for Jeanne's story – and I cannot repeat it too often – is the story of a saint, just like that of Colette of Corbie, or of Catherine of Sienna.

I have yielded frequently, perhaps too frequently, to the desire to make the reader live among the men and things of the fifteenth century. And in order not to distract him suddenly from them, I have avoided suggesting any comparison with other periods, although many such occurred to me.

My history is founded on the form and substance of ancient documents; but I have hardly ever introduced into it literal quotations; I believe that unless it possesses a certain unity of language a book is unreadable, and I want to be read.

It is neither affectation of style nor artistic taste that has led me to adhere as far as possible to the tone of the period and to prefer archaic forms of language whenever I thought they would be intelligible, it is because ideas are changed when words are changed and because one cannot substitute modern for ancient expressions without altering sentiments and characters.

I have endeavoured to make my style simple and familiar. History is too often written in a high-flown manner that renders it wearisome and false. Why should we imagine historical facts to be out of the ordinary run of things and on a scale different from every-day humanity?

The writer of a history such as this is terribly tempted to throw himself into the battle. There is hardly a modern account of these old contests, in which the author, be he ecclesiastic or professor, does not with pen behind ear, rush into the *mêlée* by the side of the Maid. Even at the risk of missing the revelation of some of the beauties of her nature, I deem it better to keep one's own personality out of the action.

I have written this history with a zeal ardent and tranquil; I have sought truth strenuously, I have met her fearlessly. Even when she assumed an unexpected aspect, I have not turned from her. I shall be reproached for audacity, until I am reproached for timidity.

I have pleasure in expressing my gratitude to my illustrious *confrères*, MM. Paul Meyer and Ernest Lavisse, who have given me valuable advice. I owe much to M. Petit Dutaillis for certain kindly observations which I have taken into consideration. I am also greatly indebted to M. Henri Jadart, Secretary of the Reims Academy; M. E. Langlois, Professor at the Faculté des Lettres of Lille; M. Camille

Bloch, some time archivist of Loiret, M. Noël Charavay, autographic expert, and M. Raoul Bonnet.

M. Pierre Champion, who albeit still young is already known as the author of valuable historical works, has placed the result of his researches at my disposal with a disinterestedness I shall never be able adequately to acknowledge. He has also carefully read the whole of my work. M. Jean Brousson has given me the advantage of his perspicacity which far surpasses what one is entitled to expect from one's secretary.

In the century which I have endeavoured to represent in this work, there was a fiend, by name Titivillus. Every evening this fiend put into a sack all the letters omitted or altered by the copyists during the day. He carried them to hell, in order that, when Saint Michael weighed the souls of these negligent scribes, the share of each one might be put in the scale of his iniquities. Should he have survived the invention of printing, surely this most properly meticulous fiend must to-day be assuming the heavy task of collecting the misprints scattered throughout the books which aspire to exactitude; it would be very foolish of him to trouble about others. As occasion requires he will place those misprints to the account of reader or author. I am infinitely indebted to my publishers and friends MM. Calmann, Lévy and to their excellent collaborators for the care and experience they have employed in lightening the burden, which Titivillus will place on my back on the Day of Judgment.

Paris, February, 1908.

JOAN OF ARC

VOLUME 1

CHAPTER I
CHILDHOOD

ROM Neufchâteau to Vaucouleurs the clear waters of the Meuse flow freely between banks covered with rows of poplar trees and low bushes of alder and willow. Now they wind in sudden bends, now in gradual curves, for ever breaking up into narrow streams, and then the threads of greenish waters gather together again, or here and there are suddenly lost to sight underground. In the summer the river is a lazy stream, barely bending in its course the reeds which grow upon its shallow bed; and from the bank one may watch its lapping waters kept back by clumps of rushes scarcely covering a little sand and moss. But in the season of heavy rains, swollen by sudden torrents, deeper and more rapid, as it rushes along, it leaves behind it on the banks a kind of dew, which rises in pools of clear water on a level with the grass of the valley.

This valley, two or three miles broad, stretches unbroken between low hills, softly undulating, crowned with oaks, maples, and birches. Although strewn with wild-flowers in the spring, it looks severe, grave, and sometimes even sad. The green grass imparts to it a monotony like that of stagnant water. Even on fine days one is conscious of a hard, cold climate. The sky seems more genial than the earth. It beams upon it with a tearful smile; it constitutes all the movement, the grace, the exquisite charm of this delicate tranquil landscape. Then when winter comes the sky merges with the earth in a kind of chaos. Fogs come down thick and clinging. The white light mists, which in summer veil the bottom of the valley, give place to thick clouds and dark moving mountains, but slowly scattered by a red, cold sun. Wanderers ranging the uplands in the early morning might dream with the mystics in their ecstasy that they are walking on clouds.

Thus, after having passed on the left the wooded plateau, from the height of which the château of Bourlémont dominates the valley of the Saonelle, and on the right Coussey with its old church, the winding river flows between le Bois Chesnu on the west and the hill of Julien on the east. Then on it goes, passing the adjacent villages of Domremy and Greux on the west bank and separating Greux from Maxey-sur-Meuse. Among other hamlets nestling in the hollows of the hills or rising on the high ground, it passes Burey-la-Côte, Maxey-sur-Vaise, and Burey-en-Vaux, and flows on to water the beautiful meadows of Vaucouleurs.[147]

In this little village of Domremy, situated at least seven and a half miles further down the river than Neufchâteau and twelve and a half above Vaucouleurs, there was born, about the year 1410 or 1412,[148] a girl who was destined to live a remarkable life. She was born poor. Her father,[149] Jacques or Jacquot d'Arc, a native of the village of Ceffonds in Champagne,[150] was a small farmer and himself drove his horses at the plough.[151] His neighbours, men and women alike, held him to be a good Christian and an industrious workman.[152] His wife came from Vouthon, a village nearly four miles northwest of Domremy, beyond the woods of Greux. Her name being Isabelle or Zabillet, she received at some time, exactly when is uncertain, the surname of Romée.[153] That name was given to those who had been to Rome or on some other important pilgrimage;[154] and it is possible that Isabelle may have acquired her name of Romée by assuming the pilgrim's shell and staff.[155] One of her brothers was a parish priest, another a tiler; she had a nephew who was a carpenter.[156] She had already borne her husband three children: Jacques or Jacquemin, Catherine, and Jean.[157]

Jacques d'Arc's house was on the verge of the precincts of the parish church, dedicated to Saint Remi, the apostle of Gaul.[158] There was only the graveyard to cross when the child was carried to the font. It is said that in those days and in that country the form of exorcism pronounced by the priest during the baptismal ceremony was much longer for girls than for boys.[159] We do not know whether Messire Jean Minet,[160] the parish priest, pronounced it over the child in all its literal fullness, but we notice the custom as one of the numerous signs of the Church's invincible mistrust of woman.

According to the custom then prevailing the child had several godfathers and godmothers.[161] The men-gossips were Jean Morel, of Greux,[162] husbandman; Jean Barrey, of Neufchâteau; Jean Le Langart or Lingui, and Jean Rainguesson; the women, Jeannette, wife of Thévenin le Royer, called Roze, of Domremy; Béatrix, wife of Estellin,[163] husbandman in the same village; Edite, wife of Jean Barrey; Jeanne, wife of Aubrit, called Jannet and described as Maire Aubrit when he was appointed secretary to the lords of Bourlémont; Jeannette, wife of Thiesselin de Vittel, a scholar of Neufchâteau. She was the most learned of all, for she had heard stories read out of books. Among the godmothers there are mentioned also the wife of Nicolas d'Arc, Jacques' brother, and two obscure Christians, one called Agnes, the other Sibylle.[164] Here, as in every group of good Catholics, we have a number of Jeans, Jeannes, and Jeannettes. St. John the Baptist was a saint of high repute; his festival, kept on the 24th of June, was a red-letter day in the calendar, both civil and religious; it marked the customary date for leases, hirings, and contracts of all kinds. In the opinion of certain ecclesiastics, especially of the mendicant orders, St. John the Evangelist, whose head had rested on the Saviour's breast and who was to return to earth when the ages should have run their course, was the greatest saint in Paradise.[165] Wherefore, in honour of the Precursor of the Saviour or of his best beloved disciple, when babes were baptised the name Jean or Jeanne was frequently preferred to all others. To render these holy names more in keeping with the helplessness of childhood and the humble destiny awaiting most of us, they were given the diminutive forms of Jeannot and Jeannette. On the banks of the Meuse the peasants had a particular liking for these diminutives at once unpretentious and affectionate: Jacquot, Pierrollot, Zabillet, Mengette, Guillemette.[166] After the wife of the scholar, Thiesselin, the child was named Jeannette. That was the name by which she was known in the village. Later, in France, she was called Jeanne.[167]

She was brought up in her father's house, in Jacques' poor dwelling.[168] In the front there were two windows admitting but a scanty light. The stone roof forming one side of a gable on the garden side sloped almost to the ground. Close by the door, as was usual in that country, were the dung-heap, a pile of firewood, and the farm tools covered with rust and mud. But the humble enclosure, which served as orchard and kitchen-garden, in the spring bloomed in a wealth of pink and white flowers.[169]

These good Christians had one more child, the youngest, Pierre, who was called Pierrelot.[170]

Fed on light wine and brown bread, hardened by a hard life, Jeanne grew up in an unfruitful land, among people who were rough and sober. She lived in perfect liberty. Among hard-working peasants the children are left to themselves. Isabelle's daughter seems to have got on well with the village children.

A little neighbour, Hauviette, three or four years younger than she, was her daily companion. They liked to sleep together in the same bed.[171] Mengette, whose parents lived close by, used to come and spin at Jacques d'Arc's house. She helped Jeanne with her household duties.[172] Taking her distaff with her, Jeanne used often to go and pass the evening at Saint-Amance, at the house of a husbandman Jacquier, who had a young daughter.[173] Boys and girls grew up as a matter of course side by side. Being neighbours, Jeanne and Simonin Musnier's son were brought up together. When Musnier's son was still a child he fell ill, and Jeanne nursed him.[174]

In those days it was not unprecedented for village maidens to know their letters. A few years earlier Maître Jean Gerson had counselled his sisters, peasants of Champagne, to learn to read, and had promised, if they succeeded, to give them edifying books.[175] Albeit the niece of a parish priest, Jeanne did not learn her horn-book, thus resembling most of the village children, but not all, for at Maxey there was a school attended by boys from Domremy.[176]

From her mother she learnt the Paternoster, Ave Maria, and the credo.[177] She heard a few beautiful stories of the saints. That was her whole education. On holy days, in the nave of the church, beneath the pulpit, while the men stood round the wall, she, in the manner of the peasant women, squatted on her toes, listening to the priest's sermon.[178]

As soon as she was old enough she laboured in the fields, weeding, digging, and, like the Lorraine maidens of to-day, doing the work of a man.[179]

The river meadows were the chief source of wealth to the dwellers on the banks of the Meuse. When the hay harvest was over, according to his share of the arable land, each villager in Domremy had the right to turn so many head of cattle into the meadows of the village. Each family took its turn at watching the flocks and herds in the meadows. Jacques d'Arc, who had a little grazing land of his own, turned out his oxen and his horses with the others. When his turn came to watch them, he delegated the task to his daughter Jeanne, who went off into the meadow, distaff in hand.[180]

But she would rather do housework or sew or spin. She was pious. She swore neither by God nor his saints; and to assert the truth of anything she was content to say: "There's no mistake."[181] When the bells rang for the *Angelus*, she crossed herself and knelt.[182] On Saturday, the Holy Virgin's day, she climbed the hill overgrown with grass, vines, and fruit-trees, with the village of Greux nestling at its foot, and gained the wooded plateau, whence she could see on the east the green valley and the blue hills. On the brow of the hill, barely two and a half miles from the village, in a shaded dale full of murmuring sounds, from beneath beeches, ash-trees, and oaks gush forth the clear waters of the Saint-Thiébault spring, which cure fevers and heal wounds. Above the spring rises the chapel of Notre-Dame de Bermont. In fine weather it is pervaded by the scent of fields and woods, and winter wraps this high ground in a mantle of sadness and silence. In those days, clothed in a royal cloak and wearing a crown, with her divine child in her arms, Notre-Dame de Bermont received the prayers and the offerings of young men and maidens. She worked miracles. Jeanne used to visit her with her sister Catherine and the boys and girls of the neighbourhood, or quite alone. And as often as she could she lit a candle in honour of the heavenly lady.[183]

A mile and a quarter west of Domremy was a hill covered with a dense wood, which few dared enter for fear of boars and wolves. Wolves were the terror of the countryside. The village mayors gave rewards for every head of a wolf or wolf-cub brought them.[184] This wood, which Jeanne could see from her threshold, was the Bois Chesnu, the wood of oaks, or possibly the hoary *chenu* wood, the old forest.[185] We shall see later how this Bois Chesnu was the subject of a prophecy of Merlin the Magician.

At the foot of the hill, towards the village, was a spring[186] on the margin of which gooseberry bushes intertwined their branches of greyish green. It was called the Gooseberry Spring or the Blackthorn Spring.[187] If, as was thought by a graduate of the University of Paris,[188] Jeanne described it as *La Fontaine-aux-Bonnes-Fées-Notre-Seigneur*, it must have been because the village people called it by that name. By making use of such a term it would seem as if those rustic souls were trying to Christianise the nymphs of the woods and waters, in whom

49

certain teachers discerned the demons which the heathen once worshipped as goddesses.[189] It was quite true. Goddesses as much feared and venerated as the Parcæ had come to be called Fates,[190] and to them had been attributed power over the destinies of men. But, fallen long since from their powerful and high estate, these village fairies had grown as simple as the people among whom they lived. They were invited to baptisms, and a place at table was laid for them in the room next the mother's. At these festivals they ate alone and came and went without any one's knowing; people avoided spying upon their movements for fear of displeasing them. It is the custom of divine personages to go and come in secret. They gave gifts to new-born infants. Some were very kind, but most of them, without being malicious, appeared irritable, capricious, jealous; and if they were offended even unintentionally, they cast evil spells. Sometimes they betrayed their feminine nature by unaccountable likes and dislikes. More than one found a lover in a knight or a churl; but generally such loves came to a bad end. And, when all is said, gentle or terrible, they remained the Fates, they were always the Destinies.[191]

Near by, on the border of the wood, was an ancient beech, overhanging the highroad to Neufchâteau and casting a grateful shade.[192] The beech was venerated almost as piously as had been those trees which were held sacred in the days before apostolic missionaries evangelised Gaul.[193] No hand dared touch its branches, which swept the ground. "Even the lilies are not more beautiful,"[194] said a rustic. Like the spring the tree had many names. It was called *l'Arbre-des-Dames*, *l'Arbre-aux-Loges-les-Dames*, *l'Arbre-des-Fées*, *l'Arbre-Charmine-Fée-de-Bourlémont*, *le Beau-Mai*.[195]

Every one at Domremy knew that fairies existed and that they had been seen under *l'Arbre-aux-Loges-les-Dames*. In the old days, when Berthe was spinning, a lord of Bourlémont, called Pierre Granier,[196] became a fairy's knight, and kept his tryst with her at eve under the beech-tree. A romance told of their loves. One of Jeanne's godmothers, who was a scholar at Neufchâteau, had heard this story, which closely resembled that tale of Melusina so well known in Lorraine.[197] But a doubt remained as to whether fairies still frequented the beech-tree. Some believed they did, others thought they did not. Béatrix, another of Jeanne's godmothers, used to say: "I have heard tell that fairies came to the tree in the old days. But for their sins they come there no longer."[198]

This simple-minded woman meant that the fairies were the enemies of God and that the priest had driven them away. Jean Morel, Jeanne's godfather, believed the same.[199]

The House of Joan of Arc at Domremy in 1419

Indeed on Ascension Eve, on Rogation days and Ember days, crosses were carried through the fields and the priest went to *l'Arbre-des-Fées* and chanted the Gospel of St. John. He chanted it also at the Gooseberry Spring and at the other springs in the parish.[200] For the exorcising of evil spirits there was nothing like the Gospel of St. John.[201]

My Lord Aubert d'Ourches held that there had been no fairies at Domremy for twenty or thirty years.[202] On the other hand there were those in the village who believed that Christians still held converse with them and that Thursday was the trysting day.

Yet another of Jeanne's godmothers, the wife of the mayor Aubrit, had with her own eyes seen fairies under the tree. She had told her goddaughter. And Aubrit's wife was known to be no witch or soothsayer but a good woman and a circumspect.[203]

In all this Jeanne suspected witchcraft. For her own part she had never met the fairies under the tree. But she would not have said that she had not seen fairies elsewhere.[204] Fairies are not like angels; they do not always appear what they really are.[205]

Every year, on the fourth Sunday in Lent, – called by the Church "*Lætare* Sunday," because during the mass of the day was chanted the passage beginning *Lætare Jerusalem*, – the peasants of Bar held a rustic festival. This was their well-dressing when they went together to drink from some spring and to dance on the grass. The peasants of Greux kept their festival at the Chapel of Notre-Dame de Bermont; those of Domremy at the Gooseberry Spring and at *l'Arbre-des-Fées*.[206] They used to recall the days when the lord and lady of Bourlémont themselves led the young people of the village. But Jeanne was still a babe in arms when Pierre de Bourlémont, lord of Domremy and Greux, died childless, leaving his lands to his niece Jeanne de Joinville, who lived at Nancy, having married the chamberlain of the Duke of Lorraine.[207]

At the well-dressing the young men and maidens of Domremy went to the old beech-tree together. After they had hung it with garlands of flowers, they spread a cloth on the grass and supped off nuts, hard-boiled eggs, and little rolls of a curious form, which the housewives had kneaded on purpose.[208] Then they drank from the Gooseberry Spring, danced in a ring, and returned to their own homes at nightfall.

Jeanne, like all the other damsels of the countryside, took her part in the well-dressing. Although she came from the quarter of Domremy nearest Greux, she kept her feast, not at Notre-Dame de Bermont, but at the Gooseberry Spring and *l'Arbre-des-Fées*.[209]

In her early childhood she danced round the tree with her companions. She wove garlands for the image of Notre-Dame de Domremy, whose chapel crowned a neighbouring hill. The maidens were wont to hang garlands on the branches of *l'Arbre-des-Fées*. Jeanne, like the others, bewreathed the tree's branches; and, like the others, sometimes she left her wreaths behind and sometimes she carried them away. No one knew what became of them; and it seems their disappearance was such as to cause wise and learned persons to wonder. One thing, however, is sure: that the sick who drank from the spring were healed and straightway walked beneath the tree.[210]

To hail the coming of spring they made a figure of May, a mannikin of flowers and foliage.[211]

Close by *l'Arbre-des-Dames*, beneath a hazel-tree, there was a mandrake. He promised wealth to whomsoever should dare by night, and according to the prescribed rites, to tear him from the ground,[212] not fearing to hear him cry or to see blood flow from his little human body and his forked feet.

The tree, the spring, and the mandrake caused the inhabitants of Domremy to be suspected of holding converse with evil spirits. A learned doctor said plainly that the country was famous for the number of persons who practised witchcraft.[213]

When quite a little girl, Jeanne journeyed several times to Sermaize in Champagne, where dwelt certain of her kinsfolk. The village priest, Messire Henri de Vouthon, was her uncle on her mother's side. She had a cousin there, Perrinet de Vouthon, by calling a tiler, and his son Henri.[214]

Full thirty-seven and a half miles of forest and heath lie between Domremy and Sermaize. Jeanne, we may believe, travelled on horseback, riding behind her brother on the little mare which worked on the farm.[215]

At each visit the child spent several days at her cousin Perrinet's house.[216]

With regard to feudal overlordship the village of Domremy was divided into two distinct parts. The southern part, with the château on the Meuse and some thirty homesteads, belonged to the lords of Bourlémont and was in the domain of the castellany of Grondrecourt, held in fief from the crown of France. It was a part of Lorraine and of Bar. The northern half of the village, in which the monastery was situated, was subject to the provost of Montéclaire and Andelot and was in the bailiwick of Chaumont in Champagne.[217] It was sometimes called Domremy de Greux because it seemed to form a part of the village of Greux adjoining it on the highroad in the direction of Vaucouleurs.[218] The serfs of Bourlémont were separated from the king's men by a brook, close by towards the west, flowing from a threefold source and hence called, so it is said, the Brook of the Three Springs. Modestly the stream flowed beneath a flat stone in front of the church, and then rushed down a rapid incline into the Meuse, opposite Jacques d'Arc's house, which it passed on the left, leaving it in the land of Champagne and of France.[219] So far we may be fairly certain; but we must beware of knowing more than was known in that day. In 1429 King Charles' council was uncertain as to whether

Jacques d'Arc was a freeman or a serf.[220] And Jacques d'Arc himself doubtless was no better informed. On both banks of the brook, the men of Lorraine and Champagne were alike peasants leading a life of toil and hardship. Although they were subject to different masters they formed none the less one community closely united, one single rural family. They shared interests, necessities, feelings – everything. Threatened by the same dangers, they had the same anxieties.

Lying at the extreme south of the castellany of Vaucouleurs, the village of Domremy was between Bar and Champagne on the east, and Lorraine on the west.[221] They were terrible neighbours, always warring against each other, those dukes of Lorraine and Bar, that Count of Vaudémont, that Damoiseau of Commercy, those Lord Bishops of Metz, Toul, and Verdun. But theirs were the quarrels of princes. The villagers observed them just as the frog in the old fable looked on at the bulls fighting in the meadow. Pale and trembling, poor Jacques saw himself trodden underfoot by these fierce warriors. At a time when the whole of Christendom was given up to pillage, the men-at-arms of the Lorraine Marches were renowned as the greatest plunderers in the world. Unfortunately for the labourers of the castellany of Vaucouleurs, close to this domain, towards the north, there lived Robert de Saarbruck, Damoiseau of Commercy, who, subsisting on plunder, was especially given to the Lorraine custom of marauding. He was of the same way of thinking as that English king who said that warfare without burnings was no good, any more than chitterlings without mustard.[222] One day, when he was besieging a little stronghold in which the peasants had taken refuge, the Damoiseau set fire to the crops of the neighbourhood and let them burn all night long, so that he might see more clearly how to place his men.[223]

In 1419 this baron was making war on the brothers Didier and Durand of Saint-Dié. It matters not for what reason. For this war as for every war the villagers had to pay. As the men-at-arms were fighting throughout the whole castellany of Vaucouleurs, the inhabitants of Domremy began to devise means of safety, and in this wise. At Domremy there was a castle built in the meadow at the angle of an island formed by two arms of the river, one of which, the eastern arm, has long since been filled up.[224] Belonging to this castle was a chapel of Our Lady, a courtyard provided with means of defence, and a large garden surrounded by a moat wide and deep. This castle, once the dwelling of the Lords of Bourlémont, was commonly called the

Fortress of the Island. The last of the lords having died without children, his property had been inherited by his niece Jeanne de Joinville. But soon after Jeanne d'Arc's birth she married a Lorraine baron, Henri d'Ogiviller, with whom she went to reside at the castle of Ogiviller and at the ducal court of Nancy. Since her departure the fortress of the island had remained uninhabited. The village folk decided to rent it and to put their tools and their cattle therein out of reach of the plunderers. The renting was put up to auction. A certain Jean Biget of Domremy and Jacques d'Arc, Jeanne's father, being the highest bidders, and having furnished sufficient security, a lease was drawn up between them and the representatives of Dame d'Ogiviller. The fortress, the garden, the courtyard, as well as the meadows belonging to the domain, were let to Jean Biget and Jacques d'Arc for a term of nine years beginning on St. John the Baptist's Day, 1419, and in consideration of a yearly rent of fourteen *livres tournois*[225] and three *imaux* of wheat.[226] Besides the two tenants in chief there were five sub-tenants, of whom the first mentioned was Jacquemin, the eldest of Jacques d'Arc's sons.[227]

The precaution proved to be useful. In that very year, 1419, Robert de Saarbruck and his company met the men of the brothers Didier and Durand at the village of Maxey, the thatched roofs of which were to be seen opposite Greux, on the other bank of the Meuse, along the foot of wooded hills. The two sides here engaged in a battle, in which the victorious Damoiseau took thirty-five prisoners, whom he afterwards liberated after having exacted a high ransom, as was his wont. Among these prisoners was the Squire Thiesselin de Vittel, whose wife had held Jacques d'Arc's second daughter over the baptismal font. From one of the hills of her village, Jeanne, who was then seven or a little older, could see the battle in which her godmother's husband was taken prisoner.[228]

Meanwhile matters grew worse and worse in the kingdom of France. This was well known at Domremy, situated as it was on the highroad, and hearing the news brought by wayfarers.[229] Thus it was that the villagers heard of the murder of Duke John of Burgundy on the Bridge at Montereau, when the Dauphin's Councillors made him pay the price of the blood he had shed in the Rue Barbette. These Councillors, however, struck a bad bargain; for the murder on the Bridge brought their young Prince very low. There followed the war between the Armagnacs and the Burgundians. From this war the English, the obstinate enemies of the kingdom, who for two hundred years had held Guyenne and carried on a prosperous trade there,[230] sucked no small advantage. But Guyenne was far away, and perhaps no one at Domremy knew that it had once been a part of the domain of the kings of France. On the other hand every one was aware that during the recent trouble the English had recrossed the sea and had been welcomed by my Lord Philip, son of the late Duke John. They occupied Normandy, Maine, Picardy, l'Île-de-France, and Paris the great city.[231] Now in France the English were bitterly hated and greatly feared on account of their reputation for cruelty. Not that they were really more wicked than other nations.[232] In Normandy, their king, Henry, had caused women and property to be respected in all places under his dominion. But war is in itself cruel, and whosoever wages war in a country is rightly hated by the people of that country. The English were accused of treachery, and not always wrongly accused, for good faith is rare among men. They were ridiculed in various ways. Playing upon their name in Latin and in French, they were called angels. Now if they were angels they were assuredly bad angels. They denied God, and their favourite oath *Goddam*[233] was so often on their lips that they were called *Godons*. They were devils. They were said to be *coués*, that is, to have tails behind.[234] There was mourning in many a French household when Queen Ysabeau delivered the kingdom of France to the *coués*,[235] making of the noble French lilies a litter for the leopard. Since then, only a few days apart, King Henry V of Lancaster and King Charles VI of Valois, the victorious king and the mad king, had departed to present themselves before God, the Judge of the good and the evil, the just and the unjust, the weak and the powerful. The castellany of Vaucouleurs was French.[236] Dwelling there were clerks and nobles who pitied that later Joash, torn from his enemies in childhood, an orphan spoiled of his heritage, in whom centred the hope of the kingdom. But how can we imagine that poor husbandmen had leisure to ponder on these things? How can we really believe that the peasants of Domremy were loyal to the Dauphin Charles, their lawful lord, while the Lorrainers of Maxey, following their Duke, were on the side of the Burgundians?

Only the river divided Maxey on the right bank from Domremy. The Domremy and Greux children went there to school. There were quarrels between them; the little Burgundians of Maxey fought pitched battles with the little Armagnacs of Domremy. More than once Joan, at the Bridge end in the evening, saw the lads of her village returning covered with blood.[237] It is quite possible that, passionate as she was, she may have gravely espoused these quarrels and conceived therefrom a bitter hatred of the Burgundians. Nevertheless, we must beware of finding an indication of public opinion in these boyish games played by the sons of villeins. For centuries the brats of these two parishes were to fight and to insult each other.[238] Insults and stones fly whenever and wherever children gather in bands, and those of one village meet those of another. The peasants of Domremy, Greux, and Maxey, we may be sure, vexed themselves little about the affairs of dukes and kings. They had learnt to be as much afraid of the captains of their own side as of the captains of the opposite party, and not to draw any distinction between the men-at-arms who were their friends and those who were their enemies.

In 1429 the English occupied the bailiwick of Chaumont and garrisoned several fortresses in Bassigny. Messire Robert, Lord of Baudricourt and Blaise, son of the late Messire Liébault de Baudricourt, was then captain of Vaucouleurs and bailie of Chaumont for the Dauphin Charles. He might be reckoned a great plunderer, even in Lorraine. In the spring of this year, 1420, the Duke of Burgundy having sent an embassy to the Lord Bishop of Verdun, as the ambassadors were returning they were taken prisoners by Sire Robert in league with the Damoiseau of Commercy. To avenge this offence the Duke of Burgundy declared war on the Captain of Vaucouleurs, and the castellany was ravaged by bands of English and Burgundians.[239]

In 1423 the Duke of Lorraine was waging war with a terrible man, one Étienne de Vignolles, a Gascon soldier of fortune already famous under the dreaded name of La Hire,[240] which he was to leave after his death to the knave of hearts in those packs of cards marked by the greasy fingers of many a mercenary. La Hire was nominally on the side of the Dauphin Charles, but in reality he only made war on his own account. At this time he was ravaging Bar west and south, burning churches and laying waste villages.

While he was occupying Sermaize, the church of which was fortified, Jean, Count of Salm, who was governing the Duchy of Bar for the Duke of Lorraine, laid siege to it with two hundred horse. Collot Turlaut, who two years before had married Mengette, daughter of Jean de Vouthon and Jeanne's cousin-german,[241] was killed there by a bomb fired from a Lorraine mortar.

Jacques d'Arc was then the elder (*doyen*) of the community. Many duties fell to the lot of the village elder, especially in troubled times. It was for him to summon the mayor and the aldermen to the council meetings, to cry the decrees, to command the watch day and night, to guard the prisoners. It was for him also to collect taxes, rents, and feudal dues, an ungrateful office in a ruined country.[242]

Under pretence of safeguarding and protecting them, Robert de Saarbruck, Damoiseau of Commercy, who for the moment was Armagnac, was plundering and ransoming the villages belonging to Bar, on the left bank of the Meuse.[243] On the 7th of October, 1423, Jacques d'Arc, as elder, signed below the mayor and sheriff the act by which the Squire extorted from these poor people the annual payment of two *gros* from each complete household and one from each widow's household, a tax which amounted to no less than two hundred and twenty golden crowns, which the elder was charged to collect before the winter feast of Saint-Martin.[244]

The following year was bad for the Dauphin Charles, for the French and Scottish horsemen of his party met with the worst possible treatment at Verneuil. This year the Damoiseau of Commercy turned Burgundian and was none the better or the worse for it.[245] Captain La Hire was still fighting in Bar, but now it was against the young son of Madame Yolande, the Dauphin Charles's brother-in-law, René d'Anjou, who had lately come of age and was now invested with the Duchy of Bar. At the point of the lance Captain La Hire was demanding certain sums of money that the Cardinal Duke of Bar owed him.[246]

At the same time Robert, Sire de Baudricourt, was fighting with Jean de Vergy, lord of Saint-Dizier, Seneschal of Burgundy.[247] It was a fine war. On both sides the combatants laid hands on bread, wine, money, silver-plate, clothes, cattle big and little, and what could not be carried off was burnt. Men, women, and children were put to ransom. In most of the villages of Bassigny agriculture was suspended, nearly all the mills were destroyed.[248]

Ten, twenty, thirty bands of Burgundians were ravaging the castellany of Vaucouleurs, laying it waste with fire and sword. The peasants hid their horses by day, and by night got up to take them to graze. At Domremy life was one perpetual alarm.[249] All day and all night there was a watchman stationed on the square tower of the monastery. Every villager, and, if the prevailing custom were observed, even the priest, took his turn as watchman, peering for the glint of lances through the dust and sunlight down the white ribbon of the road, searching the horrid depths of the wood, and by night trembling to see the villages on the horizon bursting into flame. At the approach of men-at-arms the watchman would ring a noisy peal of those bells, which in turn celebrated births, mourned for the dead, summoned the people to prayer, dispelled storms of thunder and lightning, and warned of danger. Half clothed the awakened villagers would rush to stable, to cattle-shed, and pell-mell drive their flocks and herds to the castle between the two arms of the River Meuse.[250]

One day in the summer of 1425, there fell upon the villages of Greux and Domremy a certain chief of these marauding bands, who was murdering and plundering throughout the land, by name Henri d'Orly, known as Henri de Savoie. This time the island fortress was of no use to the villagers. Lord Henri took all the cattle from the two villages and drove them fifteen or twenty leagues[251] away to his *château* of Doulevant. He had also captured much furniture and other property; and the quantity of it was so great that he could not store it all in one place; wherefore he had part of it carried to Dommartin-le-Franc, a neighbouring village, where there was a *château* with so large a court in front that the place was called Dommartin-la-Cour. The peasants cruelly despoiled were dying of hunger. Happily for them, at the news of this pillage, Dame d'Ogiviller sent to the Count of Vaudémont in his *château* of Joinville, complaining to him, as her kinsman, of the wrong done her, since she was lady of Greux and Domremy. The *château* of Doulevant was under the immediate suzerainty of the Count of Vaudémont. As soon as he received his kinswoman's message he sent a man-at-arms with seven or eight soldiers to recapture the cattle. This man-at-arms, by name Barthélemy de Clefmont, barely twenty years of age, was well skilled in deeds of war. He found the stolen beasts in the *château* of Dommartin-le-Franc, took them and drove them to Joinville. On the way he was pursued and attacked by Lord d'Orly's men and stood in great danger of death. But so valiantly did he defend himself that he arrived safe and sound at Joinville, bringing the cattle, which the Count of Vaudémont caused to be driven back to the pastures of Greux and Domremy.[252]

Unexpected good fortune! With tears the husbandman welcomed his restored flocks and herds. But was he not likely to lose them for ever on the morrow?

At that time Jeanne was thirteen or fourteen. War everywhere around her, even in the children's play; the husband of one of her godmothers taken and ransomed by men-at-arms; the husband of her cousin-german Mengette killed by a mortar;[253] her native land overrun by marauders, burnt, pillaged, laid waste, all the cattle carried off; nights of terror, dreams of horror, – such were the surroundings of her childhood.

CHAPTER II
JEANNE'S VOICES

NOW, when she was about thirteen, it befell one summer day, at noon, that while she was in her father's garden she heard a voice that filled her with a great fear. It came from the right, from towards the church, and at the same time in the same direction there appeared a light. The voice said: "I come from God to help thee to live a good and holy life.[254] Be good, Jeannette, and God will aid thee."

It is well known that fasting conduces to the seeing of visions. Jeanne was accustomed to fast. Had she abstained from food that morning and if so when had she last partaken of it? We cannot say.[255]

On another day the voice spoke again and repeated, "Jeannette, be good."

The child did not know whence the voice came. But the third time, as she listened, she knew it was an angel's voice and she even recognised the angel to be St. Michael. She could not be mistaken, for she knew him well. He was the patron saint of the duchy of Bar.[256] She sometimes saw him on the pillar of church or chapel, in the guise of a handsome knight, with a crown on his helmet, wearing a coat of mail, bearing a shield, and transfixing the devil with his lance.[257] Sometimes he was represented holding the scales in which he weighed souls, for he was provost of heaven and warden of paradise;[258] at once the leader of the heavenly hosts and the angel of judgment.[259] He loved high lands.[260] That is why in Lorraine a chapel had been dedicated to him on Mount Sombar, north of the town of Toul. In very remote times he had appeared to the Bishop of Avranches and commanded him to build a church on Mount Tombe, in such a place as he should find a bull hidden by thieves; and the site of the building was to include the whole area overtrodden by the bull. The Abbey of Mont-Saint-Michel-au-Péril-de-la-Mer was erected in obedience to this command.[261]

About the time when the child was having these visions, the defenders of Mont-Saint-Michel discomfited the English who were attacking the fortress by land and sea. The French attributed this victory to the all-powerful intercession of the archangel.[262] And why should he not have favoured the French who worshipped him with peculiar devoutness? Since my Lord St. Denys had permitted his abbey to be taken by the English, my Lord St. Michael, who carefully guarded his, was in a fair way to become the true patron saint of the kingdom.[263] In the year 1419 the Dauphin Charles had had escutcheons painted, representing St. Michael fully armed, holding a naked sword and in the act of slaying a serpent.[264] The maid of Domremy, however, knew but little of the miracles worked by my Lord St. Michael in Normandy. She recognised the angel by his weapons, his courtesy, and the noble words that fell from his lips.[265]

One day he said to her: "Saint Catherine and Saint Margaret will come to thee. Act according to their advice; for they are appointed to guide thee and counsel thee in all thou hast to do, and thou mayest believe what they shall say unto thee." And these things came to pass as the Lord had ordained.[266]

This promise filled her with great joy, for she loved them both. Madame Sainte Marguerite was highly honoured in the kingdom of France, where she was a great benefactress. She helped women in labour,[267] and protected the peasant at work in the fields. She was the patron saint of flax-spinners, of procurers of wet-nurses, of vellum-dressers, and of bleachers of wool. Her precious relics in a reliquary, carried on a mule's back, were paraded by ecclesiastics through towns and villages. Plenteous alms[268] were showered upon the exhibitors in return for permission to touch the relics. Many times had Jeanne seen Madame Sainte Marguerite at church, painted life-size, a holy-water sprinkler in her hand, her foot on a dragon's head.[269] She was acquainted with her history as it was related in those days, somewhat on the lines of the following narrative.

The blessed Margaret was born at Antioch. Her father, Theodosius, was a priest of the Gentiles. She was put out to nurse and secretly baptised. One day when she was in her fifteenth year, as she was watching the flock belonging to her nurse, the governor Olibrius saw her, and, struck by her great beauty, conceived a great passion for her. Wherefore he said to his servants: "Go, bring me that girl, in order that if she be free I may marry her, or if she be a slave I may take her into my service."

And when she was brought he inquired of her her country, her name, and her religion. She replied that she was called Margaret and that she was a Christian.

And Olibrius said unto her: "How comes it that so noble and beautiful a girl as you can worship Jesus the Crucified?"

And because she replied that Jesus Christ was alive for ever, the governor in wrath had her thrown into prison.

The next day he summoned her to appear before him and said: "Unhappy girl, have pity on your own beauty and for your own sake worship our gods. If you persist in your blindness I will have your body rent in pieces."

And Margaret made answer: "Jesus suffered death for me, and I would fain die for him."

Then the governor commanded her to be hung from the wooden horse, to be beaten with rods, and her flesh to be torn with iron claws. And the blood flowed from the virgin's body as from a pure spring of fresh water.

Those who stood by wept, and the governor covered his face with his cloak that he might not see the blood. And he commanded to unloose her and take her back to prison.

There she was tempted by the Spirit, and she prayed the Lord to reveal to her the enemy whom she had to withstand. Thereupon a huge dragon, appearing before her, rushed forward to devour her, but she made the sign of the cross and he disappeared. Then, in order to seduce her, the devil assumed the form of a man. He came to her gently, took her hands in his and said: "Margaret, what you have done sufficeth." But she seized him by the hair, threw him to the ground, placed her right foot upon his head and cried: "Tremble, proud enemy, thou liest beneath a woman's foot."

The next day, in the presence of the assembled people, she was brought before the judge, who commanded her to sacrifice to idols. And when she refused he had her body burned with flaming pine-wood, but she seemed to suffer no pain. And fearing lest, amazed at this miracle, all the people should be converted, Olibrius commanded that the blessed Margaret should be beheaded. She spoke unto the executioner and said: "Brother, take your axe and strike me." With one blow he struck off her head. Her soul took flight to heaven in the form of a dove.[270]

This story had been told in songs and mysteries.[271] It was so well known that the name of the governor, jestingly vilified and fallen into ridicule, was in common parlance bestowed on braggarts and blusterers. A fool who posed as a wicked person was called *an olibrius*.[272]

Madame Sainte Catherine, whose coming the angel had announced to Jeanne at the same time as that of Madame Sainte Marguerite, was the protectress of young girls and especially of servants and spinsters.

Orators and philosophers too had chosen as their patron saint the virgin who had confounded the fifty doctors and triumphed over the magi of the east. In the Meuse valley rhymed prayers like the following were addressed to her:

Ave, très sainte Catherine,
Vierge pucelle nette et fine.[273]

This fine lady was no stranger to Jeanne; she had her church at Maxey, on the opposite bank of the river; and her name was borne by Isabelle Romée's eldest daughter.[274]

Jeanne certainly did not know the story of Saint Catherine as it was known to illustrious clerks; as, for example, about this time it was committed to writing by Messire Jean Miélot, the secretary of the Duke of Burgundy. Jean Miélot told how the virgin of Alexandria controverted the subtle arguments of Homer, the syllogisms of Aristotle, the very learned reasonings of the famous physicians Æsculapius and Galen, practised the seven liberal arts, and disputed according to the rules of dialectics.[275] Jacques d'Arc's daughter had heard nothing of all that; she knew Saint Catherine from stories out of some history written in the vulgar tongue, in verse or in prose, so many of which were in circulation at that time.[276]

Catherine, daughter of King Costus and Queen Sabinella, as she grew in years, became proficient in the arts, and a skilful embroiderer in silk. While her body was resplendent with beauty, her soul was clouded by the darkness of idolatry. Many barons of the empire sought her in marriage; she scorned them and said: "Find me a husband wise, handsome, noble, and rich." Now in her sleep she had a vision.

Holding the Child Jesus in her arms, the Virgin Mary appeared unto her and said: "Catherine, will you take him for your husband? And you, my sweet son, will you have this virgin for your bride?"

The Child Jesus made answer: "Mother, I will not have her; bid her depart from you, for she is a worshipper of idols. But if she will be baptised I will consent to put the nuptial ring on her finger."

Desiring to marry the King of Heaven, Catherine went to ask for baptism at the hands of the hermit Ananias, who lived in Armenia on Mount Negra. A few days afterwards, when she was praying in her room, she saw Jesus Christ appear in the midst of a numerous choir of angels and of saints. He drew near unto her and placed his ring upon her finger. Then only did Catherine know that her bridal was a spiritual bridal.

In those days Maxentius was Emperor of the Romans. He commanded the people of Alexandria to offer great sacrifices to the idols. Catherine, as she was at prayer in her oratory, heard the chanting of the priests and the bellowing of the victims. Straightway she went to the public square, and beholding Maxentius at the gate of the temple, she said unto him: "How comes it that thou art so foolish as to command this people to offer incense to idols? Thou admirest this temple built by the hands of thy workmen. Thou admirest these ornaments which are but dust blown away by the wind. Thou shouldest rather admire the sky, and the earth, and the sea, and all that is therein. Thou shouldest rather admire the ornaments of the heavens: the sun, the moon, and the stars, and those circling planets, which from the beginning of the world move from the west and return to the east and never grow weary. And when thou hast observed all these things, ask and learn who is their Creator. It is our God, the Lord of Hosts, and the God of gods."

"Woman," replied the emperor, "leave us to finish our sacrifice; afterwards we will make answer unto thee."

And he commanded Catherine to be taken into the palace and strictly guarded, because he marvelled at the great wisdom and the wonderful beauty of this virgin. He summoned fifty doctors well versed in the knowledge of the Egyptians and the liberal arts; and, when they were gathered together, he said unto them: "A maiden of subtle mind maintains that our gods are but demons. I could have forced her to sacrifice or have made her pay the penalty of her disobedience; I judged it better that she should be confounded by the power of your reasoning. If you triumph over her, you will return to your homes laden with honours."

And the wise men made answer: "Let her be brought, that her rashness may be made manifest, that she may confess that never until now has she met men of wisdom."

And when she learned that she was to dispute with wise men, Catherine feared lest she should not worthily defend the gospel of Jesus Christ. But an angel appeared to her and said: "I am the Archangel Saint Michael, sent by God to make known unto thee that from this strife thou shalt come forth victorious and worthy of our Lord Jesus Christ, the hope and crown of those who strive for him."

And the virgin disputed with the doctors. When they maintained that it was impossible for God to become man, and be acquainted with grief, Catherine showed how the birth and passion of Jesus Christ had been announced by the Gentiles themselves, and prophesied by Plato and the Sibyl.

The doctors had nothing to oppose to arguments so convincing. Therefore the chief among them said to the emperor: "Thou knowest that up till now no one has disputed with us without being straightway confounded. But this maid, through whom the Spirit of God speaks, fills us with wonder, and we know nothing nor dare we say anything against Christ. And we boldly confess that if thou hast no stronger arguments to bring forth in favour of the gods, whom hitherto we have worshipped, we will all of us embrace the Christian religion."

On hearing these words, the tyrant was so transported with wrath that he had the fifty doctors burned in the middle of the town. But as a sign that they suffered for the truth, neither their garments nor the hairs of their heads were touched by the fire.

Afterwards Maxentius said unto Catherine: "O virgin, issue of a noble line, and worthy of the imperial purple, take counsel with thy youth, and sacrifice to our gods. If thou dost consent, thou shalt take rank in my palace after the empress, and thy image, placed in the middle of the town, shall be worshipped by all the people like that of a goddess."

But Catherine answered: "Speak not of such things. The very thought of them is sin. Jesus Christ hath chosen me for his bride. He is my love, my glory, and all my delight."

Finding it impossible to flatter her with soft words, the tyrant hoped to reduce her to obedience through fear; therefore he threatened her with death.

Catherine's courage did not waver. "Jesus Christ," she said, "offered himself to his Father as a sacrifice for me; it is my great joy to offer myself as an agreeable sacrifice to the glory of his name."

Straightway Maxentius commanded that she should be scourged with rods, and then cast into a dark dungeon and left there without food. Thereupon, at the call of urgent affairs, Maxentius set out for a distant province.

Now the empress, who was a heathen, had a vision, in which Saint Catherine appeared to her surrounded by a marvellous light. Angels clad in white were with her, and their faces could not be looked upon by reason of the brightness that proceeded from them. And Catherine told the empress to draw near. Taking a crown from the hand of one of the angels who attended her, she placed it upon the head of the empress, saying: "Behold a crown sent down to thee from heaven, in the name of Jesus Christ, my God, and my Lord."

The heart of the empress was troubled by this wonderful dream. Wherefore, attended by Porphyrius, a knight who was commander-in-chief of the army, in the early hours of night she repaired to the prison in which Catherine was confined. Here in her cell a dove brought her heavenly food, and angels dressed the virgin's wounds. The empress and Porphyrius found the dungeon bathed in a light so bright that it filled them with a great fear, and they fell prostrate on the ground. But there straightway filled the dungeon an odour marvellously sweet, which comforted them and gave them courage.

"Arise," said Catherine, "and be not afraid, for Jesus Christ calleth you."

They arose, and beheld Catherine in the midst of a choir of angels. The saint took from the hands of one among them a crown, very beautiful and shining like gold, and she put it upon the empress's head. This crown was the sign of martyrdom. For indeed the names of this queen and of the knight Porphyrius were already written in the book of eternal rewards.

On his return Maxentius commanded Catherine to be brought before him, and said unto her: "Choose between two things: to sacrifice and live, or to die in torment."

Catherine made answer: "It is my desire to offer to Jesus Christ my flesh and my blood. He is my lover, my shepherd, and my husband."

Then the provost of the city of Alexandria, whose name was Chursates, commanded to be made four wheels furnished with very sharp iron spikes, in order that upon these wheels the blessed Catherine should die a miserable and a cruel death. But an angel broke the machine, and with such violence that the parts of it flying asunder killed a great number of the Gentiles. And the empress, who beheld these things from the top of her tower, came down and reproached the emperor for his cruelty. Full of wrath, Maxentius commanded the empress to sacrifice; and when she refused, he commanded her breasts to be torn out and her head to be cut off. And while she was being taken to the torturer, Catherine exhorted her, saying: "Go, rejoice, queen beloved of God, for to-day thou shalt exchange for a perishable kingdom an everlasting empire, and a mortal husband for an immortal lover."

And the empress was taken to suffer death outside the walls. Porphyrius carried away the body and had it buried reverently as that of a servant of Jesus Christ. Wherefore Maxentius had Porphyrius put to death, and his body cast to the dogs. Then, summoning Catherine before him, he said unto her: "Since, by thy magic arts thou hast caused the empress to perish, now if thou repent thou shalt be first in my palace. To-day, therefore, sacrifice to the gods, or thy head shall be struck off."

She made answer: "Do as thou hast resolved that I may take my place in the band of maidens who are around the Lamb of God."

The emperor sentenced her to be beheaded. And when they had led her outside the city of Alexandria, to the place of death, she raised her eyes to heaven and said: "Jesus, hope and salvation of the faithful, glory and beauty of virgins, I pray thee to listen and to answer the prayer of whomsoever, in memory of my martyrdom, shall invoke me in death or in peril whatsoever."

And a voice from heaven made answer: "Come, my beloved bride; the gate of heaven is open to thee. And to those who shall invoke me through thy intercession, I promise help from on high." From the riven neck of the virgin flowed forth milk instead of blood.

Thus Madame Sainte Catherine passed from this world to celestial happiness, on the twenty-fifth day of the month of November, which was a Friday.[277]

My Lord Saint Michael, the Archangel, did not forget his promise. The ladies Saint Catherine and Saint Margaret came as he had said. On their very first visit the young peasant maid vowed to them to preserve her virginity as long as it should please God.[278] If there were any meaning in such a promise, Jeanne, however old she may then have been, could not have been quite a child. And it seems probable that the angel and the saints appeared to her first when she was on the threshold of womanhood, that is, if she ever became a woman.[279]

The saints soon entered into familiar relations with her.[280] They came to the village every day, and often several times a day. When she saw them appear in a ray of light coming down from heaven, shining and clad like queens, with golden crowns on their heads, wearing rich and precious jewels, the village maiden crossed herself devoutly and curtsied low.[281] And because they were ladies of good breeding, they returned her salutation. Each one had her own particular manner of greeting, and it was by this manner that Jeanne distinguished one from the other, for the dazzling light of their countenances rendered it impossible for her to look them in the face. They graciously permitted their earth-born friend to touch their feet, to kiss the hems of their garments, and to inhale rapturously the sweet perfume they emitted.[282] They addressed her courteously,[283] as it seemed to Jeanne. They called the lowly damsel daughter of God. They taught her to live well and go to church. Without always having anything very new to say to her, since they came so constantly, they spoke to her of things which filled her with joy, and, after they had disappeared, Jeanne ardently pressed her lips to the ground their feet had trodden.[284]

Oftentimes she received the heavenly ladies in her little garden, close to the precincts of the church. She used to meet them near the spring; often they even appeared to their little friend surrounded by heavenly companies. "For," Isabelle's daughter used to say, "angels are wont to come down to Christians without being seen, but I see them."[285] It was in the woods, amid the light rustling of the leaves, and especially when the bells rang for matins or compline, that she heard the sweet words most distinctly. And so she loved the sound of the bells, with which her Voices mingled. So, when at nine o'clock in the evening, Perrin le Drapier, sexton of the parish, forgot to ring for compline, she reproached him with his negligence, and scolded him for not doing his duty. She promised him cakes if in the future he would not forget to ring the bells.[286]

She told none of these things to her priest; for this, according to some good doctors, she must be censured, but, according to others equally excellent, she must be commended. For if on the one hand we are to consult our ecclesiastical superiors in matters of faith, on the other, where the gift of the Holy Ghost is poured out, there reigns perfect liberty.[287]

Since the two saints had been visiting Jeanne, my Lord Saint Michael had come less often; but he had not forsaken her. There came a time when he talked to her of love for the kingdom of France, of that love which she felt in her heart.[288]

And the holy visitants, whose voices grew stronger and more ardent as the maiden's soul grew holier and more heroic, revealed to her her mission. "Daughter of God," they said, "thou must leave thy village, and go to France."[289]

Had this idea of a holy militant mission, conceived by Jeanne through the intermediary of her Voices, come into her mind spontaneously without the intervention of any outside will, or had it been suggested to her by some one who was influencing her? It would be impossible to solve this problem were there not a slight indication to direct us. Jeanne at Domremy was acquainted with a prophecy foretelling that France would be ruined by a woman and saved by a maiden.[290] It made an extraordinary impression upon her; and later she came to speak in a manner which proved that she not only believed it, but was persuaded that she herself was the maiden designated by the prophecy.[291] Who taught her this? Some peasant? We have reason to believe that the peasants did not know it, and that it was current among ecclesiastics.[292] Besides, it is important to notice in this connection that Jeanne was acquainted with a particular form of this prophecy, obviously arranged for her benefit, since it specified that the Maiden Redemptress should come from the borders of Lorraine. This local addition is not the work of a cowherd; it suggests rather a mind apt to direct souls and to inspire deeds. It is no longer possible to doubt that the prophecy thus revised is the work of an ecclesiastic whose intentions may be easily divined. Henceforth one is conscious of an idea agitating and possessing the young seer of visions.

On the banks of the Meuse, among the humble folk of the countryside, some churchman, preoccupied with the lot of the poor people of France, directed Jeanne's visions to the welfare of the kingdom and to the conclusion of peace. He carried the ardour of his pious zeal so far as to collect prophecies concerning the salvation of the French crown, and to add to them with an eye to the accomplishment of his design. For such an ecclesiastic we must seek among the priests of Lorraine or Champagne upon whom the national misfortunes imposed cruel sufferings.[293] Merchants and artizans, crushed under the burden of taxes and subsidies, and ruined by changes in the coinage,[294] peasants, whose houses, barns, and mills had been destroyed, and whose fields had been laid waste, no longer contributed to the expenses of public worship.[295] Canons and ecclesiastics, deprived both of their feudal dues and of the contributions of the faithful, quitted the religious houses and set out to beg their bread from door to door, leaving behind in the monasteries only two or three old monks, and a few children. The fortified abbeys attracted captains and soldiers of both sides. They entrenched themselves within the walls; they plundered and burnt. When one of those holy houses succeeded in remaining standing, the wandering village folk made it their place of refuge, and it was impossible to prevent the refectories and dormitories from being invaded by women.[296] In the midst of this obscure throng of souls afflicted by the sufferings and the scandals of the Church may be divined the prophet and the director of the Maid.

We shall not be tempted to recognise him in Messire Guillaume Frontey, priest of Domremy. The successor of Messire Jean Minet, if we may judge from his conversation which has been preserved, was as simple as his flock.[297] Jeanne saw many priests and monks. She was in the habit of visiting her uncle, the priest of Sermaize, and of seeing in the Abbey of Cheminon,[298] her cousin, a young ecclesiastic in minor orders, who was soon to follow her into France. She was in touch with a number of priests who would be very quick to recognise her exceptional piety, and her gift of beholding things invisible to the majority of Christians. They engaged her in conversations, which, had they been preserved, would doubtless present to us one of the sources whence she derived inspiration for her marvellous vocation. One among them, whose name will never be known, raised up an angelic deliverer for the king and the kingdom of France.

Meanwhile Jeanne was living a life of illusion. Knowing nothing of the influences she was under, incapable of recognising in her Voices the echo of a human voice or the promptings of her own heart, she responded timidly to the saints when they bade her fare forth into France: "I am a poor girl, and know not how to ride a horse or how to make war."[299]

As soon as she began to receive these revelations she gave up her games and her excursions. Henceforth she seldom danced round the fairies' tree, and then only in play with the children.[300] It would seem that she also took a dislike to working in the fields, and especially to herding the flocks. From early childhood she had shown signs of piety. Now she gave herself up to extreme devoutness; she confessed frequently, and communicated with ecstatic fervour; she heard mass in her parish church every day. At all hours she was to be found in church, sometimes prostrate on the ground, sometimes with her hands clasped, and her face turned towards the image of Our Lord or of Our Lady. She did not always wait for Saturday to visit the chapel at Bermont. Sometimes, when her parents thought she was tending the herds, she was kneeling at the feet of the miracle-working Virgin. The village priest, Messire Guillaume Frontey, could do nothing but praise the most guileless of his parishioners.[301] One day he happened to say with a sigh: "If Jeannette had money she would give it to me for the saying of masses."[302]

As for the good man, Jacques d'Arc, it is possible that he may have occasionally complained of those pilgrimages, those meditations, and those other practices which ill accorded with the ordinary tenor of country life. Every one thought Jeanne odd and erratic. Mengette and her friends, when they found her so devout, said she was too pious.[303] They scolded her for not dancing with them. Among others, Isabellette, the young wife of Gérardin d'Epinal, the mother of little Nicholas, Jeanne's godson, roundly condemned a girl who cared so little for dancing.[304] Colin, son of Jean Colin, and all the village lads made fun of her piety. Her fits of religious ecstasy raised a smile. She was regarded as a little mad. She suffered from this persistent raillery.[305] But with her own eyes she beheld the dwellers in Paradise. And when they left her she would cry and wish that they had taken her with them.

"Daughter of God, thou must leave thy village and go forth into France."[306]

And the ladies Saint Catherine and Saint Margaret spoke again and said: "Take the standard sent down to thee by the King of Heaven, take it boldly and God will help thee." As she listened to these words of the ladies with the beautiful crowns, Jeanne was consumed with a desire for long expeditions on horseback, and for those battles in which angels hover over the heads of the warriors. But how was she to go to France? How was she to associate with men-at-arms? Ignorant and generously impulsive like herself, the Voices she heard merely revealed to her her own heart, and left her in sad agitation of mind: "I am a poor girl, knowing neither how to bestride a horse nor how to make war."[307]

Jeanne's native village was named after the blessed Remi;[308] the parish church bore the name of the great apostle of the Gauls, who, in baptising King Clovis, had anointed with holy oil the first Christian prince of the noble House of France, descended from the noble King Priam of Troy.

Thus runs the legend of Saint Remi as it was told by churchmen. In those days the pious hermit Montan, who lived in the country of Laon, beheld a choir of angels and an assembly of saints; and he heard a voice full and sweet saying: "The Lord hath looked down upon the earth. That he might hear the groans of them that are in fetters: that he might release the children of the slain: that they may declare the name of the Lord in Sion: and his praise in Jerusalem. When the people assemble together, and kings to serve the Lord.[309] And Cilinia shall bring forth a son for the saving of the people."

Now Cilinia was old, and her husband Emilius was blind. Yet Cilinia, having conceived, brought forth a son; and with the milk with which she nourished her babe she rubbed the eyes of the father, and straightway his eyes were opened, and he saw.

This child, whose birth had been foretold by angels, was called Remi, which, being interpreted, means oar; for by his teaching, as with a well-cut oar, he was to guide the Church of God, and especially the church of Reims, over the stormy sea of life, and by his merits and his prayers bring it into the heaven of eternal salvation.

In retirement and in the practice of holy and Christian observances, Cilinia's son passed his pious youth at Laon. Hardly had he entered his twenty-second year, when the episcopal seat of Reims fell vacant on the death of the blessed Bishop Bennade. An immense concourse of people nominated Remi the shepherd of the flock. He refused a burden which he said was too heavy for the weakness of his youth. But suddenly there fell upon his forehead a ray of celestial light, and a divine liquid was shed upon his hair, and scented it with a strange perfume. Wherefore, without further delay, the bishops of the province of Reims, with one consent, consecrated him their bishop. Established in the seat of Saint Sixtus, the blessed Remi revealed himself liberal in almsgiving, assiduous in vigilance, fervent in prayer, perfect in charity, marvellous in doctrine, and holy in all his conversation. Like a city built on the top of a mountain, he was admired of all men.

In those days, Clovis, King of France, was a heathen, with all his knights. But he had won a great victory over the Germans by invoking the name of Christ. Wherefore, at the entreaty of the saintly Queen Clotilde, his wife, he resolved to ask baptism at the hands of the blessed Bishop of Reims. When this pious desire had been made known to him, Saint Remi taught the King and his subjects that, renouncing Satan and his pomps and his works, they must believe in God and in Jesus Christ his Son. And as the solemn festival of Easter was approaching, he commanded them to fast according to the custom of the faithful. On the day of the Passion of Our Lord, the eve of the day on which Clovis was to be baptised, early in the morning the Bishop went to the King and Queen and led them to an oratory dedicated to the blessed Peter, Prince of the Apostles. Suddenly the chapel was filled with a light so brilliant that the sunshine became as shadow, and from the midst of this light there came a voice saying: "Peace be with you, it is I, fear not and abide in my love." After these words the light faded, but there remained in the chapel an odour of ineffable sweetness. Then, with his face shining like the countenance of Moses, and illuminated within by a divine brightness, the holy Bishop prophesied and said: "Clovis and Clotilde, your descendants shall set back the boundaries of the kingdom. They shall raise the church of Jesus Christ and triumph over foreign nations provided they fall not from virtue and depart not from the way of salvation, neither enter upon the sinful road leading to destruction and to those snares of deadly vices which overthrow empires and cause dominion to pass from one nation to another."

Meanwhile the way is being prepared from the King's palace to the baptistery; curtains and costly draperies are hung up: the houses on each side of the street are covered with hangings; the church is decorated, and the baptistery is strewn with balsam and all manner of sweet-smelling herbs. Overwhelmed with the Lord's favour the people seem already to taste the delights of Paradise. The procession sets out from the palace; the clergy lead with crosses and banners, singing hymns and sacred canticles; then comes the Bishop leading the King by the hand; and lastly the Queen follows with the people. By the way the King asked the Bishop if yonder was the kingdom of God he had promised him. "No," answered the blessed Remi, "but it is the beginning of the road that leads to it." When they had reached the baptistery, the priest who bore the holy chrism was hindered by the crowd from reaching the sacred font; so that, as God had ordained, there was no holy oil for the benediction at the font. Then the Pontiff raises his eyes to heaven, and prays in silence and in tears. Straightway there descends a dove white as snow, bearing in its beak an ampulla full of chrism sent from heaven. The heavenly oil emits a delicious perfume, which intoxicates the multitude with a delight such as they had never experienced before that hour. The holy Bishop takes the ampulla, sprinkles the baptismal water with chrism, and straightway the dove vanishes.

At the sight of so great a miracle of grace, the King, transported with joy, renounces Satan and his pomps and his works. He demands instant baptism, and bends over the fountain of life.[310]

Ever since then the kings of France have been anointed with the divine oil which the dove brought down from heaven. The holy ampulla containing it is kept in the church of Saint Remi at Reims. And by God's grace on the day of the King's anointing this ampulla is always found full.[311]

Such was the clerks' story; and doubtless the peasants of Domremy on a humbler note might have said as much or even more. We may believe that they used to sing the complaint of Saint Remi. Every year, when on the 1st of October the festival of the patron saint came round, the priest was wont to pronounce an eulogium on the saint.[312]

About this time a mystery was performed at Reims in which the miracles of the apostle of Gaul were fully represented.[313]

And among them were some which would appeal strongly to rustic souls. In his mortal life my Lord Saint Remi had healed a blind man possessed of devils. A man bestowed his goods on the chapter of Reims for the salvation of his soul and died; ten years after his death Saint Remi restored him to life, and made him declare his gift. Being entertained by persons who had nothing to drink, the saint filled their cask with miraculous wine. He received from King Clovis the gift of a mill; but when the miller refused to yield it up to him, my Lord Saint Remi, by the power of God, threw down the mill, and cast it into the centre of the earth. One night when the Saint was alone in his chapel, while all his clerks were asleep, the glorious apostles Peter and Paul came down from Paradise to sing matins with him.

Who better than the folk of Domremy should know of the baptism of King Clovis of France, and of the descent of the Holy Ghost, at the singing of Veni Creator Spiritus, bearing in its beak the holy ampulla, full of chrism blessed by Our Lord?[314]

Who better than they should understand the words addressed to the very Christian King, by my Lord Saint Remi, not doubtless in the Church's Latin, but in the good tongue of the people and very much like the following: "Now, Sire, take knowledge and serve God faithfully and judge justly, that thy kingdom may prosper. For if justice depart from it then shall this kingdom be in danger of perdition."[315]

In short, in one way or another, whether through the clerks who directed her or through the peasants among whom she dwelt, Jeanne had knowledge of the good Archbishop Remi, who so dearly cherished the royal blood in the holy ampulla at Reims, and of the anointing of the very Christian kings.[316]

And the Angel appeared unto her and said: "Daughter of God, thou shalt lead the Dauphin to Reims that he may there receive worthily his anointing."[317]

The maid understood. The scales fell from her eyes; a bright light was shed abroad in her mind. Behold wherefore God had chosen her. Through her the Dauphin Charles was to be anointed at Reims. The white dove, which of old was sent to the blessed Remi, was to come down again at the Virgin's call. God, who loves the French, marks their king with a sign, and when there is no sign the royal power has departed. The anointing alone makes the king, and Messire Charles de Valois had not been anointed. Notwithstanding the father lies becrowned and besceptred in the basilica of Saint-Denys in France, the son is but the dauphin and will not enter into his inheritance till the day when the oil of the inexhaustible ampulla shall flow over his forehead. And God has chosen her, a young, ignorant peasant maid, to lead him, through the ranks of his enemies, to Reims, where he shall receive the unction poured upon Saint Louis. Unfathomable ways of God! The humble maid, knowing not how to ride a horse, unskilled in the arts of war, is chosen to bring to Our Lord his temporal vicar of Christian France.

Henceforth Jeanne knew what great deeds she was to bring to pass. But as yet she discerned not the means by which she was to accomplish them.

"Thou must fare forth into France," Saint Catherine and Saint Margaret said to her.

"Daughter of God, thou shalt lead the Dauphin to Reims[318] that he may there receive worthily his anointing," the Archangel Michael said to her.

She must obey them – but how? If at that time there were not just at hand some devout adviser to direct her, one incident quite personal and unimportant, which then occurred in her father's house, may have sufficed to point out the way to the young saint.

Tenant-in-chief of the Castle on the island in 1419, and in 1423 elder of the community, Jacques d'Arc was one of the notables of Domremy. The village folk held him in high esteem and readily entrusted him with difficult tasks. Towards the end of March, 1427, they sent him to Vaucouleurs as their authorised proxy in a lawsuit they were conducting before Robert de Baudricourt. It was a question of the payment of damages required at once from the lord and the inhabitants of Greux and Domremy by a certain Guyot Poignant, of Montigny-le-Roi. These damages went back four years to when, as a return for his protection, the Damoiseau of Commercy had extorted from Greux and Domremy a sum amounting to two hundred and twenty golden crowns.

Guyot Poignant had become security for this sum which had not been paid by the time fixed. The Damoiseau seized Poignant's wood, hay, and horses to the value of one hundred and twenty golden crowns, which amount the said Poignant reclaimed from the nobles and villeins of Greux and Domremy. The suit was still pending in 1427, when the community nominated Jacques d'Arc its authorised proxy, and sent him to Vaucouleurs. The result of the dispute is not known; but it is sufficient to note that Jeanne's father saw Sire Robert and had speech with him.[319]

On his return home he must have more than once related these interviews, and told of the manners and words of so great a personage.

And doubtless Jeanne heard many of these things. Assuredly she must have pricked up her ears at the name of Baudricourt. Then it was that her dazzling friend, the Archangel Knight, came once more to awaken the obscure thought slumbering within her: "Daughter of God," he said, "go thou to the Captain Robert de Baudricourt, in the town of Vaucouleurs, that he may grant unto thee men who shall take thee to the gentle Dauphin."[320]

Resolved to obey faithfully the behest of the Archangel which accorded with her own desire, Jeanne foresaw that her mother, albeit pious, would grant her no aid in her design and that her father would strongly oppose it. Therefore she refrained from confiding it to them.[321]

She thought that Durand Lassois would be the man to give her the succour of which she had need. In consideration of his age she called him uncle, – he was her elder by sixteen years.

Their kinship was by marriage: Lassois had married one Jeanne, daughter of one Le Vauseul, husbandman, and of Aveline, sister of Isabelle de Vouthon, and consequently cousin-german of Isabelle's daughter.[322]

With his wife, his father-in-law, and his mother-in-law, Lassois dwelt at Burey-en-Vaulx, a hamlet of a few homesteads, lying on the left bank of the Meuse, in the green valley, five miles from Domremy, and less than two and a half miles from Vaucouleurs.[323]

Jeanne went to see him, told him of her design, and showed him that she must needs see Sire Robert de Baudricourt. That her kind kinsman might the more readily believe in her, she repeated to him the strange prophecy, of which we have already made mention: "Was it not known of old," she said, "that a woman should ruin the kingdom of France and that a woman should re-establish it?"[324]

This prognostication, it appears, caused Durand Lassois to reflect. Of the two facts foretold therein, the first, the evil one, had come to pass in the town of Troyes, when Madame Ysabeau had given the Kingdom of the Lilies and Madame Catherine of France to the King of England. It only remained to hope that the second, the good, would likewise come to pass. If in the heart of Durand Lassois there were any love for the Dauphin Charles, such must have been his desire; but on this point history is silent.

During this visit to her cousin, Jeanne met with others besides her kinsfolk, the Vouthons and their children. She visited a young nobleman, by name Geoffroy de Foug, who dwelt in the parish of Maxey-sur-Vayse, of which the hamlet of Burey formed part. She confided to him that she wanted to go to France. My Lord Geoffroy did not know much of Jeanne's parents; he was ignorant even of their names. But the damsel seemed to him good, simple, pious, and he encouraged her in her marvellous undertaking.[325] A week after her arrival at Burey she attained her object: Durand Lassois consented to take her to Vaucouleurs.[326]

Before starting she asked a favour from her aunt Aveline who was with child; she said to her: "If the babe you bear is a daughter, call her Catherine in memory of my dead sister."

Catherine, who had married Colin de Greux, had just died.[327]

CHAPTER III

FIRST VISIT TO VAUCOULEURS – FLIGHT TO NEUFCHÂTEAU – JOURNEY TO TOUL – SECOND VISIT TO VAUCOULEURS

ROBERT de Baudricourt, who in those days commanded the town of Vaucouleurs for the Dauphin Charles, was the son of Liébault de Baudricourt deceased, once chamberlain of Robert, Duke of Bar, governor of Pont-à-Mousson, and of Marguerite d'Aunoy, Lady of Blaise in Bassigny. Fourteen or fifteen years earlier he had succeeded his two uncles, Guillaume, the Bastard of Poitiers, and Jean d'Aunoy as Bailie of Chaumont and Commander of Vaucouleurs. His first wife had been a rich widow; after her death he had married, in 1425, another widow, as rich as the first, Madame Alarde de Chambley. And it is a fact that the peasants of Uruffe and of Gibeaumex stole the cart carrying the cakes ordered for the wedding feast. Sire Robert was like all the warriors of his time and country; he was greedy and cunning; he had many friends among his enemies and many enemies among his friends; he fought now for his own side, now against it, but always for his own advantage. For the rest he was no worse than his fellows, and one of the least stupid.[328]

Clad in a poor red gown,[329] but her heart bright with mystic love, Jeanne climbed the hill dominating the town and the valley. Without any difficulty she entered the castle, for its gates were opened as freely as if it had been a fair; and she was led into the hall where was Sire Robert among his men-at-arms. She heard the Voice saying to her: "That is he!"[330] And immediately she went straight to him, and spoke to him fearlessly, beginning, doubtless, by saying what she deemed to be most urgent: "I am come to you, sent by Messire," she said, "that you may send to the Dauphin and tell him to hold himself in readiness, but not to give battle to his enemies."[331]

Assuredly she must thus have spoken, prompted by a new revelation from her Voices. And it is important to notice that she repeated word for word what had been said seventy-five years earlier, not far from Vaucouleurs, by a peasant of Champagne who was a vavasour, that is, a freeman. This peasant's career had begun like Jeanne's, but had come to a much more abrupt conclusion. Jacques d'Arc's daughter had not been the first to say that revelations had been made to her concerning the war. Periods of great distress are the times when inspired persons most commonly appear. Thus it came to pass that in the days of the Plague and of the Black Prince the vavasour of Champagne heard a voice coming forth from a beam of light.

While he was at work in the fields the voice had said to him: "Go thou, and warn John, King of France, that he fight not against any of his enemies." It was a few days before the Battle of Poitiers.[332]

Then the counsel was wise; but in the month of May, 1428, it seemed less wise, and appeared to have little bearing on the state of affairs at that time. Since the disaster of Verneuil, the French had not felt equal to giving battle to their enemies; and they were not thinking of it. Towns were taken and lost, skirmishes were fought, sallies were attempted, but the enemy was not engaged in pitched battles. There was no need to restrain the Dauphin Charles, whom in those days nature and fortune rendered unadventurous.[333] About the time that Jeanne was uttering these words before Sire Robert, the English in France were preparing an expedition, and were hesitating, unable to decide whether to march on Angers or on Orléans.[334]

Jeanne gave utterance according to the promptings of her Archangel and her Saints, and touching warfare and the condition of the kingdom they knew neither more nor less than she. But it is not surprising that those who believe themselves sent by God should ask to be waited for. And again in the damsel's fear lest the French knights should once more give battle after their own guise there was much of the sound common sense of the people. They were only too well acquainted with knightly warfare.

Perfectly calm and self-possessed, Jeanne went on and uttered a prophecy concerning the Dauphin: "Before mid Lent my Lord will grant him aid." Then straightway she added: "But in very deed the realm belongs not to the Dauphin. Nonetheless it is Messire's will that the Dauphin should be king and receive the kingdom in trust – *en commande*.[335] Notwithstanding his enemies, the Dauphin shall be king; and it is I who shall lead him to his anointing."

Doubtless the title Messire, in the sense in which she employed it, sounded strange and obscure, since Sire Robert, failing to understand it, asked: "Who is Messire?"

"The King of Heaven," the damsel answered.

She had made use of another term, concerning which, as far as we know, Sire Robert made no remark; and yet it is suggestive.[336]

That word *commande* employed in matters connected with inheritance signified something given in trust.[337] If the King received the kingdom *en commande* he would merely hold it in trust. Thus the maid's utterance agreed with the views of the most pious concerning Our Lord's government of kingdoms. By herself she could not have happened on the word or the idea; she had obviously been instructed by one of those churchmen whose influence we have discerned already[338] in the Lorraine prophecy, but the trace of whom has completely vanished.

Touching things spiritual Jeanne held converse with several priests; among others with Messire Arnolin, of Gondrecourt-le-Château, and Messire Dominique Jacob, priest of Moutier-sur-Saulx, who was her confessor.[339] It is a pity we do not know what these ecclesiastics thought of the insatiable cruelty of the English, of the pride of my Lord Duke of Burgundy, of the misfortunes of the Dauphin, and whether they did not hope that one day Our Lord Jesus Christ at the prayer of the common folk would condescend to grant the kingdom *en commande* to Charles, son of Charles. It was possibly from one of these that Jeanne derived her theocratic ideas.[340]

While she was speaking to Sire Robert there was present, and not by chance merely, a certain knight of Lorraine, Bertrand de Poulengy, who possessed lands near Gondrecourt and held an office in the provostship of Vaucouleurs.[341] He was then about thirty-six years of age. He was a man who associated with churchmen; at least he was familiar with the manner of speech of devout persons.[342] Perhaps he now saw Jeanne for the first time; but he must certainly have heard of her; and he knew her to be good and pious. Twelve years before he had frequently visited Domremy; he knew the country well; he had sat beneath *l'Arbre des Dames*, and had been several times to the house of

Jacques d'Arc and Romée, whom he held to be good honest farmer folk.[343]

It may be that Bertrand de Poulengy was struck by the damsel's speech and bearing; it is more likely that the knight was in touch with certain ecclesiastics unknown to us, who were instructing the peasant seeress with an eye to rendering her better able to serve the realm of France and the Church. However that may be, in Bertrand she had a friend who was to be her strong support in the future.

For the nonce, however, if our information be correct, he did nothing and spoke not a word. Perhaps he judged it best to wait until the commander of the town should be ready to grant a more favourable hearing to the saint's request. Sire Robert understood nothing of all this; one point only appeared plain to him, that Jeanne would make a fine camp-follower and that she would be a great favourite with the men-at-arms.[344]

In dismissing the villein who had brought her, he gave him a piece of advice quite in keeping with the wisdom of the time concerning the chastising of daughters: "Take her back to her father and box her ears well."

Sire Robert held such discipline to be excellent, for more than once he urged Uncle Lassois to take Jeanne home well whipped.[345]

After a week's absence she returned to the village. Neither the Captain's contumely nor the garrison's insults had humiliated or discouraged her. Imagining that her Voices had foretold them,[346] she held them to be proofs of the truth of her mission. Like those who walk in their sleep she was calm in the face of obstacles and yet quietly persistent. In the house, in the garden, in the meadow, she continued to sleep that marvellous slumber, in which she dreamed of the Dauphin, of his knights, and of battles with angels hovering above.

She found it impossible to be silent; on all occasions her secret escaped from her. She was always prophesying, but she was never believed. On St. John the Baptist's Eve, about a month after her return, she said sententiously to Michel Lebuin, a husbandman of Burey, who was quite a boy: "Between Coussey and Vaucouleurs is a girl who in less than a year from now will cause the Dauphin to be anointed King of France."[347]

One day meeting Gérardin d'Epinal, the only man at Domremy not of the Dauphin's party, whose head according to her own confession she would willingly have cut off, although she was godmother to his son, she could not refrain from announcing even to him in veiled words her mystic dealing with God: "Gossip, if you were not a Burgundian there is something I would tell you."[348]

The good man thought it must be a question of an approaching betrothal and that Jacques d'Arc's daughter was about to marry one of the lads with whom she had broken bread under *l'Arbre des Fées* and drunk water from the Gooseberry Spring.

Alas! how greatly would Jacques d'Arc have desired the secret to be of that nature. This upright man was very strict; he was careful concerning his children's conduct; and Jeanne's behaviour caused him anxiety. He knew not that she heard Voices. He had no idea that all day Paradise came down into his garden, that from Heaven to his house a ladder was let down, on which there came and went without ceasing more angels than had ever trodden the ladder of the Patriarch Jacob; neither did he imagine that for Jeannette alone, without any one else perceiving it, a mystery was being played, a thousand times richer and finer than those which on feast days were acted on platforms, in towns like Toul and Nancy. He was miles away from suspecting such incredible marvels. But what he did see was that his daughter was losing her senses, that her mind was wandering, and that she was giving utterance to wild words. He perceived that she could think of nothing but cavalcades and battles. He must have known something of the escapade at Vaucouleurs. He was terribly afraid that one day the unhappy child would go off for good on her wanderings. This agonising anxiety haunted him even in his sleep. One night he dreamed that he saw her fleeing with men-at-arms; and this dream was so vivid that he remembered it when he awoke. For several days he said over and over again to his sons, Jean and Pierre: "If I really believed that what I dreamed of my daughter would ever come true, I would rather see her drowned by you; and if you would not do it I would drown her myself."[349]

Isabelle repeated these words to her daughter hoping that they might alarm her and cause her to correct her ways. Devout as she was, Jeanne's mother shared her father's fears. The idea that their daughter was in danger of becoming a worthless creature was a cruel thought to these good people. In those troubled times there was a whole multitude of these wild women whom the men-at-arms carried with them on horseback. Each soldier had his own.

It is not uncommon for saints in their youth by the strangeness of their behaviour to give rise to such suspicions. And Jeanne displayed those signs of sainthood. She was the talk of the village. Folk pointed at her mockingly, saying: "There goes she who is to restore France and the royal house."[350]

The neighbours had no difficulty in finding a cause for the strangeness which possessed the damsel. They attributed it to some magic spell. She had been seen beneath the *Beau Mai* bewreathing it with garlands. The old beech was known to be haunted as well as the spring near by. It was well known, too, that the fairies cast spells. There were those who discovered that Jeanne had met a wicked fairy there. "Jeannette has met her fate beneath *l'Arbre des Fées*,"[351] they said. Would that none but peasants had believed that story!

On the 22nd of June, from the Duke of Bedford, Regent of France for Henry VI, Antoine de Vergy, Governor of Champagne, received a commission to furnish forth a thousand men-at-arms for the purpose of bringing the castellany of Vaucouleurs into subjection to the English. Three weeks later, commanded by the two Vergy, Antoine and Jean, the little company set forth. It consisted of four knights-banneret, fourteen knights-bachelor, and three hundred and sixty-three men-at-arms. Pierre de Trie, commander of Beauvais, Jean, Count of Neufchâtel and Fribourg, were ordered to join the main body.[352]

On the march, as was his custom, Antoine de Vergy laid waste all the villages of the castellany with fire and sword. Threatened once again with a disaster with which they were only too well acquainted, the folk of Domremy and Greux already beheld their cattle captured, their barns set on fire, their wives and daughters ravished. Having experienced before that the Castle on the Island was not secure enough, they determined to flee and seek refuge in their market town of Neufchâteau, only five miles away from Domremy. Thus they set out towards the middle of July. Abandoning their houses and fields and driving their cattle before them, they followed the road, through the fields of wheat and rye and up the vine-clad hills to the town, wherein they lodged as best they could.[353]

The d'Arc family was taken in by the wife of Jean Waldaires, who was called La Rousse. She kept an inn, where lodged soldiers, monks, merchants, and pilgrims. There were some who suspected her of harbouring bad women.[354] And there is reason to believe that certain of her women customers were of doubtful reputation. Albeit she herself was of good standing, that is to say, she was rich. She had money enough to lend sometimes to her fellow-citizens.[355] Although Neufchâteau belonged to the Duke of Lorraine, who was of the Burgundian party, it has been thought that the hostess of this inn inclined towards the Armagnacs; but it is vain to attempt to discover the sentiments of La Rousse concerning the troubles of the kingdom of France.[356]

At Neufchâteau as at Domremy Jeanne drove her father's beasts to the field and kept his flocks.[357] Handy and robust she used also to help La Rousse in her household duties.[358] This circumstance gave rise to the malicious report set on foot by the Burgundians that she had been serving maid in an inn frequented by drunkards and bad women.[359] The truth is that Jeanne, when she was not tending the cattle, and helping her hostess, passed all her time in church.[360]

There were two fine religious houses in the town, one belonging to the Grey Friars, the other to the Sisters of St. Claire, the sons and daughters of good St. Francis.[361] The monastery of the Grey Friars had been built two hundred years earlier by Mathieu II of Lorraine. The reigning duke had recently added richly to its endowments. Noble ladies, great lords, and among others a Bourlémont lord of Domremy and Greux lay there beneath brasses.[362]

In the flower of their history these mendicant monks of old had welcomed to their third order crowds of citizens and peasants as well as multitudes of princes and kings.[363] Now they languished corrupt and decadent among the French friars. Quarrels and schisms were frequent. Notwithstanding Colette of Corbie's attempted restoration of the rule, the old discipline was nowhere observed.[364] These mendicants distributed leaden medals, taught short prayers to serve as charms, and vowed special devotion to the holy name of Jesus.[365]

During the fortnight Jeanne spent in the town of Neufchâteau,[366] she frequented the church of the Grey Friars monastery, and two or three times confessed to brethren of the order.[367] It has been stated that she belonged to the third order of St. Francis, and the inference has been drawn that her affiliation dated from her stay at Neufchâteau.[368]

Such an inference is very doubtful; and in any case the affiliation cannot have been very ceremonious. It is difficult to see how in so short a time the friars could have instructed her in the practices of Franciscan piety. She was far too imbued with ecclesiastical notions concerning the spiritual and the temporal power, she was too full of mysteries and revelations to imbibe their spirit. Besides, her sojourn at Neufchâteau was troubled by anxiety and broken by absences.

In this town she received a summons to appear before the official of Toul, in whose jurisdiction she was, as a native of Domremy-de-Greux. A young bachelor of Domremy alleged that a promise of marriage had been given him by Jacques d'Arc's daughter. Jeanne denied it. He persisted in his statement, and summoned her to appear before the official.[369] To this ecclesiastical tribunal such cases belonged; it pronounced judgment on questions of nullity of marriage or validity of betrothal.

The curious part of Jeanne's case is that her parents were against her, and on the side of the young man. It was in defiance of their wishes that she defended the suit and appeared before the official. Later she declared that in this matter she had disobeyed them, and that it was the only time she had failed in the submission she owed her parents.[370]

The journey from Neufchâteau to Toul and back involved travelling more than twenty leagues on foot, over roads infested with bands of armed men, through a country desolated by fire and sword, from which the peasants of Domremy had recently fled in a panic. To such a journey, however, she made up her mind against the will of her parents.

Possibly she may have appeared before the judge at Toul, not once but two or three times. And there was a great chance of her having to journey day and night with her so-called betrothed, for he was passing over the same road at the same time. Her Voices bade her fear nothing. Before the judge she swore to speak the truth, and denied having made any promise of marriage.

She had done nothing wrong. But an evil interpretation was set upon conduct which proceeded alone from an innocence both singular and heroic. At Neufchâteau it was said that on those journeys she had consumed all her substance. But what was her substance? Alas! she had set out with nothing. She may have been driven to beg her bread from door to door. Saints receive alms as they give them: for the love of God. There was a story that her betrothed seeing her living during the trial in company with bad women, had abandoned his demand for justice, renouncing a bride of such bad repute.[371] Such calumnies were only too readily believed.

After a fortnight's sojourn at Neufchâteau, Jacques d'Arc and his family returned to Domremy. The orchard, the house, the monastery, the village, the fields, – in what a state of desolation did they behold them! The soldiers had plundered, ravaged, burnt everything. Unable to exact ransom from the villeins who had taken flight, the men-at-arms had destroyed all their goods. The monastery once as proud as a fortress, with its watchman's tower, was now nothing but a heap of blackened ruins. And now on holy days the folk of Domremy must needs go to hear mass in the church of Greux.[372]

So full of danger were the times that the villagers were ordered to keep in fortified houses and castles.[373]

Meanwhile the English were laying siege to the town of Orléans, which belonged to their prisoner Duke Charles. By so doing they acted badly, for, having possession of his body, they ought to have respected his property.[374] They built fortified towers round the city of Orléans, the very heart of France; and it was said that they had entrenched themselves there in great strength.[375] Now Saint Catherine and Saint Margaret loved the Land of the Lilies; they were the sworn friends and gentle cousins of the Dauphin Charles. They talked to the shepherd maid of the misfortunes of the kingdom and continued to say: "Leave thy village and go into France."[376]

Jeanne was all the more impatient to set forth because she had herself announced the time of her arrival in France, and that time was drawing near. She had told the Commander of Vaucouleurs that succour should come to the Dauphin before mid Lent. She did not want to make her Voices lie.[377]

Towards the middle of January occurred the opportunity she was looking for of returning to Burey. At this time Durand Lassois' wife, Jeanne le Vauseul, was brought to bed.[378] It was the custom in the country for the young kinswomen and friends of the mother to attend and wait upon her and her babe. A good and kindly custom, followed all the more readily because of the opportunity it gave of pleasant meetings and cheerful gossip.[379] Jeanne urged her uncle to ask her father that she might be sent to tend the sick woman, and Lassois consented: he was always ready to do what his niece asked him, and perhaps his complaisance was encouraged by pious persons of some importance.[380] But how this father, who shortly before had said that he would throw his daughter into the Meuse rather than that she should go off with men-at-arms, should have allowed her to go to the gates of the town, protected by a kinsman of whose weakness he was well aware, is hard to understand. However so he did.[381]

Leaving the home of her childhood, which she was never to see again, Jeanne, in company with Durand Lassois, passed down her native valley in its winter bareness. As she went by the house of the husbandman Gérard Guillemette of Greux, whose children and Jacques d'Arc's were great friends, she cried: "Good-bye! I am going to Vaucouleurs."[382]

A few paces further she saw her friend Mengette: "Good-bye, Mengette," she said. "God bless thee."[383]

And by the way, on the doorsteps of the houses, whenever she saw faces she knew, she bade them farewell.[384] But she avoided Hauviette with whom she had played and slept in childhood and whom she dearly loved. If she were to bid her good-bye she feared that her heart would fail her. It was not till later that Hauviette heard of her friend's departure and then she wept bitterly.[385]

On her second arrival at Vaucouleurs, Jeanne imagined that she was setting foot in a town belonging to the Dauphin, and, in the language of the day, entering the royal antechamber.[386] She was mistaken. Since the beginning of August, 1428, the Commander of Vaucouleurs had yielded the fortress to Antoine de Vergy, but had not yet surrendered it to him.

It was one of those promises to capitulate at the end of a given time. They were not uncommon in those days, and they ceased to be valid if the fortress were relieved before the day fixed for its surrender.[387]

Jeanne went to Sire Robert in his castle just as she had done nine months before; and this was the revelation she made to him: "My Lord Captain," she said, "know that God has again given me to wit, and commanded me many times to go to the gentle Dauphin, who must be and who is the true King of France, and that he shall grant me men-at-arms with whom I shall raise the siege of Orléans and take him to his anointing at Reims."[388]

This time she announces that it is her mission to deliver Orléans. And the anointing is not to come to pass until this the first part of her task shall have been accomplished. We cannot fail to recognise the readiness and the tact with which the Voices altered their commands previously given, according to the necessities of the moment. Robert's manner towards Jeanne had completely changed. He said nothing about boxing her ears and sending her back to her parents. He no longer treated her roughly; and if he did not believe her announcement at least he listened to it readily.

In one of her conversations with him she spoke of strange matters: "Once I have accomplished the behest Messire has given me, I shall marry and I shall bear three sons, the eldest of whom shall be pope, the second emperor, and the third king."

Sire Robert answered gayly: "Since thy sons are to be such great personages, I should like to give thee one. Thereby should I myself have honour."

Jeanne replied: "Nay, gentle Robert, nay. It is not yet time. The Holy Ghost shall appoint the time."[389]

To judge from the few of her words handed down to us, in the early days of her mission the young prophetess spoke alternately two different languages. Her speech seemed to flow from two distinct sources. The one ingenuous, candid, naïve, concise, rustically simple, unconsciously arch, sometimes rough, alike chivalrous and holy, generally bearing on the inheritance and the anointing of the Dauphin and the confounding of the English. This was the language of her Voices, her own, her soul's language. The other, more subtle, flavoured with allegory and flowers of speech, critical with scholastic grace, bearing on the Church, suggesting the clerk and betraying some outside influence. The words she uttered to Sire Robert touching the children she should bear are of the second sort. They are an allegory. Her triple birth signifies that the peace of Christendom shall be born of her work, that after she shall have fulfilled her divine mission, the Pope, the Emperor, and the King – all three sons of God – shall cause concord and love to reign in the Church of Jesus Christ. The apologue is quite clear; and yet a certain amount of intelligence is necessary for its comprehension. The Captain failed to understand it; he interpreted it literally and answered accordingly, for he was a simple fellow and a merry.[390]

Jeanne lodged in the town with humble folk, Henri Leroyer and his wife Catherine, friends of her cousin Lassois. She used to occupy her time in spinning, being a good spinster; and the little she had she gave to the poor. With Catherine she went to the parish church.[391] In the morning, in her most devout moods, she would climb the hill, round the foot of which cluster the roofs of the town, and enter the chapel of Sainte Marie-de-Vaucouleurs. This collegiate church, built in the reign of Philippe VI, adjoined the *château* wherein dwelt the Commander of Vaucouleurs. The venerable stone nave rose up boldly towards the east, overlooking the vast extent of hills and meadows, and dominating the valley where Jeanne had been born and bred. She used to hear mass and remain long in prayer.[392]

Under the chapel, in the crypt, there was an image of the Virgin, ancient and deeply venerated, called Notre-Dame-de-la-Voûte.[393] It worked miracles, but especially on behalf of the poor and needy. Jeanne delighted to remain in this dark and lonely crypt, where the saints preferred to visit her.

One day a young clerk, barely more than a child, who waited in the chapel, saw the damsel motionless, with hands clasped, head thrown back, eyes full of tears raised to heaven; and as long as he lived the vision of that rapture remained imprinted on his mind.[394]

She confessed often, usually to Jean Fournier, priest of Vaucouleurs.[395]

Her hostess was touched by the goodness and gentleness of her manner of life; but she was profoundly agitated when one day the damsel said to her: "Dost thou not know it hath been prophesied that France ruined by a woman shall be saved by a maiden from the Lorraine Marches?"

Leroyer's wife knew as well as Durand Lassois that Madame Ysabeau, as full of wickedness as Herodias, had delivered up Madame Catherine of France and the Kingdom of the Lilies to the King of England. And henceforth she was almost persuaded to believe that Jeanne was the maid announced by the prophecy.[396]

This pious damsel held converse with devout persons and also with men of noble rank. To all alike she said: "I must to the gentle Dauphin. It is the will of Messire, the King of Heaven, that I wend to the gentle Dauphin. I am sent by the King of Heaven. I must go even if I go on my knees."[397]

Revelations of this nature she made to Messire Aubert, Lord of Ourches. He was a good Frenchman and of the Armagnac party, since four years earlier he had made war against the English and Burgundians. She told him that she must go to the Dauphin, that she demanded to be taken to him, and that to him should redound profit and honour incomparable.

91

At length through her illuminations and her prophecies, her fame was spread abroad in the town; and her words were found to be good.[398]

In the garrison there was a man-at-arms of about twenty-eight years of age, Jean de Novelompont or Nouillompont, who was commonly called Jean de Metz. By rank a freeman, albeit not of noble estate, he had acquired or inherited the lordship of Nouillompont and Hovecourt, situate in that part of Barrois which was outside the Duke's domain; and he bore its name.[399] Formerly in the pay of Jean de Wals, Captain and Provost of Stenay, he was now, in 1428, in the service of the Commander of Vaucouleurs.

Of his morals and manner of life we know nothing, except that three years before he had sworn a vile oath and been condemned to pay a fine of two *sols*.[400] Apparently when he took the oath he was in great wrath.[401] He was more or less intimate with Bertrand de Poulengy, who had certainly spoken to him of Jeanne.

One day he met the damsel and said to her: "Well, *ma mie*, what are you doing here? Must the King be driven from his kingdom and we all turn English?"[402]

Such words from a young Lorraine warrior are worthy of notice. The Treaty of Troyes did not subject France to England; it united the two kingdoms. If war continued after as before, it was merely to decide between the two claimants, Charles de Valois and Henry of Lancaster. Whoever gained the victory, nothing would be changed in the laws and customs of France. Yet this poor freebooter of the German Marches imagined none the less that under an English king he would be an Englishman. Many French of all ranks believed the same and could not suffer the thought of being Anglicised; in their minds their own fates depended on the fate of the kingdom and of the Dauphin Charles.

Jeanne answered Jean de Metz: "I came hither to the King's territory to speak with Sire Robert, that he may take me or command me to be taken to the Dauphin; but he heeds neither me nor my words."

Then, with the fixed idea welling up in her heart that her mission must be begun before the middle of Lent: "Notwithstanding, ere mid Lent, I must be before the Dauphin, were I in going to wear my legs to the knees."[403]

A report ran through the towns and villages. It was said that the son of the King of France, the Dauphin Louis, who had just entered his fifth year, had been recently betrothed to the daughter of the King of Scotland, the three-year-old Madame Margaret, and the common people celebrated this royal union with such rejoicings as were possible in a desolated country.[404] Jeanne, when she heard these tidings, said to the man-at-arms: "I must go to the Dauphin, for no one in the world, no king or duke or daughter of the King of Scotland, can restore the realm of France."

Then straightway she added: "In me alone is help, albeit for my part, I would far rather be spinning by my poor mother's side, for this life is not to my liking. But I must go; and so I will, for it is Messire's command that I should go."

She said what she thought. But she did not know herself; she did not know that her Voices were the cries of her own heart, and that she longed to quit the distaff for the sword.

Jean de Metz asked, as Sire Robert had done: "Who is Messire?"

"He is God," she replied.

Then straightway, as if he believed in her, he said with a sudden impulse: "I promise you, and I give you my word of honour, that God helping me I will take you to the King."

He gave her his hand as a sign that he pledged his word and asked: "When will you set forth?"

"This hour," she answered, "is better than to-morrow; to-morrow is better than after to-morrow."

Jean de Metz himself, twenty-seven years later, reported this conversation.[405] If we are to believe him, he asked the damsel in conclusion whether she would travel in her woman's garb. It is easy to imagine what difficulties he would foresee in journeying with a peasant girl clad in a red frock over French roads infested with lecherous fellows, and that he would deem it wiser for her to disguise herself as a boy. She promptly divined his thought and replied: "I will willingly dress as a man."[406]

There is no reason why these things should not have occurred. Only if they did, then a Lorraine freebooter suggested to the saint that idea concerning her dress which later she will think to have received from God.[407]

93

Of his own accord, or rather, acting by the advice of some wise person, Sire Robert desired to know whether Jeanne was not being inspired by an evil spirit. For the devil is cunning and sometimes assumes the mark of innocence. And as Sire Robert was not learned in such matters, he determined to take counsel with his priest.

Now one day when Catherine and Jeanne were at home spinning, they beheld the Commander coming accompanied by the priest, Messire Jean Fournier. They asked the mistress of the house to withdraw; and when they were left alone with the damsel, Messire Jean Fournier put on his stole and pronounced some Latin words which amounted to saying: "If thou be evil, away with thee; if thou be good, draw nigh."[408]

It was the ordinary formula of exorcism or, to be more exact, of conjuration. In the opinion of Messire Jean Fournier these words, accompanied by a few drops of holy water, would drive away devils, if there should unhappily be any in the body of this village maiden.

Messire Jean Fournier was convinced that devils were possessed by an uncontrollable desire to enter the bodies of men, and especially of maidens, who sometimes swallowed them with their bread. They dwelt in the mouth under the tongue, in the nostrils, or penetrated down the throat into the stomach. In these various abodes their action was violent; and their presence was discerned by the contortions and howlings of the miserable victims who were possessed.

Pope St. Gregory, in his Dialogues, gives a striking example of the facility with which devils insinuate themselves into women. He tells how a nun, being in the garden, saw a lettuce which she thought looked tender. She plucked it, and, neglecting to bless it by making the sign of the cross, she ate of it and straightway fell possessed. A man of God having drawn near unto her, the demon began to cry out: "It is I! It is I who have done it! I was seated upon that lettuce. This woman came and she swallowed me." But the prayers of the man of God drove him out.[409]

The caution required in such a matter was therefore not exaggerated by Messire Jean Fournier. Possessed by the idea that the devil is subtle and woman corrupt, carefully and according to prescribed rules he proceeded to solve a difficult problem. It was generally no easy matter to recognise one possessed by the devil and to distinguish between a demoniac and a good Christian. Very great saints had not been spared the trial to which Jeanne was to be subjected.

Having recited the formula and sprinkled the holy water, Messire Jean Fournier expected, if the damsel were possessed, to see her struggle, writhe, and endeavour to take flight. In such a case he must needs have made use of more powerful formulæ, have sprinkled more holy water, and made more signs of the cross, and by such means have driven out the devils until they were seen to depart with a terrible noise and a noxious odour, in the shape of dragons, camels, or fish.[410]

There was nothing suspicious in Jeanne's attitude. No wild agitation, no frenzy. Merely anxious and intreating, she dragged herself on her knees towards the priest. She did not flee before God's holy name. Messire Jean Fournier concluded that no devil was within her.

Left alone in the house with Catherine, Jeanne, who now understood the meaning of the ceremony, showed strong resentment towards Messire Jean Fournier. She reproached him with having suspected her: "It was wrong of him," she said to her hostess, "for, having heard my confession, he ought to have known me."[411]

She would have thanked the priest of Vaucouleurs had she known how he was furthering the fulfilment of her mission by subjecting her to this ordeal. Convinced that this maiden was not inspired by the devil, Sire Robert must have been driven to conclude that she might be inspired by God; for apparently he was a man of simple reasoning. He wrote to the Dauphin Charles concerning the young saint; and doubtless he bore witness to the innocence and goodness he beheld in her.[412]

Although it looked as if the Captain would have to resign his command to my Lord de Vergy, Sire Robert did not intend to quit his country where he had dealings with all parties. Indeed he cared little enough about the Dauphin Charles, and it is difficult to see what personal interest he can have had in recommending him a prophetess. Without pretending to discover what was passing in his mind, one may believe that he wrote to the Dauphin on Jeanne's behalf at the request of some of those persons who thought well of her, probably of Bertrand de Poulengy and of Jean de Metz. These two men-at-arms, seeing that the Dauphin's cause was lost in the Lorraine Marches, had every reason for proceeding to the banks of the Loire, where they might still fight with the hope of advantage.

On the eve of setting out, they appeared disposed to take the seeress with them, and even to defray all her expenses, reckoning on repaying themselves from the royal coffers at Chinon, and deriving honour and advantage from so rare a marvel. But they waited to be assured of the Dauphin's consent.[413]

Meanwhile Jeanne could not rest. She came and went from Vaucouleurs to Burey and from Burey to Vaucouleurs. She counted the days; time dragged for her as for a woman with child.[414]

At the end of January, feeling she could wait no longer, she resolved to go to the Dauphin Charles alone. She clad herself in garments belonging to Durand Lassois, and with this kind cousin set forth on the road to France.[415] A man of Vaucouleurs, one Jacques Alain, accompanied them.[416] Probably these two men expected that the damsel would herself realise the impossibility of such a journey and that they would not go very far. That is what happened. The three travellers had barely journeyed a league from Vaucouleurs, when, near the Chapel of Saint Nicholas, which rises in the valley of Septfonds, in the middle of the great wood of Saulcy, Jeanne changed her mind and said to her comrades that it was not right of her to set out thus. Then they all three returned to the town.[417]

At length a royal messenger brought King Charles's reply to the Commander of Vaucouleurs. The messenger was called Colet de Vienne.[418] His name indicates that he came from the province which the Dauphin had governed before the death of the late King, and which had remained unswervingly faithful to the unfortunate prince. The reply was that Sire Robert should send the young saint to Chinon.[419]

That which Jeanne had demanded and which it had seemed impossible to obtain was granted. She was to be taken to the King as she had desired and within the time fixed by herself. But this departure, for which she had so ardently longed, was delayed several days by a remarkable incident. The incident shows that the fame of the young prophetess had gone out through Lorraine; and it proves that in those days the great of the land had recourse to saints in their hour of need.

Jeanne was summoned to Nancy by my Lord the Duke of Lorraine. Furnished with a safe-conduct that the Duke had sent her, she set forth in rustic jerkin and hose on a nag given her by Durand Lassois and Jacques Alain. It had cost them twelve francs which Sire Robert repaid them later out of the royal revenue.[420] From Vaucouleurs to Nancy is twenty-four leagues. Jean de Metz accompanied her as far as Toul; Durand Lassois went with her the whole way.[421]

Before going to the Duke of Lorraine's palace, Jeanne ascended the valley of the Meurthe and went to worship at the shrine of the great Saint Nicholas, whose relics were preserved in the Benedictine chapel of Saint-Nicholas-du-Port. She did well; for Saint Nicholas was the patron saint of travellers.[422]

CHAPTER IV
THE JOURNEY TO NANCY – THE ITINERARY OF VAUCOULEURS – TO SAINTE-CATHERINE-DE-FIERBOIS

B Y giving his eldest daughter, Isabelle, the heiress of Lorraine, in marriage to René, the second son of Madame Yolande, Queen of Sicily and of Jerusalem, and Duchess of Anjou,[423] Duke Charles II of Lorraine, who was in alliance with the English, had recently done his cousin and friend, the Duke of Burgundy, a bad turn. René of Anjou, now in his twentieth year, was a man of culture as much in love with sound learning as with chivalry, and withal kind, affable, and gracious. When not engaged in some military expedition and in wielding the lance he delighted to illuminate manuscripts. He had a taste for flower-decked gardens and stories in tapestry; and like his fair cousin the Duke of Orléans he wrote poems in French.[424] Invested with the duchy of Bar by the Cardinal Duke of Bar, his great-uncle, he would inherit the duchy of Lorraine after the death of Duke Charles which could not be far off. This marriage was rightly regarded as a clever stroke on the part of Madame Yolande. But he who reigns must fight. The Duke of Burgundy, ill content to see a prince of the house of Anjou, the brother-in-law of Charles of Valois, established between Burgundy and Flanders, stirred up against René the Count of Vaudémont, who was a claimant of the inheritance of Lorraine. The Angevin policy rendered a reconciliation between the Duke of Burgundy and the King of France difficult. Thus was René of Anjou involved in the quarrels of his father-in-law of Lorraine. It befell that in this year, 1429, he was waging war against the citizens of Metz, the War of the Basketful of Apples.[425] It was so called because the cause of war was a basketful of apples which had been brought into the town of Metz without paying duty to the officers of the Duke of Lorraine.[426]

Meanwhile René's mother was sending convoys of victuals from Blois to the citizens of Orléans, besieged by the English.[427] Although she was not then on good terms with the counsellors of her son-in-law, King Charles, she was vigilant in opposing the enemies of the kingdom when they threatened her own duchy of Anjou. René, Duke of Bar, had therefore ties of kindred, friendship, and interest binding him at the same time to the English and Burgundian party as well as to the party of France. Such was the situation of most of the French nobles. René's communications with the Commander of Vaucouleurs were friendly and constant.[428] It is possible that Sire Robert may have told him that he had a damsel at Vaucouleurs who was prophesying concerning the realm of France. It is possible that the Duke of Bar, curious to see her, may have had her sent to Nancy, where he was to be towards the 20th of February. But it is much more likely that René of Anjou thought less about the Maid of Vaucouleurs, whom he had never seen, than about the little Moor and the jester who enlivened the ducal palace.[429] In this month of February, 1429, he was neither desirous nor able to concern himself greatly with the affairs of France; and although brother-in-law to King Charles, he was preparing not to succour the town of Orléans, but to besiege the town of Metz.[430]

Old and ill, Duke Charles dwelt in his palace with his paramour Alison du Mai, a bastard and a priest's daughter, who had driven out the lawful wife, Dame Marguerite of Bavaria. Dame Marguerite was pious and high-born, but old and ugly, while Madame Alison was pretty. She had borne Duke Charles several children.[431]

The following story appears the most authentic. There were certain worthy persons at Nancy who wanted Duke Charles to take back his good wife. To persuade him to do so they had recourse to the exhortations of a saint, who had revelations from Heaven, and who called herself the Daughter of God. By these persons the damsel of Domremy was represented to the enfeebled old Duke as being a saint who worked miracles of healing. By their advice he had her summoned in the hope that she possessed secrets which should alleviate his sufferings and keep him alive.

As soon as he saw her he asked whether she could not restore him to his former health and strength.

She replied that "of such things" she knew nothing. But she warned him that his ways were evil, and that he would not be cured until he had amended them. She enjoined upon him to send away Alison, his concubine, and to take back his good wife.[432]

No doubt she had been told to say something of this kind; but it also came from her own heart, for she loathed bad women.

Jeanne had come to the Duke because it was his due, because a little saint must not refuse when a great lord wishes to consult her, and because in short she had been brought to Nancy. But her mind was elsewhere; of nought could she think but of saving the realm of France.

Reflecting that Madame Yolande's son with a goodly company of men-at-arms would be of great aid to the Dauphin, she asked the Duke of Lorraine, as she took her leave, to send this young knight with her into France.

"Give me your son," she said, "with men-at-arms as my escort. In return I will pray to God for your restoration to health."

The Duke did not give her men-at-arms; neither did he give her the Duke of Bar, the heir of Lorraine, the ally of the English, who was nevertheless to join her soon beneath the standard of King Charles. But he gave her four francs and a black horse.[433]

Perhaps it was on her return from Nancy that she wrote to her parents asking their pardon for having left them. The fact that they received a letter and forgave is all that is known.[434] One cannot forbear surprise that Jacques d'Arc, all through the month that his daughter was at Vaucouleurs, should have remained quietly at home, when previously, after having merely dreamed of her being with men-at-arms, he had threatened that if his sons did not drown her he would with his own hands. For he must have been aware that at Vaucouleurs she was living with men-at-arms. Knowing her temperament, he had displayed great simplicity in letting her go. One cannot help supposing that those pious persons who believed in Jeanne's goodness, and desired her to be taken into France for the saving of the kingdom, must have undertaken to reassure her father and mother concerning their daughter's manner of life; perhaps they even gave the simple folk to understand that if Jeanne did go to the King her family would derive therefrom honour and advantage.

Before or after her journey to Nancy (which is not known), certain of the townsfolk of Vaucouleurs who believed in the young prophetess either had made, or purchased for her ready made, a suit of masculine clothing, a jerkin, cloth doublet, hose laced on to the coat, gaiters, spurs, a whole equipment of war. Sire Robert gave her a sword.[435]

She had her hair cut round like a boy.[436] Jean de Metz and Bertrand de Poulengy, with their servants Jean de Honecourt and Julien, were to accompany her as well as the King's messenger, Colet de Vienne, and the bowman Richard.[437] There was still some delay and councils were held, for the soldiers of Antoine de Lorraine, Lord of Joinville, infested the country. Throughout the land there was nothing but pillage, robbery, murder, cruel tyranny, the ravishing of women, the burning of churches and abbeys, and the perpetration of horrible crimes. Those were the hardest times ever known to man.[438] But the damsel was not afraid, and said: "In God's name! take me to the gentle Dauphin, and fear not any trouble or hindrance we may meet."[439]

At length, on a day in February, so it is said, the little company issued forth from Vaucouleurs by La Porte de France.[440]

A few friends who had followed her so far watched her go. Among them were her hosts, Henri Leroyer and Catherine, and Messire Jean Colin, canon of Saint-Nicolas, near Vaucouleurs, to whom Jeanne had confessed several times.[441] They trembled for their saint as they thought of the perils of the way and the length of the journey.

"How can you," they asked her, "set forth on such a journey when there are men-at-arms on every hand?" But out of the serene peace of her heart she answered them:

"I do not fear men-at-arms; my way has been made plain before me. If there be men-at-arms my Lord God will make a way for me to go to my Lord Dauphin. For that am I come."[442]

Sire Robert was present at her departure. According to the customary formula he took an oath from each of the men-at-arms that they would surely and safely conduct her whom he confided to them. Then, being a man of little faith, he said to Jeanne in lieu of farewell: "Go! and come what may."[443] And the little company went off into the mist, which at that season envelops the meadows of the Meuse.

They were obliged to avoid frequented roads and to beware especially of passing by Joinville, Montiers-en-Saulx and Sailly, where there were soldiers of the hostile party. Sire Bertrand and Jean de Metz were accustomed to such stealthy expeditions; they knew the byways and were acquainted with useful precautions, such as binding up the horses' feet in linen so as to deaden the sound of hoofs on the ground.[444]

At nightfall, having escaped all danger, the company approached the right bank of the Marne and reached the Abbey of Saint-Urbain.[445] From time immemorial it had been a place of refuge, and in those days its abbot was Arnoult of Aulnoy, a kinsman of Robert of Baudricourt.[446] The gate of the plain edifice opened for the travellers who passed beneath the groined vaulting of its roof.[447] The abbey included a building set apart for strangers. There they found the resting-place of the first stage of their journey.

On the right of the outer door was the abbey church wherein were preserved the relics of Pope Saint Urbain. On the 24th of February, in the morning, Jeanne attended conventual mass there.[448] Then she and her companions took horse again. Crossing the Marne by the bridge opposite Saint-Urbain, they pressed on towards France.

They had still one hundred and twenty-five leagues to cover and three rivers to cross, in a country infested with brigands. Through fear of the enemy they journeyed by night.[449] When they lay down on the straw the damsel, keeping her hose laced to her coat, slept in her clothes, under a covering, between Jean de Metz and Bertrand de Poulengy in whom she felt confidence. They said afterwards that they never desired the damsel because of the holiness they beheld in her;[450] that may or may not be believed.

Jean de Metz was filled with no such ardent faith in the prophetess, since he inquired of her: "Will you really do what you say?"

To which she replied: "Have no fear. I do what I am commanded to do. My brethren in Paradise tell me what I have to do. It is now four or five years since my brethren in Paradise and Messire told me that I must go forth to war to deliver the realm of France."[451]

These rude comrades did not all preserve an attitude of religious respect in her presence. Certain mocked her and diverted themselves by talking before her as if they belonged to the English party. Sometimes, as a joke, they got up a false alarm and pretended to turn back. Their jests were wasted. She believed them, but she was not afraid, and would say gravely to those who thought to frighten her with the English: "Be sure not to flee. I tell you in God's name, they will not harm you."[452]

Ever at the approach of danger whether real or feigned, there came to her lips the words of encouragement: "Do not be afraid. You will see how graciously the fair Dauphin will look upon us when we come to Chinon."[453]

Her greatest grief was that she could not pray in church as often as she would like. Every day she repeated: "If we could, we should do well to hear mass."[454]

As they avoided high roads they were not often in the way of bridges; and they were frequently forced to ford rivers in flood. They crossed the Aube, near Bar-sur-Aube, the Seine near Bar-sur-Seine, the Yonne opposite Auxerre, where Jeanne heard mass in the church of Saint-Etienne; then they reached the town of Gien, on the right bank of the Loire.[455]

At length these Lorrainers beheld a French town loyal to the King of France. They had travelled seventy-five leagues through the enemy's country without being attacked or molested. Afterwards this was considered miraculous. But was it impossible for seven or eight Armagnac horsemen to traverse English and Burgundian lands without misadventure? The Commander of Vaucouleurs frequently sent letters to the Dauphin which reached him, and the Dauphin was in the habit of despatching messengers to the Commander; Colet de Vienne had just borne his message.[456]

In point of fact the followers of the Dauphin ran risks well nigh as great in the provinces under his sway as in lands subject to other masters.[457]

Freebooters in the pay of King Charles, when they pillaged travellers and held them to ransom, did not stay to ask whether they were Armagnacs or Burgundians. Indeed, it was after their passage of the Loire that Bertrand de Poulengy and his companions found themselves exposed to the greatest danger.

Informed of their approach, certain men-at-arms of the French party went before and lay in ambush, waiting to surprise them. They intended to capture the damsel, cast her into a pit, and keep her there beneath a great stone, in the hope that the King who had sent for her would give a large sum for her rescue.[458] It was the custom for freebooters and mercenaries thus to cast travellers into pits delivering them on payment of ransom. Eighteen years before, at Corbeil, five men had been kept in a pit on bread and water by Burgundians. Three of them died, being unable to pay the ransom.[459] Such a fate very nearly befell Jeanne. But the wretches who were lying in wait for her, at the moment when they should have struck did nothing, wherefore is unknown, perhaps because they were afraid of not being the stronger.[460]

From Gien, the little company followed the northern boundary of the duchy of Berry, crossed into Blésois, possibly passed through Selles-sur-Cher and Saint-Aignan, then, having entered Touraine, reached the green slopes of Fierbois.[461] There one of the two heavenly ladies, who daily discoursed familiarly with the peasant girl, had her most famous sanctuary; there it was that Saint Catherine received multitudes of pilgrims and worked great miracles. According to popular belief the origin of her worship in this place was warlike and national and dated back to the beginning of French history. It was known that after his victory over the Saracens at Poitiers Charles Martel had placed his sword in the oratory of the Blessed Catherine.[462] But it must be admitted that since then the sanctuary had long suffered from desertion and neglect. Rather more than forty years before the coming of the damsel from Domremy, its walls in the depths of a wood were overrun by briers and brambles.

In those days it was not uncommon for saints of both sexes, if they had suffered from some unjust neglect, to come and complain to some pious person of the wrong being done them on earth. They appeared possibly to a monk, to a peasant or a citizen, denounced the impiety of the faithful in terms urgent and sometimes violent, and commanded him to reinstate their worship and restore their sanctuary. And this is what Madame Saint Catherine did. In the year 1375 she entrusted a knight of the neighbourhood of Fierbois, one Jean Godefroy, who was blind and paralysed, with the restoration of her oratory to its old brilliance and fame, promising to cure him if he would pray for nine days in the place where Charles Martel had put his sword. Jean Godefroy had himself carried to the deserted chapel, but beforehand his servants must perforce hew a way through the thicket with their axes. Madame Saint Catherine restored to Jean Godefroy the use of his eyes and his limbs, and it was by this benefit that she recalled to the people of Touraine the glory they had slighted. The oratory was repaired; the faithful again wended their way thither, and miracles abounded. At first the saint healed the sick; then, when the land was ravaged by war, it was her office more especially to deliver from the hands of the English such prisoners as had recourse to her. Sometimes she rendered captives invisible to their guards; sometimes she broke bonds, chains, and locks; to wit, those of a nobleman by name Cazin du Boys, who in 1418 was taken with the garrison of Beaumont-sur-Oise. Locked in an iron cage, bound with a strong rope on which slept a Burgundian, he thought on Madame Saint Catherine, and dedicated himself to this glorious virgin. Immediately the cage was opened. Sometimes she even constrained the English to unchain their prisoners themselves and set them free without ransom. That was a great miracle. One no less great was worked by her on Perrot Chapon, of Saint-Sauveur, near Luzarches. For a month Perrot had been in bonds in an English prison, when he dedicated himself to Saint Catherine and fell asleep. He awoke, still bound, in his own house.

Generally she helped those who helped themselves. Such was the case of Jean Ducoudray, citizen of Saumur, a prisoner in the castle of Bellême in 1429. He commended his soul devoutly to Saint Catherine, then leapt forth, throttled the guard, climbed the ramparts, dropped the height of two lances, and went out a free man into the country.[463]

Perhaps these miracles would have been less frequent had the English been in greater force in France; but their men were few: in Normandy they intrenched themselves in towns, abandoning the open country to soldiers of fortune who ranged the district and captured convoys, thus greatly promoting the intervention of Madame Saint Catherine.[464]

The prisoners, who had become her votaries and whom she had delivered, discharged their vows by making the pilgrimage to Fierbois. In her chapel there, they hung the cords and chains with which they had been bound, their armour, and sometimes, in special cases, the armour of the enemy.

This had been done nine months before Jeanne's coming to Fierbois by a certain knight, Jean du Chastel. He had escaped from the hands of a captain, who accused him of having committed treason thereby, alleging that du Chastel had given him his word of honour. Du Chastel on the other hand maintained that he had not sworn, and he challenged the captain to meet him in single combat. The issue of the combat proved right to be on the side of the French knight; for with the aid of Madame Saint Catherine he was victorious. In return he came to Fierbois to offer to his holy protectress the armour of the vanquished Englishman, in the presence of my Lord, the Bastard of Orléans, of Captain La Hire and several other nobles.[465]

Jeanne must have delighted to hear tell of such miracles, or others like them, and to see so many weapons hanging from the chapel walls. She must have been well pleased that the saint who visited her at all hours and gave her counsel should so manifestly appear the friend of poor soldiers and peasants cast into bonds, cages and pits, or hanged on trees by the *Godons*.

She prayed in the chapel and heard two masses.[466]

CHAPTER V
THE SIEGE OF ORLÉANS FROM THE 12TH OF
OCTOBER, 1428, TILL THE 6TH OF MARCH, 1429

INCE the victory of Verneuil and the conquest of Maine, the English had advanced but little in France and their actual possessions there were becoming less and less secure.[467] If they spared the lands of the Duke of Orléans it was not on account of any scruple. Albeit on the banks of the Loire it was held dishonourable to seize the domains of a noble when he was a prisoner,[468] everything is fair in war. The Regent had not scrupled to seize the duchy of Alençon when its duke was a prisoner.[469] The truth is that by bribes and entreaties the good Duke Charles dissuaded the English from attacking his duchy. From 1424 until 1426 the citizens of Orléans purchased peace by money payments.[470] The *Godons*, not being in a position to take the field, were all the more ready to enter into such agreements. During the minority of their half English and half French King, the Duke of Gloucester, the brother and deputy of the Regent, and his uncle, the Bishop of Winchester, Chancellor of the Kingdom, were tearing out each other's hair, and their disputes were the occasion of bloodshed in the London streets.[471] Towards the end of the year 1425 the Regent returned to England, where he spent seventeen months reconciling uncle and nephew and restoring public peace. By dint of craft and vigour he succeeded so far as to render his fellow countrymen desirous and hopeful of completing the conquest of France. With that object, in 1428, the English Parliament voted subsidies.[472]

Now the most cunning, the most expert, the most fortunate in arms of all the English captains and princes was Thomas Montacute, Earl of Salisbury and of Perche.[473] He had long waged war in Normandy, in Champagne, and in Maine. At present he was gathering an army in

England, intended for the banks of the Loire. He got as many bowmen as he wanted; but of horse and men-at-arms he was disappointed. Only those of low estate were willing to go and fight in a land ravaged by famine.[474] At length the noble earl, the fair cousin of King Henry, crossed the sea with four hundred and forty-nine men-at-arms and two thousand two hundred and fifty archers.[475] In France he found troops recruited by the Regent, four hundred horse of whom two hundred were Norman, with three bowmen to each horseman, according to the English custom.[476] He led his men to Paris where irrevocable resolutions were taken.[477] Hitherto the plan had been to attack Angers; at the last moment it was decided to lay siege to Orléans.[478]

View of Orléans, 1428-1429

Between la Beauce and la Sologne, at the entrance to the loyal provinces Touraine, Blésois, and Berry, the ducal city confronted the enemy, lying on a bend of the Loire, just as the arrow's point is lodged on the taut bow.[479] Bishopric, university, market of the country far and wide, on its belfries, towers, and steeples it raised proudly towards heaven the cross of Our Lord, the three *cœurs de lis* of the city and the three *fleurs de lis* of the dukes. Beneath the high slate roofs of its houses of stone or wood, built along winding streets or dark alleys, Orléans sheltered fifteen thousand souls. There were to be found officers of justice and of the treasury, goldsmiths, druggists, grocers, tanners, butchers, fishmongers, rich citizens as delicate as amber, who loved fine clothes, fine houses, music and dancing; priests, canons, wardens, and fellows of the university; booksellers, scriveners, illuminators, painters, scholars who were not all founts of learning, but who played prettily on the flute; monks of every habit, Black-friars, Grey-friars, Mathurins, Carmelites, Augustinians, and artisans and labourers to boot, smiths, coopers, carpenters, boatmen, fishermen.[480]

Of Roman origin, the form of the town was still the same as in the days of the Emperor Aurelian. The southern side along the Loire and the northern side extended to some three thousand feet. The eastern and western boundaries were only one hundred and fifty feet long. The city was surrounded by walls six feet thick and from eighteen to thirty-three feet high above the moat. These walls were flanked by thirty-four towers, pierced with five gates and two posterns.[481] The following is the description of the situation of these gates, posterns, and towers, with the names of those which became famous during the siege.

Passing from the south east to the south west angle of the wall, were: La Tour Neuve, round and huge, washed by the Loire; three other towers on the river bank; the postern Chesneau, the only one opening on to the water and defended by a portcullis; the tower of La Croiche-Meuffroy, so called from the crook or spur which protruded from the foot of the tower into the river; two other towers washed by the Loire; La Port du Pont, with drawbridge and flanked by two towers; La Tour de l'Abreuvoir; la Tour de Notre-Dame, deriving its name from a chapel built against the city walls; la Tour de la Barre-Flambert, the last on this side, at the south west angle of the ramparts and commanding the river. All along the Loire the walls had a stone parapet with machicolated battlements, whence paving stones could be thrown, and whence, when attempts were made to scale the walls, the enemy's ladders could be hurled down. The distance between the towers was about a bow-shot.

On the western side were first three towers, then two gate towers called Regnard or Renard from the name of citizens to whom had once belonged the adjoining palace, where in 1428 dwelt Jacques Boucher, Treasurer of the Duke of Orléans. Then came another tower and lastly La Porte Bernier or Bannier, at the north west angle of the ramparts. On this side the walls had been constructed in the days of the cross-bow, which shot a greater distance than the bow. The towers here, therefore, were farther apart at the distance of a cross-bow shot one from the other, and the walls were lower than elsewhere. On the northern side, looking towards the forest, were ten towers at a bow-shot's interval. The second, that of Saint-Samson, was used as an arsenal. The sixth and seventh flanked the Paris Gate.

On the eastern side were likewise ten towers at the same distance one from the other as those on the north. The fifth and sixth were those of the Burgundian Gate, also called the Gate of Saint-Aignan, because it was close to the church of Saint-Aignan without the walls; the last was the great corner tower, called La Tour Neuve, which thus comes to have been twice counted.

The stone bridge lined with houses which led from the town to the left bank of the Loire was famous all over the world. It had nineteen arches of varying breadth. The first, on leaving the town by La Porte du Pont, was called l'Allouée or Pont Jacquemin-Rousselet; here was a drawbridge. The fifth arch abutted on an island which was long, narrow, and in the form of a boat, like all river islands. Above the bridge it was called Motte-Saint-Antoine, from a chapel built upon it dedicated to that saint; and below, Motte-des-Poissonniers, because in order to keep captured fish alive boats with holes in them were moored to it. In 1447, to provide against the occupation of this island by the enemy, the people of Orléans had constructed a tower, the tower or fortress of Saint-Antoine, beyond the sixth arch and occupying the whole breadth of the bridge. On the buttress between the eleventh and twelfth arch was a cross of gilded bronze, supported by a pedestal of stone. It was indeed what it was called, the Cross Beautiful, – La Belle-Croix. The buttresses of the eighteenth arch were extended, and on the abutment there rose a little castle formed of two towers joined by a vaulted porch. This little castle was called Les Tourelles. Between the nineteenth and the twentieth arch as in the first was a drawbridge. Outside it was Le Portereau; and thence ran the road to Toulouse, which beyond the Loiret on the heights of Olivet joined the road to Blois.[482]

In those days the lazy waters of the Loire flowed midst osier-beds and birchen thickets, since removed for purposes of navigation. Two and a half miles east of Orléans, on the height of Chécy, l'Île aux Bourdons was separated from the Sologne bank by a thin arm of the river and by a narrow channel from l'Île Charlemagne and l'Île-aux-Bœufs, with their green grass and underwood facing Combleux on the La Beauce bank. A boat dropping down the river would next come to the two islands Saint-Loup, and, doubling La Tour Neuve, would glide between the two Martinet Islets on the right and l'Île-aux-Toiles on the left. Thence it would pass under the bridge which overspanned, as we have seen, an island called above bridge Motte-Saint-Antoine and below, Motte-des-Poissonniers. At length, below the ramparts, opposite Saint-Laurent-des-Orgerils, it would come to two islets Biche-d'Orge and another, the name of which is unknown, possibly it was nameless.[483]

The suburbs of Orléans were the finest in the kingdom. On the south the fishermen's suburb of Le Portereau, with its Augustinian church and monastery, extended along the river at the foot of the vineyards of Saint-Jean-le-Blanc, which produced the best wine in the country.[484] Above, on the gentle slopes ascending to the bleak plateau of Sologne, the Loiret, with its torrential springs, its limpid waters, its shady banks, the gardens and the brooks of Olivet, smiled beneath a mild and showery sky.

The *faubourg* of the Burgundian gate stretching eastwards was the best built and the most populous. There were the wonderful churches of Saint-Michel and of Saint-Aignan. The cloister of the latter was held to be marvellous.[485] Leaving this suburb and passing by the vineyards along the sandy branch of the Loire extending between the bank of the river and l'Île-aux-Bœufs about a quarter of a league further on, one comes to the steep slope of Saint-Loup; and, advancing still further towards the east, the belfries of Saint-Jean-de-Bray, Combleux and Chécy may be seen rising one beyond the other between the river and the Roman road from Autun to Paris. On the north of the city were fine monasteries and beautiful churches, the chapel of Saint-Ladre, in the cemetery; the Jacobins, the Cordeliers, the church of Saint-Pierre-Ensentelée. Directly north, the *faubourg* of La Porte Bernier lay along the Paris road, and close by there stretched the sombre city of the wolves, the deep forest of oaks, horn-beams, beeches, and willows, wherein were hidden, like wood-cutters and charcoal-burners, the villages of Fleury and Samoy.[486]

Towards the west the *faubourg* of La Porte Renard stretched out into the fields along the road to Châteaudun, and the hamlet of Saint-Laurent along the road to Blois.[487]

These *faubourgs* were so populous and so extensive that when, on the approach of the English, the people from the suburbs took refuge within the city the number of its inhabitants was doubled.[488]

The inhabitants of Orléans were resolved to fight, not for their honour indeed; in those days no honour redounded to a citizen from the defence of his own city; his only reward was the risk of terrible danger. When the town was captured the great and wealthy had but to pay ransom and the conqueror entertained them well; the lesser and poorer nobility ran greater risks. In this year, 1428, the knights, who defended Melun and surrendered after having eaten their horses and their dogs, were drowned in the Seine. "Nobility was worth nothing," ran a Burgundian song.[489]

But generally being of noble birth saved one's life. As for those burghers brave enough to defend themselves, they were likely to perish. There were no fixed rules with regard to them; sometimes several were hanged; sometimes only one, sometimes all. It was also lawful to cut off their heads or to throw them into the water, sewn in a sack. In that same year, 1428, Captains La Hire and Poton had failed in their assault on Le Mans and decamped just in time. The citizens who had aided them were beheaded in the square du Cloître-Saint-Julien, on the Olet stone, by order of William Pole, Earl of Suffolk, who had already arrived at Olivet, and of John Talbot, the most courteous of English knights, who was shortly to come there too.[490] Such an example was sufficient to warn the people of Orléans.

Notwithstanding that it was under the control of the Governor, the town administered its own affairs by means of twelve magistrates elected for two years by the citizens, subject to the governor's approbation.[491] These magistrates risked more than the other citizens. One of them, as he passed the monastery of Saint-Sulpice, where was the place of execution, might well reflect that before the year was out he might have justice executed on him there for having defended his lord's inheritance. Yet the twelve were resolved to defend this inheritance; and they acted for the common weal with promptness and with wisdom.

The people of Orléans were not taken by surprise. Their fathers had watched the English closely, and put their city in a state of defence. They themselves, in the year 1425, had so firmly expected a siege that they had collected arms in the Tower of Saint-Samson, while all, rich and poor alike, had been required to dig dykes and build ramparts.[492] War has always been costly. They devoted three quarters of the yearly revenue of the town to keeping up the ramparts and other preparations for war. Hearing of the approach of the Earl of Salisbury, with marvellous energy they prepared to receive him.

The walls, except those along the river, were devoid of breastwork; but in the shops were stakes and cross-beams intended for the manufacture of balustrades. These were put up on the fortifications to form parapets, with barbicans of a pent-house shape so as to provide with cover the defenders firing from the walls.[493] At the entrance to each suburb wooden barriers were erected, with a lodge for the porter whose duty it was to open and shut them. On the tops of the ramparts and in the towers were seventy-one pieces of artillery, including cannons and mortars, without counting culverins. The quarry of Montmaillard, three leagues from the town, produced stones which were made into cannon balls. At great expense there were brought into the city lead, powder, and sulphur which the women prepared for use in the cannons and culverins. Every day there were manufactured in thousands, arrows, darts, stacks of bolts,[494] armed with iron points and feathered with parchment, numbers of *pavas*, great shields made of pieces of wood mortised one into the other and covered with leather. Corn, wine, and cattle were purchased in great quantities both for the inhabitants and the men-at-arms, the King's men, and adventurers who were expected.[495]

By a jealously guarded privilege the inhabitants had the right of defending the ramparts. According to their trades they were divided into as many companies as there were towers. Thus defending themselves they had the right to refuse to admit any garrison within the walls. They held to this right because it delivered them from the pillage, the rapine, the burnings and constant molestations inflicted by the King's men. But now they were eager to renounce it; for they realised that alone with only the town bands and those from the neighbouring villages, mere peasants, they could not sustain the siege; to resist the enemy they must have horsemen, skilled in wielding the lance, and foot, skilled in the use of the cross-bow. While their Governor the Sire de Gaucourt and my Lord, the Bastard of Orléans, the King's Lieutenant General, went to Chinon and Poitiers to obtain supplies of men and money[496] from the King, the citizens in commissions of two and two went forth asking help of the towns, travelling as far as Bourbonnais and Languedoc.[497] The magistrates appealed to those soldiers of fortune who held the neighbouring country for the King of France. By the mouths of the two heralds of the city, Orléans and Cœur-de-Lis, they proclaimed that within the city walls were gold and silver in abundance and such good provision of victuals and arms as would nourish and accoutre two thousand combatants for two years, and that every gentle, honest knight who would might share in the defence of the city and wage battle to the death.[498]

The inhabitants of Orléans feared God. In those days God was greatly to be feared; he was almost as terrible as in the days of the Philistines. The poor fisher folk were afraid of being repulsed if they addressed him in their affliction; they thought it better to take a roundabout road and to seek the intercession of Our Lady and the saints. God respected his Mother and sought to please her on every occasion. Likewise he deferred to the wishes of the Blessed, seated on his right hand and on his left in Paradise, and he inclined his ear to listen to the petitions they presented to him. Thus in cases of dire necessity it was customary to solicit the favour of the saints by presenting prayers and offerings. Then also did the citizens of Orléans remember Saint Euverte and Saint-Aignan, the patrons of their town. In very ancient days Saint Euverte had sat upon that episcopal seat, now, in 1428, occupied by a Scot. Messire Jean de Saint Michel, and Saint Euverte had shone with all the glory of apostolic virtue.[499] His successor, Saint-Aignan had prayed to God. He had regarded the city in a peril like unto that of which it was now in danger.

The following is his story as it was known to the people of Orléans. When still young, Saint-Aignan had withdrawn to a solitary place near Orléans. There Saint Euverte, at that time bishop of the city, discovered him. He ordained him priest, appointed him Abbot of Saint-Laurent-des-Orgerils, and elected him to succeed him in the government of the faithful. And when Saint Euverte had passed from this life to the other, the blessed Aignan, with the consent of the people of Orléans, was proclaimed bishop by the voice of a little child. For God, who is praised out of the mouths of babes, permitted one of them, borne in his swaddling clothes to the altar, to speak and say: "Aignan, Aignan is chosen of God to be bishop of this town." Now in the sixtieth year of his pontificate, the Huns invaded Gaul, led by their King Attila, who boasted that wherever he went the stars fell and the earth trembled beneath him, that he was the hammer of the world, *stellas pre se cadere, terram tremere, se malleum esse universi orbis.* Every town on his march had been destroyed by him, and now he was advancing against Orléans. Then the blessed Aignan went forth into the city of Arles, to the Patrician Aëtius, who commanded the Roman army, and implored his aid in so great a peril. Having obtained of the Patrician promise of succour, Aignan returned to his episcopal see, which he found surrounded by barbarian warriors. The Huns, having made breaches in the walls, were preparing an assault. The blessed saint went up on to the ramparts, knelt and prayed, and then, having prayed, spat upon the enemy. By God's will that drop of his saliva was followed by all the raindrops in the sky. A tempest arose: the rain fell in such torrents on the barbarians that their camp was flooded; their tents were overturned by the power of the winds, and many among them perished by lightning. The rain lasted for three days, after which time Attila assailed the ramparts with powerful engines of war. When they saw the walls fall down the inhabitants were terrified. All hope of resistance being at an end, the holy bishop, clad in his episcopal robes, went to the King of the Huns and adjured him to take pity on the people of Orléans, threatening him with the wrath of God if he dealt hardly with the conquered. These prayers and these threats did not soften Attila's heart. On his return to the faithful, the bishop warned them that henceforth nothing remained to them but trust in God; divine succour, however, would not fail them. And soon, according to the promise he had given them, God delivered the town by means of the Romans and the Franks, who defied the Huns in a great battle. Not long after the miraculous deliverance of his beloved city, Saint Aignan fell asleep in the Lord.[500]

Wherefore, in this great peril of the English, the citizens of Orléans resorted to Saint Euverte and Saint-Aignan for succour and relief. According to the marvels accomplished by Saint-Aignan in this mortal life they measured his power of working miracles now that he was in Paradise. These two confessors had each his church in the faubourg de Bourgogne, wherein their bodies were jealously guarded.[501] In those days the bones of martyrs and confessors were devoutly worshipped. It was said that sometimes they shed abroad a healing odour which represented the virtues proceeding from them. They were enclosed in gilded reliquaries adorned with precious stones, and no miracle was thought too great to be accomplished by these holy relics. On the 6th of August, 1428, the clergy of the city went to the church wherein was the reliquary of Saint Euverte and bore it round the walls, that they might be strengthened. And the holy reliquary made the round of the whole city, followed by all the people. On the 8th of September a *tortis* weighing one hundred and ten livres[502] was offered to Saint-Aignan. In time of need the favour of the saints was solicited by all kinds of gifts, garments, jewels, coins, houses, lands, woods, ponds; but natural wax was thought to be especially grateful to them. A *tortis* was a wheel of wax on which candles were placed and two escutcheons bearing the arms of the city.[503]

Thus did the people of Orléans strive to provision and protect their town.

Adventurers from all parts responded to the magistrates' appeal. The first to hasten to the city were: Messire Archambaud de Villars, Governor of Montargis; Guillaume de Chaumont, Lord of Guitry; Messire Pierre de la Chapelle, a baron of La Beauce; Raimond Arnaud de Corraze, knight of Béarn; Don Matthias of Aragon; Jean de Saintrailles and Poton de Saintrailles. The Abbot of Cerquenceaux, sometime student at the University of Orléans, arrived at the head of a band of followers.[504] Thus the number of friends who entered the city was well-nigh as great as that of the expected foe. The defenders were paid; they were furnished with bread, meat, fish, forage in plenty, and casks of wine were broached for them. In the beginning the inhabitants treated them like their own children. The citizens all contributed to the entertainment of the strangers, and gave them what they had. But this concord did not long endure. Whatever tradition alleges as to the friendly relations subsisting between the citizens and their military guests,[505] affairs in Orléans were in truth not different from what they were in other besieged towns; before long the inhabitants began to complain of the garrison.

On the 5th of September the Earl of Salisbury reached Janville, having taken with ease towns, fortified churches or castles to the number of forty. But that was not his greatest achievement; for, although he had left but few men in each place, he had by that means rid himself on the march of that portion of his army which had already shown itself ready to drop away.[506]

From Janville he sent two heralds to Orléans to summon the inhabitants to surrender. The magistrates lodged these heralds honourably in the faubourg Bannier, at the Hôtel de la Pomme and confided to them a present of wine for the Earl of Salisbury; they knew their duty to so great a prince. But they refused to open their gates to the English garrison, alleging, doubtless, as was the custom of citizens in those days, that they were not able to open them, having those within who were stronger than they.[507]

Now that the danger was drawing near, on the 6th of October, priests, burgesses, notables, merchants, mechanics, women and children walked in solemn procession with crosses and banners, singing psalms and invoking the heavenly guardians of the city.[508]

On Tuesday, the 12th of this month, at the news that the enemy was coming through Sologne, the magistrates sent soldiers to pull down the houses of Le Portereau, the suburb on the left bank, also the Augustinian church and monastery of that suburb, as well as all other buildings in which the enemy might lodge or entrench himself. But the soldiers were taken by surprise. That very day the English occupied Olivet and appeared in Le Portereau.[509] With them were the victors of Verneuil, the flower of English knighthood: Thomas, Lord of Scales and of Nucelles, Governor of Pontorson, whom the King of England called cousin; William Neville; Baron Falconbridge; William Gethyn, a Welsh knight, Bailie of Évreux; Lord Richard Gray, nephew of the Earl of Salisbury; Gilbert Halsall, Richard Panyngel, Thomas Guérard, knights, and many others of great renown.

Over the two hundred lances from Normandy there floated the standards of William Pole, Earl of Suffolk, and of John Pole, two brothers descended from a comrade-in-arms of Duke William; of Thomas Rampston, knight banneret, the Regent's chamberlain; of Richard Walter, squire, Governor of Conches, Bailie and Captain of Évreux; of William Mollins, knight; of William Glasdale, whom the French called Glacidas, squire, Bailie of Alençon, a man of humble birth.[510]

The archers were all on horseback. There were practically no foot-soldiers. In carts drawn by oxen were barrels of powder, cross-bows, arrows, cannon-balls, and guns of all kinds, muskets, fowling-pieces, and large cannon. The two English master-gunners, Philibert de Moslant and William Appleby, accompanied the troops. There were also two masters of mining with thirty-eight workmen. Of women there were not a few, some of them acting as spies.[511]

When the army arrived it was greatly diminished by desertions, having shed runaways at each victory. Some returned to England, others roamed through the realm of France robbing and plundering. That very 12th of October orders had been despatched from Rouen to the Bailies and Governors of Normandy to arrest those English who had departed from the company of my Lord, the Earl of Salisbury.[512]

The fort of Les Tourelles and its outworks barred the entrance to the bridge. The English established themselves in Le Portereau, placed their cannon and their mortars on the rising ground of Saint-Jean-le-

Blanc,[513] and, on the following Sunday, they hurled down upon the city a shower of stone cannon-balls, which did great damage to the houses, but killed no one save a woman of Orléans, named Belles, who dwelt near the Chesneau postern on the river bank. Thus the siege, which was to be ended by a woman's victory, began with a woman's death.

That same week the English cannon destroyed twelve water mills near La Tour Neuve. Whereupon the people of Orléans constructed within the city eleven mills worked by horses,[514] in order that there might be no lack of flour. There were a few skirmishes at the bridge. Then on Thursday, the 21st of October, the English attempted to storm the outworks of Les Tourelles. The little band of adventurers in the service of the town and the city troops made a gallant defence. The women helped; throughout the four hours that the assault lasted long lines of gossips might be seen hurrying to the bridge, bearing their pots and pans filled with burning coals and boiling oil and fat, frantic with joy at the idea of scalding the *Godons*.[515] The attack was repulsed; but two days later the French perceived that the outworks were undermined; the English had dug subterranean passages, to the props of which they had afterwards set fire. The outworks having become untenable in the opinion of the soldiers, they were destroyed and abandoned. It was deemed impossible to defend Les Tourelles thus dismantled. Those towers which would once have arrested an army's progress for a whole month were now useless against cannon. In front of La Belle Croix the townsfolk erected a rampart of earth and wood. Beyond this outwork two arches of the bridge were cut and replaced by a movable platform. And when this was done, the fort of Les Tourelles was abandoned to the English with no great regret. The latter set up a rampart of earth and faggots on the bridge, breaking two of its arches, one in front, the other behind their earthwork.[516]

On the Sunday, towards evening, a few hours after the flag of St. George had been planted on the fort, the Earl of Salisbury, with William Glasdale and several captains, went up one of the towers to observe the lie of the city. Looking from a window he beheld the walls armed with cannon; the towers vanishing into pinnacles or with terraces on their flat roofs; the battlements dry and grey; the suburbs adorned for a few days longer with the fine stone-work of their churches and monasteries; the vineyards and the woods yellow with autumn tints; the Loire and its oval-shaped islands, – all slumbering in the evening calm. He was looking for the weak point in the ramparts, the place where he might make a breach and put up his scaling ladders.

For his plan was to take Orléans by assault. William Glasdale said to him, "My Lord, look well at your city. You have a good bird's-eye view of it from here."

At this moment a cannon-ball breaks off a corner of the window recess, a stone from the wall strikes Salisbury, carrying away one eye and one side of his face. The shot had been fired from La Tour Notre-Dame. That at least was generally believed. It was never known who had fired it. A townsman, alarmed by the noise, hastened to the spot, saw a child coming out of the tower and the cannon deserted. It was thought that the hand of an innocent child had fired the bullet by the permission of the Mother of God, who had been irritated by the Earl of Salisbury's despoiling monks and pillaging the Church of Notre Dame de Cléry. It was said also that he was punished for having broken his oath, for he had promised the Duke of Orléans to respect his lands and his towns. Borne secretly to Meung-sur-Loire, he died there on Wednesday the 27th of October; and the English were very sorrowful.[517] Most of them felt that loss to be irreparable which had deprived them of a chief who was conducting the siege vigorously, and who in less than twelve days had captured Les Tourelles, the very corner-stone of the city's defence. But there were others who reflected that he must have been very simple to imagine that thick ramparts could be overthrown by stone balls, the force of which had already been spent in crossing the wide stretches of the river, and that he must have been mad to attempt to storm a city which could only be reduced by famine. Then they thought: "He is dead. God receive his soul! But he has brought us into a sorry plight."

Men told how Maître Jean de Builhons, a famous astrologer, had prophesied this death,[518] and how in the night before the fatal day, the Earl of Salisbury himself had dreamed that he was being clawed by a wolf. A Norman clerk composed two songs on this sad death, one against the English, the other for them. The first, which is the better, closes with a couplet, worthy in its profound wisdom of King Solomon himself:[519]

Certes le duc de Bedefort
Se sage est, il se tendra
Avec sa femme en un fort,
Chaudement le mieulx520 que il porra,
De bon ypocras finera,

119

Garde son corps, lesse la guerre:
Povre et riche porrist en terre.[521]

The day after the taking of Les Tourelles and when its loss had been remedied as best might be, the King's lieutenant-general entered the town. He was le Seigneur Jean, Count of Porcien and of Montaing, Grand Chamberlain of France, son of Duke Louis of Orléans, who had been assassinated in 1407 by order of Jean-Sans-Peur, and whose death had armed the Armagnacs against the Burgundians. Dame de Cany was his mother, but he ought to have been the son of the Duchess of Orléans since the Duke was his father. Not only was it no drawback to children to be born outside wedlock and of an adulterous union, but it was a great honour to be called the bastard of a prince. There have never been so many bastards as during these wars, and the saying ran: "Children are like corn: sow stolen wheat and it will sprout as well as any other."[522] The Bastard of Orléans was then twenty-six at the most. The year before, with a small company, he had hastened to revictual the inhabitants of Montargis, who were besieged by the Earl of Warwick. He had not only revictualled the town; but with the help of Captain La Hire had driven away the besiegers. This augured well for Orléans.[523] The Bastard was the cleverest baron of his day. He knew grammar and astrology, and spoke more correctly than any one.[524] In his affability and intelligence he resembled his father, but he was more cautious and more temperate. His amiability, his courtesy and his discretion caused it to be said that he was in favour with all the ladies, even with the Queen.[525] In everything he was apt, in war as well as in diplomacy, marvellously adroit, and a consummate dissembler.

My Lord the Bastard brought in his train several knights, captains, and squires of renown, that is to say, of high birth or of great valour: the Marshal de Boussac, Messire Jacques de Chabannes, Seneschal of Bourbonnais, the Lord of Chaumont, Messire Théaulde of Valpergue, a Lombard knight, Captain La Hire, wondrous in war and in pillage, who had lately done so well in the relief of Montargis, and Jean, Sire de Bueil, one of those youths who had come to the King on a lame horse and who had taken lessons from two wise women, Suffering and Poverty. These knights came with a company of eight hundred men, archers, arbalesters, and Italian foot, bearing broad shields like those of St. George in the churches of Venice and Florence. They represented all the nobles and free-lances who for the moment could be gathered together.[526]

After the death of its chief, Salisbury's army was paralysed by disunion and diminished by desertions. Winter was coming: the captains, seeing there was nothing to be done for the present, broke up their camp, and, with such men as remained to them, went off to shelter behind the walls of Meung and Jargeau.[527] On the evening of the 8th of November all that remained before the city was the garrison of Les Tourelles, consisting of five hundred Norman horse, commanded by William Molyns and William Glasdale. The French might besiege and take them: they would not budge. The Governor, the old Sire de Gaucourt, had just fallen on the pavement in La Rue des Hôtelleries and broken his arm; he couldn't move.[528] But what about the rest of the defenders?

The truth is, no one knew what to do. These warriors were doubtless acquainted with many measures for the succour of a besieged town, but they were all measures of surprise.[529] Their only devices were sallies, ambuscades, skirmishes, and other such valiant feats of arms. Should they fail in raising a siege by surprise, then they remained inactive, – at the end of their ideas and of their resources. Their most experienced captains were incapable of any common effort, – of any concerted action, of any enterprise in short, requiring a continuous mental effort and the subordination of all to one. Each was for his own hand and thought of nothing but booty. The defence of Orléans was altogether beyond their intelligence.

For twenty-one days Captain Glasdale remained entrenched, with his five hundred Norman horse, under the battered walls of Les Tourelles, between his earthworks on Le Portereau side, which couldn't have become very formidable as yet, and his barrier on the bridge, which being but wood, a spark could easily have set on fire.

Meanwhile the citizens were at work. After the departure of the English they performed a huge and arduous task. Concluding, and rightly, that the enemy would return not through La Sologne this time, but through La Beauce, they destroyed all their suburbs on the west, north, and east, as they had already destroyed or begun to destroy Le Portereau. They burned and pulled down twenty-two churches and monasteries, among others the church of Saint-Aignan and its monastery, so beautiful that it was a pity to see it spoiled, the church of Saint Euverte, the church of Saint-Laurent-des-Orgerils, not without promising the blessed patrons of the town that when they should have delivered the city from the English, the citizens would build them new and more beautiful churches.[530]

On the 30th of November Captain Glasdale beheld Sir John Talbot approaching Les Tourelles. He brought three hundred men furnished with cannon, mortars, and other engines of war. Thenceforward the bombardment was resumed more violently than before: roofs were broken through, walls were battered, but there was more noise than work. In La Rue Aux-Petits-Souliers a cannon-ball fell on to a table, round which five persons were dining, and no one was hurt. It was thought to have been a miracle of Our Lord worked at the intercession of Saint Aignan, the patron saint of the city.[531] The people of Orléans had wherewith to answer the besiegers. For the seventy cannon and mortars, of which the city artillery consisted, there were twelve professional gunners with servants to wait on them. A very clever founder named Guillaume Duisy had cast a mortar which from its position at the crook or spur by the Chesneau postern, hurled stone bullets of one hundred and twenty *livres* on to Les Tourelles. Near this mortar were two cannon, one called Montargis because the town of Montargis had lent it, the other named *Rifflart*[532] after a very popular demon. A culverin firer, a Lorrainer living at Angers, had been sent by the King to Orléans, where he was paid twelve *livres*[533] a month. His name was Jean de Montesclère. He was held to be the best master of his trade. He had in his charge a huge culverin which inflicted great damage on the English.[534]

A jovial fellow was Maître Jean. When a cannon-ball happened to fall near him he would tumble to the ground and be carried into the town to the great joy of the English who believed him dead. But their joy was short-lived, for Maître Jean soon returned to his post and bombarded them as before.[535] These culverins were loaded with leaden bullets by means of an iron ramrod. They were tiny cannon or rather large guns on gun-carriages. They could be moved easily.[536] And so Maître Jean's culverin was brought wherever it was needed.

On the 25th of December a truce was proclaimed for the celebration of the Nativity of Our Lord. Of one faith and one religion, on feast days the hostility of the combatants ceased, and courtesy reconciled the knights of the two camps whenever the calendar reminded them that they were Christians. Noël is a gay feast. Captain Glasdale wanted to celebrate it with carol singing according to the English custom. He asked my Lord Jean, the Bastard of Orléans, and

Marshal de Boussac to send him a band of musicians, which they graciously did. The Orléans players went forth to Les Tourelles with their clarions and their trumpets; and they played the English such carols as rejoiced their hearts. To the folk of Orléans, who came on to the bridge to listen to the music, it sounded very melodious; but no sooner had the truce expired than every man looked to himself. For from one bank to the other the cannon burst from their slumber, hurling balls of stone and copper with renewed vigour.[537]

That which the people of Orléans had foreseen happened on the 30th of December. On that day the English came in great force through La Beauce to Saint-Laurent-des-Orgerils.[538] All the French knights went out to meet them and performed great feats of arms; but the English occupied Saint-Laurent, and then the siege really began. They erected a bastion on the left bank of the Loire, west of Le Portereau, in a place called the Field of Saint-Privé. Another they erected in the little island to the right of Saint-Laurent-des-Orgerils.[539] On the right bank, at Saint-Laurent, they constructed an entrenched camp. At a bow-shot's distance on the road to Blois, in a place called la Croix-Boissée, they built another bastion. Two bow-shots away, towards the north on the road to Mans, at a spot called Les Douze-Pierres, they raised a fort which they called London.[540]

By these works half of Orléans was invested, which was as good as saying that it was not invested at all. People went in and out as they pleased. Small relieving companies despatched by the King arrived without let or hindrance. On the 5th of January, 1429, Admiral de Culant with five hundred men-at-arms crosses the Loire opposite Saint-Loup and enters the city by the Burgundian Gate. On the 8th of February there enters William Stuart, brother of the Constable of Scotland, at the head of a thousand combatants well accoutred, and accompanied by several knights and squires. On the morrow they are followed by three hundred and twenty soldiers. Victuals and ammunition are constantly arriving; on the 3rd of January, nine hundred and fifty-four pigs and four hundred sheep; on the 10th, powder and victuals; on the 12th, six hundred pigs; on the 24th, six hundred head of fat cattle and two hundred pigs; on the 31st, eight horses loaded with oil and fat.[541]

It became evident to Lord Scales, William Pole, and Sir John Talbot, who since Salisbury's[542] death had been conducting the siege, that months and months must elapse ere the investment could be completed and the city surrounded by a ring of forts connected by a moat. Meanwhile the miserable *Godons*, up to the ears in mud and snow, were freezing in their wretched hovels, – mere shelters of wood and earth. If things went on thus they were in danger of being worse off and more starved than the besieged. Therefore, following the example of the late Earl, from time to time they tried to bring matters to a crisis; without great hope of success they endeavoured to take the town by assault.[543]

On the side of the Renard Gate the wall was lower than elsewhere; and, as their strongest force lay in this direction, they preferred to attack this part of the ramparts. They stormed the Renard Gate, rushing against the barriers with loud cries of Saint George; but the king's men and the city bands drove them back to their bastions.[544] Each of these ill planned and useless assaults cost them many men. And they already lacked both soldiers and horses.

Neither had they succeeded in alarming the people of Orléans by their double bombardment on the south and on the west. There was a joke in the town that a great cannon-ball had fallen near La Porte Bannière into the midst of a crowd of a hundred people without touching one, except a fellow who had his shoe taken off by it, but suffered no further hurt than having to put it on again.[545]

Meanwhile the French, English, and Burgundian knights took delight in performing valiant deeds of prowess. Whenever the whim took them, and under the slightest protest, they sallied forth into the country, but always with the object of capturing some booty, for they thought of little else. One day, for instance, towards the end of January, when it was bitterly cold, a little band of English marauders entered the vineyards of Saint-Ladre and Saint-Jean-de-la-Ruelle to gather sticks for firewood. The watchman no sooner announces them than behold all the banners flying to the wind. Marshal de Boussac, Messire Jacques de Chabannes, Seneschal of Bourbonnais, Messire Denis de Chaîlly, and many another baron, and with them captains and free-lances, make forth into the fields. Not one of them can have commanded as many as twenty men.[546]

The King's council was making every effort to succour Orléans. The King summoned the nobles of Auvergne. They had been true to the Lilies ever since the day when the Dauphin, Canon of Notre-Dame-d'Ancis, and barely more than a child, had travelled over wild peaks to subdue two or three rebellious barons.[547] At the royal call the nobles of Auvergne came forth from their mountains. Beneath the standard of the Count of Clermont, in the early days of February, they reached Blois, where they joined the Scottish force of John Stuart of Darnley, the Constable of Scotland, and a company from Bourbonnais, under the command of the barons La Tour-d'Auvergne and De Thouars.[548]

Just at this time tidings were received of a convoy of victuals and ammunition which Sir John Fastolf was bringing from Paris to the English at Orléans. With two hundred men-at-arms the Bastard started from Orléans to concert measures with the Count of Clermont. It was decided to attack the convoy. Commanded by the Count of Clermont and the Bastard the whole army from Blois marched towards Étampes with the object of encountering Sir John Fastolf.[549]

On the 11th of February there sallied forth from Orléans fifteen hundred fighting men commanded by Messire Guillaume d'Albret, Sir William Stuart, brother of the Constable of Scotland, the Marshal de Boussac, the Lord of Gravelle, the two Captains Saintrailles, Captain La Hire, the Lord of Verduzan, and sundry other knights and squires. They were summoned by the Bastard and ordered to join the Count of Clermont's army on the road to Étampes, at the village of Rouvray-Saint-Denis, near Angerville.[550]

The next day, Saturday, the eve of the first Sunday in Lent, when the Count of Clermont's army was still some distance away, they reached Rouvray. There, early in the morning, the Gascons of Poton and La Hire perceived the head of the convoy advancing into the plain, along the Étampes road.

There they were, a line of three hundred carts and wagons full of arms and victuals conducted by English soldiers and merchants and peasants from Normandy, Picardy, and Paris, fifteen hundred men at the most, all tranquil and unsuspecting. There naturally occurred to the Gascons the idea of falling upon these people and making short work with them at the moment when they least expected it.[551] In great haste they sent to the Count of Clermont for permission to attack. As handsome as Absalom and Paris of Troy, full of words and eaten up of vanity, the Count of Clermont, who was but a lad and none of the wisest, had that very day received his spurs and was at his first engagement.[552] He foolishly sent word to the Gascons not to attack before his arrival. The Gascons obeyed greatly disappointed; they saw what was being lost by waiting. And at length, perceiving that they have walked into the lion's mouth, the English leaders, Sir John Fastolf, Sir Richard Gethyn, Bailie of Évreux, Sir Simon Morhier, Provost of Paris, place themselves in good battle array. With their wagons they make a long narrow enclosure in the plain. There they entrench their horsemen, posting the archers in front, behind stakes planted in the ground with their points inclined towards the enemy.[553] Seeing these preparations, the Constable of Scotland loses patience and leads his four hundred horsemen in a rush upon the stakes, where the horses' legs are broken.[554] The English, discovering that it is only a small company they have to deal with, bring out their cavalry and charge with such force that they overthrow the French and slay three hundred. Meanwhile the men of Auvergne had reached Rouvray and were scouring the village, draining the cellars. The Bastard left them and came to the help of the Scots with four hundred fighting men. But he was wounded in the foot, and in great danger of being taken.[555]

There fell in this combat Lord William Stuart and his brother, the Lords of Verduzan, of Châteaubrun, of Rochechouart, Jean Chabot with many others of high nobility and great valour.[556] The English, not yet satiated with slaughter, scattered in pursuit of the fugitives. La Hire and Poton, beholding the enemy's standards dispersed over the plain, gathered together as many men as they could, between sixty and eighty, and threw themselves on a small part of the English force, which they overcame. If at this juncture the rest of the French had rallied they might have saved the honour and advantage of the day.[557] But the Count of Clermont, who had not attempted to come to the aid of the Bastard and the Constable of Scotland, displayed his unfailing cowardice to the end. Having seen them all slain, he returned with his army to Orléans, where he arrived well on into the night of the 12th of February.[558] There followed him with their troops in disorder, the Baron La Tour-d'Auvergne, the Viscount of Thouars, the Marshal de Boussac, the Lord of Gravelle and the Bastard, who with the greatest difficulty kept in the saddle. Jamet du Tillay, La Hire, and Poton came last, watching to see that the English did not complete their discomfiture by falling upon them from the forts.[559]

Because the Lenten fast was beginning, the victuals which Sir John Fastolf was bringing from Paris to the English round Orléans, consisted largely of red herrings, which had suffered during the battle from the casks containing them having been broken in. To honour the French for having discomfited so many natives of Dieppe the delighted English merrily named the combat the Battle of the Herrings.[560]

Albeit the Count of Clermont was the King's cousin, the people of Orléans received him but coldly. He was held to have acted shamefully and treacherously; and there were those who let him know what they thought. On the morrow he made off with his men of Auvergne and Bourbonnais amidst the rejoicings of the townsfolk who did not want to support those who would not fight.[561] At the same time there left the city Sire Louis de Culant, High Admiral of France and Captain La Hire, with two thousand men-at-arms. At their departure there arose from the citizens such howls of displeasure, that to appease them it was necessary to explain that the captains were going to fetch fresh supplies of men and victuals, which was the actual truth. My Lord Regnault de Chartres, the date of whose arrival at Orléans is uncertain, departed with them; but he could not be reproached for going, since as Chancellor of France his place was in the King's Council. But what must indeed have appeared strange was that my Lord Saint-Michel, the successor of Saint-Euverte and Saint-Aignan, should quit his episcopal see and desert his afflicted spouse.[562] When the rats go the vessel is on the point of sinking. Only the Lord Bastard and the Marshal de Boussac were left in the city. And even the Marshal was not to stay long. A month later he went, saying that the King had need of him and that he must go and take possession of broad lands fallen to him through his wife, by the death of his brother-in-law, the Lord of Châteaubrun, at the Battle of the Herrings.[563] The townsfolk deemed the reason a good one. He promised to return before long, and they were content. Now the Marshal de Boussac was one of the barons who had the welfare of the kingdom most at heart.[564] But he who has lands must needs do his duty by them.

Believing that they were betrayed and abandoned, the citizens bethought them of securing their own safety. Since the King was not able to protect them, they resolved that in order to escape from the English, they would give themselves to one more powerful than he. Therefore, to Lord Philip, Duke of Burgundy, they despatched Captain Poton of Saintrailles, who was known to him because he had been his prisoner, and two magistrates of the city, Jean de Saint-Avy and Guion du Fossé. Their mission was to pray and entreat the Duke to look favourably on the town, and for the sake of his good kinsman, their Lord, Charles, Duke of Orléans, a prisoner in England, and thus prevented from defending his own domain, to induce the English to

127

raise the siege until such time as the troubles of the realm should be set at rest.[565] Thus they were offering to place their town as a pledge in the hands of the Duke of Burgundy. Such an offer was in accordance with the secret desire of the Duke, who, having sent a few hundred Burgundian horse to the walls of Orléans, was helping the English, and did not intend to do it for nothing.[566]

Pending the uncertain and distant day when they might be thus protected, the people of Orléans continued to protect themselves as best they could. But they were anxious and not without reason. For although they might prevent the enemy from entering within the city, they could devise no means for speedily driving him away. In the early days of March they observed with concern that the English were digging a ditch to serve them as cover in passing from one bastion to another, from la Croix-Boissée to Saint-Ladre. This work they attempted to destroy. They vigorously attacked the *Godons* and took a few prisoners. With two shots from his culverin Maître Jean killed five persons, including Lord Gray, the nephew of the late Earl of Salisbury.[567] But they could not hinder the English from completing their work. The siege continued with terrible vigour. Agitated by doubts and fears, consumed with anxiety, without sleep, without rest, and succeeding in nothing, they began to despair. Suddenly a strange rumour arises, spreads, and gains credence.

It is told that there had lately passed through the town of Gien a maid (*une pucelle*), who proclaimed that she was on her way to Chinon to the gentle Dauphin, and said that she had been sent by God to raise the siege of Orléans and take the King to his anointing at Reims.[568]

In colloquial language, a maid (*une pucelle*) was a girl of humble birth, who earned her livelihood by manual work and was generally a servant. Thus the leaden pumps used in kitchens were usually called *pucelles*. The term was doubtless vulgar, but it had no evil meaning. In spite of Clopinel's naughty saying: "*Je lègue ma pucelle à mon curé,*" it was used to describe a respectable girl of good morals.[569]

The tidings that a little saint of lowly origin, one of Our Lord's poor, was bringing divine help to Orléans made a great impression on minds excited by the fevers of the siege and rendered religious through fear. The Maid inspired them with a burning curiosity, which the Lord Bastard, like a wise man, deemed it prudent to encourage. He despatched to Chinon two knights charged to inquire concerning the damsel. One was Sire Archambaud of Villars, Governor of Montargis, whom the Bastard had already sent to the King during the siege; he was an aged knight, once the intimate friend of Duke Louis of Orléans, and one of the seven Frenchmen who fought against the seven Englishmen at Montendre,[570] in 1402: an Orléans citizen of the early days, notwithstanding his great age he had vigourously defended Les Tourelles on the 21st of October. The other, Messire Jamet du Tillay, a Breton squire, had recently won great honour by covering the retreat of Rouvray with his men. They set forth and the whole town anxiously awaited their return.[571]

CHAPTER VI
THE MAID AT CHINON – PROPHECIES

ROM the village of Sainte-Catherine-de-Fierbois, Jeanne dictated a letter to the King, for she did not know how to write. In this letter she asked permission to come to him, and told him that to bring him aid she had travelled over one hundred and fifty leagues, and that she knew of many things for his good. She was said to have added that were he hidden amidst many others she would recognise him;[572] but later, when she was questioned on this matter, she replied that she had no recollection of it.

Towards noon, when the letter had been sealed, Jeanne and her escort set out for Chinon.[573] She went to the King, just as in those days there went to him the sons of poor widows of Azincourt and Verneuil riding lame horses found in some meadow, – fifteen-year-old lads coming forth from their ruined towers to mend their own fortunes and those of France; just as Loyalty, Desire, and Famine went to him.[574] Charles VII was France, the image and symbol of France. Yet he was but a poor creature withal, the eleventh of the miserable children born to the mad Charles VI and his prolific Bavarian Queen.[575] He had grown up among disasters, and had survived his four elder brethren. But he himself was badly bred, knock-kneed, and bandy-legged;[576] a veritable king's son, if his looks only were considered, and yet it was impossible to swear to his descent.[577] Through his presence on the bridge at Montereau on that day, when, according to a wise man, it were better to have died than to have been there,[578] he had grown pale and trembling, looking dully at everything going to wrack and ruin around him. After their victory of Verneuil and their partial conquest of Maine, the English had left him four years' respite. But his friends, his defenders, his deliverers had alike been terrible. Pious and humble, well content with his plain wife, he led a sad, anxious life in his châteaux on the Loire. He was timid. And well might he be so, for no sooner did he show friendship towards or confidence in one of the nobility than that noble was killed. The Constable de Richemont and the Sire de la Trémouille had drowned the Lord de Giac after a mock trial.[579] The Marshal de Boussac, by order of the Constable, had slain Lecamus de Beaulieu with even less ceremony. Lecamus was riding his mule in a meadow on the bank of the Clain, when he was set upon, thrown down, his head split open, and his hand cut off. The favourite's mule was taken back to the King.[580] The Constable de Richemont had given Charles in his stead La Trémouille, a very barrel of a man, a toper, a kind of Gargantua who devoured the country. La Trémouille having driven away Richemont, the King kept La Trémouille until the Constable, of whom he was greatly in dread, should return. And indeed so meek and fearful a prince had reason to dread this Breton, always defeated, always furious, bitter, ferocious, whose awkwardness and violence created an impression of rude frankness.[581]

In 1428 Richemont wanted to resume his influence over the King. The Counts of Clermont and of Pardiac united to aid him. The King's mother-in-law, Yolande of Aragon, the kingdomless Queen of Sicily and Jerusalem, and the Duchess of Anjou, took the part of the discontented barons.[582] The Count of Clermont took prisoner the Chancellor of France, the first minister of the crown, and held him to ransom. The King had to pay for the restoration of his Chancellor.[583] In Poitou the Constable was warring against the King's men, while the provinces which remained loyal were being wasted by free lances in the King's pay, while the English were advancing towards the Loire.

In the midst of such miseries, King Charles, thin, dwarfed in mind and body, cowering, timorous, suspicious, cut a sorry figure. Yet he was as good as another; and perhaps at that time he was just the king that was needed. A Philippe of Valois or a Jean le Bon would have amused himself by losing his provinces at the point of the sword. Poor King Charles had neither their means nor their desire to perform deeds of prowess, or to press to the front of the battle by riding down the common herd. He had one good point: he did not love feats of prowess and it was impossible for him to be one of those chivalrous knights who make war for the love of it. His grandfather before him, who had been equally lacking in chivalrous graces, had greatly damaged the English. The grandson had not Charles V's wisdom, but he also was not free from guile and was inclined to believe that more may be gained by the signing of a treaty than at the point of the lance.[584]

Concerning his poverty ridiculous stories were in circulation. It was said that a shoemaker, to whom he could not pay ready money, had torn from his leg the new gaiter he had just put on, and gone off, leaving the King with his old ones.[585] It was related how one day La Hire and Saintrailles, coming to see him, had found him dining with the Queen, with two chickens and a sheep's tail as their only entertainment.[586] But these were merely good stories. The King still possessed domains wide and rich; Auvergne, Lyonnais, Dauphiné, Touraine, Anjou, all the provinces south of the Loire, except Guyenne and Gascony.[587]

His great resource was to convoke the States General. The nobility gave nothing, alleging that it was beneath their dignity to pay money. When, notwithstanding their poverty, the clergy did contribute something, it was still, always the third estate that bore more than its share of the financial burden. That extraordinary tax, the *taille*,[588] became annual. The King summoned the Estates every year, sometimes twice a year. They met not without difficulty.[589] The roads were dangerous. At every corner travellers might be robbed or murdered. The officers, who journeyed from town to town collecting the taxes, had an armed escort for fear of the Scots and other men-at-arms in the King's service.[590]

In 1427 a free lance, Sabbat by name, in garrison at Langeais, was the terror of Touraine and Anjou. Thus the representatives of the towns were in no hurry to present themselves at the meeting of the Estates. It might have been different had they believed that their money would be employed for the good of the realm. But they knew that the King would first use it to make gifts to his barons. The deputies were invited to come and devise means for the repression of the pillage and plunder from which they were suffering;[591] and, when at the risk of their lives they did come to the royal presence, they were forced to consent to the *taille* in silence. The King's officers threatened to have them drowned if they opened their mouths. At the meeting of the Estates held at Mehun-sur-Yèvre in 1425 the men from the good towns said they would be glad to help the King, but first they desired that an end be put to pillage, and my Lord Bishop of Poitiers, Hugues de Comberel, said likewise. On hearing his words the Sire de Giac said to the King: "If my advice were taken, Comberel would be thrown into the river with the others of his opinion." Whereupon the men from the good towns voted two hundred and sixty thousand livres.[592] In September, 1427, assembled at Chinon, they granted five hundred thousand livres for the war.[593] By writs issued on the 8th of January, 1428, the King summoned the States General to meet six months hence, on the following 18th of July, at Tours.[594] On the 18th of July no one attended. On the 22nd of July came a new summons from the King, commanding the Estates to meet at Tours on the 10th of September.[595] But the meeting did not take place until October, at Chinon, just when the Earl of Salisbury was marching on the Loire. The States granted five hundred thousand livres.[596]

But the time could not be far off when the good people would be unable to pay any longer. In those days of war and pillage many a field was lying fallow, many a shop was closed, and few were the merchants ambling on their nags from town to town.[597]

The tax came in badly, and the King was actually suffering from want of money. To extricate himself from this embarrassment he employed three devices, of which the best was useless. First, as he owed every one money, – the Queen of Sicily,[598] La Trémouille,[599] his Chancellor,[600] his butcher,[601] the chapter of Bourges, which provided him with fresh fish,[602] his cooks,[603] his footmen,[604] – he made over the proceeds of the tax to his creditors.[605] Secondly, he alienated the royal domain: his towns and his lands belonged to every one save himself.[606] Thirdly, he coined false money. It was not with evil intent, but through necessity, and the practice was quite usual.[607]

The only title borne by La Trémouille was that of Conseiller-Chambellan, but he was also the Grand Usurer of the kingdom. His debtors were the King and a multitude of nobles high and low.[608] He was therefore a powerful personage. In those difficult days he rendered the crown services self-interested, but none the less valuable. From January to August, 1428, he advanced sums amounting to about twenty-seven thousand livres for which he received lands and castles as security.[609] Fortunately the Royal Council included a number of Jurists and Churchmen who were good business men. One of them, an Angevin, Robert Le Maçon, Lord of Trèves, of plebeian birth, had entered the Council during the Regency. He was the first among those of lowly origin who served Charles VII so ably that he came to be called The Well Served (*Le Bien Servi*).[610] Another, the Sire de Gaucourt, had aided his King in war.[611]

There is yet a third whom we must learn to know as well as possible. For he will play an important part in this story; and his part would appear greater still if it were laid bare in its entirety. This is Regnault de Chartres, whom we have already seen promoted to be minister of finance.[612] Son of Hector de Chartres, master of Woods and Waters in Normandy, he took orders, became archdeacon of Beauvais, then chamberlain of Pope John XXIII, and in 1414, at about thirty-four, was raised to the archiepiscopal see of Reims.[613] The following year three of his brothers fell on the gory field of Azincourt. In 1418 Hector de Chartres perished at Paris, assassinated by the Butchers.[614] Regnault himself, cast into prison by the Cabochiens, expected to be put to death. He vowed that if he escaped he would fast every Wednesday, and drink water for breakfast every Friday and Saturday, for the rest of his life.[615] One must not judge a man by an act prompted by fear. Nevertheless we may well hesitate to rank the author of this vow with those Epicureans who did not believe in God, of whom there were said to be many among the clerks. We may conclude rather that his intelligence submitted to the common beliefs.

A tragic fidelity, an inherited loyalty to the Armagnacs recommended my Lord Regnault to the Dauphin, who entrusted him with important missions to various parts of Christendom, Languedoc, Scotland, Brittany, and Burgundy.[616] The Archbishop of Reims acquitted himself with rare skill and indefatigable zeal. In December he prayed the Holy Father to dispense him from the fulfilment of the vow taken in the Butchers' prison,[617] on the grounds of his feeble health and his services rendered to the Dauphin, who required him to undertake frequent journeys and arduous embassies.

In 1425, when the King and the kingdom were governed by President Louvet,[618] a learned lawyer, who may well have been a rogue, my Lord Regnault was appointed Chancellor of France in the place of my Lord Martin Gouges of Charpaigne, Bishop of Clermont.[619] But shortly afterwards, when the Constable of France, Arthur of Brittany, had dismissed Louvet, Regnault sold his appointment to Martin Gouges for a pension of two thousand five hundred *livres tournois.*[620]

The Reverend Father in God, my Lord the Archbishop of Reims, was not as rich, far from it, as my Lord de la Trémouille; but he made the best of what he had. Like the Sire de la Trémouille he lent money to the King.[621] But in those days who did not lend the King money?

Charles VII gave him the town and castle of Vierzon in payment of a debt of sixteen thousand *livres tournois*.[622] When La Trémouille had treated the Constable as the Constable had treated Louvet, Regnault de Chartres became Chancellor again. He entered into his office on the 8th of November, 1428. By this time the Council had sent men-at-arms and cannon to Orléans. No sooner was my Lord of Reims appointed than he threw himself into the city and spared no trouble.[623] He was keenly attached to the goods of this world and might pass for a miser.[624] But there can be no doubt of his devotion to the royal cause, nor of his hatred of those who fought under the Leopard and the Red Cross.[625]

After eleven days' journey, Jeanne reached Chinon on the 6th of March.[626] It was the fourth Sunday in Lent, that very Sunday on which the lads and lasses of Domremy went forth in bands, into the country still grey and leafless, to eat their nuts and hard-boiled eggs, with the rolls their mothers had kneaded. That was what they called their well-dressing. But Jeanne was not to recollect past well-dressings nor the home she had left without a word of farewell.[627] Ignoring those rustic, well-nigh pagan festivals which poor Christians introduced into the penance of the holy forty days, the Church had named this Sunday *Lætare* Sunday, from the first word in the introit for the day: *Lætare, Jerusalem*. On that Sunday the priest, ascending the altar steps, says low mass; and at high mass the choir sings the following words from Scripture: "*Lætare, Jerusalem; et conventum facite, omnes qui diligitis eam* ...: Rejoice ye with Jerusalem, and be glad with her, all ye that love her: rejoice for joy with her all ye that mourn for her: That ye may suck, and be satisfied with the breasts of her consolations; ..."[628] That day priests, monks, and clerks versed in holy Scripture, as in the churches with the people assembled they sang *Lætare, Jerusalem*, had present before their minds the virgin announced by prophecy, raised up for the deliverance of the kingdom, marked with a sign, who was then making her humble entrance into the town. Perhaps more than one applied what that passage of Scripture says of the Holy Nation to the realm of France, and in the coincidence of that liturgical text and the happy coming of the Maid found occasion for hope. *Lætare, Jerusalem!* Rejoice ye, O people, in your true King and your rightful sovereign. *Et conventum facite*: and come together. Unite all your strength against the enemy. *Gaudete cum laetitia, qui in tristitia fuistis*: after your long mourning, rejoice. The Lord sends you succour and consolation.

By the intercession of Saint Julien, and probably with the aid of Collet de Vienne, the King's messenger, Jeanne found a lodging in the town, near the castle, in an inn kept by a woman of good repute.[629] The spits were idle. And the guests, deep in the chimney-corner, were watching the grilling of Saint Herring, who was suffering worse torments than Saint Lawrence.[630] In those times no one in Christendom neglected the Church's injunctions concerning the fasts and abstinences of Holy Lent. Following the example of Our Lord Jesus Christ who fasted forty days in the desert, the faithful observed the fast from Quadragesima Sunday until Easter Sunday, making forty days after abstracting the Sundays when the fast was broken but not the abstinence. Thus fasting and with her soul comforted, Jeanne listened to the soft whisper of her Voices.[631] The two days she spent in the inn were passed in retirement, on her knees.[632] The banks of the Vienne and the broad meadows, still in their black wintry garb, the hill-slopes over which light mists floated, did not tempt her. But when, on her way to church, climbing up a steep street, or merely grooming her horse in the inn yard, she raised her eyes to the north, there on a mountain close at hand, just about the distance that would be traversed by one of those stone cannon-balls which had been in use for the last fifty or sixty years, she saw the towers of the finest castle of the realm. Behind its proud walls there breathed that King to whom she had journeyed, impelled by a miraculous love.

There were three castles merging before her into one long mass of embattled walls, of keeps, towers, turrets, curtains, barbicans, ramparts, and watch-towers; three castles separated one from the other by dykes, barriers, posterns, and portcullis. On her left, towards sunset, crowded, one behind the other, the eight towers of Coudray, one of which had been built for a king of England, while the newest were more than two hundred years old. On the right could be plainly seen the middle castle, with its ancient walls and its towers crowned with machicolated battlements. There was the chamber of Saint Louis, the King's chamber, the apartment of him whom Jeanne called the Gentle Dauphin. And there also, close to the rush-strewn room, was the great hall in which she was to be received. Towards the town the site of the hall was indicated by an adjoining tower, square and very old. On the right extended a vast bailey or stronghold, intended as a lodging for the garrison, and a defence of the middle part of the castle. Near by a large chapel raised its roof, in the form of an inverted keel, above the ramparts. This chapel, built by Henry II of England, was under the patronage of Saint George, and from it the bailey received its name of Fort Saint George.[633] In those days every one knew the story of Saint George the valiant knight, who with his lance transfixed a dragon and delivered a King's daughter, and then suffered martyrdom confessing his faith. Like Saint Catherine he had been bound to a wheel with sharp spikes, and the wheel had been miraculously broken like that on which the executioners had bound the Virgin of Alexandria. And like her Saint George had suffered death by means of an axe, thus proving that he was a great saint.[634] In one thing, however, he was wrong; he was of the party of the *Godons*, who for more than three hundred years had kept his feast as that of all the English. They held him to be their patron saint and invoked him before all other saints. Thus his name was pronounced as constantly by the vilest Welsh archer as by a knight of the Garter. In truth no one knew what he thought and whether he did not condemn all these marauders who were fighting for a bad cause; but there was reason to fear that such great honours would affect him. The saints of Paradise are generally ready to take the side of those who invoke them most devoutly. And Saint George, after all, was just as English as Saint Michael was French. That glorious archangel had appeared as the most vigilant protector of the Lilies ever since my Lord Saint Denys, the patron saint of the kingdom, had permitted his abbey to be taken. And Jeanne knew it.

Meanwhile the despatches brought from the Commander of Vaucouleurs by Colet de Vienne were presented to the King.[635] These despatches instructed him concerning the deeds and sayings of the damsel. This was one of those countless matters to be examined by the Council, one which, it appears, the King must himself investigate, as pertaining to his royal office and as interesting him especially, since it might be a question of a damsel of remarkable piety, and he was himself the highest ecclesiastical personage in France.[636] His grandfather, wise prince that he was, would have been far from scorning the counsel of devout women in whom was the voice of God. About the year 1380 he had summoned to Paris Guillemette de la Rochelle, who led a solitary and contemplative life, and acquired such great power therefrom, so it was said, that during her transports she raised herself more than two feet from the ground. In many a church King Charles V had beautiful oratories built, where she might pray for him.[637] The grandson should do no less, for his need was still greater. There were still more recent examples in his family of dealings between kings and saints. His father, the poor King Charles VI, when he was passing through Tours, had caused Louis, Duke of Orléans, to present to him Dame Marie de Maillé. She had taken a vow of virginity and had transformed the spouse, who approached her like a devouring lion, into a timorous lamb. She revealed secrets to the King, and he was pleased with her, for three years later he wanted to see her again at Paris. This time they talked long together in private, and she revealed more secrets to the King, so that he sent her away with gifts.[638] This same Prince had granted an audience to a poor knight of Caux, one Robert le Mennot, to whom, when he was in danger of shipwreck near the coast of Syria, had been vouchsafed a vision. He proclaimed that God had sent him to restore peace.[639] Still more favourably had the King received a woman, Marie Robine, who was commonly called la Gasque of Avignon.[640] In 1429, there were those at court who remembered the prophetess sent to Charles VI to confirm him in his subjection to Pope Benedict XIII. This pope was held to be an antipope; nevertheless, La Gasque was regarded as a prophetess. Like Jeanne she had had many visions concerning the desolation of the realm of France; and she had seen weapons in the sky.[641] The kings of England were no less ready than the kings of France to heed the words of those saintly men and women, multitudes of whom were at that time uttering prophecies. Henry V consulted the hermit of Sainte-Claude, Jean de Gand, who foretold the King's approaching death; and on his death-bed he again had the stern prophet summoned.[642] It was the custom of saints to speak to kings and of kings to listen to them. How could a pious prince disdain so miraculous a source of counsel? Had he done so he would have incurred the censure of the wisest.

King Charles read the Commander of Vaucouleur's letters, and had the damsel's escort examined before him. Of her mission and her miracles they could say nothing. But they spoke of the good they had seen in her during the journey, and affirmed that there was no evil in her.[643]

Of a truth, God speaketh through the mouths of virgins. But in such matters it is necessary to act with extreme caution, to distinguish carefully between the true prophetesses and the false, not to take for messengers from heaven the heralds of the devil. The latter sometimes create illusions. Following the example of Simon the Magician, who worked wonders vying with the miracles of St. Peter, these creatures have recourse to diabolical arts for the seduction of men. Twelve years before, there had prophesied a woman, likewise from the Lorraine Marches, Catherine Suave, a native of Thons near Neufchâteau, who lived as a recluse at Port de Lates, yet most certainly did the Bishop of Maguelonne know her to be a liar and a sorceress, wherefore she was burned alive at Montpellier in 1417.[644] Multitudes of women, or rather of females, *mulierculæ*,[645] lived like this Catherine and ended like her.

Certain ecclesiastics briefly interrogated Jeanne and asked her wherefore she had come. At first she replied that she would say nothing save to the King. But when the clerks represented to her that they were questioning her in the King's name, she told them that the King of Heaven had bidden her do two things: one was to raise the siege of Orléans, the other to lead the King to Reims for his anointing and his coronation.[646] Just as at Vaucouleurs before Sire Robert, so before these Churchmen she repeated very much what the vavasour of Champagne had said formerly, when he had been sent to Jean le Bon, as she was now sent to the Dauphin Charles.

Having journeyed as far as the Plain of Beauce, where King John, impatient for battle, was encamped with his army, the vavasour of Champagne entered the camp and asked to see the wisest and best of the King's liegemen at court. The nobles, to whom this request was carried, began to laugh. But one among them, who had with his own eyes seen the vavasour, recognised at once that he was a good, simple man and without guile. He said to him: "If thou hast any advice to give, go to the King's chaplain." The vavasour therefore went to King John's chaplain and said to him: "Obtain for me an audience of the King; I have something to tell that I will say to no one but to him." "What is it?" asked the chaplain. "Tell me what is in your heart." But the good man would not reveal his secret. The chaplain went to King John and said to him: "Sire, there is a worthy man here who seems to me wise in his way. He desires to say to you something that he will tell to you alone." King John refused to see the good man. He summoned his confessor, and, accompanied by the chaplain, sent him to learn the vavasour's secret. The two priests went to the man and told him that the King had appointed them to hear him. At this announcement, despairing of ever seeing King John, and trusting to the Confessor and the chaplain not to reveal his secret to any but the King, he uttered these words: "While I was alone in the fields, a voice spake unto me three times, saying: 'Go unto King John of France and warn him that he fight not with any of his enemies.' Obedient to that voice am I come to bring the tidings to King John." Having heard the vavasour's secret the confessor and the chaplain took him to the King, who laughed at him. With his comrades-in-arms he advanced to Poitiers, where he met the Black Prince. He lost his whole army in battle, and, twice wounded in the face, was taken prisoner by the English.[647]

The ecclesiastics, who had examined Jeanne, held various opinions concerning her. Some declared that her mission was a hoax, and that the King ought to beware of her.[648] Others on the contrary held that, since she said she was sent of God, and that she had something to tell the King, the King should at least hear her.

Two priests who were then with the King, Jean Girard, President of the Parlement of Grenoble, and Pierre l'Hermite, later subdean of Saint-Martin-de-Tours, judged the case difficult and interesting enough to be submitted to Messire Jacques Gélu, that Armagnac prelate who had long served the house of Orléans and the Dauphin of France both in council and in diplomacy. When he was nearly sixty, Gélu had withdrawn from the Council, and exchanged the archiepiscopal see of Tours for the bishopric of Embrun, which was less exalted and more retired. He was illustrious and venerable.[649] Jean Girard and Pierre l'Hermite informed him of the coming of the damsel in a letter, wherein they told him also that, having been questioned in turn by three professors of theology, she had been found devout, sober, temperate, and in the habit of participating once a week in the sacraments of confession and communion. Jean Girard thought she might have been sent by the God who raised up Judith and Deborah, and who spoke through the mouths of the Sibyls.[650]

Charles was pious, and on his knees devoutly heard three masses a day. Regularly at the canonical hours he repeated the customary prayers in addition to prayers for the dead and other orisons. Daily he confessed, and communicated on every feast day.[651] But he believed in foretelling events by means of the stars, in which he did not differ from other princes of his time. Each one of them had an astrologer in his service.[652]

The late Duke of Burgundy had been constantly accompanied by a Jewish soothsayer, Maître Mousque. On that day, the end of which he was never to see, as he was going to the Bridge of Montereau, Maître Mousque counselled him not to advance any further, prophesying that he would not return. The Duke continued on his way and was killed.[653] The Dauphin Charles confided in Jean des Builhons, in Germain de Thibonville and in all others of the peaked cap.[654]

He always had two or three astrologers at court. These almanac makers drew up schemes of nativity, cast horoscopes and read in the sky the approach of wars and revolutions. One of them, Maître Rolland the Scrivener, a fellow of the University of Paris, was one night, at a certain hour, observing the heavens from his roof, when he saw the apex of Virgo in the ascendant, Venus, Mercury, and the sun half way up the sky.[655] This his colleague, Guillaume Barbin of Geneva, interpreted to mean that the English would be driven from France and the King restored by the hand of a mere maid.[656] If we may believe the Inquisitor Bréhal, some time before Jeanne's coming into France, a clever astronomer of Seville, Jean de Montalcin by name, had written to the King among other things the following words: "By a virgin's counsel thou shalt be victorious. Continue in triumph to the gates of Paris."[657]

At that very time the Dauphin Charles had with him at Chinon an old Norman astrologer, one Pierre, who may have been Pierre de Saint-Valerien, canon of Paris. The latter had recently returned from Scotland, whither, accompanied by certain nobles, he had gone to fetch the Lady Margaret, betrothed to the Dauphin Louis. Not long afterwards this Maître Pierre was, rightly or wrongly, believed to have read in the sky that the shepherdess from the Meuse valley was appointed to drive out the English.[658]

Jeanne had not long to wait in her inn. Two days after her arrival, what she had so ardently desired came to pass: she was taken to the King.[659] In the last century near the Grand-Carroy, opposite a wooden-fronted house, there was shown a well on the edge of which, according to tradition, Jeanne set foot when she alighted from her horse, before climbing the steep ascent leading to the Castle. Through La Vieille Porte,[660] she was already crossing the moat when the King was still hesitating as to whether he would receive her. Many of his familiar advisers, and those not the least important, counselled him to beware of a strange woman whose designs might be evil. There were others who put it before him that this shepherdess was introduced by letters from Robert de Baudricourt carried through hostile provinces; that in journeying to the King she had forded many rivers in a manner almost miraculous. On these considerations the King consented to receive her.[661]

The great hall was crowded. As at every audience given by the King the room was close with the breath of the assembled multitude. The vast chamber presented that aspect of a market-house or of a rout which was so familiar to courtiers. It was evening; fifty torches flamed beneath the painted beams of the roof.[662] Men of middle age in robes and furs, young, smooth-faced nobles, thin and narrow shouldered, of slender build, their lean legs in tight hose, their feet in long, pointed shoes; barons fully armed to the number of three hundred, according to Aulic custom, pushed, crowded and elbowed each other while the usher was here and there striking the courtiers on the head with his rod.[663]

Besides the two ambassadors from Orléans, Messire Jamet du Tillay and the old baron Archambaud de Villars, governor of Montargis, there were present Simon Charles, Master of Requests, as well as certain great nobles, the Count of Clermont, the Sire de Gaucourt, and probably the Sire de La Trémouille and my Lord the Archbishop of Reims, Chancellor of the kingdom.[664] On hearing of Jeanne's approach, King Charles buried himself among his retainers, either because he was still mistrustful and hesitating, or because he had other persons to speak to, or for some other reason.[665] Jeanne was presented by the Count of Vendôme.[666] Robust, with a firm, short neck, her figure appeared full, although confined by her man's jerkin. She wore breeches like a man,[667] but still more surprising than her hose was her head-gear and the cut of her hair. Beneath a woollen hood, her dark hair hung cut round in soup-plate fashion like a page's.[668] Women of all ranks and all ages were careful to hide their hair so that not one lock of it should escape from beneath the coif, the veil, or the high head-dress which was then the mode. Jeanne's flowing locks looked strange to the folk of those days.[669] She went straight to the King, took off her cap, curtsied, and said: "God send you long life, gentle Dauphin."[670]

Afterwards there were those who marvelled that she should have recognised him in the midst of nobles more magnificently dressed than he. It is possible that on that day he may have been poorly attired. We know that it was his custom to have new sleeves put to his old doublets.[671] And in any case he did not show off his clothes. Very ugly, knock-kneed, with emaciated thighs, small, odd, blinking eyes, and a large bulbous nose, on his bony, bandy legs tottered and trembled this prince of twenty-six.[672]

That Jeanne should have seen his picture already and recognised him by it is hardly likely. Portraits of princes were rare in those days. Jeanne had never handled one of those precious books in which King Charles may have been painted in miniature as one of the Magi offering gifts to the Child Jesus.[673] It was not likely that she had ever seen one of those figures painted on wood in the semblance of her King, with hands clasped, beneath the curtains of his oratory.[674] And if by chance some one had shown her one of these portraits her untrained eyes could have discerned but little therein. Neither need we inquire whether the people of Chinon had described to her the costume the King usually wore and the shape of his hat: for like every one else he kept his hat on indoors even at dinner. What is most probable is that those who were kindly disposed towards her pointed out the King. At any rate he was not difficult to distinguish, since those who saw her go up to him were in no wise astonished.

When she had made her rustic curtsey, the King asked her name and what she wanted. She replied: "Fair Dauphin, my name is Jeanne the Maid; and the King of Heaven speaks unto you by me and says that you shall be anointed and crowned at Reims, and be lieutenant of the King of Heaven, who is King of France." She asked to be set about her work, promising to raise the siege of Orléans.[675]

The King took her apart and questioned her for some time. By nature he was gentle, kind to the poor and lowly, but not devoid of mistrust and suspicion.

It is said that during this private conversation, addressing him with the familiarity of an angel, she made him this strange announcement: "My Lord bids me say unto thee that thou art indeed the heir of France and the son of a King; he has sent me to thee to lead thee to Reims to be crowned there and anointed if thou wilt."[676] Afterwards the Maid's chaplain reported these words, saying he had received them from the Maid herself. All that is certain is that the Armagnacs were not slow to turn them into a miracle in favour of the Line of the Lilies. It was asserted that these words spoken by God himself, by the mouth of an innocent girl, were a reply to the carking, secret anxiety of the King. Madame Ysabeau's son, it was said, distracted and saddened by the thought that perhaps the royal blood did not flow in his veins, was ready to renounce his kingdom and declare himself a usurper, unless by some heavenly light his doubts concerning his birth should be dispelled.[677] Men told how his face shone with joy[678] when it was revealed to him that he was the true heir of France.

Doubtless the Armagnac preachers were in the habit of speaking of Queen Ysabeau as "*une grande gorre*" and a Herodias of licentiousness; but one would like to know whence her son derived his curious misgiving. He had not manifested it on entering into his inheritance; and, had occasion required, the jurists of his party would have proved to him by reasons derived from laws and customs that he was by birth the true heir and the lawful successor of the late King; for filiation must be proved not by what is hidden, but by what is manifest, otherwise it would be impossible to assign the legal heir to a kingdom or to an acre of land. Nevertheless it must be borne in mind that the King was very unfortunate at this time. Now misfortune agitates the conscience and raises scruples; and he might well doubt the justice of his cause since God was forsaking him. But if he were indeed assailed by painful doubts, how can he have been relieved from them by the words of a damsel who, as far as he then knew, might be mad or sent to him by his enemies? It is hard to reconcile such credulity with what we know of his suspicious nature. The first thought that occurred to him must have been that ecclesiastics had instructed the damsel.

A few moments after he had dismissed her, he assembled the Sire de Gaucourt and certain other members of his Council and repeated to them what he had just heard: "She told me that God had sent her to aid me to recover my kingdom."[679] He did not add that she had revealed to him a secret known to himself alone.[680]

The King's Counsellors, knowing little of the damsel, decided that they must have her before them to examine her concerning her life and her belief.[681]

The Sire de Gaucourt took her from the inn and lodged her in a tower of that Castle of Coudray, which for the last three days she had seen dominating the town.[682] One of the three castles, Le Coudray was only separated from the middle château in which the King dwelt by a moat and fortifications.[683] The Sire de Gaucourt confided her to the care of the lieutenant of the Town of Chinon, Guillaume Bellier, the King's Major Domo.[684] He gave her for her servant one of his own pages, a child of fifteen, Immerguet, sometimes called Minguet, and sometimes Mugot. His real name was Louis de Coutes, and he came of an old warrior family which had been in the service of the house of Orléans for a century. His father, Jean, called Minguet, Lord of Fresnay-le-Gelmert, of la Gadelière and of Mitry, Chamberlain to the Duke of Orléans, had died in great poverty the year before. He had left a widow and five children, three boys and two girls, one of whom, Jeanne by name, had since 1421 been the wife of Messire Florentin d'Illiers, Governor of Châteaudun. Thus the little page, Louis de Coutes, and his mother, Catherine le Mercier, Dame de Noviant, who came of a noble Scottish family, were both in a state of penury, albeit the Duke of Orléans in acknowledgment of his Chamberlain's faithful services had from his purse granted aid to the Lady of Noviant.[685] Jeanne kept Minguet with her all day, but at night she slept with the women.

The wife of Guillaume Bellier, who was good and pious, at least so it was said, watched over her.[686] At Coudray the page saw her many a time on her knees. She prayed and often wept many tears.[687] For several days persons of high estate came to speak with her. They found her dressed as a boy.[688]

Since she had been with the King, divers persons asked her whether there were not in her country a wood called "Le Bois-Chenu."[689] This question was put to her because a prophecy of Merlin concerning a maid who should come from "Le Bois-Chenu" was then in circulation. And folk were impressed by it; for in those days every one gave heed to prophecies and especially to those of Merlin the Magician.[690]

Begotten of a woman by the Devil, it was from him that Merlin derived his profound wisdom. To the science of numbers, which is the key to the future, he added a knowledge of physics, by means of which he worked his enchantments. Thus it was easy for him to transform rocks into giants. And yet he was conquered by a woman; the fairy Vivien enchanted the enchanter and kept him in a hawthorn bush under a spell. This is only one of many examples of the power of women.

Famous doctors and illustrious masters held that Merlin had laid bare many future events and prophesied many things which had not yet happened. To such as were amazed that the son of the Devil should have received the gift of prophecy they replied that the Holy Ghost is able to reveal his secrets to whomsoever he pleases, for had he not caused the Sibyls to speak, and opened the mouth of Balaam's ass?

Merlin had seen in a vision Sire Bertrand du Guesclin in the guise of a warrior bearing an eagle on his shield. This was remembered after the Constable had wrought his great deeds.[691]

In the prophecies of this Wise Man the English believed no less firmly than the French. When Arthur of Brittany, Count of Richemont, was taken prisoner, held to ransom, and brought before King Henry, the latter, when he perceived a boar on the arms of the Duke, broke forth into rejoicing; for he called to mind the words of Merlin who had said, "A Prince of Armorica, called Arthur, with a boar for his crest, shall conquer England, and when he shall have made an end of the English folk he shall re-people the land with a Breton race."[692]

Now during the Lent of 1429 there was circulated among the Armagnacs this prophecy, taken from a book of the prophecies of Merlin: "From the town of the Bois-Chenu there shall come forth a maid for the healing of the nation. When she hath stormed every citadel, with her breath she shall dry up all the springs. Bitter tears shall she shed and fill the Island with a terrible noise. Then shall she be slain by the stag with ten antlers, of which six branches shall bear crowns of gold, and the other six shall be changed into the horns of oxen; and with a horrible sound they shall shake the Isles of Britain. The forest of Denmark shall rise up and with a human voice say: 'Come, Cambria, and take Cornwall unto thyself.'"[693]

In these mysterious words Merlin dimly foretells that a virgin shall perform great and wonderful deeds before perishing by the hand of the enemy. On one point only is he clear, or so it seems; that is, when he says that this virgin shall come from the town of the Bois-Chenu.

If this prophecy had been traced back to its original source and read in the fourth book of the *Historia Britonum*, where it is to be found under the title of *Guyntonia Vaticinium*, it would have been seen to refer to the English city of Winchester, and it would have appeared that in the version then in circulation in France, the original meaning had been garbled, distorted, and completely metamorphosed. But no one thought of verifying the text. Books were rare and minds uncritical. This deliberately falsified prophecy was accepted as the pure word of Merlin and numerous copies of it were spread abroad.

Whence came these copies? Their origin doubtless will remain a mystery for ever; but one point is certain: they referred to La Romée's daughter, to the damsel who, from her father's house, could see the edge of "Le Bois-Chenu." Thus they came from close at hand and were of recent circulation.[694] If this amended prophecy of Merlin be not the one that reached Jeanne in her village, forecasting that a Maid should come from the Lorraine Marches for the saving of the kingdom, then it was closely related to it. The two prognostications have a family likeness.[695] They were uttered in the same spirit and with the same intention; and they indicate that the ecclesiastics of the

Meuse valley and those of the Loire had agreed to draw attention to the inspired damsel of Domremy.

As Merlin had foretold the works of Jeanne, so Bede must also have predicted them, for Bede and Merlin were always together in matters of prophecy.

The Monk of Wearmouth, the Venerable Bede, who had been dead six centuries, had been a veritable mine of knowledge in his lifetime. He had written on theology and chronology; he had discoursed of night and day, of weeks and months, of the signs of the zodiac, of epacts, of the lunar cycle, and of the movable feasts of the Church. In his book *De temporum ratione* he had treated of the seventh and eighth ages of the world, which were to follow the age in which he lived. He had prophesied. During the siege of Orléans, churchmen were circulating these obscure lines attributed to him, and foretelling the coming of the Maid:

Bis sex cuculli, bis septem se sociabunt,[696]
Gallorum pulli Tauro nova bella parabunt
Ecce beant bella, tunc fert vexilla Puella.

The first of these lines is a chronogram, that is, it contains a date. To decipher it you take the numeral letters of the line and add them together; the total gives the date.

bIs seX CVCVLLI, bIs septeM se soCIabVnt.

$1 + 10 + 100 + 5 + 100 + 5 + 50 + 50 + 1 + 1 + 1000 + 100 + 1 + 5 = 1429.$

Had any one sought these lines in the works of the Venerable Bede they would not have found them, because they are not there; but no one thought of looking for them any more than they thought of looking for the Forêt Chenue in Merlin.[697] And it was understood that both Bede and Merlin had foretold the coming of the Maid. In those days prophecies, chronograms, and charms flew like pigeons from the banks of the Loire and spread abroad throughout the realm. Not later than the May or June of this year the pseudo Bede will reach Burgundy. Earlier still he will be heard of in Paris. The aged Christine de Pisan, living in retirement in a French abbey, before the last day of July, 1429, will write that Bede and Merlin had beheld the Maid in a vision.[698]

The clerks, who were busy forging prophecies for the Maid's benefit, did not stop at a pseudo Bede and a garbled Merlin. They were truly indefatigable, and by a stroke of good luck we possess a piece of their workmanship which has escaped the ravages of time. It is a short Latin poem written in the obscure prophetic style, of which the following is a translation through the old French.

"A virgin clothed in man's attire, with the body of a maid, at God's behest goes forth to raise the downcast King, who bears the lilies, and to drive out his accursed enemies, even those who now beleaguer the city of Orléans and strike terror into the hearts of its inhabitants. And if the people will take heart and go out to battle, the treacherous English shall be struck down by death, at the hand of the God of battles who fights for the Maid, and the French shall cause them to fall, and then shall there be an end of the war; and the old covenants and the old friendship shall return. Pity and righteousness shall be restored. There shall be a treaty of peace, and all men shall of their own accord return to the King, which King shall weigh justice and administer it unto all men and preserve his subjects in beautiful peace. Henceforth no English foe with the sign of the leopard shall dare to call himself King of France and adopt the arms of France, which arms are borne by the holy Maid."[699]

These false prophecies give some idea of the means employed for the setting to work of the inspired damsel. Such methods may be somewhat too crafty for our liking. These clerks had but one object, – the peace of the realm and of the church. The miraculous deliverance of the people had to be prepared. We must not be too hasty to condemn those pious frauds without which the Maid could not have worked her miracles. Much art and some guile are necessary to contrive for innocence a hearing.

Meanwhile, on a steep rock, on the bank of the Durance, in the remote see of Saint-Marcellin, Jacques Gélu remained faithful to the King he had served and careful for the interests of the house of Orléans and of France. To the two churchmen, Jean Girard and Pierre l'Hermite, he replied that, for the sake of the orphan and the oppressed, God would doubtless manifest himself, and would frustrate the evil designs of the English; yet one should not easily and lightly believe the words of a peasant girl bred in solitude, for the female sex was frail and easily deceived, and France must not be made ridiculous in the eyes of the foreigner. "The French," he added, "are already famous for the ease with which they are duped." He ended by advising Pierre l'Hermite that it would be well for the King to fast and do penance so that Heaven might enlighten him and preserve him from error.[700]

But the mind of the oracle and ex-councillor could not rest. He wrote direct to King Charles and Queen Marie to warn them of the danger. To him it seemed that there could be no good in the damsel. He mistrusted her for three reasons: first, because she came from a country in the possession of the King's enemies, Burgundians and Lorrainers; secondly, she was a shepherdess and easily deceived; thirdly, she was a maid. He cited as an example Alexander of Macedon, whom a Queen endeavoured to poison. She had been fed on venom by the King's enemies and then sent to him in the hope that he would fall a victim to the wench's[701] wiles. But Aristotle dismissed the seductress and thus delivered his prince from death. The Archbishop of Embrun, as wise as Aristotle, warned the King against conversing with the damsel in private. He advised that she should be kept at a distance and examined, but not repulsed.

A prudent answer to those letters reassured Gélu. In a new epistle he testified to the King his satisfaction at hearing that the damsel was regarded with suspicion and left in uncertainty as to whether she would or would not be believed. Then, with a return to his former misgivings, he added: "It behoves not that she should have frequent access to the King until such time as certainty be established concerning her manner of life and her morals."[702]

King Charles did indeed keep Jeanne in uncertainty as to what was believed of her. But he did not suspect her of craftiness and he received her willingly. She talked to him with the simplest familiarity. She called him gentle Dauphin, and by that term she implied nobility and royal magnificence.[703] She also called him her *oriflamme*, because he was her *oriflamme*, or, as in modern language she would have expressed it, her standard.[704] The *oriflamme* was the royal banner. No one at Chinon had seen it, but marvellous things were told of it. The *oriflamme* was in the form of a gonfanon with two wings, made of a costly silk, fine and light, called *sandal*,[705] and it was edged with tassels of green silk. It had come down from heaven; it was the banner of Clovis and of Saint Charlemagne. When the King went to war it was carried before him. So great was its virtue that the enemy at its approach became powerless and fled in terror. It was remembered how, when in 1304 Philippe le Bel defeated the Flemings, the knight who bore it was slain. The next day he was found dead, but still clasping the standard in his arms.[706] It had floated in front of King Charles VI before his misfortunes, and since then it had never been unfurled.

One day when the Maid and the King were talking together, the Duke of Alençon entered the hall. When he was a child, the English had taken him prisoner at Verneuil and kept him five years in the Crotoy Tower.[707] Only recently set at liberty, he had been shooting quails near Saint-Florent-lès-Saumur, when a messenger had brought the tidings that God had sent a damsel to the King to turn the English out of France.[708] This news interested him as much as any one because he had married the Duke of Orléans' daughter; and straightway he had come to Chinon to see for himself. In the days of his graceful youth the Duke of Alençon appeared to advantage, but he was never renowned for his wisdom. He was weak-minded, violent, vain, jealous, and extremely credulous. He believed that ladies find favour by means of a certain herb, the mountain-heath; and later he thought himself bewitched. He had a disagreeable, harsh voice; he knew it, and the knowledge annoyed him.[709] As soon as she saw him approaching, Jeanne asked who this noble was. When the King replied that it was his cousin Alençon, she curtsied to the Duke and said: "Be welcome. The more representatives of the blood royal are here the better."[710] In this she was completely mistaken. The Dauphin smiled bitterly at her words. Not much of the royal blood of France ran in the Duke's veins.

On the next day Jeanne went to the King's mass. When she approached her Dauphin she bowed before him. The King took her into a room and sent every one away except the Sire de la Trémouille and the Duke of Alençon.

Then Jeanne addressed to him several requests. More especially did she ask him to give his kingdom to the King of Heaven. "And afterwards," she added, "the King of Heaven will do for you what he has done for your predecessors and will restore you to the condition of your fathers."[711]

In discoursing thus of things spiritual, in giving utterance to those precepts of reformation and of a new life, she was repeating what the clerks had taught her. Nevertheless she was by no means imbued with this doctrine. It was too subtle for her, and it was shortly to fade from her mind and give place to an ardour less monastic but more chivalrous.

That same day she rode out with the King and threw a lance in the meadow with so fine a grace that the Duke of Alençon, marvelling, made her a present of a horse.[712]

A few days later this young noble took her to the Abbey of Saint-Florent-lès-Saumur,[713] the church of which was so greatly admired that it was called La Belle d'Anjou. Here in this abbey there dwelt at that time his mother and his wife. It is said that they were glad to see Jeanne. But they had no great faith in the issue of the war. The young Dame of Alençon said to her: "Jeannette, I am full of fear for my husband. He has just come out of prison, and we have had to give so much money for his ransom that gladly would I entreat him to stay at home." To which Jeanne replied: "Madame, have no fear. I will bring him back to you in safety, and either such as he is now or better."[714]

She called the Duke of Alençon her fair Duke,[715] and loved him for the sake of the Duke of Orléans, whose daughter he had married. She loved him also because he believed in her when all others doubted or denied, and because the English had done him wrong. She loved him too because she saw he had a good will to fight. It was told how when he was a captive in the hands of the English at Verneuil, and they proposed to give him back his liberty and his goods if he would join their party, he had rejected their offer.[716] He was young like her; she thought that he like her must be sincere and noble. And perhaps in those days he was, for doubtless he was not then seeking to discover powders with which to dry up the King.[717]

It was decided that Jeanne should be taken to Poitiers to be examined by the doctors there.[718] In this town the Parlement met. Here also were gathered together many famous clerks learned in theology, secular as well as regular,[719] and grave doctors and masters were summoned to join them. Jeanne set out under escort. At first she thought she was being taken to Orléans. Her faith was like that of the ignorant but believing folk, who, having taken the cross, went forth and thought every town they approached was Jerusalem. Half way she inquired of her guides where they were taking her. When she heard that it was to Poitiers: "In God's name!" she said, "much ado will be there, I know. But my Lord will help me. Now let us go on in God's strength!"[720]

CHAPTER VII
THE MAID AT POITIERS

OR fourteen years the town of Poitiers had been the capital of that part of France which belonged to the French. The Dauphin Charles had transferred his Parlement there, or rather had assembled there those few members who had escaped from the Parlement of Paris. The Parlement of Poitiers consisted of two chambers only. It would have judged as wisely as King Solomon had there been any questions on which to pronounce judgment, but no litigants presented themselves – they were afraid of being captured on the way by freebooters and captains in the King's pay; besides, in the disturbed state of the kingdom justice had little to do with the settlement of disputes. The councillors, who for the most part had lands near Paris, were hard put to it for food and clothing. They were rarely paid and there were no perquisites. In vain they had inscribed their registers with the formula: *Non deliberetur donec solvantur species*; no payments were forthcoming from the suitors.[721] The Attorney General, Messire Jean Jouvenel des Ursins, who owned rich lands and houses in Île-de-France, Brie, and Champagne, was filled with pity at the sight of that good and honourable lady his wife, his eleven children, and his three sons-in-law going barefoot and poorly clad through the streets of the town.[722] As for the doctors and professors who had followed the King's fortunes, in vain were they wells of knowledge and springs of clerkly learning, since, for lack of a University to teach in, they reaped no advantage from their eloquence and their erudition. The town of Poitiers, having become the first city in the realm, had a Parlement but no University, like a lady highly born but one-eyed withal, for the Parlement and the University are the two eyes of a great city. Thus in their doleful leisure they were consumed with a desire, if it were God's will, to restore the King's fortunes as well as their own. Meanwhile, shivering with cold and emaciated with hunger, they groaned and lamented. Like Israel in the desert they sighed for the day when the Lord, inclining his ear to their supplications, should say: "At even ye shall eat flesh, and in the morning ye shall be filled with bread: and ye shall know that I am the Lord your God." *Vespere comedetis carnes et mane saturabimini panibus: scietisque quod ego sum Dominus deus vester.* (Exodus xvi, 12.) It was from among these poor and faithful servants of a poverty-stricken King that were chosen for the most part the doctors and clerks charged with the examination of the Maid. They were: the Lord Bishop of Poitiers;[723] the Lord Bishop of Maguelonne;[724] Maître Jean Lombard, doctor in theology, sometime professor of theology at the University of Paris;[725] Maître Guillaume le Maire, bachelor of theology, canon of Poitiers;[726] Maître Gérard Machet, the King's Confessor;[727] Maître Jourdain Morin;[728] Maître Jean Érault, professor of theology;[729] Maître Mathieu Mesnage, bachelor of theology;[730] Maître Jacques Meledon;[731] Maître Jean Maçon, a very famous doctor of civil law and of canon law;[732] Brother Pierre de Versailles, a monk of Saint-Denys in France, of the order of Saint Benedict, professor of theology, Prior of the Priory of Saint-Pierre de Chaumont, Abbot of Talmont in the diocese of Laon, Ambassador of his most Christian Majesty the King of France;[733] Brother Pierre Turelure, of the Order of Saint Dominic, Inquisitor at Toulouse;[734] Maître Simon Bonnet;[735] Brother Guillaume Aimery, of the Order of Saint-Dominic, doctor and professor of theology;[736] Brother Seguin of Seguin of the Order of Saint Dominic, doctor and professor of theology;[737] Brother Pierre Seguin, Carmelite;[738] several of the King's Councillors, licentiates of civil as well as of canon law.

Here was a large assembly of doctors for the cross-examination of one shepherdess. But we must remember that in those days theology subtle and inflexible dominated all human knowledge and forced the secular arm to give effect to its judgment. Therefore, as soon as an ignorant girl caused it to be believed that she had seen God, the Virgin, the saints, and the angels, she must either pass from miracle to miracle, through an edifying death to beatification, or from heresy to heresy through an ecclesiastical prison, to be burnt as a witch. And, as the holy inquisitors were fully persuaded that the Devil easily entered into a woman, the unhappy creature was more likely to be burnt alive than to die in an odour of sanctity. But Jeanne before the doctors at Poitiers was an exception; she ran no risk of being suspected in matters of faith. Even Brother Pierre Turelure himself had no desire to find in her one of those heretics he zealously sought to discover at Toulouse. In her presence the illustrious masters drew in their theological claws. They were churchmen, but they were Armagnacs, for the most part business men, diplomatists, old councillors of the Dauphin.[739] As priests, doubtless they were possessed of a certain body of dogma and morality, and of a code of rules for judging matters of faith. But now it was a question not of curing the disease of heresy, but of driving out the English. Jeanne was in favour with my Lord the Duke of Alençon and with my Lord the Bastard; the inhabitants of Orléans were looking to her for their deliverance. She promised to take the King to Reims; and it happened that the cleverest and the most powerful man in France, the Chancellor of the kingdom, my Lord Regnault de Chartres, was Archbishop and Count of Reims; and that had great weight.[740]

If it should be as she said, if God had verily sent her to the aid of the Lilies, to the mind of whomsoever possessed sense and learning it appeared marvellous but not incredible. No one denied that God could directly intervene in the affairs of kingdoms, for he himself had said: *Per me reges regnant.*

In this Church holy and indivisible, there were the doctors of Poitiers who deliberately pronounced God to be on the side of the Dauphin, while the University of Paris as deliberately pronounced God to be on the side of the Burgundians and the English. His messenger need not necessarily be an angel. He might employ a creature human or not human, like the raven that fed Elijah. And that a woman should engage in war accorded with what was written in books concerning Camilla, the Amazons, and Queen Penthesilea, and with what the Bible says of the strong women, Deborah, Jahel, Judith of Bethulia, raised up by God for the salvation of Israel. For it is written: "The mighty one did not fall by the young men, neither did the sons of Titans smite him, nor high giants set upon him; but Judith the daughter of Merari weakened him with the beauty of her countenance."[741]

Jeanne was taken to the mansion where dwelt Maître Jean Rabateau, not far from the law-courts, in the heart of the town.[742] Maître Jean Rabateau was Lay Attorney General; all criminal cases went to him, while civil cases went to the ecclesiastical Attorney General, Jean Jouvenel. Alike King's advocates, in the King's service, they both represented him in cases wherein he was concerned. The King was an unprofitable client. For representing him in criminal trials

Maître Jean Rabateau received four hundred livres a year. He was forbidden to appear in any but crown cases; and no one suspected him of receiving many bribes. If in addition he held the office of Councillor to the Duke of Orléans he gained little by it. Like most Parlement officials he was for the moment very poor. A stranger in Poitiers, he had no house there, but lodged in a mansion, which, because it belonged to a family named Rosier, was called the Hôtel de la Rose. It was a large dwelling. Witnesses whom it was necessary to keep securely and deal with honourably were entertained there. Jeanne was taken there although the Parlement had nothing to do with her cross-examination.[743] Once again she was placed in charge of a man who served both the Duke of Orléans and the King of France.

Jean Rabateau's wife, in common with the wives of all lawyers, was a woman of good reputation.[744] While she was at La Rose, Jeanne would stay long on her knees every day after dinner. At night she would rise from her bed to pray, and pass long hours in the little oratory of the mansion. It was in this house that the doctors conducted her examination. When their coming was announced she was seized with cruel anxiety. The Blessed Saint Catherine was careful to reassure her.[745] She likewise had disputed with doctors and confounded them. True, those doctors were heathen, but they were learned and their minds were subtle; for in the life of the Saint it is written: "The Emperor summoned fifty doctors versed in the lore of the Egyptians and the liberal arts. And when she heard that she was to dispute with the wise men, Catherine feared lest she should not worthily defend the Gospel of Jesus Christ. But an angel appeared unto her and said: 'I am the Archangel Saint Michael, and I am come to tell thee that thou shalt come forth from the strife victorious and worthy of Our Lord Jesus Christ, the hope and crown of those who strive for him.' And the Virgin disputed with the doctors."[746]

The grave doctors and masters and the principal clerks of the Parlement of Poitiers, in companies of two and three, repaired to the house of Jean Rabateau, and each one of them in turn questioned Jeanne. The first to come were Jean Lombard, Guillaume le Maire, Guillaume Aimery, Pierre Turelure, and Jacques Meledon. Brother Jean Lombard asked: "Wherefore have you come? The King desires to know what led you to come to him."

Jeanne's reply greatly impressed these clerks: "As I kept my flocks a *Voice appeared to me*. The Voice said: 'God has great pity on the people of France. Jeanne, thou must go into France.' On hearing these words I began to weep. Then the Voice said unto me: 'Go to Vaucouleurs. There shalt thou find a captain, who will take thee safely into France, to the King. Fear not.' I did as I was bidden, and I came to the King without hindrance."[747]

Then the word fell to Brother Guillaume Aimery: "According to what you have said, the Voice told you that God will deliver the people of France from their distress; but if God will deliver them he has no need of men-at-arms."

"In God's name," replied the Maid, "the men-at-arms will fight, and God will give the victory."

Maître Guillaume declared himself satisfied.[748]

On the 22nd of March, Maître Pierre de Versailles and Maître Jean Érault went together to Jean Rabateau's lodging. The squire, Gobert Thibault, whom Jeanne had already seen at Chinon, came with them. He was a young man and very simple, one who believed without asking for a sign. As they came in Jeanne went to meet them, and, striking the squire on the shoulder, in a friendly manner, she said: "I wish I had many men as willing as you."[749]

With men-at-arms she felt at her ease. But the doctors she could not tolerate, and she suffered torture when they came to argue with her. Although these theologians showed her great consideration, their eternal questions wearied her; their slowness and heaviness exasperated her. She bore them a grudge for not believing in her straightway, without proof, and for asking her for a sign, which she could not give them, since neither Saint Michael nor Saint Catherine nor Saint Margaret appeared during the examination. In retirement, in the oratory, and in the lonely fields the heavenly visitants came to her in crowds; angels and saints, descending from heaven, flocked around her. But when the doctors came, immediately the Jacob's ladder was drawn up. Besides, the clerks were theologians, and she was a saint. Relations are always strained between the heads of the Church Militant and those devout women who communicate directly with the Church Triumphant. She realised that the revelations granted to her so abundantly inspired her most favourable judges with doubts, suspicion, and even mistrust. She dared not confide to them much of the mystery of her Voices, and when the Churchmen were not present she told Alençon, her fair Duke, that she knew more and could do more than she had ever told all those clerks.[750] It was not to them she had been sent; it was not for them that she had come. She felt awkward in their presence, and their manners were the occasion of that irritation which is discernible in more than one of her replies.[751] Sometimes when they questioned her she retreated to the end of her bench and sulked.

"We come to you from the King," said Maître Pierre de Versailles.

She replied with a bad grace: "I am quite aware that you are come to question me again. I don't know A from B."[752] But to the question: "Wherefore do you come?" she made answer eagerly: "I come from the King of Heaven to raise the siege of Orléans, and take the King to be crowned and anointed at Reims. Maître Jean Érault, have you ink and paper? Write what I shall tell you." And she dictated a brief manifesto to the English captains: "You, Suffort, Clasdas, and La Poule, in the name of the King of Heaven I call upon you to return to England."[753]

Maître Jean Érault, who wrote at her dictation, was, like most of the clerks, favourably disposed towards her. Further, he had his own ideas. He recollected that Marie of Avignon, surnamed La Gasque, had uttered true and memorable prophecies to King Charles VI. Now La Gasque had told the King that the realm was to suffer many sorrows; and she had seen weapons in the sky. Her story of her vision had concluded with these words: "While I was afeard, believing myself called upon to take these weapons, a voice comforted me, saying: 'They are not for thee, but for a Virgin, who shall come and with these weapons deliver the realm of France.'" Maître Jean Érault meditated on these marvellous revelations and came to believe that Jeanne was the Virgin announced by Marie of Avignon.[754]

Maître Gérard Machet, the King's Confessor, had found it written that a Maid should come to the help of the King of France. He remarked on it to Gobert Thibault, the Squire, who was no very great personage;[755] and he certainly spoke of it to several others. Gérard Machet, Doctor of Theology, sometime Vice Chancellor of the University, from which he was now excluded, was regarded as one of the lights of the Church. He loved the court,[756] although he would not admit it, and enjoyed the favour of the King, who had just rewarded his services by giving him money with which to purchase a mule.[757] All doubts concerning the disposition of these doctors are removed by the discovery that the King's Confessor himself put into circulation those prophecies which had been distorted in favour of the Maid from the Bois-Chenu.

The damsel was interrogated concerning her Voices, which she called her Council, and her saints, whom she imagined in the semblance of those sculptured or painted figures peopling the churches.[758] The doctors objected to her having cast off woman's clothing and had her hair cut round in the manner of a page. Now it is written: "The woman shall not wear that which pertaineth unto a man, neither shall a man put on a woman's garment: for all that do so are abomination unto the Lord thy God" (Deuteronomy xxii, 5). The Council of Gangres, held in the reign of the Emperor Valens, had anathematised women who dressed as men and cut short their hair.[759] Many saintly women, impelled by a strange inspiration of the Holy Ghost, had concealed their sex by masculine garb. At Saint-Jean-des-Bois, near Compiègne, was preserved the reliquary of Saint Euphrosyne of Alexandria, who lived for thirty-eight years in man's attire in the monastery of the Abbot Theodosius.[760] For these reasons, and because of these precedents, the doctors argued: since Jeanne had put on this clothing not to offend another's modesty but to preserve her own, we will put no evil interpretation on an act performed with good intent, and we will forbear to condemn a deed justified by purity of motive.

Certain of her questioners inquired why she called Charles Dauphin instead of giving him his title of King. This title had been his by right since the 30th of October, 1422; for on that day, the ninth since the death of the King his father, at Mehun-sur-Yèvre, in the chapel royal, he had put off his black gown and assumed the purple robe, while the heralds, raising aloft the banner of France, cried: "Long live the King!"

She answered: "I will not call him King until he shall have been anointed and crowned at Reims. To that city I intend to take him."[761]

Without this anointing there was no king of France for her. Of the miracles which had followed that anointing she had heard every year from the mouth of her priest as he recited the glorious deeds of the Blessed Saint Remi, the patron saint of her parish. This reply was such as to satisfy the interrogators because, both for things spiritual and temporal, it was important that the King should be anointed at Reims.[762] And Messire Regnault de Chartres must have ardently desired it.

Contradicted by the clerks, she opposed the Church's doctrine by the inspiration of her own heart, and said to them: "There is more in the Book of Our Lord than in all yours."[763]

This was a bold and biting reply, which would have been dangerous had the theologians been less favourably inclined to her. Otherwise they might have held it to be trespassing on the rights of the Church, who, as the guardian of the Holy Books, is their jealous interpreter, and does not suffer the authority of Scripture to be set up against the decisions of Councils.[764] What were those books, which without having read she judged to be contrary to those of Our Lord, wherein with mind and spirit she seemed to read plainly? They would seem to be the Sacred Canons and the Sacred Decretals. This child's utterance sapped the very foundations of the Church. Had the doctors of Poitiers been less zealously Armagnac they would henceforth have mistrusted Jeanne and suspected her of heresy. But they were loyal servants of the houses of Orléans and of France. Their cassocks were ragged and their larders empty;[765] their only hope was in God, and they feared lest in rejecting this damsel they might be denying the Holy Ghost. Besides, everything went to prove that these words of Jeanne were uttered without guile and in all ignorance and simplicity. No doubt that is why the doctors were not shocked by them.

Brother Seguin of Seguin in his turn questioned the damsel. He was from Limousin, and his speech betrayed his origin. He spoke with a drawl and used expressions unknown in Lorraine and Champagne. Perhaps he had that dull, heavy air, which rendered the folk of his province somewhat ridiculous in the eyes of dwellers on the Loire, the Seine, and the Meuse. To the question: "What language do your Voices speak?" Jeanne replied: "A better one than yours."[766]

Even saints may lose patience. If Brother Seguin did not know it before, he learnt it that day. And what business had he to doubt that Saint Catherine and Saint Margaret, who were on the side of the French, spoke French? Such a doubt Jeanne could not bear, and she gave her questioner to understand that when one comes from Limousin one does not inquire concerning the speech of heavenly ladies. Notwithstanding he pursued his interrogation: "Do you believe in God?" "Yes, more than you do," said the Maid, who, knowing nothing of the good Brother, was somewhat hasty in esteeming herself better grounded in the faith than he.

But she was vexed that there should be any question of her belief in God, who had sent her. Her reply, if favourably interpreted, would testify to the ardour of her faith. Did Brother Seguin so understand it? His contemporaries represented him as being of a somewhat bitter disposition. On the contrary, there is reason to believe that he was good-natured.[767]

"But after all," he said, "it cannot be God's will that you should be believed unless some sign appear to make us believe in you. On your word alone we cannot counsel the King to run the risk of granting you men-at-arms."

"In God's name," she answered, "it was not to give a sign that I came to Poitiers. But take me to Orléans and I will show you the signs wherefore I am sent. Let me be given men, it matters not how many, and I will go to Orléans."

And she repeated what she was continually saying: "The English shall all be driven out and destroyed. The siege of Orléans shall be raised and the city delivered from its enemies, after I shall have summoned it to surrender in the name of the King of Heaven. The Dauphin shall be anointed at Reims, the town of Paris shall return to its allegiance to the King, and the Duke of Orléans shall come back from England."[768]

Long did the doctors and masters, following the example of Brother Seguin of Seguin, urge her to show a sign of her mission. They thought that if God had chosen her to deliver the French nation he would not fail to make his choice manifest by a sign, as he had done for Gideon, the son of Joash. When Israel was sore pressed by the Midianites, and when God's chosen people hid from their enemies in the caves of the mountains, the Angel of the Lord appeared to Gideon under an oak, and said unto him: "Surely I will be with thee and thou shalt smite the Midianites as one man." To which Gideon made answer: "If now I have found grace in thy sight, then shew me a sign that thou talkest with me." And Gideon made ready a kid and kneaded unleavened cakes; the flesh he put in a basket, and he put the broth in a pot and brought the pot and the basket beneath the oak. Then the Angel of God said unto him: "Take the flesh and the unleavened cakes, and lay them upon this rock, and pour out the broth." And he did so. Then the angel of the Lord put forth the end of the staff that was in his hand, and touched the flesh and the unleavened cakes; and there rose up fire out of the rock, and consumed the flesh and the unleavened cakes. When Gideon perceived that he had seen an angel of the Lord, he cried out: "Alas, O Lord God! for because I have seen an angel of the Lord face to face."[769] With three hundred men Gideon subdued the Midianites. This example the doctors had before their minds.[770]

But for the Maid the sign of victory was victory itself. She said without ceasing: "The sign that I will show you shall be Orléans relieved and the siege raised."[771]

Such persistency made an impression on most of her interrogators. They determined to make of it, not a stone of stumbling, but rather an example of zeal and a subject of edification. Since she promised them a sign it behoved them in all humility to ask God to send it, and, filled with a like hope, joining with the King and all the people, to pray to the God, who delivered Israel, to grant them the banner of victory. Thus were overcome the arguments of Brother Seguin and of those who, led away by the precepts of human wisdom, desired a sign before they believed.

After an examination which had lasted six weeks, the doctors declared themselves satisfied.[772]

There was one point it was necessary to ascertain; they must know whether Jeanne was, as she said, a virgin. Matrons had indeed already examined her on her arrival at Chinon. Then there was a doubt as to whether she were man or maid; and it was even feared that she might be an illusion in woman's semblance, produced by the art of demons, which scholars considered by no means impossible.[773] It was not long since the death of that canon who held that now and again knights are changed into bears and spirits travel a hundred leagues in one night, then suddenly become sows or wisps of straw.[774] Suitable measures had therefore been taken. But they must be carried out exactly, wisely, and cautiously, for the matter was of great importance.

CHAPTER VIII
THE MAID AT POITIERS (CONTINUED)

A BELIEF, common to learned and ignorant alike, ascribed special virtues to the state of virginity. Such ideas had been handed down from a remote antiquity; their origin was pre-Christian; they were an immemorial inheritance, one part of which came from the Gauls and Germans, the other from the Romans and Greeks. In the land of Gaul there still lingered a memory of the sacred beauty of the white priestesses of the forest; and sometimes in the Island of Sein, along the misty shores of the Ocean, there wandered the shades of those nine sisters at whose bidding, in days of yore, the tempest raged and was stilled.

According to these beliefs, which had dawned in the childhood of races, the gift of prophecy is bestowed on virgins alone. It is the heritage of a Cassandra or a Velleda. It was said that Sibyls had prophesied the coming of Jesus Christ. In the Church they were considered the first witnesses of Christ among the Gentiles, and they were venerated as the august sisters of the prophets of Israel. The *Dies Iræ* mentions one of them in the same breath with King David himself. By what pious frauds their fame for prophecy was established, we cannot tell any more than Jean Gerson or Gérard Machet. With the doctors of the fifteenth century we must look upon these virgins as speaking the word of truth to the nations, who venerated but did not understand them. Such was the ancient tradition of the Christian Church. The most ancient fathers of the Church, Justin, Origen, Clement of Alexandria, frequently made use of the Sibylline oracles; and the heathen were at a loss for a reply when Lactantius confronted them with these prophetesses of the nations. Trusting in the word of Varro, Saint Jerome firmly believed in their existence. Into *The City of*

God Saint Augustine introduces the Erythrean Sibyl, who, he says, faithfully foretold the Life of the Saviour. As early as the thirteenth century, these virgins of old had their places in cathedrals by the side of patriarchs and prophets. But it was not until the fifteenth century that multitudes of them were represented; sculptured on church porches, carved on choir stalls, painted on chapel walls or glass windows. Each one has her distinctive attribute. The Persian holds the lantern and the Libyan the torch, which illuminated the darkness of the Gentiles. The Agrippine, the European, and Erythrean are armed with the sword; the Phrygian bears the Paschal cross; the Hellespontine presents a rose tree in flower; the others display the visible signs of the mystery they foretell: the Cumæan a manger; the Delphian, the Samian, the Tiburtine, the Cimmerian a crown of thorns, a sceptre of reeds, scourges, a cross.[775]

The very economy of the Christian religion – the ordering of its mysteries, wherein humanity is represented as ruined by a woman and saved by a virgin, and all flesh is involved in Eve's curse – led to the triumph of virginity and the exaltation of a condition which, in the words of a Father of the Church, is in the flesh, yet not of the flesh.

"It is because of virginity," says Saint Gregory of Nyssa, "that God vouchsafes to dwell with men. It is virginity which gives men wings to soar towards heaven." Celibacy raises the Apostle John above the Prince of the Apostles himself. At the funeral of the Virgin Mary, Peter gave John a palm branch, saying: "It becometh one who is celibate to bear the Virgin's palm."[776]

Throughout western Christendom the Virgin Mary – the Virgin *par excellence* – had been the object of zealous devout worship[777] ever since the twelfth century. The great cathedrals of northern France, dedicated to Our Lady, celebrated the feast of their patron saint on the day of the Assumption. On the sculptured pillar of the central porch was the Virgin, with her divine Child and the Virgin's lily. Sometimes Eve figured beneath, in order to represent at once sin and its redemption: the second Eve redeeming the first, the Virgin exalted the woman humbled. Marvellous scenes are portrayed on the tympanums of porches. The Virgin is kneeling; at her side is a flowering lily in a vase. The Angel, book in hand, greets her with an AVE, thus transposing the name EVA, *mutans Evæ nomen*. Or again, with her feet resting on the crescent moon, she rises to the highest heaven: *Exaltata est super choros angelorum*. Further, from Jesus Christ she receives the precious crown: *Posuit in capite ejus coronam de lapide pretioso*. In gems of painted glass, church windows portrayed the figures of Mary's virginity; the stone which Daniel saw dug from the mountain by no human hand, Gideon's fleece, Moses' burning bush, and Aaron's budding rod.

In an inexhaustible flow of images, expressed in hymns, sequences, and litanies, she was the Mystic Rose, the Ivory Tower, the Ark of the Covenant, the Gate of Heaven, the Morning Star. She was the Well of Living Water, the Fountain of the Garden, the Walled Orchard, the Bright and Shining Stone, the Flower of Virtue, the Palm of Sweetness, the Myrtle of Temperance, the Sweet Ointment.

In the Golden Legend, images rich and charming clothed the idea that grace and power resided in virginity. The hagiographers burst forth in loving praise of the brides of Jesus Christ; of those especially who put on the white robe of virginity and the red roses of martyrdom. It was during the passion of virgins that miracles of the most abounding grace were worked. Angels bring down to Dorothea celestial roses, which she scatters over her executioners. Virgin martyrs exercise their power over beasts. The lions of the amphitheatre lick the feet of Saint Thecla. The wild beasts of the circus gather together, and with tails interlaced, prepare a throne for Saint Euphemia; in the pit, aspics form a pleasing necklace for Saint Christina. It is not the will of the divine Spouse for whom they endure anguish that they should suffer in their modesty. When the executioner tears off Saint Agnes's garments, her hair grows thicker and clothes her in a miraculous garment. When Saint Barbara is to be taken naked through the streets, an angel brings her a white tunic. These Agneses and these Dorotheas, these Catherines and these Margarets, this legion of innocent conquerors prepared men's minds to believe in the miracle of a virgin stronger than armed men. Had not Saint Geneviève turned away Attila and his barbarian warriors from Paris?

The fable of the Maid and the Unicorn, so widely known in those days, is a lively expression of this belief in a special virtue residing in the state of virginity.

The unicorn was half goat and half horse, of immaculate whiteness; it bore a marvellous sword upon its forehead. Hunters, when they saw it pass in the thicket, had never been able to reach it, so rapid was its course. But if a virgin in the forest called the unicorn, the creature obeyed, came and laid its head on her lap, and allowed such feeble hands to take and bind it. If however a damsel corrupt and no longer a maid approached it, the unicorn slew her immediately.[778]

It was even said that a virgin had the power to cure king's evil, by reciting, fasting and naked, certain magic words; but they were not words from the Gospel.[779]

While mystics and visionaries were glorifying virginity, the Church, bent on governing the body as well as the soul, condemned opinions denying the lawfulness of marriage, which she had constituted a sacrament. Those who would anathematise all works of the flesh she held to be abominable and impious. A maid deserved praise for preserving her virginity, provided always that her motives were praiseworthy. Two hundred years before the reign of Charles VII, a young girl of Reims realised that a grave sin may be committed against the Church of God by refusing the solicitations of a clerk in a vineyard. Here is the damsel's story as related by the canon Gervais.

"On a day, Guillaume with the White Hands, Uncle of King Philippe of France, for his pleasure rode forth from his town. A clerk of his following, Gervais by name, who was in the heat of youth, saw a maiden walking alone in a vineyard. He went to her, greeted her and asked: 'What are you doing in such great haste?' And with fitting words he courteously solicited her.

"Without even looking at him, calmly and gravely she replied: 'God forbid, youth, that I should ever be yours or any man's, for if I were to lose my virginity and my body its purity, I should inevitably fall into eternal damnation.'

"Such words caused the clerk to suspect that the maiden belonged to the impious sect of the Cathari, whom the Church was in those days pursuing relentlessly and punishing severely. One of the errors of these heretics was indeed to condemn all carnal intercourse. Impatient to resolve his doubts, Gervais straightway provoked the damsel to a discussion on the Church's teaching in this matter. Meanwhile, the Archbishop, Guillaume with the White Hands, turned his steed, and, followed by his monks, came to the vineyard where the clerk and the maiden were disputing together. When he learnt the cause of their disagreement he ordered the maiden to be seized and brought into the town. There he exhorted her, and, in charity, endeavoured to convert her to the Catholic Faith.

"She would not submit, however. 'I am not well enough grounded in doctrine to defend myself,' she said to him. 'But in the town I have a mistress, who, with good reasons, will easily refute all your arguments. She it is who lodges in that house.'

"The Archbishop Guillaume straightway sent to inquire after this woman; and, having questioned her, perceived that what the maiden had said concerning her was true. The very next day he convoked an assembly of clerks and nobles to judge the two women. Both of them were condemned to be burnt. The mistress contrived to escape, but promises and persuasions having failed to turn the maiden from the pernicious error of her ways, she was delivered up to the executioner. She died without shedding a tear, without uttering a complaint."[780]

In the year 1416 there was a certain woman, a native of the Duchy of Bar, Catherine Sauve by name. She was then a solitary, living at Montpellier, on the road to Lattes. Having been publicly accused, she was examined by the Inquisitor's Vicar, Maître Raymond Cabasse, and found to be infected with the heresy of the Cathari. Among other errors she maintained that all carnal intercourse is sinful, even in wedlock. Wherefore she was delivered to the secular arm and burned at the stake on the 2nd of November in that year.[781]

It was then commonly believed that such maidens as gave themselves to the devil were straightway stripped of their virginity; and that thus he obtained power over these unhappy creatures.[782] Such ways accorded with what was known of his libidinous disposition. These pleasures were tempered to his woeful state. And thereby he gained a further advantage, – that of unarming his victim, – for virginity is as a coat of mail against which the darts of hell are but blades of straw. Hence it was all but certain that a soul vowed to the devil could not reside within a maid.[783] Wherefore, there was one infallible way of proving that the peasant girl from Vaucouleurs was not given up to magic or to sorcery, and had made no pact with the Evil One. Recourse was had to it.

Jeanne was seen, visited, privately inspected, and thoroughly examined by wise women, *mulieres doctas*; by knowing virgins, *peritas virgines*; by widows and wives, *viduas et conjugates*. First among these matrons were: the Queen of Sicily and of Jerusalem, Duchess of Anjou; Dame Jeanne de Preuilly, wife of the Sire de Gaucourt, Governor of Orléans, who was about fifty-seven years of age; and Dame Jeanne de Mortemer, wife of Messire Robert le Maçon, Lord of Trèves, a man full of years.[784] The last was only eighteen, and one would have expected her to be better acquainted with the

Calendrier des Vieillards than with the formulary of matrons. It is strange with what assurance the good wives of those days undertook the solution of a problem which had appeared difficult to King Solomon in all his wisdom.

Jeanne of Domremy was found to be a maid pure and intact.[785]

While she herself was being subjected to the interrogatories of doctors and the examination of matrons, certain clerics who had been despatched to her native province were there prosecuting an inquiry concerning her birth, her life, and her morals.[786] The ecclesiastics had been chosen from those mendicant Friars[787] who could pass freely along the highways and byways of the enemy's country without exciting the suspicion of English and Burgundians. And, indeed, they were in no way molested. From Domremy and from Vaucouleurs they brought back sure testimony to the humility, the devotion, the honesty, and the simplicity of Jeanne. But, most important, they had found no difficulty in gleaning certain pious tales, such as commonly adorned the childhood of saints. To these monks we must attribute an important share in the development of those legends of Jeanne's early years, which were so soon to become popular. From this time, apparently, dates the story that when Jeanne was in her seventh year, wolves spared her sheep, and birds of the woods came at her call and ate crumbs from her lap.[788] Such saintly flowers suggest a Franciscan origin; among them are the wolf of Gubbio and the birds preached to by Saint Francis. These mendicants may also have furnished examples of the Maid's prophetic gift. They may have spread abroad the story that, when she was at Vaucouleurs, on the day of the Battle of the Herrings, she knew of the great hurt inflicted on the French at Rouvray.[789] The success of such little stories was immediate and complete.

After this examination and inquiry, the doctors came to the following conclusions: "The King, beholding his own need and that of his realm, and considering the constant prayers to God of his poor subjects and all others who love peace and justice, ought not to repulse or reject the Maid who says that God has sent her to bring him succour, albeit these promises may be nothing[790] but the works of man; neither ought he lightly or hastily to believe in her. But, according to Holy Scripture he must try her in two ways: to wit, with human wisdom, by inquiring of her life, her morals, and her motive, as saith Saint Paul the Apostle: *Probate spiritus, si ex Deo sunt*; and by earnest prayer to ask for a sign of her work and her divine hope, by which to tell whether it is by God's will that she is come. Thus God commanded Ahaz that he should ask for a sign when God promised him victory, saying unto him: *Pete signum a Domino*; and Gideon did likewise when he asked for a sign and many others, etc. Since the coming of the said Maid, the King hath observed her in the two manners aforesaid: to wit, by trial of human wisdom and by prayer, asking God for a sign. As for the first, which is trial by human wisdom, he has tested the said Maid in her life, her origin, her morals, her intention; and has kept her near him for the space of six weeks to show her to all people, whether clerks, ecclesiastics, monks, men-at-arms, wives, widows or others. In public and in private she hath conversed with persons of all conditions. But there hath been found no evil in her, nothing but good, humility, virginity, devoutness, honesty, simplicity. Of her birth, as well as of her life, many marvellous things are related."

"As for the second ordeal, the King asked her for a sign, to which she replied that before Orléans she would give it, but neither earlier nor elsewhere, for thus it is ordained of God.

"Now, seeing that the King hath made trial of the aforesaid Maid as far as it was in his power to do, that he findeth no evil in her, and that her reply is that she will give a divine sign before Orléans; seeing her persistency, and the consistency of her words, and her urgent request that she be sent to Orléans to show there that the aid she brings is divine, the King should not hinder her from going to Orléans with men-at-arms, but should send her there in due state trusting in God. For to fear her or reject her when there is no appearance of evil in her would be to rebel against the Holy Ghost, and to render oneself unworthy of divine succour, as Gamaliel said of the Apostles in the Council of the Jews."[791]

In short, the doctors' conclusion was that as yet nothing divine appeared in the Maid's promises, but that she had been examined and been found humble, a virgin, devout, honest, simple, and wholly good; and that, since she had promised to give a sign from God before Orléans, she must be taken there, for fear that in her the gift of the Holy Ghost should be rejected.

Of these conclusions a great number of copies were made and sent to the towns of the realm as well as to the princes of Christendom. The Emperor Sigismond, for example, received a copy.[792]

If the doctors of Poitiers had intended this six weeks inquiry, culminating in a favourable and solemn conclusion, to bring about the glorification of the Maid and the heartening of the French people by the preparation and announcement of the marvel they had before them, then they succeeded perfectly.[793]

That prolonged investigation, that minute examination reassured those doubting minds among the French, who suspected a woman dressed as a man of being a devil; they flattered men's imaginations with the hope of a miracle; they appealed to all hearts to judge favourably of the damsel who came forth radiant from the fire of ordeal and appeared as if glorified with a celestial halo. Her vanquishing the doctors in argument made her seem like another Saint Catherine.[794] But that she should have met difficult questions with wise answers was not enough for a multitude eager for marvels. It was imagined that she had been subjected to a strange probation from which she had come forth by nothing short of a miracle. Thus a few weeks after the inquiry, the following wonderful story was related in Brittany and in Flanders: when at Poitiers she was preparing to receive the communion, the priest had one wafer that was consecrated and another that was not. He wanted to give her the unconsecrated wafer. She took it in her hand and told the priest that it was not the body of Christ her Redeemer, but that the body was in the wafer which the priest had covered with the corporal.[795] After that there could be no doubt that Jeanne was a great saint.

At the termination of the inquiries, a favourable opportunity for introducing the Maid into Orléans arrived in the beginning of April. For her arming and her accoutring she was sent first to Tours.[796]

Sixty-six years later, an inhabitant of Poitiers, almost a hundred years old, told a young fellow-citizen that he had seen the Maid set out for Orléans on horseback, in white armour.[797] He pointed to the very stone from which she had mounted her horse in the corner of the Rue Saint-Etienne. Now, when Jeanne was at Poitiers, she was not in armour. But the people of Poitou had named the stone "the Maid's mounting stone." With what a glad eager step the Saint must have leapt from that stone on to the horse which was to carry her away from those furred cats to the afflicted and oppressed whom she was longing to succour.[798]

CHAPTER IX
THE MAID AT TOURS

A T Tours the Maid lodged in the house of a dame commonly called Lapau.[799] She was Eléonore de Paul, a woman of Anjou, who had been lady-in-waiting to Queen Marie of Anjou. Married to Jean du Puy, Lord of La Roche-Saint-Quentin, Councillor of the Queen of Sicily, she had remained in the service of the Queen of France.[800]

The town of Tours belonged to the Queen of Sicily, who grew richer and richer as her son-in-law grew poorer and poorer. She aided him with money and with lands. In 1424, the duchy of Touraine with all its dependencies, except the castellany of Chinon, had come into her possession.[801] The burgesses and commonalty of Tours earnestly desired peace. Meanwhile they made every effort to escape from pillage at the hands of men-at-arms. Neither King Charles nor Queen Yolande was able to defend them, so they must needs defend themselves.[802] When the town watchmen announced the approach of one of those marauding chiefs who were ravaging Touraine and Anjou, the citizens shut their gates and saw to it that the culverins were in their places. Then there was a parley: the captain from the brink of the moat maintained that he was in the King's service and on his way to fight the English; he asked for a night's rest in the town for himself and his men. From the heights of the ramparts he was politely requested to pass on; and, in case he should be tempted to force an entry, a sum of money was offered him.[803] Thus the citizens fleeced themselves for fear of being robbed. In like manner, only a few days before Jeanne's coming, they had given the Scot, Kennedy, who was ravaging the district, two hundred livres to go on. When they had got rid of their defenders, their next care was to fortify themselves against the English. On the 29th of February of this same year, 1429, these citizens lent one hundred crowns to Captain La Hire, who was then doing his best for Orléans. And even on the approach of the English they consented to receive forty archers belonging to the company of the Sire de Bueil, only on condition that Bueil should lodge in the castle with twenty men, and that the others should be quartered in the inns, where they were to have nothing without paying for it. Thus it was or was not; and the Sire de Bueil went off to defend Orléans.[804]

In Jean du Puy's house, Jeanne was visited by an Augustinian monk, one Jean Pasquerel. He was returning from the town of Puy-en-Velay where he had met Isabelle Romée and certain of those who had conducted Jeanne to the King.[805]

In this town, in the sanctuary of Anis, was preserved an image of the Mother of God, brought from Egypt by Saint Louis. It was of great antiquity and highly venerated, for the prophet Jeremiah had with his own hands carved it out of sycamore wood in the semblance of the virgin yet to be born, whom he had seen in a vision.[806] In holy week, pilgrims flocked from all parts of France and of Europe, – nobles, clerks, men-at-arms, citizens and peasants; and many, for penance or through poverty, came on foot, staff in hand, begging their bread from door to door. Merchants of all kinds betook themselves thither; and it was at once the most popular of pilgrimages and one of the richest fairs in the world. All round the town the stream of travellers overflowed from the road on to vineyards, meadows, and gardens. On the day of the Festival, in the year 1407, two hundred persons perished, crushed to death in the throng.[807]

In certain years the feast of the conception of Our Lord fell on the same day as that of his death; and thus there coincided the promise and the fulfilment of the promise of the greatest of mysteries. Then Holy Friday became still holier. It was called Great Friday, and on that day such as entered the sanctuary of Anis received plenary indulgence. On that day the crowd of pilgrims was greater than usual. Now, in the year 1429, Good Friday fell on the 25th of March, the day of the Annunciation.[808]

There is, therefore, nothing extraordinary in Brother Pasquerel's meeting Jeanne's relatives at Puy during Holy Week. That a peasant woman should travel two hundred and fifty miles on foot, through a country infested with soldiers and other robbers, in a season of snows and mist, to obtain an indulgence, was an every-day matter if we remember the surname which had for long been hers.[809] This was not

La Romée's first pilgrimage. As we do not know which members of the Maid's escort the good Brother met, we are at liberty to conjecture that Bertrand de Poulengy was among them. We know little about him, but his speech would suggest that he was a devout person.[810]

Jeanne's comrades, having made friends with Pasquerel, said to him: "You must go with us to Jeanne. We will not leave you until you have taken us to her." They travelled together. Brother Pasquerel went with them to Chinon, which Jeanne had left; then he went on to Tours, where his convent was.

The Augustinians, who claimed to have received their rule from St. Francis himself, wore the grey habit of the Franciscans. It was from their order that in the previous year the King had chosen a chaplain for his young son, the Dauphin Louis. Brother Pasquerel held the office of reader (*lector*) in his monastery.[811] He was in priest's orders. Quite young doubtless and of a wandering disposition, like many mendicant monks of those days, he had a taste for the miraculous, and was excessively credulous.

Jeanne's comrades said to her: "Jeanne, we have brought you this good father. You will like him well when you know him."

She replied: "The good father pleases me. I have already heard tell of him, and even to-morrow will I confess to him." The next day the good father heard her in confession, and chanted mass before her. He became her chaplain, and never left her.[812]

In the fifteenth century Tours was one of the chief manufacturing towns of the kingdom. The inhabitants excelled in all kinds of trades. They wove tissues of silk, of gold, and of silver. They manufactured coats of mail; and, while not competing with the armourers of Milan, of Nuremberg, and of Augsburg, they were skilled in the forging and hammering of steel.[813] Here it was that, by the King's command, the master armourer made Jeanne a suit of mail.[814] The suit he furnished was of wrought iron; and, according to the custom of that time, consisted of a helmet, a cuirass in four parts, with epaulets, armlets, elbow-pieces, fore-armlets, gauntlets, cuisses, knee-pieces, greaves and shoes.[815] The maker had doubtless no thought of accentuating the feminine figure. But the armour of that period, full in the bust, slight in the waist, with broad skirts beneath the corselet, in its slender grace and curious slimness, always has the air of a woman's armour, and seems made for Queen Penthesilea or for the Roman Camilla. The Maid's armour was white and unadorned, if one may judge from its modest price of one hundred *livres tournois*. The two suits of mail, made at the same time by the same armourer for Jean de Metz and his comrade, were together worth one hundred and twenty-five *livres tournois*.[816] Possibly one of the skilful and renowned drapers of Tours took the Maid's measure for a *houppelande* or loose coat in silk or cloth of gold or silver, such as captains wore over the cuirass. To look well, the coat, which was open in front, must be cut in scallops that would float round the horseman as he rode. Jeanne loved fine clothes but still more fine horses.[817]

The King invited her to choose a horse from his stables. If we may believe a certain Latin poet, she selected an animal of illustrious origin, but very old. It was a war horse, which Pierre de Beauvau, Governor of Maine and Anjou, had given to one of the King's two brothers; who had both been dead, the one thirteen years, the other twelve.[818] This steed, or another, was brought to Lapau's house and the Duke of Alençon went to see it. The horse must likewise be accoutred, it must be furnished with a chanfrin to protect its head and one of those wooden saddles with broad pommels which seemed to encase the rider.[819] A shield was out of the question. Since chain-armour, which was not proof against blows, had been succeeded by that plate-armour, on which nothing could make an impression, they had ceased to be used save in pageants. As for the sword, – the noblest part of her accoutrement and the bright symbol of strength joined to loyalty, – Jeanne refused to take that from the royal armourer; she was resolved to receive it from the hand of Saint Catherine herself.

We know that on her coming into France she had stopped at Fierbois and heard three masses in Saint Catherine's chapel.[820] Therein the Virgin of Alexandria had many swords, without counting the one Charles Martel was said to have given her, and which it would not have been easy to find again. A good Touranian in Touraine, Saint Catherine was an Armagnac ever on the side of those who fought for the Dauphin Charles. When captains and soldiers of fortune stood in danger of death, or were prisoners in the hands of their enemies, she was the saint they most willingly invoked; for they knew she wished them well. She did not save them all, but she aided many. They came to render her thanks; and as a sign of gratitude they offered her their armour, so that her chapel looked like an armoury.[821] The walls bristled with swords; and, as gifts had been flowing in for half a century, ever since the days of King Charles V, the sacristans were probably in the habit of taking down the old weapons to make room for the new, hoarding the old steel in some store-house until an opportunity arrived for selling it.[822] Saint Catherine could not refuse a sword to the damsel, whom she loved so dearly that every day and every hour she came down from Paradise to see and talk with her on earth, – a maiden who in return had shown her devotion by travelling to Fierbois to do the Saint reverence. For we must not omit to state that Saint Catherine in company with Saint Margaret had never ceased to appear to Jeanne both at Chinon and at Tours. She was present at all those secret assemblies, which the Maid called sometimes her Council but oftener her Voices, doubtless because they appealed more to her ears and her mind than to her eyes, despite the burst of light which sometimes dazzled her, and notwithstanding the crowns she was able to discern on the heads of the saints. The Voices indicated one sword among the multitude of those in the Chapel at Fierbois. Messire Richard Kyrthrizian and Brother Gille Lecourt, both of them priests, were then custodians of the chapel. Such is the title they assumed when they signed the accounts of miracles worked by their saint. Jeanne in a letter caused them to be asked for the sword, which had been revealed to her. In the letter she said that it would be found underground, not very deep down, and behind the altar. At least these were all the directions she was able to give afterwards, and then she could not quite remember whether it was behind the altar or in front. Was she able to give the custodians of the chapel any signs by which to recognise the sword? She never explained this point, and her letter is lost.[823]

It is certain, however, that she believed the sword had been shown to her in a vision and in no other manner. An armourer of Touraine, whom she did not know (afterwards she maintained that she had never seen him), was appointed to carry the letter to Fierbois. The custodians of the chapel gave him a sword marked with five crosses, or with five little swords on the blade, not far from the hilt. In what part of the chapel had they found it? No one knows. A contemporary says it was in a coffer with some old iron. If it had been buried and hidden it was not very long before, because the rust could easily be removed by rubbing. The priests were careful to offer it to the Maid with great ceremony[824] before giving it to the armourer who had come for it. They enclosed it in a sheath of red velvet, embroidered with the royal flowers de luce. When Jeanne received it she recognised it to be the one revealed to her in a celestial vision and promised her by her Voices, and she failed not to let the little company of monks and soldiers who surrounded her know that it was so. This they took to be a good omen and a sign of victory.[825] To protect Saint Catherine's sword the priests of the town gave her a second sheath; this one was of black cloth. Jeanne had a third made of very tough leather.[826]

The story of the sword spread far and wide and was elaborated by many a curious fable. It was said to be the sword of the great Charles Martel, long buried and forgotten. Many believed it had belonged to Alexander and the knights of those ancient days. Every one thought well of it and esteemed it likely to bring good fortune. When the English and the Burgundians heard tell of the matter, there soon occurred to them the idea that the Maid had discovered what was hidden beneath the earth by taking counsel of demons; or they suspected her of having herself craftily hidden the sword in the place she had indicated in order to deceive princes, clergy, and people. They wondered anxiously whether those five crosses were not signs of the devil.[827] Thus there began to arise conflicting illusions, according to which Jeanne appeared either saint or sorceress.[828]

The King had given her no command. Acting according to the counsel of the doctors, he did not hinder her from going to Orléans with men-at-arms. He even had her taken there in state in order that she might give the promised sign. He granted her men to conduct her, not for her to conduct. How could she have conducted them since she did not know the way? Meanwhile she had a standard made according to the command of Saint Catherine and Saint Margaret, who had said: "Take the standard in the name of the King of Heaven!" It was of a coarse white cloth, or buckram, edged with silk fringe. At the bidding of her Voices, Jeanne caused a painter of the town to represent on it what she called "the World,"[829] that is, Our Lord seated upon his throne, blessing with his right hand, and in his left holding the globe of the world. On his right and on his left were angels, both painted as they were in churches, and presenting Our Lord with flowers de luce. Above or on one side were the names Jhesus – Maria, and the background was strewn with the royal lilies in gold.[830] She also had a coat-of-arms painted: on an azure shield a silver dove, holding in its beak a scroll on which was written: *"De par le Roi du Ciel."*[831] This coat-of-arms she had painted on the reverse of the standard bearing on the front the picture of Our Lord. A servant of the Duke of Alençon, Perceval de Cagny, says that she ordered to be made another and a smaller standard, a banner, on which was the picture of Our Lady receiving the angel's salutation. The Tours painter Jeanne employed came from Scotland and was called Hamish Power. He provided the material and executed the paintings of the two escutcheons, of the small one as well as of the large. For this he received from the keeper of the war treasury twenty-five *livres tournois*.[832] Hamish Power had a daughter, Héliote by name, who was about to be married and to whom Jeanne afterwards showed kindness.[833]

The standard was the signal for rallying. For long only kings, emperors, and leaders in war had had the right of raising it. The feudal suzerain had it carried before him; vassals ranged themselves beneath their lord's banners. But in 1429 banners had ceased to be used save in corporations, guilds, and parishes, borne only before the armies of peace. In war they were no longer needed. The meanest captain, the poorest knight had his own standard. When fifty French men-at-arms went forth from Orléans against a handful of English marauders, a crowd of banners like a swarm of butterflies waved over the fields. "To raise one's standard" came to be a figure of speech for "to be puffed up."[834] So indeed it was permissible for a freebooter to raise his standard when he commanded scarce a score of men-at-arms and half-naked bowmen. Even if Jeanne, as she may have done, held her standard to be a sign of sovereign command, and if, having received it from the King of Heaven, she thought to raise it above all others, was there a soul in the realm to say her nay? What had become of all those feudal banners which for eighty years had been in the vanguard of defeat; sown over the fields of Crécy; collected beneath bushes and hedges by Welsh and Cornish swordsmen; lost in the vineyards of Maupertuis, trampled underfoot by English archers on the soft earth into which sank the corpses of Azincourt; gathered in handfuls under the walls of Verneuil by Bedford's marauders? It was because all these banners had miserably fallen, it was because at Rouvray a prince of the blood royal had shamefully trailed his nobles' banners in flight, that the peasant now raised her banner.

CHAPTER X
THE SIEGE OF ORLÉANS FROM THE 7TH OF MARCH TO
THE 28TH OF APRIL, 1429

INCE the terrible and ridiculous discomfiture of the King's men in the Battle of the Herrings, the citizens of Orléans had lost all faith in their defenders.[835] Their minds agitated, suspicious and credulous were possessed by phantoms of fear and wrath. Suddenly and without reason they believe themselves betrayed. One day it is announced that a hole big enough for a man to pass through has been made in the town wall just where it skirts the outbuildings of the Aumône.[836] A crowd of people hasten to the spot; they see the hole and a piece of the wall which had been restored, with two loop-holes; they fail to understand, and think themselves sold and betrayed into the enemy's hands; they rave and break forth into howls, and seek the priest in charge of the hospital to tear him to pieces.[837] A few days after, on Holy Thursday, a similar rumour is spread abroad: traitors are about to deliver up the town into the hands of the English. The folk seize their weapons; soldiers, burgesses, villeins mount guard on the outworks, on the walls and in the streets. On the morrow, the day after that on which the panic had originated, fear still possesses them.[838]

In the beginning of March the besiegers saw approaching the Norman vassals, summoned by the Regent. But they were only six hundred and twenty-nine lances all told, and they were only bound to serve for twenty-six days. Under the leadership of Scales, Pole, and Talbot, the English continued the investment works as best they could.[839] On the 10th of March, two and a half miles east of the city, they occupied without opposition the steep slope of Saint-Loup and began to erect a bastion there, which should command the upper river and the two roads from Gien and Pithiviers, at the point where they meet near the Burgundian gate.[840] On the 20th of March they completed the bastion named London, on the road to Mans. Between the 9th and 15th of April two new bastions were erected towards the west, Rouen nine hundred feet east of London, Paris nine hundred feet from Rouen. About the 20th they fortified Saint-Jean-le-Blanc across the Loire and established a watch to guard the crossing of the river.[841] This was but little in comparison with what remained to be done, and they were short of men; for they had less than three thousand round the town. Wherefore they fell upon the peasants. Now that the season for tending the vines was drawing near, the country folk went forth into the fields thinking only of the land; but the English lay in wait for them, and when they had taken them prisoners, set them to work.[842]

In the opinion of those most skilled in the arts of war, these bastions were worthless. They were furnished with no stabling for horses. They could not be built near enough to render assistance to each other; the besieger was in danger of being himself besieged in them. In short, from these vexatious methods of warfare the English reaped nothing but disappointment and disgrace. The Sire de Bueil, one of the defenders, perceived this when he was reconnoitring.[843] In fact it was so easy to pass through the enemy's lines that merchants were willing to run the risk of taking cattle to the besieged. There entered into the town, on the 7th of March, six horses loaded with herrings; on the 15th, six horses with powder; on the 29th, cattle and victuals; on the 2nd of April, nine fat oxen and horses; on the 5th, one hundred and one pigs and six fat oxen; on the 9th, seventeen pigs, horses, sucking-pigs, and corn; on the 13th, coins with which to pay the garrison; on the 16th, cattle and victuals; on the 23rd, powder and victuals. And more than once the besieged had carried off, in the very faces of the English, victuals and ammunition destined for the besiegers and including casks of wine, game, horses, bows, forage, and even twenty-six head of large cattle.[844]

The siege was costing the English dear, – forty thousand *livres tournois* a month.[845] They were short of money; they were obliged to resort to the most irritating expedients. By a decree of the 3rd of March King Henry had recently ordered all his officers in Normandy to lend him one quarter of their pay.[846] In their huts of wood and earth, the men-at-arms, who had endured much from the cold, now began to suffer hunger.

The wasted fields of La Beauce, of l'Île-de-France, and of Normandy could furnish them with no great store of sheep or oxen. Their food was bad, their drink worse. The vintage of 1427 had been bad, that of the following year was poor and weak – more like sour grapes than wine.[847] Now an old English author has written of the soldiers of his country:

> *"They want their porridge and their fat bull-beeves:*
> *Either they must be dieted like mules*
> *And have their provender tied to their mouths*
> *Or piteous they will look, like drowned mice."*[848]

A sudden humiliation still further weakened the English. Captain Poton de Saintrailles and the two magistrates, Guyon du Fossé and Jean de Saint-Avy, who had gone on an embassy to the Duke of Burgundy, returned to Orléans on the 17th of April. The Duke had granted their request and consented to take the town under his protection. But the Regent, to whom the offer had been made, would not have it thus.

He replied that he would be very sorry if after he had beaten the bush another should go off with the nestlings.[849] Therefore the offer was rejected. Nevertheless the embassy had been by no means useless, and it was something to have raised a new cause of quarrel between the Duke and the Regent. The ambassadors returned accompanied by a Burgundian herald who blew his trumpet in the English camp, and, in the name of his master, commanded all combatants who owed allegiance to the Duke to raise the siege. Some hundreds of archers and men-at-arms, Burgundians, men of Picardy and of Champagne, departed forthwith.[850]

On the next day, at four o'clock in the morning, the citizens emboldened and deeming the opportunity a good one, attacked the camp of Saint-Laurent-des-Orgerils. They slew the watch and entered the camp, where they found piles of money, robes of martin, and a goodly store of weapons. Absorbed in pillage, they paid no heed to defending themselves and were surprised by the enemy, who in great force had hastened to the place. They fled pursued by the English who slew many. On that day the town resounded with the lamentations of women weeping for a father, a husband, a brother, kinsmen.[851]

Within those walls, in a space where there was room for not more than fifteen thousand inhabitants, forty thousand[852] were huddled together, one vast multitude agonised by all manner of suffering;

depressed by domestic sorrow; racked with anxiety; maddened by constant danger and perpetual panic. Although the wars of those days were not so sanguinary as they became later, the sallies of the inhabitants of Orléans were the occasion of constant and considerable loss of life. Since the middle of March the English bullets had fallen more into the centre of the town; and they were not always harmless. On the eve of Palm Sunday one stone, fired from a mortar, killed or wounded five persons; another, seven.[853] Many of the inhabitants, like the provost, Alain Du Bey, died of fatigue or of the infected air.[854]

In the Christendom of those days all men were taught to believe that earthquakes, wars, famine, pestilence are punishments for wrong-doing. Charles, the Fair Duke of Orléans, good Christian that he was, held that great sorrows had come upon France as chastisement for her sins, to wit: swelling pride, gluttony, sloth, covetousness, lust, and neglect of justice, which were rife in the realm; and in a ballad he discoursed of the evil and its remedy.[855] The people of Orléans firmly believed that this war was sent to them of God to punish sinners, who had worn out his patience. They were aware both of the cause of their sorrows and of the means of remedying them. Such was the teaching of the good friars preachers; and, as Duke Charles put it in his ballad, the remedy was to live well, to amend one's life, to have masses said and sung for the souls of those who had suffered death in the service of the realm, to renounce the sinful life, and to ask forgiveness of Our Lady and the saints.[856] This remedy had been adopted by the people of Orléans. They had had masses said in the Church of Sainte-Croix for the souls of nobles, captains, and men-at-arms killed in their service, and especially for those who had died a piteous death in the Battle of the Herrings. They had offered candles to Our Lady and to the patron saints of the town, and had carried the shrine of Saint-Aignan round the walls.[857]

Every time they felt themselves in great danger, they brought it forth from the Church of Sainte-Croix, carried it in grand procession round the town and over the ramparts,[858] then, having brought it back to the cathedral, they listened to a sermon preached in the porch by a good monk chosen by the magistrates.[859] They said prayers in public and resolved to amend their lives. Wherefore they believed that in Paradise Saint Euverte and Saint-Aignan, touched by their piety, must be interceding for them with Our Lord; and they thought they could hear the voices of the two pontiffs. Saint Euverte was saying, "All-powerful Father, I pray and entreat thee to save the city of Orléans. It is mine. I was its bishop. I am its patron saint. Deliver it not up to its enemies."

Then afterwards spoke Saint-Aignan: "Give peace to the people of Orléans. Father, thou who by the mouth of a child didst appoint me their shepherd, grant that they fall not into the hands of the enemy."

The inhabitants of Orléans expected that the Lord would not at once answer the prayers of the two confessors. Knowing the sternness of his judgments they feared lest he would reply: "For their sins are the French people justly chastised. They suffer because of their disobedience to Holy Church. From the least to the greatest in the realm each vies with the other in evil-doing. The husbandmen, citizens, lawyers and priests are hard and avaricious; the princes, dukes and noble lords are proud, vain, cursers, swearers, and traitors. The corruptness of their lives infects the air. It is just that they suffer chastisement."

That the Lord should speak thus must be expected, because he was angry and because the people of Orléans had greatly sinned. But now, behold, Our Lady, she who loves the King of the Lilies, prays for him and for the Duke of Orléans to the Son, whose pleasure it is to do her will in all things: "My Son, with all my heart I entreat thee to drive the English from the land of France; they have no right to it. If they take Orléans, then they will take the rest at their pleasure. Suffer it not, O my Son, I beseech thee." And Our Lord, at the prayer of his holy Mother, forgives the French and consents to save them.[860]

Thus in those days, according to their ideas of the spiritual world, did men represent even the councils of Paradise. There were folk not a few, and those not unlearned, who believed that as the result of these councils Our Lord had sent his Archangel to the shepherdess. And it might even be possible that he would save the kingdom by the hand of a woman. Is it not in the weak things of the world that he maketh his power manifest?

Did he not allow the child David to overthrow the giant Goliath, and did he not deliver into the hands of Judith the head of Holophernes? In Orléans itself was it not by the mouth of a babe that he had caused to be named that shepherd who was to deliver the besieged town from Attila?[861]

The Lord of Villars and Messire Jamet du Tillay, having returned from Chinon, reported that they had with their own eyes seen the Maid; and they told of the marvels of her coming. They related how she had travelled far, fording rivers, passing by many towns and villages held by the English, as well as through those French lands wherein were rife pillage and all manner of evils. Then they went on to tell how, when she was taken to the King, she had spoken fair words to him as she curtsied, saying: "Gentle Dauphin, God sends me to help and succour you. Give me soldiers, for by grace divine and by force of arms, I will raise the siege of Orléans and then lead you to your anointing at Reims, according as God hath commanded me, for it is his will that the English return to their country and leave in peace your kingdom which shall remain unto you. Or, if they do not quit the land, then will God cause them to perish." Further, they told how, interrogated by certain prelates, knights, squires, and doctors in law, her bearing had been found honest and her words wise. They extolled her piety, her candour, that simplicity which testified that God dwelt with her, and that skill in managing a horse and wielding weapons which caused all men to marvel.[862]

At the end of March, tidings came, that, taken to Poitiers, she had there been examined by doctors and famous masters, and had replied to them with an assurance equal to that of Saint Catherine before the doctors at Alexandria. Because her words were good and her promises sure, it was said that the King, trusting in her, had caused her to be armed in order that she might go to Orléans, where she would soon appear, riding on a white horse, wearing at her side the sword of Saint Catherine and holding in her hand the standard she had received from the King of Heaven.[863]

To the ecclesiastics what was told of Jeanne seemed marvellous but not incredible, since parallel instances were to be found in sacred history, which was all the history they knew. To those who were lettered among them their erudition furnished fewer reasons for denial than for doubt or belief. Those who were simple frankly wondered at these things.

Certain of the captains, and certain even of the people, treated them with derision. But by so doing they ran the risk of ill usage. The inhabitants of the city believed in the Maid as firmly as in Our Lord. From her they expected help and deliverance. They summoned her in a kind of mystic ecstasy and religious frenzy. The fever of the siege had become the fever of the Maid.[864]

Nevertheless, the use made of her by the King's men proved that, following the counsel of the theologians, they were determined to adopt only such methods as were prompted by human prudence. She was to enter the town with a convoy of victuals, then being prepared at Blois by order of the King assisted by the Queen of Sicily.[865] In all the loyal provinces a new effort was being made for the relief and deliverance of the brave city. Gien, Bourges, Blois, Châteaudun, Tours sent men and victuals; Angers, Poitiers, La Rochelle, Albi, Moulins, Montpellier, Clermont sulphur, saltpetre, steel, and arms.[866] And if the citizens of Toulouse gave nothing it was because their city, as the notables consulted by the *capitouls*[867] ingenuously declared, had nothing to give – *non habebat de quibus*.[868]

The King's councillors, notably my Lord Regnault de Chartres, Chancellor of the Realm, were forming a new army. What they had failed to accomplish, by means of the men of Auvergne, they would now attempt with troops from Anjou and Le Mans. The Queen of Sicily, Duchess of Touraine and Anjou, willingly lent her aid. Were Orléans taken she would be in danger of losing lands by which she set great store. Therefore she spared neither men, money, nor victuals. After the middle of April, a citizen of Angers, one Jean Langlois, brought letters informing the magistrates of the imminent arrival of the corn she had contributed. The town gave Jean Langlois a present, and the magistrates entertained him at dinner at the Écu Saint-Georges. This corn was a part of that large convoy which the Maid was to accompany.[869]

Towards the end of the month, by order of my Lord the Bastard, the captains of the French garrisons of La Beauce and Gâtinais, betook themselves to the town to reinforce the army of Blois, the arrival of which was announced. On the 28th, there entered my Lord Florent d'Illiers,[870] Governor of Châteaudun, with four hundred fighting men.[871]

What was to become of Orléans? The siege, badly conducted, was causing the English the most grievous disappointments. Further, their captains perceived they would never succeed in taking the town by means of those bastions, between which anything, either men, victuals, or ammunition, could pass, and with an army miserably quartered in mud hovels, ravaged by disease, and reduced by desertions to three thousand, or at the most to three thousand two hundred men. They had lost nearly all their horses. Far from being able to continue the attack it was hard for them to maintain the defensive and to hold out in those miserable wooden towers, which, as Le Jouvencel said, were more profitable to the besieged than to the besiegers.[872]

Their only hope, and that an uncertain and distant one, lay in the reinforcements, which the Regent was gathering with great difficulty.[873] Meanwhile, time seemed to drag in the besieged town. The warriors who defended it were brave, but they had come to the end of their resources and knew not what more to do. The citizens were good at keeping guard, but they would not face fire. They did not suspect the miserable condition to which the besiegers had been reduced. Hardship, anxiety, and an infected atmosphere depressed their spirits. Already they seemed to see *Les Coués* taking the town by storm, killing, pillaging, and ravaging. At every moment they believed themselves betrayed. They were not calm and self-possessed enough to recognise the enormous advantages of their situation. The town's means of communication, whereby it could be indefinitely reinforced and revictualled, were still open. Besides, a relieving army, well in advance of that of the English, was on the point of arriving. It was bringing a goodly drove of cattle, as well as men and ammunition enough to capture the English fortresses in a few days.

With this army the King was sending the Maid who had been promised.

CHAPTER XI
THE MAID AT BLOIS – THE LETTER TO THE ENGLISH –
THE DEPARTURE FOR ORLÉANS

ITH an escort of soldiers of fortune the Maid reached Blois at the same time as my Lord Regnault de Chartres, Chancellor of France, and the Sire de Gaucourt, Governor of Orléans.[874] She was in the domain of the Prince, whom it was her great desire to deliver: the people of Blois owed allegiance to Duke Charles, a prisoner in the hands of the English. Merchants were bringing cows, rams, ewes, herds of swine, grain, powder and arms into the town.[875] The Admiral, De Culant, and the Lord Ambroise de Loré had come from Orléans to superintend the preparations. The Queen of Sicily herself had gone to Blois. Notwithstanding that at this time the King consulted her but seldom, he now sent to her the Duke of Alençon, commissioned to concert with her measures for the relief of the city of Orléans.[876] There came also the Sire de Rais, of the house of Laval and of the line of the Dukes of Brittany, a noble scarce twenty-four, generous and magnificent, bringing in his train, with a goodly company from Maine and Anjou, organs for his chapel, choristers, and little singing-boys from the choir school.[877] The Marshal de Boussac, the Captains La Hire and Poton came from Orléans.[878] An army of seven thousand men assembled beneath the walls of the town.[879] All that was now waited for was the money necessary to pay the cost of the victuals and the hire of the soldiers. Captains and men-at-arms did not give their services on credit. As for the merchants, if they risked the loss of their victuals and their life, it was only for ready money.[880] No cash, no cattle – and the wagons stayed where they were.

In the month of March, Jeanne had dictated to one of the doctors at Poitiers a brief manifesto intended for the English.[881] She expanded it into a letter, which she showed to certain of her companions and afterwards sent by a Herald from Blois to the camp of Saint-Laurent-des-Orgerils. This letter was addressed to King Henry, to the Regent and to the three chiefs, who, since Salisbury's death, had been conducting the siege, Scales, Suffolk, and Talbot. The following is the text of it:[882]

Jhesus † Maria

King of England, and you, Duke of Bedford, who call yourself Regent of the realm of France, – you, Guillaume de la Poule, Earl of Sulford; Jehan, Sire de Talebot, and you Thomas, Sire d'Escales, who call yourselves Lieutenants of the said Duke of Bedfort, do right in the sight of the King of Heaven. Surrender to the Maid sent hither by God, the King of Heaven, the keys of all the good[883] towns in France that you have taken and ravaged.[884] She is come here in God's name to claim the Blood Royal.[885] She is ready to make peace if so be you will do her satisfaction by giving and paying back to France what you have taken from her.[886] And you, archers, comrades-in-arms, gentle and otherwise,[887] who are before the town of Orléans, go ye hence into your own land, in God's name. And if you will not, then hear the wondrous works[888] of the Maid who will shortly come upon you to your very great hurt. And you, King of England, if you do not thus, I am a Chieftain of war, – and in whatsoever place in France I meet with your men, I will force them to depart willy nilly; and if they will not, then I will have them all slain. I am sent hither by God, the King of Heaven, body for body, to drive them all out of the whole of France. And if they obey, then will I show them mercy. And think not in your heart that you will hold the kingdom of France [from] God, the King of Heaven, Son of the Blessed Mary, for it is King Charles, the true heir, who shall so hold it. God, the King of Heaven, so wills it, and he hath revealed it unto King Charles by the Maid. With a goodly company the King shall enter Paris. If ye will not believe these wondrous works wrought by God and the Maid, then, in whatsoever place ye shall be, there shall we fight. And if ye do me not right, there shall be so great a noise as hath not been in France for a thousand years. And know ye that the King of Heaven will send such great power to the Maid, to her and to her good soldiers, that ye will not be able to overcome her in any battle; and in the end the God of Heaven will reveal who has the better right. You, Duke of Bedfort, the Maid prays and beseeches you that you bring not destruction upon yourself.

If you do her right, you may come in her company where the French will do the fairest deed ever done for Christendom. And if ye will have peace in the city of Orléans, then make ye answer; and, if not, then remember it will be to your great hurt and that shortly. Written this Tuesday of Holy Week.

Such is the letter. It was written in a new spirit; for it proclaimed the kingship of Jesus Christ and declared a holy war. It is hard to tell whether it proceeded from Jeanne's own inspiration or was dictated to her by the council of ecclesiastics. On first thoughts one might be inclined to attribute to the priests the idea of a summons, which is a literal application of the precepts of Deuteronomy:

"When thou comest nigh unto a city to fight against it, then proclaim peace unto it.

"And it shall be, if it make thee answer of peace, and open unto thee, then it shall be, that all the people that is found therein shall be tributaries unto thee, and they shall serve thee.

"And if it will make no peace with thee, but will make war against thee, then thou shalt besiege it:

"And when the Lord thy God hath delivered it into thine hands, thou shalt smite every male thereof with the edge of the sword:

"But the women, and the little ones, and the cattle, and all that is in the city, even all the spoil thereof, shalt thou take unto thyself." (Deuteronomy xx, 10-14.)

But at least it is certain that on this occasion the Maid is expressing her own sentiments. Afterwards we shall find her saying: "I asked for peace, and when I was refused I was ready to fight."[889] But, as she dictated the letter and was unable to read it, we may ask whether the clerks who held the pen did not add to it.

Two or three passages suggest the ecclesiastical touch. Afterwards the Maid did not remember having dictated "body for body," which is quite unimportant. But she declared that she had not said: "I am chief in war" and that she had dictated: "Surrender to the King" and not "Surrender to the Maid."[890] Possibly her memory failed her; it was not always faithful. Nevertheless she appeared very certain of what she said, and twice she repeated that "chief in war" and "surrender to the Maid" were not in the letter. It may have been that the monks who were with her used these expressions. To these wandering priests a dispute over fiefs mattered little, and it was not their first concern to bring King Charles into the possession of his inheritance. Doubtless they desired the good of the kingdom of France; but certainly they desired much more the good of Christendom; and we shall see that, if those mendicant monks, Brother Pasquerel and later Friar Richard, follow the Maid, it will be in the hope of employing her to the Church's advantage. Thus it would be but natural that they should declare her at the outset commander in war, and even invest her with a spiritual power superior to the temporal power of the King, and implied in the phrase: "Surrender to the Maid ... the keys of the good towns."

This very letter indicates one of those hopes which among others she inspired. They expected that after she had fulfilled her mission in France, she would take the cross and go forth to conquer Jerusalem, bringing all the armies of Christian Europe in her train.[891] At this very time a disciple of Bernardino of Siena, Friar Richard, a Franciscan lately come from Syria,[892] and who was shortly to meet the Maid, was preaching at Paris, announcing the approach of the end of the world, and exhorting the faithful to fight against Antichrist.[893] It must be remembered that the Turks, who had conquered the Christian knights at Nicopolis and at Semendria, were threatening Constantinople and spreading terror throughout Europe. Popes, emperors, kings felt the necessity of making one great effort against them.

In England it was said that between Saint-Denys and Saint-George there had been born to King Henry V and Madame Catherine of France a boy, half English and half French, who would go to Egypt and pluck the Grand Turk's beard.[894] On his death-bed the conqueror Henry V was listening to the priests repeating the penitential psalms. When he heard the verse: *Benigne fac Domine in bona voluntate tua ut ædificentur muri Jerusalem*, he murmured with his dying breath: "I have always intended to go to Syria and deliver the holy city out of the hand of the infidel."[895] These were his last words. Wise men counselled Christian princes to unite against the Crescent. In France, the Archbishop of Embrun, who had sat in the Dauphin's Council, cursed the insatiable cruelty of the English nation and those wars among Christians which were an occasion of rejoicing to the enemies of the Cross of Christ.[896]

To summon the English and French to take the cross together, was to proclaim that after ninety-one years of violence and crime the cycle of secular warfare had come to an end. It was to bid Christendom return to the days when Philippe de Valois and Edward Plantagenet promised the Pope to join together against the infidel.

But when the Maid invited the English to unite with the French in a holy and warlike enterprise, it is not difficult to imagine with what kind of a reception the *Godons* would greet such an angelic summons. And at the time of the siege of Orléans, the French on their side had good reasons for not taking the cross with the *Coués*.[897]

The learned did not greatly appreciate the style of this letter. The Bastard of Orléans thought the words very simple; and a few years later a good French jurist pronounced it coarse, heavy, and badly arranged.[898] We cannot aspire to judge better than the jurist and the Bastard, both men of erudition. Nevertheless, we wonder whether it were not that her manner of expression seemed bad to them, merely because it differed from the style of legal documents. True it is that the letter from Blois indicates the poverty of the French prose of that time when not enriched by an Alain Chartier; but it contains neither term nor expression which is not to be met with in the good authors of the day. The words may not be correctly ordered, but the style is none the less vivacious. There is nothing to suggest that the writer came from the banks of the Meuse; no trace is there of the speech of Lorraine or Champagne.[899] It is clerkly French.

While Isabelle de Vouthon had gone on a pilgrimage to Puy, her two youngest children, Jean and Pierre, had set out for France to join their sister, with the intention of making their fortunes through her or the King. Likewise, Brother Nicolas of Vouthon, Jeanne's cousin german, a monk in priest's orders in the Abbey of Cheminon, joined the young saint.[900] To have thus attracted her kinsfolk before giving any sign of her power, Jeanne must have had witnesses on the banks of the Meuse; and certain venerable ecclesiastical personages, as well as noble lords of Lorraine, must have answered for her reputation in France. Such guarantors of the truth of her mission were doubtless those who had instructed her in and accredited her by prophecy. Perhaps Brother Nicolas of Vouthon was himself of the number.

In the army she was regarded as a holy maiden. Her company consisted of a chaplain, Brother Jean Pasquerel;[901] two pages, Louis de Coutes and Raymond;[902] her two brethren, Pierre and Jean; two heralds, Ambleville and Guyenne;[903] two squires, Jean de Metz and Bertrand de Poulengy.

Jean de Metz kept the purse which was filled by the crown.[904] She had also certain valets in her service. A squire, one Jean d'Aulon, whom the King gave her for a steward, joined her at Blois.[905] He was the poorest squire of the realm. He was entirely dependent on the Sire de La Trémouille, who lent him money; but he was well known for his honour and his wisdom.[906] Jeanne attributed the defeats of the French to their riding forth accompanied by bad women and to their taking God's holy name in vain. And this opinion, far from being held by her alone, prevailed among persons of learning and religion; according to whom the disaster of Nicopolis was occasioned by the presence of prostitutes in the army, and by the cruelty and dissoluteness of the knights.[907]

On several occasions, between 1420 and 1425, the Dauphin had forbidden cursing and denying and blaspheming the name of God, of the Virgin Mary and of the saints under penalty of a fine and of corporal punishment in certain cases. The decrees embodying this prohibition asserted that wars, pestilence, and famine were caused by blasphemy and that the blasphemers were in part responsible for the sufferings of the realm.[908] Wherefore the Maid went among the men-at-arms, exhorting them to turn away the women who followed the army, and to cease taking the Lord's name in vain. She besought them to confess their sins and receive divine grace into their souls, maintaining that their God would aid them and give them the victory if their souls were right.[909]

Jeanne took her standard to the Church of Saint-Sauveur and gave it to the priests to bless.[910] The little company formed at Tours was joined at Blois by ecclesiastics and monks, who, on the approach of the English, had fled in crowds from the neighbouring abbeys, and were now suffering from cold and hunger. It was generally thus. Monks were for ever flocking to the armies. Many churches and most abbeys had been reduced to ruin. Those of the mendicants, built outside the towns, had all perished, – plundered and burnt by the English or pulled down by the townsfolk; for, when threatened with siege, the inhabitants always dealt thus with the outlying portions of their town. The homeless monks found no welcome in the cities, which were sparing of their goods; they must needs take the field with the soldiers and follow the army. From such a course their rule suffered and piety gained nothing. Among mercenaries, sumpters and camp followers, these hungry nomad monks lived an edifying life. Those who accompanied the Maid were doubtless neither worse nor better than the rest, and as they were very hungry their first care was to eat.[911]

The men-at-arms were much too accustomed to seeing monks and nuns mingling side by side in the army to feel any surprise at the sight of the holy damsel in the midst of a band so disreputable. It is true that the damsel was said to work wonders. Many believed in them; others mocked and said aloud: "Behold the brave champion and captain who comes to deliver the realm of France."[912]

The Maid had a banner made for the monks to assemble beneath and summon the men-at-arms to prayer. This banner was white, and on it were represented Jesus on the Cross between Our Lady and Saint John.[913] The Duke of Alençon went back to the King to make known to him the needs of the company at Blois. The King sent the necessary funds; and at length they were ready to set out.[914] At the start there were two roads open, one leading to Orléans along the right bank of the Loire, the other along the left bank. At the end of twelve or fourteen miles the road along the right bank came out on the edge of the Plain of La Beauce, occupied by the English who had garrisons at Marchenoir, Beaugency, Meung, Montpipeau, Saint-Sigismond, and Janville. In that direction lay the risk of meeting the army, which was coming to the aid of the English round Orléans. After the experience of the Battle of the Herrings such a meeting was to be feared. If the road along the left bank were taken, the march would lie through the district of La Sologne, which still belonged to King Charles; and if the river were left well on one side, the army would be out of sight of the English garrisons of Beaugency and of Meung. True, it would involve crossing the Loire, but by going up the river five miles east of the besieged city a crossing could conveniently be effected between Orléans and Jargeau. On due deliberation it was decided that they should go by the left bank through La Sologne. It was decided to take in the victuals in two separate lots for fear the unloading near the enemy's bastions should take too long.[915] On Wednesday, the 27th of April, they started.[916] The priests in procession, with a banner at their head, led the march, singing the *Veni creator Spiritus*.[917] The Maid rode with them in white armour, bearing her standard. The men-at-arms and the archers followed, escorting six hundred wagons of victuals and ammunition and four hundred head of cattle.[918] The long line of lances, wagons, and herds defiled over the Blois bridge into the vast plain beyond. The first day the army covered twenty miles of rutty road. Then at curfew, when the setting sun, reflected in the Loire, made the river look like a sheet of copper between lines of dark reeds, it halted,[919] and the priests sang *Gabriel angelus.*

That night they encamped in the fields. Jeanne, who had not been willing to take off her armour, awoke aching in every limb.[920] She heard mass and received communion from her chaplain, and exhorted the men-at-arms always to confess their sins.[921] Then the army resumed its march towards Orléans.

CHAPTER XII
THE MAID AT ORLÉANS

N the evening of Thursday, the 28th of April, Jeanne was able to discern from the heights of Olivet the belfries of the town, the towers of Saint-Paul and Saint-Pierre-Empont, whence the watchmen announced her approach. The army descended the slopes towards the Loire and stopped at the Bouchet wharf, while the carts and the cattle continued their way along the bank as far as l'Île-aux-Bourdons, opposite Chécy, two and a half miles further up the river.[922] There the unloading was to take place. At a signal from the watchmen my Lord the Bastard, accompanied by Thibaut de Termes and certain other captains, left the town by the Burgundian Gate, took a boat at Saint-Jean-de-Braye, and came down to hold counsel with the Lords de Rais and de Loré, who commanded the convoy.[923]

Meanwhile the Maid had only just perceived that she was on the Sologne bank,[924] and that she had been deceived concerning the line of march. Sorrow and wrath possessed her. She had been misled, that was certain. But had it been done on purpose? Had they really intended to deceive her? It is said that she had expressed a wish to go through La Beauce and not through La Sologne, and that she had received the answer: "Jeanne, be reassured; we will take you through La Beauce."[925]

Is it possible? Why should the barons have thus trifled with the holy damsel, whom the King had confided to their care, and who already inspired most of them with respect? Certain of them, it is true, believing her not to be in earnest, would willingly have turned her to ridicule; but if one of them had played her the trick of representing La Beauce as La Sologne, how was it there was no one to undeceive her? How could Brother Pasquerel, her chaplain, her steward, and the honest squire d'Aulon, have become the accomplices of so clumsy a jest? It is all very mysterious, and, when one comes to think of it, what is most mysterious is that Jeanne should have expressly asked to go to Orléans through La Beauce. Since she was so ignorant of the way that when crossing the Blois bridge she never suspected that she was going into La Sologne, there is not much likelihood of her realising so exactly the lie of Orléans as to choose between entering it from the south or the west. A damsel knowing naught beyond the name of the gate through which she is to enter the city, and who is yet persuaded by malicious captains to take one road rather than another, sounds too much like a Mother Goose's tale.

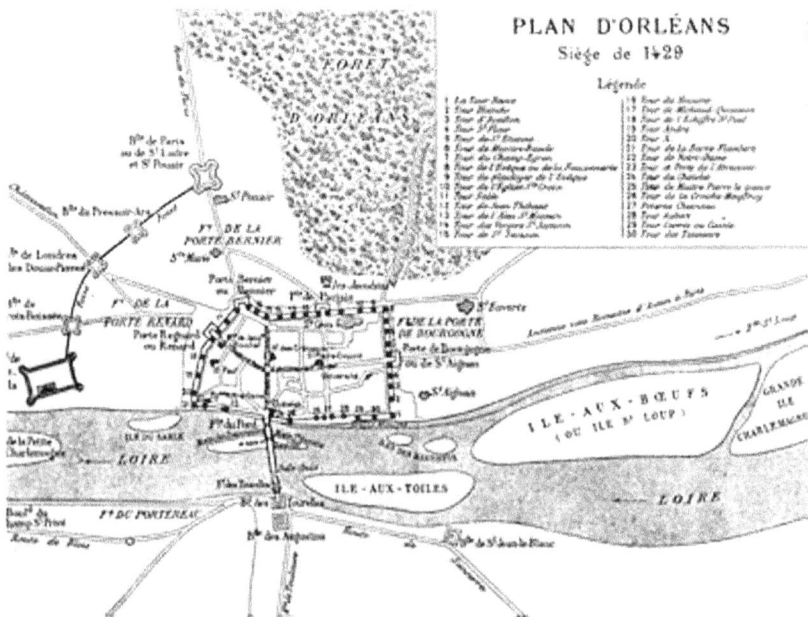

Plan d'Orléans
(siège de 1429)

Jeanne knew no more of Orléans than she did of Babylon. We may therefore conjecture that there was a misunderstanding. She had spoken neither of Sologne nor of Beauce. Her Voices had told her that the English would not budge. They had not shown her a picture of the town, they had not given her either maps or plans: soldiers did not use them. Doubtless Jeanne had said to the captains and priests what she

194

was soon to repeat to the Bastard: "I must go to Talbot and the English." And the priests and soldiers had replied quite frankly: "Jeanne, we are going to Talbot and the English."[926] They had thought they were speaking the truth, since Talbot, who was conducting the siege, would be before them, so to speak, from whatever side they approached the town. But apparently they had not thoroughly understood what the Maid said, and the Maid had not understood what they had replied. For now she was angry and sad at finding herself separated from the town by the sands and waters of the river. What was there to vex her in this? Those who were with her then did not discover; and perhaps her reasons were misunderstood because they were spiritual and mystic. She certainly could not have judged that a military mistake had been made by the bringing of troops and victuals through La Sologne. As she did not know the roads, it was impossible for her to tell which was the best. She was ignorant alike of the enemy's position, of the outworks of the besiegers, and of the defences of the besieged. She had just learnt on what bank of the river the town was situated, yet she must have thought she had good ground for complaint; for she approached the Lord Bastard and inquired sharply: "Are you the Bastard of Orléans?" "I am he. I rejoice at your coming." "Was it through your counsel that I came hither on this side of the river, and that I did not go straight to where Talbot and the English are?" "It was I and those wiser than I who gave this counsel, believing we acted for the best and for the greatest safety." But Jeanne retorted: "In God's name! Messire's counsel is better and wiser than yours. You thought to deceive me, but you deceive yourselves. For I bring you surer aid than ever came yet to knight or city; it is the aid of the King of Heaven and comes from God himself, who not merely for my sake but at the prayer of Saint Louis and Saint Charlemagne has had pity upon the town of Orléans, and will not suffer the enemy to hold at once both the body and the city of the Duke."[927]

One may conclude that what really vexed her was that she had not been taken straight to Talbot and the English. She had just heard that Talbot with his camp was on the right bank. And when she spoke of Talbot and the English she meant only those English who were with Talbot. For, as she came down into the Loire valley, near the ford of Saint-Jean-le-Blanc, she must have seen the bastion of Les Augustins and Les Tourelles at the end of the bridge; and she must have known that there were also English on the left bank. But still, it is not clear why she should have desired to appear first before Talbot and his

English, and why she was now so annoyed at being separated from him by the Loire. Did she think that the entrenched camp, Saint-Laurent-des-Orgerils, commanded by Scales, Suffolk, and Talbot would be attacked immediately? Such an idea would never of itself have occurred to her, since she did not know the place, and no soldier would ever have put such madness into her head as an attack on an entrenched camp by a convoy of cattle and wagons. Neither, as has so often been asserted, can she have thought of forcing a passage between the bastion Saint-Pouair and the outskirts of the wood, since of the bastions and of the forest she knew as little as of the rest. If such had been her intention she would have announced it plainly to the Bastard; for she knew how to make her meaning clear, and even educated persons considered that she spoke well. Then what was her idea? It is not impossible to discover it if one remembers what must have been in the saint's mind at that time, or if one merely recollects by what words and deeds Jeanne had announced and prepared her mission. She had said to the doctors of Poitiers: "The siege of Orléans shall be raised and the town delivered from the enemy after I have summoned it to surrender in God's name."[928] In the name of the King of Heaven she had called upon Scales, Suffolk, and Talbot to raise the siege. She had written that she was ready to make peace, and had bidden them return to England. Now she asked Talbot, Suffolk, and Scales for an answer. Since the English had not sent back her herald she herself came to their leaders as the herald of Messire. She came to require them to make peace, and if they would not make peace she was ready to fight. It was not until they had refused that she could be certain of conquering, not for any human reason, but because her Council had so promised her. Perhaps even she may have hoped that by appearing to the English captains, her standard in hand, accompanied by Saint Catherine and Saint Margaret and Saint Michael the Archangel, she would persuade them to leave France. She may have believed that Talbot, falling on his knees, would obey not her, but Him who sent her; that thus she would accomplish that for which she came, without shedding one drop of that French blood which was so dear to her; neither would the English whom she pitied lose their bodies or their souls. In any case God must be obeyed and charity shown: it was only at such a price that victory could be gained. A victory so spiritual, a conquest so angelic, she had come to win; but now it was snatched from her by the false wisdom of the leaders of her party. They were hindering her from fulfilling her mission, – perhaps from giving the promised sign, – and they were involving her with themselves in enterprises less certain of success and less noble in spirit. Hence her sorrow and her wrath.

Even after the discomfiture of her arrival, in order that she might please God, she did not consider herself freed from the obligation of offering peace to her enemies.[929] And since she could not go straight to Talbot's camp she wanted to appear before the fort of Saint-Jean-le-Blanc.[930]

There was no one left behind the palisades. But if she had gone and found any of the enemy there she would first have offered them peace. Of this her subsequent behaviour within the city walls is positive proof. Her mission was not to contribute to the defence of Orléans plans of campaign or stratagems of war; her share in the work of deliverance was higher and nobler. To suffering men, weak, unhappy, and selfish, she brought the invincible forces of love and faith, the virtue of sacrifice.

My Lord the Bastard who regarded Jeanne's mission as purely religious, and who would have been greatly astonished had any one told him that he ought to consult this peasant on military matters,[931] appeared as if he did not understand the reproaches she addressed to him. And he went away to see that operations were carried out according to the plans he had made.

Everything had been carefully concerted and prepared, but a slight obstacle occurred. The barges that the people of Orléans were to send for the victuals were not yet unmoored.[932] They were sailing vessels, and, as the wind was blowing from the east, they could not set out. No one knew how long they would be delayed, and time was precious. Jeanne said confidently to those who were growing anxious: "Wait a little, for in God's name everything shall enter the town."[933]

She was right. The wind changed: the sails were unfurled, and the barges were borne up the river by a favourable wind, so strong that one boat was able to tow two or three others.[934] Without hindrance they passed the Saint-Loup bastion. My Lord the Bastard sailed in one of these boats with Nicole de Giresme, Grand Prior of France of the order of Rhodes. And the flotilla came to the port of Chécy, where it remained at anchor all night.[935] It was decided that the relieving army should that night encamp at the port of Bouchet and guard the convoy by watching down the river, while one detachment was stationed near the Islands of Chécy to watch up the river in the direction of Jargeau.

In company with certain captains, and with a body of men-at-arms and archers, the Maid followed the bank as far as l'Île-aux-Bourdons.[936]

The lords who had brought the convoy decided that they would set out immediately after the unloading. Having accomplished the first part of its task, the army would return to Blois to fetch the remaining victuals and ammunition, for everything had not been brought at once. Hearing that the soldiers, with whom she had come, were going away, Jeanne wished to go with them; and, after having so urgently asked to be taken to Orléans, now that she was before the gates of the city, her one idea was to go back.[937] Thus is the soul of the mystic blown hither and thither by the breath of the Spirit. Now as always Jeanne was guided by impulses purely spiritual. She would not be parted from these soldiers because she believed they had made their peace with God, and she feared that she might not find others as contrite. For her, victory or defeat depended absolutely on whether the combatants were in a state of grace or of sin. To lead them to confession was her only art of war; no other science did she know, whether for fighting behind ramparts or in the open field.[938]

"As for entering the town," she said, "it would hurt me to leave my men, and I ought not to do it. They have all confessed, and in their company I should not fear the uttermost power of the English."[939]

In reality, as one may well imagine, whether or no they had confessed, whether they were near or far from her, these mercenaries committed all the sins compatible with the simplicity of their minds. But the innocent damsel did not see them. Sensitive to things invisible, her eyes were closed to things material.

She was confirmed in her resolution to return to Blois by the captains who had brought her and who wanted to take her back, alleging the King's command. They wished to keep her because she brought good luck. My Lord the Bastard, however, saw serious obstacles and even dangers in the way of her return.[940] In the state in which he had left the people of Orléans, if their Maid were not straightway brought before them they would rise in fury and despair, with cries, threats, rioting, and violence; everything was to be feared, even massacres. He entreated the captains, in the King's interest, to agree to Jeanne's entering Orléans; and without great difficulty, he induced them to return to Blois without her. But Jeanne did not give in so quickly. He besought her to decide to cross the Loire. She refused and with such insistence that he must have realised how difficult it is to influence a saint. It was necessary for one of the lords who had brought her, the Sire de Rais or the Sire de Loré, to join his entreaties to those of the Bastard, and to say to her: "Assuredly you must go, for we promise to return to you shortly."[941]

At last, when she heard that Brother Pasquerel would go with them to Blois, accompanied by the priests and bearing her standard, believing that her men would have a good spiritual director, she consented to stay.[942] She crossed the Loire with her brothers, her little company, the Bastard, the Marshal de Boussac, the Captain La Hire, and reached Chécy, which was then quite a town, with two churches, an infirmary, and a lepers' hospital.[943] She was received by a rich burgess, one Guy de Cailly, in whose manor of Reuilly she passed the night.[944]

On the morning of the 29th the barges, which had been anchored at Chécy, crossed the Loire, and those who were with the convoy loaded them with victuals, ammunition, and cattle.[945] The river was high.[946] The barges were able to drift down the navigable channel near the left bank. The birches and osiers of l'Île-aux-Bœufs hid them from the English in the Saint-Loup bastion. Besides, at that moment, the enemy was occupied elsewhere. The town garrison was skirmishing with them in order to distract their attention. The fighting was somewhat hard. There were slain and wounded; prisoners were taken on both sides; and the English lost a banner.[947] Beneath the deserted[948] watch of Saint-Jean-le-Blanc the barges passed unprotected. Between l'Île-aux-Bœufs and the Islet of Les Martinets they turned starboard, to go down again, following the right bank, under l'Île-aux-Toiles, as far as La Tour Neuve, the base of which was washed by the Loire, at the south-eastern corner of the town. Then they took shelter in the moat near the Burgundian Gate.[949]

The whole day the manor of Reuilly was besieged by a procession of citizens, who could not forbear coming at the risk of their lives to see the promised Maid. It was six o'clock in the evening before she left Chécy. The captains wanted her to enter the town at nightfall for fear of disorders and lest the crush around her should be too great.[950] Doubtless they passed along the broad valleys leading from Semoy towards the south, on the borders of the parishes of Saint-Marc and Saint-Jean-de-Braye. On the way she said to those who rode with her: "Fear nothing. No harm shall happen to you."[951] And indeed the only danger was for pedestrians. Horsemen ran little risk of being pursued by the English, who were short of horses in their bastions.

On that Friday, the 29th of April, in the darkness, she entered Orléans, by the Burgundian Gate. She was in full armour and rode a white horse.[952] A white horse was the steed of heralds and archangels.[953] The Bastard had placed her on his right. Before her was borne her standard, on which figured two angels, each holding a flower de luce, and her pennon, painted with the picture of the Annunciation. Then came the Marshal de Boussac, Guy de Cailly, Pierre and Jean d'Arc, Jean de Metz, and Bertrand de Poulengy, the Sire d'Aulon, and those lords, captains, men-of-war, and citizens who had come to meet her at Chécy.[954] Bearing torches and rejoicing as heartily as if they had seen God himself descending among them, the townsfolk of Orléans pressed around her.[955] They had suffered great privations, they had feared that help would never come; but now they were heartened and felt as if the siege had been raised already by the divine virtue, which they had been told resided in this Maid. They looked at her with love and veneration; elbowing and pushing each other, men, women, and children rushed forward to touch her and her white horse, as folk touch the relics of saints. In the crush a torch set her pennon on fire. The Maid, beholding it, spurred on her horse and galloped to the flame, which she extinguished with a skill apparently miraculous; for everything in her was marvellous.[956] Men-at-arms and citizens, enraptured, accompanied her in crowds to the Church of Sainte-Croix, whither she went first to give thanks, then to the house of Jacques Boucher, where she was to lodge.[957]

Jacques or Jacquet Boucher, as he was called, had been the Duke of Orléans' treasurer for several years. He was a very rich man and had married the daughter of one of the most influential burgesses of the city.[958] Having stayed in the town throughout the siege, he contributed to the defence by gifts of wheat, oats, and wine, and by advancing funds for the purchase of ammunition and weapons. As the care of the ramparts fell to the burgesses, it was Jacques' duty to keep in repair and ready for defence the Renard Gate, where he dwelt, which was the most exposed to the English attack. His mansion, one of the finest and largest in the town, once inhabited by Regnart or Renard, the family which had given its name to the gate, was in the Rue des Talmeliers, quite near the fortifications. The captains held their councils of war there, when they did not meet at the house of Chancellor Guillaume Cousinot in the Rue de la Rose.[959] Jacques

Boucher's dwelling was doubtless well furnished with silver plate and storied tapestry. It would appear that in one of the rooms there was a picture representing three women and bearing this inscription: *Justice, Peace, Union.*[960]

Into this house the Maid was received with her two brothers, the two comrades who had brought her to the King, and their valets. She had her armour taken off.[961] Jacques Boucher's wife and daughter passed the night with her. Jeanne shared the child's bed. She was nine years old and was called Charlotte after Duke Charles, who was her father's lord.[962] It was the custom in those days for the host to share his bed with his man guest and the hostess with her woman guest. This was the rule of courtesy; kings observed it as well as burgesses. Children were taught how to behave towards a sleeping companion, to keep to their own part of the bed, not to fidget, and to sleep with their mouths shut.[963]

Thus the Duke's treasurer took the Maid into his house and entertained her at the town's expense. Jeanne's horses were stabled by a burgess named Jean Pillas.

As for the D'Arc brothers, they did not stay with their sister, but lodged in the house of Thévenin Villedart. The town paid all their expenses; for example it furnished them with the shoes and gaiters they needed and gave them a few gold crowns. Three of the Maid's comrades, who were very destitute and came to see her at Orléans, received food.[964]

On the next day, the 30th of April, the town bands of Orléans were early afoot. From morn till eve everything in the town was topsy-turvy; the rebellion, which had been repressed so long, now broke forth. As early as February the citizens had begun to mistrust and hate the knights;[965] now at last they shook off their yoke and broke it.[966] Henceforth they would recognise no King's lieutenant, no governor, no lords, no generals; there was but one power and one defence: the Maid.[967] The Maid was the people's captain. This damsel, this shepherdess, this nun did the knights the greatest injury they ever experienced: she reduced them to nothing. On the morning of the 30th they must have been convinced that the popular revolution had taken place. The town bands were waiting for the Maid to put herself at their head, and with her to march immediately against the *Godons*. The captains endeavoured to make them understand that they must wait for the army from Blois and the company of Marshal de Boussac, who that night had set out to meet the army. The citizens in arms would listen to nothing, and with loud cries clamoured for the Maid. She did not appear. My Lord the Bastard, who was honey-tongued, had advised her to keep away.[968] This was the last advantage the leaders gained over her. And now as before, when she appeared to give way to them, she was merely doing as she liked. As for the citizens, with the Maid or without her, they were determined to fight. The Bastard could not hinder them. They sallied forth,[969] accompanied by the Gascons of Captain La Hire and the men of Messire Florent d'Illiers. They bravely attacked the bastion Saint-Pouair, which the English called Paris, and which was about eight hundred yards from the walls. They overcame the outposts and approached so close to the bastion that they were already clamouring for faggots and straw to be brought from the town to set fire to the palisades. But at the cry "Saint George!" the English gathered themselves together, and after a sore and sanguinary fight repulsed the attack of the citizens and free-lances.[970]

The Maid had known nothing of it. Sent from God, on her white horse, a messenger armed yet peaceful, she held it neither just nor pious to fight the English before they had refused her offers of peace. On that day as before her one wish was to go in true saintly wise straight to Talbot. She asked for tidings of her letter and learnt that the English captains had paid no heed to it, and had detained her herald, Guyenne.[971] This is what had happened:

That letter, which the Bastard deemed couched in vulgar phrase, produced a marvellous impression on the English. It filled them with fear and rage. They kept the herald who had brought it; and, although use and custom insisted on the person of such officers being respected, alleging that a sorceress's messenger must be a heretic, they put him in chains, and after some sort of a trial condemned him to be burnt as the accomplice of the seductress.[972]

They even put up the stake to which he was to be bound. And yet, before executing the sentence, they judged it well to consult the University of Paris, as in like manner the Bishop of Beauvais was to consult it eighteen months later.[973] Their evil disposition arose from fear. These unfortunates, who were treated as devils, were afraid of devils. They suspected the subtle French of being necromancers and sorcerers. They said that by repeating magic lines the Armagnacs had compassed the death of the great King, Henry V. Fearing lest their enemies should make use of sorcery and enchantment against them, in order to protect themselves from all evil influences, they wore bands of parchment inscribed with the formulæ of conjuration and called *periapts.*[974] The most efficacious of these amulets was the first chapter of the Gospel of St. John. At this time the stars were unfavourable to them, and astrologers were reading their approaching ruin in the sky. Their late King, Henry V, when he was studying at Oxford, had learnt there the rules of divination by the stars. For his own special use he kept in his coffers two astrolabes, one of silver and one of gold. When his queen, Catherine of France, was about to be confined, he himself cast the horoscope of the expected child. And further, as there was a prophecy in England[975] which said that Windsor would lose what Monmouth had gained, he determined that the Queen should not be confined at Windsor. But destiny cannot be thwarted. The royal child was born at Windsor. His father was in France when he heard the tidings. He held them to be of ill omen, and summoned Jean Halbourd of Troyes, minister general of the Trinitarians or Mathurins, "excellent in astrology," who, having drawn up the scheme of nativity, could only confirm the King in his doleful presentiments.[976] And now the time had come. Windsor reigned; all would be lost. Merlin had predicted that they would be driven out of France and by a Virgin utterly undone. When the Maid appeared they grew pale with fright, and fear fell upon captains and soldiers.[977] Those whom no man could make afraid, trembled before this girl whom they held to be a witch. They could not be expected to regard her as a saint sent of God. The best they could think of her was that she was a very learned sorceress.[978] To those she came to help she appeared a daughter of God, to those she came to destroy she appeared a horrid monster in woman's form. In this double aspect lay all her strength: angelic for the French, devilish for the English, to one and the other she appeared invincible and supernatural.

In the evening of the 30th she sent her herald, Ambleville, to the camp of Saint-Laurent-des-Orgerils to ask for Guyenne, who had borne the letter from Blois and had not returned. Ambleville was also instructed to tell Sir John Talbot, the Earl of Suffolk, and the Lord Scales that in God's name the Maid required them to depart from France and go to England; otherwise they would suffer hurt. The English sent back Ambleville with an evil message.

"The English," he said to the Maid, "are keeping my comrade to burn him."

She made answer: "In God's name they will do him no harm." And she commanded Ambleville to return.[979]

She was indignant, and, no doubt, greatly disappointed. In truth, she had never anticipated that Talbot and the leaders of the siege would give such a welcome to a letter inspired by Saint Catherine and Saint Margaret and Saint Michael; but so broad was her charity that she was still willing to offer peace to the English. In her innocence she may have believed that her proclamations in God's name were misunderstood after all. Besides, whatever happened, she was determined to go through with her duty to the end. At night she sallied forth from the Bridge Gate and went as far as the outwork of La Belle-Croix. It was not unusual for the two sides to address each other. La Belle-Croix was within ear-shot of Les Tourelles. The Maid mounted the rampart and cried to the English: "Surrender in God's name. I will grant you your lives only."

But the garrison and even the Captain, William Glasdale himself, hurled back at her coarse insults and horrible threats.

"Milk-maid! If ever we get you, you shall be burned alive."[980]

She answered that it was a lie. But they were in earnest and sincere. They firmly believed that this damsel was arming legions of devils against them.

On Sunday, the 1st of May, my Lord the Bastard went to meet the army from Blois.[981] He knew the country; and, being both energetic and cautious, he was desirous to superintend the entrance of this convoy as he had done that of the other. He set out with a small escort. He did not dare to take with him the Saint herself; but, in order, so to speak, to put himself under her protection and tactfully to flatter the piety and affections of the folk of Orléans, he took a member of her suite, her steward, Sire Jean d'Aulon.[982] Thus he grasped the first opportunity of showing his good will to the Maid, feeling that henceforth nothing could be done except with her or under her patronage.

The fervour of the citizens was not abated. That very day, in their passionate desire to see the Saint, they crowded round Jacques Boucher's house as turbulently as the pilgrims from Puy pressed into the sanctuary of La Vierge Noire. There was a danger of the doors being broken in. The cries of the townsfolk reached her. Then she appeared: good, wise, equal to her mission, one born for the salvation of the people. In the absence of captains and men-at-arms, this wild multitude only awaited a sign from her to throw itself in tumult on the bastions and perish there. Notwithstanding the visions of war that haunted her, that sign she did not give. Child as she was, and as ignorant of war as of life, there was that within her which turned away disaster. She led this crowd of men, not to the English bastions, but to the holy places of the city. Down the streets she rode, accompanied by many knights and squires; men and women pressed to see her and could not gaze upon her enough. They marvelled at the manner of her riding and of her behaviour, in every point like a man-at-arms; and they would have hailed her as a veritable Saint George had they not suspected Saint George of turning Englishman.[983]

That Sunday, for the second time, she went forth to offer peace to the enemies of the kingdom. She passed out by the Renard Gate and went along the Blois Road, through the suburbs that had been burnt down, towards the English bastion. Surrounded by a double moat, it was planted on a slope at the crossroads called La Croix Boissée or Buissée, because the townsfolk of Orléans had erected a cross there, which every Palm Sunday they dressed with a branch of box blessed by the priest. Doubtless she intended to reach this bastion, and perhaps to go on to the camp of Saint-Laurent-des-Orgerils situated between La Croix Boissée and the Loire, where, as she had said, were Talbot and the English. For she had not yet given up hope of gaining a hearing from the leaders of the siege. But at the foot of the hill, at a place called La Croix-Morin, she met some *Godons* who were keeping watch. And there, in tones grave, pious, and noble, she summoned them to retreat before the hosts of the Lord. "Surrender, and your lives shall be spared. In God's name go back to England. If ye will not I will make you suffer for it."[984]

These men-at-arms answered her with insults as those of Les Tourelles had done. One of them, the Bastard of Granville, cried out to her: "Would you have us surrender to a woman?"

The French, who were with her, they dubbed pimps and infidels, to shame them for being in the company of a bad woman and a witch.[985] But whether because they thought her magic rendered her invulnerable, or because they held it dishonourable to strike a messenger, now, as on other occasions, they forbore to fire on her.

That Sunday, Jacquet le Prestre, the town varlet, offered the Maid wine.[986] The magistrates and citizens could not have more highly honoured her whom they regarded as their captain. Thus they treated barons, kings and queens when they were entertained in the city. In those days wine was highly valued on account of its beneficent power. Jeanne, when she emphasised a wish, would say: "If I were never to drink wine between now and Easter!..."[987] But in reality she never drank wine except mixed with water, and she ate little.[988]

Throughout this time of waiting the Maid never rested for a moment. On Monday, May 2nd, she mounted her horse and rode out into the country to view the English bastions. The people followed her in crowds; they had no fear and were glad to be near her. And when she had seen all that she wanted, she returned to the city, to the cathedral church, where she heard vespers.[989]

On the morrow, the 3rd of May, the day of the Invention of the Holy Cross, which was the Cathedral Festival, she followed in the procession, with the magistrates and the townsfolk. It was then that Maître Jean de Mâcon, the precentor of the cathedral,[990] greeted her with these words: "My daughter, are you come to raise the siege?"

She replied: "Yea, in God's name."[991]

The people of Orléans all believed that the English round the city were as innumerable as the stars in the sky; the notary, Guillaume Girault, expected nothing short of a miracle.[992] Jean Luillier, woollen draper[993] by trade, thought it impossible for the citizens to hold out longer against an enemy so enormously their superior.[994] Messire Jean de Mâcon was likewise alarmed at the power and the numbers of the *Godons*.

"My daughter," he said to the Maid, "their force is great and they are strongly intrenched. It will be a difficult matter to turn them out."[995]

If notary Guillaume Girault, if draper Jean Luillier, if Messire Jean de Mâcon, instead of fostering these gloomy ideas, had counted the numbers of the besieged and the besieging, they would have found that the former were more numerous than the latter; and that the army of Scales, of Suffolk, of Talbot appeared mean and feeble when compared with the great besieging armies of the reign of King Henry V. Had they looked a little more closely they would have perceived that the bastions, with the formidable names of London and of Paris, were powerless to prevent either corn, cattle, pigs, or men-at-arms being brought into the city; and that these gigantic dolls were being mocked at by the dealers, who, with their beasts, passed by them daily. In short, they would have realised that the people of Orléans were for the moment better off than the English. But they had examined nothing for themselves. They were content to abide by public opinion which is seldom either just or correct. The Maid did not share Messire Jean de Mâcon's illusions. She knew no more of the English than he did; yet because she was a saint, she replied tranquilly: "With God all things are possible."[996] And Maître Jean de Mâcon thought it well that such should be her opinion.

What aggravated the trouble, the danger, and the panic of the situation, was that the citizens believed they were betrayed. They recollected the Count of Clermont at the Battle of the Herrings, and they suspected the King's men of deserting them once again. After having done so much and spent so much they saw themselves given up to the English. This idea made them mad.[997] There was a rumour that the Marshal de Boussac, who had started with my Lord the Bastard to meet the second convoy of supplies, and who was to return on Tuesday the 3rd, would not come back. It was said that the Chancellor of France wanted to disband the army. It was absurd. On the contrary, great efforts for the deliverance of the city were being made by the King's Council and that of the Queen of Sicily. But the people's brains had been turned by their long suffering and their terrible danger. A more reasonable fear was lest any mishap should occur on the road from Blois like that which had overtaken the force at Rouvray. The Maid's comrades were infected with the anxieties of the townsfolk; one of them betrayed his fears to her, but she was not affected by them. With the radiant tranquillity of the illuminated, she said:[998] "The Marshal will come. I am confident that no harm will happen to him."[999]

On that day there entered into the city the little garrisons of Gien, of Château-Regnard, and of Montargis.[1000] But the Blois army did not come. On the morrow, at daybreak, it was descried in the plain of La Beauce. And, indeed, the Sire de Rais and his company, escorted by the Marshal de Boussac and my Lord the Bastard, were skirting the Forest of Orléans.[1001] At these tidings the citizens must needs exclaim that the Maid had been right in wishing to march straight against Talbot since the captains now followed the very road she had indicated. But in reality it was not just as they thought. Only one part of the Blois army had risked forcing its way between the western bastions; the convoy, with its escort, like the first convoy, was coming through La Sologne and was to enter the town by water. Those arrangements for the entrance of supplies, which, in the first instance, had proved successful, were naturally now repeated.[1002]

Captain La Hire and certain other commanders, who had remained in the city with five hundred fighting men, went out to meet the Sire de Rais, the Marshal de Boussac and the Bastard. The Maid mounted her horse and went with them. They passed through the English lines; and, a little further on, having met the army, they returned to the town together. The priests, and among them Brother Pasquerel bearing the banner, were the first to pass beneath the Paris bastion, singing psalms.[1003]

Jeanne dined at Jacques Boucher's house with her steward, Jean d'Aulon. When the table was cleared, the Bastard, who had come to the treasurer's house, talked with her for a moment. He was gracious and polite, but spoke with restraint.

"I have heard on good authority," he remarked, "that Fastolf is soon to join the English who are conducting the siege. He brings them supplies and reinforcements and is already at Janville."

At these tidings Jeanne appeared very glad and said, laughing: "Bastard, Bastard, in God's name, I command thee to let me know as soon as thou shalt hear of Fastolf's arrival. For should he come without my knowledge, I warn thee thou shalt lose thy head."[1004]

Far from betraying any annoyance at so rude a jest, he replied that she need have no fear, he would let her know.[1005]

The approach of Sir John Fastolf had already been announced on the 26th of April. It was expressly in order to avoid him that the army had come through La Sologne. It is possible that on the 4th of May the tidings of his coming had no surer foundation. But the Bastard knew something else. The corn of the second convoy, like that of the first, was coming down the river. It had been resolved, in a council of war, that in the afternoon the captains should attack the Saint-Loup bastion, and divert the English as had been done on the 29th of April.[1006] The attack had already begun. But of this the Bastard breathed not a word to the Maid. He held her to be the one source of strength in the town. But he believed that in war her part was purely spiritual.[1007]

After he had withdrawn, Jeanne, worn out by her morning's expedition, lay down on her bed with her hostess for a short sleep. Sire Jean d'Aulon, who was very weary, stretched himself on a couch in the same room, thinking to take the rest he so greatly needed. But scarce had he fallen asleep when the Maid leapt from her bed and roused him with a great noise. He asked her what she wanted.

"In God's name," she answered in great agitation, "my Council have told me to go against the English; but I know not whether I am to go against their bastions or against Fastolf, who is bringing them supplies."[1008]

In her dreams she had been present at her Council, that is to say, she had beheld her saints. She had seen Saint Catherine and Saint Margaret. There had happened to her what always happens. The saints had told her no more than she herself knew. They had revealed to her nothing of what she needed to know. They had not informed her how, at that very moment, the French were attacking the Saint-Loup bastion and suffering great hurt. And the Blessed Ones had departed leaving her in error and in ignorance of what was going on, and in uncertainty as to what she was to do. The good Sire d'Aulon was not the one to relieve her from her embarrassment. He, too, was excluded from the Councils of War. Now he answered her nothing, and set to arming himself as quickly as possible. He had already begun when they heard a great noise and cries coming up from the street. From the passers-by, they gleaned that there was fighting near Saint-Loup and that the enemy was inflicting great hurt on the French. Without staying to inquire further, Jean d'Aulon went straightway to his squire to have his armour put on. Almost at the same time Jeanne went down and asked: "Where are my armourers? The blood of our folk is flowing."[1009]

In the street she found Brother Pasquerel, her chaplain, with other priests, and Mugot, her page, to whom she cried: "Ha! cruel boy, you did not tell me that the blood of France was being shed!... In God's name, our people are hard put to it."[1010]

She bade him bring her horse and leave the wife and daughter of her host to finish arming her. On his return the page found her fully accoutred. She sent him to fetch her standard from her room. He gave it her through the window. She took it and spurred on her horse into the high street, towards the Burgundian Gate, at such a pace that sparks flashed from the pavement.

"Hasten after her!" cried the treasurer's wife.[1011]

Sire d'Aulon had not seen her start. He imagined, why, it is impossible to say, that she had gone out on foot, and, having met a page on horseback in the street, had made him dismount and give her his horse.[1012] The Renard Gate and the Burgundian Gate were on opposite sides of the town. Jeanne, who for the last three days had been going up and down the streets of Orléans, took the most direct way. Jean d'Aulon and the page, who were hastily pursuing her, did not come up with her until she had reached the gate. There they met a wounded man being brought into the town. The Maid asked his bearers who the man was. He was a Frenchman, they replied. Then she said: "I have never seen the blood of a Frenchman flow without feeling my heart stand still."[1013]

The Maid and Sire d'Aulon, with a few fighting men of their company, pressed on through the fields to Saint-Loup. On the way they saw certain of their party. The good squire, unaccustomed to great battles, never remembered having seen so many fighting men at once.[1014]

For an hour the Sire de Rais' Bretons and the men from Le Mans had been skirmishing before the bastion. As the custom was those who had arrived last were keeping watch.[1015] But if these combatants, who had reached the town only that very morning, had attacked without taking time to breathe, they must have been hard pressed. They were doing what had been done on the 29th of April, and for the same reason:[1016] namely, occupying the English while the barges corn-laden were coming down the river to the moat. On the top of their high hill, in their strong fortress, the English had easily held out albeit they were but few; and the French King's men can hardly have been able to make head against them, since the Maid and Sire d'Aulon found them scattered through the fields. She gathered them together and led them back to the attack. They were her friends: they had journeyed together: they had sung psalms and hymns together: together they had heard mass in the fields. They knew that she brought good luck: they followed her. As she marched at their head her first idea was a religious one. The bastion was built upon the church and convent of the Ladies of Saint-Loup. With the sound of a trumpet she had it proclaimed that nothing should be taken from the church.[1017] She remembered how Salisbury had come to a bad end for having pillaged the Church of Notre Dame de Cléry; and she desired to keep her men from an evil death.[1018] This was the first time she had seen fighting; and no sooner had she entered into the battle than she became the leader because she was the best. She did better than others, not because she knew more; she knew less. But her heart was nobler. When every man thought of himself, she alone thought of others: when every man took heed to defend himself, she defended herself not at all, having previously offered up her life. And thus this child, – who feared suffering and death like every human being, who knew by her Voices and her presentiments that she would be wounded, – went straight on and stood beneath showers of arrows and cannon-balls on the edge of the moat, her standard in hand, rallying her men.[1019] Through her what had been merely a diversion became a serious attack. The bastion was stormed.

When he heard that the fort of Saint-Loup was being attacked, Sir John Talbot sallied forth from the camp of Saint-Laurent-des-Orgerils. In order to reach the threatened bastion he had some distance to go down his lines and along the border of the forest. He set out, and on his way was reinforced by the garrisons of the western bastions. The town watchmen observed his movements and sounded the alarm. Marshal Boussac passing through the Parisis Gate, went out to meet Talbot on the north, towards Fleury. The English captain was preparing to break through the French force when he saw a thick cloud of smoke rising over the fort Saint-Loup. He understood that the French had captured and set fire to it; and sadly he returned to the camp of Saint-Laurent-des-Orgerils.[1020]

The attack had lasted three hours. After the burning of the bastion the English climbed into the church belfry. The French had difficulty in dislodging them; but they ran no danger thereby. Of prisoners, they took two score, and the rest they slew. The Maid was very sorrowful when she saw so many of the enemy dead. She pitied these poor folk who had died unconfessed.[1021] Certain *Godons*, wearing the ecclesiastical habit and ornaments, came to meet her. She perceived that they were soldiers disguised in stoles and hoods taken from the sacristy of the Abbaye aux Dames. But she pretended to take them for what they represented themselves to be. She received them and had them conducted to her house without allowing any harm to come to them. With a charitable jest she said: "One should never question priests."[1022]

Before leaving the fort she confessed to Brother Pasquerel, her chaplain. And she charged him to make the following announcement to all the men-at-arms: "Confess your sins and thank God for the victory. If you do not, the Maid will never help you more and will not remain in your company."[1023]

The Saint-Loup bastion, attacked by fifteen hundred French, had been defended by only three hundred English. That they made no vigorous defence is indicated by the fact that only two or three

Frenchmen were slain.[1024] It was not by any severe mental effort or profound calculation that the French King's men had gained this advantage. It had cost them little, and yet it was immense. It meant the cutting off of the besiegers' communications with Jargeau: it meant the opening of the upper Loire: it was the first step towards the raising of the siege. Better still, it afforded positive proof that these devils who had inspired such fear were miserable creatures, who might be entrapped like mice and smoked out like wasps in their nest. Such unhoped-for good fortune was due to the Maid. She had done everything, for without her nothing would have been done. She it was, who, in ignorance wiser than the knowledge of captains and free-lances, had converted an idle skirmish into a serious attack and had won the victory by inspiring confidence.

That very evening the magistrates sent workmen to Saint-Loup to demolish the captured fortifications.[1025]

When at night she returned to her lodging, Jeanne told her chaplain that on the morrow, which was the day of the Ascension of Our Lord, she would keep the Festival by not wearing armour and by abstaining from fighting. She commanded that no one should think of quitting the town, of attacking or making an assault, until he had first confessed. She added that the men-at-arms must pay heed that no dissolute women followed in their train for fear lest God should cause them to be defeated on account of their sins.[1026]

When need was the Maid herself saw that her orders concerning bad women and blasphemers were scrupulously obeyed. More than once she drove away the camp-followers. She rebuked men-at-arms who swore and blasphemed. One day, in the open street, a knight began to swear and take God's name in vain. Jeanne heard him. She seized him by the throat, exclaiming, "Ah, Sir! dare you take in vain the name of Our Lord and Master? In God's name you shall take back those words before I move from this place."

A citizen's wife, passing down the street at that moment, beheld this man, who seemed to her to be a great baron, humbly receiving the Saint's reproaches and testifying his repentance.[1027]

On the morrow, which was Ascension Day, the captains held a council-of-war in the house of Chancellor Cousinot in the Rue de la Rose.[1028] There were present, as well as the Chancellor, my Lord the Bastard, the Sire de Gaucourt, the Sire de Rais, the Sire de Graville, Captain La Hire, my Lord Ambroise de Loré and several others. It was decided that Les Tourelles, the chief stronghold of the besiegers, should be attacked on the morrow. Meanwhile, it would be necessary to hold in check the English of the camp of Saint-Laurent-des-Orgerils. On the previous day, when Talbot set out from Saint-Laurent, he had not been able to reach Saint-Loup in time because he had been obliged to make a long circuit, going round the town from west to east. But, although, on that previous day, the enemy had lost command of the Loire above the town, they still held the lower river. They could cross it between Saint-Laurent and Saint-Privé[1029] as rapidly as the French could cross it by the Île-aux-Toiles; and thus the English might gather in force at Le Portereau. This, the French must prevent and, if possible, draw off the garrisons from Les Augustins and Les Tourelles to Saint-Laurent-des-Orgerils. With this object it was decided that the people of Orléans with the folk from the communes, that is, from the villages, should make a feigned attack on the Saint-Laurent camp, with mantelets, faggots, and ladders. Meanwhile, the nobles would cross the Loire by l'Île-aux-Toiles, would land at Le Portereau under the watch of Saint-Jean-le-Blanc which had been abandoned by the English, and attack the bastion of Les Augustins; and when that was taken, the fort of Les Tourelles.[1030] Thus there would be one assault made by the citizens, another by the nobles; one real, the other feigned; both useful, but only one glorious and worthy of knights. When the plan was thus drawn up, certain captains were of opinion that it would be well to send for the Maid and tell her what had been decided.[1031] And, indeed, on the previous day, she had done so well that there was no longer need to hold her aloof. Others deemed that it would be imprudent to tell her what was contemplated concerning Les Tourelles. For it was important that the undertaking should be kept secret, and it was feared that the holy damsel might speak of it to her friends among the common people. Finally, it was agreed that she should know those decisions which affected the train-bands of Orléans, since, indeed, she was their captain, but that such matters as could not be safely communicated to the citizens should be concealed from her.

Jeanne was in another room of the house with the Chancellor's wife. Messire Ambroise de Loré went to fetch her; and, when she had come, the Chancellor told her that the camp of Saint-Laurent-des-Orgerils was to be attacked on the morrow. She divined that something was being kept back; for she possessed a certain acuteness. Besides, since they had hitherto concealed everything, it was natural she should suspect that something was still being kept from her. This mistrust annoyed her. Did they think her incapable of keeping a secret? She said bitterly: "Tell me what you have concluded and ordained. I could keep a much greater secret than that."[1032]

And refusing to sit down she walked to and fro in the room.

My Lord the Bastard deemed it well to avoid exasperating her by telling her the truth. He pacified her without incriminating anybody: "Jeanne, do not rage. It is impossible to tell you everything at once. What the Chancellor has said has been concluded and ordained. But if those on the other side [of the water, the English of La Sologne] should depart to come and succour the great bastion of Saint-Laurent and the English who are encamped near this part of the city, we have determined that some of us shall cross the river to do what we can against those on the other side [those of Les Augustins and Les Tourelles]. And it seems to us that such a decision is good and profitable."

The Maid replied that she was content, that such a decision seemed to her good, and that it should be carried out in the manner determined.[1033]

It will be seen that by this proceeding the secrecy of the deliberations had been violated, and that the nobles had not been able to do what they had determined or at least not in the way they had determined. On that Ascension Day the Maid for the last time sent a message of peace to the English, which she dictated to Brother Pasquerel in the following terms: *Ye men of England, who have no right in the realm of France, the King of Heaven enjoins and commands you by me, Jeanne the Maid, to leave your forts and return to your country. If ye will not I will make so great a noise as shall remain for ever in the memory of man: This I write to you for the third and last time, and I will write to you no more.*

Signed thus: Jhesus † Maria. Jeanne the Maid.

And below: I should have sent to you with more ceremony. But you keep my heralds. You kept my herald Guyenne. If you will send him back to me, I will send you some of your men taken at the bastion Saint-Loup; they are not all dead.[1034]

Jeanne went to La Belle Croix, took an arrow, and tied her letter to it with a string, then told an archer to shoot it to the English, crying: "Read! This is the message."

The English received the arrow, untied the letter, and having read it they cried: "This a message from the Armagnac strumpet."

When she heard them, tears came into Jeanne's eyes and she wept. But soon she beheld her saints, who spoke to her of Our Lord, and she was comforted. "I have had a message from my Lord," she said joyfully.[1035]

My Lord the Bastard himself demanded the Maid's herald, threatening that if he were not sent back he would keep the heralds whom the English had sent to treat for the exchange of prisoners. It is asserted that he even threatened to put those prisoners to death. But Ambleville did not return.[1036]

CHAPTER XIII

THE TAKING OF LES TOURELLES AND THE
DELIVERANCE OF ORLÉANS

O N the morrow, Friday the 6th of May, the Maid rose at daybreak. She confessed to her chaplain and heard mass sung before the priests and fighting men of her company.[1037] The zealous townsfolk were already up and armed. Whether or no she had told them, the citizens, who were strongly determined to cross the Loire and attack Les Tourelles themselves, were pressing in crowds to the Burgundian Gate. They found it shut. The Sire de Gaucourt was guarding it with men-at-arms. The nobles had taken this precaution in case the citizens should discover their enterprise and wish to take part in it. The gate was closed and well defended. Bent on fighting and themselves recovering their precious jewel, Les Tourelles, the citizens had recourse to her before whom gates opened and walls fell; they sent for the Saint. She came, frank and terrible. She went straight to the old Sire de Gaucourt, and, refusing to listen to him, said: "You are a wicked man to try to prevent these people from going out. But whether you will or no, they will go and will do as well as they did the other day."[1038]

Excited by Jeanne's voice and encouraged by her presence, the citizens, crying slaughter, threw themselves on Gaucourt and his men-at-arms. When the old baron perceived that he could do nothing with them, and that it was impossible to bring them to his way of thinking, he himself joined them. He had the gates opened wide and cried out to the townsfolk: "Come, I will be your captain."

And with the Lord of Villars and Sire d'Aulon he went out at the head of the soldiers, who had been keeping the gate, and all the train-bands of the town. At the foot of La Tour-Neuve, at the eastern corner of the ramparts, there were boats at anchor. In them l'Île-aux-Toiles was reached, and thence on a bridge formed by two boats they crossed over the narrow arm of the river which separates l'Île-aux-Toiles from the Sologne bank.[1039] Those who arrived first entered the abandoned fort of Saint-Jean-le-Blanc, and, while waiting for the others, amused themselves by demolishing it.[1040] Then, when all had passed over, the townsfolk gayly marched against Les Augustins. The bastion was situated in front of Les Tourelles, on the ruins of the monastery; and the bastion would have to be taken before the fortifications at the end of the bridge could be attacked. But the enemy came out of their entrenchments and advanced within two bow-shots of the French, upon whom from their bows and cross-bows they let fly so thick a shower of arrows that the men of Orléans could not stand against them. They gave way and fled to the bridge of boats: then, afraid of being cast into the river, they crossed over to l'Île-aux-Toiles.[1041] The fighting men of the Sire de Gaucourt were more accustomed to war. With the Lord of Villars, Sire d'Aulon, and a valiant Spaniard, Don Alonzo de Partada, they took their stand on the slope of Saint-Jean-le-Blanc and resisted the enemy. Although very few in number, they were still holding out when, about three o'clock in the afternoon, Captain La Hire and the Maid crossed the river with the free-lances. Seeing the French hard put to it, and the English in battle array, they mounted their horses, which they had brought over with them, and holding their lances in rest spurred on against the enemy. The townsfolk, taking heart, followed them and drove back the English. But at the foot of the bastion they were again repulsed.[1042] In great agitation the Maid galloped from the bastion to the bank, and from the bank to the bastion, calling for the knights; but the knights did not come. Their plans had been upset, their order of battle reversed, and they needed time to collect themselves. At last she saw floating over the island the banners of my Lord the Bastard, the Marshal de Boussac, and the Lord de Rais. The artillery came too, and Master Jean de Montesclère with his culverin and his gunners, bringing all the engines needed for the assault. Four thousand men assembled round Les Augustins. But much time had been lost; they were only just beginning, and the sun was going down.[1043]

The Sire de Gaucourt's men were ranged behind, to cover the besiegers in case the English from the bridge end should come to the aid of their countrymen in Les Augustins. But a quarrel arose in de Gaucourt's company. Some, like Sire d'Aulon and Don Alonzo, judged it well to stay at their post. Others were ashamed to stand idle. Hence haughty words and bravado. Finally Don Alonzo and a man-at-arms, having challenged each other to see who would do the best, ran towards the bastion hand in hand. At one single volley Maître Jean's culverin overthrew the palisade. Straightway the two champions forced their way in.[1044]

"Enter boldly!" cried the Maid.[1045] And she planted her standard on the rampart. The Sire de Rais followed her closely.

The numbers of the French were increasing. They made a strong attack on the bastion and soon took it by storm. Then one by one they had to assault the buildings of the monastery in which the *Godons* were entrenched. In the end all the English were slain or taken, except a few, who took refuge in Les Tourelles. In the huts the French found many of their own men imprisoned. After bringing them out, they set fire to the fort, and thus made known to the English their new disaster.[1046] It is said to have been the Maid who ordered the fire in order to put a stop to the pillage in which her men were mercilessly engaging.[1047]

A great advantage had been won. But the French were slow to regain confidence. When, in the darkness by the light of the fire, they beheld for the first time close to them the bulwarks of Les Tourelles, the men-at-arms were afraid. Certain said: "It would take us more than a month to capture it."[1048]

The lords, captains, and men-at-arms went back to the town to pass a quiet night. The archers and most of the townsfolk stayed at Le Portereau. The Maid would have liked to stay too, so as to be sure of beginning again on the morrow.[1049] But, seeing that the captains were leaving their horses and their pages in the fields, she followed them to Orléans.[1050] Wounded in the foot by a caltrop,[1051] overcome with fatigue, she felt weak, and contrary to her custom she broke her fast, although the day was Friday.[1052] According to Brother Pasquerel, who in this matter is not very trustworthy, while she was finishing her supper in her lodging, there came to her a noble whose name is not mentioned and who addressed her thus: "The captains have met in council.[1053] They recognise how few we were in comparison with the English, and that it was by God's great favour that we won the victory. Now that the town is plentifully supplied we may well wait for help from the King. Wherefore, the council deems it inexpedient for the men-at-arms to make a sally to-morrow."

Jeanne replied: "You have been at your council; I have been at mine. Now believe me the counsel of Messire shall be followed and shall hold good, whereas your counsel shall come to nought." And turning to Brother Pasquerel who was with her, she said: "To-morrow rise even earlier than to-day, and do the best you can. Stay always at my side, for to-morrow I shall have much ado – more than I have ever had, and to-morrow blood shall flow from my body."[1054]

It was not true that the English outnumbered the French. On the contrary they were far less numerous. There were scarce more than three thousand men round Orléans. The succour from the King having arrived, the captains could not have said that they were waiting for it. True it is that they were hesitating to proceed forthwith to attack Les Tourelles on the morrow; but that was because they feared lest the English under Talbot should enter the deserted town during the assault, since the townsfolk, refusing to march against Saint-Laurent, had all gone to Le Portereau. The Maid's Council troubled about none of these difficulties. No fears beset Saint Catherine and Saint Margaret. To doubt is to fear; they never doubted. Whatever may be said to the contrary, of military tactics and strategy they knew nothing. They had not read the treatise of Vegetius, *De re militari*. Had they read it the town would have been lost. Jeanne's Vegetius was Saint Catherine.

During the night it was cried in the streets of the city that bread, wine, ammunition and all things necessary must be taken to those who had stayed behind at Le Portereau. There was a constant passing to and fro of boats across the river. Men, women and children were carrying supplies to the outposts.[1055]

On the morrow, Saturday the 7th of May, Jeanne heard Brother Pasquerel say mass and piously received the holy sacrament.[1056] Jacques Boucher's house was beset with magistrates and notable citizens. After a night of fatigue and anxiety, they had just heard tidings which exasperated them. They had heard tell that the captains wanted to defer the storming of Les Tourelles. With loud cries they appealed to the Maid to help the townsfolk, sold, abandoned, and betrayed.[1057] The truth was that my Lord the Bastard and the captains, having observed during the night a great movement among the English on the upper Loire, were confirmed in their fears that Talbot would attack the walls near the Renard Gate while the French were occupied on the left bank. At sunrise they had perceived that during the night the English had demolished their outwork Saint Privé, south of l'Île-

Charlemagne.[1058] That also caused them to believe firmly that in the evening the English had concentrated in the Saint-Laurent camp and the bastion, London. The townsfolk had long been irritated by the delay of the King's men in raising the siege. And there is no doubt that the captains were not so eager to bring it to an end as they were.[1059] The captains lived by war, while the citizens died of it, – that made all the difference. The magistrates besought the Maid to complete without delay the deliverance she had already begun. They said to her: "We have taken counsel and we entreat you to accomplish the mission you have received from God and likewise from the King."

"In God's name, I will," she said. And straightway she mounted her horse, and uttering a very ancient phrase, she cried: "Let who loves me follow me!"[1060]

As she was leaving the treasurer's house a shad was brought her. She said to her host, smiling, "In God's name! we will have it for supper. I will bring you back a *Godon* who shall eat his share." She added: "This evening we shall return by the bridge."[1061] For the last ninety-nine days it had been impossible. But happily her words proved true.

The townsfolk had been too quick to take alarm. Notwithstanding their fear of Talbot and the English of the Saint-Laurent camp, the nobles crossed the Loire in the early morning, and at Le Portereau rejoined their horses and pages who had passed the night there with the archers and train-bands. They were all there, the Bastard, the Sire de Gaucourt, and the lords of Rais, Graville, Guitry, Coarraze, Villars, Illiers, Chailly, the Admiral de Culant, the captains La Hire, and Poton.[1062] The Maid was with them. The magistrates sent them great store of engines of war: hurdles, all kinds of arrows, hammers, axes, lead, powder, culverins, cannon, and ladders.[1063] The attack began early. What rendered it difficult was not the number of English entrenched in the bulwark and lodged in the towers: there were barely more than five hundred of them;[1064] true, they were commanded by Lord Moleyns, and under him by Lord Poynings and Captain Glasdale, who in France was called Glassidas, a man of humble birth, but the first among the English for courage.[1065] The assailants, citizens, men-at-arms and archers were ten times more numerous. That so many combatants had been assembled was greatly to the credit of the French nation; but so great an army of men could not be employed at once. Knights were not much use against earthworks; and the townsfolk although very zealous, were not very tenacious.[1066] Finally, the Bastard, who was prudent and thoughtful, was afraid of Talbot.[1067] Indeed if Talbot had known and if he had wanted he might have taken the town while the French were trying to take Les Tourelles. War is always a series of accidents, but on that day no attempt whatever was made to carry out any concerted movement. This vast army was not an irresistible force, since no one, not even the Bastard, knew how to bring it into action. In those days the issue of a battle was in the hands of a very few combatants. On the previous day everything had been decided by two or three men.

The French assembled before the entrenchments had the air of an immense crowd of idlers looking on while a few men-at-arms attempted an escalade. Notwithstanding the size of the army, for a long while the assault resolved itself into a series of single combats. Twenty times did the most zealous approach the rampart and twenty times they were forced to retreat.[1068] There were some wounded and some slain, but not many. The nobles, who had been making war all their lives, were cautious, while the soldiers of fortune were careful of their men. The townsfolk were novices in war.[1069] The Maid alone threw herself into it with heart and soul. She was continually saying: "Be of good cheer. Do not retreat. The fort will soon be yours."[1070]

At noon everyone went away to dinner. Then about one o'clock they set to work again.[1071] The Maid carried the first ladder. As she was putting it up against the rampart, she was struck on the shoulder over the right breast, by an arrow shot so straight that half a foot of the shaft pierced her flesh.[1072] She knew that she was to be wounded; she had foretold it to her King, adding that he must employ her all the same. She had announced it to the people of Orléans and spoken of it to her chaplain[1073] on the previous day; and certainly for the last five days she had been doing her best to make the prophecy come true.[1074] When the English saw that the arrow had pierced her flesh they were greatly encouraged: they believed that if blood were drawn from a witch all her power would vanish. It made the French very sad. They carried her apart. Brother Pasquerel and Mugot, the page, were with her. Being in pain, she was afraid and wept.[1075] As was usual when combatants were wounded in battle, a group of soldiers surrounded her; some wanted to charm her. It was a custom with men-at-arms to attempt to close wounds by muttering paternosters over them. Spells were cast by means of incantations and conjurations. Certain paternosters had the power of stopping haemorrhage. Papers covered with magic characters were also used. But it meant having recourse to the power of devils and committing mortal sin. Jeanne did not wish to be charmed.

"I would rather die," she said, "than do anything I knew to be sin or contrary to God's will."

Again she said: "I know that I am to die. But I do not know when or how, neither do I know the hour. If my wound may be healed without sin then am I willing to be made whole."[1076]

Her armour was taken off. The wound was anointed with olive oil and fat, and, when it was dressed, she confessed to Brother Pasquerel, weeping and groaning. Soon she beheld coming to her her heavenly counsellors, Saint Catherine and Saint Margaret. They wore crowns and emitted a sweet fragrance. She was comforted.[1077] She resumed her armour and returned to the attack.[1078]

The sun was going down; and since morning the French had been wearing themselves out in a vain attack upon the palisades of the bulwark. My Lord the Bastard, seeing his men tired and night coming on, and afraid doubtless of the English of the Saint-Laurent-des-Orgerils Camp, resolved to lead the army back to Orléans. He had the retreat sounded. The trumpet was already summoning the combatants to Le Portereau.[1079] The Maid came to him and asked him to wait a little.

"In God's name!" she said, "you will enter very soon. Be not afraid and the English shall have no more power over you."

According to some, she added: "Wherefore, rest a little; drink and eat."[1080]

While they were refreshing themselves, she asked for her horse and mounted it. Then, leaving her standard with a man of her company, she went alone up the hill into the vineyards, which it had been impossible to till this April, but where the tiny spring leaves were beginning to open. There, in the calm of evening, among the vine props tied together in sheaves and the lines of low vines drinking in the early warmth of the earth, she began to pray and listened for her heavenly voices.[1081] Too often tumult and noise prevented her from hearing what her angel and her saints had to say to her. She could only understand them well in solitude or when the bells were tinkling in the distance, and evening sounds soft and rhythmic were ascending from field and meadow.[1082]

During her absence Sire d'Aulon, who could not give up the idea of winning the day, devised one last expedient. He was the least of the nobles in the army; but in the battles of those days every man was a law unto himself. The Maid's standard was still waving in front of the bulwark. The man who bore it was dropping with fatigue and had passed it on to a soldier, surnamed the Basque, of the company of my Lord of Villars.[1083] It occurred to Sire d'Aulon, as he looked upon this standard blessed by priests and held to bring good luck, that if it were borne in front, the fighting men, who loved it dearly, would follow it and in order not to lose it would scale the bulwark. With this idea he went to the Basque and said: "If I were to enter there and go on foot up to the bulwark would you follow me?"

The Basque promised that he would. Straightway Sire d'Aulon went down into the ditch and protecting himself with his shield, which sheltered him from the stones fired from the cannon, advanced towards the rampart.[1084]

After a quarter of an hour, the Maid, having offered a short prayer, returned to the men-at-arms and said to them: "The English are exhausted. Bring up the ladders."[1085]

It was true. They had so little powder that their last volley fired in an insufficient charge carried no further than a stone thrown by hand.[1086] Nothing but fragments of weapons remained to them. She went towards the fort. But when she reached the ditch she suddenly beheld the standard so dear to her, a thousand times dearer than her sword, in the hands of a stranger. Thinking it was in danger, she hastened to rescue it and came up with the Basque just as he was going down into the ditch. There she seized her standard by the part known as its tail, that is the end of the flag, and pulled at it with all her might, crying:

"Ha! my standard, my standard!"

The Basque stood firm, not knowing who was pulling thus from above. And the Maid would not let it go. The nobles and captains saw the standard shake, took it for a sign and rallied. Meanwhile Sire d'Aulon had reached the rampart. He imagined that the Basque was following close behind. But, when he turned round he perceived that he had stopped on the other side of the ditch, and he cried out to him: "Eh! Basque, what did you promise me?"

At this cry the Basque pulled so hard that the Maid let go, and he bore the standard to the rampart.[1087]

Jeanne understood and was satisfied. To those near her she said: "Look and see when the flag of my standard touches the bulwark."

A knight replied: "Jeanne, the flag touches."

Then she cried: "All is yours. Enter."[1088]

Straightway nobles and citizens, men-at-arms, archers, townsfolk threw themselves wildly into the ditch and climbed up the palisades so quickly and in such numbers that they looked like a flock of birds descending on a hedge.[1089] And the French, who had now entered within the fortifications, saw retreating before them, but with their faces turned proudly towards the enemy, the Lords Moleyns and Poynings, Sir Thomas Giffart, Baillie of Mantes, and Captain Glasdale, who were covering the flight of their men to Les Tourelles.[1090] In his hand Glasdale was holding the standard of Chandos, which, after having waved over eighty years of victories, was now retreating before the standard of a child.[1091] For the Maid was there, standing upon the rampart. And the English, panic-stricken, wondered what kind of a witch this could be whose powers did not depart with the flowing of her blood, and who with charms healed her deep wounds. Meanwhile she was looking at them kindly and sadly and crying out, her voice broken with sobs:

"Glassidas! Glassidas! surrender, surrender to the King of Heaven. Thou hast called me strumpet; but I have great pity on thy soul and on the souls of thy men."[1092]

At the same time, from the walls of the town and the bulwark of La Belle Croix cannon balls rained down upon Les Tourelles.[1093] Montargis and Rifflart cast forth stones. Maître Guillaume Duisy's new cannon, from the Chesneau postern, hurled forth balls weighing one hundred and twenty pounds.[1094] Les Tourelles were attacked from the bridge side. Across the arch broken by the English a narrow footway was thrown, and Messire Nicole de Giresme, a knight in holy orders, was the first to pass over.[1095] Those who followed him set fire to the palisade which blocked the approach to the fort on that side. Thus the six hundred English, their strength and their weapons alike exhausted, found themselves assailed both in front and in the rear. In a crafty and terrible manner they were also attacked from beneath. The people of Orléans had loaded a great barge with pitch, tow, faggots, horse-bones, old shoes, resin, sulphur, ninety-eight pounds of olive oil and such other materials as might easily take fire and smoke. They had steered it under the wooden bridge, thrown by the enemy from Les

Tourelles to the bulwark: they had anchored the barge there and set fire to its cargo. The fire from the barge had caught the bridge just when the English were retreating. Through smoke and flames the six hundred passed over the burning platform. At length it came to the turn of William Glasdale, Lord Poynings and Lord Moleyns, who with thirty or forty captains, were the last to leave the lost bulwark; but when they set foot on the bridge, its beams, reduced to charcoal, crumbled beneath them, and they all with the Chandos standard were engulfed in the Loire.[1096]

Jeanne moved to pity wept over the soul of Glassidas and over the souls of those drowned with him.[1097] The captains, who were with her, likewise grieved over the death of these valiant men, reflecting that they had done the French a great wrong by being drowned, for their ransom would have brought great riches.[1098]

Having escaped from the French on the bulwark, across the burning planks the six hundred were set upon by the French on the bridge. Four hundred were slain, the others taken. The day had cost the people of Orléans a hundred men.[1099]

When in the black darkness, along the fire-reddened banks of the Loire, the last cries of the vanquished had died away, the French captains, amazed at their victory, looked anxiously towards Saint-Laurent-des Orgerils, for they were still afraid lest Sir John Talbot should sally forth from his camp to avenge those whom he had failed to succour. Throughout that long attack, which had lasted from sunrise to sunset, Talbot, the Earl of Suffolk and the English of Saint-Laurent had not left their entrenchments. Even when Les Tourelles were taken the conquerors remained on the watch, still expecting Talbot.[1100] But this Talbot, with whose name French mothers frightened their children, did not budge. He had been greatly feared that day, and he himself had feared lest,[1101] if he withdrew any of his troops to succour Les Tourelles, the French would capture his camp and his forts on the west.

The army prepared to return to the town. In three hours, the bridge, three arches of which had been broken, was rendered passable. Some hours after darkness, the Maid entered the city by the bridge as she had foretold.[1102] In like manner all her prophecies were fulfilled when their fulfilment depended on her own courage and determination. The captains accompanied her, followed by all the men-at-arms, the archers, the citizens and the prisoners who were brought in two by two. The bells of the city were ringing; the clergy and people sang the Te Deum.[1103] After God and his Blessed Mother, they gave thanks in all humility to Saint Aignan and Saint Euverte, who had been bishops in their mortal lives and were now the heavenly patrons of the city. The townsfolk believed that both before and during the siege they had given the saints so much wax and had paraded their relics in so many processions that they had deserved their powerful intercession, and that thereby they had won the victory and been delivered out of the enemy's hand. There was no doubt about the intervention of the saints because at the time of assault on Les Tourelles two bishops bright and shining had been seen in the sky, hovering over the fort.[1104]

Jeanne was brought back to Jacques Boucher's house, where a surgeon again dressed the wound she had received above the breast. She took four or five slices of bread soaked in wine and water, but neither ate nor drank anything else.[1105]

On the morrow, Sunday, the 8th of May, being the Feast of the Appearance of St. Michael, it was announced in Orléans, in the morning, that the English issuing forth from those western bastions which were all that remained to them, were ranging themselves before the town moat in battle array and with standards flying. The folk of Orléans, both the men-at-arms and the train-bands, greatly desired to fall upon them. At daybreak Marshal de Boussac and a number of captains went out and took up their positions over against the enemy.[1106]

The Maid went out into the country with the priests. Being unable to put on her cuirass because of the wound on her shoulder, she merely wore one of those light coats-of-mail called *jaserans*.[1107]

The men-at-arms inquired of her: "To-day being the Sabbath, is it wrong to fight?"

She replied: "You must hear mass."[1108]

She did not think the enemy should be attacked.

"For the sake of the holy Sabbath do not give battle. Do not attack the English, but if the English attack you, defend yourselves stoutly and bravely, and be not afraid, for you will overcome them."[1109]

In the country, at the foot of a cross, where four roads met, one of those consecrated stones, square and flat, which priests carried with them on their journeys, was placed upon a table. Very solemnly did the officiating ecclesiastics sing hymns, responses and prayers; and at this altar the Maid with all the priests and all the men-at-arms heard mass.[1110]

After the *Deo gratias* she recommended them to observe the movements of the English. "Now look whether their faces or their backs be towards you."

She was told that they had turned their backs and were going away.

Three times she had told them: "Depart from Orléans and your lives shall be saved." Now she asked that they should be allowed to go without more being required of them.

"It is not well pleasing to my Lord that they should be engaged to-day," she said. "You will have them another time. Come, let us give thanks to God."[1111]

The *Godons* were going. During the night they had held a council of war and resolved to depart.[1112] In order to put a bold front on their retreat and to prevent its being cut off, they had faced the folk of Orléans for an hour, now they marched off in good order.[1113] Captain La Hire and Sire de Loré, curious as to which way they would take and desiring to see whether they would leave anything behind them, rode three or four miles in pursuit with a hundred or a hundred and twenty horse. The English were retreating towards Meung.[1114]

A crowd of citizens, villeins and villagers rushed into the abandoned forts. The *Godons* had left their sick and their prisoners there. The townsfolk discovered also ammunition and even victuals, which were doubtless not very abundant and not very excellent. "But," says a Burgundian, "they made good cheer out of them, for they cost them little."[1115] Weapons, cannons and mortars were carried into the town. The forts were demolished so that they might henceforth be useless to the enemy.[1116]

On that day there were grand and solemn processions and a good friar[1117] preached. Clerks, nobles, captains, magistrates, men-at-arms and citizens devoutly went to church and the people cried: "Noël!"[1118]

Thus, on the 8th of May, in the morning, was the town of Orléans delivered, two hundred and nine days after the siege had been laid and nine days after the coming of the Maid.

CHAPTER XIV

THE MAID AT TOURS AND AT SELLES-EN-BERRY — THE TREATISES OF JACQUES GÉLU AND OF JEAN GERSON

N the morning of Sunday the 8th of May, the English departed, retreating towards Meung and Beaugency. In the afternoon of the same day, Messire Florent d'Illiers with his men-at-arms left the town and went straight to his captaincy of Châteaudun to defend it against the *Godons* who had a garrison at Marchenoir and were about to descend on Le Dunois. On the next day the other captains from La Beauce and Gâtinais returned to their towns and strongholds.[1119]

On the ninth of the same month, the combatants brought by the Sire de Rais, receiving neither pay nor entertainment, went off each man on his own account; and the Maid did not stay longer.[1120] After having taken part in the procession by which the townsfolk rendered thanks to God, she took her leave of those to whom she had come in the hour of distress and affliction and whom she now quitted in the hour of deliverance and rejoicing. They wept with joy and with gratitude and offered themselves to her for her to do with them and their goods whatever she would. And she thanked them kindly.[1121]

From Chinon the King caused to be sent to the inhabitants of the towns in his dominion and notably to those of La Rochelle and Narbonne, a letter written at three sittings, between the evening of the 9th of May and the morning of the 10th, as the tidings from Orléans were coming in. In this letter he announced the capture of the forts of Saint-Loup, Les Augustins and Les Tourelles and called upon the townsfolk to praise God and do honour to the great feats accomplished there, especially by the Maid, who "had always been present when these deeds were done."[1122] Thus did the royal power describe Jeanne's share in the victory. It was in no wise a captain's share; she held no command of any kind. But, sent by God, at least so it might be believed, her presence was a help and a consolation.

In company with a few nobles she went to Blois, stayed there two days,[1123] then went on to Tours, where the King was expected.[1124] When, on the Friday before Whitsunday, she entered the town, Charles, who had set out from Chinon, had not yet arrived. Banner in hand, she rode out to meet him and when she came to him, she took off her cap and bowed her head as far as she could over her horse. The King lifted his hood, bade her look up and kissed her. It is said that he felt glad to see her, but in reality we know not what he felt.[1125]

In this month of May, 1429, he received from Messire Jacques Gélu a treatise concerning the Maid, which he probably did not read, but which his confessor read for him. Messire Jacques Gélu, sometime Councillor to the Dauphin and now my Lord Archbishop of Embrun,[1126] had at first been afraid that the King's enemies had sent him this shepherdess to poison him, or that she was a witch possessed by demons. In the beginning he had advised her being carefully interrogated, not hastily repulsed, for appearances are deceptive and divine grace moves in a mysterious manner. Now, after having read the conclusions of the doctors of Poitiers, learnt the deliverance of Orléans, and heard the cry of the common folk, Messire Jacques Gélu no longer doubted the damsel's innocence and goodness. Seeing that the doctors were divided in their opinion of her, he drew up a brief treatise, which he sent to the King, with a very ample, a very humble, and a very worthy dedicatory epistle.

About that time, on the pavement of the cathedral of Reims a labyrinth had been traced with compass and with square.[1127] Pilgrims who were patient and painstaking followed all its winding ways. The Archbishop of Embrun's treatise is likewise a carefully planned scholastic labyrinth. Herein one advances only to retreat and retreats only to advance, but without entirely losing one's way provided one walks with sufficient patience and attention. Like all scholastics, Gélu begins by giving the reasons against his own opinion and it is not until he has followed his opponent at some length that he returns to his own argument. Into all the intricacies of his labyrinth it would take too long to follow him. But since those who were round the King consulted this theological treatise, since it was addressed to the King and since the

King and his Council may have based on it their opinion of Jeanne and their conduct towards her, one is curious to know what, on so singular an occasion, they found taught and recommended therein.

Treating first of the Church's weal, Jacques Gélu holds that God raised up the Maid to confound the heretics, the number of whom, according to him, is by no means small. "To turn to confusion those who believe in God as if they believed not," he writes, "the Almighty, who hath on His vesture and on His thigh a name written, *King of Kings and Lord of Lords*, was pleased to succour the King of France by the hand of a child of low estate." The Archbishop of Embrun discerns five reasons why the divine succour was granted to the King; to wit: the justice of his cause, the striking merits of his predecessors, the prayers of devout souls and the sighs of the oppressed, the injustice of the enemies of the kingdom and the insatiable cruelty of the English nation.

That God should have chosen a maid to destroy armies in no way surprises him. "He created insects, such as flies and fleas, with which to humble man's pride." So persistently do these tiny creatures worry and weary us that they prevent our studying or acting. However strong his self-control, a man may not rest in a room infested with fleas. By the hand of a young peasant, born of poor and lowly parents, subject to menial labour, ignorant and simple beyond saying, it hath pleased Him to strike down the proud, to humble them and make His Majesty manifest unto them by the deliverance of the perishing.

That to a virgin the Most High should have revealed His designs concerning the Kingdom of the Lilies cannot astonish us; on virgins He readily bestows the gift of prophecy. To the sibyls it pleased Him to reveal mysteries hidden from all the Gentiles. On the authority of Nicanor, of Euripides, of Chrysippus, of Nennius, of Apollodorus, of Eratosthenes, of Heraclides Ponticus, of Marcus Varro and of Lactantius, Messire Jacques Gélu teaches that the sibyls were ten in number: the Persian, the Libyan, the Delphian, the Cimmerian, the Erythrean, the Samian, the Cumæan, the Hellespontine, the Phrygian and the Tiburtine. They prophesied to the Gentiles the glorious incarnation of Our Lord, the resurrection of the dead and the consummation of the ages. This example appears to him worthy of consideration.

As for Jeanne, she is in herself unknowable. Aristotle teaches: there is nothing in the intellect which hath not first been in the senses, and the senses cannot penetrate beyond experience. But what the mind cannot grasp directly it may come to comprehend by a roundabout way. When we consider her works, as far as in our human weakness we can know, we say the Maid is of God. Albeit she hath adopted the profession of arms, she never counsels cruelty; she is merciful to her enemies when they throw themselves upon her mercy and she offers peace. Finally the Archbishop of Embrun believes that this Maid is an angel sent by God, the Lord of Hosts, for the saving of the people; not that she has the nature, but that she does the work of an angel.

Concerning the conduct to be followed in circumstances so marvellous, the doctor is of opinion that in war the King should act according to human wisdom. It is written: "Thou shalt not tempt the Lord thy God." In vain would an active mind have been bestowed on man were he not to make use of it in his undertakings. Long deliberation must precede prompt execution. It is not by a woman's desires or supplications that God's help is obtained. A prosperous issue is the fruit of action and of counsel.

But the inspiration of God must not be rejected. Wherefore the will of the Maid must be accomplished, even should that will appear doubtful and mistaken. If the words of the Maid are found to be stable, then the King must follow her and confide to her as to God the conduct of the enterprise to which she is committed. Should any doubt occur to the King, let him incline rather towards divine than towards human wisdom, for as there is no comparing the finite with the infinite so there is no comparing the wisdom of man with the wisdom of God. Wherefore we must believe that He who sent us this child is able to impart unto her a counsel superior to man's counsel. Then from this Aristotelian reasoning the Archbishop of Embrun draws the following two-headed conclusion: "On the one hand we give it to be understood that the wisdom of this world must be consulted in the ordering of battle, the use of engines, ladders and all other implements of war, the building of bridges, the sufficient despatch of supplies, the raising of funds, and in all matters without which no enterprise can succeed save by miracle.

"But when on the other hand divine wisdom is seen to be acting in some peculiar way, then human reason must be humble and withdraw. Then it is, we observe, that the counsel of the Maid must be asked for, sought after and adopted before all else. He who gives life gives wherewithal to support life. On his workers he bestows the instruments for their work. Wherefore let us hope in the Lord. He makes the King's cause his own. Those who support it he will inspire with the wisdom necessary to make it triumphant. God leaves no work imperfect."

The Archbishop concludes his treatise by commending the Maid to the King because she inspires holy thoughts and makes manifest the works of piety. "This counsel do we give the King that every day he do such things as are well pleasing in the sight of the Lord and that he confer with the Maid concerning them. When he shall have received her advice let him practise it piously and devoutly; then shall not the Lord withdraw His hand from Him but continue His loving kindness unto him."[1128]

The great doctor Gerson, former Chancellor of the University, was then ending his days at Lyon in the monastery of Les Célestins, of which his brother was prior. His life had been full of work and weariness.[1129] In 1408 he was priest of Saint-Jean-en-Grève in Paris. In that year he delivered in his parish church the funeral oration of the Duke of Orléans, assassinated by order of the Duke of Burgundy; and he roused the passions of the mob to such a fury that he ran great danger of losing his life. At the Council of Constance, possessed by a so-called "merciful cruelty"[1130] which goaded him to send a heretic to the stake, he urged the condemnation of John Huss, regardless of the safe-conduct which the latter had received from the Emperor; for in common with all the fathers there assembled he held that according to natural law both divine and human, no promise should be kept if it were prejudicial to the Catholic Faith. With a like ardour he prosecuted in the Council the condemnation of the thesis of Jean Petit concerning the lawfulness of tyrannicide. In things temporal as well as spiritual he advocated uniform obedience and the respect of established authority. In one of his sermons he likens the kingdom of France to the statue of Nebuchadnezzar, making the merchants and artisans the legs of the statue, "which are partly iron, partly clay, because of their labour and humility in serving and obeying...." Iron signifies labour, and clay humility. All the evil has arisen from the King and the great citizens being held in subjection by those of low estate.[1131]

Now, crushed by suffering and sorrow, he was teaching little children. "It is with them that reforms must begin," he said.[1132]

The deliverance of the city of Orléans must have gladdened the heart of the old Orleanist partisan. The Dauphin's Councillors, eager to set the Maid to work, had told him of the deliberations at Poitiers, and asked him, as a good servant of the house of France, for his opinion concerning them. In reply he wrote a compendious treatise on the Maid.

In this work he is careful from the first to distinguish between matters of faith and matters of devotion. In questions of faith doubt is forbidden. With regard to questions of devotion the unbeliever, to use a colloquial expression, is not necessarily damned. Three conditions are necessary if a question is to be considered as one of devotion: first, it must be edifying; second, it must be probable and attested by popular report or the testimony of the faithful; third, it must touch on nothing contrary to faith. When these conditions are fulfilled, it is fitting neither persistently to condemn nor to approve, but rather to appeal to the church.

For example, the conception of the very holy Virgin, indulgences, relics, are matters of faith and not of devotion. A relic may be worshipped in one place or another, or in several places at once. Recently the Parlement of Paris disputed concerning the head of Saint Denys, worshipped at Saint-Denys in France and likewise in the cathedral at Paris. This is a matter of devotion.[1133]

Whence it may be concluded that it is lawful to consider the question of the Maid as a matter of devotion, especially when one reflects on her motives, which are the restitution of his kingdom to her King and the very righteous expulsion or destruction of her very stubborn enemies.

And if there be those who make various statements concerning her idle talk, her frivolity, her guile, now is the time to quote the saying of Cato: "Common report is not our judge." According to the words of the Apostle, it doth not become us to call in question the servant of God. Much better is it to abstain from judgment, as is permitted, or to submit doubtful points to ecclesiastical superiors. This is the principle followed in the canonisation of saints. The catalogue of the saints is not, strictly speaking, necessarily a matter of faith, but of pious devotion. Nevertheless, it is not to be highly censured by any manner of man.

To come to the present case, the following circumstances are to be noted: First, the royal council and the men-at-arms were induced to believe and to obey; and they faced the risk of being put to shame by defeat under the leadership of a girl. Second, the people rejoice, and their pious faith seems to tend to the glory of God and the confounding of his enemies. Third, the enemy, even his princes, are in hiding and stricken with many terrors. They give way to weakness like a woman with child; they are overthrown like the Egyptians in the song sung by Miriam, sister of Moses, to the sound of the timbrel in the midst of the women who went out with her with timbrels and with dances: "Sing ye to the Lord, for he hath triumphed gloriously; the horse and his rider hath he thrown into the sea."[1134] And let us likewise sing the song of Miriam with the devotion which becometh our case.

Fourth, and in conclusion, this point is worthy of consideration: The Maid and her men-at-arms despise not the wisdom of men; they tempt not God. Wherefore it is plain that the Maid goes no further than what she interprets to be the instruction or inspiration received from God.

Many of the incidents of her life from childhood up have been collected in abundance and might be set forth; but these we shall not relate.

Here may be cited the examples of Deborah and of Saint Catherine who miraculously converted fifty doctors or rhetoricians, of Judith and of Judas Maccabeus. As is usually the case, there were many circumstances in their lives which were purely natural.

A first miracle is not always followed by the other miracles which men expect. Even if the Maid should be disappointed in her expectation and in ours (which God forbid) we ought not to conclude therefrom, that the first manifestation of her miraculous power proceeded from an evil spirit and not from heavenly grace; we should believe rather that our hopes have been disappointed because of our ingratitude and our blasphemy, or by some just and impenetrable judgment of God. We beseech him to turn away his anger from us and vouchsafe unto us his favour.

Herein we perceive lessons, first for the King and the Blood Royal, secondly for the King's forces and the kingdom; thirdly for the clergy and people; fourthly for the Maid. Of all these lessons the object is the same, to wit: a good life, consecrated to God, just towards others, sober, virtuous and temperate. With regard to the Maid's peculiar lesson, it is that God's grace revealed in her be employed not in caring for trifles, not in worldly advantage, nor in party hatred, nor in violent sedition, nor in avenging deeds done, nor in foolish self-glorification, but in meekness, prayer, and thanksgiving. And let every one contribute a liberal supply of temporal goods so that peace be established and justice once more administered, and that delivered out of the hands of our enemies, God being favourable unto us, we may serve him in holiness and righteousness.

At the conclusion of his treatise, Gerson briefly examines one point of canon law which had been neglected by the doctors of Poitiers. He establishes that the Maid is not forbidden to dress as a man.

Firstly. The ancient law forbade a woman to dress as a man, and a man as a woman. This restriction, as far as strict legality is concerned, ceases to be enforced by the new law.

Secondly. In its moral bearing this law remains binding. But in such a case it is merely a matter of decency.

Thirdly. From a legal and moral standpoint this law does not refuse masculine and military attire to the Maid, whom the King of Heaven appoints His standard-bearer, in order that she may trample underfoot the enemies of justice. In the operations of divine power the end justifies the means.

Fourthly. Examples may be quoted from history alike sacred and profane, notably Camilla and the Amazons.

Jean Gerson completed this treatise on Whit-Sunday, a week after the deliverance of Orléans. It was his last work. He died in the July of that year, 1429, in the sixty-fifth year of his age.[1135]

The treatise is the political testament of the great university doctor in exile. The Maid's victory gladdened the last days of his life. With his dying voice he sings the Song of Miriam. But with his rejoicings over this happy event are mingled the sad presentiments of keen-sighted old age. While in the Maid he beholds a subject for the rejoicing and edification of the people, he is afraid that the hopes she inspires may soon be disappointed. And he warns those who now exalt her in the hour of triumph not to forsake her in the day of disaster.

His dry close reasoning does not fundamentally differ from the ampler, more flowery argument of Jacques Gélu. One and the other contain the same reasons, the same proofs; and in their conclusions both doctors agree with the judges of Poitiers.

For the Poitiers doctors, for the Archbishop of Embrun, for the ex-chancellor of the University, for all the theologians of the Armagnac party the Maid's case is not a matter of faith. How could it be so before the Pope and the Council had pronounced judgment concerning it? Men are free to believe in her or not to believe in her. But it is a subject of edification; and it behoves men to meditate upon it, not in a spirit of prejudice, persisting in doubt, but with an open mind and according to the Christian faith. Following the counsel of Gerson, kindly souls will believe that the Maid comes from God, just as they believe that the head of Saint Denys may be venerated by the faithful either in the Cathedral Church of Paris or in the abbey-church of Saint Denys in France. They will think less of literal than of spiritual truths and they will not sin by inquiring too closely.

In short neither the treatise of Jacques Gélu nor that of Jean Gerson brought much light to the King and his Council. Both treatises abounded in exhortations, but they all amounted to saying: "Be good, pious and strong, let your thoughts be humble and prudent," Concerning the most important point, the use to be made of Jeanne in the conduct of war, the Archbishop of Embrun wisely recommended: "Do what the Maid commands and prudence directs; for the rest give yourselves to works of piety and prayers of devotion." Such counsel was somewhat embarrassing to a captain like the Sire de Gaucourt and even to a man of worth like my Lord of Trèves. It appears that the clerks left the King perfect liberty of judgment and of action, and that in the end they advised him not to believe in the Maid, but to let the people and the men-at-arms believe in her.

During the ten days he spent at Tours the King kept Jeanne with him. Meanwhile the Council were deliberating as to their line of action.[1136] The royal treasury was empty. Charles could raise enough money to make gifts to the gentlemen of his household, but he had great difficulty in defraying the expenses of war.[1137] Pay was owing to the people of Orléans. They had received little and spent much. Their resources were exhausted and they demanded payment. In May and in June the King distributed among the captains, who had defended the town, sums amounting to forty-one thousand six hundred and thirty-one livres.[1138] He had gained his victory cheaply. The total cost of the defence of Orléans was one hundred and ten thousand livres. The townsfolk did the rest; they gave even their little silver spoons.[1139]

It would doubtless have been expedient to attempt to destroy that formidable army of Sir John Fastolf which had lately terrified the good folk of Orléans. But no one knew where to find it. It had disappeared somewhere between Orléans and Paris. It would have been necessary to go forth to seek it; that was impossible, and no one thought of doing such a thing. So scientific a manœuvre was never dreamed of in the warfare of those days. An expedition to Normandy was suggested; and the idea was so natural that the King was already imagined to be at Rouen.[1140] Finally it was decided to attempt the capture of the châteaux the English held on the Loire, both below and above Orléans, Jargeau, Meung, Beaugency.[1141] A useful undertaking and one which presented no very great difficulties, unless it involved an encounter with Sir John Fastolf's army, and whether it would or no it was impossible to tell.

Without further delay my Lord the Bastard marched on Jargeau with a few knights and some of Poton's soldiers of fortune; but the Loire was high and its waters filled the trenches. Being unprovided with siege train, they retreated after having inflicted some hurt on the English and slain the commander of the town.[1142]

By the reasons of the captains the Maid set little store. She listened to her Voices alone, and they spoke to her words which were infinitely simple. Her one idea was to accomplish her mission. Saint Catherine, Saint Margaret and Saint Michael the Archangel, had sent her into France not to calculate the resources of the royal treasury, not to decree aids and taxes, not to treat with men-at-arms, with merchants and the conductors of convoys, not to draw up plans of campaign and negotiate truces, but to lead the Dauphin to his anointing. Wherefore it was to Reims that she wished to take him, not that she knew how to go there, but she believed that God would guide her. Delay, tardiness, deliberation saddened and irritated her. When with the King she urged him gently.

Many times she said to him: "I shall live a year, barely longer. During that year let as much as possible be done."[1143]

Then she enumerated the four charges which she must accomplish during that time. After having delivered Orléans she must drive the *Godons* out of France, lead the King to be crowned and anointed at Reims and rescue the Duke of Orléans from the hands of the English.[1144] One day she grew impatient and went to the King when he was in one of those closets of carved wainscot constructed in the great castle halls for intimate or family gatherings. She knocked at the door and entered almost immediately. There she found the King conversing with Maître Gérard Machet, his confessor, my Lord the Bastard, the Sire de Trèves and a favourite noble of his household, by name Messire Christophe d'Harcourt. She knelt embracing the King's knees (for she was conversant with the rules of courtesy), and said to him: "Fair Dauphin, do not so long and so frequently deliberate in council, but come straightway to Reims, there to receive your rightful anointing."[1145]

The King looked graciously upon her but answered nothing. The Lord d'Harcourt, having heard that the Maid held converse with angels and saints, was curious to know whether the idea of taking the King to Reims had really been suggested to her by her heavenly visitants. Describing them by the word she herself used, he asked: "Is it your Council who speak to you of such things?"

She replied: "Yes, in this matter I am urged forward." Straightway my Lord d'Harcourt responded: "Will you not here in the King's presence tell us the manner of your Council when they speak to you?"

At this request Jeanne blushed.

Willing to spare her constraint and embarrassment, the King said kindly: "Jeanne, does it please you to answer this question before these persons here present?"

But Jeanne addressing my Lord d'Harcourt said: "I understand what you desire to know and I will tell you willingly."

And straightway she gave the King to understand what agony she endured at not being understood and she told of her inward consolation: "Whenever I am sad because what I say by command of Messire is not readily believed, I go apart and to Messire I make known my complaint, saying that those to whom I speak are not willing to believe me. And when I have finished my prayer, straightway I hear a voice saying unto me: 'Daughter of God, go, I will be thy help.' And this voice fills me with so great a joy, that in this condition I would forever stay."[1146]

While she was repeating the words spoken by the Voice, Jeanne raised her eyes to heaven. The nobles present were struck by the divine expression on the maiden's face. But those eyes bathed in tears, that air of rapture, which filled my Lord the Bastard with amazement, was not an ecstasy, it was the imitation of an ecstasy.[1147] The scene was at once simple and artificial. It reveals the kindness of the King, who was incapable of wounding the child in any way, and the light-heartedness with which the nobles of the court believed or pretended to believe in the most wonderful marvels. It proves likewise that henceforth the little Saint's dignifying the project of the coronation with the authority of a divine revelation was favourably regarded by the Royal Council.

The Maid accompanied the King to Loches and stayed with him until after the 23rd of May.[1148]

The people believed in her. As she passed through the streets of Loches they threw themselves before her horse; they kissed the Saint's hands and feet. Maître Pierre de Versailles, a monk of Saint-Denys in France, one of her interrogators at Poitiers, seeing her receive these marks of veneration, rebuked her on theological grounds: "You do wrong," he said, "to suffer such things to which you are not entitled. Take heed: you are leading men into idolatry."

Then Jeanne, reflecting on the pride which might creep into her heart, said: "In truth I could not keep from it, were not Messire watching over me."[1149]

She was displeased to see certain old wives coming to salute her; that was a kind of adoration which alarmed her. But poor folk who came to her she never repulsed. She would not hurt them, but aided them as far as she could.[1150]

With marvellous rapidity the fame of her holiness had been spread abroad throughout the whole of France. Many pious persons were wearing medals of lead or some other metal, stamped with her portrait, according to the customary mode of honouring the memory of saints.[1151] Paintings or sculptured figures of her were placed in chapels. At mass the priest recited as a collect "the Maid's prayer for the realm of France:"

"O God, author of peace, who without bow or arrow dost destroy those enemies who hope in themselves,[1152] we beseech thee O Lord, to protect us in our adversity; and, as Thou hast delivered Thy people by the hand of a woman, to stretch out to Charles our King, Thy conquering arm, that our enemies, who make their boast in multitudes and glory in bows and arrows, may be overcome by him at this present, and vouchsafe that at the end of his days he with his people may appear gloriously before Thee who art the way, the truth and the life. Through Our Lord Jesus Christ, etc."[1153]

In those days the saintly, both men and women, were consulted in all the difficulties of life. The more they were deemed simple and innocent the more counsel was asked of them. For if of themselves they knew nothing then all the surer was it that the voice of God was to be heard in their words. The Maid was believed to have no intelligence of her own, wherefore she was held capable of solving the most difficult questions with infallible wisdom. It was observed that knowing nought of the arts of war, she waged war better than captains, whence it was concluded that everything, which in her holy ignorance she undertook, she would worthily accomplish. Thus at Toulouse it occurred to a *capitoul* to consult her on a financial question. In that city the indignation of the townsfolk had been aroused because the guardians of the mint had been ordered to issue coins greatly inferior to those which had been previously in circulation. From April till June the *capitouls* had been endeavouring to get this order revoked. On the 2nd of June, the *capitoul*, Pierre Flamenc, proposed that the Maid should be written to concerning the evils resulting from the corruption of the coinage and that she should be asked to suggest a remedy. Pierre Flamenc made this proposal at the Capitole because he thought that a saint was a good counsellor in all matters, especially in anything which concerned the coinage, particularly when, like the Maid, she was the friend of the King.[1154]

From Loches Jeanne sent a little gold ring to the Dame de Laval, who had doubtless asked for some object she had touched.[1155] Fifty-four years previously Jeanne Dame de Laval had married Sire Bertrand Du Guesclin whose memory the French venerated and who in the House of Orléans was known as the tenth of *Les Preux*. Dame Jeanne's renown, however, fell short of that of Tiphaine Raguenel, astrologer and fairy,[1156] who had been Sire Bertrand's first wife. Jeanne was a choleric person and a miser. Driven out of her domain of Laval by the English, she lived in retirement at Vitré with her daughter Anne. Thirteen years before, the latter had incurred her mother's displeasure by secretly marrying a landless younger son of a noble house. When Dame Jeanne discovered it she imprisoned her daughter in a dungeon and welcomed the younger son by shooting at him with a cross-bow. After which the two ladies dwelt together in peace.[1157]

From Loches the Maid went to Selles-en-Berry, a considerable town on the Cher. Here, shortly before had met the three estates of the kingdom; and here the troops were now gathering.[1158]

On Saturday, the 4th of June, she received a herald sent by the people of Orléans to bring her tidings of the English.[1159] As commander in war they recognised none but her.

Meanwhile, surrounded by monks, and side by side with men-at-arms, like a nun she lived apart, a saintly life. She ate and drank little.[1160] She communicated once a week and confessed frequently.[1161] During mass at the moment of elevation, at confession and when she received the body of Our Lord she used to weep many tears. Every evening, at the hour of vespers, she would retire into a church and have the bells rung for about half an hour to summon the mendicant friars who followed the army. Then she would begin to pray while the brethren sang an anthem in honour of the Virgin Mary.[1162]

While practising as far as she was able the austerities required by extreme piety, she appeared magnificently attired, like a lord, for indeed she held her lordship from God. She wore the dress of a knight, a small hat, doublet and hose to match, a fine cloak of silk and cloth of gold well lined and shoes laced on the outer side of the foot.[1163] Such attire in no wise scandalised even the most austere members of the Dauphin's party. They read in holy Scripture that Esther and Judith, inspired by the Lord, loaded themselves with ornaments; true it was for sexual reasons and in order for the salvation of Israel to attract Ahasuerus and Holophernes. Wherefore they held that when Jeanne decked herself with masculine adornments, in order to appear before the men-at-arms as an angel giving victory to the Christian King, far from yielding to the vanities of the world, she, like Esther and Judith, had nothing in her heart but the interest of the holy nation and the glory of God. The English and Burgundian clerks on the other hand converted into scandal what was a subject of edification, and maintained that she was a woman dissolute in dress and in manners.

For seven years now Saint Michael the Archangel and the Saints Catherine and Margaret, wearing rich and precious crowns, had been visiting and conversing with her. It was when the bells were ringing, at the hour of compline and of matins, that she could best hear their words.[1164] In those days bells of all kinds, large and small, metropolitan, parochial or conventual, sounded in peals, or, chiming harmoniously, in voices grave or gay, spoke to all men and of all things. Their song descended from the sky to mark the ecclesiastical and civic calendar. They called priests and people to church; they mourned for the dead and they praised God; they announced fairs and field work; they clashed portentous tidings through the sky, and in times of war they called to arms and sounded the alarm. Friendly to the husbandman they scattered the tempest, they warded off hail-storms and drove away pestilence. They put to flight those demons that, flying ceaselessly through the air, haunt the children of men; and to their blessed sound was attributed the power of calming violence.[1165] Saint Catharine, she who visited Jeanne every day, was the patron of bells and bell-ringers. Thus many bells bore her name. In the ringing of bells as in the rustling of leaves, Jeanne was wont to hear her Voices. She seldom heard them without seeing a light in the direction whence they came.[1166] Those Voices called her: "Jeanne, daughter of God!"[1167] Often the Archangel and the Saints appeared to her. When they came she did them reverence, bending her knee and bowing her head; she kissed their feet, knowing it to be a greater mark of respect than kissing the countenance. She was conscious of the fragrance and grateful warmth of their glorified bodies.[1168]

Saint Michael the Archangel did not come alone. There accompanied him angels so numerous and so tiny that they danced like sparks in the damsel's dazzled eyes. When the saints and the Archangel went away, she wept with grief because they had not taken her with them.[1169] In like manner an angel visited Judith in the camp of Holofernes.

One day Jeanne's equerry, Jean d'Aulon, asked her what her Council was, just as my Lord d'Harcourt had done. She replied that she had three councillors, one of whom was always with her. Another was constantly going and coming; the third was the one with whom the other two deliberated.

Sire d'Aulon, more curious than the King, besought and requested her to let him see this Council for once.

She replied: "Your virtues are not great enough and you are not worthy to behold it."[1170]

The good squire never asked again. If he had read the Bible he would have known that Elisha's servant did not see the angels beheld by the prophet (2 Kings VI, 16, 17).

And yet Jeanne imagined that her Council had appeared to the King and his court.

"My King," she said later, "my King and many besides saw and heard the Voices that came to me. The Count of Clermont and two or three others were with him."[1171]

She believed it was so. But in reality she never showed her Voices to anyone. Not even, despite what has been said to the contrary, to that Guy de Cailly who had been following her since Chécy.[1172]

With Brother Pasquerel Jeanne engaged in pious conversation. To him she often expressed the desire that the Church after her death should pray for her and for all the French slain in the war.

"If I were to depart from this world," she used to say to him, "I should like the King to build chantries, where prayers should be offered to Messire for the salvation of the souls of those who died in war or for the defence of the realm."[1173]

Such a wish was common to all devout souls. What Christian in those days did not hold the practice of saying masses for the dead to be good and salutary? Thus, in the matter of devotion, the Maid was in accord with Duke Charles of Orléans, who, in one of his complaints, recommends the saying and singing of masses for the souls of those who had suffered violent death in the service of the realm.[1174]

She said one day to the good brother: "There is succour that I am appointed to bring."

And Pasquerel, albeit he had studied the Bible, cried out in amazement: "Such a history as yours there hath never been before in the world. Nought like unto it can be read in any book."

Jeanne answered him even more boldly than the doctors at Poitiers: "Messire has a book in which no clerk, however perfect his learning, has ever read."[1175]

She had received her mission from God alone, and she read in a book sealed against all the doctors of the Church.

On the reverse of her standard, sprinkled by mendicants with holy water, she had had a dove painted, holding in its beak a scroll, whereon were written the words "in the name of the King of Heaven."[1176] These were the armorial bearings she had received from her Council. The emblem and the device seemed appropriate to her, since she proclaimed that God had sent her, and since at Orléans she had given the sign promised at Poitiers. The King, notwithstanding, changed this shield for arms representing a crown supported upon a sword between two flowers-de-luce and indicating clearly what was the aid that the Maid of God was bringing to the realm of France. It is said that she regretted having to abandon the arms communicated to her by divine revelation.[1177]

She prophesied, and, as happens to all prophets, she did not always foretell what was to come to pass. It was the fate of the prophet Jonah himself. And doctors explain how the prophecies of true prophets cannot be all fulfilled.

She had said: "Before Saint John the Baptist's Day, in 1429, there shall not be one Englishman, howsoever strong and valiant, to be seen throughout France, either in battle or in the open field."[1178]

The nativity of Saint John the Baptist is celebrated on the 24th of June.

CHAPTER XV

THE TAKING OF JARGEAU – THE BRIDGE OF MEUNG – BEAUGENCY

N Monday, the 6th of June, the King lodged at Saint-Aignan near Selles-en-Berry.[1179] Among the gentlemen of his company were two sons of that Dame de Laval who, in her widowhood, had made the mistake of loving a landless cadet. André, the younger, at the age of twenty, had just passed under the cloud of a disgrace common to nearly all nobles in those days; his grandmother's second husband, Sire Bertrand Du Guesclin, had experienced it several times. Taken prisoner in the château of Laval by Sir John Talbot, he had incurred a heavy debt in order to furnish the sixteen thousand golden crowns of his ransom.[1180]

Being in great need of money, the two young nobles offered their services to the King, who received them very well, gave them not a crown, but said he would show them the Maid. And as he was going with them from Saint-Aignan to Selles, he summoned the Saint,[1181] who straightway, armed at all points save her head, and lance in hand, rode out to meet the King. She greeted the two young nobles heartily and returned with them to Selles. The eldest, Lord Guy, she received in the house where she was lodging, opposite the church, and called for wine. Such was the custom among princes. Cups of wine were brought, into which the guests dipped slices of bread called sops.[1182] When offering him the wine cup, the Maid said to Lord Guy: "I will shortly give you to drink at Paris."

She told him that, three days before, she had sent a gold ring to Dame Jeanne de Laval.

"It was a small matter," she added graciously. "I should like to have sent her something of greater value, considering her reputation."[1183]

That same day, at the hour of vespers, she set out from Selles for Romorantin with a numerous company of men-at-arms and train-bands, commanded by Marshal de Boussac. She was surrounded by mendicant friars and one of her brothers went with her. She wore white armour and a hood. Her horse was brought to her at the door of her house. It was a great black charger which resolutely refused to let her mount him. She had him led to the Cross by the roadside, opposite the church, and there she leapt into the saddle. Whereupon Lord Guy marvelled; for he saw that the charger was as still as if he had been bound. She turned her horse's head towards the church porch, and in her clear woman's voice cried: "Ye priests and churchmen, walk in processions and pray to God."

Then, gaining the highroad: "Go forward, go forward," she said.

In her hand she carried a little axe. Her page bore her standard furled.[1184]

The meeting-place was Orléans. On Thursday, the 9th of June, in the evening, Jeanne passed over the bridge she had crossed on the 8th of May. Saturday, the 11th, the army set out for Jargeau.[1185] It consisted of horse brought by the Duke of Alençon, the Count of Vendôme, the Bastard, the Marshal de Boussac, Captain La Hire, Messire Florent d'Illiers, Messire Jamet du Tillay, Messire Thudal de Kermoisan of Brittany, as well as of contingents furnished by the communes, in all, perhaps eight thousand combatants, many of whom were armed with pikes, axes, cross-bows and leaden mallets.[1186] The young Duke of Alençon was placed in command. He was not remarkable for his intelligence.[1187] But he knew how to ride, and in those days that was the only knowledge indispensable to a general. Again the people of Orléans defrayed the cost of the expedition. For the payment of the fighting men they contributed three thousand livres, for their feeding, seven hogsheads of corn. At their own request, the King imposed on them a new *taille* of three thousand livres.[1188] At their own expense they despatched workmen of all trades, – masons, carpenters, smiths. They lent their artillery. They sent culverins, cannons, La Bergère, and the large mortar to which four horses were harnessed, with the gunners Megret and Jean Boillève.[1189] They furnished ammunition, engines, arrows, ladders, pickaxes, spades, mattocks; and all were marked, for they were a methodical folk. Everything for the siege was sent to the Maid. For in this undertaking she was the one commander they recognised, not the Duke of Alençon, not even the Bastard their own lord's noble brother. For the inhabitants of Orléans, Jeanne was the leader of the siege; and to Jeanne, before the besieged town, they despatched two of their citizens, – Jean Leclerc and François Joachim.[1190] After the citizens of Orléans, the Sire de Rais contributed most to the expenses of the siege of Jargeau.[1191] This unfortunate noble spent thoughtlessly right and left, while rich burgesses made great profits by lending to him at a high rate of interest. The sorry state of his affairs was shortly to bring him to attempt their readjustment by vowing his soul to the devil.

The town of Jargeau, which was shortly to be taken after a severe siege, had surrendered to the English without resistance on the 5th of October in the previous year.[1192] The bridge leading to the town from the Beauce bank was furnished with two castlets.[1193] The town itself, surrounded by walls and towers, was not strongly fortified; but its means of defence had been improved by the English. Warned that the army of the French King was coming to besiege it, the Earl of Suffolk and his two brothers threw themselves into the town, with five hundred knights, squires, and other fighting men, as well as two hundred picked bowmen.[1194] The Duke of Alençon with six hundred horse was at the head of the force, and with him, the Maid. The first night they slept in the woods.[1195] On the morrow, at daybreak, my Lord the Bastard, my Lord Florent d'Illiers, and several other captains joined them. They were in a great hurry to reach Jargeau. Suddenly they hear that Sir John Fastolf is at hand, coming from Paris with two thousand combatants, bringing supplies and artillery to Jargeau.[1196]

This was the army which had been the cause of Jeanne's anxiety on the 4th of May, because her saints had not told her where Fastolf was. The captains held a council of war. Many thought the siege ought to be abandoned and that the army should go to meet Fastolf. Some actually went off at once. Jeanne exhorted the men-at-arms to continue their march on Jargeau. Where Sir John Fastolf's army was, she knew no more than the others; her reasons were not of this world.

"Be not afraid of any armed host whatsoever," she said, "and make no difficulty of attacking the English, for Messire leads you."

And again she said: "Were I not assured that Messire leads, I would rather be keeping sheep than running so great a danger."

She gained a better hearing from the Duke of Alençon than from any of the Orléans leaders.[1197] Those who had gone were recalled and the march on Jargeau was continued.[1198]

The suburbs of the town appeared undefended; but, when the French King's men approached, they found the English posted in front of the outbuildings, wherefore they were compelled to retreat. When the Maid beheld this, she seized her standard and threw herself upon the enemy, calling on the fighting men to take courage. That night, the French King's men were able to encamp in the suburbs.[1199] They kept no watch, and yet from the Duke of Alençon's own avowal they would have been in great danger if the English had made a sally.[1200] The Maid's judgment was even more fully justified than she expected. Everything in her army depended upon the grace of God.

The very next day, in the morning the besiegers brought their siege train and their mortars up to the walls. The Orléans cannon fired upon the town and did great damage. Three of La Bergère's volleys wrecked the greatest tower on the fortifications.[1201]

The train-bands reached Jargeau on Saturday, the 11th. Straightway, without staying to take counsel, they hastened to the trenches and began the assault. They were too zealous; consequently, they went badly to work, received no aid from the men-at-arms and were driven back in disorder.[1202]

On Saturday night, the Maid, who was accustomed to summon the enemy before fighting, approached the entrenchments, and cried out to the English: "Surrender the town to the King of Heaven and to King Charles, and depart, or it will be the worse for you."[1203]

To this summons the English paid no heed, albeit they had a great desire to come to some understanding. The Earl of Suffolk came to my Lord the Bastard, and told him that if he would refrain from the attack, the town should be surrendered to him. The English asked for a fortnight's respite, after which time, they would undertake to withdraw immediately, they and their horses, provided, doubtless, that by that time they had not been relieved.[1204] On both sides such conditional surrenders were common. The Sire de Baudricourt had signed one at Vaucouleurs just before Jeanne's arrival there.[1205] In this case it was mere trickery to ask the French to enter into such an agreement just when Sir John Fastolf was coming with artillery and supplies.[1206] It has been asserted that the Bastard was taken in this snare; but such a thing is incredible; he was far too wily for that. Nevertheless, on the morrow, which was Sunday and the 12th of the month, the Duke of Alençon and the nobles, who were holding a council concerning the measures for the capture of the town, were told that Captain La Hire was conferring with the Earl of Suffolk. They were highly displeased.[1207] Captain La Hire, who was not a general, could not treat in his own name, and had doubtless received powers from my Lord the Bastard. The latter commanded for the Duke, a prisoner in the hands of the English, while the Duke of Alençon commanded for the King; and hence the disagreement.

The Maid, who was always ready to show mercy to prisoners when they surrendered and at the same time always ready to fight, said: "If they will, let them in their jackets of mail depart from Jargeau with their lives! If they will not, the town shall be stormed."[1208]

The Duke of Alençon, without even inquiring the terms of the capitulation, had Captain La Hire recalled.

He came, and straightway the ladders were brought. The heralds sounded the trumpets and cried: "To the assault."

The Maid unfurled her standard, and fully armed, wearing on her head one of those light helmets known as *chapelines*,[1209] she went down into the trenches with the King's men and the train-bands, well within reach of arrows and cannon-balls. She kept by the Duke of Alençon's side, saying: "Forward! fair duke, to the assault."

The Duke, who was not so courageous as she, thought that she went rather hastily to work; and this he gave her to understand.

Then she encouraged him: "Fear not. God's time is the right time. When He wills it you must open the attack. Go forward, He will prepare the way."

And seeing him lack confidence, she reminded him of the promise she had recently made concerning him in the Abbey of Saint-Florent-lès-Saumur. "Oh! Fair Duke, can you be afraid? Do you not remember that I promised your wife to bring you back safe and sound?"[1210]

In the thick of the attack, she noticed on the wall one of those long thin mortars, which, from the manner of its charging, was called a breechloader. Seeing it hurl stones on the very spot where the King's fair cousin was standing, she realised the danger, but not for herself. "Move away," she said quickly. "That cannon will kill you."

The Duke had not moved more than a few yards, when a nobleman of Anjou, the Sire Du Lude, having taken the place he had quitted, was killed by a ball from that same cannon.[1211] The Duke of Alençon marvelled at her prophetic gift. Doubtless the Maid had been sent to save him, but she had not been sent to save the Sire Du Lude. The angels of the Lord are sent for the salvation of some, for the destruction of others. When the French King's men reached the wall, the Earl of Suffolk cried out for a parley with the Duke of Alençon. No heed was paid to him and the assault continued.[1212]

The attack had lasted four hours,[1213] when Jeanne, standard in hand, climbed up a ladder leaning against the rampart. A stone fired from a cannon struck her helmet and knocked it with its escutcheon, bearing her arms, off her head. They thought she was crushed, but she rose quickly and cried to the fighting men: "Up, friends, up! Messire has doomed the English. They are ours at this moment. Be of good cheer."[1214]

The wall was scaled and the French King's men penetrated into the town. The English fled into La Beauce and the French rushed in pursuit of them. Guillaume Regnault, a squire of Auvergne, came up with the Earl of Suffolk on the bridge and took him prisoner.

"Are you a gentleman?" asked Suffolk.

"Yes."

"Are you a knight?"

"No."

The Earl of Suffolk dubbed him a knight and surrendered to him.[1215]

Very soon the rumour ran that the Earl of Suffolk had surrendered on his knees to the Maid.[1216] It was even stated that he had asked to surrender to her as to the bravest lady in the world.[1217] But it is more likely that he would have surrendered to the lowest menial of the army rather than to a woman whom he held to be a witch possessed of the devil.

John Pole, Suffolk's brother, was likewise taken on the bridge. The Duke's third brother, Alexander Pole, was slain in the same place or drowned in the Loire.[1218]

The garrison surrendered at discretion. Now, as always, no great harm was done during the battle, but afterwards the conquerors made up for it. Five hundred English were massacred; the nobles alone were held to ransom. And over them, the French fell to quarrelling. The French nobles kept them all for themselves; the train-bands claimed their share, and, not getting it, began to destroy everything. What the nobles could save was carried off during the night, by water, to Orléans. The town was completely sacked; the old church, which had served the *Godons* as a magazine, was pillaged.[1219]

Including killed and wounded, the French had not lost twenty men.[1220]

Without disarming, the Maid and the knights returned to Orléans. To celebrate the taking of Jargeau, the magistrates organised a public procession. An eloquent sermon was preached by a Jacobin monk, Brother Robert Baignart.[1221]

The inhabitants of Orléans presented the Duke of Alençon with six casks of wine, the Maid with four, the Count of Vendôme with two.[1222]

As an acknowledgment of the good and acceptable services rendered by the holy maiden, the councillors of the captive Duke Charles of Orléans, gave her a green cloak and a robe of crimson Flemish cloth or fine Brussels purple. Jean Luillier, who furnished the stuff, asked eight crowns for two ells of fine Brussels at four crowns the ell; two crowns for the lining of the robe; two crowns for an ell of yellowish green cloth, making in all twelve golden crowns.[1223] Jean Luillier was a young woollen draper who adored the Maid and regarded her as an angel of God. He had a good heart; but fear of the English dazzled him, and where they were concerned caused him to see double.[1224] One of his kinsfolk was a member of the council elected in 1429. He himself was to be appointed magistrate a little later.[1225]

Jean Bourgeois, tailor, asked one golden crown for the making of the robe and the cloak, as well as for furnishing white satin, taffeta, and other stuffs.[1226]

The town had previously given the Maid half an ell of cloth of two shades of green worth thirty-five *sous* of Paris to make "nettles" for her gown.[1227] Nettles were the Duke of Orléans' device, green or purple or crimson his colours.[1228] This green was no longer the bright colour of earlier days, it had gradually been growing darker as the fortunes of the house declined. It had first been a vivid green, then a brownish shade, and, finally, the tint of the faded leaf with a suggestion of black in it which signified sorrow and mourning. The Maid's colour was *feuillemort*. She, like the officers of the duchy and the men of the train-bands, wore the Orléans livery; and thus they made of her a kind of herald-at-arms or heraldic angel.

The cloak of yellowish green and the robe embroidered with nettles, she must have been glad to wear for love of Duke Charles, whom the English had treated with such sore despite. Having come to defend the heritage of the captive prince, she said that in Jesus' name, the good Duke of Orléans was on her mind and she was confident that she would deliver him.[1229] Her design was first to summon the English to give him up; then, if they refused, to cross the sea and with an army to seek him in England.[1230] In case such means failed her, she had thought of another course which she would adopt, with the permission of her saints. She would ask the King if he would let her take prisoners, believing that she could take enough to exchange for Duke Charles.[1231] Saint Catherine and Saint Margaret had promised her that thus his deliverance would take her less than three years and longer than one.[1232] Such were the pious dreams of a child lulled to sleep by the sound of her village bells! Deeming it just that she should labour and suffer to rescue her princes from trouble and weariness, she used to say, like a good servant: "I know that in matters of bodily ease God loves my King and the Duke of Orléans better than me; and I know it because it hath been revealed unto me."[1233]

Then, speaking of the captive duke she would say: "My Voices have revealed much to me concerning him. Duke Charles hath oftener been the subject of my revelations than any man living except my King."[1234]

In reality, all that Saint Catherine and Saint Margaret had done was to tell her of the well-known misfortunes of the Prince. Valentine of Milan's son and Isabelle Romée's daughter were separated by a gulf broader and deeper than the ocean which stretched between them. They dwelt at the antipodes of the world of souls, and all the saints of Paradise would have been unable to explain one to the other.

All the same Duke Charles was a good prince and a debonair; he was kind and he was pitiful. More than any other he possessed the gift of pleasing. He charmed by his grace, albeit but ill-looking and of weak constitution.[1235] His temperament was so out of harmony with his position that he may be said to have endured his life rather than to have lived it. His father assassinated by night in the Rue Barbette in Paris by order of Duke John; his mother a perennial fount of tears, dying of anger and of grief in a Franciscan nunnery; the two S's, standing for *Soupirs* (sighs) and *Souci* (care), the emblems and devices of her mourning, revealing her ingenious mind fancifully elegant even in despair; the Armagnacs, the Burgundians, the Cabochiens, cutting each other's throats around him; these were the sights he had witnessed when little more than a child. Then he had been wounded and taken prisoner at the Battle of Azincourt.

Now, for fourteen years, dragged from castle to castle, from one end to the other of the island of fogs; imprisoned within thick walls, closely guarded, receiving two or three of his countrymen at long intervals, but never permitted to converse with one except before witnesses, he felt old before his time, blighted by misfortune. "Fruit fallen in its greenness, I was put to ripen on prison straw. I am winter fruit,"[1236] he said of himself. In his captivity, he suffered without hope, knowing that on his death-bed Henry V had recommended his brother not to give him up at any price.[1237]

Kind to others, kind to himself, he took refuge in his own thoughts, which were as bright and clear as his life was dark and sad. In the gloom of the stern castles of Windsor and of Bolingbroke, in the Tower of London, side by side with his gaolers, he lived and moved in the world of phantasy of the *Romance of the Rose*. Venus, Cupid, Hope, Fair-Welcome, Pleasure, Pity, Danger, Sadness, Care, Melancholy, Sweet-Looks were around the desk, on which, in the deep embrasure of a window, beneath the sun's rays, he wrote his ballads, as delicate and fresh as an illumination on the page of a manuscript. For him it was the world of allegory that really existed. He wandered in the forest of Long Expectation; he embarked on the vessel Good Tidings. He was a poet; Beauty was his lady; and courteously did he sing of her. From his verses one would say that he was but the Captive of Lord Love.[1238]

He was left in ignorance of the affairs of his duchy; and, if he ever concerned himself about it, it was when he collected the books of King Charles V which had been bought by the Duke of Bedford and resold to London merchants;[1239] or when he commanded that on the approach of the English to Blois, its fine tapestries and his father's library should be carried off to La Rochelle. After Beauty rich hangings and delicate miniatures were what he loved most in the world.[1240] The bright sunshine of France, the lovely month of May, dancing and ladies were what he longed for most. He was cured of prowess and of chivalry.

Some have wished to believe that from his duchy news reached him of the Maid's coming. They have gone so far as to imagine that a faithful servant kept him informed of the happy incidents of May and June, 1429;[1241] but nothing is less certain. On the contrary, the probability is that the English refused to let him receive any message, and that he was totally ignorant of all that was going on in the two kingdoms.[1242]

Possibly he did not care for news of the war as much as one might expect. He hoped nothing from men-at-arms; and it was not to his fair cousins of France and to feats of prowess and battles that he looked for deliverance. He knew too much about them. It was in peace that he put his trust, both for himself and for his people. Since the fathers were dead, he thought that the sons might forgive and forget. He placed his hope in his cousin of Burgundy; and he was right, for the fortunes of the English were in the hands of Duke Philip. Charles brought himself, or at any rate he was to bring himself later, to recognise the suzerainty of the King of England. It is less important to consider the weakness of men than the force of circumstances. And the prisoner could never do enough to obtain peace: "joy's greatest treasure."[1243]

No, despite her revelations, the picture Jeanne imagined of her fair Duke was not the true one. They were never to meet; but if they had met there would have been serious misunderstandings between them, and they would have remained incomprehensible one to the other. Jeanne's elemental, straight-forward way of thinking could never have accorded with the ideas of so great a noble and so courteous a poet. They could never have understood each other because she was simple, he subtle; because she was a prophetess while he was filled with courtly knowledge and lettered grace; because she believed, and he was as one not believing; because she was a daughter of the common folk and a saint ascribing all sovereignty to God, while for him law consisted in feudal uses and customs, alliances and treaties;[1244] because, in short, they held conflicting ideas concerning life and the world. The Maid's mission, her being sent by Messire to recover his duchy for him, would never have appealed to the good Duke; and Jeanne would never have understood his behaviour towards his English and Burgundian cousins. It was better they should never meet.

The capture of Jargeau had given the French control of the upper Loire. In order to free the city of Orléans from all danger, it was necessary to make sure of the banks of the lower river. There the English still held Meung and Beaugency. On Tuesday, the 14th of June, at the hour of vespers, the army took the field.[1245]

They passed through La Sologne, and that same evening gained the Bridge of Meung, situated above the town and separated from its walls by a broad meadow. Like most bridges, it was defended by a castlet at each end; and the English had provided it with an earthen outwork, as they had done for Les Tourelles at Orléans.[1246] They defended it badly, however, and the French King's men forced their way in before nightfall. They left a garrison there, and went out to encamp in Beauce, almost under the walls. The young Duke of Alençon lodged in a church with a few men-at-arms; and, as was his wont, did not keep watch. He was surprised and ran great danger.[1247]

The town garrison, which was a small one, was commanded by Lord Scales, and "the Child of Warwick." The next day, early in the morning, the King's men, passing within a cannon shot of the town of Meung, marched straight on Beaugency, which they reached in the morning.[1248]

The ancient little town, built on the side of a hill and girt around with vineyards, gardens, and cornfields, sloped before them towards the green valley of the Ru. Straight in front of them rose its square tower of somewhat proud aspect, although it had oftentimes been taken. The suburbs were not fortified; but the French, when they entered them, were riddled by a shower of arrows of every kind, fired by archers concealed in dwellings and outhouses. On both sides there were killed and wounded. Finally, the English retreated into the castle and the bridge bastions.[1249]

The Duke of Alençon stationed sentinels in front of the castle to watch the English. Just then, he saw coming towards him, two nobles of Brittany, the Lords of Rostrenen and of Kermoisan, who said to him: "The Constable asks the besiegers for entertainment."[1250]

Arthur of Brittany, Sire de Richemont, Constable of France, had spent the winter in Poitou waging war against the troops of the Sire de La Trémouille. Now in defiance of the King's prohibition the Constable came to join the King's men.[1251] He had crossed the Loire at Amboise and arrived before Beaugency with six hundred men-at-arms and four hundred archers.[1252] His coming caused the captains great embarrassment. Some esteemed him a man of strong will and great courage. But many were dependent upon the Sire de La Trémouille, as for example the poor squire, Jean d'Aulon. The Duke of Alençon wanted to retreat, alleging that the King had commanded him not to receive the Constable.

"If the Constable comes, I shall retire," he said to Jeanne.

To the Breton nobles he replied, that if the Constable came into the camp, the Maid, and the besiegers would fight against him.[1253]

So decided was he that he mounted his horse to ride straight up to the Bretons. The Maid, out of respect for him and for the King, was preparing to follow him. But many of the captains restrained the Duke of Alençon[1254] deeming that now was not the time to break a lance with the Constable of France.

On the morrow a loud alarm was sounded in the camp. The heralds were crying: "To arms!" The English were said to be approaching in great numbers. The young Duke still wanted to retreat in order to avoid receiving the Constable. This time Jeanne dissuaded him: "We must stand together," she said.[1255]

He listened to this counsel and went forth to meet the Constable, followed by the Maid, my Lord the Bastard, and the Lords of Laval. Near the leper's hospital at Beaugency they encountered a fine company. As they approached, a thick-lipped little man, dark and frowning, alighted from his horse.[1256] It was Arthur of Brittany. The Maid embraced his knees as she was accustomed to do when holding converse with the great ones of heaven and earth. Thus did every baron when he met one nobler than himself.[1257]

The Constable spoke to her as a good Catholic, a devout servant of God and the Church, saying: "Jeanne, I have heard that you wanted to fight against me. Whether you are sent by God I know not. If you are I do not fear you. For God knows that my heart is right. If you are sent by the devil I fear you still less."[1258]

He was entitled to speak thus, for he made a point of never acknowledging the devil's power over him. His love of God he showed by seeking out wizards and witches with a greater zeal than was displayed by bishops and inquisitors. In France, in Poitou, and in Brittany he had sent more to the stake than any other man living.[1259]

The Duke of Alençon dared not either dismiss him or grant him a lodging for the night. It was the custom for new comers to keep the watch. The Constable with his company kept watch that night in front of the castle.[1260]

Without more ado the young Duke of Alençon proceeded to the attack. Here, again, those who bore the brunt of the attack and provided for the siege were the citizens of Orléans. The magistrates of the town had sent by water from Meung to Beaugency the necessary siege train, ladders, pickaxes, mattocks, and those great pent-houses beneath which the besiegers protected themselves like tortoises under their shells. They had sent also cannons and mortars. The gay gunner, Master Jean de Montesclère, was there.[1261] All these supplies were addressed to the Maid. The magistrate, Jean Boillève, brought bread and wine in a barge.[1262] Throughout Friday, the 7th, mortars and cannon hurled stones on the besieged. At the same time from the valley and from the river the attack was being made from barges. On the 17th of June, at midnight, Sir Richard Gethyn, Bailie of Évreux, who commanded the garrison, offered to capitulate. It was agreed that the English should surrender the castle and bridge, and depart on the morrow, taking with them horses and harness with each man his property to the value of not more than one silver mark. Further, they were required to swear that they would not take up arms again before the expiration of ten days. On these terms, the next day, at sunrise, to the number of five hundred, they crossed the drawbridge and retreated on Meung, where the castle, but not the bridge, remained in the hands of the English.[1263] The Constable wisely sent a few men to reinforce the garrison on the Meung Bridge.[1264] Sir Richard Gethyn and Captain Matthew Gough were detained as hostages.[1265]

The Beaugency garrison had been in too great haste to surrender. Scarce had it gone when a man-at-arms of Captain La Hire's company came to the Duke of Alençon saying: "The English are marching upon us. We shall have them in front of us directly. They are over there, full one thousand fighting men."

Jeanne heard him speak but did not seize his meaning.

"What is that man-at-arms saying?" she asked.

And when she knew, turning to Arthur of Brittany, who was close by, she said: "Ah! Fair Constable, it was not my will that you should come, but since you are here, I bid you welcome."[1266]

The force the French had to face was Sir John Talbot and Sir John Fastolf with the whole English army.

CHAPTER XVI

THE BATTLE OF PATAY – OPINIONS OF ITALIAN AND GERMAN ECCLESIASTICS – THE GIEN ARMY

AVING left Paris on the 9th of June, Sir John Fastolf was coming through La Beauce with five thousand fighting men. To the English at Jargeau he was bringing victuals and arrows in abundance. Learning by the way that the town had surrendered, he left his stores at Étampes and marched on to Janville, where Sir John Talbot joined him with forty lances and two hundred bowmen.[1267]

There they heard that the French had taken the Meung bridge and laid siege to Beaugency. Sir John Talbot wished to march to the relief of the inhabitants of Beaugency and deliver them with the aid of God and Saint George. Sir John Fastolf counselled abandoning Sir Richard Gethyn and his garrison to their fate; for the moment he deemed it wiser not to fight. Finding his own men fearful and the French full of courage, he thought the best thing the English could do would be to establish themselves in the towns, castles, and strongholds remaining to them, there to await the reinforcements promised by the Regent.

"In comparison with the French we are but a handful," he said. "If luck should turn against us, then we should be in a fair way to lose all those conquests won by our late King Henry after strenuous effort and long delay."[1268]

His advice was disregarded and the army marched on Beaugency. The force was not far from the town on Friday, the 17th of June, just when the garrison was issuing forth with horses, armour, and baggage to the amount of one silver mark's worth for each man.[1269]

Informed of the army's approach the French King's men went forth to meet it. The scouts had not far to ride before they descried the standards and pennons of England waving over the plain, about two and a half miles from Patay. Then the French ascended a hill whence they could observe the enemy. Captain La Hire and the young Sire de Termes said to the Maid: "The English are coming. They are in battle array and ready to fight."

As was her wont, she made answer: "Strike boldly and they will flee."

And she added that the battle would not be long.[1270]

Believing that the French were offering them battle, the English took up their position. The archers planted their stakes in the ground, their points inclined towards the enemy. Thus they generally prepared to fight; they had not done otherwise at the Battle of the Herrings. The sun was already declining on the horizon.[1271]

The Duke of Alençon had by no means decided to descend into the plain. In presence of the Constable, my Lord the Bastard and the captains, he consulted the holy Maid, who gave him an enigmatical answer: "See to it that you have good spurs."

Taking her to mean the Count of Clermont's spurs, the spurs of Rouvray, the Duke of Alençon exclaimed: "What do you say? Shall we turn our backs on them?"

"Nay," she replied.

On all occasions her Voices counselled unwavering confidence. "Nay. In God's name, go down against them; for they shall flee and shall not stay and shall be utterly discomfited; and you shall lose scarce any men; wherefore you will need your spurs to pursue them."[1272]

According to the opinions of doctors and masters it was well to listen to the Maid, but at the same time to follow the course marked out by human wisdom.

The commanders of the army, either because they judged the occasion unfavourable or because, after so many defeats, they feared a pitched battle, did not come down from their hill. The two heralds sent by two English knights to offer single combat received the answer: "For to-day you may go to bed, because it grows late. But to-morrow, if it be God's will, we will come to closer quarters."[1273]

The English, assured that they would not be attacked, marched off to pass the night at Meung.[1274]

On the morrow, Saturday, the 18th, Saint Hubert's day, the French went forth against them. They were not there. The *Godons* had decamped early in the morning and gone off, with cannon, ammunition, and victuals, towards Janville,[1275] where they intended to entrench themselves.

Straightway King Charles's army of twelve thousand men[1276] set out in pursuit of them. Along the Paris road they went, over the plain of Beauce, wooded, full of game, covered with thickets and brushwood, wild, but finely to the taste of English and French riders, who praised it highly.[1277]

Gazing over the infinite plain, where the earth seems to recede before one's glance, the Maid beheld the sky in front of her, that cloudy sky of plains, suggesting marvellous adventures on the mountains of the air, and she cried: "In God's name, if they were hanging from the clouds we should have them."[1278]

Now, as on the previous evening, she prophesied: "To-day our fair King shall win a victory greater than has been his for a long time. My Council has told me that they are all ours."

She foretold that there would be few, or none of the French slain.[1279]

Captain Poton and Sire Arnault de Gugem went forth to reconnoitre. The most skilled men-of-war, and among them my Lord the Bastard and the Marshal de Boussac, mounted on the finest of war-steeds, formed the vanguard. Then under the leadership of Captain La Hire, who knew the country, came the horse of the Duke of Alençon, the Count of Vendôme, the Constable of France, with archers and cross-bowmen. Last of all came the rear-guard, commanded by the lords of Graville, Laval, Rais, and Saint-Gilles.[1280]

The Maid, ever zealous, desired to be in the vanguard; but she was kept back. She did not lead the men-at-arms, rather the men-at-arms led her. They regarded her, not as captain of war but as a bringer of good luck. Greatly saddened, she must needs take her place in the rear, in the company, doubtless, of the Sire de Rais, where she had originally been placed.[1281] The whole army pressed forward for fear the enemy should escape them.

After they had ridden twelve or thirteen miles in overpowering heat, and passed Saint-Sigismond on the left and got beyond Saint-Péravy, Captain Poton's sixty to eighty scouts reached a spot where the ground, which had been level hitherto, descends, and where the road leads down into a hollow called La Retrève. They could not actually see the hollow, but beyond it the ground rose gently; and, dimly visible, scarcely two and a half miles away was the belfry of Lignerolles on the wooded plain known as Climat-du-Camp. A league straight in front of them was the little town of Patay.[1282]

It is two o'clock in the afternoon. Poton's and Gugem's horse chance to raise a stag, which darts out of a thicket and plunges down into the hollow of La Retrève. Suddenly a clamour of voices ascends from the hollow. It proceeds from the English soldiers loudly disputing over the game which has fallen into their hands. Thus informed of the enemy's presence, the French scouts halt and straightway despatch certain of their company to go and tell the army that they have surprised the *Godons* and that it is time to set to work.[1283]

Now this is what had been happening among the English. They were retreating in good order on Janville, their vanguard commanded by a knight bearing a white standard.[1284] Then came the artillery and the victuals in wagons driven by merchants; then the main body of the army, commanded by Sir John Talbot and Sir John Fastolf. The rear-guard, which was likely to bear the brunt of the attack, consisted only of Englishmen from England.[1285] It followed at some distance from the rest. Its scouts, having seen the French without being seen by them, informed Sir John Talbot, who was then between the hamlet of Saint-Péravy and the town of Patay. On this information he called a halt and commanded the vanguard with wagons and cannon to take up its position on the edge of the Lignerolles wood. The position was excellent: backed by the forest, the combatants were secure against being attacked in the rear,[1286] while in front they were able to entrench themselves behind their wagons. The main body did not advance so far. It halted some little distance from Lignerolles, in the hollow of La Retrève. On this spot the road was lined with quickset hedges. Sir John Talbot with five hundred picked bowmen stationed himself there to await the French who must perforce pass that way. His design was to defend the road until the rear-guard had had time to join the main body, and then, keeping close to the hedges, he would fall back upon the army.

The archers, as was their wont, were making ready to plant in the ground those pointed stakes, the spikes of which they turned against the chests of the enemy's horses, when the French, led by Poton's scouts, came down upon them like a whirlwind, overthrew them, and cut them to pieces.[1287]

At this moment, Sir John Fastolf, at the head of the main body, was preparing to join the vanguard. Feeling the French cavalry at his heels, he gave spur and at full gallop led his men on to Lignerolles. When those of the white standard saw him arriving thus in rout, they thought he had been defeated. They took fright, abandoned the edge of the wood, rushed into the thickets of Climat-du-Camp and in great disorder came out on the Paris road. With the main body of the army, Sir John Fastolf pushed on in the same direction. There was no battle. Marching over the bodies of Talbot's archers, the French threw themselves on the English, who were as dazed as a flock of sheep and fell before the foe without resistance. Thus the French slew two thousand of those common folk whom the *Godons* were accustomed to transport from their own land to be killed in France. When the main body of the French, commanded by La Hire, reached Lignerolles, they found only eight hundred foot whom they soon overthrew. Of the twelve to thirteen thousand French on the march, scarce fifteen hundred took part in the battle or rather in the massacre. Sir John Talbot, who had leapt on to his horse without staying to put on his spurs, was taken prisoner by the Captains La Hire and Poton.[1288] The Lords Scales, Hungerford and Falconbridge, Sir Thomas Guérard, Richard Spencer and Fitz Walter were taken and held to ransom. In all, there were between twelve and fifteen hundred prisoners.[1289]

Not more than two hundred men-at-arms pursued the fugitives to the gates of Janville. Except for the vanguard, which had been the first to take flight, the English army was entirely destroyed. On the French side, the Sire de Termes, who was present, states that there was only one killed; a man of his own company. Perceval de Boulainvilliers, Councillor and King's Chamberlain, says there were three.[1290]

The Maid arrived[1291] before the slaughter was ended.[1292] She saw a Frenchman, who was leading some prisoners, strike one of them such a blow on the head that he fell down as if dead. She dismounted and procured the Englishman a confessor. She held his head and comforted him as far as she could. Such was the part she played in the Battle of Patay.[1293] It was the part of a saintly maid.

The French spent the night in the town. Sir John Talbot, having been brought before the Duke of Alençon and the Constable, was thus addressed by the young Duke: "This morning you little thought what would happen to you."

Talbot replied: "It is the chance of war."[1294]

A few breathless *Godons* succeeded in reaching Janville.[1295] But the townsfolk, with whom on their departure they had deposited their money and their goods, shut the gates in their faces and swore loyalty to King Charles.

The English commanders of the two small strongholds in La Beauce, Montpipeau and Saint Sigismond, set fire to them and fled.[1296]

From Patay the victorious army marched to Orléans. The inhabitants were expecting the King. They had hung up tapestries ready for his entrance.[1297] But the King and his Chamberlain, fearing and not without reason, some aggressive movement on the part of the Constable, held themselves secure in the Château of Sully.[1298] Thence they started for Châteauneuf on the 22nd of June. That same day the Maid joined the King at Saint-Benoit-sur-Loire. He received her with his usual kindness and said: "I pity you because of the suffering you endure." And he urged her to rest.

At these words she wept. It has been said that her tears flowed because of the indifference and incredulity towards her that the King's urbanity implied.[1299] But we must beware of attributing to the tears of the enraptured and the illuminated a cause intelligible to human reason. To her Charles appeared clothed in an ineffable splendour like that of the holiest of kings. How, since she had shown him her angels, invisible to ordinary folk, could she for one moment have thought that he lacked faith in her?

"Have no doubt," she said to him, confidently, "you shall receive the whole of your kingdom and shortly shall be crowned."[1300]

True, Charles seemed in no great haste to employ his knights in the recovery of his kingdom. But his Council just then had no idea of getting rid of the Maid. On the contrary, they were determined to use her cleverly, so as to put heart into the French, to terrify the English, and to convince the world that God, Saint Michael, and Saint Catherine, were on the side of the Armagnacs. In announcing the victory of Patay to the good towns, the royal councillors said not one word of the Constable, neither did they mention my Lord the Bastard.[1301] They described as leaders of the army, the Maid, with the two Princes of the Blood Royal, the Duke of Alençon, and the Duke of Vendôme. In such wise did they exalt her. And, indeed, she must have been worth as much and more than a great captain, since the Constable attempted to seize her. With this enterprise, he charged one of his men, Andrieu de Beaumont, who had formerly been employed to carry off the Sire de la Trémouille. But, as Andrieu de Beaumont had failed with the Chamberlain, so he failed with the Maid.[1302]

Probably she herself knew nothing of this plot. She besought the King to pardon the Constable, – a request which proves how great was her naïveté. By royal command Richemont received back his lordship of Parthenay.[1303]

Duke John of Brittany, who had married a sister of Charles of Valois, was not always pleased with his brother-in-law's counsellors. In 1420, considering him too Burgundian, they had devised for him a Bridge of Montereau.[1304] In reality, he was neither Armagnac nor Burgundian nor French nor English, but Breton. In 1423 he recognised the Treaty of Troyes; but two years later, when his brother, the Duke of Richemont, had gone over to the French King and received the Constable's sword from him, Duke John went to Charles of Valois, at Saumur, and did homage for his duchy.[1305] In short, he extricated himself cleverly from the most embarrassing situations and succeeded in remaining outside the quarrel of the two kings who were both eager to involve him in it. While France and England were cutting each other's throats, he was raising Brittany from its ruins.[1306]

The Maid filled him with curiosity and admiration. Shortly after the Battle of Patay, he sent to her, Hermine, his herald-at-arms, and Brother Yves Milbeau, his confessor, to congratulate her on her victory.[1307] The good Brother was told to question Jeanne.

He asked her whether it was God who had sent her to succour the King.

Jeanne replied that it was.

"If it be so," replied Brother Yves Milbeau, "my Lord the Duke of Brittany, our liege lord, is disposed to proffer his service to the King. He cannot come in person for he is sorely infirm. But he is to send his son with a large army."

The good Brother was speaking lightly and making a promise for his duke which would never be kept. The only truth in it was that many Breton nobles were coming in to take service with King Charles.

On hearing these words, the little Saint made a curious mistake. She thought that Brother Yves had meant that the Duke of Brittany was her liege lord as well as his, which would have been altogether senseless. Her loyalty revolted: "The Duke of Brittany is not my liege lord," she replied sharply. "The King is my liege lord."

As far as we can tell, the Duke of Brittany's caution had produced no favourable impression in France. He was censured for having set the King's war ban at nought and made a treaty with the English. Jeanne was of that opinion and to Brother Yves she said so plainly: "The Duke should not have tarried so long in sending his men to aid the King."[1308]

A few days later, the Sire de Rostrenen, who had accompanied the Constable to Beaugency and to Patay, came from Duke John to treat of the prospective marriage between his eldest son, François, and Bonne de Savoie, daughter of Duke Amédée. With him was Comment-Qu'il-Soit, herald of Richard of Brittany, Count of Étampes. The herald was commissioned to present the Maid with a dagger and horses.[1309]

At Rome, in 1428, there was a French clerk, a compiler of one of those histories of the world so common in those days and so much alike. His cosmography, like all of them, began with the creation and came down to the pontificate of Martin V who was then Pope. "Under this pontificate," wrote the author, "the realm of France, the flower and the lily of the world, opulent among the most opulent, before whom the whole universe bowed, was cast down by its invader, the tyrant Henry, who was not even the lawful lord of the realm of England." Then this churchman vows the Burgundians to eternal infamy and hurls upon them the most terrible maledictions. "May their eyes be torn out: may they perish by an evil death!" Such language indicates a good Armagnac and possibly a clerk despoiled of his goods and driven into exile by the enemies of his country. When he learns the coming of the Maid and the deliverance of Orléans, transported with joy and wonder, he re-opens his history and consigns to its pages arguments in favour of the marvellous Maid, whose deeds appear to him more divine than human, but concerning whom he knows but little. He compares her to Deborah, Judith, Esther, and Penthesilea. "In the books of the Gentiles it is written," he says, "that Penthesilea, and a thousand virgins with her, came to the succour of King Priam and fought so valiantly that they tore the Myrmidons in pieces and slew more than two thousand Greeks." According to him, both in courage and feats of prowess, the Maid far surpasses Penthesilea. Her deeds promptly refute those who maintain that she is sent by the Devil.[1310]

In a moment the fame of the French King's prophetess had been spread abroad throughout Christendom. While in temporal affairs the people were rending each other, in spiritual matters obedience to one common head made Europe one spiritual republic with one language and one doctrine, governed by councils. The spirit of the Church was all-pervading. In Italy, in Germany, the talk was all of the Sibyl of France and her prowess which was so intimately associated with the Christian faith. In those days it was sometimes the custom of those who painted on the walls of monasteries to depict the Liberal Arts as three noble dames. Between her two sisters, Logic would be painted, seated on a lofty throne, wearing an antique turban, clothed in a sparkling robe, and bearing in one hand a scorpion, in the other a lizard, as a sign that her knowledge winds its way into the heart of the adversary's argument, and saves her from being herself entrapped. At her feet, looking up to her, would be Aristotle, disputing and reckoning up his arguments on his fingers.[1311] This austere lady formed all her disciples in the same mould. In those days nothing was more despicable than singularity. Originality of mind did not then exist. The clerks who treated of the Maid all followed the same method, advanced the same arguments, and based them on the same texts, sacred and profane. Conformity could go no further. Their minds were identical, but not their hearts; it is the mind that argues, but the heart that decides. These scholastics, dryer than their parchment, were men, notwithstanding; they were swayed by sentiment, by passion, by interests spiritual or temporal. While the Armagnac doctors were demonstrating that in the Maid's case reasons for belief were stronger than reasons for disbelief, the German or Italian masters, caring nought for the quarrel of the Dauphin of Viennois,[1312] remained in doubt, unmoved by either love or hatred.

There was a doctor of theology, one Heinrich von Gorcum, a professor at Cologne. As early as the month of June, 1429, he drew up a memorial concerning the Maid. In Germany, minds were divided as to whether the nature of the damsel were human or whether she were not rather a celestial being clothed in woman's form; as to whether her deeds proceeded from a human origin or had a supernatural source; and, if the latter, whether that source were good or bad. Meister Heinrich von Gorcum wrote his treatise to present arguments from Holy Scripture on both sides, and he abstained from drawing any conclusion.[1313]

In Italy, the same doubts and the same uncertainty prevailed concerning the deeds of the Maid. Those there were who maintained that they were mere inventions. At Milan, it was disputed whether any credence could be placed in tidings from France. To discover the truth about them, the notables of the city resolved to despatch a Franciscan friar, Brother Antonio de Rho, a good humanist and a zealous preacher of moral purity.

And Giovanni Corsini, Senator of the duchy of Arezzo, impelled by a like curiosity, consulted a learned clerk of Milan, one Cosmo Raimondi of Cremona. The following is the gist of the learned Ciceronian's reply:

"Most noble lord, they say that God's choice of a shepherdess for the restoration of a kingdom to a prince, is a new thing. And yet we know that the shepherd David was anointed king. It is told how the Maid, at the head of a small company, defied a great army. The victory may be explained by an advantageous position and an unexpected attack. But supposing we refrain from saying that the enemy was surprised and that his courage forsook him, matters which are none the less possible, supposing we admit that there was a miracle: what is there astonishing in that? Is it not still more wonderful that Samson should have slain so many Philistines with the jaw-bone of an ass?

"The Maid is said to possess the power of revealing the future. Remember the Sibyls, notably the Erythræan and the Cumæan. They were heathens. Why should not a like power be granted to a Christian? This woman is a shepherdess. Jacob, when he kept Laban's flocks, conversed familiarly with God. To such examples and to such reasons, which incline me to give credence to the rumour, I add another reason derived from physical science. In treatises on astrology I have often read that by the favourable influence of the stars, certain men of lowly birth have become the equals of the highest princes and been regarded as men divine charged with a celestial mission. Guido da Forli, a clever astronomer, quotes a great number of such instances. Wherefore I should not deem myself to be incurring any reproach if I believed that through the influence of the stars, the Maid has undertaken what is reported of her."

At the conclusion of his arguments the clerk of Cremona says that, while not absolutely rejecting the reports concerning her, he does not consider them to be sufficiently proved.[1314]

Jeanne maintained her resolution to go to Reims and take the King to his anointing.[1315] She did not stay to consider whether it would be better to wage war in Champagne than in Normandy. She did not know enough of the configuration of the country to decide such a question, and it is not likely that her saints and angels knew more of geography than she did. She was in haste to take the King to Reims for his anointing, because she believed it impossible for him to be king until he had been anointed.[1316] The idea of leading him to be anointed with the holy oil had come to her in her native village, long before the siege of Orléans.[1317] This inspiration was wholly of the spirit, and had nothing to do with the state of affairs created by the deliverance of Orléans and the victory of Patay.

The best course would have been to march straight on Paris after the 18th of June. The French were then only ninety miles from the great city, which at that juncture would not have thought of defending itself. Considering it as good as lost, the Regent shut himself up in the Fort of Vincennes.[1318] They had missed their opportunity. The French King's Councillors, Princes of the Blood, were deliberating, surprised by victory, not knowing what to do with it. Certain it is that not one of them thought of conquering, and that speedily, the whole inheritance of King Charles. The forces at their disposal, and the very conditions of the society in which they lived, rendered it impossible for them to conceive of such an undertaking. The lords of the Great Council were not like the poverty stricken monks, dreaming in their ruined cloisters[1319] of an age of peace and concord. The King's Councillors were no dreamers; they did not believe in the end of the war, neither did they desire it. But they intended to conduct it with the least possible risk and expenditure. There would always be folk enough to don the hauberk and go a-plundering they said to themselves; the taking and re-taking of towns must continue; sufficient unto the day is the evil thereof; to fight long one must fight gently; nine times out of ten more is gained by negotiations and treaties than by feats of prowess; truces must be concluded craftily and broken cautiously; some defeats must be expected, and some work must be left for the young. Such were the opinions of the good servants of King Charles.[1320]

Certain among them wished the war to be carried on in Normandy.[1321] The idea had occurred to them as early as the month of May, before the Loire campaign, and indeed there was much to be said for it. In Normandy they would cut the English tree at its root. It was quite possible that they might immediately recover a part of that province where the English had but few fighting men. In 1424 the Norman garrisons consisted of not more than four hundred lances and twelve hundred bowmen.[1322] Since then they had received but few reinforcements. The Regent was recruiting men everywhere and displaying marvellous activity, but he lacked money, and his soldiers were always deserting.[1323] In the conquered province, as soon as the *Coués* came out of their strongholds they found themselves in the enemy's territory. From the borders of Brittany, Maine, Perche as far as Ponthieu and Picardy, on the banks of the Mayenne, Orne, the Dive, the Touque, the Eure, the Seine, the partisans of the various factions held the country, watching the roads, robbing, ravaging, and murdering.[1324] Everywhere the French would have found these brave fellows ready to espouse their cause; the peasants and the village priests would likewise have wished them well. But the campaign would involve long sieges of towns, strongly defended, albeit held by but small garrisons. Now the men-at-arms dreaded the delays of sieges, and the royal treasury was not sufficient for such costly undertakings.[1325] Normandy was ruined, stripped of its crops, and robbed of its cattle. Were the captains and their men to go into this famine-stricken land? And why should the King reconquer so poor a province?

And these freebooters, who were willing to stretch out a hand to the French, were not very attractive. It was well known that brigands they were, and brigands would remain, and that Normandy once reconquered, they would have to be got rid of, to the last man, without honour and without profit. In which case would it not be better to leave them to be dealt with by the *Godons*?

Other nobles clamoured for an expedition into Champagne.[1326] And in spite of all that has been said to the contrary, the Maid's visions had no influence whatever on this determination. The King's Councillors led Jeanne and were far from being led by her. Once before they had diverted her from the road to Reims by providing her with work on the Loire. Once again they might divert her into Normandy, without her even perceiving it, so ignorant was she of the roads and of the lie of the land. If there were certain who recommended a campaign in Champagne, it was not on the faith of saints and angels, but for purely human reasons. Is it possible to discover these reasons? There were doubtless certain lords and captains who considered the interest of the King and the kingdom, but every one found it so difficult not to confound it with his own interest, that the best way to discover who was responsible for the march on Reims is to find out who was to profit by it. It was certainly not the Duke of Alençon, who would have greatly preferred to take advantage of the Maid's help for the conquest of his own duchy.[1327] Neither was it my Lord the Bastard, nor the Sire de Gaucourt, nor the King himself, for they must have desired the securing of Berry and the Orléanais by the capture of La Charité held by the terrible Perrinet Gressart.[1328] On the other hand we may conclude that the Queen of Sicily would not be unfavourable to the march of the King, her son-in-law, in a north easterly direction. This Spanish lady was possessed by the Angevin mania. Reassured for the moment concerning the fate of her duchy of Anjou, she was pursuing eagerly, and to the great hurt of the realm of France, the establishment of her son René in the duchy of Bar and in the inheritance of Lorraine. She cannot have been displeased, therefore, when she saw the King keeping her an open road between Gien and Troyes and Châlons. But since the Constable's exile she had lost all influence over her son-in-law, and it is difficult to discover who could have watched her interests in the Council of May, 1429.[1329] Besides, without seeking further, it is obvious that there was one person, who above all others must have desired the anointing of the King, and who more than any was in a position to make his opinion prevail. That person was the man on whom devolved the duty of holding in his consecrated hands the Sacred Ampulla, my Lord Regnault de Chartres, Archbishop Duke of Reims, Chancellor of the Kingdom.[1330]

He was a man of rare intelligence, skilled in business, a very clever diplomatist, greedy of wealth, caring less for empty honours than for solid advantage, avaricious, unscrupulous, one who at the age of about fifty had lost nothing of his consuming energy; he had recently displayed it by spending himself nobly in the defence of Orléans. Thus gifted, how could he fail to exercise a powerful control over the government?

Fifteen years had passed since his elevation to the archiepiscopal see of Reims; and of his enormous revenue he had not yet received one penny. Albeit the possessor of great wealth from other sources, he pleaded poverty. To the Pope he addressed heart-rending supplications.[1331] If the Maid had found favour in the eyes of the Poitiers doctors, Monseigneur Regnault had had something to do with it. Had it not been for him, the doctors at court would never have proposed her examination. And we shall not be making too bold a hypothesis if we conclude, that when the march on Reims was decided in the royal council, it was because the Archbishop, on grounds suggested by human reason, approved of what the Maid proposed by divine inspiration.[1332]

While the coronation campaign was attended with grave drawbacks and met with serious obstacles, it nevertheless brought great gain and a certain subtle advantage to the royal cause. Unfortunately it left free from attack the rest of France occupied by the English, and it gave the latter time to recover themselves and procure aid from over sea. We shall shortly see what good use they made of their opportunities.[1333] As to the advantages of the expedition, they were many and various. First, Jeanne truly expressed the sentiments of the poor priests and the common folk when she said that the Dauphin would reap great profit from his anointing.[1334] From the oil of the holy Ampulla the King would derive a splendour, a majesty which would impress the whole of France, yea, even the whole of Christendom. In those days royalty was alike spiritual and temporal; and multitudes of men believed with Jeanne that kings only became kings by being anointed with the holy oil. Thus it would not be wrong to say that Charles of Valois would receive greater power from one drop of oil than from ten thousand lances. On a consideration like this the King's Councillors must needs set great store. They had also to take into account the time and the place. Might not the ceremony be performed in some other town than Reims? Might not the so-called "mystery" take place in that city which had been delivered by the intercession of its blessed patrons, Saint-Aignan and Saint Euverte? Two kings descended from Hugh Capet, Robert the Wise and Louis the Fat, had been crowned at Orléans.[1335] But the memory of their royal coronation was lost in the mists of antiquity, while folk still retained the memory of a long procession of most Christian kings anointed in the town where the holy oil had been brought down to Clovis by the celestial dove.[1336] Besides, the lord Archbishop and Duke of Reims would never have suffered the King to receive his anointing save at his hand and in his cathedral.

Therefore it was necessary to go to Reims. It was necessary also to anticipate the English who had resolved to conduct thither their infant King that he might receive consecration according to the ancient ceremonial.[1337] But if the French had invaded Normandy they would have closed the young Henry's road to Paris and to Reims, a road which was already insecure for him; and it would be childish to maintain that the coronation could not have been postponed for a few weeks. If the conquest of Norman lands and Norman towns was renounced therefore, it was not merely for the sake of capturing the holy Ampulla. The Lord Archbishop of Reims had other objects at heart. He believed, for example, that, by pressing in between the Duke of Burgundy and his English allies, an excellent impression would be produced on the mind of that Prince and the edifying object-lesson presented to his consideration of Charles, son of Charles, King of France, riding at the head of a powerful army.

To attain the city of the Blessed Saint Remi two hundred and fifty miles of hostile country must be traversed. But for some time the army would be in no danger of meeting the enemy on the road. The English and Burgundians were engaged in using every means both fair and foul for the raising of troops. For the moment the French need fear no foe. The rich country of Champagne, sparsely wooded, well cultivated, teemed with corn and wine, and abounded in fat cattle.[1338] Champagne had not been devastated like Normandy. There was a likelihood of obtaining food for the men-at-arms, especially if, as was hoped, the good towns supplied victuals. They were very wealthy; their barns overflowed with corn. While owing allegiance to King Henry, no bonds of affection united them to the English or to the Burgundians. They governed themselves. They were rich merchants, who only longed for peace and who did their best to bring it about. Just now they were beginning to suspect that the Armagnacs were growing the stronger party. These folk of Champagne had a clergy and a *bourgeoisie* who might be appealed to. It was not a question of storming their towns with artillery, mines, and trenches, but of getting round them with amnesties, concessions to the merchants and elaborate engagements to respect the privileges of the clergy. In this country there was no risk of rotting in hovels or burning in bastions. The townsfolk were expected to throw open their gates and partly from love, partly from fear, to give money to their lord the King.

The campaign was already arranged, and that very skilfully. Communications had been opened with Troyes and Châlons. By letters and messages from a few notables of Reims it was made known to King Charles that if he came they would open to him the gates of their town. He even received three or four citizens, who said to him, "Go forth in confidence to our city of Reims. It shall not be our fault if you do not enter therein."[1339]

Such assurances emboldened the Royal Council; and the march into Champagne was resolved upon.

The army assembled at Gien; it increased daily. The nobles of Brittany and Poitou came in in great numbers, most of them mounted on sorry steeds[1340] and commanding but small companies of men. The poorest equipped themselves as archers, and in default of better service were ready to act as bowmen. Villeins and tradesmen came likewise.[1341] From the Loire to the Seine and from the Seine to the Somme the only cultivated land was round *châteaux* and fortresses. Most of the fields lay fallow. In many places fairs and markets had been suspended. Labourers were everywhere out of work. War, after having ruined all trades, was now the only trade. Says Eustache Deschamps, "All men will become squires. Scarce any artisans are left."[1342] At the place of meeting there assembled thirty thousand men, of whom many were on foot and many came from the villages, giving their services in return for food. There were likewise monks, valets, women and other camp-followers. And all this multitude was an hungered. The King went to Gien and summoned the Queen who was at Bourges.[1343]

His idea was to take her to Reims and have her crowned with him, following the example of Queen Blanche of Castille, of Jeanne de Valois, and of Queen Jeanne, wife of King John. But queens had not usually been crowned at Reims; Queen Ysabeau, mother of the present King, had received the crown from the hands of the Archbishop of Rouen in the Sainte-Chapelle, in Paris.[1344] Before her time, the wives of the kings, following the example set by Berthe, wife of Pepin the Short, generally came to Saint-Denys to receive the crown of gold, of sapphire and of pearls given by Jeanne of Évreux to the monks of the Abbey.[1345] Sometimes the queens were crowned with their husbands, sometimes alone and in a different place; many had never been crowned at all.

That King Charles should have thought of taking Queen Marie on this expedition proves that he did not anticipate great fatigue or great danger. Nevertheless, at the last moment the plan was changed. The Queen, who had come to Gien, was sent back to Bourges. The King set out without her.[1346]

Quand le roy s'en vint en France,
Il feit oindre ses houssiaulx,

> *Et la royne lui demande:*
> *Ou veult aller cest damoiseaulx?*[1347]

In reality the Queen asked nothing. She was ill-favoured and weak of will.[1348] But the song says that the King on his departure had his old gaiters greased because he had no new ones. Those old jokes about the poverty of the King of Bourges still held good.[1349] The King had not grown rich. It was customary to pay the men-at-arms a part of their wages in advance. At Gien each fighting man received three francs. It did not seem much, but they hoped to gain more on the way.[1350]

On Friday, the 24th of June, the Maid set out from Orléans for Gien. On the morrow she dictated from Gien a letter to the inhabitants of Tournai, telling them how the English had been driven from all their strongholds on the Loire and discomfited in battle. In this letter she invited them to come to the anointing of King Charles at Reims and called upon them to continue loyal Frenchmen. Here is the letter:

Jhesus † Maria

Fair Frenchmen and loyal, of the town of Tournay, from this place the Maid maketh known unto you these tidings: that in eight days, by assault or otherwise, she hath driven the English from all the strongholds they held on the River Loire. Know ye that the Earl of Suffort, Lapoulle his brother, the Sire of Tallebord, the Sire of Scallez and my lords Jean Falscof and many knights and captains have been taken, and the brother of the Earl of Suffort and Glasdas slain. I beseech you to remain good and loyal Frenchmen; and I beseech and entreat you that ye make yourselves ready to come to the anointing of the fair King Charles at Rains, where we shall shortly be, and come ye to meet us when ye know that we draw nigh. To God I commend you. God keep you and give you his grace that ye may worthily maintain the good cause of the realm of France. Written at Gien the xxvth day of June.

Addressed "to the loyal Frenchmen of the town of Tournay."[1351]

An epistle in the same tenor must have been sent by the Maid's monkish scribes to all the towns which had remained true to King Charles, and the priests themselves must have drawn up the list of them.[1352] They would certainly not have forgotten that town of the royal domain, which, situated in Flanders,[1353] in the heart of Burgundian territory, still remained loyal to its liege lord. The town of Tournai, ceded to Philip the Good by the English government, in 1423, had not recognised its new master. Jean de Thoisy, its bishop, resided at Duke Philip's court;[1354] but it remained the King's town,[1355] and the well-known attachment of its townsfolk to the Dauphin's fortunes was exemplary and famous.[1356] The Consuls of Albi, in a short note concerning the marvels of 1429, were careful to remark that this northern city, so remote that they did not exactly know where it was, still held out for France, though surrounded by France's enemies. "The truth is that the English occupy the whole land of Normandy, and of Picardy, except Tournay,"[1357] they wrote.

Indeed the inhabitants of the bailiwick of Tournai, jealously guarding the liberties and privileges accorded to them by the King of France, would not have separated themselves from the Crown on any consideration. They protested their loyalty, and in honour of the King and in the hope of his recovering his kingdom they had grand processions; but their devotion stopped there; and, when their liege Lord, King Charles, urgently demanded the arrears of their contribution, of which he said he stood in great need, their magistrates deliberated and decided to ask leave to postpone payment again, and for as long as possible.[1358]

There is no doubt that the Maid herself dictated this letter. It will be noticed that therein she takes to herself the credit and the whole credit for the victory. Her candour obliged her to do so. In her opinion God had done everything, but he had done everything through her. "The Maid hath driven the English out of all their strongholds." She alone could reveal so naïve a faith in herself. Brother Pasquerel would not have written with such saintly simplicity.

It is remarkable that in this letter Sir John Fastolf should be reckoned among the prisoners. This mistake is not peculiar to Jeanne. The King announces to his good towns that three English captains have been taken, Talbot, the Lord of Scales and Fastolf. Perceval de Boulainvilliers, in his Latin epistle to the Duke of Milan, includes Fastolf, whom he calls *Fastechat*, among the thousand prisoners taken by the folk of Dauphiné. Finally, a missive despatched about the 25th of June, from one of the towns of the diocese of Luçon, shows great uncertainty concerning the fate of Talbot, Fastolf and Scales, "who are said to be either prisoners or dead."[1359] Possibly the French had laid hands on some noble who resembled Fastolf in appearance or in name; or perhaps some man-at-arms in order to be held to ransom had given himself out to be Fastolf. The Maid's letter reached Tournai on the 7th of July. On the morrow the town council resolved to send an embassy to King Charles of France.[1360]

On the 27th of June, or about then, the Maid caused letters to be despatched to the Duke of Burgundy, inviting him to come to the King's coronation. She received no reply.[1361] Duke Philip was the last man in the world to correspond with the Maid. And that she should have written to him courteously was a sign of her goodness of heart. As a child in her village she had been the enemy of the Burgundians before being the enemy of the English, but none the less she desired the good of the kingdom and a reconciliation between Burgundians and French.

The Duke of Burgundy could not lightly pardon the ambush of Montereau; but at no time of his life had he vowed an irreconcilable hatred of the French. An understanding had become possible after the year 1425, when his brother-in-law, the Constable of France, had excluded Duke John's murderers from the Royal Council. As for the Dauphin Charles, he maintained that he had had nothing to do with the crime; but among the Burgundians he passed for an idiot.[1362] In the depths of his heart Duke Philip disliked the English. After King Henry V's death he had refused to act as their regent in France. Then there was the affair of the Countess Jacqueline which very nearly brought about an open rupture.[1363] For many years the House of Burgundy had been endeavouring to gain control over the Low Countries. At last Duke Philip attained his object by marrying his second cousin, John, Duke of Brabant to Jacqueline of Bavaria, Countess of Hainault, Holland and Zealand, and Lady of Friesland. Jacqueline, finding her husband intolerable, fled to England, and there, having had her marriage annulled by the Antipope, Benedict XIII, married the Duke of Gloucester, the Regent's brother.

Bedford, as prudent as Gloucester was headstrong, made every effort to retain the great Duke in the English alliance; but the secret hatred he felt for the Burgundians burst forth occasionally in sudden acts of rage. Whether he planned the assassination of the Duke and the Duke knew it, is uncertain. But at any rate it is alleged that one day the courteous Bedford forgot himself so far as to say that Duke Philip might well go to England and drink more beer than was good for him.[1364] The Regent had just tactlessly offended him by refusing to let him take possession of the town of Orléans.[1365] Now Bedford was biting his fingers with rage. Regretting that he had refused the Duke the key to the Loire and the heart of France, he was at present eager to offer him the province of Champagne which the French were preparing to conquer: this was indeed just the time to present some rich gift to his powerful ally.[1366]

Meanwhile the great Duke could think of nothing but the Low Countries. Pope Martin had declared the marriage of the Countess Jacqueline and Gloucester to be invalid; and Gloucester was marrying another wife. Now the Gargantua of Dijon could once more lay hands on the broad lands of the fair Jacqueline. He remained the ally of the English, intending to make use of them but not to play into their hands, and prepared, should he find it to his advantage, to make war on the French before being reconciled to them; he saw no harm in that. After the Low Countries what he cared most about were ladies and beautiful paintings, like those of the brothers Van Eyck. He would not be likely therefore to pay much attention to a letter from the Maid of the Armagnacs.[1367]

CHAPTER XVII

THE CONVENTION OF AUXERRE – FRIAR RICHARD – THE SURRENDER OF TROYES

O N the 27th of June,[1368] the vanguard, commanded by Marshal de Boussac, the Sire de Rais, the Captains La Hire and Poton, set out from Gien in the direction of Montargis with the design of pressing on to Sens, which, so they had been wrongly informed, was deemed likely to open its gates to the Dauphin. But, at the news that the town had hoisted the flag of St. Andrew, as a sign of fidelity to the English and Burgundians, the army changed its route, so little did it desire to take towns by force. The march was now directed towards Auxerre, where a more favourable reception was expected.[1369] The Maid in her impatience had not waited for the King. She rode with the company which had started first. Had she been its leader she would not have turned from a town when its cannon were directed against her.

The King set forth two days later, with the Princes of the Blood, many knights, the main battle, as it was called, and the Sire de la Trémouille, who commanded the expedition.[1370] All these troops arrived before Auxerre on the 1st of July.[1371] There on the hill-slope, encircled with vineyards and cornfields, rose the ramparts, towers, roofs, and belfries of the blessed Bishop Germain's city. That town towards which in the summer sunshine, in the company of gallant knighthood, she was now riding, fully armed like a handsome Saint Maurice, Jeanne had seen only three months before, under a dark and cloudy sky; then, clad like a stable-boy, in the company of two or three poor soldiers of fortune, she was travelling over a bad road, on her way to the Dauphin Charles.[1372]

Since 1424 the County of Auxerre had belonged to the Duke of Burgundy, upon whom it had been bestowed by the Regent. The Duke governed it through a bailie and a captain.[1373]

The lord Bishop, Messire Jean de Corbie, formerly Bishop of Mende, was thought to be on the Dauphin's side.[1374] The Chapter of the Cathedral on the other hand held to Burgundy.[1375] Twelve jurors, elected by the burgesses and other townsfolk, administered the affairs of the city. One can easily imagine that fear must have been the dominant sentiment in their hearts when they saw the royal army approaching. Men-at-arms, no matter whether they wore the white cross or the red, inspired all town dwellers with a well-grounded terror. And, in order to turn from their gates these violent and murderous thieves, the townsfolk were capable of resorting to the strongest measures, even to that of putting their hands in their purses.

The royal heralds summoned the people of Auxerre to receive the King as their natural and lawful lord. Such a summons, backed by lances, placed them in a very embarrassing position. Alike by refusing and by consenting these good folk ran great risk. To transfer their allegiance was no light matter; their lives and their goods were involved. Foreseeing this danger, and conscious of their weakness, they had entered into a league with the cities of Champagne. The object of the league was to relieve its members from the burden of receiving men-at-arms and the peril of having two hostile masters. Certain of the townsfolk therefore presented themselves before King Charles and promised him such submission as should be accorded by the towns of Troyes, Châlons, and Reims.[1376]

This was not obedience, neither was it rebellion. Negotiations were begun; ambassadors went from the town to the camp and from the camp to the town. Finally the confederates, who were not lacking in intelligence, proposed an acceptable compromise, – one that princes were constantly concluding with each other, to wit, a truce.

They said to the King: "We entreat and request you to pass on, and we ask you to agree to refrain from fighting." And, in order to secure their request being granted, they gave two thousand crowns to the Sire de la Trémouille, who, it is said, kept them without a blush. Further, the townsfolk undertook to revictual the army in return for money down; and that was worth considering, for there was famine in the camp.[1377] This truce by no means pleased the men-at-arms, who thereby lost a fine opportunity for robbery and pillage. Murmurs arose;

many lords and captains said that it would not be difficult to take the town, and that its capture should have been attempted. The Maid, who was always receiving promises of victory from her Voices, never ceased calling the soldiers to arms.[1378] Unaffected by any of these things, the King concluded the proposed truce; for he cared not by force of arms to obtain more than could be compassed by peaceful methods. Had he attacked the town he might have taken it and held it in his mercy; but it would have meant certain pillage, murder, burning, and ravishing. On his heels would have come the Burgundians, and there would have been plundering, burning, ravishing, massacring over again. How many examples had there not been already of unhappy towns captured and then lost almost immediately, devastated by the French, devastated by the English and the Burgundians, when each citizen kept in his coffer a red cap and a white cap, which he wore in turns! Was there to be no end to these massacres and abominations, resentment against which caused the Armagnacs to be cursed throughout l'Île de France, and which made it so hard for the lawful King to recover his town of Paris. The royal Council thought the time had come to put an end to these things. It was of opinion that Charles of Valois would the more easily reconquer his inheritance if, while manifesting his power, he showed himself lenient and exercised royal clemency, as in arms and yet pursuing peace, he continued his march to Reims.[1379]

After having spent three days under the walls of the town, the army being refreshed, crossed the Yonne and came to the town of Saint-Florentin, which straightway submitted to the King.[1380] On the 4th of July, they reached the village of Saint-Phal, four hours' journey from Troyes.[1381]

In this strong town there was a garrison of between five and six hundred men at the most.[1382] A bailie, Messire Jean de Dinteville, two captains, the Sires de Rochefort and de Plancy, commanded in the town for King Henry and for the Duke of Burgundy.[1383] Troyes was a manufacturing town; the source of its wealth was the cloth manufacture. True, this industry had long been declining through competition and the removal of markets; its ruin was being precipitated by the general poverty and the insecurity of the roads. Nevertheless the cloth workers' guild maintained its importance and sent a number of magistrates to the Council.[1384]

In 1420, these merchants had sworn to the treaty which promised the French crown to the House of Lancaster; they were then at the mercy of English and Burgundians. For the holding of those great fairs, to which they took their cloth, they must needs live at peace with their Burgundian neighbours, and if the *Godons* had closed the ports of the Seine against their bales, they would have died of hunger. Wherefore the notables of the town had turned English, which did not mean that they would always remain English. Within the last few weeks great changes had taken place in the kingdom; and the Gilles Laiguisés, the Hennequins, the Jouvenels did not pride themselves on remaining unchanged amidst vicissitudes of fortune which were transferring the power from one side to the other. The French victories gave them food for reflection. Along the banks of the streams, which wound through the city, there were weavers, dyers, curriers who were Burgundian at heart.[1385] As for the Churchmen, if they were thrilled by no love for the Armagnacs, they felt none the less that King Charles was sent to them by a special dispensation of divine providence.

The Bishop of Troyes was my lord Jean Laiguisé, son of Master Huet Laiguisé, one of the first to swear to the treaty of 1420.[1386] The Chapter had elected him without waiting for the permission of the Regent, who declared against the election, not that he disliked the new pontiff; Messire Jean Laiguisé had sucked hatred of the Armagnacs and respect for the Rose of Lancaster from his *alma mater* of Paris. But my Lord of Bedford could not forgive any slighting of his sovereign rights.

Shortly afterwards he incurred the censure of the whole Church of France and was judged by the bishops worse than the cruellest tyrants of Scripture – Pharaoh, Nebuchadnezzar, Artaxerxes[1387] – who, when they chastised Israel had spared the Levites. More wicked than they and more sacrilegious, my Lord of Bedford threatened the privileges of the Gallican Church, when, on behalf of the Holy See, he robbed the bishops of their patronage, levied a double tithe on the French clergy, and commanded churchmen to surrender to him the contributions they had been receiving for forty years. That he was acting with the Pope's consent made his conduct none the less execrable in the eyes of the French bishops. The episcopal lords resolved to appeal from a Pope ill informed to one with wider knowledge; for they held the authority of the Bishop of Rome to be insignificant in comparison with the authority of the Council. They groaned: the abomination of desolation was laying waste Christian

Gaul. In order to pacify the Church of France thus roused against him, my lord of Bedford convoked at Paris the bishops of the ecclesiastical province of Sens, which included the dioceses of Paris, Troyes, Auxerre, Nevers, Meaux, Chartres, and Orléans.[1388]

Messire Jean Laiguisé attended this Convocation. The Synod was held at Paris, in the Priory of Saint-Eloi, under the presidency of the Archbishop, from the 1st of March till the 23rd of April, 1429.[1389] The assembled bishops represented to my Lord the Regent the sorry plight of the ecclesiastical lords: the peasants, pillaged by soldiers, no longer paid their dues; the lands of the Church were lying waste; divine service had ceased to be held because there was no money with which to support public worship. Unanimously they refused to pay the Pope and the Regent the double tithe; and they threatened to appeal from the Pope to the Council. As for despoiling the clergy of all the contributions they had received during the last forty years, that, they declared, would be impious; and with great charity they reminded my Lord of Bedford of the fate reserved by God's judgment for the impious even in this world. "The Prince," they said, "should beware of the miseries and sorrows already fallen upon a multitude of princes, who with such demands had oppressed the Church which God redeemed with his own precious blood: some had perished by the sword, some had been driven into exile, others had been despoiled of their illustrious sovereignties. Wherefore such as set themselves to enslave the Church, the Bride of God, may not hope to deserve the grace of his divine Majesty."[1390]

Jean Laiguisé's sentiments towards the English Regent were those of the Synod. It would be wrong, however, to conclude that the Bishop of Troyes desired the death of the sinner, or even that he was hostile to the English.[1391] The Church is usually capable of temporising with the powers of this world. Wide is her mercy, and great her longsuffering. She threatens oft before striking and receives the repentance of the sinner at the first sign of contrition. But we may believe that if Charles of Valois were to win the power and show the will to protect the Church of France, the Lord Bishop and the Chapter of Troyes would fear lest if they resisted him they might be resisting God himself, since all power comes from God who *deposuit potentes*.

King Charles had not ventured to enter Champagne without taking measures for his safety; he knew on what he could rely in the town of Troyes. He had received information and promises; he maintained secret relations with several burgesses of the city, and those none of the least.[1392] During the first fortnight of May, a royal notary, ten clerks and leading merchants, on their way to the king, were arrested just outside the walls, on the Paris road, by the Sire de Chateauvillain,[1393] a captain in the English service. This mission was probably fulfilled by others more fortunate. It is easy to divine what questions were discussed at these audiences. The merchants would ask whether Charles, if he became their Lord, would guarantee absolute freedom to their trade; the clerks would ask his promise to respect the goods of the Church. And the King doubtless was not sparing of his pledges.

The Maid, with one division of the army, halted before the stronghold of Saint-Phal, belonging to Philibert de Vaudrey, commander of the town of Tonnerre, in the service of the Duke of Burgundy.[1394] In that place of Saint-Phal, Jeanne beheld approaching her a Franciscan friar, who was crossing himself and sprinkling holy water, for he feared lest she were the devil, and dared not draw near without having first exorcised the evil spirit. It was Friar Richard who was coming from Troyes.[1395] It will be interesting to see who this monk was as far as we can tell.

The place of his birth is unknown.[1396] A disciple of Brother Vincent Ferrier and of Brother Bernardino of Sienna, like them, he taught the imminent coming of Antichrist and the salvation of the faithful by the adoration of the holy name of Jesus.[1397] After having been on a pilgrimage to Jerusalem, he returned to France, and preached at Troyes, during the Advent of 1428. Advent, sometimes called Saint Martin's Lent, begins on the Sunday which falls between the 27th of November and the 3rd of December. It lasts four weeks, which Christians spend in making themselves ready to celebrate the mystery of the Nativity.

"Sow, sow your seed, my good folk," he said. "Sow beans ready for the harvest, for He who is to come will come quickly."[1398]

By beans he meant the good works to be performed before Our Lord should come in the clouds to judge the quick and the dead. Now it was important to sow those good works quickly, for the harvest-tide was drawing nigh. The coming of Antichrist was but shortly to precede the end of the world and the consummation of the ages. In the month of April, 1429, Friar Richard went to Paris; the Synod of the Province of Sens was then holding its final session. It is possible that the good Friar was summoned to the great city by the Bishop of

Troyes who was present at the Synod; but at any rate it would appear that it was not the rights of the Gallican Church the wandering monk went there to defend.[1399]

On the 16th of April, he preached his first sermon at Sainte-Geneviève; on the next and the following days, until Sunday, the 24th, he preached every morning, from five until ten or eleven o'clock, in the open air, on a platform, erected against the charnel-house of the Innocents, on the spot whereon was celebrated the dance of death. Around the platform, about nine feet high, there crowded five or six thousand persons, to whom he announced the speedy coming of Antichrist and the end of the world.[1400] "In Syria," he said, "I met bands of Jews; I asked them whither they were going, and they replied: 'We are wending in a multitude towards Babylon, for of a truth the Messiah is born among men, and he will restore unto us our inheritance, and he will bring us again to the land of promise.' Thus spake those Syrian Jews. Now Scripture teaches us that He, whom they call the Messiah, is in truth that Antichrist, of whom it is said he shall be born in Babylon, capital of the kingdom of Persia, he shall be brought up at Bethsaida and in his youth he shall dwell at Chorazin. Wherefore our Lord said: 'Woe unto thee, Chorazin! woe unto thee, Bethsaida.' The year 1430," added Friar Richard, "shall witness greater marvels than have ever been seen before.[1401] The time draweth nigh. He is born, the man of sin, the child of perdition, the wicked one, the beast vomited forth from the abyss, the abomination of desolation; he came out of the tribe of Dan, of whom it is written: 'Dan shall be a serpent by the way, an adder in the path.' Soon shall return to the earth the prophets Elijah and Enoch, Moses, Jeremiah and Saint John the Evangelist; and soon shall dawn that day of wrath which shall grind the age in a mill and beat it in a mortar, according to the testimony of David and the Sibyl."[1402] Then the good Brother concluded by calling upon them to repent, to do penance and to renounce empty riches. In short, in the opinion of the clerks, he was a man of worship and an orator. His sermons produced more devoutness among the people, it was thought, than those of all the sermonizers who for the last century had been preaching in the town. And it was time that he came, for in those days the folk of Paris were greatly addicted to games of chance; yea, even priests unblushingly indulged in them, and seven years before, a canon of Saint-Merry, a great lover of dice was known to have gamed in his own house.[1403] Despite war and famine, the women of Paris loaded themselves with ornaments. They troubled more about their beauty than about the salvation of their souls.

Friar Richard thundered most loudly against the draught boards of the men and the ornaments of the women. One day notably, when he was preaching at Boulogne-la-Petite, he cried down dice and *hennins*,[1404] and spoke with such power that the hearts of those who listened were changed. On returning to their homes, the citizens threw into the streets gaming-tables, draught-boards, cards, billiard cues and balls, dice and dice-boxes, and made great fires before their doors. More than one hundred of these fires continued burning in the streets for three or four hours. Women followed the good example set by the men that day, and the next they burnt in public their head-dresses, pads, ornaments, and the pieces of leather or whalebone on which they mounted the fronts of their hoods. Young misses threw off their horns[1405] and their tails,[1406] ashamed to clothe themselves in the devil's garb.[1407]

The good Brother likewise caused to be burnt the mandrake roots which many folk kept in their houses.[1408] Those roots are sometimes in the form of an ugly little man, of a curious and devilish aspect. On that account possibly, singular virtues are attributed to them. These mannikins were dressed in fine linen and silk and were kept in the belief that they would bring good luck and procure wealth. Witches made much of them; and those who believed that the Maid was a witch accused her of carrying a mandrake on her person. Friar Richard hated these magic roots all the more strongly because he believed in their power of attracting wealth, the root of all evil. Once again his word was obeyed; and many a Parisian threw away his mandrake in horror, albeit he had bought it dear from some old wife who knew more than was good for her.[1409] Friar Richard caused the Parisians to replace these evil treasures by objects of greater edification, – pewter medals, on which was stamped the name of Jesus, to the worship of whom he was especially devoted.[1410]

Having preached ten times in the town and once in the village of Boulogne, the good Brother announced his return to Burgundy and took his leave of the Parisians.

"I will pray for you," he said; "pray for me. Amen."

Whereupon all the folk, high and lowly, wept bitterly and copiously, as if each one were bearing to the grave his dearest friend. He wept with them and consented to delay his departure for a little.[1411]

On Sunday, the 1st of May, he was to preach to the devout Parisians for the last time. Montmartre, the very spot where Saint Denis had suffered martyrdom, was the place chosen for the meeting of the faithful. In those unhappy days the hill was well-nigh uninhabited. But on the evening before that day more than six thousand people flocked to the mount to be certain of having good places; and there they passed the night, some in deserted hovels, but the majority in the open, under the stars. When the morning came no Friar Richard appeared, and in vain they waited for him. Disappointed and sad, at length they learnt that the Friar had been forbidden to preach.[1412] He had said nothing in his sermons to offend the English. The Parisians who had heard him believed him to be a good friend to the Regent and to the Duke of Burgundy. Perhaps he had taken flight owing to a report that the theologians of the University intended to proceed against him. His views concerning the end of the world were indeed both singular and dangerous.[1413]

Friar Richard had gone off to Auxerre. Thence he went preaching through Burgundy and Champagne. If he was on the King's side he did not let it appear. For in the month of June the folk of Champagne, and the inhabitants of Châlons especially, deemed him a worthy man and attached to the Duke of Burgundy.[1414] And we have seen that on the 4th of July he suspected the Maid of being either the devil or possessed by a devil.[1415]

She understood. When she saw the good Brother crossing himself and sprinkling holy water she knew that he took her for something evil, – for a phantom fashioned by the spirit of wickedness, or at least for a witch.[1416] However, she was by no means offended as she had been by the suspicions of Messire Jean Fournier. The priest, to whom she had confessed, could not be forgiven for having doubted whether she were a good Christian.[1417] But Friar Richard did not know her, had never seen her. Besides, she was growing accustomed to such treatment. The Constable, Brother Yves Milbeau, and many others who came to her asked whether she were from God or the devil.[1418] It was without a trace of anger, although in a slightly ironical tone, that she said to the preacher: "Approach boldly, I shall not fly away."[1419]

Meanwhile Friar Richard, by the ordeal of holy water and by the sign of the cross, had proved that the damsel was not a devil and that there was no devil in her. And when she said she had come from God he believed her with all his heart and esteemed her an angel of the Lord.[1420]

He confided to her the reason for his coming.[1421] The inhabitants of Troyes doubted whether she were of God; to resolve their doubts he had come to Saint-Phal. Now he knew she was of God, and he was not amazed; for he knew that the year 1430 would witness greater marvels than had ever been seen before, and one day or other he was expecting to behold the Prophet Elias walking and conversing with men.[1422] From that moment he threw in his lot with the party of the Maid and the Dauphin. It was not the Maid's prophecies concerning the realm of France that attracted him to her. The world was too near its end for him to take any interest in the re-establishment of the madman's son in his inheritance. But he expected that once the kingdom of Jesus Christ had been established in the Land of the Lilies, Jeanne, the prophetess, and Charles, the temporal vicar of Jesus Christ, would lead the people of Christendom to deliver the Holy Sepulchre. That would be a meritorious work and one which must be accomplished before the consummation of the ages.

To the burgesses and inhabitants of the town of Troyes Jeanne dictated a letter. Herein, calling herself the servant of the King of Heaven and speaking in the name of God Himself, in terms gentle yet urgent, she called upon them to render obedience to King Charles of France, and warned them that whether they would or no she with the King would enter into all the towns of the holy kingdom and bring them peace. Here is the letter:[1423]

Jhesus † Maria

Good friends and beloved, an it please you, ye lords, burgesses and inhabitants of the town of Troies, Jehanne the Maid doth call upon and make known unto you on behalf of the King of Heaven, her sovereign and liege Lord, in whose service royal she is every day, that ye render true obedience and fealty to the Fair King of France. Whosoever may come against him, he shall shortly be in Reins and in Paris, and in his good towns of his holy kingdom, with the aid of King Jhesus. Ye loyal Frenchmen, come forth to King Charles and fail him not. And if ye come have no fear for your bodies nor for your goods. An if ye come not, I promise you and on your lives I maintain it, that with God's help we shall enter into all the towns of the holy kingdom and shall there establish peace, whosoever may oppose us. To God I commend you. God keep you if it be his will. Answer speedily. Before

287

the city of Troyes, written at Saint-Fale, Tuesday the fourth day of July.[1424]

On the back:

"To the lords and burgesses of the city of Troyes."

The Maid gave this letter to Friar Richard, who undertook to carry it to the townsfolk.[1425]

From Saint-Phal the army advanced towards Troyes along the Roman road.[1426] When they heard of the army's approach, the Council of the town assembled on Tuesday, the 5th, early in the morning, and sent the people of Reims a missive of which the following is the purport:

"This day do we expect the enemies of King Henry and the Duke of Burgundy who come to besiege us. In view of the design of these our foes and having considered the just cause we support and the aid of our princes promised unto us, we have resolved in council, no matter what may be the strength of our enemies, to continue in our obedience waxing ever greater to King Henry and to the Duke of Burgundy, even until death. And this have we sworn on the precious body of Our Lord Jesus Christ. Wherefore we pray the citizens of Reims to take thought for us as brethren and loyal friends, and to send to my Lord the Regent and the Duke of Burgundy to beseech and entreat them to take pity on their poor subjects and come to their succour."[1427]

On that same day, in the morning, from his lodging at Brinion-l'Archevêque, King Charles despatched his heralds bearing closed letters, signed by his hand, sealed with his seal, addressed to the members of the Council of the town of Troyes. Therein he made known unto them that by the advice of his Council, he had undertaken to go to Reims, there to receive his anointing, that his intention was to enter the city of Troyes on the morrow, wherefore he summoned and commanded them to render the obedience they owed him and prepare to receive him. He wisely made a point of reassuring them as to his intentions, which were not to avenge the past. Such was not his will, he said, but let them comport themselves towards their sovereign as they ought, and he would forget all and maintain them in his favour.[1428]

The Council refused to admit King Charles' heralds within the town; but they received his letters, read them, deliberated over them, and made known to the heralds the result of their deliberations which was the following:

"The lords, knights and squires who are in the town, on behalf of King Henry and the Duke of Burgundy, have sworn with us, inhabitants of the city, that we will not receive into the town any who are stronger than we, without the express command of the Duke of Burgundy. Having regard to their oath, those who are in the town would not dare to admit King Charles."

And the councillors added for their excuse:

"Whatever we the citizens may wish we must consider the men of war in the city who are stronger than we."[1429]

The councillors had King Charles' letter posted up and below it their reply.

In council they read the letter the Maid had dictated at Saint-Phal and entrusted to Friar Richard. The monk had not prepared them to give it a favourable reception, for they laughed at it heartily. "There is no rhyme or reason in it," they said. "'Tis but a jest."[1430] They threw it in the fire without sending a reply. Jeanne was a braggart,[1431] they said. And they added: "We certify her to be mad and possessed of the devil."[1432]

That same day, at nine o'clock in the morning, the army began to march by the walls and take up its position round the town.[1433]

Those who encamped to the south west could thence admire the long walls, the strong gates, the high towers and the belfry of the city rising in the midst of a vast plain. On their right they would see above the roofs the church of Saint-Pierre, the huge structure of which was devoid of tower and steeple.[1434] It was there that eight years before had been celebrated the betrothal of King Henry V of England to the Lady Catherine of France. For in that town of Troyes, Queen Ysabeau and Duke Jean had made King Charles VI, bereft of sense and memory, sign away the Kingdom of the Lilies to the King of England and put his name to the ruin of Charles of Valois. At her daughter's betrothal, Madame Ysabeau was present wearing a robe of blue silk damask and a coat of black velvet lined with the skins of fifteen hundred minevers.[1435] After the ceremony she caused to be brought for her entertainment her singing birds, goldfinches, chaffinches, siskins and linnets.[1436]

When the French arrived, most of the townsfolk were on the ramparts looking more curious than hostile and apparently fearing nothing. They desired above all things to see the King.[1437]

The town was strongly defended. The Duke of Burgundy had long been keeping up the fortifications. In 1417 and 1419 the people of Troyes, like those of Orléans in 1428, had pulled down their suburbs and destroyed all the houses outside the town for two or three hundred paces from the ramparts. The arsenal was well furnished; the stores overflowed with victuals; but the Anglo-Burgundian garrison amounted only to between five and six hundred men.[1438]

On that day also, at five o'clock in the afternoon, the Councillors of the town of Troyes sent to inform the people of Reims of the arrival of the Armagnacs, and despatched to them copies of the letter from Charles of Valois, of their reply to it and of the Maid's letter, which they cannot therefore have burned immediately. They likewise communicated to them their resolution to resist to the death in case they should receive succour. In like manner they wrote to the people of Châlons to tell them of the Dauphin's coming; and to them they made known that the letter of Jeanne the Maid had been brought to Troyes by Friar Richard the preacher.[1439]

These writings amounted to saying: like all citizens in such circumstances, we are in danger of being hanged either by the Burgundians or by the Armagnacs, which would be very grievous. To avoid this calamity as far as in us lies, we give King Charles of Valois to understand that we do not open our gates to him because the garrison prevents us and that we are the weaker, which is true. And we make known to our Lords, the Regent and the Duke of Burgundy, that the garrison being too weak to defend us, which is true, we ask for succour, which is loyal; and we trust that the succour will not be sent, for if it were we should have to endure a siege, and risk being taken by assault which for us merchants would be grievous. But, having asked for succour and not receiving it, we may then surrender without reproach. The important point is to cause the garrison, fortunately a small one, to make off. Five hundred men are too few for defence, but too many for surrender. As for enjoining the citizens of Reims to demand succour for themselves and for us, that is merely to prove our good-will to the Duke of Burgundy; and we risk nothing by it, for we know that our trusty comrades of Reims will take care that when they ask for succour they do not receive it, and that they will await a favourable opportunity for opening their gates to King Charles, who comes with a strong army. And now to conclude, we will resist to the death if we are succoured, which God forbid!

Such were the crafty thoughts of those dwellers in Champagne. The citizens fired a few stone bullets on to the French. The garrison skirmished awhile and returned into the town.[1440]

Meanwhile King Charles' army was stricken with famine.[1441] The Archbishop of Embrun's counsel to provide the army with victuals by means of human wisdom was easier to give than to follow. There were between six and seven thousand men in camp who had not broken bread for a week. The men-at-arms were reduced to feeding on pounded ears of corn still green and on the new beans they found in abundance. Then they called to mind how during Saint Martin's Lent Friar Richard had said to the folk of Troyes: "Sow beans broadcast: He who is to come shall come shortly." What the good brother had said of the spiritual seed-time was interpreted literally: by a curious misunderstanding, what had been uttered concerning the coming of the Messiah was applied to the coming of King Charles. Friar Richard was held to be the prophet of the Armagnacs and the men-at-arms really believed that this evangelical preacher had caused the beans they gathered to grow; thus had he provided for their nourishment by his excellence, his wisdom and his penetration into the counsels of God, who gave manna unto the people of Israel in the desert.[1442]

The King, who had been lodging at Brinion since the 4th of July, arrived before Troyes in the afternoon of Friday the 8th.[1443] That very day he held council of war with the commanders and princes of the blood to decide whether they should remain before the town until by dint of promises[1444] or threats they obtained its submission, or whether they should pass on, leaving it to itself, as they had done at Auxerre.[1445]

The discussion had lasted long when the Maid arrived and prophesied:

"Fair Dauphin," said she, "command your men to attack the town of Troyes and delay no further in councils too prolonged, for, in God's name, before three days, I will cause you to enter the town, which shall be yours by love or by force and courage. And false Burgundy shall look right foolish."[1446]

Wherefore had they contrary to their custom summoned her to the Council? It was merely a question of firing a few cannon balls and pretending to scale the walls, in short, of making a false attack. Such a feigned assault was due to the people of Troyes, who could not decently surrender save to some display of force; and besides the lower orders must be frightened, for they remained at heart

Burgundian. Probably my Lord of Trèves[1447] or another judged that the little Saint by appearing beneath the ramparts of Troyes would strike a religious terror into the weavers of the city.

They had only to leave her to go her own way. The Council over, she mounted her horse, and lance in hand hurried to the moat, followed by a crowd of knights, squires, and craftsmen.[1448] The point of attack was to be the north west wall, between the Madeleine and the Comporté Gates.[1449] Jeanne, who firmly believed that the town would be taken by her, spent the night inciting her people to bring faggots and put the artillery in position. "To the assault," she cried, and signed to them to throw hurdles into the trenches.[1450]

This threat had the desired effect. The lower orders, imagining the town already taken, and expecting the French to come to pillage, massacre and ravish, as was the custom, took refuge in the churches. As for the clerics and notables, this was just what they wanted.[1451]

Being assured by Charles of Valois that they might come to him in safety, the Lord Bishop Jean Laiguisé, my Lord Guillaume Andouillette, Master of the Hospital, the Dean of the Chapter, the clergy and the notables went to the King.[1452]

Jean Laiguisé was the spokesman. He came to do homage to the King and to offer excuse for the townsfolk.

It is not their fault, he said, if the King enter not according to his good pleasure. The Bailie and those of the garrison, some three or four hundred, guard the gates, and forbid their being opened. Let it please the King to have patience until I have spoken to those of the town. I trust that as soon as I have spoken to them, they will open the gates and render the King such obedience as he shall be pleased withal.[1453]

In replying to the Bishop, the King set forth the reasons for the expedition and the rights he held over the town of Troyes.

Without exception, he said, I will forgive all the deeds of past times, and, according to the example of Saint Louis,[1454] I will maintain the people of Troyes in peace and liberty.

Jean Laiguisé demanded that such revenues and patronage as had been bestowed on churchmen by the late King, Charles VI, should be retained by them, and that those who had received the same from King Henry of England should be given charters by King Charles authorizing them to keep their benefices, even in cases where the King had bestowed them on others.

The King consented and the Lord Bishop beheld in him a new Cyrus. This conference he reported to the Council of the Town. Thereupon it deliberated and resolved to render allegiance to the King, in consideration of his legal right and provided he would grant an amnesty for all offences, would leave no garrison in the city and would abolish all aids, save the *gabelle*.[1455] Whereupon the Council sent letters to the citizens of Reims making known to them this resolution and exhorting them to take a similar one:

"Thus," they said, "we shall have the same lord over us. You will keep your lives and your goods, as we have done. For otherwise we should all be lost. We do not regret our submission. Our only grief is that we delayed so long. You will be right glad to follow our example; for King Charles is a prince of greater discretion, understanding and valour than any who for many a long year have arisen in the noble house of France."[1456]

Friar Richard went to find the Maid. As soon as he saw her, and when he was still afar off, he knelt before her. When she saw him, she likewise knelt before him, and they bowed low to each other. When he returned to the town, the good Friar preached to the folks at length and exhorted them to obey King Charles. "God is preparing his way," he said. "To accompany him and to lead him to his anointing God hath sent him a holy Maid, who, as I firmly believe, is as able to penetrate the mysteries of God as any saint in Paradise, save Saint John the Evangelist."[1457] The good Brother found himself obliged to recognise as superior to Jeanne at least one saint, – one who was the first of saints, the apostle who had lain with his head on Jesus' breast, the prophet who was ere long to return to earth, when the ages should have been consummated.

"If she wished," continued Friar Richard, "she could bring in all the King's men-at-arms, over the walls or in any other manner that pleased her. And many other things can she do."

The townsfolk had great faith and confidence in this good Brother who spoke so eloquently. What he said of the Maid appeared to them admirable, and won their obedience to a king so powerfully accompanied. With one voice they all cried aloud, "Long live King Charles of France!"[1458]

But now it was necessary to treat with the Bailie. He was not unapproachable, seeing that he had suffered this going and coming from the town to the camp and the camp to the town; and with him

293

must be devised some honest means of getting rid of the garrison. With this object the commonalty, preceded by the Lord Bishop, went in great numbers to the Bailie and the Captains, and called upon them to provide for the safety of the town.[1459] This demand they were incapable of granting, for to safeguard a city against its will and to drive out thirty thousand French was beyond their power.

As the townsfolk had anticipated, the Bailie was greatly embarrassed. Beholding his perplexity, the Councillors of the town said to him, "If you will not keep the treaty you have made for the public weal, then will we bring the King's men into the city, whether you will or no."

The Bailie and the Captains refused to betray their English and Burgundian masters, but they consented to go. That was all that was required of them.[1460]

The town opened its gates to Charles. On Sunday, the 10th of July, very early in the morning, the Maid entered first into Troyes and with her the common folk whom she so dearly loved. Friar Richard accompanied her. She posted archers along the streets which the procession was to follow, so that the King of France should pass through the town between a double row of those foot soldiers of his army who had so nobly aided him.[1461]

While Charles of Valois was entering by one gate, the Burgundian garrison was going out by the other.[1462] As had been agreed, the men of King Henry and Duke Philip bore away their arms and other possessions. Now, in their possessions they included such French prisoners as they were holding to ransom. And, according to the use and custom of war, it would seem that they were not altogether wrong; but pitiful it was to see King Charles's men led away captive just as their lord was arriving. The Maid heard of it, and her kind heart was touched. She hurried to the gate of the town, where with arms and baggage the fighting men were assembled. She found there the lords of Rochefort and Philibert de Moslant. She challenged them and called to them to leave the Dauphin's men. But the Captains thought otherwise.

"Thus to proceed against the treaty is fraudulent and wicked," they said to her.

Meanwhile the prisoners on their knees were entreating the Saint to keep them.

"In God's name," she cried, "they shall not go."[1463]

During this altercation there was standing apart a certain Burgundian squire, and through his mind were passing concerning the Maid of the Armagnacs certain reflections to which he was to give utterance later. "By my faith," he was thinking, "it is the simplest creature that ever I saw. There is neither rhyme nor reason in her, no more than in the greatest stupid. To so valiant a woman as Madame d'Or, I will not compare her, and the Burgundians do but jest when they appear afraid of her."[1464]

To taste the full flavour of this joke it must be explained that Madame d'Or, about as high as one's boot, held the office of fool to my Lord Philip.[1465]

The Maid failed to come to an understanding with the Lords de Rochefort and de Moslant concerning the prisoners. They had right on their side. She had only the promptings of her kind heart. This discussion afforded great entertainment to the men-at-arms of both parties. When King Charles was informed of it, he smiled and said that to settle the dispute he would pay the prisoners' ransom, which was fixed at one silver mark per head. On receiving this sum the Burgundians extolled the generosity of the King of France.[1466]

On that same Sunday, about nine o'clock in the morning, King Charles entered the city. He had put on his festive robes, gleaming with velvet, with gold, and with precious stones. The Duke of Alençon and the Maid, holding her banner in her hand, rode at his side. He was followed by all the knighthood. The townsfolk lit bonfires and danced in rings. The little children cried, "Noël!" Friar Richard preached.[1467]

The Maid prayed in the churches. In one church she held a babe over the baptismal font. Like a princess or a holy woman, she was frequently asked to be godmother to children she did not know and was never to see again. She generally named the children Charles in honour of the King, and to the girls she gave her own name of Jeanne. Sometimes she called the children by names chosen by their mothers.[1468]

On the morrow, the 11th of July, the army, which had remained outside the walls, under the command of Messire Ambroise de Loré, passed through the town. The entrance of men-at-arms was a scourge, of which the citizens were as much afraid as of the Black Death.[1469] King Charles, being careful to spare the citizens, took measures to control this scourge. By his command the heralds cried that under pain of hanging no soldier must enter the houses or take anything against the will of the townsfolk.[1470]

CHAPTER XVIII

THE SURRENDER OF CHÂLONS AND OF REIMS – THE CORONATION

EAVING Troyes, the royal army entered into the poorer part of Champagne, crossed the Aube near Arcis, and took up its quarters at Lettrée, twelve and a half miles from Châlons. From Lettrée the King sent his herald Montjoie to the people of Châlons to ask them to receive him and render him obedience.[1471]

The towns of Champagne were as closely related as the fingers of one hand. When the Dauphin was at Brinion-l'Archevêque, the people of Châlons had heard of it from their friends of Troyes. The latter had even told them that Friar Richard, the preacher, had brought them a letter from Jeanne the Maid. Whereupon the folk of Châlons wrote to those of Reims:

"We are amazed at Friar Richard. We esteemed him a man right worthy. But he has turned sorcerer. We announce unto you that the citizens of Troyes are making war against the Dauphin's men. We are resolved to resist the enemy with all our strength."[1472]

They thought not one word of what they wrote, and they knew that the citizens of Reims would believe none of it. But it was important to display great loyalty to the Duke of Burgundy before receiving another master.

The Count Bishop of Châlons came out to Lettrée to meet the King and gave up to him the keys of the town. He was Jean de Montbéliard-Saarbrück, one of the Sires of Commercy.[1473]

On the 14th of July the King and his army entered the town of Châlons.[1474] There the Maid found four or five peasants from her village come to see her, and with them Jean Morel, who was her kinsman. By calling a husbandman, and about forty-three years of age, he had fled with the d'Arc family to Neufchâteau on the passing of the men-at-arms. Jeanne gave him a red gown which she had worn.[1475] At Châlons also she met another husbandman, younger than Morel by about ten years, Gérardin from Épinal, whom she called her *compeer*,[1476] just as she called Gérardin's wife Isabellette her *commère*[1477] because she had held their son Nicolas over the baptismal font and because a godmother is a mother in the spirit. At home in the village Jeanne mistrusted Gérardin because he was a Burgundian. At Châlons she showed more confidence in him and talked to him of the progress of the army, saying that she feared nothing except treason.[1478] Already she had dark forebodings; doubtless she felt that henceforth the frankness of her soul and the simplicity of her mind would be hardly assailed by the wickedness of men and the confusing forces of circumstance. Already the words of Saint Michael, Saint Catherine and Saint Margaret had lost some of their primitive clearness, for they had come to treat of those French and Burgundian state secrets which were not heavenly matters.

The people of Châlons, following the example of their friends of Troyes, wrote to the inhabitants of Reims that they had received the King of France and that they counselled them to do likewise. In this letter they said they had found King Charles kind, gracious, pitiful, and merciful; and of a truth the King was dealing leniently with the towns of Champagne. The people of Châlons added that he had a great mind and a fine bearing.[1479] That was saying much.

The citizens of Reims acted with extreme caution. On the arrival of the King of France in the neighbourhood of the town, while they sent informing him that their gates should be opened to him, to their Lord Philip and likewise to the Burgundians and English captains, they sent word of the progress of the royal army as far as they knew it, and called upon them to oppose the enemy's march.[1480] But they were in no hurry to obtain succour, reckoning that, should they receive none, they could surrender to King Charles without incurring any censure from the Burgundians, and that thus they would have nothing to fear from either party. For the moment they preserved their loyalty to the two sides, which was wise in circumstances so difficult and so dangerous. While observing the craft with which these towns of Champagne practised the art of changing masters, it is well to remember that their lives and possessions depended on their knowledge of that art.

As early as the 1st of July Captain Philibert de Moslant wrote to them from Nogent-sur-Seine, where he was with his Burgundian company, that if they needed him he would come to their help like a good Christian.[1481] They feigned not to understand. After all, the Lord Philibert was not their captain. What he proposed to do was, as he said, only out of Christian charity. The notables of Reims, who did not wish for deliverance, had to beware, above all, of their natural deliverer, the Sire de Chastillon, Grand Steward of France, the commander of the town.[1482] And they must needs request help in such a manner as not to obtain their request, for fear of being like the Israelites, of whom it is written: *Et tribuit eis petitionem eorum.*

When the royal army was yet before the walls of Troyes, a herald appeared at the gates of Reims, bearing a letter given by the King, at Brinion-l'Archevêque, on Monday, the 4th of July. This letter was delivered to the Council. "You may have heard tidings," said the King to his good people of Reims, "of the success and victory it hath pleased God to vouchsafe unto us over our ancient enemies, the English, before the town of Orléans and since then at Jargeau, Beaugency, and Meung-sur-Loire, in each of which places our enemies have received grievous hurt; all their leaders and others to the number of four thousand have been slain or taken prisoners. Such things having happened, more by divine grace than human skill, we, according to the advice of our Princes of the Blood and the members of our Great Council, are coming to the town of Reims to receive our anointing and coronation. Wherefore we summon you, on the loyalty and obedience you owe us, to dispose yourselves to receive us in the accustomed manner as you have done for our predecessors."[1483]

And King Charles, adopting towards the citizens of Reims that same wise benignity he had shown to the citizens of Troyes, promised them full pardon and oblivion.

"Be not deterred," he said, "by matters that are past and the fear that we may remember them. Be assured that if now ye act towards us as ye ought, ye shall be dealt with as becometh good and loyal subjects."

He even asked them to send notables to treat with him. "If, in order to be better informed concerning our intentions, certain citizens of Reims would come to us with the herald, whom we send, we should be well pleased. They may come in safety and in such numbers as shall seem good to them."[1484]

On the delivery of this letter the Council was convoked, but it so befell that there were not enough aldermen to deliberate; hence the Council was relieved from a serious embarrassment. Whereupon the common folk were assembled in the various quarters of the city, and from the citizens thus consulted was obtained the following crafty declaration: "It is our intention to live and die with the Council and the Notables. According to their advice we shall act in concord and in peace, without murmuring or making answer, unless it be by the counsel and decree of the Commander of Reims and his Lieutenant."[1485]

The Sire de Chastillon, Commander of the town, was then at Château-Thierry with his lieutenants, Jean Cauchon and Thomas de Bazoches, both of them knights. The citizens of Reims deemed it wise that he should see King Charles's letter. Their Bailie, Guillaume Hodierne, went to the Lord Captain and showed it to him. Most faithfully did the Bailie express the sentiments of the people of Reims: he asked the Sire de Chastillon to come to their deliverance, but he asked in such a manner that he did not come. That was the all-important point; for by not appealing to him they laid themselves open to a charge of treason, while if he did come they risked having to endure a siege grievous and dangerous.

With this object the Bailie declared that the citizens of Reims, desirous to communicate with their captains, were willing to receive him if he were accompanied by no more than fifty horse. Herein they displayed their good will, being entitled to refuse to receive a garrison within their walls; this privilege notwithstanding, they consented to admit fifty horse, which meant about two hundred fighting men. As the citizens had foreseen, the Sire de Chastillon judged such a number insufficient for his safety. He demanded as the conditions of his coming, that the town should be victualled and put in a state of defence, that he should enter it with three or four hundred combatants, that the defence of the city as well as of the castle should be entrusted to him, and that there should be delivered up to him five or six notables as hostages. On these conditions he declared himself ready to live and die for them.[1486]

He marched with his company to within a short distance of the town, and then made known to the townsfolk that he had come to succour them.[1487]

The English were indeed recruiting troops wherever they could and pressing all manner of folk into their service. They were said to be arming even priests; and the Regent was certainly pressing into his service the crusaders disembarked in France, whom the Cardinal of Winchester was intending to lead against the Hussites.[1488] As we may imagine, King Henry's Council did not fail to inform the inhabitants of Reims of the armaments which were being assembled. On the 3rd of July they were told that the troops were crossing the sea, and on the 10th Colard de Mailly, Bailie of Vermandois, announced that they had landed. But these tidings failed to inspire the folk of Champagne with any great confidence in the power of the English. While the Sire de Chastillon was promising that in forty days they should have a fine large army from beyond the seas, King Charles with thirty thousand combatants was but a few miles from their gates. The Sire de Chastillon perceived, what he had previously suspected, that he was tricked. The citizens of Reims refused to admit him. Nothing remained for him but to turn round and join the English.[1489]

On the 12th of July, from my Lord Regnault de Chartres, Archbishop and Duke of Reims, the townsfolk received a letter requesting them to make ready for the King's coming.[1490]

The Council of the city having assembled on that day, the clerk proceeded to draw up an official report of its deliberations:

"... After having represented to my Lord of Chastillon that he is the Commander and that the lords and the mass of the people who...."[1491]

He wrote no more. Finding it difficult to protest their loyalty to the English while making ready King Charles's coronation, and considering it imprudent to recognize a new prince without being forced to it, the citizens abruptly renounced the silver of speech and took refuge in the gold of silence.

On Saturday, the 16th, King Charles took up his quarters in the Castle of Sept-Saulx, ten miles from the city where he was to be crowned. This fortress had been erected two hundred years before by the warlike predecessors of my Lord Regnault. Its proud keep commanded the crossing of the Vesle.[1492] There the King received the citizens of Reims, who came in great numbers to do him homage.[1493] Then, with the Maid and his whole army, he resumed his march. Having traversed the last stage of the highroad which wound along the bank of the Vesle, he entered the great city of Champagne at nightfall.

The southern gate, called Dieulimire, lowered its drawbridge and raised its two portcullises to let him pass.[1494]

Charles VII, King of France
(from an old engraving)

According to tradition the coronation should take place on a Sunday. This rule was found mentioned in a ceremonial which was believed to have served for the coronation of Louis VIII and was considered authoritative.[1495] The citizens of Reims worked all night in order that everything might be ready on the morrow.[1496] They were urged on by their sudden affection for the King of France and likewise by their fear lest he and his army[1497] should spend many days in their city. Their horror of receiving and maintaining men-at-arms within their gates they shared with the citizens of all towns, who in their panic were incapable of distinguishing Armagnac soldiers from English and Burgundians. Wherefore in all things were they diligent, but with the firm intention of paying as little as possible. Seeing that to them the coronation brought neither profit nor honour, the aldermen were accustomed to throw the burden of it on the Archbishop, who, they said, as peer of France,[1498] would receive the emoluments.

The royal ornaments, which, after the coronation of the late King, had been deposited in the sacristy of Saint-Denys, were in the hands of the English. The crown of Charlemagne, brilliant with rubies, sapphires and emeralds, adorned with four flowers-de-luce, which the Kings of France received on their coronation, the English wished to place on the head of their King Henry. This child King they were preparing to gird with the sword of Charlemagne, the illustrious Joyeuse, which in its sheath of violet velvet slept in the keeping of the Burgundian Abbot of Saint-Denys. In English hands likewise were the sceptre surmounted by a golden Charlemagne in imperial robes, the rod of justice terminated by a hand in horn of unicorn, the golden clasp of Saint Louis' mantle, and the golden spurs and the Pontifical, containing within its enamelled binding of silver-gilt the ceremonial of the coronation.[1499] The French must needs make shift with a crown kept in the sacristy of the cathedral.[1500] The other signs of royalty handed down from Clovis, from Saint Charlemagne and Saint Louis must be represented as well as could be. After all, it was not unfitting that this coronation, won by a single expedition, should be expressive of the labour and suffering it had cost. It was well that the ceremony should suggest something of the heroic poverty of the men-at-arms and the common folk who had brought the Dauphin thither.

Kings were anointed with oil, because oil signifies renown, glory, and wisdom. In the morning the Sires de Rais, de Boussac, de Graville and de Culant were deputed by the King to go and fetch the Holy Ampulla.[1501]

It was a crystal flask which the Grand Prior of Saint-Remi kept in the tomb of the Apostle, behind the high altar of the Abbey Church. This flask contained the sacred chrism with which the Blessed Remi had anointed King Clovis. It was enclosed in a reliquary in the form of a dove, because the Holy Ghost in the semblance of a dove had been seen descending with the oil for the anointing of the first Christian King.[1502] Of a truth in ancient books it was written that an angel had come down from heaven with the miraculous ampulla,[1503] but men were not disturbed by such inconsistencies, and among Christian folk no one doubted that the sacred chrism was possessed of miraculous power. For example, it was known that with use the oil became no less, that the flask remained always full, as a premonition and a pledge that the kingdom of France would endure for ever. According to the observation of witnesses, at the time of the coronation of the late King Charles, the oil had not diminished after the anointing.[1504]

At nine o'clock in the morning Charles of Valois entered the church with a numerous retinue. The king-at-arms of France called by name the twelve peers of the realm to come before the high altar. Of the six lay peers not one replied. In their places came the Duke of Alençon, the Counts of Clermont and of Vendôme, the Sires de Laval, de La Trémouille, and de Maillé.

Of the six ecclesiastical peers, three replied to the summons of the king-at-arms, – the Archbishop Duke of Reims, the Bishop Count of Châlons, the Bishop Duke of Laon. For the missing bishops of Langres and Noyon were substituted those of Seez and Orléans. In the absence of Arthur of Brittany, Constable of France, the sword was held by Charles, Sire d'Albret.[1505]

In front of the altar was Charles of Valois, wearing robes open on the chest and shoulders. He swore, first, to maintain the peace and privileges of the Church; second, to preserve his people from exactions and not to burden them too heavily; third, to govern with justice and mercy.[1506]

From his cousin d'Alençon he received the arms of a knight.[1507] Then the Archbishop anointed him with the holy oil, with which the Holy Ghost makes strong priests, kings, prophets and martyrs. So this new Samuel consecrated the new Saul, making manifest that all power is of God, and that, according to the example set by David, kings are pontiffs, the ministers and the witnesses of the Lord. This pouring out of the oil, with which the Kings of Israel were anointed, had rendered the kings of most Christian France burning and shining lights since the time of Charlemagne, yea, even since the days of Clovis; for though it was baptism and confirmation rather than anointing that Clovis received at the hands of the Blessed Saint Remi, yet he was anointed Christian and King by the blessed bishop, and at the same time and with that same holy oil which God himself had sent to this prince and to his successors.[1508]

And Charles received the anointing, the sign of power and victory, for it is written in the Book of Samuel:[1509] "And Samuel took a vial of oil and poured it upon his head and kissed him, and said, 'Is it not because the Lord hath anointed thee to be captain over his inheritance and to deliver his people from their enemies round about. *Ecce unxit te Dominus super hereditatem suam in principem, et liberabis populum suum de manibus inimicorum ejus, qui in circuitu ejus sunt.*'" (Reg. 1. x. 1. 6.)

During the mystery, as it was called in the old parlance,[1510] the Maid stayed by the King's side. Her white banner, before which the ancient standard of Chandos had retreated, she held for a moment unfurled. Then others in their turn held her standard, her page Louis de Coutes, who never left her, and Friar Richard the preacher, who had followed her to Châlons and to Reims.[1511] In one of her dreams she had lately given a crown to the King; she was looking for this crown to be brought into the church by heavenly messengers.[1512] Did not saints commonly receive crowns from angels' hands? To Saint Cecilia an angel offered a crown with garlands of roses and lilies. To Catherine, the Virgin, an angel gave an imperishable crown, which she placed upon the head of the Empress of Rome. But the crown curiously rich and magnificent that Jeanne looked for came not.[1513]

From the altar the Archbishop took the crown of no great value provided by the chapter, and with both hands raised it over the King's head. The twelve peers, in a circle round the prince, stretched forth their arms to hold it. The trumpets blew and the folk cried: "Noël."[1514]

Thus was anointed and crowned Charles of France issue of the royal line of Priam, great Troy's noble King.

Two hours after noon the mystery came to an end.[1515] We are told that then the Maid knelt low before the King, and, weeping said:

"Fair King, now is God's pleasure accomplished. It was His will that I should raise the siege of Orléans and bring you to this city of

Reims to receive your holy anointing, making manifest that you are the true King and he to whom the realm of France should belong."[1516]

The King made the customary gifts. To the Chapter he presented hangings of green satin as well as ornaments of red velvet and white damask. Moreover, he placed upon the altar a silver vase with thirteen golden crowns. Regardless of the claims asserted by the canons, the Lord Archbishop took possession of it, but it profited him little, for he had to give it up.[1517] After the ceremony King Charles put the crown on his head and over his shoulders the royal mantle, blue as the sky, flowered with lilies of gold; and on his charger he passed down the streets of Reims city. The people in great joy cried, "Noël!" as they had cried when my Lord the Duke of Burgundy entered. On that day the Sire de Rais was made marshal of France and the Sire de la Trémouille count. The eldest of Madame de Laval's two sons, he to whom the Maid had offered wine at Selles-en-Berry, was likewise made count. Captain La Hire received the county of Longueville with such parts of Normandy as he could conquer.[1518]

King Charles dined in the archiepiscopal palace in the ancient hall of Tau, and was served by the Duke of Alençon and the Count of Clermont.[1519] As was customary, the royal table extended into the street, and there was feasting throughout the town. It was a day of free drinking and fraternity. In the houses, at the doors, by the wayside, folk made good cheer, and the kitchens were busy; there were that day consumed oxen in dozens, sheep in hundreds, chicken and rabbits in thousands. Folk stuffed themselves with spices, and (for it was a thirsty day) they quaffed full many a beaker of wine of Burgundy, and especially of that wine of delicate flavour that comes from Beaune. At every coronation the ancient stag, made of bronze and hollow, which stood in the courtyard of the archiepiscopal palace was carried into the Rue du Parvis; it was filled with wine and the people drank from it as from a fountain. Finally the burgesses and all the inhabitants of Blessed Saint Remi's city, rich and poor alike, stuffed and satiated with good wine, having howled "Noël!" till they were hoarse, fell asleep over the wine-casks and the victuals, the remains of which were to be a cause of bitter dispute between the grim aldermen and the King's men on the morrow.[1520]

Jacques d'Arc had come to see the coronation for which his daughter had so zealously laboured. He lodged at the Sign of *L'Ane Rayé* in the Rue du Parvis in a hostelry kept by Alix, widow of Raulin

Morieau. As well as his daughter, he saw once more his son Pierre.[1521] The cousin, whom Jeanne called uncle and who had accompanied her to Vaucouleurs to Sire Robert, had likewise come hither to the coronation. He spoke to the King and told him all he knew of his cousin.[1522] At Reims also Jeanne found her young fellow-countryman, Husson Le Maistre, coppersmith of the village of Varville, about seven miles from Domremy. She did not know him; but he had heard tell of her, and he was very familiar with Jacques and Pierre d'Arc.[1523]

Jacques d'Arc was one of the notables and perhaps the best business man of his village.[1524] It was not merely to see his daughter riding through the streets in man's attire that he had come to Reims. He had come doubtless for himself and on behalf of his village to ask the King for an exemption from taxation. This request, presented to the King by the Maid, was granted. On the 31st of the month the King decreed that the inhabitants of Greux and of Domremy should be free from all *tailles*, aids, subsidies, and subventions.[1525] Out of the public funds the magistrates of the town paid Jacques d'Arc's expenses, and when he was about to depart they gave him a horse to take him home.[1526]

During the five or six days she spent at Reims the Maid appeared frequently before the townsfolk. The poor and humble came to her; good wives took her by the hand and touched their rings with hers.[1527] On her finger she wore a little ring made of a kind of brass, sometimes called electrum.[1528] Electrum was said to be the gold of the poor. In place of a stone the ring had a collet inscribed with the words "Jhesus Maria" with three crosses. Oftentimes she reverently fixed her gaze upon it, for once she had had it touched by Saint Catherine.[1529] And that the Saint should have actually touched it was not incredible, seeing that some years before, in 1413, Sister Colette, who was vowed to virginal chastity, had received from the Virgin apostle a rich golden ring, as a sign of her spiritual marriage with the King of Kings. Sister Colette permitted the nuns and monks of her order to touch this ring, and she confided it to the messengers she sent to distant lands to preserve them from perils by the way.[1530] The Maid ascribed great powers to her ring, albeit she never used it to heal the sick.[1531]

She was expected to render those trifling services which it was usual to ask from holy folk and sometimes from magicians. Before the coronation ceremony the nobles and knights had been given gloves, according to the custom. One of them lost his; he asked the Maid to find them, or others asked her for him. She did not promise to do it; notwithstanding the matter became known, and various interpretations were placed upon it.[1532]

After the King's coronation, jostled by the crowd in the Rue du Parvis, one can imagine some thoughtful clerk raising his eyes to the glorious façade of the Cathedral, that Bible in stone, already appearing ancient to men, who, knowing naught of the chronicles, measured time by the span of human existence. Such a clerk would have certainly beheld on the left of the pointed arch above the rose window the colossal image of Goliath rising proudly in his coat of mail, and that same figure repeated on the right of the arch in the attitude of a man tottering and ready to fall.[1533] Then this clerk must have remembered what is written in the first book of Kings:[1534]

"And there went out a man base-born from the camp of the Philistines, named Goliath, of Geth, whose height was six cubits and a span. And he had a helmet of brass upon his head and he was clothed with a coat of mail with scales; and the weight of his coat of mail was five thousand sicles of brass. And standing he cried out to the bands of Israel and said to them: I bring reproach unto the armies of Israel. Choose out a man of you, and let him come down and fight hand to hand.

"Now David had gone to feed his Father's sheep at Bethlehem. But he arose in the morning and gave the charge of the flock to the keeper. And he came to the place of Magala and to the army which was going out to fight. And, seeing Goliath, he asked: 'Who is this uncircumcised Philistine that he should defy the armies of the living God?'

"And the words which David spoke, were rehearsed before Saul; and he sent for him. David said to Saul, 'Let not any man's heart be dismayed in him; I, thy servant, will go and fight against this Philistine.' And Saul said to David 'Thou art not able to withstand this Philistine nor to fight against him; for thou art but a boy, but he is a warrior from his youth.' And David made answer, 'I will go against him and I will take away the reproach from Israel.' Then Saul said to David, 'Go and the Lord be with thee.'

"And David took his staff which he had always in his hands, and chose him five smooth stones out of the brook, and he took a sling in his hand; and went forth against the Philistine.

"And when the Philistine looked and beheld David, he despised him. For he was a young man, and ruddy, and of a comely countenance. And the Philistine said to David: 'Am I a dog, that thou comest to me with a staff?' Then said David to the Philistine: 'Thou comest to me with a sword, and with a spear and with a shield: but I come to thee in the name of the Lord of Hosts, the God of the armies of Israel, which thou hast defied. This day will the Lord deliver thee into mine hand that all the earth may know that the Lord saveth not with sword and spear: for it is his battle, and he will deliver you into our hands.'

"And when the Philistine arose and was coming and drew nigh to meet David, David made haste and ran to the fight to meet the Philistine. And he put his hand into his scrip and took a stone, and cast it with the sling and fetching it about struck the Philistine in the forehead, and the stone was fixed in his forehead and he fell on his face upon the earth."[1535]

Then the clerk, meditating on these words of the Book, would reflect how God, the Unchanging, who saved Israel and struck down Goliath by the sling of a shepherd lad, had raised up the daughter of a husbandman for the deliverance of the most Christian realm and the reproach of the Leopard.[1536]

From Gien, about June the 27th, the Maid had had a letter written to the Duke of Burgundy, calling upon him to come to the King's anointing. Having received no reply, on the day of the coronation she dictated a second letter to the Duke. Here it is:

Jhesus † Maria

"High and greatly to be feared Prince, Duke of Burgundy, Jehanne the Maid, in the name of the King of Heaven, her rightful and liege lord, requires you and the King of France to make a good peace which shall long endure. Forgive one another heartily and entirely as becometh good Christians; an if it please you to make war, go ye against the Saracens. Prince of Burgundy, I pray you, I entreat you, I beseech you as humbly as lieth in my power, that ye make war no more against the holy realm of France, and that forthwith and speedily ye withdraw those your men who are in any strongholds and fortresses of the said holy kingdom; and in the name of the fair King of France, he is ready to make peace with you, saving his honour if that be necessary. And in the name of the King of Heaven, my Sovereign liege Lord, for your good, your honour and your life, I make known unto you, that ye will never win in battle against the loyal French and that all they who wage war against the holy realm of France, will be warring against King Jhesus, King of Heaven and of the world, my lawful liege lord. And with clasped hands I beseech and entreat you that ye make no battle nor wage war against us, neither you, nor your people, nor your subjects; and be assured that whatever number of folk ye bring against us, they will gain nothing, and it will be sore pity for the great battle and the blood that shall be shed of those that come against us. And three weeks past, I did write and send you letters by a herald, that ye should come to the anointing of the King, which to-day, Sunday, the 17th day of this present month, is made in the city of Reims: to which letter I have had no answer, neither news of the said herald. To God I commend you; may he keep you, if it be his will; and I pray God to establish good peace. Written from the said place of Reims, on the said seventeenth of July."

Addressed: "to the Duke of Burgundy."[1537]

Had Saint Catherine of Sienna been at Reims she would not have written otherwise. Albeit the Maid liked not the Burgundians, in her own way she realized forcibly how desirable was peace with the Duke of Burgundy. With clasped hands she entreats him to cease making war against France. "An it please you to make war then go ye against the Saracens." Already she had counselled the English to join the French and go on a crusade. The destruction of the infidel was then the dream of gentle peace-loving souls; and many pious folk believed that the son of the knight, who had been vanquished at Nicopolis, would make the Turks pay dearly for their former victory.[1538]

In this letter, the Maid, in the name of the King of Heaven, tells Duke Philip that if he fight against the King, he will be conquered. Her voices had foretold to her the victory of France over Burgundy; they had not revealed to her that at the very moment when she was dictating her letter the ambassadors of Duke Philip were at Reims; that was so, notwithstanding.[1539]

Esteeming King Charles, master of Champagne, to be a prince worthy of consideration, Duke Philip sent to Reims, David de Brimeu, Bailie of Artois, at the head of an embassy, to greet him and open negotiations for peace.[1540] The Burgundians received a hearty welcome from the Chancellor and the Council. It was hoped that peace would be concluded before their departure. The Angevin lords announced it to their queens, Yolande and Marie.[1541] By so doing they showed how little they knew the consummate old fox of Dijon. The French were not strong enough yet, neither were the English weak enough. It was agreed that in August an embassy should be sent to the Duke of Burgundy in the town of Arras. After four days negotiation, a truce for fifteen days was signed and the embassy left Reims.[1542] At the same time, the Duke at Paris solemnly renewed his complaint against Charles of Valois, his father's assassin, and undertook to bring an army to the help of the English.[1543]

Leaving Antoine de Hellande, nephew of the Duke-Archbishop[1544] to command Reims, the King of France departed from the city on the 20th of July and went to Saint-Marcoul-de-Corbeny, where on the day after their coronation, the Kings were accustomed to touch for the evil.[1545]

Saint Marcoul cured the evil.[1546] He was of royal race, but his power, manifested long after his death, came to him especially from his name, and it was believed that Saint Marcoul was able to cure those afflicted with marks on the neck, as Saint Clare was to give sight to the blind, and Saint Fort to give strength to children. The King of France shared with him the power of healing scrofula; and as the power came to him from the holy oil brought down from heaven by a dove, it was thought that this virtue would be more effectual at the time of the anointing, all the more because by lewdness, disobedience to the Christian Church, and other irregularities, he stood in danger of losing it. That is what had happened to King Philippe I.[1547] The Kings of England touched for the evil; notably King Edward III worked wondrous cures on scrofulous folk who were covered with scars. For these reasons scrofula was called Saint Marcoul's evil or King's evil. Virgins as well as kings could cure this royal malady.

King Charles worshipped and presented offerings at the shrine of Saint Marcoul, and there touched for the evil. At Corbeny he received the submission of the town of Laon. Then, on the morrow, the 22nd, he went off to a little stronghold in the valley of the Aisne, called Vailly, which belonged to the Archbishop Duke of Reims. At Vailly he received the submission of the town of Soissons.[1548] In the words of an Armagnac prophet of the time: "the keys of the war gates knew the hands that had forged them."[1549]

Chapter XIX
Rise of the Legend

T is always difficult to ascertain what happens in war. In those days it was quite impossible to form any clear idea of how things came about. At Orléans, doubtless, there were certain who were keen enough to perceive that the numerous and ingenious engines of war, gathered together by the magistrates, had been of great service; but folk generally prefer to ascribe results to miraculous causes, and the merit of their deliverance the people of Orléans attributed first to their Blessed Patrons, Saint Aignan and Saint Euverte, and after them to Jeanne, the Divine Maid, believing that there was no easier, simpler, or more natural explanation of the deeds they had witnessed.[1550]

Guillaume Girault, former magistrate of the town and notary at the Châtelet, wrote and signed, with his own hand, a brief account of the deliverance of the city. Herein he states that on Wednesday, Ascension Eve, the bastion of Saint-Loup was stormed and taken as if by miracle, "there being present, and aiding in the fight, Jeanne the Maid, sent of God;" and that, on the following Saturday, the siege laid by the English to Les Tourelles at the end of the bridge was raised by the most obvious miracle since the Passion. And Guillaume Girault testifies that the Maid led the enterprise.[1551] When eye-witnesses, participators in the deeds themselves, had no clear idea of events, what could those more remote from the scene of action think of them?

The tidings of the French victories flew with astonishing rapidity.[1552] The brevity of authentic accounts was amply supplemented by the eloquence of loquacious clerks and the popular imagination. The Loire campaign and the coronation expedition were scarcely known at first save by fabulous reports, and the people only thought of them as supernatural events.

In the letters sent by royal secretaries to the towns of the realm and the princes of Christendom, the name of Jeanne the Maid was associated with all the deeds of prowess. Jeanne herself, by her monastic scribe, made known to all the great deeds which, it was her firm belief, she had accomplished.[1553]

It was believed that everything had been done through her, that the King had consulted her in all things, when in truth the King's counsellors and the Captains rarely asked her advice, listened to it but seldom, and brought her forth only at convenient seasons. Everything was attributed to her alone. Her personality, associated with deeds attested and seemingly marvellous, became buried in a vast cycle of astonishing fables and disappeared in a forest of heroic stories.[1554]

Contrite souls there were in those days, who, ascribing all the woes of the kingdom to the sins of the people, looked for salvation to humility, repentance, and penance.[1555] They expected the end of iniquity and the kingdom of God on earth. Jeanne, at least in the beginning, was one of those pious folk. Sometimes, speaking as a mystic reformer, she would say that Jesus is King of the holy realm of France, that King Charles is his lieutenant, and does but hold the kingdom "in fief."[1556] She uttered words which would create the impression that her mission was all charity, peace, and love, – these, for example, "I am sent to comfort the poor and needy."[1557] Such gentle penitents as dreamed of a world pure, faithful, and good, made of Jeanne their saint and their prophetess. They ascribed to her edifying words she had never uttered.

"When the Maid came to the King," they said, "she caused him to make three promises: the first was to resign his kingdom, to renounce it and give it back to God, from whom he held it; the second, to pardon all such as had turned against him and afflicted him; the third, to humiliate himself so far as to receive into favour all such as should come to him, poor and rich, friend and foe."[1558]

Or again, in apologues, simple and charming, like the following, they represented her accomplishing her mission:

"One day, the Maid asked the King to bestow a present upon her; and when he consented, she claimed as a gift the realm of France. Though astonished, the King did not withdraw his promise. Having received her present, the Maid required a deed of gift to be solemnly drawn up by four of the King's notaries and read aloud. While the King listened to the reading, she pointed him out to those that stood by, saying: 'Behold the poorest knight in the kingdom.' Then, after a short time, disposing of the realm of France, she gave it back to God. Thereafter, acting in God's name, she invested King Charles with it and commanded that this solemn act of transmission should be recorded in writing."[1559]

It was believed that Jeanne had prophesied that on Saint John the Baptist's Day, 1429, not an Englishman should be left in France.[1560] These simple folk expected their saint's promises to be fulfilled on the day she had fixed. They maintained that on the 23rd of June she had entered the city of Rouen, and that on the morrow, Saint John the Baptist's day, the inhabitants of Paris had of their own accord, opened their gates to the King of France. In the month of July these stories were being told in Avignon.[1561] Reformers, numerous it would seem in France and throughout Christendom, believed that the Maid would organise the English and French on monastic lines and make of them one nation of pious beggars, one brotherhood of penitents. According to them, the following were the intentions of the two parties and the clauses of the treaty:

"King Charles of Valois bestows universal pardon and is willing to forget all wrongs. The English and French, having turned to contrition and repentance, are endeavouring to conclude a good and binding peace. The Maid herself has imposed conditions upon them. Conforming to her will, the English and French for one year or for two will wear a grey habit, with a little cross sewn upon it; on every Friday they will live on bread and water; they will dwell in unity with their wives and will seek no other women. They promise God not to make war except for the defence of their country."[1562]

During the coronation campaign, nothing being known of the agreement between the King's men and the people of Auxerre, towards the end of July, it was related that the town having been taken by storm, four thousand five hundred citizens had been killed and likewise fifteen hundred men-at-arms, knights as well as squires belonging to the parties of Burgundy and Savoy. Among the nobles slain were mentioned Humbert Maréchal, Lord of Varambon, and a very famous warrior, le Viau de Bar. Stories were told of treasons and massacres, horrible adventures in which the Maid was associated with that knave of hearts who was already famous. She was said to have had twelve traitors beheaded.[1563] Such tales were real romances of chivalry. Here is one of them:

About two thousand English surrounded the King's camp, watching to see if they could do him some hurt. Then the Maid called Captain La Hire and said to him: "Thou hast in thy time done great prowess, but to-day God prepares for thee a deed greater than any thou hast yet performed. Take thy men and go to such and such a wood two leagues herefrom, and there shalt thou find two thousand English, all lance in hand; them shalt thou take and slay."

La Hire went forth to the English and all were taken and slain as the Maid had said.[1564]

Such were the fairy-stories told of Jeanne to the joy of simple primitive folk, who delighted in the idea of a maid slayer of giants and remover of mountains.

There was a rumour that after the sack of Auxerre, the Duke of Burgundy had been defeated and taken in a great battle, that the Regent was dead and that the Armagnacs had entered Paris.[1565] Prodigies were said to have attended the capitulation of Troyes. On the coming of the French, it was told how the townsfolk beheld from their ramparts a vast multitude of men-at-arms, some five or six thousand, each man holding a white pennon in his hand. On the departure of the French, they beheld them again, ranged but a bow-shot behind King Charles. These knights with white pennons vanished when the King had gone; for they were as miraculous as those white-scarfed knights, whom the Bretons had seen riding in the sky but shortly before.[1566]

All that the people of Orléans beheld when their siege was suddenly raised, all that Armagnac mendicants and the Dauphin's clerks related was greedily received, accredited, and amplified. Three months after her coming to Chinon, Jeanne had her legend, which grew and increased and extended into Italy, Flanders, and Germany.[1567] In the summer of 1429, this legend was already formed. All the scattered parts of what may be described as the gospel of her childhood existed.

At the age of seven Jeanne kept sheep; the wolves did not molest her flock; the birds of the field, when she called them, came and ate bread from her lap. The wicked had no power over her. No one beneath her roof need fear man's fraud or ill-will.[1568]

When it is a Latin poet who is writing, the miracles attending Jeanne's birth assume a Roman majesty and are clothed with the august dignity of ancient myths. Thus it is curious to find a humanist of 1429 summoning the Italian muse to the cradle of Zabillet Romée's daughter.

"The thunder rolled, the ocean shuddered, the earth shook, the heavens were on fire, the universe rejoiced visibly; a strange transport mingled with fear moved the enraptured nations. They sing sweet verses and dance in harmonious motion at the sign of the salvation prepared for the French people by this celestial birth."[1569]

Moreover an attempt was made to represent the wonders that had heralded the nativity of Jesus as having been repeated on the birth of Jeanne. It was imagined that she was born on the night of the Epiphany. The shepherds of her village, moved by an indescribable joy, the cause of which was unknown to them, hastened through the darkness towards the marvellous mystery. The cocks, heralds of this new joy, sing at an unusual season and, flapping their wings, seem to prophesy for two hours. Thus the child in her cradle had her adoration of the shepherds.[1570]

Of her coming into France there was much to tell. It was related that in the Château of Chinon she had recognised the King, whom she had never seen before, and had gone straight to him, although he was but poorly clad and surrounded by his baronage.[1571] It was said that she had given the King a sign, that she had revealed a secret to him; and that on the revelation of the secret, known to him alone, he had been illuminated with a heavenly joy. Concerning this interview at Chinon, while those present had little to say, the stories of many who were not there were interminable.[1572]

On the 7th of May, at four o'clock in the afternoon, a white dove alighted on the Maid's standard; and on the same day, during the assault, two white birds were seen to be flying over her head.[1573] Saints were commonly visited by doves. One day when Saint Catherine of Sienna was kneeling in the fuller's house, a dove as white as snow perched on the child's head.[1574]

A tale then in circulation is interesting as showing the idea which prevailed concerning the relations of the King and the Maid; it serves, likewise, as an example of the perversions to which the story of an actual fact is subject as it passes from mouth to mouth. Here is the tale as it was gathered by a German merchant.

On a day, in a certain town, the Maid, hearing that the English were near, went into the field; and straightway all the men-at-arms, who were in the town, leapt to their steeds and followed her.

Meanwhile, the King, who was at dinner, learning that all were going forth in company with the Maid, had the gates of the town closed.

The Maid was told, and she replied without concern: "Before the hour of nones, the King will have so great need of me, that he will follow me immediately, spurless, and barely staying to throw on his cloak."

And thus it came to pass. For the men-at-arms shut up in the town besought the King to open the gates forthwith or they would break them down. The gates were opened and all the fighting men hastened to the Maid, heedless of the King, who threw on his cloak and followed them.

On that day a great number of the English were slain.[1575]

Such is the story which gives a very inaccurate representation of what happened at Orléans on the 6th of May. The citizens hastened in crowds to the Burgundian Gate, resolved to cross the Loire and attack Les Tourelles. Finding the gate closed, they threw themselves furiously on the Sire de Gaucourt who was keeping it. The aged baron had the gate opened wide and said to them, "Come, I will be your captain."[1576] In the story the citizens have become men-at-arms, and it is not the Sire de Gaucourt but the King who maliciously closes the gates. But the King gained nothing by it; and it is astonishing to find that so early there had grown up in the minds of the people the idea that, far from aiding the Maid to drive out the English, the King had put obstacles in her way and was always the last to follow her.

Seen through this chaos of stories more indistinct than the clouds in a stormy sky, Jeanne appeared a wondrous marvel. She prophesied and many of her prophecies had already been fulfilled. She had foretold the deliverance of Orléans and Orléans had been delivered. She had prophesied that she would be wounded, and an arrow had pierced her above the right breast. She had prophesied that she would take the King to Reims, and the King had been crowned in that city. Other prophecies had she uttered touching the realm of France, to wit, the deliverance of the Duke of Orléans, the entering into Paris, the driving of the English from the holy kingdom, and their fulfilment was expected.[1577]

Every day she prophesied and notably concerning divers persons who had failed in respect towards her and had come to a bad end.[1578]

At Chinon, when she was being taken to the King, a man-at-arms who was riding near the château, thinking he recognised her, asked,

"Is not that the Maid? By God, an I had my way she should not be a maid long."

Then Jeanne prophesied and said "Ha, thou takest God's name in vain, and thou art so near thy death!"

Less than an hour later the man fell into the water and was drowned.[1579]

Straightway this miracle was related in Latin verse. In the poem which records this miraculous history of Jeanne up to the deliverance of Orléans, the lewd blasphemer, who like all blasphemers, came to a bad end, is noble and by name Furtivolus.[1580]

> *... generoso sanguine natus,*
> *Nomine Furtivolus, veneris moderator iniquus.*

Captain Glasdale called Jeanne strumpet and blasphemed his Maker. Jeanne prophesied that he would die without shedding blood; and Glasdale was drowned in the Loire.[1581]

Many of these tales were obvious imitations of incidents in the lives of the saints, which were widely read in those days. A woman, who was a heretic, pulled the cassock of Saint Ambrose, whereupon the blessed bishop said to her, "Take heed lest one day thou be chastised of God." On the morrow the woman died, and the Blessed Ambrose conducted her to the grave.[1582]

A nun, who was then alive and who was to die in an odour of sanctity, Sister Colette of Corbie, had met her Furtivolus and had punished him, but less severely. On a day when she was praying in a church of Corbie, a stranger drew near and spoke to her libidinous words: "May it please God," she said, "to bring home to you the hideousness of the words you have just uttered." The stranger in shame went to the door. But an invisible hand arrested him on the threshold. Then he realised the gravity of his sin; he asked pardon of the saint and was free to leave the church.[1583]

After the royal army had departed from Gien, the Maid was said to have prophesied that a great battle would be fought between Auxerre and Reims.[1584] When such predictions were not fulfilled they were forgotten. Besides, it was admitted that true prophets might sometimes utter false prophecies. A subtle theologian distinguished between prophecies of predestination which are always fulfilled and those of condemnation, which being conditioned, may not be fulfilled and that without reflecting untruthfulness on the lips that uttered them.[1585] Folk wondered that a peasant child should be able to forecast the future, and with the Apostle they cried, "I praise thee, O Father, because thou hast hidden those things from the wise and prudent and revealed them unto babes."

The Maid's prophecies were speedily spread abroad throughout the whole of Christendom.[1586] A clerk of Spiers wrote a treatise on her, entitled *Sibylla Francica*, divided into two parts. The first part was drawn up not later than July, 1429. The second is dated the 17th of September, the same year. This clerk believes that the Maid practised the art of divination by means of astrology. He had heard a French monk of the order of the Premonstratensians[1587] say that Jeanne delighted to study the heavens by night. He observes that all her prophecies concerned the kingdom of France; and he gives the following as having been uttered by the Maid: "After having ruled for twenty years, the Dauphin will sleep with his fathers. After him, his eldest son, now a child of six, will reign more gloriously, more honourably, more powerfully than any King of France since Charlemagne."[1588]

The Maid possessed the gift of beholding events which were taking place far away.

At Vaucouleurs, on the very day of the Battle of the Herrings, she knew the Dauphin's army had suffered grievous hurt.[1589]

On a day when she was dining, seated near the King, she began to laugh quietly. The King, perceiving, asked her: "My beloved, wherefore laugh ye so merrily?"

She made answer that she would tell him when the repast was over. And, when the ewer was brought her, "Sire," she said, "this day have been drowned in the sea five hundred English, who were crossing to your land to do you hurt. Therefore did I laugh. In three days you will know that it is true."

And so it was.[1590]

Another time, when she was in a town some miles distant from the château where the King was, as she prayed before going to sleep, it was revealed to her that certain of the King's enemies wished to poison him at dinner. Straightway she called her brothers and sent them to the King to advise him to take no food until she came.

When she appeared before him, he was at table surrounded by eleven persons.

"Sire," she said, "have the dishes brought."

She gave them to the dogs, who ate from them and died forthwith.

Then, pointing to a knight, who was near the King and to two other guests: "Those persons," she said, "wished to poison you."

The knight straightway confessed that it was true; and he was dealt with according to his deserts.[1591]

It was borne in upon her that a certain priest kept a concubine;[1592] and one day, meeting in the camp a woman dressed as a man, it was revealed to her that the woman was pregnant and that having already had one child she had made away with it.[1593]

She was likewise said to possess the power of discovering things hidden. She herself had claimed this power when she was at Tours. It had been revealed to her that a sword was buried in the ground in the chapel of Saint Catherine of Fierbois, and that was the sword she wore. Some deemed it to be the sword with which Charles Martel had defeated the Saracens. Others suspected it of being the sword of Alexander the Great.[1594]

In like manner it was said that before the coronation Jeanne had known of a precious crown, hidden from all eyes. And here is the story told concerning it:

A bishop kept the crown of Saint Louis. No one knew which bishop it was, but it was known that the Maid had sent him a messenger, bearing a letter in which she asked him to give up the crown. The bishop replied that the Maid was dreaming. A second time she demanded the sacred treasure, and the bishop made the same reply. Then she wrote to the citizens of the episcopal city, saying that if the crown were not given up to the King, the Lord would punish the town, and straightway there fell so heavy a storm of hail that all men marvelled. Wizards commonly caused hail storms. But this time the hail was a plague sent by the God who afflicted Egypt with ten plagues. After which the Maid despatched to the citizens a third letter in which she described the form and fashion of the crown the bishop was hiding, and warned them that if it were not given up even worse things would happen to them. The bishop, who believed that the wondrous circlet of gold was known to him alone, marvelled that the form and fashion thereof should be described in this letter. He repented of his wickedness, wept many tears, and commanded the crown to be sent to the King and the Maid.[1595]

It is not difficult to discern the origin of this story. The crown of Charlemagne, which the kings of France wore at the coronation ceremony, was at Saint-Denys in France, in the hands of the English. Jeanne boasted of having given the Dauphin at Chinon a precious crown, brought by angels. She said that this crown had been sent to Reims for the coronation, but that it did not arrive in time.[1596] As for the hiding of the crown by the bishop, that idea arose probably from the well-known cupidity of my Lord Regnault de Chartres, Archbishop of Reims, who had appropriated the silver vase intended for the chapter and placed by the King upon the high altar after the ceremony.[1597]

There was likewise talk of gloves lost at Reims and of a cup that Jeanne had found.[1598]

Maiden, at once a warrior and a lover of peace, *béguine*, prophetess, sorceress, angel of the Lord, ogress, every man beholds her according to his own fashion, creates her according to his own image. Pious souls clothe her with an invincible charm and the divine gift of charity; simple souls make her simple too; men gross and violent figure her a giantess, burlesque and terrible. Shall we ever discern the true features of her countenance? Behold her, from the first and perhaps for ever enclosed in a flowering thicket of legends!

† END OF VOLUME I †

REFERENCES TO VOLUME I

1. "De mon cœur l'orgueilleuse faiblesse," Racine, Iphigénie en Aulide, Act i, sc. i. – (W.S.)

2. Le P. Lelong, *Bibliothèque historique de la France*, Paris, 1768 (5 vols. folio), II, n. 17172-17242. Potthast, *Bibliotheca medii œvi*, Berlin, 1895, 8vo, vol. i, pp. 643 *seq*. U. Chevalier, *Répertoire des sources historiques du Moyen Âge*, Paris, 8vo, 1877, pp. 1247-1255; *Jeanne d'Arc, bibliographie*, Montbéliard, 1878 selections.; *Supplément au Répertoire*, Paris, 1883, pp. 2684-2686, 8vo. Lanéry d'Arc, *Le livre d'or de Jeanne d'Arc, bibliographie raisonnée et analytique des ouvrages relatifs à Jeanne d'Arc*, Paris, 1894, large 8vo, and supplement. A. Molinier, *Les sources de l'histoire de France des origines aux guerres d'Italie, IV: Les Valois, 1328-1461*, Paris, 1904, pp. 310-348.

3. Jules Quicherat, *Procès de condamnation et de réhabilitation de Jeanne d'Arc*, Paris, 8vo, 1841, vol. i. (Called hereafter *Trial*. – W.S.)

4. *Trial*, vol. i, p. 93, *passim*.

5. *Ibid.*, vol. iii, pp. 89, 142, 161, 176, 178, 201.

6. *Trial*, vol. i, pp. 478 *et seq*.

7. Cf. J. Quicherat, Aperçus nouveaux sur l'histoire de Jeanne d'Arc, Paris, 1880, pp. 138-144.

8. Evidence of G. Manchon, *Trial*, vol. ii, p. 14.

9. *Ne donnoit point d'argent pour soy faire mettre ès croniques*. – Jean de Bueil, *Le Jouvencel*, ed. C. Fabre and L. Lecestre, Paris, 1887, 8vo, vol. ii, p. 283.

10. Perceval de Cagny, *Chroniques*, published by H. Moranvillé, Paris, 1902, 8vo.

11. Le sens, mémoire, ne l'abillité de savoir faire metre par escript ce, ne autre chose mendre de plus de la moitié, Perceval de Cagny, p. 31.

12. *Trial*, vol. iv, p. 1.

13. *Ibid.*, pp. 40-50. D. Godefroy, *Histoire de Charles VII*, Paris, 1661, fol. pp. 369-474.

14. Jean Chartier, *Chronique de Charles VII, roi de France*, ed. Vallet de Viriville, Paris, 1858, 3 vols., 18mo. (*Bibliothèque Elzévirienne*).

15. Lequel Luxembourg la vendit aux Angloix, qui la menèrent à Rouen, où elle fut durement traictée; et tellement que, après grant dillacion de temps, sans procez, maiz de leur voulenté indeue, la firent ardoir en icelle ville de Rouen publiquement ... qui fut bien inhumainement fait, veu la vie et gouvernement dont elle vivoit, car elle se confessoit et recepvoit par chacune sepmaine le corps de Nostre Seigneur, comme bonne catholique. – Jean Chartier, Chronique de Charles VII, roi de France, vol. i, p. 122.

16. Jean Chartier, Chronique de Charles VII, roi de France, vol. i, p. 122.

17. Par l'admonestement de ladite Pucelle, Jean Chartier, vol. i, p. 87.

18. *Fut cause, ibid.*, vol. i, p. 97.

19. This revolt of the French nobles was so named because various risings of a similar nature had taken place in the city of Prague. – W.S.

20. *Journal du siège d'Orléans* (1428-1429), ed. P. Charpentier and C. Cuissart, Orléans, 1896, 8vo.

21. The oldest copy extant is dated 1472 (MS. fr. 14665).

22. *Journal du siège d'Orléans* (1428-1429), p. 87. *Trial*, vol. iv, p. 162, note.

23. *Journal du siège*, p. 97. *Trial*, vol. iii, p. 215.

24. Chronique de la Pucelle, or Chronique de Cousinot, ed. Vallet de Viriville, Paris, 1859, 16mo. (Bibliothèque Gauloise).

25. *Mystère du Siège d'Orléans*, first published by MM. F. Guessard and E. de Certain, Paris, 1862, 4to, according to the only manuscript, which is preserved in the Vatican Library. – *Cf. Étude sur le mystère du siège d'Orléans*, by H. Tivier, Paris, 1868, 8vo.

26. *Trial*, vol. v, p. 309.

27. The Abbé E. Bossard and de Maulde, *Gilles de Rais, Maréchal de France, dit Barbe-Bleue* (1404-1440), 2nd edition, Paris, 1886, 8vo, pp. 94-113.

28. Un estandart et bannière qui furent à Monseigneur de Reys pour faire la manière de l'assaut comment les Tourelles furent prinses sur les Anglois Mistère du siège, p. viii.

29. *Mistère du siège*, preface, p. x.

30.

> Quant est de l'ostel de mon père,
> Il est en pays de Barois;
> Gentilhomme et de noble afaire
> Honneste et loyal François.

Mistère du siège, pp. 397-398.

31.

> ... Ayez en souvenance....
> Comment Orléans eult délivrance....
> L'an mil iiijc xxix;
> Faites en mémoire tous dis;
> Des jours de may ce fut le neuf.

Mistère du siège, lines 14375-14381, p. 559.

32. *Trial*, vol. v, pp. 285 *et seq.*

33. Relation inédite sur Jeanne d'Arc, extraite du livre noir de l'hôtel de ville de La Rochelle, ed. J. Quicherat, Orléans, 1879, 8vo, and La Revue Historique, vol. iv, 1877, pp. 329-344.

34. Bibl. Nat. fr. 23018: J. Quicherat, *Supplément aux témoignages contemporains sur Jeanne d'Arc*, in *Revue Historique*, vol. xix, May-June, 1882, pp. 72-83.

35. Pierre Champion, *Guillaume de Flavy*, Paris, 1906, in 8vo, pp. xi, xii.

36. *Chronique d'Antonio Morosini*, introduction and commentary by Germain Lefèvre-Pontalis, text established by Léon Dorez, vol. iii, 1901, p. 302, and vol. iv, supplement xxi.

37. Enguerrand de Monstrelet, *Chronique*, ed. Doüet-d'Arcq, Paris, 1857-1861, 6 vols. in 8vo.

38. Rabelais, Urquhart's Trans., ii-49, in Bohn's edition, 1849 (W.S.). *Plus baveux que ung pot de moutarde.* – Rabelais, *Pantagruel*, bk. iii, chap. xxiv.

39. Jehan de Wavrin, *Anchiennes croniques d'Engleterre*, ed. Mademoiselle Dupont, Paris, 1858-1863, 3 vols., 8vo.

40. Wavrin's additions to Monstrelet in *Trial*, vol. iv, p. 407.

41. *Chronique de Jean le Fèvre, seigneur de Saint-Rémy*, ed. François Morand, Paris, 1876-1881, 2 vols. in 8vo.

42. *Chroniques des ducs de Bourgogne*, Paris, 1827, 2 vols. in 8vo; vols. xlii and xliii of the *Collection des Chroniques françaises*, by Buchon. *Œuvres de Georges Chastellain*, ed. Kervyn de Lettenhove, Brussels, 1863, 8 vols. in 8vo.

43. *Journal d'un bourgeois de Paris* (1405-1449), ed. A. Tuetey, Paris, 1881, in 8vo.

44. *Chronique d'Antonio Morosini*, ed. Léon Dorez and Germain Lefèvre-Pontalis, Paris, 1900-1902, 4 vols. in 8vo.

45. G. Lefèvre-Pontalis, *Les sources allemandes de l'histoire de Jeanne d'Arc*, Eberhard Windecke, Paris, 1903, in 8vo.

46. *Trial*, vols. ii to iii, 1844-1845 (vols. v and vi, 1846-1847, contain the evidence).

47. Lanéry d'Arc, *Mémoires et consultations en faveur de Jeanne d'Arc*, 1889, in 8vo. *Trial*, vol. iii, pp. 411-468.

48. *Trial*, vol. ii, pp. 378-463.

49. J. Quicherat, *Histoire du costume*, Paris, 1875, large 8vo, *passim*. G. Demay, *Le costume au moyen âge d'après les sceaux*, Paris, 1880, p. 121, figs. 76 and 77.

50. *Trial*, vol. iii, p. 34.

51. *Ibid.*, p. 100.

52. We must notice, however, that Brother Pasquerel, who was not present either at Chinon or at Poitiers, is careful to say that he knows nothing of Jeanne's sojourn in these two towns save what she herself has told him. Now we are surprised to find that she herself placed the examination at Poitiers before the audience at Chinon, since she says in her trial that at Chinon, when she gave her King a sign, the clerks ceased to contend with her. – *Trial*, vol. i, p. 145.

53. Expectando succursum regis, Trial, vol. iii, p. 109.

54. *Trial*, vol. iii, p. 105.

55. *Ibid.*, pp. 2 *et seq.*

56. *Trial*, vol. iii, p. 13.

57. *Ibid.*, p. 15.

58. *Ibid.*, p. 12.

59. *Ibid.*, vol. ii, pp. 15, 161, 329; vol. iii, pp. 41 and *passim*.

60. *Ibid.*, vol. iii, p. 23.

61. L. Jarry, *Le compte de l'armée anglaise au siège d'Orléans* (1428-1429), Orléans, 1892, in 8vo.

62. *Trial*, vol. iii, p. 20.

63. *Ibid.*, p. 87.

64. *Trial*, vol. iii, p. 85.

65. *Ibid.*, p. 100. On the other hand see the evidence of Dunois (vol. iii, p. 16), "licet dicta Johanna aliquotiens *jocose* loqueretur de facto armorum, pro animando armatos ... tamen quando loquebatur seriose de guerra ... nunquam affirmative asserebat nisi quod erat missa ad levandum obsidionem Aurelianensem."

66. *Trial*, vol. ii, pp. 438, 457; vol. iii, pp. 100, 219.

67. *Trial*, vol. ii, p. 438; vol. iii, pp. 15, 76, 100, 219, and 457.

68. *Trial*, vol. iii, pp. 89 and 121.

69. *Trial*, vol. iii, pp. 2 and 35.

70. *Trial*, vol. iii, pp. 100 *et seq.*

71. Siméon Luce, Jeanne d'Arc à Domremy, recherches critiques sur les origines de la mission de la Pucelle, Paris, 1886, in 8vo; La France pendant la guerre de cent ans: épisodes historiques et vie privée aux xive et xve siècles, Paris, 1890, in 12mo.

72. D. Lottin, Recherches sur la ville d'Orléans, Orléans, 7 vols. in 8vo; Boucher de Molandon, Les comptes de ville d'Orléans des xive et xve siècles, 1880, in 8vo; Jules Loiseleur, Compte des dépenses faites par Charles VII pour secourir Orléans pendant le siège de 1428, Orléans, 1868, in 8vo; Louis Jarry, Le compte de l'armée anglaise au siège d'Orléans, Orléans, 1892, in 8vo; Couret, Un fragment inédit des anciens registres de la prévôté d'Orléans, relatif au règlement des frais du siège de 1428-1429, Orléans, 1697, in 8vo (extract from the Mémoires de l'Académie de Sainte Croix).

73. Rymer, Fœdera, conventiones...., ed. tercia, Hagae Comitis, 1739-1745, 10 vols. in folio; Delpit, Collection de documents français qui se trouvent en Angleterre, Paris, 1847, in 4to; J. Stevenson, Letters and Papers illustrative of the Wars of the English in France during the reign of Henry VI, 1861-1864, 3 parts, in 2 vols. in 8vo; Charles Gross, The Sources and Literature of English History, 1900, in 8vo.

74. Varin, *Archives législatives de la ville de Reims*, 2nd part; *Statuts*, vol. i, p. 596; *Trial*, vol. iv, pp. 284 *et seq.*

75. E. Robillard de Beaurepaire, Recherches sur le procès de condamnation de Jeanne d'Arc, Rouen, 1869, in 8vo Précis des travaux de l'Académie de Rouen, 1867-1868, pp. 321-448.; Notes sur les juges et les assesseurs du procès de condamnation de Jeanne d'Arc, Rouen, 1890, in 8vo Précis des travaux de l'Académie de Rouen, 1888-1889, pp. 375-504..

76. *Trial*, vol. v, pp. 342 *et seq.*

77. *Trial*, vol. iii, p. 19.

78. Brière de Boismont, De l'hallucination historique, ou étude médico-psychique sur les voix et les révélations de Jeanne d'Arc, 1861, in 8vo. Le Vicomte de Mouchy, Jeanne d'Arc, étude historique et psychologique, Montpellier, 1868, in 8vo, 67 pp.

79. Vol. ii, Appendix i.

80. *Acta Sanctorum*, 1675, April, iii, 851.

81. *Ibid.*, March 1, 1532.

82. Le Père Hugues de Saint-François, *Les grandeurs de Sainte Anne*, Rennes, 1657, in 8vo; L'abbé Max Nicol, *Sainte-Anne-d'Auray*, Paris, Brussels, s.d., in 8vo, pp. 37 *et seq*. M. le Docteur G. de Closmadeuc has kindly lent me his valuable work, as yet unpublished, on Yves Nicolazic, which is characterised by the same exactness of information and of criticism as are to be found in his studies of local history.

83. Recueil des ouvrages de la célèbre Mademoiselle Labrousse, du Bourg de Vauxains, en Périgord, canton de Ribeirac de la Dordogne, actuellement prisonnière au château Saint-Ange, à Rome, Bordeaux, 1797, in 8vo; E. Lairtullier, Les femmes célèbres de 1789 à 1795, Paris, 1842, in 8vo, vol. i, pp. 212 et seq.; Abbé Chr. Moreau, Une mystique révolutionnaire Suzette Labrousse, Paris, 1886, in 8vo; A. France, Susette Labrousse, Paris, 1907, in 12mo.

84. Vol. ii, Appendices ii and iii.

85. Le P. Ayroles, *La vraie Jeanne d'Arc*, 5 vols. in large 8vo, Paris, 1894-1902. Writing of this book in a study of *L'Abjuration de Jeanne d'Arc* (Paris, 1902, pp. 7 and 8, note), Canon Ulysse Chevalier, author of a valuable *Répertoire des sources du moyen âge*, displays boldness and sound sense. "From the dimensions of these five volumes," he says, "one might expect this work to be the fullest history of Jeanne d'Arc; it is nothing of the sort. It is a chaos of memoranda translated or rendered into modern French, reflections and arguments against free-thought as represented by Michelet, H. Martin, Quicherat, Vallet de Viriville, Siméon Luce, and Joseph Fabre. Two headings will suffice to give an idea of the book's tone: *The Pseudo-theologians, executioners of Jeanne d'Arc, executioners of the Papacy* (vol. i, p. 87); *The University of Paris and the Brigandage of Rouen* (p. 149). The author too often judges the fifteenth century by the standards of the nineteenth. Is he quite sure that if he had been a member of the University of Paris in 1431 he would have thought and pronounced in favour of Jeanne, and in opposition to his colleagues?"

86. *Trial*, vol. ii, p. 456.

87. Le P. Denifle, La désolation des églises, monastères hôpitaux en France vers le milieu du xv^{ieme} siècle, Mâcon, 1897, in 8vo.

88. O. Raguenet, Les juges de Jeanne d'Arc à Poitiers, membres du Parlement ou gens d'Église? in Lettres et mémoires de l'Académie de Sainte-Croix d'Orléans VII, 1894, pp. 339-442; D. Lacombe, L'hôte de Jeanne d'Arc à Poitiers, maître Jean Rabateau, Président au Parlement de Poitiers in Revue du Bas-Poitou, 1891, pp. 46-66.

89. Mr. Andrew Lang (*La Jeanne d'Arc de M. Anatole France*, p. 60) misreads this passage when he takes it to mean that the English withdrew their garrisons from these places. That their ultimate surrender became inevitable after the English retreat from Orléans is what the writer intends to convey. – W.S.

90. *Trial*, vol. i, p. 146.

91. *Ibid.*, vol. iii, p. 13.

92. *Ibid.*, p. 100. See *ante*, p. xxvi (note 4).

93. Letter from Alain Chartier in the *Trial*, vol. v, pp. 135, 136; Capitaine P. Marin, *Jeanne d'Arc tacticien et stratégiste*, Paris, 1889, 4 vols. in 12mo; Le Général Canonge, *Jeanne d'Arc guerrière*, Paris, 1907, in 8vo.

94. *Rossel et la légende de Jeanne d'Arc* in *la Petite République* of July 15, 1896; *Jeanne d'Arc soldat* by Art Roë, in *le Temps* of May 8, 1907. See also the works of Captain Marin, always so praiseworthy for their carefulness and good faith.

95. *Trial*, vol. iii, p. 16.

96. Alain Chartier, *Œuvres*, ed. André du Chesne, p. 412.

97. Jean Chartier, *Chronique de Charles VII*, vol. i, p. 121.

98. See the deliberations of the Commons on December 2, 1421, in Bréquigny, *Lettres de rois, reines et autres personnages des cours de France et d'Angleterre*, Paris, 1847 (2 vols. in 4to), vol. ii, pp. 393 *et seq.*

99. For the origin of this term see *post*, vol. i, p. 22 and note 2. – W.S.

100. For the origin of this term see *ibid.* and note 1. – W.S.

101. The Reverend Father M. Fornier, *Histoire des Alpes-Maritimes*, Paris, 1890, in 8vo, vol. ii, p. 324; Lanéry d'Arc, *Mémoires et consultations*, pp. 565 *et seq.*

102. *Trial*, vol. iii, p. 117; *Perceval de Cagny*, p. 168; Marquis de Gaucourt, *Le sire de Gaucourt*, Orléans, 1855, in 8vo.

103. *Perceval de Cagny*, pp. 168, 170, 171; *Cronicques de Normendie*, ed. Hellot, pp. 77, 78.

104. *Perceval de Cagny*, pp. 170, 171; *Chronique de la Pucelle*, p. 313; Héraut Berry, in *Trial*, vol. iv, p. 48.

105. H. Martin, *Jeanne d'Arc*, Paris, 1856, in 12mo; J. Quicherat, *Nouvelles preuves des trahisons essuyées par la Pucelle* in *Revue de Normandie*, vol. vi (1866), pp. 396-401.

106. Even when the canons who took part in the trial are severally considered. *Cf.* Ch. de Beaurepaire, *Recherches sur le procès de condamnation de Jeanne d'Arc*, Rouen, 1869, in 8vo.

107. Or at least the conclusions of the doctors which have been preserved. As for the register itself it could not have contained anything of great importance. From their evidence at the rehabilitation trial we see that the Poitiers clerks were not desirous for much to be said of their inquiry.

108. Aug. Vallet, Observation sur l'ancien monument érigé à Orléans, Paris, 1858, in 8vo.

109. See a curious project for the decoration of the platform of the Pont-Neuf addressed to Louis XIV (B.N.V., p. [zz]338, in fol.). A Sieur Dupuis, Aide des Cérémonies, proposes that thereon shall be erected statues to "those great and illustrious captains who from reign to reign have valiantly maintained the dignity of the crown.... Artus of Bretagne, Constable, Jean, Count of Dunois, Jeanne Dark, Maid of Orléans, Roger de Gramont, Count of Guiche, Guillaume, Count of Chaumont, Amaury de Severac, Vignoles, called La Hire...." (Communications of M. Paul Lacombe, *Bulletin de la Société de l'Histoire de Paris*, 1894, p. 115, June 11, 1907. *Ibid.*)

110. Puellæ Aureliensis causa adversariis orationibus disceptata auctore Jacobo Jolio, Parisiis apud Julianum Bertant, 1609.

111. Jean Hordal, Heroinae nobilissimae Ioannæ Darc Lotharingæ vulgo aurelianensis puellæ historia, Ponti-Mussi, 1612, in 8vo.

112. Rabelais, *Gargantua*, chap. vi; Abbé Thiers, *Traité des superstitions selon l'Écriture sainte*, Paris, 1697, vol. i, p. 109.

113. Edmond Richer, *Histoire de la Pucelle d'Orléans en 4 livres*, MS. Biblioth. Nat. f. Fr. 10448, fol. 12mo.

114. "The Life of Saint Catherine, virgin and martyr, is fabulous throughout from beginning to end," *Valesiana*, p. 48. "M. de Launoy, doctor of theology, had cut Saint Catherine, virgin and martyr, out of his calendar. He said that her life was a myth, and to

show that he placed no faith in it, every year when the feast of the saint came round, he said a Requiem mass. This curious circumstance I learn from his own telling," *Ibid.*, p. 36.

115. Jean Chapelain, *La Pucelle ou la France délivrée*, Paris, 1656, in fol.

116. *Œuvres de messire Jacques-Bénigne Bossuet*, Paris, in 4to, vol. xi, 1749, numbered pages; vol. xii, pp. 234 *et seq.* Cf. what he says of inspired persons in *l'Instruction sur les états d'oraison*, Paris, 1697, in 8vo.

117. "This girl called Jeanne d'Arq ... had been a servant in an inn," *loc. cit.*, p. 233.

118. We must not be too severe on a tutor's note-books. But Bossuet, who places the rehabilitation under the date 1431, does not tell us that it was only pronounced twenty-five years later. On the contrary, as far as he is concerned, we might conclude that it occurred before the deliverance of Compiègne. The following are his words: "In execution of this sentence, she was burned alive at Rouen in 1431. The English spread the rumour that at the last she had admitted the revelations which she had so loudly boasted to be false. But some time afterwards the Pope appointed commissioners. Her trial was solemnly revised and her conduct approved of by a final sentence which the Pope himself confirmed. The Burgundians were forced to raise the siege of Compiègne," *loc. cit.* p. 236. Mézeray is more credulous than Bossuet; he mentions "the Saints Catherine and Margaret, who purified her soul with heavenly conversations, wherefore she venerated them with a particular devotion." In relating the trial, he like Bossuet, ignores the Vice-Inquisitor (*Histoire de France*, vol. ii, 1746, in folio, pp. 11 *et seq.*)

119. Voltaire ed. Beuchot, vol. xxvi. *Cf.* also *Essai sur les mœurs*, chap. lxxx. "Finally, being accused of having once resumed man's dress, which had been left near her on purpose to tempt her, her judges ... declared her a relapsed heretic and caused to be burnt at the stake one who in heroic ages, when men erected altars to their liberators, would have had an altar raised to her for having served her King. Afterwards Charles VII rehabilitated her memory, which her death itself had sufficiently honoured."

120. L'Abbé Lenglet du Fresnoy, Histoire de Jeanne d'Arc, vierge, héroïne et martyre d'État suscitée par la Providence pour rétablir la monarchie française, tirée des procès et pièces originales du temps, Paris, 1753-1754, 3 vols. in 12mo.

121. F. de L'Averdy, Mémorial lu au comité des manuscrits concernant la recherche à faire des minutes originales des différentes affaires qui ont eu lieu par rapport à Jeanne d'Arc, appelée communément la Pucelle d'Orléans, Paris, Imprimerie Royale, 1787, in 4to; Notices et extraits des manuscrits de la Bibliothèque du roi, lus au comité établi par sa Majesté dans l'Académie royale des Inscriptions et Belles Lettres, Paris, Imp. Royale, 1790, vol. iii.

122. "Modern times present but two fine subjects for an epic poem, the Crusades and the Discovery of the New World" (ed. 1802, Paris, vol. ii, p. 7).

123. "The illustrious Jeanne d'Arc has proved that there is no miracle which the French genius is incapable of working when national independence is at stake" (*Moniteur* of 10 Pluviose, year XI, January 30, 1803). For the approval of the First Consul: facsimile in A. Sarrazin, *Jeanne d'Arc et la Normandie*, p. 600. Original taken from the Reiset collection..

124. Le Brun de Charmettes, *Histoire de Jeanne d'Arc surnommée la Pucelle d'Orléans*, Paris, 1817, 4 vols. in 8vo.

125. Michelet, *Histoire de France*, vol. v.

126. Vallet de Viriville, *Histoire de Charles VII*, vol. ii, Paris, 1863, in 8vo.

127. H. Wallon, *Jeanne d'Arc*, Paris, 1860, 2 vols. in 8vo.

128. M. Sepet, *Jeanne d'Arc*, with an introduction by Léon Gautier, Tours, 1869, in 8vo.

129. Chanoine Dunand, *Histoire de Jeanne d'Arc*, Toulouse, 1898-1899, 3 vols. in 8vo.

130. Joseph Fabre, *Jeanne d'Arc libératrice de la France*, new edition, Paris, 1894, in 12mo.

131. *Procès de condamnation de Jeanne d'Arc....*, translated with commentary by J. Fabre, new edition, Paris, 1895, in 18mo.

132. Jeanne d'Arc à Domremy, op. cit.; La France pendant la guerre de Cent Ans, op. cit.

133. Lanéry d'Arc, *Le livre d'Or de Jeanne d'Arc*, Nos. 2080 to 2112.

134. A. Thomas, Le mot "Patrie" et Jeanne d'Arc in Revue des Idées, July 15, 1906.

135. *Les œuvres de Maistre Alain Chartier*, published by André Duchesne, Paris, 1642, in 4to, p. 410.

136. *Trial*, vol. ii, p. 436. See *post*, vol. i, p. 82.

137. Froissart, *Chroniques*, book i, chap. 128.

138. Jean Juvénal des Ursins in Buchon, *Choix des Chroniques*, iv.

139. Rymer, *Fœdera*, vol. ix, p. 427.

140. *Pantagruel*, book iv, chap. lxvii.

141. *La Pucelle*, Preface.

142. Germain Lefèvre-Pontalis, Les sources allemandes de l'histoire de Jeanne d'Arc, p. 93.

143. Imitation velvet.

144. See the picture of 1581, preserved in the Orléans Museum and reproduced in Wallon's *Jeanne d'Arc*, p. 466.

145. *La Danse des Morts*, painted at Berne between 1515 and 1520 by Nicolas Manuel, lithographed by Guillaume Stettler, s.d. in folio oblong, engraving xx. M. Salomon Reinach believes this prototype may be found in the Judiths of Cranach.

146. Lanéry d'Arc, *Le livre d'Or de Jeanne d'Arc*, Iconography, Nos. 2080-2112.

147. J. Ch. Chappellier, *Étude historique et géographique sur Domremy, pays de Jeanne d'Arc*, Saint-Dié, 1890, in 8vo. É. Hinzelin, *Chez Jeanne d'Arc*, Paris, 1894, in 18mo.

148. This may be inferred from vol. i, p. 46, of the *Trial*. But Jeanne did not know how old she was when she left her father's house (*Trial*, vol. i, p. 51). I have ignored the letter of Perceval de Boulainvilliers, p. 116, vol. v, of the *Trial*. It is quite unauthentic and is too much in the manner of a hagiologist. See post, p. 468, note 1.

149. Darc (*Trial*, vol. i, p. 191; vol. ii, p. 82). Dars (Siméon Luce, *Jeanne d'Arc à Domremy*, p. 360). Day (*Trial*, vol. v, p. 150). Daiz (furnished by M. Pierre Champion). This document appears to justify the pronunciation *Jeanne d'Arc*. Concerning the orthography of the name d'Arc, cf. Lanéry d'Arc, *Livre d'or de Jeanne d'Arc*, notes 647-657.

150. *Trial*, vol. i, pp. 46, 208. E. de Bouteiller and G. de Braux, *La famille de Jeanne d'Arc*, Paris, 1878, in 8vo, p. 185; *Nouvelles recherches sur la famille de Jeanne d'Arc*, Paris, Orléans, 1879, in 12mo, p. x, *passim*. Boucher de Molandon, *Jacques d'Arc, père de la Pucelle*, Orléans, 1885, in 8vo.

151. See post, pp. 57, 451, 452.

152. *Trial*, vol. ii, pp. 378 *et seq.*

153. *Ibid.*, vol. i, pp. 191, 208; vol. ii, p. 74, note 1. Armand Boucher de Crèvecœur, *Les Romée et les de Perthes, famille maternelle de Jeanne*

d'Arc, Abbeville, 1891, in 8vo. Lanéry d'Arc, *Livre d'or*, notes 1278-1308.

154. Du Cange, *Glossaire*, under the word *Romeus*. G. de Braux, *Jeanne d'Arc à Saint-Nicolas*, Nancy, 1889, p. 8. *Revue catholique des institutions et du droit*, August, 1886. E. de Bouteiller, *Nouvelles recherches*, p. xii. Vallet de Viriville, *Histoire de Charles VII*, vol. ii, p. 43.

155. Probably before Jeanne's birth. "My surname is d'Arc or Romée," said Jeanne (*Trial*, vol. i, p. 191). Thus she indiscriminately assumes either her father's or her mother's surname, although she says (*Trial*, vol. i, p. 191) that in her country girls are called by their mother's surname.

156. Trial, vol. v, p. 252. E. de Bouteiller and G. de Braux, Nouvelles recherches sur la famille de Jeanne d'Arc, Paris, 1879, pp. 3-20. Ch. du Lys, Traité sommaire tant du nom et des armes que de la naissance et parenté de la Pucelle d'Orléans et de ses frères, ed. Vallet de Viriville, Paris, 1857, p. 28. E. Georges, Jeanne d'Arc considérée au point de vue Franco-Champenois, Troyes, 1893, in 8vo, p. 101.

157. The order of the births of Jacques d'Arc's children is extremely doubtful (*Trial*, index, under the word *Arc*).

158. *Trial*, vol. ii, p. 393, *passim*. S. Luce, *Jeanne d'Arc à Domremy*, vol. xvi, p. 357.

159. A. Monteil, *Histoire des Français*, 1853, in 18mo, vol. ii, p. 194.

160. *Trial*, vol. i, p. 46. Jean Minet was a native of Neufchâteau.

161. J. Corblet, Parrains et marraines, in Revue de l'art chrétien, 1881, vol. xiv, pp. 336 et seq.

162. Siméon Luce, *Jeanne d'Arc à Domremy*, proofs and illustrations, li, p. 98.

163. *Ibid.*, p. clxxix, note.

164. Cf. *Trial*, index, under *parrains* and *marraines*. It is not always possible to assign to these personages the names they bore and the position they occupied at the exact date when they are introduced.

165. *Relation du greffier de La Rochelle*, in the *Revue Historique*, vol. iv, p. 342. Cf. Eustache Deschamps, ballad 354, vol. iii, p. 83, ed. Queux de Saint Hilaire.

166. *Trial*, vol. ii, pp. 74-388; vol. v, pp. 151, 220, *passim*.

167. *Ibid.*, vol. i, p. 46. Henri Lepage, *Jeanne d'Arc est-elle Lorraine?* Nancy, 1852, pp. 57-79.

168. *Trial*, vol. v, pp. 244 *et seq.* Jacques d'Arc's house doubtless looked on to the road; the Du Lys, or rather the Thiesselins, pulled it down and erected in its place a house no longer existing. The shields which ornamented its façade have been placed upon the door of the building now shown as Jeanne's house. What is represented as Jeanne's room is the bakehouse (É. Hinzelin, *Chez Jeanne d'Arc*, p. 74). See an article by Henri Arsac in *L'écho de l'Est*, 26 July, 1890. A whole literature has been written on this subject (Lanéry d'Arc, *Livre d'or*, pp. 330 *et seq.*).

169. Émile Hinzelin, *Chez Jeanne d'Arc, passim.*

170. *Trial*, vol. v, pp. 151, 220.

171. Ibid., vol. ii, p. 417: "Jacuit amorose in domo patris sui."

172. *Ibid.*, p. 429.

173. *Ibid.*, p. 408.

174. *Ibid.*, p. 423.

175. E. Georges, *Jeanne d'Arc considérée au point de vue Franco-Champenois*, p. 115. De La Fons-Mélicocq, *Documents inédits pour servir à l'histoire de l'instruction publique en France et à l'histoire des mœurs au XV*ieme *siècle*, in the Bulletin de la Société des Antiquaires de la Morinie, vol. iii, pp. 460 et seq.

176. Trial, vol. i, pp. 65-66. (Item: je donne à Oudinot, à Richard et à Gérard, clercz enfantz du maistre de l'escole de Marcey dessoubz Brixey, doubz escus pour priier pour mi et pour dire les sept psaulmes.) (Item: I give to the boys, Oudinot, Richard, and Gérard, scholars of the school-master at Marcey below Brixey, twelve crowns to pray for me and to repeat the seven psalms.) The will of Jean de Bourlémont, 23 October, 1399, in S. Luce, *Jeanne d'Arc à Domremy*, document in facsimile xiii.

177. *Trial*, vol. i, pp. 46, 47.

178. *Ibid.*, vol. ii, p. 402. See in Montfaucon's *Monuments de la Monarchie Française*, vol. iii, the second miniature, the "Douze périls d'enfer" (the twelve perils of hell).

179. *Trial*, vol. ii, pp. 409, 415, 420.

180. *Trial*, vol. i, pp. 51, 66; vol. ii, p. 404. S. Luce, *Jeanne d'Arc à Domremy*, p. lij.

181. *Trial*, vol. ii, p. 404.

182. *Ibid.*, vol. i, p. 423.

183. *Trial*, index, at the word *Bermont*. Du Haldat, *Notice sur la chapelle de Belmont*, in the *Mémoires de l'Académie Stanislas de Nancy*, 1833-1834, p. 96. É. Hinzelin, *Chez Jeanne d'Arc*, p. 95. Lanéry d'Arc, *Livre d'or*, p. 330.

184. Alexis Monteil, *Histoire des François*, vol. i, p. 91.

185. *Trial*, index, under the words *Bois Chesnu*.

186. *Ibid.*, index, under the words *Fontaine des Groseilliers*.

187. *Ibid.*, vol. i, pp. 67-210; vol. ii. pp. 391 *et seq.*

188. Journal d'un bourgeois de Paris, ed. Tuetey, p. 267.

189. *Trial*, vol. i, p. 209.

190. *Trial*, vol. i, pp. 67, 187, 209; vol. ii, pp. 390, 404, 450.

191. Wolf, Mythologie des fées et des elfes, 1828, in 8vo. A. Maury, Les fées au moyen âge, 1843, in 18mo, and Croyances et légendes du moyen âge, Paris, 1896, in 8vo.

192. Richer, *Histoire manuscrite de Jeanne d'Arc*, ms. fr. 10,448, fols. 14, 15.

193. For tree worship, see an article by M. Henry Carnoy in *La tradition*, 15 March, 1889.

194. *Trial*, vol. ii, p. 422.

195. *Ibid.*, index, under the words *Arbre des Fées*.

196. *Ibid.*, vol. ii, p. 404.

197. Ibid., p. 404, passim. Simple Crayon de la noblesse des ducs de Lorraine et de Bar, in Le Brun des Charmettes' Histoire de Jeanne d'Arc, vol. i, p. 266. Jules Baudot, Les princesses Yolande et les ducs de Bar de la famille des Valois, first part. Mélusine, Paris, 1901, in 8vo, p. 121.

198. *Propter eorum peccata*, in the *Trial*, vol. ii, p. 396. There is no doubt as to the meaning of these words.

199. *Trial*, vol. ii, p. 390.

200. *Trial*, vol. ii, p. 397.

201. *Ibid.*, p. 390. Bergier, *Dictionnaire de théologie*, under the word *Conjuration*.

202. *Trial*, vol. i, p. 187.

203. *Ibid.*, pp. 67, 209.

204. *Ibid.*, pp. 178, 209 *et seq.*

205. For the traditions of fairies at Domremy and for Jeanne's opinion of them, see *Trial*, index, under the word *Fées*.

206. Concerning the Sunday and the Festival of the Well-Dressing at Domremy, see *Trial*, index, under the word *Fontaine*.

207. *Trial*, vol. i, pp. 67, 212, 404 *et seq.* S. Luce, *Jeanne d'Arc à Domremy*, pp. xx-xxii.

208. *Trial*, vol. ii, pp. 407, 411, 413, 421.

209. *Ibid.*, pp. 391-462.

210. *Trial*, vol. i, pp. 67, 209, 210.

211. *Ibid.*, vol. ii, p. 434.

212. Atropa Mandragor, female mandragora, main de gloire, herbe aux magiciens. Trial, vol. i, pp. 89, 213. Journal d'un bourgeois de Paris, p. 236.

213. *Trial*, vol. i, p. 209.

214. This is probable but not certain. *Trial*, vol. ii, pp. 74, 388; vol. v, p. 252. E. de Bouteiller and G. de Braux, *Nouvelles recherches sur la famille de Jeanne d'Arc*, pp. xviii *et seq.*; 7, 8, 10, *passim.* C. Gilardoni, *Sermaize et son église*, published at Vitry-le-François, 1893, 8vo.

215. Capitaine Champion, *Jeanne d'Arc écuyère*, Paris, 1901, 12mo, p. 28.

216. Boucher de Molandon, *La famille de Jeanne d'Arc*, p. 627. E. de Bouteiller et G. de Braux, *Nouvelles recherches*, pp. 9 and 10. S. Luce, *Jeanne d'Arc à Domremy*, pp. xlv *et seq.*

217. E. Misset, *Jeanne d'Arc champenoise*, Paris, s.d. (1894), 8vo. Concerning the nationality of Joan of Arc there is a whole literature extremely rich, the bibliography of which it is impossible to give here. Cf. Lanéry d'Arc, *Livre d'or*, pp. 295 *et seq.*

218. *Trial*, vol. i, p. 208.

219. P. Jollois, *Histoire abrégée de la vie et des exploits de Jeanne d'Arc*, Paris, 1821, engraving I, p. 190. A. Renard, *La patrie de Jeanne d'Arc*, Langres, 1880, in 18mo, p. 6. S. Luce, *Jeanne d'Arc à Domremy*, supplement with proofs and illustrations, pp. 281, 282.

220. *Trial*, vol. v, p. 152.

221. Colonel de Boureulle, Le pays de Jeanne d'Arc, Saint-Dié, 1890, in 8vo, 28 small engravings. J. Ch. Chappellier, Étude historique sur Domremy, pays de Jeanne d'Arc, 2 plans; C. Niobé, Le pays de Jeanne d'Arc, in Mémoires de la Société académique de l'Aube, 1894, 3d series, vol. xxxi, pp. 307 et seq.

222. Juvénal des Ursins, in the *Collection Michaud et Poujoulat*, col. 561.

223. A. Tuetey, *Les écorcheurs sous Charles VII*, Montbéliard, 1874, vol. i, p. 87.

224. *Trial*, vol. i, pp. 66, 215.

225. In 1390 one *livre tournois* was worth £7 5s of present money; in 1488, £5. Cf. Avenel, *Histoire économique*, 1894 (W.S.).

226. "*Imal*," says Le Trévoux, "is a measure of corn used at Nancy." There are two *imaux* in a quarter, and four quarters in a *réal*, which contains fifteen bushels, according to the Paris measure.

227. The Archives of the department of Meurthe-et-Moselle, collection Ruppes II, No. 28. The farm lease, dated 2nd of April, 1420, was first published by M. J. Ch. Chappellier in *Le Journal de la Société d'Archéologie Lorraine*, Jan.-Feb., 1889; and *Deux actes inédits du XV siècle sur Domremy*, Nancy, 1889, 8vo, 16 pages. S. Luce, *La France pendant la guerre de cent ans*, 1890, 18mo, pp. 274 *et seq*. Lefèvre-Pontalis, *Étude historique et géographique sur Domremy, pays de Jeanne d'Arc*, in *Bibliothèque de l'École des Chartes*, vol. lvi, pp. 154-168.

228. *Trial*, vol. ii, pp. 420-426. S. Luce, *Jeanne d'Arc à Domremy*, p. lxiv.

229. Liénard, Dictionnaire topographique de la Meuse, introduction, p. x.

230. Dom Devienne, *Histoire de Bordeaux*, pp. 98, 103. L. Bachelier, *Histoire du commerce de Bordeaux*, Bordeaux, 1862, in 8vo, p. 45. D. Brissaud, *Les Anglais en Guyenne*, Paris, 1875, in 8vo.

231. Ch. de Beaurepaire, De l'administration de la Normandie sous la domination Anglaise, Caen, 1859, in 4to; and États de Normandie sous la domination Anglaise, Évreux, 1859, in 8vo. De Beaucourt, Histoire de Charles VII, vol. v, pp. 40-56, 261-286.

232. Thomas Basin, *Histoire de Charles VII et de Louis XI*, ed. Quicherat, vol. i, p. 27.

233. La Curne, under the words *Anglois* and *Goddons*.

234. Voragine, *La légende de Saint-Grégoire*. Du Cange, *Glossaire*, under the word *Caudatus*. Le Roux de Lincy, *Recueil de chants historiques français*, Paris, 1851, vol. i, pp. 300, 301. This oath is to be found current as early as Eustache Deschamps; it was still in use in the seventeenth century (*Sommaire tant du nom et des armes que de la naissance et parenté de la Pucelle*, ed. Vallet de Viriville).

235. S. Luce, *Jeanne d'Arc à Domremy*, ch. iii. Carlier, *Histoire du Valois*, vol. ii, pp. 441 *et seq*.

236. Dom Calmet, *Histoire de Lorraine*, vol. ii, col. 631. Bonnabelle, *Notice sur la ville de Vaucouleurs*, Bar-le-Duc, 1879, in 8vo, 75 pages.

237. *Trial*, vol. i, pp. 65, 66. S. Luce, *Jeanne d'Arc à Domremy*, pp. 18 *et seq.*

238. N. Villiaumé, *Histoire de Jeanne d'Arc*, 1864, in 8vo, p. 52, note 1.

239. S. Luce, *Jeanne d'Arc à Domremy*, ch. iii.

240. Pierre d'Alheim, *Le jargon Jobelin*, Paris, 1892, in 18mo: glossary, under the word *Hirenalle*, p. 61, and the verbal communication of M. Marcel Schwob. *Cronique Martiniane*, ed. P. Champion, p. 8, note 3; *Journal d'un bourgeois de Paris*, p. 270; De Montlezun, *Histoire de Gascogne*, 1847, in 8vo, p. 143; A. Castaing, *La patrie du valet de cœur*, in *Revue de Gascogne*, 1869, vol. x, pp. 29-33.

241. S. Luce, *Jeanne d'Arc à Domremy*, pp. lxxiii, 87, note 1. E. de Bouteiller and G. de Braux, *Nouvelles recherches*, pp. 4-15.

242. Bonvalot, Le tiers état d'après la charte de Beaumont et ses filiales, Paris, 1886, p. 412.

243. S. Luce, Jeanne d'Arc à Domremy, pp. lxxi et seq.

244. *Ibid.*, proofs and illustrations, li, p. 97.

245. De Beaucourt, *Histoire de Charles VII*, vol. ii, pp. 16, 17.

246. S. Luce, *Jeanne d'Arc à Domremy*, appendix, lxii.

247. Du Chesne, Génealogie de la maison de Vergy, Paris, 1625, folio. Nouvelle biographie générale, vol. xlv, p. 1125.

248. S. Luce, Domremy and Vaucouleurs, from 1412 to 1425, in *Jeanne d'Arc à Domremy*, ch. iii.

249. *Trial*, vol. i, p. 66.

250. *Trial*, vol. i, p. 66. S. Luce, *Jeanne d'Arc à Domremy*, p. lxxxvi, and appendix, xiv, p. 20.

251. A league is two and a half English miles (W.S.).

252. S. Luce, Jeanne d'Arc à Domremy, pp. 275 et seq.

253. E. de Bouteiller and G. de Braux, *Nouvelles recherches*, pp. 4-15.

254. *Trial*, vol. i, pp. 52, 72, 73, 89, 170.

255. The manuscript runs: *non jejunaverat die præcedenti*. Quicherat omits *non*. *Trial*, vol. i, p. 52. Cf. *Revue critique*, March, 1908, p. 215.

256. V. Servais, *Annales historiques du Barrois*, Bar-le-Duc, 1865, vol. i, engraving 2.

257. P. Ch. Cahier, *Caractéristique des saints dans l'art populaire*, vol. i, p. 363. Quicherat, *Aperçus nouveaux*, p. 50. S. Luce, *Jeanne d'Arc à Domremy*, pp. xcv, xcvi, and proofs and illustrations, xxiv, p. 74.

258. *Mystère de Saint Remi*, the Arsenal Library, ms. 3.364, folios 4 and 108.

259. "Sed signifer Sanctus Michael representet eas (animas) in lucem sanctam." Prayer from the mass for the dead.

260. A. Maury, Croyances et légendes du moyen âge, pp. 171 et seq. Barbier de Montault, Traité d'iconographie chrétienne, vol. i, p. 191.

261. AA. SS., 1672, vol. iii, i, pp. 85 *et seq.* Dom. J. Huynes, *Histoire générale de l'abbaye du Mont-Saint-Michel*, ed. R. de Beaurepaire, Rouen, 1872, pp. 61 *et seq.* A. Forgeais, *Collection de plombs* (seals) *historiés trouvés dans la Seine*, Paris, 1864, vol. iii, p. 197. S. Luce, *Jeanne d'Arc à Domremy*, ch. iv. *Chronique du Mont-Saint-Michel* (1343-1468), ed. S. Luce, Paris, 1880-1886 (2 vols. in 8vo), vol. i, pp. 26, 146, 163 *et seq.*

262. Lanéry d'Arc, *Mémoires et consultations en faveur de Jeanne d'Arc*, p. 272 (opinion of Jean Bochard, called de Vaucelle, Bishop of Avranches). Dom. J. Huynes, *loc. cit.*, ch. viii, p. 105.

263. Dom Félibien, *Histoire de l'abbaye royale de Saint-Denis....* Paris, 1706, in folio, p. 341.

264. Richer, *Histoire manuscrite de la Pucelle*, ms. fr. 10,448, fol. 13. S. Luce, *Jeanne d'Arc à Domremy*, proofs and illustrations, xxiv.

265. *Trial*, vol. i, pp. 173, 248, 249.

266. *Ibid.*, p. 170.

267. *La vierge Marguerite substituée à la Lucine antique*, analysis of an unpublished poem of the fifteenth century, Paris, 1885, in 8vo, p. 2. Rabelais, *Gargantua*, vol. i, ch. vi. L'Abbé J.B. Thiers, *Traité des superstitions qui regarde les sacrements selon l'Écriture sainte*, Paris, 1697 (4 vols. in 12mo), vol. i, p. 109.

268. S. Luce, *Jeanne d'Arc à Domremy*, proofs and illustrations, ccxxxiv, p. 272.

269. Abbé Bourgaut, *Guide du pélerin à Domremy*, Nancy, 1878, in 12mo, p. 60. É. Hinzelin, *Chez Jeanne d'Arc*, pp. 65-72.

270. Voragine, *La légende dorée* (Légende de Sainte Marguerite). Douhet, *Dictionnaire des légendes*, pp. 824-836.

271. Gaston Paris, *La littérature française au moyen âge*, 1890, in 16mo, p. 212.

340

272. La Curne, *Dictionnaire de l'ancien langage français,* under the word *Olibrius.* Olibrius figures also in the legend of Saint Reine, where he is governor of the Gallic Provinces. The legend of Saint Reine is only a somewhat ancient variant of the legend of Saint Margaret.

273.　　　　Hail,　　　　thou　　　　holy　　　　Catherine, Virgin Maid so pure and fine.

Bibliothèque Mazarine, manuscrit, 515. *Recueil de prières,* folio 55. This manuscript comes from the banks of the Meuse.

274. S. Luce, *loc. cit.,* proofs and illustrations, xiii, p. 19, note 2. E. de Bouteiller and G. de Braux, *Nouvelles recherches sur la famille de Jeanne d'Arc,* pp. xvi and 62. *Guide et souvenir du pélerin à Domremy,* Nancy, 1878, in 18mo, p. 60.

275. J. Miélot, *Vie de sainte Cathérine,* text revised by Marius Sepet, 1881, in large 8vo.

276. Gaston Paris, La littérature française au moyen âge, pp. 82, 213.

277. Voragine, *La légende dorée,* 1846, pp. 789-797. Douhet, *Dictionnaire des légendes,* 1855, pp. 824-836.

278. *Trial,* vol. i, p. 128. Hinzelin, *Chez Jeanne d'Arc,* p. 29. When we come to the trial, we shall consider whether it be possible to reconcile Jeanne's assertions with regard to this vow.

279. *Trial,* vol. i, p. 128; vol. iii, p. 219.

280. *Ibid.,* index, under the words, *Voices, Catherine,* and *Marguerite.*

281. *Ibid.,* vol. i, pp. 71-85, 167 *seq.,* 186 *seq.*

282. *Ibid.,* pp. 185, 186.

283. In the French, humblement. In old French humblement means courteously. In Froissart there is a passage quoted by La Curne: "Li contes de Hainaut rechut ces seigneurs d'Engleterre, l'un après l'autre, moult humblement."

284. *Trial,* vol. i, p. 130.

285. *Ibid.,* p. 130.

286. *Ibid.,* vol. ii, p. 413, note 2.

287. *Trial,* vol. i, p. 52, marginal comment of the d'Urfé MS.: *Celavit visiones curato, patri et matri et cuicumque,* in the *Trial,* vol. i, p. 128, note. Lanéry d'Arc, *Mémoires et consultations en faveur de Jeanne d'Arc,* p. 471.

288. *Trial,* vol. i, p. 171: "*Et luy racontet l'angle la pitié qui estoit ou royaume de France.*" *Pitié* means here occasion for tenderness and love. The angel is thinking especially of the Dauphin. For the

meaning and use of this word, cf. Monstrelet, vol. iii, p. 74: "... *et le peuple plorant de pitié et de joie qu'ils avoient à regarder leur seigneur.*" Gérard de Nevers in La Curne: "*Pitié estoit de voir festoyer leur seigneur; on ne pourroit retenir ses larmes en voyant la joie qu'ils marquoient de recevoir leur seigneur.*"

289. *Trial*, vol. i, p. 53.

290. *Trial*, vol. ii, p. 444.

291. "Nonne alias dictum fuit quod Francia per mulierem desolaretur, et postea per Virginem restaurari debebat?" Evidence given by Durand Lassois in Trial, vol. ii, p. 444.

292. *Trial*, vol. ii, p. 447. Nevertheless the woman Le Royer of Domremy remembered it and was astonished by it. *Et hunc ipsa testis hæc audisse recordata est et stupefacta fuit.*

293. Monstrelet, vol. iii, p. 180. Jean Chartier, *Chronique latine*, ed. Vallet de Viriville, vol. i, p. 13. Th. Basin, *Histoire de Charles VII et de Louis XI*, vol. i, pp. 44 *et seq.*

294. Alain Chartier, *Quadriloge invectif*, ed. André Duchesne, Paris, 1617, pp. 440 *et seq. Ordonnances*, vol. xi, pp. 101 *et seq.* Viutry, *Les monnaies sous les trois premiers Valois*, Paris, 1881, in 8vo, *passim*. De Beaucourt, *Histoire de Charles VII*, vol. i, ch. xi.

295. Juvénal des Ursins and *Journal d'un bourgeois de Paris, passim*. Letter from Nicholas de Clemangis to Gerson, in *Clemangis opera omnia*, 1613, in 4to, vol. ii, pp. 159 *et seq.*

296. Le P. Denifle, *La désolation des églises, monastères*, Mâcon, 1897, in 8vo, introduction.

297. *Trial*, vol. ii, pp. 402, 434.

298. These two persons, however, are only known to us through somewhat doubtful genealogical documents. *Trial*, vol. v, p. 252. Boucher de Molandon, *La famille de Jeanne d'Arc*, p. 127. G. de Braux and E. de Bouteiller, *Nouvelles recherches*, pp. 7 *et seq.*

299. *Trial*, vol. i, pp. 52, 53.

300. *Ibid.*, vol. ii, pp. 404, 407, 409, 411, 414, 416, *passim*.

301. *Trial*, vol. ii, pp. 402, 434.

302. *Ibid.*, p. 402. Concerning Jeanne's religious observances, see *Ibid.*, index, under the words *Messe, Vierge, Cloche*.

303. *Ibid.*, vol. ii, p. 429.

304. *Ibid.*, p. 427.

305. *Trial*, vol. ii, p. 432.

306. *Ibid.*, vol. i, pp. 52, 53.

307. *Ibid.*, p. 53.

308. *Ibid.*, vol. ii, pp. 393, 400, *passim*.

309. Psalm ci, 20-23. *Vulgate*, Douai Version (W.S.).

310. Grégoire de Tours, Le livre des miracles, ed. Bordier, 1864, in 8vo, vol. ii, pp. 27, 31. Hincmar, Vita sancti Remigii in the Patrologie de Migne, vol. cxxv, pp. 1130 et seq. H. Jadart, Bibliographie des ouvrages concernant la vie et le culte de saint Remi, évêque de Reims, 1891, in 8vo.

311. Froissart, Bk. II, ch. lxxiv. Le doyen de Saint-Thibaud, p. 328. Vertot, *Dissertation au sujet de la sainte ampoule conservée à Reims*, in *Mémoires de l'Académie des Inscriptions et Belles-Lettres*, 1736, vol. ii, pp. 619-633; vol. iv, pp. 1350-1365. Leber, *Des cérémonies du sacre ou recherches historiques et critiques sur les mœurs, les coutumes dans l'ancienne monarchie*, Paris, Reims, 1825, in 8vo, pp. 255 *et seq.*

312. A. Monteil, *Histoire des Français*, 1853, vol. ii, p. 194.

313. *Mystère de saint Remi*, Arsenal Library, ms. no. 3.364. This mystery dates from the fifteenth century, from the time of the wars in Champagne. The following lines relate to the misfortunes of the kingdom:

SAINT-ESTIENNE

O Jhesucrist, qui les sains cieulx
As de lumiere environnez,
Soleil et lune enluminés,
Et ordonnez à ta plaisance;
Pour le tres doulz païs de France
Les martirs, non pas un mais tous,
A jointes mains et à genoux
Te requierent que tu effaces
La grant doleur de France; et faces
Par ta sainte digne vertu
Qu'ilz aient paix; adfin que tu,
Ta doulce mere et tous les sains,
Et ceulx qui sont de pechiez sains,
Devotement servis y soient!...

SAINT STEPHEN

O Jesus Christ who hast surrounded the heavens with light and kindled the sun and the moon, command, if it be thy will, the martyrs, not one only but all, to clasp their hands and on bended knee to implore thee to remove the great sorrow from France; and by thy holy and august merit ordain that they may have peace, that thou, thy sweet mother and all the saints and those who are cleansed from sin may be served devoutly!...

SAINT-NICOLAS

Dieu tout puissant fay tant qu'il ysse
Hors du doulz païs sans amer
Que toutes gens doivent amer
C'est France, où sont les bons Chrestiens
S'on les confort; si les soustiens
Car l'engin de leur adversaire
Et son faulx art les tire à faire
Contre ta sainte voulenté.
Ayez pitié de Crestienté
Beau sire Dieux
Tant en France qu'en autres lieux!
Ce seroit Pitié à oultrance
Que si noble roiaume, comme France,
Fust par male temptacion
Mis du tout à perdicion....
Fol. 3, verso.

SAINT NICHOLAS

God all powerful grant that he may issue forth from that sweet land which all must love, all France, where are good Christians, and may they be comforted, and may they be sustained; for the power of their adversary and his false art tempt them to withstand thy holy will. Have pity on Christendom, good lord God, on other lands as well as on France! It would be the worst of pities if so noble a kingdom as France were through much temptation to fall into perdition....

314. *Mystère de Saint Remi*, Arsenal Library, ms. no. 3.364, fol. 69, verso.

315. *Mystère de Saint Remi*, fol. 71, verso.

316.

Le bon archevesque Remy,
Qui tant aime le sang royal,
Qui tant a son conseil loyal,
Qui tant aime Dieu et l'Église.

Mystère de Saint Remi, fol. 77.

The good Archbishop Remi, who so dearly cherishes the *royal* blood, so faithful in counsel, so devout a lover of God and the Church.

317. *Trial*, vol. i, p. 53.

318. *Trial*, vol. i, p. 130; vol. ii, p. 456; vol. iii, p. 3, *passim*.

319. S. Luce, Jeanne d'Arc à Domremy, pp. cliv, clv, clvi, 97, 359 et seq.; La France pendant la guerre de cent ans, p. 287.

320. *Trial*, vol. i, p. 53.

321. *Trial*, vol. i, p. 128.

322. *Ibid.*, vol. ii, p. 443. Boucher de Molandon, *La famille de Jeanne d'Arc*, p. 146. E. de Bouteiller and G. de Braux, *Nouvelles recherches sur la famille de Jeanne d'Arc*, introduction, pp. xxi, xxii.

323. *Trial*, vol. ii, pp. 411, 431, 439. S. Luce, *Jeanne d'Arc à Domremy*, p. clxi. Hinzelin, *Chez Jeanne d'Arc*, p. 92.

324. *Trial*, vol. ii, pp. 443, 444.

325. *Trial*, vol. ii, p. 442.

326. *Ibid.*, vol. i, pp. 53, 221; vol. ii, p. 443.

327. Genealogical Inquiry made by the Bailie of Chaumont concerning Jehan Royer (8 October, 1555) in E. de Bouteiller and G. de Braux, *Nouvelles recherches sur la famille de Jeanne d'Arc*, p. 62. Document of doubtful authenticity..

328. *Chronique de la Pucelle*, p. 271. Jean Chartier, *Chronique*, vol. i, p. 67. Le R.P. Benoît, *Histoire ecclésiastique et politique de la ville et du diocèse de Toul*, Toul, 1707, p. 529. S. Luce, *Jeanne d'Arc à Domremy*, pp. clxii, clxiii. Léon Mougenot, *Jeanne d'Arc, le Duc de Lorraine et le Sire de Baudricourt*, 1895, in 8vo. E. de Bouteiller and G. de Braux, *Nouvelles recherches*, p. xviii. G. Nioré, *Le pays de Jeanne d'Arc*, in *Mémoires de la Société académique de l'Aube*, 1894, vol. xxxi, pp. 307-320. De Pange, *Le Pays de Jeanne d'Arc; Le fief et l'arrière-fief. Les Baudricourt*, Paris, 1903, in 8vo.

329. *Trial*, vol. ii, p. 436.

330. *Ibid.*, vol. i, p. 53.

331. *Ibid.*, vol. ii, p. 456.

332. *Chronique des quatre premiers Valois*, ed. S. Luce, Paris, 1861, in 8vo, pp. 46-48.

333. P. de Fénin, *Mémoires*, ed. Mademoiselle Dupont, Paris, 1837, pp. 195, 222, 223.

334. L. Jarry, *Le compte de l'armée anglaise au siège d'Orléans*, Orléans, 1892, in 8vo, pp. 75, 76.

335. *Et quod aberet in commendam: illud regnum, Trial,* vol. ii, p. 456 (evidence of Bertrand de Poulengy).

336. *Trial,* vol. ii, p. 456.

337. See La Curne and Godefroy for the word *commande.* Durand de Maillane, *Dictionnaire de droit canonique,* 1770, vol. i, pp. 567 *et seq.*

338. See *ante,* p. 59, *post,* pp. 177, 178.

339. *Trial,* vol. ii, pp. 392, 393, 458, 459.

340. As for Nicolas de Vouthon, priest of the Abbey of Cheminon, what is stated concerning him in the evidence of the 2nd and 3rd November, 1476, seems improbable. *Trial,* vol. v, p. 252. E. de Bouteiller and G. de Braux, *Nouvelles recherches sur la famille de Jeanne d'Arc,* pp. xviii *et seq.,* 9.

341. *Trial,* vol. ii, p. 475. Servais, in *Mémoires de la Société des Lettres, Sciences et Arts de Bar-le-Duc,* vol. vi, p. 139. E. de Bouteiller and G. de Braux, *Nouvelles recherches,* p. xxviii. S. Luce, *Jeanne d'Arc à Domremy,* proofs and illustrations xcv, p. 143 and note 3. De Beaucourt, *Histoire de Charles VII,* vol. ii, p. 204.

342. This appears from the manner in which he reports Jeanne's words.

343. *Trial,* vol. ii, pp. 451, 458.

344. Chronique de la Pucelle, p. 72. Journal du siège, p. 35.

345. Trial, vol. ii, p. 444. L. Mougenot, Jeanne d'Arc, le Duc de Lorraine et le Sire de Baudricourt, Nancy, 1895, in 8vo.

346. *Trial,* vol. i, p. 53.

347. *Ibid.,* p. 440.

348. *Ibid.,* p. 423.

349. *Trial,* vol. i, pp. 131, 132, 219.

350. *Trial,* vol. ii, p. 421, cf. p. 433, "*et alii juvenes de ea deridebant,*" said Colin's son, referring to her piety.

351. *Ibid.,* vol. i, p. 68.

352. Report of André d'Epernon in S. Luce, *Jeanne d'Arc à Domremy,* p. clxvii and proofs and illustrations, pp. 217, 218, 220.

353. *Trial,* vol. i, pp. 51, 214; vol. ii, pp. 391-454. S. Luce, *Jeanne d'Arc à Domremy,* p. clxxvi.

354. *Trial,* vol. i, p. 214.

355. S. Luce, *Jeanne d'Arc à Domremy,* p. clxxvii.

356. *Trial,* vol. i, pp. 51, 214; vol. ii, p. 402.

357. *Ibid.*, vol. ii, pp. 409, 423, 428, 463.

358. *Ibid.*, pp. 416, 417.

359. Monstrelet, vol. iii, p. 314.

360. *Trial*, vol. i, p. 51.

361. S. Luce, *Jeanne d'Arc à Domremy*, p. clxxvii.

362. Expilly, Dictionnaire géographique de la France, under the word Neufchâteau.

363. S.M. de Vernon, *Histoire générale et particulière du tiers-ordre de Saint-François*, Paris, 1667, 3 vols. in 8vo. Hilarion de Nolay, *Histoire du tiers-ordre*, Lyon, 1694, in 4to.

364. Acta Sanctorum, March, vol. i, p. 549.

365. Wadding, *Annales Minorum*, vol. v, p. 183.

366. Jean Morel declares that she was at Neufchâteau four days, and he adds: "What I tell you I know, for I was with the others at Neufchâteau" (*Trial*, vol. ii, p. 392); Gérard Guillemette speaks of four or five days (*Ibid.*, p. 414); Nicolas Bailly of three or four (*Ibid.*, p. 451). But Jeanne told her judges at Rouen that she stayed a fortnight at Neufchâteau (*Ibid.*, vol. i, p. 51). When she gave her evidence, the event was less remote, and doubtless her recollection of it was more accurate.

367. *Ibid.*, vol. i, p. 51.

368. S. Luce, *Jeanne d'Arc à Domremy*, chs. ix, x, xi. Abbé V. Mourot, *Jeanne d'Arc et le tiers-ordre de Saint-François*, Saint-Dié, 1886, in 8vo. L. de Kerval, *Jeanne d'Arc et les Franciscains*, Vanves, 1893, in 18mo. *E iera begina*, says a correspondent of Morosini, edited by Lefèvre-Pontalis, vol. iii, p. 92 and note 2.

369. *Trial*, vol. i, pp. 128, 219. E. Misset, *Jeanne d'Arc Champenoise*, 1895, in 8vo, p. 28.

370. Trial, vol. i, p. 219: quibus obediebat in omnibus, nisi in processu Tullensi.

371. *Trial*, vol. i, p. 215. Article 9 of the deed of accusation is drawn up as the result of an inquiry made at Neufchâteau.

372. *Trial*, vol. ii, p. 396, *passim*.

373. S. Luce, *Jeanne d'Arc à Domremy*, pp. clxxx, 230.

374. Mistère du siège, v, 497.

375. *Chronique de la Pucelle*, chs. xxxiv, xxxv. Jean Chartier, *Chronique*, chs. xxxii, xxxv; *Journal du siège*, pp. 2 *et seq.*

376. *Trial*, vol. i, pp. 52, 216.

377. *Ibid.*, vol. ii, p. 456.

378. *Trial*, vol. ii, pp. 428, 434. S. Luce, *Jeanne d'Arc à Domremy*, p. clxxx. E. de Bouteiller and G. de Braux, *Nouvelles recherches*, p. xxiii.

379. *Les caquets de l'accouchée*, new edition by E. Fournier and Le Roux de Lincy, Paris, 1855, in 16mo, introduction.

380. *Trial*, vol. i, p. 53; vol. ii, p. 443.

381. *Ibid.*, vol. ii, pp. 428, 430, 434.

382. *Ibid.*, p. 416.

383. *Ibid.*, p. 431.

384. *Trial*, vol. ii, p. 418.

385. Ibid., p. 419: dixit quod nescivit recessum dictæ Johannæ; quæ testis propter hoc multum flebat, quia eam multum propter suam bonitatem diligebat et quod sua socia erat.

386. *Ibid.*, vol. ii, p. 436.

387. S. Luce, *Jeanne d'Arc à Domremy*, pp. clxviii, 222, 234.

388. *Chronique de la Pucelle*, p. 273; *La Chronique de Lorraine* in Dom Calmet, *Histoire de Lorraine*, vol. iii, col. vj, gives an amplified version of these words, the authenticity of which is doubtful.

389. *Trial*, vol. i, pp. 219, 220. The source is doubtful. Nevertheless the accusation here lays stress on these facts produced by the inquiry. If Jeanne denied having spoken these words, it was because she had forgotten them, or because they had been so changed that she could disavow the form in which they were presented to her.

390. See *ante*, page 66.

391. *Trial*, vol. ii, p. 446.

392. *Trial*, vol. ii, p. 461.

393. S. Luce, *Jeanne d'Arc à Domremy*, p. cxcxiv.

394. *Trial*, vol. ii, pp. 460, 461 (evidence of Jean le Fumeux in the rehabilitation trial).

395. *Ibid.*, p. 446.

396. *Ibid.*, p. 447.

397. *Trial*, vol. ii, p. 448.

398. Quæ puella multum bene loquebatur. Trial, vol. ii, p. 450. S. Luce, Jeanne d'Arc à Domremy, p. 103.

399. *Ibid.*, vol. v, p. 363; *Journal du siège*, p. 45. S. Luce, *Jeanne d'Arc à Domremy*, pp. xcv, cxi, cxxvj. De Beaucourt, *Histoire de Charles VII*, vol. ii, p. 204, note. E. de Bouteiller and G. de Braux, *Nouvelles recherches*, pp. xxv *et seq.*

400. *A sol tournois* is the twentieth part of a *livre tournois* (W.S.).

401. S. Luce, *Jeanne d'Arc à Domremy*, pp. cxc, 160, 161.

402. *Trial*, vol. ii, pp. 435-457. E. de Bouteiller and G. de Braux, *Nouvelles recherches*, pp. xxvi, xxvii.

403. *Trial*, vol. ii, p. 436. De Beaucourt, *Histoire de Charles VII*, vol. ii, pp. 396 *et seq.*

404. *Trial*, vol. ii, p. 436. S. Luce, *Jeanne d'Arc à Domremy*, p. cxci.

405. *Trial*, vol. ii, p. 436.

406. *Ibid.*, p. 436, 437.

407. *Ibid.*, vol. i, pp. 161, 176, 332. *Journal du siège*, p. 45. *Chronique de la Pucelle*, p. 372.

408. *Trial*, vol. ii, p. 446.

409. Voragine, *La légende dorée*, in the Festival of the Exaltation of the Holy Cross.

410. Migne, *Dictionnaire des sciences occultes*, Paris, 2 vols. in large 8vo, under the word *Exorcisme*.

411. *Trial*, vol. ii, p. 446.

412. *Trial*, vol. iii, p. 115. *Journal du siège*, p. 48. *Mirouer des femmes vertueuses* in the *Trial*, vol. iv, p. 267.

413. Extract from the eighth report of Guillaume Charrier, in the *Trial*, vol. v, pp. 257 *et seq.*

414. *Trial*, vol. ii, p. 447.

415. *Ibid.*, vol. i, p. 53; vol. ii, pp. 443 *et seq.*

416. *Ibid.*, vol. ii, pp. 445-447.

417. *Ibid.*, pp. 447-457.

418. *Ibid.*, p. 406. S. Luce, *Jeanne d'Arc à Domremy*, p. 160, note 6.

419. Monstrelet, vol. iv, pp. 314, 315. Anonymous poem on the arrival of the Maid, in the *Trial*, vol. v, p. 30.

420. Durand Lassois says it cost twelve francs, Jean de Metz, sixteen. "*Ce serait aujourd'hui un cheval de cent écus.*" It would be a horse worth one hundred crowns to-day (L. Champion, *Jeanne d'Arc écuyère*, 1901, p. 55). According to the reckoning of P. Clément, from 400 to 800 francs (*Jacques Cœur et Charles VII*, 1873, p. lxvi).

421. *Trial*, vol. i, pp. 54, 222; vol. ii, pp. 391, 406, 432, 437, 442-450, 456, 457; vol. iii, pp. 87, 115. Extract from the eighth account of Guillaume Charrier and from the thirteenth account of Hémon Raguier, in the *Trial*, vol. v, pp. 257 *et seq.*

422. Et postquam ipsa Johanna fuit in peregrinacio in Sancto Nicolas et exstitit versus dominum ducem Lotharingiae, says Bertrand de Poulengy, Trial, vol. ii, p. 457. Cf. The Evidence of J. Robert, in E. de Bouteiller and G. de Braux, Nouvelles recherches sur la famille de Jeanne d'Arc, pp. 33, 34. It is impossible to find in the text of the Trial a redundancy such as the evidence of D. Lannois and the woman Le Royer would lead us to expect. A. Renard, Jeanne d'Arc. Examen d'une question de lieu, Orléans, 1861, in 8vo, 16 pages. G. de Braux, Jeanne d'Arc à Saint-Nicolas, Nancy, 1889, in 8vo. De Pimodan, La première étape de Jeanne d'Arc, 1890, in 8vo, with maps.

423. Le Père Anselme, *Histoire généalogique de la maison de France*, vol. ii, p. 218. Ludovic Drapeyron, *Jeanne d'Arc et Philippe le Bon*, in *Revue de Géographie*, November, 1886, p. 236. S. Luce, *Jeanne d'Arc à Domremy*, pp. lxvi, cxcix.

424. *Œuvres du Roi René*, by Le Comte de Quatrebarbes, Angers, 1845, vol. i, preface, pp. lxxvi *et seq.* Lecoy de la Marche, *Le Roi René, sa vie, son administration, ses travaux artistiques et littéraires*, Paris, 1875, 2 vols. in 8vo, and Giry, Review in the *Revue critique*.

425. La guerre de la hottée de pommes.

426. Dom Calmet, *Histoire de Lorraine*, vol. ii, col. 695, 703.

427. *Trial*, vol. iii, p. 93.

428. S. Luce, *Jeanne d'Arc à Domremy*, pp. cxcvii, clxxxvii, clxxxviii, and 236. The register of the Archives of La Meuse, B. 1051, bears trace of a regular correspondence between the Duke of Bar and Baudricourt.

429. *Chronique du doyen de Saint-Thibaud*, in Dom Calmet, *Histoire de Lorraine*, proofs and illustrations, vol. ii, col. cxcix. S. Luce, *Jeanne d'Arc à Domremy*, pp. cxcvii *et seq.*

430. Letter from Jean Desch, Secretary of the town of Metz, in the *Trial*, vol. v, p. 355. Dom Calmet, *Histoire de Lorraine*, vol. ii, proofs and illustrations, col. cxcix.

431. S. Luce, *Jeanne d'Arc à Domremy*, p. cc, note.

432. *Trial*, vol. iii, p. 87. Dom Calmet, *Histoire de Lorraine*, vol. iii, proofs and illustrations, col. vj.

433. *Trial*, vol. ii, pp. 391, 444.

434. *Ibid.*, vol. i, p. 129.

435. *Trial*, vol. i, p. 54; vol. ii, pp. 438, 445, 447, 457. *Relation du greffier de La Rochelle*, in the *Revue historique*, vol. iv, p. 336.

436. Relation du greffier de La Rochelle, in the Revue historique, ibid.

437. *Trial*, vol. ii, pp. 406, 432, 442, 457; vol. iii, p. 209. S. Luce, *Jeanne d'Arc à Domremy*, pp. xcv, 143 note 3. G. de Braux and E. de Bouteiller, *Nouvelles recherches*, pp. xxix *et seq.*

438. Les routiers en Lorraine, in the Journal de la Société archéologique de Lorraine, 1866, p. 161. Dr. A. Lapierre, La guerre de cent ans dans l'Argonne et le Rethélois, Sedan, 1900, in 8vo.

439. *Journal du siège* (interpolation); *Chronique de la Pucelle*, p. 272 (a document of doubtful authority owing to its hagiographical character).

440. Trial, vol. i, p. 54; vol. ii, p. 437. Chronique du Mont-Saint-Michel, vol. i, p. 30. De Boismarmin, Mémoire sur la date de l'arrivée de Jeanne d'Arc à Chinon, in the Bulletin du comité des travaux historiques et scientifiques, 1892, pp. 350-359. Ulysse Chevalier, L'abjuration de Jeanne d'Arc, p. 10, note 1. Jeanne had returned to Vaucouleurs about the first Sunday in Lent, the 13th of February, 1429 (Trial, vol. iii, p. 437). Bertrand de Poulengy says that the journey to Chinon (6th March) lasted eleven days, and that sometimes they travelled by night only (ibid.). It is difficult to admit that they started from Vaucouleurs on the 23rd of February, and that about 660 kilometres were traversed in eleven days.

441. *Trial*, vol. ii, pp. 431, 446.

442. *Ibid.*, p. 449.

443. *Ibid.*, vol. i, p. 55.

444. De Pimodan, *La première étape de Jeanne d'Arc*, Paris, 1891, in 8vo, with maps.

445. *Trial*, vol. i, p. 54.

446. Jolibois, Dictionnaire historique de la Haute-Marne, p. 492.

447. De Pimodan, La première étape de Jeanne d'Arc, loc. cit.

448. *Trial*, vol. i, pp. 54, 55.

449. *Ibid.*, vol. iii, p. 437. According to the somewhat improbable testimony of Bertrand de Poulengy. *See ante*, p. 96, note 6.

450. *Trial*, vol. ii, p. 457.

451. *Ibid.*, pp. 437, 438.

452. *Ibid.*, vol. iii, p. 199.

453. *Ibid.*, vol. ii, p. 458.

454. *Trial*, vol. ii, p. 438.

455. *Ibid.*, vol. i, p. 54; vol. ii, p. 437.

456. *Ibid.*, vol. ii, pp. 406, 432, 445, 448, 457.

457. Monstrelet, vol. v, p. 269. Th. Basin, vol. i, p. 44. Bueil, *Le jouvencel*, introduction. Royal Pardons, in E. Boutaric, *Institutions militaires de la France avant les armées permanentes....* 1863, in 8vo, p. 266. *Récit du prieur de Droillet*, ed. Quicherat, in *Bibliothèque de l'École des Chartes*, fourth series, vol. iii, p. 359. Mantellier, *Histoire de la communauté des marchands fréquentant la rivière de Loire*, vol. i, p. 195. Le P. H. Denifle, *La désolation des églises, monastères, hôpitaux en France, vers le milieu du XVe siècle*, Mâcon, in 8vo.

458. *Trial*, vol. iii, p. 203.

459. Abbé J.-J. Bourassé, *Les miracles de Madame Sainte Katerine de Fierboys en Touraine, d'après un manuscrit de la Bibliothèque Impériale*, Paris, in 12mo, 1858, p. 28.

460. I have here interwoven the account given by Seguin, *Trial*, vol. iii, p. 203, with that of Touroulde, *Trial*, vol. iii, pp. 86, 87. It seems to me the same incident reported summarily by the former, inexactly by the latter.

461. *Trial*, vol. i, pp. 56, 75; vol. iii, pp. 3, 21; vol. v, p. 378.

462. That Saint Catherine was known in the west shortly before the Crusades is possible, but not that her worship should date back to Charles Martel; at any rate it flourished in the days of Jeanne d'Arc. Cf. H. Moranvillé, *Un pèlerinage en Terre sainte et au Sinaï au XVe siècle*, in the *Bibliothèque de l'École des Chartes*, vol. lxvi (1905), pp. 70 *et seq.*

463. *Les miracles de Madame Sainte Katerine*, passim. G. Launay, Article in Bull. soc. archéol. du Vendômois, 1880, vol. xix, pp. 23-25.

464. G. Lefèvre-Pontalis, *La guerre des partisans dans la Haute Normandie* (1424-1429), in *Bibliothèque de l'École des Chartes* (1893-1896).

465. *Les miracles de Madame Sainte Katerine*, passim.

466. *Trial*, vol. i, p. 75.

467. Journal d'un bourgeois de Paris, p. 190. Alain Chartier, *L'espérance ou consolation des trois vertus*, in Œuvres, p. 271. Jean Chartier, *Chronique*, vol. i, p. 14.

468. *Mistère du siège*, line 497.

469. Perceval de Cagny, pp. 21, 22.

470. Chronique de la Pucelle, p. 255. Chronique de l'établissement de la fête in the Trial, vol. v, p. 286. Le Maire, Histoire et antiquités de la ville et duché d'Orléans, Orléans, 1645, in 4to, pp. 129 et seq. Lottin, Recherches historiques sur la ville d'Orléans, Orléans, 1836-1845 (7 vols. in 8vo), vol. i, p. 197.

471. Joseph Stevenson, *Letters and Papers*, Introduction, vol. i, p. xlvii. De Beaucourt, *Histoire de Charles VII*, vol. ii, p. 17.

472. Rymer, *Fœdera*, vol. iv, part iv, p. 135. Mademoiselle A. de Villaret, *Campagne des Anglais dans l'Orléanais, la Beauce chartraine et le Gâtinais (1421-1428)*, Orléans, 1893, in 8vo, original documents, p. 134. Stevenson, *Letters and Papers*, vol. i, pp. 403 *et seq.*

473. Monstrelet, vol. iv, p. 300.

474. L. Jarry, Le compte de l'armée anglaise au siège d'Orléans, 1428-1429, Orléans, 1892, in 8vo, pp. 59 et seq.

475. Monstrelet, vol. iv, p. 293. Rymer, *Fœdera*, vol. iv, part iv, pp. 132, 135, 138.

476. L. Jarry, *Le compte de l'armée anglaise*, pp. 26, 27.

477. Monstrelet, vol. iv, p. 294. Stevenson, *Letters and Papers*, p. lxii.

478. Boucher de Molandon and A. de Beaucorps, *L'armée anglaise vaincue par Jeanne d'Arc sous les murs d'Orléans*, Orléans, 1892, in 8vo, p. 61. L. Jarry, *loc. cit.*

479. Le Maire, *Antiquités*, p. 29.

480. Astesan in *Paris et ses historiens*, by Le Roux de Lincy and Tisserand, pp. 528 *et seq.* Le Maire, *Antiquités*, ch. xix, pp. 75 *et seq.* P. Mantellier, *Histoire du siège d'Orléans*, in 18mo, pp. 22, 24. E. Fournier, *Le Conteur orléanais*, p. 111. C. Cuissard, *Étude sur la musique dans l'Orléanais*, Orléans, 1886, p. 50. Jodocius Sincere, *Itirerarium Galliae*, Amstelodami, 1655, pp. 24, 25. Paul Charpentier et Cuissard, *Histoire du siège d'Orléans, mémoire inédite de M. l'Abbé Dubois*, Orléans, 1894, in 8vo, p. 129. De Buzonnière, *Histoire architecturale de la ville d'Orléans*, 1849 (2 vols. in 8vo), vol. i, p. 76.

481. Jollois, *Histoire du siège d'Orléans*, Paris, 1833, in 4to, with plans. Lottin, *Recherches*, vol. i, pp. 183 *et seq.*

482. Jollois, Lettre à Messieurs les membres de la Société des Antiquaires de France, sur l'emplacement du fort des Tourelles de l'ancien pont d'Orléans, Paris, 1834, in folio with illustrations. Abbé

Dubois, Histoire du siège, dissertation, v. Lottin, Recherches, vol. i, pp. 15-18. Vergniaud Romagnési, Des différentes enceintes de la ville d'Orléans, pp. 17-19. A. Collin, Le Pont des Tourelles à Orléans, Orléans, 1895, in 8vo. Morosini, vol. iii, p. 13, note 2.

483. For some unknown reason modern historians have named the little island to the right of Saint-Laurent l'Île Charlemagne, which causes it to be confused with the Île Charlemagne lying to the East of l'Île-aux-Bœufs. On the accompanying plan we indicate the little island just below Biche-d'Orge by the name of Petite Île Charlemagne. Jollois, *Histoire du siège*, engraving 1. Abbé Dubois, *Histoire du siège*, pp. 193, 199. Boucher de Molandon, *Première expédition de Jeanne d'Arc*, p. 16. Manuscript of M. A. Cagnieul, librarian at Orléans.

484. Symphorien Guyon, *Histoire de l'église et diocèse d'Orléans*, Orléans, 1647, vol. i, preface. Le Maire, *Antiquités*, p. 36.

485. *Journal du siège*, pp. 13, 15. *Chronique de la Pucelle*, p. 270. Hubert, *Antiquités historiques de l'église royale d'Orléans*, Orléans, 1661, in 8vo. Le Maire, *Antiquités*, p. 284. Abbé Dubois, *Histoire du siège*, pp. 133, 205, 277, *passim*. Jollois, *Histoire du siège*, p. 21. H. Baraude, *Le siège d'Orléans et Jeanne d'Arc*, Paris, 1906, pp. 10 *et seq.*

486. Le Maire, *Antiquités*, p. 43.

487. Abbé Dubois, Histoire du siège, p. 296. Boucher de Molandon, Première expédition de Jeanne d'Arc, le ravitaillement d'Orléans, nouveaux documents, Orléans, 1874, in large 8vo, with topographical plan: Orléans, la Loire et ses îles en 1429.

488. Abbé Dubois, *Histoire du siège*, pp. 391, 399. Jollois, *Histoire du siège*, pp. 41, 44. P. Mantellier, *Histoire du siège*, Orléans, 1867, in 8vo, p. 24. Lottin, *Recherches sur Orléans*, vol. i, p. 141.

489. Le Roux de Lincy, Chants historiques et populaires du temps de Charles VII, Paris, 1862, in 18mo, p. 28.

490. Journal d'un bourgeois de Paris, pp. 225, 226. Geste des nobles, p. 202. Chronique de la Pucelle, p. 251. Jean Chartier, Chronique, vol. i, p. 59. Jarry, Le compte de l'armée anglaise, pp. 107, 112.

491. Lottin, *Recherches*, vol. i, pp. 164, 171. P. Mantellier, *Histoire du siège*, p. 25.

492. *The Monk of Dunfermline*, in *Trial*, vol. v, p. 341. Le Maire, *Antiquités*, pp. 283 *et seq.* Lottin, *Recherches*, vol. i, pp. 160, 161.

493. Jollois, *Histoire du siège*, p. 6. Lottin, *Recherches*, vol. i, pp. 202-205.

494. An arrow shot from the long-bow, the feathers of the arrow were spirally arranged to produce a spinning movement in its flight (W.S.).

495. The accounts of the fortresses, in Journal du siège, pp. 301 et seq. Jollois, Histoire du siège, p. 12. P. Mantellier, Histoire du siège, pp. 15-17. Loiseleur, Comptes des dépenses faites par Charles VII pour secourir Orléans pendant le siège de 1428, Orléans, 1868, in 8vo, p. 113. Boucher de Molandon et de Beaucorps, L'armée anglaise vaincue par Jeanne d'Arc, p. 81.

496. Accounts of Hémon Raguier, Bibl. Nat. Fr. 7858, fol. 41. Loiseleur, *Comptes des dépenses*, p. 65. Pallet, *Nouvelle histoire du Berry*, vol. iii, pp. 78-80. Vallet de Viriville, in *Bulletin de la Société d'histoire de France. Cabinet historique*, vol. v, part ii, p. 107. P. Mantellier, *Histoire du siège*, p. 15.

497. A. Thomas, Le siège d'Orléans, Jeanne d'Arc et les capitouls de Toulouse, in Annales du Midi, April, 1889, p. 232. M. Boudet, Villandrando et les écorcheurs à Saint-Flour, pp. 18, 19. A. de Villaret, Campagne des Anglais, p. 61.

498. The monk of Dunfermline in the *Trial*, vol. v, p. 341.

499. *Journal du siège*, p. 51. *Chronique de la fête* in the *Trial*, vol. v, p. 296. Lottin, *Recherches*, vol. i, pp. 27-31.

500. Hubert, Antiquitez historiques de l'église royale de Saint-Aignan d'Orléans, 1661, in 8vo, pp. 1-15.

501. *Trial*, vol. iii, p. 32. *Journal du siège*, p. 14. Hubert, *loc. cit.*, chs. iii, iv. Lottin, *Recherches*, vol. i, pp. 82, 83.

502. A livre varied in weight from province to province; generally it was about seventeen ounces (W.S.).

503. Le Maire, *Antiquités*, p. 285. P. Mantellier, *Histoire du siège*, p. 16.

504. Chronique de la Pucelle, pp. 257, 258. Journal du siège, pp. 6, 7. Lottin, Recherches, vol. i, p. 204. J. Devaux, Le Gâtinais au temps de Jeanne d'Arc, in Ann. Soc. hist. et arch. du Gâtinais, vol. v, 1887, p. 220.

505. Journal du siège, p. 92.

506. Geste des Nobles, p. 204. Chronique de la Pucelle, p. 256. Letter from Salisbury to the Commons of London, in Delpit, Collection de documents français qui se trouvent en Angleterre, pp. 236, 237. Jarry, Le compte de l'armée anglaise, pp. 79-89.

507. Abbé Dubois, Histoire du siège, p. 11. Jarry, Le compte de l'armée anglaise, p. 82. Boucher de Molandon, Les comptes de ville d'Orléans des quatorzième et quinzième siècles, Orléans, 1880, in 8vo, pp. 91 et seq.

508. Lottin, *Recherches*, vol. i, p. 205. P. Mantellier, *Histoire du siège*, p. 17.

509. Journal du siège, p. 4.

510. *Journal du siège*, pp. 2-4. Boucher de Molandon et de Beaucorps, *L'armée anglaise vaincue par Jeanne d'Arc*, p. 129.

511. L. Jarry, *Le compte de l'armée anglaise*, pp. 26, 28, 29. Boucher de Molandon and de Beaucorps, *L'armée anglaise vaincue par Jeanne d'Arc*, pp. 50 et seq. Mademoiselle A. de Villaret, *Campagne des anglais*, ch. iv, pp. 39, 53; Accounts of the siege, nos. 30, 31, p. 214. Lottin, *Recherches*, vol. i, p. 205.

512. L. Jarry, Le compte de l'armée anglaise, p. 61.

513. *Chronique de la Pucelle*, p. 258. Jean Chartier, *Chronique*, p. 66. Jean Raoulet in Chartier, *Chronique*, vol. iii, p. 198. *Journal du siège*, pp. 1, 2. Abbé Dubois, *Histoire du siège*, p. 246. P. Mantellier, *Histoire du siège*, p. 27. H. Baraude, *Le siège d'Orléans et Jeanne d'Arc*, p. 31.

514. Journal du siège, p. 4.

515. *Ibid.*, pp. 7-8. Lottin, *Recherches*, vol. i, pp. 208, 210.

516. *Journal du siège*, pp. 5-8.

517. *Journal du siège*, pp. 10, 12. *Chronique de la Pucelle*, p. 264. Monstrelet, vol. iv, p. 298. Jean Chartier, *Chronique*, vol. i, p. 63. *Mistère d'Orléans*, line 3104 et seq. *Chronique de la fête* in *Trial*, vol. v, p. 288. Morosini, vol. iii, p. 131. Lorenzo Buonincontro in Muratori, *Rerum Italicarum Scriptores*, vol. xxi, col. 136. Jarry, *Le compte de l'armée anglaise*, pp. 85, 86.

518. *Trial*, vol. iv, p. 345. *Chronique de la Pucelle*, p. 263. *Journal du siège*, p. 10. Vallet de Viriville, *Histoire de Charles VII*, vol. ii, p. 32.

519. L. Jarry, *Deux chansons normandes*, Orléans, 1894, in 8vo, p. 11.

520. The text published by M. Jarry has *mielux*.

521. Certes that wise man the Duke of Bedford, will keep himself in a fortress with his wife as snug as may be. He will drink good hypocras (a kind of wine). He looks after himself, leaves warfare and the poor and rich to rot in the ground.

522. Vallet de Viriville, *Histoire de Charles VII*, vol. i, p. 25; vol. ii, p. 389.

523. Monstrelet, vol. iv, pp. 273, 274. *Chronique de la Pucelle*, pp. 243, 247. Jean Chartier, *Chronique*, vol. i, p. 54. *Journal d'un bourgeois de Paris*, p. 221. *Cronique Martiniane*, p. 7.

524. Jean Chartier, *Chronique*, vol. ii, p. 105.

525. Mathieu d'Escouchy, *Chronique*, ed. Beaucourt, Paris, 1863, vol. i, p. 186. De Beaucourt, *Histoire de Charles VII*, vol. ii, p. 236.

526. Journal du siège, pp. 10, 12. Cronique Martiniane, p. 8. Le jouvencel, p. 277. Loiseleur, Comptes des dépenses, pp. 90, 91.

527. *Journal du siège*, pp. 12, 13. Abbé Dubois, *Histoire du siège*, p. 245. Boucher de Molandon et de Beaucorps, *L'armée anglaise vaincue par Jeanne d'Arc*, pp. 92, 111. Jean de Bueil, *Le jouvencel, passim*.

528. Journal du siège, p. 7.

529. *Le jouvencel*, vol. i, p. 142.

530. *Journal du siège*, p. 19. *Chronique de la Pucelle*, p. 270. Jean Chartier, *Chronique*, vol. i, p. 61. Le P. Denifle, *La désolation des églises de France*, petition C.

531. *Journal du siège*, pp. 16, 17.

532. *Ibid.*, p. 17. J.L. Micqueau, *Histoire du siège d'Orléans par les Anglais*, translated by Du Breton, Paris, 1631, p. 27. Abbé Dubois, *Histoire du siège*, p. 287. Lottin, *Recherches*, vol. i, pp. 209, 210.

533. *Livre*, if it were of Paris, was equivalent to one shilling, if of Tours, to ten pence (W.S.).

534. Journal du siège, p. 18. S. Luce, Jeanne d'Arc à Domremy, p. clxxxv. Loiseleur, Compte des dépenses faites par Charles VII pour secourir Orléans, in Mém. Soc. Arch. de l'Orléanais, vol. xi, pp. 114, 186.

535. *Journal du siège*, p. 28. Lottin, *Recherches*, vol. i, p. 214.

536. Loiseleur, *Comptes*, p. 114. P. Mantellier, *Histoire du siège*, p. 33.

537. *Journal du siège*, pp. 15, 18.

538. To the number of 2500. *Journal du siège*, p. 20. *Chronique de la Pucelle*, p. 265. Abbé Dubois, *Histoire du siège*, p. 252. Jollois, *Histoire du siège*, pp. 26, 27.

539. Cf. *ante*, p. 112, note 1. On the plan this island is called Petite Île Charlemagne.

540. G. Girault's report in the *Trial*, vol. iv, p. 283. Morosini, vol. iii, p. 16, note 5; vol. iv, supplement xiii.

541. *Journal du siège*, pp. 22, 23, 24, 25, 27, 34.

542. Boucher de Molandon and A. de Beaucorps, *L'armée anglaise vaincue par Jeanne d'Arc*, pp. 3 *et seq.* Jarry, *Le compte de l'armée anglaise*, proofs and illustrations v, p. 233.

543. Jan. 1, 2. *Journal du siège*, pp. 21, 22, 30.

544. 4-27 Jan. *Journal du siège*, pp. 21, 22, 30.

545. 17 Jan. *Ibid.*, p. 26.

546. *Ibid.*, p. 32.

547. *Gallia Christiana*, vol. ii, p. 732. Vallet de Viriville, *Histoire de Charles VII*, vol. i, p. 213; vol. ii, p. 6, note 2. S. Luce, *Jeanne d'Arc à Domremy*, p. ccxcv.

548. *Journal du siège*, pp. 21, 36-38. The accounts of Hémon Raguier, Bibl. Nat. Fr. 7858, fol. 41. Loiseleur, *Comptes des dépenses de Charles VII pour secourir Orléans*, *loc. cit.*

549. Journal du siège, p. 37.

550. Journal d'un bourgeois de Paris, p. 231. Chronique de la Pucelle, pp. 266, 267. Journal du siège, pp. 37, 38.

551. *Journal du siège*, pp. 38, 39. *Chronique de la Pucelle*, pp. 267, 268. *Mistère du siège*, line 8867. Dom Plancher, *Histoire de Bourgogne*, vol. iv, p. 127.

552. Monstrelet, vol. iv, p. 312. *Journal du siège*, p. 43. Chastellain, ed. Kervyn de Lettenhove, vol. ii, p. 164.

553. Monstrelet, vol. iv, p. 311. *Journal du siège*, p. 39. *Journal d'un bourgeois de Paris*, p. 232. *Chronique de la Pucelle*, pp. 267, 268. Perceval de Cagny, pp. 137, 139.

554. *Journal du siège*, pp. 40, 41.

555. Ibid., p. 43. Journal d'un bourgeois de Paris, p. 232.

556. *Journal du siège*, p. 43. *Chronique de la Pucelle*, p. 269. Monstrelet, vol. iv, p. 313.

557. *Journal du siège*, p. 42. Jean Chartier, *Chronique*, vol. i, p. 63.

558. Journal du siège, p. 44.

559. *Ibid.*, pp. 43, 44.

560. *Journal d'un bourgeois de Paris*, pp. 230-233. Monstrelet, vol. iv, p. 313. Jean Chartier, *Chronique*, vol. ii, p. 62. Symphorien Guyon, *Histoire de la ville d'Orléans*, vol. ii, p. 195. Vallet de Viriville, *Histoire de Charles VII*, vol. ii, p. 37.

561. 18 Feb. *Journal du siège*, pp. 50, 52.

562. *Ibid.*, p. 51.

563. 16 March. *Ibid.*, p. 59.

564. Thaumas de la Thaumassière, *Histoire du Berry*, Bourges, 1689, in fol., pp. 648-656.

565. Journal du siège, p. 52.

566. Monstrelet, vol. iv, p. 317. *Journal du siège*, p. 52. *Chronique de la Pucelle*, p. 269. Jean Chartier, *Chronique*, vol. i, p. 65. Morosini, pp. 16, 17, vol. iv, supplement xiv. Du Tillet, *Recueil des traités*, p. 221.

567. 3 March. *Journal du siège*, p. 54.

568. Trial, vol. iii, pp. 21, 23. Journal du siège, pp. 46 et seq. Chronique de la Pucelle, p. 278.

569. La Curne, under the word *Pucelle*; Du Cange, ad. v. *Pucella*.

> *Je laisse cent sols de deniers*
> *A ceulx qui boivent voluntiers*
> *Et s'ay laissié a mon curé*
> *Ma pucelle quand je mourrai,*

says Eustache Deschamps (quoted by La Curne); Du Cange cites a will of 1274: "afterwards I leave to Laurence *ma pucelle* and twelve *livres* of Paris."

570. Relation contemporaine du combat de Montendre, in Bulletin de la Société de l'Histoire de France, 1834, pp. 109-113.

571. *Trial*, vol. iii, pp. 3, 125, 215. *Journal du siège*, pp. 5, 6, 31, 44. *Nouvelle biographie générale*, articles by Vallet de Viriville.

572. *Trial*, vol. i, pp. 56, 75.

573. *Ibid.*, p. 56.

574. Bueil, *Le jouvencel*, vol. i, p. 32, and Tringant, xv; Jean Chartier, *Chronique*, ch. cxxxviii.

575. Vallet de Viriville, Isabeau de Bavière, 1859, in 8vo, and Notes sur l'état civil des princes et princesses nés d'Isabeau de Bavière in the Bibliothèque de l'École des Chartes, vol. xix, pp. 473-482.

576. Th. Basin, *Histoire de Charles VII et de Louis XI*, vol. i, p. 312. Chastellain, ed. Kervyn de Lettenhove, vol. ii, p. 178.

577. Chronique du religieux de Saint-Denis, vol. i, pp. 28, 43. Docteur A. Chevreau, De la maladie de Charles VI, roi de France, et des médecins qui ont soigné ce prince, in l'Union Médicale, February, March, 1862. De Beaucourt, Histoire de Charles VII, vol. i, p. 4, note.

578. Monstrelet, vol. iii, p. 347.

579. Gruel, ed. Le Vavasseur, pp. 46 *et seq. Chronique de la Pucelle*, p. 239. Berry, p. 374. Pierre de Fénin, *Mémoires*, ed. Mademoiselle Dupont, pp. 222, 223. Vallet de Viriville, *Histoire de Charles VII*, vol. i, p. 453. De Beaucourt, *Histoire de Charles VII*, vol. ii, p. 432.

580. Gruel, pp. 53, 193. *Geste des nobles*, p. 200. Jean Chartier, *Chronique*, vol. i, pp. 23, 24, 54. De Beaucourt, *Histoire de Charles VII*, vol. ii, p. 132. E. Cosneau, *Le connétable de Richemont*, Paris, 1886, in 8vo, p. 131.

581. Gruel, p. 231. *Chronique de la Pucelle*, pp. 200, 248. Jean Chartier, *Chronique*, vol. i, p. 54; vol. iii, p. 189. De Beaucourt, *Histoire de Charles VII*, vol. ii, p. 142. E. Cosneau, *Le connétable de Richemont*, p. 140.

582. De Beaucourt, *op. cit.*, vol. ii, pp. 143, 144 *et seq.* E. Cosneau, *op. cit.*, pp. 142 *et seq.*

583. Dom Morice, *Preuves de l'histoire de Bretagne*, vol. ii, col. 1199. De Beaucourt, *op. cit.*, vol. ii, p. 150. E. Cosneau, *op. cit.*, p. 144.

584. P. de Fénin, *Mémoires*, p. 222. De Beaucourt, *Histoire de Charles VII*, Introduction. E. Charles, *Le caractère de Charles VII*, in *Revue contemporaine*, vol. xxii, pp. 300-328.

585. Le doyen de Saint-Thibaud, *Tableau des rois de France*, in *Trial*, vol. iv, p. 325.

586. Martial d'Auvergne, *Les vigiles de Charles VII*, ed. Coustelier, 1724 (2 vols. in 12mo), vol. i, p. 56.

587. L. Drapeyron, *Jeanne d'Arc et Philippe le Bon*, in *Revue de géographie*, November, 1886, p. 331.

588. *Taille*, so called from a notched stick (Eng. tally), used by the tax-collector, the number of notches indicating the amount of the tax due. There were two *tailles*: *la taille seigneuriale*, a contribution paid by serfs to their lord; and *la taille royale*, paid by the third estate to the King. The latter was first levied by Philippe le Bel (1285-1314), but was only an occasional tax until the reign of Charles VII, who converted it into a regular impost. But although collected at stated intervals its amount varied from reign to reign, becoming intolerably burdensome under the spendthrift kings, while wise rulers, like Henri IV, considerably reduced it. It was not abolished until the Revolution (W.S.).

589. *Recueil des ordonnances*, vol. xiii, p. xcix, and the index of this volume under the word *Impôts*. Loiseleur, *Compte des dépenses*, pp. 51 *et seq.* A. Thomas, *Les états généraux sous Charles VII* in the

Cabinet historique, vol. xxiv, 1878. *Les états provinciaux de la France centrale sous Charles VII*, Paris, 1879, 2 vols. in 8vo, *passim*.

590. Jean Chartier, *Chronique*, vol. iii, p. 318. Vallet de Viriville, *Histoire de Charles VII*, vol. i, p. 390. De Beaucourt, *Histoire de Charles VII*, vol. i, p. 428; vol. ii, pp. 646 *et seq.*

591. *Le Jouvencel*, vol. i, Introduction, pp. xix, xx.

592. Chronique de la Pucelle, p. 237. Loiseleur, Compte des dépenses, p. 61. Vallet de Viriville, Mémoire sur les institutions de Charles VII, in Bibliothèque de l'École des Chartes, vol. xxxiii, p. 37.

593. Dom Vaissette, *Histoire du Languedoc*, vol. iv, p. 471.

594. De Beaucourt, *Histoire de Charles VII*, vol. ii, p. 167.

595. Dom Vaissette, *Histoire du Languedoc*, vol. iv, p. 471. A. Thomas, *Les états généraux sous Charles VII*, pp. 49, 50.

596. Dom Vaissette, *Histoire du Languedoc*, vol. iv, p. 472. Raynal, *Histoire du Berry*, vol. iii, p. 20. Loiseleur, *Comptes des dépenses*, pp. 63 *et seq.* De Beaucourt, *Histoire de Charles VII*, vol. ii, pp. 170 *et seq.*

597. Th. Basin, Histoire de Charles VII, Bk. II, ch. vi. Antoine Loysel, Mémoires des pays, villes, comtés et comtes de Beauvais et Beauvoisis, Paris, 1618, p. 229. P. Mantellier, Histoire de la communauté des marchands fréquentant la rivière de Loire, vol. i, p. 195.

598. Dom Morice, *Preuves de l'histoire de Bretagne*, vol. ii, cols. 1145, 1194. *Ordonnances*, vol. xv, p. 147.

599. Vallet de Viriville, Histoire de Charles VII, vol. i, p. 373. De Beaucourt, Histoire de Charles VII, vol. ii, p. 175. Duc de la Trémoïlle, Chartier de Thouars, Documents historiques et généalogiques, p. 17. Les La Trémoïlle pendant cinq siècles, vol. i, p. 175.

600. De Beaucourt, *Histoire de Charles VII*, vol. ii, p. 632.

601. Jean Chartier, *Chronique*, vol. iii. Accounts, p. 316. *Cabinet historique*, June, 1858, p. 176.

602. *Cabinet historique*, September and October, 1858, p. 263.

603. Vallet de Viriville, *Histoire de Charles VII*, vol. i, p. 374.

604. De Beaucourt, *Histoire de Charles VII*, vol. ii, p. 632.

605. Loiseleur, *Compte des dépenses*, p. 57.

606. De Beaucourt, *Histoire de Charles VII*, vol. ii, p. 634.

607. Vuitry, *Les monnaies sous les trois premiers Valois*, Paris, 1881, in 8vo, pp. 29 *et seq.* Loiseleur, *Compte des dépenses*, p. 47. Vallet de Viriville, *Histoire de Charles VII*, vol. i, p. 243. De Beaucourt, *Histoire de Charles VII*, vol. ii, pp. 620 *et seq.*

608. Clairambault, *Titres, Scellés*, vol. 205, pp. 8769, 8771, 8773, *passim.* De Beaucourt, *Histoire de Charles VII*, vol. ii, p. 293.

609. Archives nationales, J. 183, no. 142. Duc de La Trémoïlle, *Les La Trémoïlle pendant cinq siècles*, vol. i, p. 177. De Beaucourt, *Histoire de Charles VII*, vol. ii, p. 198.

610. Le P. Anselme, Histoire généalogique et chronologique de la maison de France, vol. vi, p. 399. Vallet de Viriville, in Nouvelle biographie générale. De Beaucourt, Histoire de Charles VII, vol. i, p. 63.

611. Marquis de Gaucourt, *Le Sire de Gaucourt*, Orléans, 1855, in 8vo.

612. Le P. Anselme, *Histoire généalogique et chronologique de la maison de France*, vol. vi, p. 339. *Gallia Christiana*, vol. ix, col. 135. Hermant, *Histoire ecclésiastique de Beauvais* (Bibl. nat. fr. 8581), fol. 15 *et seq.* Article by Vallet de Viriville, in *Nouvelle biographie générale* and *Histoire de Charles VII*, vol. ii, pp. 160 *et seq.*

613. Le P. Denifle, *Cartularium Universitatis Parisiensis*, vol. iv, p. 275.

614. *Journal d'un bourgeois de Paris*, p. 109. In 1411 the Butchers of Paris, led by Jean-Simonnet Caboche, rose in favour of the Duke of Burgundy (W.S.).

615. Le P. Denifle, La désolation des églises, vol. i, pp. 594, 595. Garnier, Documents relatifs à la surprise de Paris par les Bourguignons en Mai, 1418, in Bulletin de la Société de l'Histoire de Paris, 1877, p. 51.

616. De Beaucourt, *Histoire de Charles VII*, vol. i, pp. 268, 276, 339. P. Champion, *Guillaume de Flavy*, p. 4, and proofs and illustrations, lxxj.

617. Le P. Denifle, *La désolation des églises, loc. cit.* According to a "legitimist" fiction he pleads the service he had rendered to King Charles VI, and his son the Dauphin "... *tam propter sue persone debilitatem, quam etiam propter assidua viagia et ambassiatas, que ipse serviendo Carolo Francorum regi et Carolo, ejusdem regis unigenito filio, dalphino Viennensi....*"

618. Vallet de Viriville, *Nouvelle biographie générale*. De Beaucourt, *Histoire de Charles VII*, vol. i, pp. 64 *et seq.*

619. F. Duchesne, Histoire des chanceliers et gardes des sceaux de France, 1680, in fol., p. 483.

620. The *livre* of Tours was worth ten pence, while that of Paris was worth one shilling (W.S.). National Archives, p. 2298.

621. De Beaucourt, *Histoire de Charles VII*, vol. ii, p. 632.

622. Le P. Anselme, Histoire généalogique de la maison de France, vol. i, p. 407.

623. Journal du siège, p. 51.

624. Le P. Denifle, *La désolation des églises*, introduction. *Cf.* the collection of official receipts in the National Library, fr. 20,887, original documents 693, Clairambault, *deeds, seals*, vol. 29.

625. F. Duchesne, Histoire des chanceliers et garde des sceaux de France, p. 487.

626. *Trial*, vol. i, p. 56.

627. *Ibid.*, vol. ii, pp. 394, 462.

628. Isaiah, ch. 66, verse 10 (W.S.).

629. *Trial*, vol. i, p. 143.

630. La vie de saint Harenc glorieux martir et comment il fut pesché en la mer et porté à Dieppe, in Recueil des poésies françaises des XVe et XVIe siècles, by A. de Montaiglon, vol. ii, pp. 325-332.

631. Still if Jeanne were the age she is said to have been, about eighteen, she was under no obligation to fast, but only to be abstinent. Nevertheless, when imprisoned at Rouen, she fasted during Lent; but we do not know how old her judges considered her to be.

632. *Trial*, vol. i, p. 143.

633. G. de Cougny, Notice archéologique et historique sur le château de Chinon, Chinon, 1860, in 8vo.

634. *La légende dorée*, translated by Gustave Brunet, 1846, pp. 259, 264. Douhet, *Dictionnaire des légendes*, pp. 426, 436.

635. Chronique de la Pucelle, p. 273. Journal du siège, pp. 46, 47.

636. Epître de Jouvenel des Ursins, in De Beaucourt, Histoire de Charles VII vol. v, p. 206, note 1.

637. Vallet de Viriville, *Histoire de Charles VII*, vol. ii, p. x.

638. *Acta sanctorum*, vol. iii, March, p. 742. Abbé Pétin, *Dictionnaire hagiographique*, 1850, vol. ii, p. 1516.

639. Froissart, *Chroniques*, Bk. IV, ch. xliii *et seq.*

640. *Trial*, vol. iii, p. 83, note 2. Vallet de Viriville, *Procès de condamnation de Jeanne d'Arc*, Paris, 1867, in 8vo, pp. xxxi *et seq.*

641. *Le songe du vieil Pélerin*, by Philippe de Maizières (Bibl. Nat. French collection, no. 22,542).

642. Chastellain, ed. Buchon, pp. 114, 116. *Acta Sanctorum Junii*, vol. 1, p. 648. Le P. De Buck, *Le bienheureux Jean de Gand*, Brussels, 1862, in 8vo, 40 pages. Le P. Chapotin, *La guerre de cent ans; Jeanne d'Arc et les Dominicains*, Évreux, 1888, in 8vo, p. 89.

643. Chronique de la Pucelle, p. 273. Journal du siège, p. 46.

644. *Parvus Thalamus*, ed. Archæological Society of Montpellier, p. 464. Th. de Bèze, *Histoire ecclésiastique*, 1580, vol. i, p. 217. A. Germain, *Catherine Suave*, Montpellier, 1853, in 4to, 16 pages. H.C. Lea, *A History of the Inquisition in the Middle Ages* (1906), vol. ii, p. 157. Vallet de Viriville, *Histoire de Charles VII*, vol. ii, p. x.

645. Jean Nider, *Formicarium*, in the *Trial*, vol. iv, p. 502.

646. *Trial*, vol. iii, p. 22. These facts were known at Lyons on the 22nd of April, 1429. (Clerk of the Chambre des Comptes of Brabant, in *Trial*, vol. iv, p. 426.)

647. S. Luce, *Chronique des quatre premiers Valois*, Paris, 1861, in 8vo, pp. 46, 48.

648. *Trial*, vol. iii, p. 115. Thomassin, *Registre Delphinal*, in the *Trial*, vol. iv, p. 304. *Chronique de la Pucelle*, p. 273. *Journal du siège*, p. 47.

649. *Gallia Christiana*, vol. iii, col. 1089.

650. Le R.P. Marcellin Fornier, *Histoire générale des Alpes Maritimes ou Cottiennes*, ed. by the Abbé Paul Guillaume, Paris, 1890-1892 (3 vols. in 8vo), vol. ii, pp. 313 *et seq.*

651. The Monk of Dunfermline, in the *Trial*, vol. v, p. 340. Vallet de Viriville, *Histoire de Charles VII*, vol. i, pp. 265 *et seq.* De Beaucourt, *Histoire de Charles VII*, vol. i, p. 243.

652. Simon de Phares, *Recueil des plus célèbres astrologues*, fr. ms. 1357. Vallet de Viriville, *Histoire de Charles VII*, vol. i, p. 306; vol. ii, p. 345, note. De Beaucourt, *Histoire de Charles VII*, vol. vi, p. 399.

653. Chastellain, vol. iii, p. 446.

654. Vallet de Viriville, *Histoire de Charles VII*, vol. i, p. 173.

655. I here correct the text of Simon de Phares (*Trial*, vol. iv, p. 536) according to the written opinion of M. Camille Flammarion.

656. *Trial*, vol. iv, p. 536.

657. *Ibid.*, vol. iii, p. 341.

658. Recueil de Simon de Phares, in the *Trial*, vol. v, p. 32, note.

659. *Ibid.*, vol. i, p. 143.

660. The kerb was removed during the Second Empire. Moreover it is admitted that no faith should be put in such traditions. G. de Cougny, *Charles VII et Jeanne d'Arc à Chinon*, Tours, 1877, in 8vo.

661. *Trial*, vol. i, p. 75; vol. iii, p. 115. *Chronique de la Pucelle*, p. 273. *Journal du siège*, pp. 46, 47. Th. Basin, *Histoire de Charles VII et de Louis XI*, vol. i, p. 68.

662. *Trial*, vol. i, pp. 75, 141.

663. Le Curial, in *Les œuvres de Maistre Alain Chartier*, ed. Du Chesne, Paris, 1642, in 4to, p. 398.

664. According to Jeanne there were present La Trémoïlle and the Archbishop of Reims, but she also mentions the Duke of Alençon, who was certainly not there.

665. *Trial*, vol. iii, p. 115.

666. *Ibid.*, pp. 102-103.

667. *Ibid.*, p. 219. *Chronique de la Pucelle*, in *Trial*, vol. iv, p. 205. Mathieu Thomassin, *ibid.*, p. 304. *Chronique de Lorraine*, *ibid.*, p. 330. Philippe de Bergame, *ibid.*, p. 523.

668. Relation du greffier de La Rochelle, in the Revue historique, vol. iv, p. 336.

669. St. Paul, Second Epistle to the Corinthians. Labbe, *Collection des conciles*, vol. vii, p. 978. Saumaise, *Epistola ad Andream Colvium super cap. xi, I ad Corynth. de cæsarie virorum et mulierum coma.* Lugd-Batavor ex off. Elz. 1644, in 12mo. *Quelques notes d'archéologie sur la chevelure féminine*, in *Comptes rendus de l'Académie des Inscriptions et Belles Lettres*, 1888, vol. xvi, pp. 419, 425.

670. *Trial*, vol. i, p. 75; vol. iii, pp. 17, 92, 115. Jean Chartier, *Chronique*, vol. i, p. 67. *Chronique de la Pucelle*, p. 273. *Journal du siège*, p. 46.

671. De Beaucourt, *Histoire de Charles VII*, vol. ii, p. 195.

672. Th. Basin, vol. i, p. 312. Chastellain, vol. ii, p. 178. *Portrait historique du roi Charles VII*, by Henri Baude, published by Vallet de Viriville in *Nouvelles recherches sur Henri Baude*, p. 6. De Beaucourt, *Histoire de Charles VII*, p. 83.

673. As in the miniature painted by Jean Fouquet, more than ten years later. Gruyer, *Les Quarante Fouquet de Chantilly*, Paris, 1897, in 4to.

674. Note sur un ancien portrait de Charles VII, conservé au Louvre, in the Bulletin de la Société des Antiquaires de France, 1862, pp. 67 et seq.

675. *Trial*, vol. ii, p. 103. *Relation du greffier de La Rochelle*, p. 337. *Chronique de la Pucelle*, p. 273. Jean Chartier, *Chronique*, vol. i, pp. 67, 68.

676. *Trial*, vol. iii, p. 103 (evidence of Brother Pasquerel).

677. The Abridger of the *Trial*, in *Trial*, vol. iv, pp. 258, 259. Basin, *Histoire de Charles VII et de Louis XI*, vol. i, p. 67. *Journal du siège*, p. 48.

678. *Trial*, vol. iii, p. 116 (evidence of S. Charles). S. Luce, *Jeanne d'Arc à Domremy*, p. lxi.

679. *Trial*, vol. iii, pp. 17, 209. As early as April the promised deliverance of Orléans and coronation at Reims had been heard of at Lyons (*Trial*, vol. iv, p. 426).

680. Pasquerel alone of the witnesses mentions this (*Trial*, vol. iii, p. 103). Cf. the anecdote of the Sire de Boissy related by P. Sala in his collection, *Les hardiesses des grands rois et empereurs* (*Trial*, vol. iv, p. 278).

681. *Trial*, vol. iii, p. 209.

682. *Ibid.*, p. 66.

683. G. de Cougny, *Charles VII et Jeanne d'Arc à Chinon*, Tours, 1877, p. 40.

684. *Trial*, vol. iii, p. 17.

685. *Ibid.*, pp. 65, 73. Mademoiselle A. de Villaret, *Louis de Coutes, page de Jeanne d'Arc*, Orléans, 1890, in 8vo.

686. *Trial*, vol. iii, p. 17.

687. *Ibid.*, p. 66.

688. *Chronique de la Pucelle*, pp. 274 *et seq.* Jean Chartier, *Chronique*, p. 68.

689. *Trial*, vol. i, p. 68.

690. *Ibid.*, vol. iii, pp. 133, 340. Thomassin, in *Trial*, vol. iv, p. 395. Walter Bower, in *Trial*, vol. iv, p. 489. Christine de Pisan, in *Trial*, vol. v, p. 12. La Borderie, *Les véritables prophéties de Merlin, examen des poèmes bretons attribués à ce barde*, in the *Revue de Bretagne*, 1883, vol. liii.

691. Cuvelier, Le poème de Du Guesclin, l. 3285. Francisque-Michel and Th. Wright, Vie de Merlin attribuée à Geoffroy de Monmouth, suivie des prophéties de ce barde tirées de l'histoire des Bretons, Paris, 1837, in 8vo, pp. 67 et seq. La Villemarqué, Myrdhin ou Merlin l'Enchanteur, son histoire, ses œuvres, son influence, n. ed., Paris,

1862, in 12mo. D'Arbois de Jubainville, Merlin est-il un personnage réel? in the Revue des questions historiques, 1868, pp. 559-568. Lefèvre-Pontalis, Morosini, vol. iv, supplement xvi. "Geoffrey of Monmouth. represented Merlin as having prophesied all the events of the history of Britain until the year 1135 in which he wrote. The Historia Regum was very popular in the ecclesiastical world. Its legends were held to be facts. The exactness with which its prognostications had been fulfilled down to 1135 was marvelled at, and an attempt was made to interpret the prophecies relating to subsequent times." Gaston Paris, La littérature française au moyen age, 1890, pp. 86-104.

692. Le Baud, *Histoire de Bretagne*, Paris, 1638, in fol., p. 451.

693. *Trial*, vol. iii, pp. 340-342.

694. Morosini, vol. iv, p. 324.

695. Pierre Migiet weaves the two prophecies into one, which he says he has read in a book, *Trial*, vol. iii, p. 133.

696. Adopting the emendation made by M. Germain Lefèvre-Pontalis in his *Chronique d'Antonio Morosini*, vol. iii, pp. 126, 127; vol. iv, pp. 316 *et seq.*

697. The Complete Works of the Venerable Bede, ed. Giles, London, 1843-1844, 12 vols., in 8vo, in Patres Ecclesiæ Anglicanæ.

698. Christine de Pisan, in *Trial*, vol. v, p. 12. Morosini, vol. iii, p. 126. The Dean of Saint Thibaud, in *Trial*, vol. iv, p. 423. Herman Korner, in Le P. Ayroles, *La vraie Jeanne d'Arc*, pp. 279 *et seq.* Walter Bower, in *Trial*, vol. iv, p. 481.

699. Buchon, *Math. d'Escouchy*, etc., p. 537. G. Lefèvre-Pontalis, Eberhard Windecke, pp. 21-31. A Latin text of this prophecy is to be found on the fly-leaf of the Cartulary of Thérouanne.

700. *Trial*, vol. iii, pp. 393-407; vol. v, p. 473. Marcellin Fornier, *Histoire des Alpes-Maritimes ou Cottiennes*, vol. ii, pp. 313, 314.

701. In the original French *garce..* The text has *grace*, which is not possible. I have conjectured that the word should be *garce*.

702. M. Fornier, *Histoire des Alpes-Maritimes ou Cottiennes*, vol. ii, pp. 313, 314.

703. Clerk of the Town Hall of Albi, in *Trial*, vol. iv, p. 300.

704. Thomassin, in *Trial*, vol. iv, p. 304.

705. *Sandal* or *cendal*, a silk bearing some resemblance to taffetas. Cf. Godefroy, *Lexique de l'ancien français* (W.S.).

706. Du Cange, *Glossaire*, under the word *auriflamma*. Le Roux de Lincy and Tisserand, *Paris et ses historiens*, pp. 150, 251, 257, 259. *Histoire générale de Paris.*.

707. Perceval de Cagny, p. 136. *Chronique de la Pucelle*, pp. 224, 249.

708. *Trial*, vol. iii, p. 91.

709. Vallet de Viriville, *Histoire de Charles VII*, vol. iii, pp. 408, 409. De Beaucourt, *Histoire de Charles VII*, vol. vi, pp. 43, 44.

710. *Trial*, vol. iii, p. 91.

711. *Ibid.*, pp. 91, 92. Eberhard Windecke, pp. 152 *et seq.*

712. *Trial*, vol. iii, p. 92.

713. Perceval de Cagny, p. 148.

714. *Trial*, vol. iii, p. 96.

715. Perceval de Cagny, p. 151, *passim*.

716. Monstrelet, vol. iv, p. 240.

717. Cf. 1 Kings xiii, 4 (W.S.). P. Dupuy, *Procès de Jean II, duc d'Alençon, 1458-1474*, 1658, in 4to. Michelet, *Histoire de France*, vol. v, p. 382. Docteur Chereau, *Médecins du quinzième siècle*, in *l'Union Médicale*, vol. xiv, August, 1862. Joseph Guibert, *Jean II duc d'Alençon*, in *Les positions de l'École des Chartes*, 1893.

718. *Trial*, vol. iii, pp. 116, 209.

719. Bélisaire Ledain, *Jeanne d'Arc à Poitiers*, Saint-Maixent, 1891, in 8vo, 15 pages. Neuville, *Le Parlement royal à Poitiers*, in the *Revue historique*, vol. vi, p. 284.

720. *Chronique de la Pucelle*, p. 275. *Journal du siège*, p. 48. Monstrelet, vol. iv, p. 316.

721. Neuville, *Le Parlement royal à Poitiers*, in the *Revue historique*, vol. vi, p. 18. De Beaucourt, *Histoire de Charles VII*, vol. ii, pp. 571 *et seq.*

722. Louis Battifol, *Jean Jouvenel, prévôt des marchands de la ville de Paris*, Paris, 1894, in 8vo. Juvénal des Ursins, *Histoire de Charles VI*, pp. 359, 360.

723. *Trial*, vol. iii, p. 92. *Gallia Christiana*, vol. ii, col. 1198.

724. *Trial*, vol. iii, p. 92. Le P. Ayroles, *La Pucelle devant l'Église de son temps*, p. 6.

725. *Trial*, vol. iii, pp. 203, 204.

726. *Ibid.*, pp. 19, 203.

727. *Ibid.*, pp. 74, 75. Launoy, *Historia Collegii Navarrici*, lib. ii, *passim*.

728. *Trial*, vol. iii, pp. 92, 102.

729. *Ibid.*, pp. 74, 75.

730. *Ibid.*, pp. 74, 92, 102.

731. *Ibid.*, vol. ii, p. 203.

732. *Ibid.*, vol. iii, pp. 27, 28.

733. *Ibid.*, pp. 19, 74, 92, 203. *Gallia Christiana*, vol. iii, col. 1128.

734. *Trial*, vol. iii, p. 203. *Gallia Christiana*, vol. iii, col. 1129.

735. *Trial*, vol. iii, p. 92.

736. *Ibid.*, pp. 19, 83, 203.

737. Ibid., pp. 19, 203. Le P. Chapotin, La guerre de cent ans; Jeanne d'Arc et les Dominicains, p. 132.

738. Canon Dunand, *La légende anglaise de Jeanne*, Paris, 1903, in 8vo, p. 118.

739. O. Raguenet de Saint-Albin, Les juges de Jeanne d'Arc à Poitiers, membres du Parlement ou gens d'Église, Orléans, 1894, in 8vo, 46 pages.

740. See *ante*, pp. 153, 154.

741. Judith, xvi, 7 (W.S.).

742. *Trial*, vol. iii, pp. 19, 74, 82, 203. *Chronique de la Pucelle*, p. 275. B. Ledain, *Jeanne d'Arc à Poitiers*, Saint-Maixent, 1891, in 8vo.

743. Nevertheless see *Le mistère du siège*, pp. 397-406.

744. There can be no reason for suspecting this lady of not living up to her reputation, for nothing is known of her, not even whether she were Maître Jean Rabateau's first or second wife, for he had two. The first was the daughter of Benoît Pidelet. Cf. B. Ledain, *La maison de Jeanne d'Arc à Poitiers, Maître Jean Rabateau* (*Revue du Bas-Poitou*, April, 1891, pp. 48, 66). A. Barbier, *Jeanne d'Arc et l'hôtellerie de la Rose*, Poitiers, 1892, in 8vo.

745. *Trial*, vol. iii, p. 82.

746. Voragine, *La légende dorée* (Vie de Sainte Catherine).

747. *Trial*, vol. iii, p. 204 (evidence of Brother Seguin).

748. *Ibid.*, pp. 203, 204.

749. *Ibid.*, p. 74.

750. *Trial*, vol. iii, p. 92.

751. Chronique de la Pucelle, p. 275.

752. *Trial*, vol. iii, p. 74 (evidence of Gobert Thibault).

753. *Trial*, vol. iii, p. 74. Boucher de Molandon and A. de Beaucorps, *L'armée anglaise*, p. 111. La Poule, as he is called here, is identical with Suffort, and is none other than William Pole, Earl of Suffolk, unless John Pole, William's brother, be intended, but he was not one of the three organisers of the siege. As for Clasdas or Glasdale, as the French called him, he served under the orders of the Commander of Les Tourelles. These errors may have been Jeanne's, or possibly they were made by the witness. They do not recur in the letter to the English.

754. *Trial*, vol. iii, p. 83.

755. *Ibid.*, p. 75.

756. *Lettres de Gérard Machet*, Bibl. nat. Latin documents, no. 8577. Launoy, *Regii Navarrœ Gymnasii Parisiensis historia*, Paris, 1682 (2 vols. in 4to), vol. ii, pp. 533, 557. Du Boulay, *Hist. Univ. Parisiensis*, vol. v, p. 875. Vallet de Viriville, in *Nouvelle biographie générale*.

757. De Beaucourt, Extrait du catalogue des actes de Charles VII, p. 18.

758. *Trial*, vol. i, pp. 71, 72, 73, 171.

759. Labbe, *Sacro-Sancta Consilia* (1671), vol. ii, pp. 413, 434.

760. Surius, Vitæ S.S. (1618), vol. i, pp. 21-24. Gabriel Brosse, Histoire abrégée de la vie et de la translation de Sainte Euphrosine, Vierge d'Alexandrie, patronne de l'abbaye de Beaulieu-lès-Compiègne, Paris, 1649, in 8vo.

761. *Trial*, vol. iii, p. 20.

762. It may be noticed that during the consultation of the doctors, according to the report of it given by Thomassin in *Le registre Delphinal*, Charles of Valois is designated alike by the title of King and by that of Dauphin (*Trial*, vol. iv, p. 303).

763. *Trial*, vol. iii, p. 86.

764. Le Père Didon, *Vie de Jésus*, vol. i, Preface.

765. Juvénal des Ursins, *Histoire de Charles VI*, p. 359.

766. *Trial*, vol. iii, p. 204.

767. It seems to have been the fate of the inhabitants of Limousin to be jeered at by the French of Champagne and of l'Île de France. After Brother Seguin we have the student from Limousin to whom Pantagruel says: "Thou art Limousin to the bone and yet here thou wilt pass thyself off as a Parisian." It is the lot of M. de Pourceaugnac. La Fontaine, in 1663, writes from Limoges to his wife that the people of Limousin are by no means afflicted; neither do

they labour under Heaven's displeasure "as the folk of our provinces imagine." But he adds that he does not like their habits. It would seem that at first Brother Seguin was annoyed by Jeanne's mocking vivacious repartees. But he cherished no ill-will against her. "The Limousin's good nature does not permit the endurance of any unfriendly feeling," says Abel Hugo in *La France pittoresque: Haute-Vienne*. Cf. A. Précicou, *Rabelais et les Limousins*, Limoges, 1906, in 8vo.

768. *Trial*, vol. iii, p. 205.

769. Judges, ch. vi. (W.S.).

770. *Trial*, vol. iii, p. 20.

771. Ibid., pp. 20, 205. Chronique de la Pucelle, p. 278. Journal du siège, p. 49.

772. *Trial*, vol. iii, pp. 19, 20.

773. *Ibid.*, vol. i, p. 95; vol. iii, p. 209.

774. Mary Darmesteter, *Froissart*, Paris, 1894, in 12mo, p. 96.

775. Jean Philippe de Lignan, Rome, 1481 (not paginated), leaf 10 and the following. For the comparison of Jeanne d'Arc to the ancient Sibyl, see the Clerk of Spire, *Sibylla Francica*, in the *Trial*, vol. iii, p. 422. Christine de Pisano in the *Trial*, vol. v, p. 12. Lanéry d'Arc, *Mémoires et consultations en faveur de Jeanne d'Arc*, pp. 8-10. Barbier de Montault, *Iconographie des Sibylles*, in the *Revue de l'art chrétien*, xiii-xiv (1869-1870). Barraud, *Notice sur les attributs avec lesquelles on représente les Sibylles aux XVe et XVIe siècles*, in the *Bulletin archéologique de la Commission historique des arts mon.*, vol. iv (1848). Cf. Morosini, vol. iv, supplement xiv, p. 319.

776. Voragine, *La légende dorée* (Assomption de la Vierge).

777. Le Curé de Saint-Sulpice, *Notre Dame de France ou histoire du culte de la Sainte Vierge en France*, Paris, 1862, 7 vols. in 8vo. Abbé Mignard, *La Sainte Vierge*, Paris, 1877, in 8vo, pp. 382 *et seq.*

778. *De l'unicorne qu'une jeune fille séduit*, in the *Bestiaire* of R. de Fournival (Paulin Paris, *Manuscrits français*, vol. iv, p. 25). Berger de Xivrey, *Traditions tératologiques*, p. 559. J. Doublet, *Histoire de l'abbaye de Saint-Denys*, vol. i, p. 320. Vallet de Viriville, *Nouvelles recherches sur Agnès Sorel*, in *Bulletin de la Société des Antiquaires de Picardie*, vol. vi, p. 621. A. Maury, *Croyances et légendes du moyen âge*, pp. 262 *et seq.*

779. Leber, *Des cérémonies du sacre*, Paris, 1825, in 8vo, p. 459.

780. L. Tanon, Histoire des tribunaux de l'inquisition en France, Paris, 1893, in 8vo, p. 293.

781. Germain, Catherine Sauve, in Académie des sciences et lettres de Montpellier, Lettres, vol. i, 1854, in 4to, pp. 539-552.

782. Du Cange, Glossaire, under the word Matrimonium.

783. Pierre Le Loyer, Livre des spectres, 1586, in 4to, pp. 527, 551.

784. Trial, vol. iii, p. 102. Vallet de Viriville, article Le Maçon, in Nouvelle biographie générale.

785. Trial, vol. iii, p. 210. Eberhard Windecke, p. 157. Morosini, p. 99.

786. Trial, vol. iii, p. 82.

787. Siméon Luce, Jeanne d'Arc à Domremy, p. cxliii. Trial, vol. ii, p. 397.

788. Letter from Perceval de Boulainvilliers to the Duke of Milan, in the Trial, vol. v, pp. 115, 121. Journal d'un bourgeois de Paris, p. 237.

789. Journal du siège, p. 48. Chronique de la Pucelle, p. 275.

790. The word seules in the text is doubtful.

791. Trial, vol. iii, pp. 391, 392.

792. Eberhard Windecke, pp. 32, 41.

793. The conclusions of the Poitiers commission were circulated everywhere. Traces of them are to be found in Brittany (Buchon and Chronique de Morosini), in Flanders (Chronique de Tournai and Chronique de Morosini), in Germany (Eb. Windecke), in Dauphiné (Buchon).

794. "Altra santa Catarina" (Morosini, vol. iii, p. 52). There is no doubt that here she is compared to Saint Catherine of Alexandria and not to Saint Catherine of Sienna.

795. Morosini, vol. iii, p. 101.

796. Trial, vol. iii, pp. 66, 210.

797. Jean Bouchet, Annales d'Aquitaine, in the Trial, vol. iv, pp. 536, 537.

798. Guilbert, Histoire des villes de France, vol. iv, Poitiers. Cf. B. Ledain, La Maison de Jeanne d'Arc à Poitiers, Saint-Maixent, 1892, in 8vo. According to M. Ledain the Hôtel de la Rose was on the spot now occupied by a house, number 13 in La Rue Notre-Dame-la-Petite.

799. Trial, vol. iii, p. 66.

800. Vallet de Viriville, Notices et extraits de chartes et de manuscrits appartenant au British Museum de Londres, in the Bibliothèque de l'École des Chartes, vol. viii, pp. 139, 140.

801. De Beaucourt, Histoire de Charles VII, vol. ii, p. 77.

802. Vallet de Viriville, *Analyse et fragments tirés des Archives municipales de Tours* in *Cabinet historique*, vol. v, pp. 102-121.

803. Quicherat, *Rodrigue de Villandrando*, Paris, 1879, in 8vo, pp. 14 *et seq.*

804. *Le Jouvencel*, vol. i, Introduction, p. xxii, note 1.

805. *Trial*, vol. iii, p. 101.

806. Francisque Mandet, *Histoire du Velay*, Le Puy, 1860-1862 (7 vols. in 12mo), vol. i, pp. 590 *et seq.* S. Luce, *Jeanne d'Arc à Domremy*, ch. xii.

807. Jean Juvénal des Ursins, 1407.

808. Nicole de Savigni, *Notes sur les exploits de Jeanne d'Arc et sur divers évènements de son temps*, in the *Bulletin de la Société de l'Histoire de Paris*, 1, 1874, p. 43. Chanoine Lucot, *Jeanne d'Arc en Champagne*, Châlons, 1880, pp. 12, 13.

809. *Trial*, vol. i, p. 191; vol. ii, p. 74, note. La Romée may have received her surname for an entirely different reason. Most of our knowledge of Jeanne's mother is derived from documents of very doubtful authenticity.

810. Francis C. Lowell considers the idea of La Romée's pilgrimage to Puy as a "characteristic example of the madness" of Siméon Luce (*Joan of Arc*, Boston, 1896, in 8vo, p. 72, note). Nevertheless, after considerable hesitation, I, like Luce, have rejected the corrections proposed by Lebrun de Charmettes and Quicherat, and adopted unamended the text of the *Trial*.

811. *Trial*, vol. iii, p. 101. For the meaning of *Lector*, professor of theology, cf. Du Cange.

812. *Trial*, vol. iii, pp. 101 *et seq.*

813. E. Giraudet, *Histoire de la ville de Tours*, Tours, 1874, 2 vols. in 8vo, *passim*.

814. *Trial*, vol. iii, pp. 67, 94, 210; vol. iv, pp. 3, 301, 363.

815. J. Quicherat, *Histoire du costume en France*, Paris, 1875, large 8vo, pp. 270, 271.

816. *Trial*, vol. iii, pp. 67, 94, 210. *Relation du greffier de La Rochelle*, p. 60. "The white armour of fifteenth century soldiers, simple as it was, was expensive; it cost about ten thousand francs of our present money. But the complete horse's armour was included in this" (Maurice Maindron, *Pour l'histoire de l'armure*, in *Le monde moderne*, 1896). According to the calculation of P. Clément (*Jacques*

Cœur et Charles VII, 1873, p. lxvi), 100 livres would be equal to 4000 francs of present money.

817. *Trial*, vol. i, p. 76. Letter from Perceval de Boulainvilliers, *ibid.*, vol. v, p. 120. Greffier de la Chambre des comptes of Brabant, *ibid.*, vol. iv, p. 428. Le Fèvre de Saint-Rémy, *ibid.*, p. 439.

818. Anonymous poem in the *Trial*, vol. v, p. 38 and note.

819. Capitaine Champion, *Jeanne d'Arc écuyère*, pp. 146 *et seq.*

820. *Trial*, vol. i, pp. 56, 75, 76, 77.

821. Abbé Bourassé, *Les miracles de madame sainte Katerine de Fierboys en Touraine (1375-1446)*, Tours, 1858, in 8vo, *passim*.

822. *Chronique de la Pucelle*, p. 277. Jean Chartier, *Chronique*, vol. i, p. 69.

823. *Trial*, vol. i, p. 77. *Les miracles de madame sainte Katerine*, *passim*.

824. *Trial*, vol. i, pp. 76, 234, 236. *Chronique de la Pucelle*, p. 277. *Journal du siège*, p. 49. Jean Chartier, *Chronique*, vol. i, pp. 69, 70. Guerneri Berni, in the *Trial*, vol. iv, p. 519. *Journal d'un bourgeois de Paris*, p. 267. Morosini, vol. iii, p. 109. *Relation du greffier de La Rochelle*, pp. 337, 338. *Chronique Messine*, edition Bouteiller, 1878, Orléans, in 8vo, 26 pages.

825. *Trial*, vol. i, pp. 75, 235.

826. *Ibid.*, p. 76.

827. Morosini, vol. iii, pp. 108, 109. *Chronique de Lorraine*, in the *Trial*, vol. iv, p. 332. Eberhard Windecke, p. 101. Cf. *Journal du siège*, p. 49.

828. Jean Chartier, vol. i, p. 122.

829. *Trial*, vol. i, pp. 77, 179, 236; vol. iii, p. 103.

830. *Ibid.*, pp. 78, 117.

831. *Ibid.*, pp. 78, 117, 181, 300. *Relation du greffier de La Rochelle*, p. 338. Morosini, vol. iii, p. 110; vol. iv, supplement, xv, pp. 313, 315.

832. Perceval de Cagny, p. 150. *Journal du siège*, p. 76. *Relation du greffier d'Albi*, in the *Trial*, vol. iv, p. 301. *Relation du greffier de La Rochelle*, p. 338. *Chronique du doyen de Saint-Thibaud de Metz*, in the *Trial*, vol. iv, p. 322. Extract from the thirteenth account of Hémon Raguier, in the *Trial*, vol. v, p. 258.

833. Vallet de Viriville, *Histoire de Charles VII*, vol. ii, p. 65; *Un épisode de la vie de Jeanne d'Arc*, in *Bibliothèque de l'École des Chartes*, vol. iv, first series, p. 488.

834. In Beaudouin de Sebourg (xx, 249) is the passage:

Il est cousin au conte
Il en fait estandart

quoted by Godefroy. Cf. La Curne and Littré.

835. *"Pourquoy la Hire, Poton et plusieurs autres vaillants hommes qui moult enviz s'en alloient ainsi honteusement," Journal du siège,* p. 42.

836. The hospital of Orléans, close to the cathedral.

837. 9 March. *Journal du siège,* pp. 56, 57.

838. *Journal du siège,* p. 64.

839. Boucher de Molandon, *L'armée anglaise vaincue par Jeanne d'Arc,* ch. ii. Jarry, *Le compte de l'armée anglaise,* pp. 60, 107, 110, 112.

840. *Journal du siège,* pp. 57, 58. Abbé Dubois, *Histoire du siège,* dissertation vi.

841. *Chronique de la Pucelle,* pp. 265, 267. Morosini, vol. iv, supplement xiii.

842. *Journal du siège,* p. 58.

843. *Le Jouvencel,* vol. i, p. xxii; vol. ii, p. 44.

844. *Journal du siège,* pp. 56, 62.

845. Jarry, *Le compte de l'armée anglaise,* pp. 50, 58.

846. Pierre Sureau's account in Jarry, *Le compte de l'armée anglaise,* proofs and illustrations, no. vi, pp. 45, 46.

847. *Journal d'un bourgeois de Paris,* pp. 221, 222 *et seq.*

848. Shakespeare, *Henry VI,* part i, act i, scene ii. According to M. G. Duval the first part of this play was adapted from one of Shakespeare's predecessors.

849. Jean Chartier, *Chronique,* vol. i, p. 65.

850. *Journal du siège,* pp. 69, 70. *Chronique de la Pucelle,* p. 270. Monstrelet, vol. iv, pp. 317 *et seq.* Morosini, vol. iii, pp. 19, 20, 21; vol. iv, supplement xiv, p. 311. Jarry, *Le compte de l'armée anglaise,* pp. 68 *et seq.* Boucher de Molandon, *L'armée anglaise vaincue par Jeanne d'Arc,* p. 145.

851. *Journal du siège,* p. 70.

852. Jollois, *Histoire du siège,* part vi, ch. i. Abbé Dubois, *Histoire du siège,* dissertation ix. Loiseleur, *Compte des dépenses de Charles VII,* ch. v. Lottin, *Recherches historiques sur la ville d'Orléans,* vol. ii, p. 205. Morosini, vol. iii, p. 25, note 2.

853. *Journal du siège,* p. 64.

854. *Ibid.*, p. 59.

855. Charles d'Orléans, *Poésies*, edited by A. Champollion-Figeac, Paris, 1842, in 8vo, p. 176.

856. Miniature in the MS. of the poems of Charles d'Orléans, in the British Museum, Royal 16 F. ii, fol. 73 v°.

857. *Journal du siège*, p. 43. Symphorien Guyon, *Histoire de la ville d'Orléans*, vol. ii, p. 43.

858. *Chronique de la fête*, in the *Trial*, vol. v, p. 297.

859. Accounts of the Commune, *passim*, in *Journal du siège*, pp. 210 *et seq.*

860. *Mistère du siège*, lines 6964 *et seq.*

861. Aug. Theiner, *Saint Aignan ou le siège d'Orléans par Attila, notice historique suivie de la vie de ce saint, tirée des MSS. de la Bibliothèque du Roi*, Paris, 1832, in 8vo.

862. *Journal du siège*, p. 46. *Chronique de la Pucelle*, p. 278. Jean Chartier, *Chronique*, p. 66.

863. *Journal du siège*, pp. 47, 48. P. Mantellier, *Histoire du siège*, pp. 61 *et seq.*

864. *Journal du siège*, p. 77.

865. *Trial*, vol. iii, p. 93. *Geste des nobles*, in *La chronique de la Pucelle*, p. 250. The Accounts of fortresses (1428-1430), in Boucher de Molandon, *Première expédition de Jeanne d'Arc*, pp. 30 *et seq.*

866. *Chronique de la Pucelle*, p. 287. *Journal du siège*, p. 81. Boucher de Molandon, *Première expédition de Jeanne d'Arc*, pp. 28, 29. P. Mantellier, *Histoire du siège*, p. 230.

867. The name by which the town councillors of Toulouse were called.

868. *Le siège d'Orléans, Jeanne d'Arc et les capitouls de Toulouse*, by A. Thomas, in *Annales du Midi*, 1889, p. 232. It would appear that Saint-Flour, although solicited, did not contribute: it had enough to do to defend itself from the freebooters who were constantly hovering round. Cf. *Villandrando et les écorcheurs à Saint-Flour* by M. Boudet, Clermont-Ferrand, 1895, in 8vo, pp. 18 *et seq.*

869. Receipts of the town of Orléans in 1429, in Boucher de Molandon, *Première expédition de Jeanne d'Arc*, p. 36.

870. Florent d'Illiers, descended from an old family of the Chartres country, had married Jeanne, daughter of Jean de Coutes and sister of the little page whom the Sire de Gaucourt had given the Maid (A. de Villaret).

871. *Journal du siège*, p. 73. *Chronique de la Pucelle*, p. 278.

872. *Le Jouvencel*, vol. ii, p. 44.

873. Jarry, *Le compte de l'armée anglaise*, pp. 75 *et seq.*

874. *Trial*, vol. iii, p. 4.

875. *Journal du siège, passim. Chronique de Tournai*, ed. Smedt (vol. iii, in the *Recueil des chroniques de Flandre*), p. 409.

876. *Trial*, vol. iii, p. 93.

877. Wavrin, in the *Trial*, vol. iv, p. 407. Monstrelet, vol. iv, p. 316. *Chronique de la Pucelle*, p. 278. Jean Chartier, *Chronique*, p. 68. *Mistère du siège*, lines 11,431 *et seq.* Abbé Bossard, *Gilles de Rais, Maréchal de France, dit Barbe-Bleue* (1404-1440), Paris, 1886, 8vo, pp. 31, 106.

878. *Trial*, vol. iii, p. 74.

879. Jeanne says (in her *Trial*) from 10,000 to 12,000 men; Monstrelet says, 7000; Eberhard Windecke, 3000; Morosini, 12,000.

880. "*Car vous ne trouverez nulz marchans qu'ils se mettent en ceste peine ne en ce danger, s'ilz n'ont l'argent contant.*" ("For you will find no merchants who will take that trouble, and run that risk, unless they are paid ready money.") *Le Jouvencel*, vol. i, p. 184.

881. *Trial*, vol. iii, p. 74.

882. There are eight ancient texts of this letter: (1) the text used in the Rouen trial (*Trial*, i, p. 240); (2) a text probably written by a Knight of the Order of St. John of Jerusalem; the original document has been lost, but there are two copies dating from the 18th century (*Ibid.*, v, p. 95); (3) the text contained in *Le journal du siège* (*Ibid.*, iv, p. 139); (4) the text in *La chronique de la Pucelle* (*Ibid.*, iv, p. 215); (5) the text in Thomassin's *Registre Delphinal* (*Ibid.*, iv, p. 306); (6) the text of the Greffier de La Rochelle (*Revue historique*, vol. iv); (7) the text of the Tournai Chronicle (*Recueil des chroniques de Flandre*, vol. iii, p. 407); (8) the text in *Le mistère du siège*. There may be mentioned also a German contemporary translation by Eberhard Windecke.

The text from the *Trial* is the one quoted here. It is a reproduction of the original. The others differ from it and from original too widely for it to be possible to indicate the differences except by giving the whole of each text. And after all these variations are of no great importance.

883. The King of France himself designated as *good* such of his towns as he wished to honour.

884. Compare: "Et ardirent la ville et *violèrent l'abbaye*." ("And burnt the town and *violated the abbey*.") Froissart, quoted by Littré. As early as *Le chanson de Roland* we find: "*Les castels pris, les cités violées*." ("The castles taken, the cities violated.")

885. The deliverance of the Duke of Orléans. *Réclamer* in the French. M. S. Reinach proposes to substitute *relever*, which is plausible (cf. *Trial*, vol. ii, p. 421).

886. *Le journal du siège* omits the word *France* and thus renders the phrase unintelligible. This omission proceeds from a text of great antiquity on which are based notably *La chronique de la Pucelle* and the account of the Greffier de La Rochelle whom this mangled phrase visibly embarrassed.

887. *Gentle* is here in opposition to *villein*. Gentle and otherwise: nobles and villeins. Here we must interpret the terms *comrades* and *gentle* according to their true meaning and not consider them as used ironically, as in the following passage from Froissart: "*Il (le duc de Lancastre) entendit comme il pourroit estre saisy de quatre gentils compaignons qui estranglé avoyent son oncle, le duc de Glocestre, au chasteau de Calais*." "He (the Duke of Lancaster) realised how he might be seized by the four gentle comrades who had strangled his uncle, the Duke of Gloucester, in the Castle of Calais." (Froissart in La Curne.)

888. French. *Attendez les nouvelles de la Pucelle* and further on: *Si vous ne voulés croire lez nouvelles de par Dieu de la Pucelle....* This word *Nouvelles* then as now meant *tidings*, but it also had a sense of *marvels* as in the following phrase: "*En celle année apparurent maintes nouvelles à Rosay en Brie; le vin fut mué en sang et le pain en chair sensiblement ou (au) sacrement de l'autel*." ("In that year many *marvels* were wrought at Rosay in Brie; the wine was turned to blood and the bread to flesh visibly at the sacrament of the altar.") (*Chroniques de Saint Denys*, in La Curne.)

889. *Trial*, vol. i, pp. 55, 84, 240.

890. *Ibid.*, pp. 55, 56, 84.

891. Morosini, vol. iii, pp. 64, 82 *et seq.* Christine de Pisan, in the *Trial*, vol. v, p. 16. Concerning the subject of the Crusade, cf. N. Jorga, Philippe de Mezières, 1896, in 8vo: *Notes et extraits pour servir à l'histoire des Croisades au XVe siècle*, Paris, 1899-1902, 3 vols. in 8vo (taken from *La revue de l'Orient Latin*).

892. *Pii Secundi commentarii*, 1614 edition, p. 440. Wadding, *Annales Minorum*, vol. v, pp. 130 *et seq.*

893. *Journal d'un bourgeois de Paris*, p. 233. S. Luce, *Jeanne d'Arc à Domremy*, pp. xv, ccxxxvii. See the pictures in the numerous fifteenth century little popular books concerning Antichrist. (Brunet, *Manuel du libraire*, vol. i, col. 316.)

894. Félix Rabbe, *Jeanne d'Arc en Angleterre*, Paris, 1891, p. 12.

895. Monstrelet, vol. iv, p. 112. Vallet de Viriville, *Histoire de Charles VII*, vol. i, p. 340.

896. Le P. Marcellin Fornier, *Histoire des Alpes, Maritimes ou Cottiennes*, vol. ii, pp. 315 *et seq.*

897. In all extant copies of the Letter to the English, except that of the Trial, at the passage "you may come" *Encore que pourrez venir.* the text is completely illegible.

898. *Per unam litteram suo materno idiomate confectam, verbis bene simplicibus*, *Trial*, vol. iv, p. 7, evidence of the Bastard of Orléans. Mathieu Thomassin, *Registre Delphinal*, in the *Trial*, vol. iv, p. 306.

899. On the contrary it contains forms which would never have been penned by a native of Picardy, Burgundy, Lorraine, or Champagne, such as the participle *envoyée*. Both the grammar and the writing are those of a French clerk. (Contributed by M. E. Langlois.)

900. *Trial*, vol. v, p. 252. E. de Bouteiller and G. de Braux, *Nouvelles recherches sur la famille de Jeanne d'Arc*, pp. xx, 9, 10. Document of very doubtful authenticity..

901. *Trial*, vol. iii, p. 101.

902. *Ibid.*, pp. 65, 67, 124. *Chronique de la Pucelle*, p. 277. A. de Villaret, *Louis de Coutes, page de Jeanne d'Arc*, Orléans, 1890, 8vo.

903. *Trial*, vol. iii, pp. 26, 27.

904. Extracts from the Accounts of Hémon Raguier, *Trial*, vol. v, pp. 257, 258.

905. *Trial*, vol. iii, p. 211. D'Aulon had seen her at Poitiers.

906. *Ibid.*, p. 15. De Beaucourt, *Histoire de Charles VII*, vol. ii, p. 292, note 3. The loans mentioned occurred later, but there is no reason to believe that they were the first. Duc de La Tremoïlle, *Les La Trémouille pendant cinq siècles, Guy VI et Georges (1346-1446)*, Nantes, 1890, pp. 196, 201.

907. Juvénal des Ursins, year 1396.

908. *Ordonnances des rois de France*, vol. xi, p. 105; vol. xiii, p. 247. S. de Bouillerie, *La répression du blasphème dans l'ancienne législation*, in the *Revue historique et archéologique du Maine*, 1884, pp. 369 *et seq.* De Beaucourt, *Histoire de Charles VII*, vol. i, p. 370; vol. ii, p. 189. A. Longnon, *Paris pendant la domination anglaise*, Paris, 1878, in 8vo, pp. 11, 56.

909. *Trial*, vol. iii, pp. 78, 104, 105. *Chronique de la Pucelle*, p. 283. Very early she was mentioned in connection with La Hire, the most valiant of the French, and it was imagined that she taught him to confess and to cease swearing. These are pretty stories (*Trial*, vol. iii, p. 32; vol. iv, p. 327).

910. *Trial*, vol. iii, p. 103. Boucher de Molandon, *Première expédition de Jeanne d'Arc*, p. 47. L.A. Bossebœuf, *Jeanne d'Arc en Touraine*, Tours, 1899, pp. 34 *et seq.*

911. Le P. Denifle, *La désolation des églises, monastères, hôpitaux, en France, vers le milieu du XVe siècle*, Mâcon, 1897, in 8vo, introduction.

912. *Trial*, vol. iv, p. 327. Tringant, *Le Jouvencel*, vol. ii, p. 277, merely says that few soldiers went willingly to the relief of Orléans, which is not strictly accurate.

913. *Trial*, vol. iii, p. 104 (Brother Pasquerel's evidence). *Chronique de la Pucelle*, p. 281. Morosini, vol. iii, pp. 110, 111; vol. iv, pp. 313-315. G. Martin, *L'étendard de Jeanne d'Arc*, in *Notes d'art et d'arch.*, 1834, pp. 65-71, 81-88, illustrated.

914. *Trial*, vol. iii, p. 93. *Chronique du doyen de Saint-Thibaud*, in *Trial*, vol. iv, p. 327.

915. *Trial*, vol. iii, pp. 5, 67, 78, 105, 212. Martial d'Auvergne, *ibid.*, vol. v, p. 53. *Chronique de la fête, ibid.*, p. 290. *Chronique de la Pucelle*, p. 281. Jean Chartier, *Chronique*, vol. i, p. 71. Boucher de Molandon, *Première expédition de Jeanne d'Arc*, pp. 38 *et seq.*

916. The 28th of April, according to Eberhard Windecke, p. 165. The 27th, if, as Pasquerel says, the army spent two nights on the march.

917. *Trial*, vol. iii, p. 105.

918. Eberhard Windecke, p. 167.

919. *Trial*, vol. iii, p. 104 (Brother Pasquerel's evidence).

920. *Ibid.*, p. 67 (evidence of Louis de Coutes).

921. *Ibid.*, p. 67. Pasquerel says (vol. iii, p. 105) that the soldiers of fortune were permitted to join the congregation if they had confessed.

922. *Trial*, vol. iii, pp. 4, 5. Boucher de Molandon, *Bulletin de la Société archéologique de l'Orléanais*, vol. iv, p. 427; vol. ix, p. 73. The same author, *Première expédition de Jeanne d'Arc*, pp. 41 *et seq. Mistère du siège*, lines 11,480 *et seq. Chronique de l'établissement de la fête*, in *Trial*, vol. v, p. 289.

923. *Journal du siège*, p. 75. *Chronique de la Pucelle*, p. 283.

924. "*Et cuidoit bien qu'ils deussent passer par devers les bastides du siège devers la Beausse.*" *Chronique de la Pucelle*, p. 281.

925. *Chronique de la Pucelle*, p. 285 (the Chronicle here amplifies the evidence of Dunois, vol. iii, p. 67).

926. *Trial*, vol. iii, pp. 5, 6.

927. *Trial*, vol. iii, pp. 5, 6. *Chronique de la Pucelle*, p. 284. Boucher de Molandon, *Première expédition de Jeanne d'Arc*, p. 49.

928. *Chronique de la Pucelle*, p. 273.

929. Opinion of Martin Berruyer, in Lanéry d'Arc, *Mémoires et consultations*, ch. vii.

930. *Trial*, vol. iii, pp. 78, 214.

931. *Trial*, vol. iii, p. 16.

932. *Ibid.*, p. 78. *Journal du siège*, pp. 74, 75. *Chronique de la fête*, in *Trial*, vol. v, p. 290.

933. *Trial*, vol. iii, p. 105. *Chronique du la Pucelle*, p. 284.

934. Boucher de Molandon, *La délivrance d'Orléans et l'institution de la fête du 8 mai, Chronique anonyme du XVe siècle*, Orléans, 1883, in 8vo, pp. 28, 29.

935. *Trial*, vol. iii, p. 6. *Journal du siège*, p. 75.

936. *Chronique de la fête*, in the *Trial*, vol. v, p. 290. Morosini, vol. iii, p. 23, note 5. Boucher de Molandon, *Première expédition de Jeanne d'Arc*, pp. 52-56.

937. *Chronique de la Pucelle*, p. 285. This document very untrustworthy as a whole is in certain passages a better authority than *Le journal du siège*.

938. *Trial*, vol. iii, pp. 104, 105 (Pasquerel's evidence).

939. *Chronique de la Pucelle*, pp. 284, 285.

940. "*Ex tunc dictus deponens habuit bonam spem de ea et plus quam ante,*" *Trial,* vol. iii, p. 6.

941. *Timens ne recedere vellent et quod opus remaneret imperfectum,* *Trial,* vol. iii, p. 78. *Chronique de la Pucelle,* p. 286. *Chronique de la fête,* in the *Trial,* vol. v, p. 285. Boucher de Molandon, *Première expédition de Jeanne d'Arc,* pp. 61, 62.

942. *Trial,* vol. iii, p. 105. *Mistère du siège,* line 11,616.

943. Boucher de Molandon, *Première expédition de Jeanne d'Arc,* pp. 62, 99, note xiv, and in *Bulletin de la Société archéologique de l'Orléanais,* vol. iv, p. 429; vol. ix, p. 73.

944. *Journal du siège,* p. 75. Ch. du Lys, *Traité sommaire tant du nom et des armes que de la naissance et parenté de la Pucelle d'Orléans et de ses frères,* Paris, 1628, in 4to, p. 50. Abbé Dubois, *Histoire du siège,* p. 344. P. Mantellier, *Histoire du siège,* p. 86. Boucher de Molandon, *Première expédition de Jeanne d'Arc,* p. 65, proofs and illustrations, note xv.

945. *Journal du siège,* pp. 75, 76.

946. Boucher de Molandon, *Première expédition de Jeanne d'Arc,* p. 68.

947. *Chronique de la Fête,* in *Trial,* vol. v, p. 290.

948. *Journal du siège,* pp. 74, 75. Jean Chartier, *Chronique,* vol. i, p. 69. *Chronique de la Pucelle,* pp. 284, 285.

949. Boucher de Molandon, *Première expédition de Jeanne d'Arc,* pp. 51 *et seq.*

950. *Journal du siège,* p. 75.

951. *Ibid.,* p. 76.

952. *Journal du siège,* pp. 74, 75.

953. And even now trumpeters ride white horses (*Histoire de Jeanne d'Arc,* by Lebrun de Charmettes, 1817, in 8vo, vol. ii, p. 21).

954. *Trial,* vol. iii, p. 7. *Journal du siège,* p. 76. *Chronique de la Pucelle,* p. 287. Jean Chartier, *Chronique,* vol. i, p. 72. Morosini, vol. iii, pp. 28, 30.

955. "*Comme se ilz veissent Dieu descendre entre eulx,*" says *Le journal du siège,* p. 76. Luillier (*Trial,* vol. iii, p. 24) calls her "the angel of the Lord" (*l'ange de Dieu*).

956. *Journal du siège,* pp. 76, 77.

957. *Chronique de l'établissement de la fête,* p. 28.

958. *Trial*, vol. i, p. 101; vol. iii, pp. 34, 68, 124 *et seq.*, 211. *Chronique de la Pucelle*, p. 285. Boucher de Molandon, *Jacques Boucher, sieur de Guilleville, trésorier général du district d'Orléans....* in *Mémoires de la Société archéologique de l'Orléanais*, vol. xxii, 1889, p. 373. Boucher de Molandon, *Première expédition de Jeanne d'Arc*, p. 101, note xvi; proofs and illustrations, p. 108.

959. Jean Chartier, *Chronique*, vol. i, p. 73. *Chronique de la Pucelle*, ed. Vallet de Viriville, p. 20. Note on G. Cousinot the Chancellor.. Cf. *Nouvelle biographie générale*. Vallet de Viriville, *Essais critiques sur les historiens originaux du règne de Charles VII*, in *Bibliothèque de l'École des Chartes*, 1857, fourth series, vol. iii, pp. 11-14, 105-111.

960. *Trial*, vol. i, p. 101; vol. iii, pp. 68, 124 *et seq.*; vol. iv, pp. 153, 219, 227. *Journal du siège*, pp. 77, 78. Boucher de Molandon, *Première expédition de Jeanne d'Arc*, pp. 69, 107, note xvi.

961. G. Lefèvre-Pontalis (*Chronique d'Antonio Morosini*, vol. iii, p. 101, note) discovers in *La chronique de la Pucelle* (xliv, p. 285) a wrong use of an incident cited by Dunois in his evidence, which must be allowed to have happened on the 7th of May, as Dunois cited it (*Trial*, vol. iii, p. 9).

962. *Trial*, vol. iii, pp. 34, 68.

963. Franklin, *La vie privée d'autrefois*, vols. ii, xix, *passim*. H. Havard, *Dictionnaire de l'ameublement*, under the word *lit*.

964. Accounts of the fortress in *Trial*, vol. v, pp. 259, 260.

965. *Journal du siège*, pp. 43, 44.

966. *Ibid.*, pp. 78, 79.

967. See the evidence of S. Charles (vol. iii, pp. 116, 117) and certain details in *La chronique de la Pucelle*.

968. *Trial*, vol. iii, pp. 7, 211; vol. iv, pp. 221, 222. *Chronique de la Pucelle*, pp. 250, 251, 287. Jean Chartier, *Chronique*, vol. i, pp. 74, 75.

969. *Journal du siège*, pp. 78, 79.

970. *Ibid.*, p. 78. *Chronique de la fête*, in *Trial*, vol. v, pp. 291, 292. Cf. Letter written from Germany, in *Trial*, vol. v, p. 349.

971. *Trial*, vol. iii, pp. 27, 108. *Journal du siège*, p. 79.

972. *Chronique de la Pucelle*, p. 284. *Trial*, vol. iii, pp. 26, 27.

973. Martial de Paris, called d'Auvergne, *Vigiles de Charles VII*, ed. Coustelier, 1724, vol. i, p. 98.

974. La Curne, under the word *Periapt*. Shakespeare, *Henry VI*, part i, act v, sc. iii.

975. Shakespeare, *Henry VI*, part i, act iii, sc. i.

976. Vallet de Viriville, *Histoire de Charles VII*, vol. i, p. 306. Carlier, *Histoire du Valois*, vol. ii, p. 442.

977. Jarry, *Le compte de l'armée anglaise*, p. 61.

978. Shakespeare, *Henry VI*, part i, act i, sc. ii.

979. *Trial*, vol. iii, p. 27. *Journal du siège*, p. 79. *Chronique de la Pucelle*, pp. 285, 286.

980. *Journal du siège*, p. 79. *Chronique de la Pucelle*, p. 290.

981. *Trial*, vol. iii, p. 7. *Journal du siège*, p. 79.

982. *Trial*, vol. iii, p. 211.

983. *Journal du siège*, p. 80. P. Mantellier, *Histoire du siège*, pp. 92, 95.

984. 1 May. *Journal du siège*, p. 80.

985. *Trial*, vol. iii, p. 68 (evidence of Louis de Coutes).

986. Extracts from fortress accounts, in the *Trial*, vol. v, p. 259.

987. *Trial*, vol. i, p. 64.

988. *Ibid.*, vol. iii, pp. 9, 15, 18, 22, 60; vol. v, p. 120. *Chronique de la Pucelle*, p. 285. Morosini, p. 101. *Relation du greffier de La Rochelle*, p. 337.

989. *Journal du siège*, p. 80. P. Mantellier, *Histoire du siège*, p. 95.

990. Charles Cuissard, *Notes chronologiques sur Jean de Mâcon*, in *Mémoires de la Société archéologique de l'Orléanais*, vol. xi, 1897, pp. 529, 545.

991. *Chronique de la fête*, in *Trial*, vol. v, p. 291. Lottin, *Recherches*, vol. i, p. 30.

992. Note by Guill. Girault, notary in the *Trial*, vol. iv, p. 282. *Journal du siège*, p. 135.

993. *Trial*, vol. v, pp. 112, 113.

994. *Ibid.*, vol. iii, p. 24. Cf. *Ibid.*, pp. 7, 8 (the evidence of Dunois amounts to much the same).

995. *Chronique de la fête*, in *Trial*, vol. v, p. 291.

996. *Chronique de la fête*, in *Trial*, vol. v, p. 291.

997. *Journal du siège*, pp. 51, 52.

998. Beaucroix, in his evidence, says it was Jean d'Aulon (*Trial*, vol. iii, p. 79); but, according to his own testimony, d'Aulon was then following the Bastard (*Ibid.*, vol. iii, p. 210).

999. *Ibid.*, vol. iii, p. 79. *Chronique de la Pucelle*, p. 286. P. Mantellier, *Histoire du siège*, p. 85.

1000. *Chronique de la Pucelle*, p. 287.

1001. *Ibid.*, p. 287. *Journal du siège*, p. 81. Abbé Dubois, *Histoire du siège*, dissertation ix. Lottin, *Recherches*, vol. i, p. 205. Loiseleur, *Comptes des dépenses*, ch. vii.

1002. On the 4th of May, as on the 29th of April, the corn was brought down the Loire. Indeed there exists a bill which makes mention of "sailors who brought the corn which came from Blois on the 4th day of May," "*nottoniers qui amenèrent les blés qui furent amenés de Blois le iiij^e jour de may*" (Boucher de Molandon, *Première expédition de Jeanne d'Arc*, pp. 58, 59).

1003. The 4th of May, *Trial*, vol. iii, pp. 105, 211. *Journal du siège*, p. 81. *Chronique de la Pucelle*, p. 287.

1004. *Trial*, vol. iii, p. 212 (Jean d'Aulon's evidence).

1005. *Ibid.*, p. 212.

1006. *Ibid.*, p. 212. *Journal du siège*, p. 78.

1007. I have followed the account of Jean Chartier, vol. i, p. 73 (amplified in *La chronique de la Pucelle*, p. 288), which is more plausible than that of *Le journal du siège*.

1008. *Trial*, vol. iii, pp. 212, 213 (Jean d'Aulon's evidence).

1009. *Ibid.*, vol. iii, p. 106.

1010. *Trial*, vol. iii, p. 68 (evidence of Louis de Coutes).

1011. *Ibid.*, p. 69.

1012. *Ibid.*, p. 212.

1013. *Ibid.*, pp. 212, 213 (Jean d'Aulon's evidence).

1014. *Trial*, vol. iii, p. 213.

1015. Gruel, *Chronique d'Arthur de Richemont*, p. 72.

1016. *Journal du siège*, p. 75.

1017. *Trial*, vol. iii, pp. 124, 126. Abbé Dubois, *Histoire du siège*, dissertation vi. Morosini, vol. iv, supplement xiii. *Journal du siège*, pp. 83, 84. Jean Chartier, *Chronique*, vol. i, p. 72.

1018. Robert Blondel, *De reductione Normanniæ*, in *Trial*, vol. iv, p. 347. *Journal du siège*, p. 13. *Chronique de la fête*, in *Trial*, vol. v, pp. 286 *et seq.*

1019. *Trial*, vol. iii, pp. 109, 127. *Chronique de la Pucelle*, p. 295. Clerk of the Chambre des Comptes de Brabant, in *Trial*, vol. iv, p. 426. Eberhard Windecke, p. 172.

1020. Perceval de Cagny says: "Soon after the arrival of the Maid on the edge of the entrenchments. those in the fort wished to surrender to her: she would not take them for ransom and said she would capture them in any event, and redoubled the attack. And straightway the fort was taken and almost all put to death." This is hard to believe. The English would sooner have surrendered to the humblest menial in the Armagnac host than to the Maid: and it is not likely that she would have refused to hold them as prisoners for ransom. Besides, Perceval de Cagny has not the remotest idea of what happened on the 4th of May. For example, he believes that the Maid opened the attack. Perceval de Cagny, pp. 144 *et seq. Journal du siège*, p. 82. *Chronique de la Pucelle*, p. 289. *Chronique de la fête*, in *Trial*, vol. v, p. 294.

1021. *Trial*, vol. iii, p. 106.

1022. *Chronique de la Pucelle*, p. 289.

1023. *Trial*, vol. iii, p. 106.

1024. At the capture of the Saint-Loup bastion:

	Number of French engaged.	Number of French slain.
Journal du Siège	1,500 without counting nobles.	
Letter of Charles VII		2
Morosini's correspondent	3,500	
Eberhard Windecke		2

	Number of English engaged.	Number of English slain.
Brother Pasquerel	100 picked men	100 slain or taken
Jean d'Aulon		all killed or taken
G. Girault		120 killed or taken
Charles VII's letter		all killed or taken
Journal du siège		114 killed, 40 taken
Relation de la fête du 8 Mai	From 120 to 140	all killed or taken
Perceval de Cagny	3,000	all killed or taken
Chronique de la Pucelle		160 killed

	Number of English engaged.	Number of English slain.
Monstrelet	From 300 to 400	all killed or taken
Eberhard Windecke		170 killed, 1,300 taken
Les Vigiles de Charles VII		60 killed, 22 taken

1025. The accounts of the fortress in *Journal du siège*, p. 284.

1026. *Trial*, vol. iii, p. 107. *Chronique de la Pucelle*, pp. 289, 290.

1027. *Trial*, vol. iii, pp. 34, 35 (evidence of the widow Huré).

1028. May 5th. Quicherat is mistaken when he says (*Trial*, vol. iv, p. 57, note) that this council was held at Jacques Boucher's. Cf. *Journal du siège*, p. 83. Jean Chartier, *Chronique*, p. 73. Boucher de Molandon in *Mémoires de la Société archéologique de l'Orléanais*, vol. xxii, p. 373.

1029. By the little island without a name which is marked on the plan as Petite Île Charlemagne. The English had fortified it. See plan.

1030. Jean Chartier, *Chronique*, vol. i, p. 74.

1031. *Ibid.*, pp. 74, 75. These statements are very doubtful.

1032. Jean Chartier, *Chronique*, vol. i, pp. 74, 75. Very doubtful.

1033. *Ibid.*, p. 75. *Journal du siège*, pp. 82, 83. Cf. the evidence of S. Charles (*Trial*, vol. iii, pp. 116, 117).

1034. May 5th. *Trial*, vol. iii, p. 107 (Pasquerel's evidence).

1035. *Ibid.*, p. 108.

1036. *Chronique de la Pucelle*, p. 286. *Journal du siège*, p. 79, gives a different account of this episode.

1037. *Trial*, vol. iii, p. 108 (Pasquerel's evidence).

1038. *Ibid.*, pp. 116, 117. Evidence of S. Charles. P. Mantellier, *Histoire du siège*, p. 105.

1039. *Journal du siège*, pp. 83, 84. Abbé Dubois, *Histoire du siège*, p. 535. Jollois, *Histoire du siège*, p. 39.

1040. *Chronique de la Pucelle*, p. 290.

1041. Jean Chartier, *Chronique*, vol. i, p. 76. *Journal du siège*, pp. 84, 85.

1042. "Et les rebouterent ils par maintes fois et tresbucherent de hault en bas." *Journal du siège*, p. 85.

1043. *Trial*, vol. iii, pp. 214, 215 (Jean d'Aulon's evidence).

1044. *Trial*, vol. iii, p. 215 (Jean d'Aulon's evidence).

1045. *Ibid.*, p. 78 (evidence of Beaucroix). *Journal du siège*, p. 86.

1046. *Chronique de la Pucelle*, p. 291. Jean Chartier, *Chronique*, vol. i, p. 72. *Journal du siège*, pp. 84, 85. Of doubtful authenticity.

1047. *Chronique de la Pucelle*, p. 291.

1048. Perceval de Cagny, p. 146.

1049. *Trial*, vol. iii, p. 79 (evidence of Beaucroix).

1050. *Ibid.*, p. 70. *Chronique de la fête*, p. 33.

1051. *Chronique de la Pucelle*, p. 291.

1052. *Trial*, vol. iii, p. 108.

1053. The council is mentioned in *La chronique de la Pucelle*, p. 292; but this document is a mere echo of Brother Pasquerel's evidence.

1054. *Trial*, vol. iii, pp. 108, 109. Brother Pasquerel, whom I follow here, reports Jeanne's saying in the following terms: *Exibit crastina die sanguis a corpore meo supra mammam.* I suspect him of having added to the prophecy. He was too fond of miracles and prophecies. On the 28th of April the Maid says that the wind will change, and it changed. Brother Pasquerel is not satisfied with so moderate a marvel. He relates that Jeanne raised the waters of the Loire. We know on other authority that the Loire was high. It cannot be denied that long before this Jeanne had foretold that she would be wounded. This fact, stated in a letter from Lyon, dated the 22nd of April, 1429, was recorded in a register of La Cour des Comptes of Brabant. But she did not specify the day. *Dixit ... quod ipsa ante Aureliam in conflictu telo vulnerabitur* (*Trial*, vol. iv, p. 426).

1055. *Journal du siège*, p. 84.

1056. *Trial*, vol. iii, p. 109. *Chronique de la Pucelle*, p. 295.

1057. *Chronique de la Pucelle*, p. 292. *Trial*, vol. iii, p. 215. *Journal du siège*, pp. 84, 85.

1058. *Chronique de la fête*, in *Trial*, vol. v, p. 293.

1059. "*Par l'accord et consentement des bourgeois d'Orléans mais contre l'opinion et volonté de tous les chefs et capitaines,*" *Chronique de la Pucelle*, p. 292.

1060. *Chronique de l'établissement de la fête*, in *Trial*, vol. v, p. 293. Le Roux de Lincy, *Proverbes*, vol. ii, p. 395.

1061. *Trial*, vol. iii, p. 124 (evidence of the woman P. Milet). *Chronique de la Pucelle*, p. 292.

1062. Berry, in *Trial*, vol. iv, pp. 43, 44.

1063. *Chronique de la Pucelle*, p. 292. *Journal du siège*, p. 284, *passim*.

1064. *Journal du siège*, p. 87. Letter from Charles VII to the people of Narbonne (10 May, 1429), in *Trial*, vol. v, pp. 101 *et seq. Chronique de la fête*, in *Trial*, vol. v, p. 294. Jean Chartier, *Chronique*, vol. i, p. 77. Morosini, vol. iii, p. 32, note 1.

1065. Jarry, *Le compte de l'armée anglaise*, pp. 94, 95, 136, 206. Boucher de Molandon, *L'armée anglaise*, pp. 94 *et seq.*

1066. They were employed chiefly in carrying munitions of war. *Chronique de la Pucelle*, p. 292.

1067. *Trial*, vol. iii, p. 5.

1068. *Journal du siège*, p. 85. *Chronique de la Pucelle*, p. 293. Jean Chartier, *Chronique*, vol. i, p. 77. Morosini, vol. iii, pp. 31 *et seq.*

1069. Accounts of fortresses in *Journal du siège*, pp. 296, 300. Vergniaud-Romagnési, *Notice historique sur le fort des Tourelles*, Paris, in 8vo, 1832, p. 50.

1070. *Chronique de la Pucelle*, p. 293.

1071. "Post prandium," says Brother Pasquerel (*Trial*, vol. iii, p. 108). Cf. the evidence of Dunois (*Ibid.*, p. 8).

1072. *Trial*, vol. i, p. 79. Eberhard Windecke, p. 172.

1073. *Trial*, vol. iii, p. 109.

1074. *Chronique de la Pucelle*, p. 292. Clerk of *La Chambre des Comptes* of Brabant, in *Trial*, vol. iv, p. 426.

1075. *Trial*, vol. iii, p. 109. *Chronique de la Pucelle*, pp. 292, 293.

1076. *Trial*, vol. iii, p. 109 (Pasquerel's evidence).

1077. *Ibid.*, vol. i, p. 79; vol. iii, p. 110.

1078. *Chronique de la Pucelle*, p. 293.

1079. *Trial*, vol. iii, p. 216 (Jean d'Aulon's evidence), p. 25; (evidence of J. Luillier). *Chronique de la Pucelle*, p. 293.

1080. *Trial*, vol. iii, p. 25. *Journal du siège*, pp. 85, 86. Eberhard Windecke, p. 173.

1081. *Trial*, vol. iii, p. 8 (evidence of Dunois). I emphatically reject the facts alleged by Charles du Lys, concerning Guy de Cailly, who is said to have accompanied Jeanne into the vineyard and seen the angels coming down to her. Guy de Cailly's patent of nobility is apocryphal. Charles du Lys, *Traité sommaire*, pp. 50, 52.

1082. *Trial*, vol. i, pp. 52, 62, 153, 480; vol. ii, pp. 420, 424.

1083. *Ibid.*, vol. iii, p. 216. The Count Couret, *Un fragment inédit des anciens registres de la Prévoté d'Orléans*, Orléans, 1897, pp. 12, 20, 21, *passim*.

1084. *Trial*, vol. iii, p. 216.

1085. *Journal du siège*, p. 86.

1086. *Chronique de la Pucelle*, p. 293.

1087. *Trial*, vol. iii, pp. 216, 217.

1088. *Journal du siège*, p. 86. *Chronique de la Pucelle*, p. 293.

1089. *Chronique de la fête*, in the *Trial*, vol. v, p. 294.

1090. *Journal du siège*, p. 87.

1091. Letter from Charles VII to the inhabitants of Narbonne, 10 May, 1429, in *Trial*, vol. v, p. 103. Monstrelet, in *Trial*, vol. iv, p. 365.

1092. *Trial*, vol. iii, p. 110 (Pasquerel's evidence).

1093. *Chronique de la Pucelle*, pp. 293, 294. Morosini, vol. iii, p. 31.

1094. *Journal du siège*, p. 17. Jollois, *Histoire du siège*, p. 12.

1095. *Journal du siège*, p. 87. *Chronique de la Pucelle*, p. 294. *Chronique de la fête*, in *Trial*, vol. v, p. 294.

1096. *Trial*, vol. iii, pp. 9, 25, 80. *Chronique de l'établissement de la fête*, in *Trial*, vol. v, p. 294. *Chronique de la Pucelle*, p. 294. *Journal du siège*, pp. 87, 88. Jean Chartier, *Chronique*, vol. i, p. 78. Perceval de Cagny, p. 145. Eberhard Windecke, p. 173. Monstrelet, vol. iv, p. 321. Morosini, vol. iii, pp. 31 *et seq.*

1097. *Trial*, vol. iii, p. 110 (Pasquerel's evidence).

1098. *Journal du siège*, p. 87.

1099. The number of the English who defended Les Tourelles is given in *Le journal du siège* as 400 or 500; in Charles VII's letter as 600; in *La relation de la fête du 8 mai* as 800; in *La chronique de la Pucelle* as 500. It is impossible to fix exactly the number of the French, but they were more than ten times as many as the English.

The English losses, by Guillaume Girault, are said to have been 300 slain and taken; by Berry, 400 or 500 slain and taken; by Jean Chartier, about 400 slain, the rest taken; by *La chronique de la Pucelle*, 300 slain, 200 taken; by *Le journal du siège*, 400 or 500 slain besides a few taken. By Monstrelet, in the MSS., 600 or 800 slain or taken; in the printed editions, 1000; by Bower, 600 and more slain.

The losses of the French are said by Perceval de Cagny to have been 16 to 20 slain; by Eberhard Windecke, 5 slain and a few wounded; by

Monstrelet, about 100. The Maid estimated that in the various engagements at Orléans in which she took part "one hundred and even more" of the French were wounded.

1100. *Journal du siège*, p. 88.

1101. Perceval de Cagny, p. 147. *Chronique de la Pucelle*, p. 295.

1102. *Journal du siège*, p. 88. *Chronique de la Pucelle*, p. 295. Jean Chartier, *Chronique*, vol. i, p. 78.

1103. *Chronique de l'établissement de la fête*, in *Trial*, vol. v, pp. 294 *et seq.*

1104. *Trial*, vol. iv, p. 163.

1105. *Chronique de la Pucelle*, p. 295.

1106. *Journal du siège*, p. 89. *Chronique de la Pucelle*, p. 296. Jean Chartier, *Chronique*, vol. i, pp. 78, 79. *Le Jouvencel*, vol. i, p. 208. The passage beginning with the words, "The Sire of Rocquencourt said," must be taken as historical.

1107. *Trial*, vol. iii, p. 9 (evidence of Dunois).

1108. *Ibid.*, p. 29 (evidence of J. de Champeaux).

1109. *Journal du siège*, p. 89.

1110. *Chronique de la Pucelle*, p. 296.

1111. *Chronique de la Pucelle*, p. 296.

1112. *Chronique de l'établissement de la fête*, in *Trial*, vol. v, pp. 294, 295. *Chronique de la Pucelle*, p. 296.

1113. *Chronique de la Pucelle*, p. 296.

1114. *Trial*, vol. iii, pp. 71, 97, 110. *Journal du siège*, p. 89. *Chronique de la Pucelle*, p. 297. Morosini, vol. iii, p. 34. Walter Bower, *Scotichronicon*, in *Trial*, vol. iv, pp. 478, 479. Eberhard Windecke, p. 177.

1115. Charles VII's letter to the people of Narbonne, in the *Trial*, vol. v, p. 101. Monstrelet, vol. iv, p. 323.

1116. *Journal du siège*, pp. 209 *et seq.*

1117. *Ibid.*, p. 216. *Chronique de la fête*, in *Trial*, vol. v, p. 295.

1118. *Trial*, vol. iii, p. 110. *Journal du siège*, p. 92.

1119. *Journal du siège*, p. 91. G. Met-Gaubert, *Notice sur Florent d'Illiers*, Chartres, 1864, in 8vo.

1120. *Chronique de la Pucelle*, p. 298.

1121. *Journal du siège*, pp. 91, 92. Jean Chartier, *Chronique*, vol. i, p. 71.

1122. *Charles VII's Letter to the Inhabitants of Narbonne*, in *Trial*, vol. v, pp. 101, 104. Arcère, *Histoire de La Rochelle*, vol. i, p. 271 (1756). Moynès, *Inventaire des archives de l'Aude*, supplement, p. 390. *Procession d'actions de grâces à Brignoles (Var) en l'honneur de la délivrance d'Orléans par Jeanne d'Arc* (1429). Communication made to the Congress of learned Societies at the Sorbonne (April, 1893) by F. Mireur, Draguignan, 1894, in 8vo, p. 175.

1123. *Trial*, vol. iii, p. 80. *Journal du siège*, p. 91.

1124. *Ibid.*, vol. iii, pp. 72, 76, 80.

1125. *Trial*, vol. iii, p. 116 (evidence of S. Charles). Eberhard Windecke, p. 177, and *Chronique de Tournai*, edition Smedt, pp. 407 *et seq.* (vol. iii of *Les chroniques de Flandre*).

1126. *Trial*, vol. iii, pp. 394, 407; vol. v, p. 413. Le P. Marcellin Fornier, *Histoire des Alpes-Maritimes ou Cottiennes*, vol. ii, p. 320. Le P. Ayroles, *La Pucelle devant l'Église de son temps*, pp. 39, 52.

1127. L. Paris, *Notice sur le dédale ou labyrinthe de l'église de Reims*, in *Ann. des Inst. provinc.*, 1857, vol. ix, p. 233.

1128. Bibl. Nat. Latin Collection, no. 6199, folio 36. *Trial*, vol. iii, pp. 395-410. Lanéry d'Arc, *Mémoires et consultations*, pp. 365 *et seq.* Le P. Ayroles, *La Pucelle devant l'Église de son temps*, pp. 31-52.

1129. Launoy, *Historia Navarrici Gymasii*, book iv, ch. v. J.B. Lecuy, *Essai sur la vie de Jean Gerson, chancelier de l'église et de l'université de Paris, sur sa doctrine, sur ses écrits....* Paris, 1832, 2 vols. in 8vo. Vallet de Viriville, *Histoire de Charles VII*, vol. ii, p. 94. A.L. Masson, *Jean Gerson, sa vie, son temps, ses œuvres*, Lyon, 1894, 8vo.

1130. *Par une cruauté miséricordieuse.* Du Boulay, *Historia Universitatis Parisiensis*, vol. iv, p. 270.

1131. Gerson, *Opera*, vol. iv, pp. 668-678.

1132. Gerson, *Adversus corruptionem Juventutis*. A. Lafontaine, *De Johanne Gersonio puerorum adulescentiumque institutore....* La Chapelle-Montligeon, 1902, in 8vo.

1133. *Gallia Christiana*, vol. vii, col. 142. Jean Juvénal des Ursins, year 1406.

1134. Exodus, xv, 20, 21 (W.S.).

1135. *Œuvres de Gerson*, ed. Ellies Dupin, Paris, 1706, in folio, vol. iv, p. 864. *Trial*, vol. iii, p. 298; vol. v, p. 412. Le P. Ayroles, *La Pucelle devant l'Église de son temps*, p. 24.

1136. *Trial*, vol. iii, pp. 12, 72, 76, 80. *Chronique de la Pucelle*, p. 298. *Journal du siège*, p. 93. *Chronique de la fête*, in *Trial*, vol. v, p. 299. Letter written by the agents of a German town, in *Trial*, vol. v, p. 349. *Chronique de Tournai (Recueil des chroniques de Flandre*, vol. iii, p. 412). Eberhard Windecke, p. 177. De Beaucourt, *Histoire de Charles VII*, vol. ii, p. 215.

1137. De Beaucourt, *Histoire de Charles VII*, pp. 634 *et seq.*

1138. Loiseleur, *Compte des dépenses*, pp. 147 *et seq.*

1139. *Trial*, vol. v, pp. 256 *et seq.*, and taken from the Commune and Fortress Accounts in *Journal du siège*. A. de Villaret, *loc. cit.* p. 61. Couret, *Un fragment inédit des anciens registres de la Prévôté d'Orléans*.

1140. Morosini, vol. iii, p. 61.

1141. *Trial*, vol. iii, pp. 9, 10.

1142. *Journal du siège*, p. 93. *Chronique de la Pucelle*, p. 300.

1143. *Trial*, vol. iii, p. 99.

1144. *Ibid.*, p. 99 (evidence of the Duke of Alençon).

1145. *Trial*, vol. iii, p. 12. *Journal du siège*, p. 93. *Chronique de la Pucelle*, p. 299.

1146. *Trial*, vol. iii, p. 12 (evidence of Dunois).

1147. *Ibid.*, p. 12.

1148. *Ibid.*, p. 116, vol. iv, p. 245.

1149. *Trial*, vol. iii, p. 84.

1150. *Ibid.*, vol. i, p. 102.

1151. *Ibid.*, pp. 290, 291. A. Forgeais, *Collection de plombs historiés trouvés dans la Seine*, Paris, 1869 (5 vol. in 8vo), vol. ii, iv, and *passim*. Vallet de Viriville, *Notes sur deux médailles de plomb relatives à Jeanne d'Arc*, Paris, 1861, in 8vo, 30 p. Taken from *La revue archéologique*. N. Valois, *Un nouveau témoignage sur Jeanne d'Arc*, pp. 8, 13. Cf. Appendix iv.

1152. *Trial*, vol. v, p. 104. I read *in se sperantes*.

1153. *Trial*, vol. v, p. 104. Lanéry d'Arc, *Le culte de Jeanne d'Arc au XVe siècle*, 1886, in 8vo.

1154. A. Thomas, *Le siège d'Orléans, Jeanne d'Arc et les capitouls de Toulouse*, in *Annales du Midi*, 1889, pp. 235, 236.

1155. Letter from the Lavals, in *Trial*, vol. v, p. 109. Bertrand de Broussillon, *La maison de Laval, les Montfort-Laval*, Paris, 1900, in

8vo, vol. iii, p. 75. Quicherat is mistaken when (*Trial*, vol. v, p. 105) he gives the name of Anne to Du Guesclin's widow and calls the mother of Guy and of André Jeanne.

1156. Cuvelier, *Poème de Duguesclin*, line 2325 *et seq.*

1157. Bertrand de Broussillon, *La maison de Laval* in 8vo, 1900, vol. iii, *loc. cit.*

1158. Letter from Gui de Laval, in *Trial*, vol. v, p. 105. Lucien Jeny and P. Lanéry d'Arc, *Jeanne d'Arc en Berry*, Paris, s.d. in 8vo, p. 53.

1159. Fortress accounts in *Trial*, vol. v, p. 262.

1160. *Ibid.*, vol. iii, pp. 3, 9, 15, 18, 22, 69, 219, *passim.*

1161. *Ibid.*, vol. v, under the words *Confession* and *Communion.* The Duke of Alençon says twice a week (*Ibid.*, vol. iii, p. 100).

1162. *Ibid.*, vol. iii, p. 14; vol. ii, pp. 420, 424.

1163. *Ibid.*, vol. i, pp. 220, 253; vol. ii, pp. 294, 438. *Relation du greffier de La Rochelle*, p. 60. Analysis of a letter from Regnault de Chartres in Rogier (*Trial*, vol. v, pp. 168-169). Martin le Franc, *Le champion des dames*, in *Trial*, vol. v, p. 48.

1164. *Trial*, vol. i, pp. 61, 62, 481.

1165. P. Blavignac, *La cloche*, Geneva, 1877, in 8vo. L. Morillot, *Étude sur l'emploi des clochettes*, in *Bulletin hist. archéolog. du diocèse de Dijon*, 1887, in 8vo.

1166. *Trial*, vol. i, pp. 52, 64, 153, *passim.*

1167. *Ibid.*, p. 130.

1168. *Ibid.*, p. 186.

1169. *Ibid.*, pp. 72, 75.

1170. *Trial*, vol. iii, pp. 219, 220.

1171. *Ibid.*, vol. i, p. 57.

1172. *Ibid.*, vol. v, p. 342. Guy de Cailly's patent of nobility cannot be regarded as authentic. Vallet de Viriville, *Petit traité....* p. 92.

1173. *Trial*, vol. iii, p. 112.

1174. *Trial*, vol. iii, p. 112. *Poésies de Charles d'Orléans*, ed. A. Champollion-Figeac, p. 174.

1175. *Trial*, vol. iii, pp. 108, 109.

1176. *Ibid.*, vol. i, pp. 78, 117, 182.

1177. *Ibid.*, pp. 117, 300; vol. v, p. 227.

1178. Letter written from Germany, in *Trial*, vol. v, p. 351. Morosini, vol. iii, pp. 33, 46, 62.

1179. Letter from Gui and André de Laval to the Ladies de Laval, in *Trial*, vol. v, p. 106. L. Jeny and Lanéry d'Arc, *Jeanne D'Arc en Berry*, Paris, 1892, in 8vo, p. 54.

1180. Bertrand de Broussillon, *La maison de Laval*, vol. iii, p. 21.

1181. Letter from Gui and André de Laval, in *Trial*, vol. v, pp. 106 *et seq.*

1182. N. Villiaumé, *Histoire de Jeanne d'Arc*, p. 88.

1183. *Recommandation* in French. The esteem in which she was held. Compare Froissart cited by La Curne, Glossary, *ad v.* *"Six bourgeois de la ville de Calais et de plus grande recommandation."* ("Six citizens of Calais and of the highest reputation.")

1184. Letter from Gui and André de Laval, in *Trial*, vol. v, pp. 106, 107.

1185. *Trial*, vol. iii, p. 94; vol. iv, p. 12.

1186. *Mistère du siège*, line 15,761. *Journal du siège*, p. 95. *Chronique de la Pucelle*, p. 299. Jean Chartier, *Chronique*, vol. i, p. 81. Monstrelet, vol. iii, p. 338.

1187. See *ante*, p. 211. A. Duveau, *Le jugement du duc d'Alençon*, in *Bull. soc. archéol. du Vendômois* (1874), vol. xiii, pp. 132 *et seq.*

1188. Loiseleur, *Compte des dépenses faites par Charles VII pour secourir Orléans*, p. 158.

1189. *Journal du siège*, p. 97.

1190. Taken from the Book of Accounts, in *Trial*, vol. v, pp. 262, 263. A. de Villaret, *Campagnes de Jeanne d'Arc sur la Loire*, pp. 77-80. Loiseleur, *Compte des dépenses*, p. 149.

1191. *Trial*, vol. v, p. 261.

1192. *Chronique de la Pucelle*, p. 258.

1193. Berry, in the *Trial*, vol. iv, p. 45.

1194. *Journal du siège*, p. 96. *Chronique de la Pucelle*, p. 299. *Chronique de la fête*, in *Trial*, vol. v, p. 295. Jean Chartier, *Chronique*, vol. i, p. 82. Berry, in *Trial*, vol. iv, p. 44. Monstrelet, vol. iv, p. 325.

1195. *Trial*, vol. iii, p. 94. Perceval de Cagny, pp. 150, 151.

1196. *Journal du siège*, *Chronique de la Pucelle*, Berry, Jean Chartier, *loc. cit.* Wavrin du Forestel, *Anciennes chroniques*, vol. i, p. 284. Falconbridge, in *Trial*, vol. iv, p. 452.

1197. Perceval de Cagny, p. 148, *passim*. *Chronique de la Pucelle*, p. 300.

1198. *Trial*, vol. iii, p. 95.

1199. The night of Friday, the 10th to 11th of June.

1200. *Trial*, vol. iii, p. 95.

1201. *Ibid. Journal du siège*, p. 97.

1202. Perceval de Cagny, p. 150.

1203. *Ibid.*

1204. *Trial*, vol. i, pp. 79, 95.

1205. S. Luce, *Jeanne d'Arc à Domremy*, p. clxviii.

1206. *Journal du siège, Chronique de la Pucelle*, J. Chartier, Monstrelet, *loc. cit.*

1207. *Trial*, vol. iii, p. 95.

1208. *Ibid.*, vol. i, pp. 79-80, 234.

1209. *Ibid.*, vol. iii, p. 97. Perceval de Cagny, pp. 150-151.

1210. *Trial*, vol. iii, pp. 95-96.

1211. *Ibid.*, pp. 96, 97. *Chronique de la Pucelle*, p. 301. *Journal du siège*, p. 97.

1212. *Trial*, vol. iii, p. 97.

1213. *Journal du siège*, p. 100.

1214. *Trial*, vol. iii, p. 97. *Journal du siège*, p. 98. *Chronique de la Pucelle*, pp. 301-302. Perceval de Cagny, pp. 150-151.

1215. *Journal du siège*, p. 99. *Chronique de la Pucelle*, p. 302. Jean Chartier, *Chronique*, vol. i, p. 82. Berry, in *Trial*, vol. iv, p. 65.

1216. Fragment of a letter concerning the wonders which happened in Poitou, in *Trial*, vol. v, p. 122.

1217. *Relation du greffier de La Rochelle*, p. 340. Morosini, vol. iii, p. 70. *Trial*, vol. v, pp. 121-122.

1218. *Trial*, vol. iii, p. 72. Perceval de Cagny, p. 151. *Journal du siège*, p. 99. Monstrelet, vol. iv, p. 328. Morosini, vol. iii, pp. 128, 129.

1219. *Journal du siège*, p. 99.

1220. Perceval de Cagny, p. 151. *Chronique de la Pucelle*, p. 302. Jean Chartier, *Chronique*, vol. i, pp. 82, 83. Berry, in *Trial*, vol. iv, p. 65.

1221. Accounts of the town of Orléans at the end of *Le Journal du siège*, ed. Charpentier and Cuissard, p. 229. Le R.P. Chapotin, *La guerre de cent ans, Jeanne d'Arc et les Dominicains*, Paris, 1889, 8vo, p. 82.

1222. A. de Villaret, *Campagne des Anglais*, proofs and illustrations, p. 51.

1223. *Trial*, vol. v, pp. 112-113.

1224. *Ibid.*, vol. iii, p. 23.

1225. *Ibid.*, vol. v, p. 306.

1226. *Ibid.*, pp. 112, 114.

1227. *Accounts of the Fortress*, in *Trial*, vol. v, p. 259.

1228. *Trial*, vol. v, pp. 106, 259. *Catalogue des Arch. de Joursanvault*, vol. i, p. 129, nos. 603, 607, 619, 645, 772. Dambreville, *Abrégé de l'histoire des ordres de chevalerie*, p. 167. P. Mantellier, *Histoire du siège*, p. 92.

1229. *Trial*, vol. i, p. 55, 258.

1230. *Ibid.*, p. 254.

1231. *Ibid.*, p. 133.

1232. *Ibid.*, pp. 133, 254.

1233. *Ibid.*, p. 258.

1234. *Ibid.*, p. 55.

1235. Bibliothèque Nationale, ms. fr. 966, fol. 1.

1236. *Les poésies de Charles d'Orléans*, ed. Guichard, 1842, in 12mo, p. 145.

1237. A. Champollion-Figeac, *Louis et Charles, ducs d'Orléans, leur influence sur les arts, la littérature et l'ésprit de leur siècle*, Paris, 1844, 1 vol. in 8vo, with an atlas, pp. 300-337.

1238. *Les poésies de Charles d'Orléans*, ed. A. Champollion-Figeac, Paris, 1842, 8vo. Pierre Champion, *Le manuscrit autographe des poésies de Charles d'Orléans*, Paris, 1907, 8vo.

1239. L. Delisle, *Recherches sur la librairie de Charles V* (1907), vol. i, p. 140.

1240. Le Roux de Lincy, *La bibliothèque de Charles d'Orléans à son château de Blois, en 1427*, Paris, 1843, 8vo, pp. 5-7. Comte de Laborde, *Les ducs de Bourgogne, études sur les lettres, les arts et l'industrie pendant le XVe siècle*, Paris, 1852, vol. iii, pp. 235 *et seq.* – *Inventaires et documents relatifs aux joyaux et tapisseries des princes d'Orléans-Valois*, Paris, 1894, 8vo.

1241. *Chronique de la Pucelle*, Introduction by Vallet de Viriville, pp. 8, 19 *et seq.*

1242. With regard to the year 1433, this is well established (*Poésies complètes de Charles d'Orléans*, ed. Charles d'Héricault, Paris, 1874, 2 vols. 8vo, introduction).

1243. *Poésies de Charles d'Orléans*, ed. A. Champollion-Figeac, pp. 175-176.

1244. For him every treaty of peace was a good treaty, even that of 1420, the Treaty of Troyes (Pierre Champion, *Le manuscrit autographe des poésies de Charles d'Orléans*, Paris, 1907, 8vo, p. 32).

1245. Perceval de Cagny, p. 152: "*Je veux demain, après dîner, aller voir ceux de Meung.*" "To-morrow after dinner I will go to the people of Meung.". The turn of expression which this chronicle attributes to Jeanne is really that of the clerk who wrote it.

1246. *Trial*, vol. iii, pp. 71, 97, 110. *Chronique de la Pucelle*, p. 305. *Journal du siège*, p. 101. Berry, in *Trial*, vol. iv, p. 44. Walter Bower, *Scotichronicon*, in *Trial*, vol. iv, p. 479. Eberhard Windecke, p. 176.

1247. *Trial*, vol. iii, p. 97.

1248. *Ibid.*, pp. 97, 98.

1249. *Journal du siège*, p. 101. *Chronique de la Pucelle*, p. 304. Jean Chartier, *Chronique*, vol. i, p. 83.

1250. *Trial*, vol. iii, pp. 97, 98. Gruel, *Chronique de Richemont*, p. 70.

1251. E. Cosneau, *Le connétable de Richemont*, pp. 93 *et seq.*

1252. *Trial*, vol. iii, pp. 315, 516. Jean Chartier, *Chronique*, vol. i, p. 84. *Journal du siège*, pp. 101, 102. Perceval de Cagny, p. 153.

1253. *Trial*, vol. iii, p. 98. E. Cosneau, *Le connétable de Richemont*, p. 168.

1254. Gruel, *Chronique de Richemont*, pp. 70 *et seq.*

1255. *Trial*, vol. iii, p. 98.

1256. Gruel, *Chronique de Richemont*, p. 71. Cf. E. Cosneau, *Le connétable de Richemont*, pp. 169, 583. See a drawing in the Gaignières collection reproduced by J. Lair, *Essai sur la bataille de Formigny*, 1903, 8vo.

1257. *Lors le saluèrent et le vinrent accoller par les jambes.* (Then they saluted him and embraced his knees.) J. de Bueil, *Le Jouvencel*, vol. i, p. 191.

1258. Gruel, *Chronique de Richemont*, pp. 71-72. I have here followed Gruel, who is not generally very trustworthy, but whose account in this particular seems probable, at least he is no mere hagiographer.

1259. *Ibid.*, p. 228.

1260. *Ibid.*, p. 72. E. Cosneau, *Le connétable de Richemont*, p. 170.

1261. *Journal du siège*, p. 97. *Chronique de la Pucelle*, p. 301.

1262. A. de Villaret, *Campagne des Anglais*, pp. 87-88, and proofs and illustrations, pp. 153, 158.

1263. *Chronique de la Pucelle*, p. 305. *Journal du siège*, p. 102. Jean Chartier, *Chronique*, vol. i, p. 84. Wavrin du Forestel, *Anciennes chroniques*, vol. i, pp. 279, 282. Monstrelet, vol. iii, pp. 325 *et seq.*

1264. Gruel, *Chronique de Richemont*, p. 72.

1265. Wavrin du Forestel, *Anciennes chroniques*, vol. i, p. 279.

1266. *Trial*, vol. iii, p. 98.

1267. Wavrin du Forestel, *Anciennes chroniques*, ed. Dupont, vol. i, p. 281. Berry, in *Trial*, vol. iv, p. 44. Jean Chartier, *Chronique*, vol. i, p. 85. *Journal du siège*, pp. 102, 103. *Chronique de la Pucelle*, p. 306. Gruel, *Chronique de Richemont*, p. 72. Falconbridge, in *Trial*, vol. iv, p. 452. Morosini, vol. iii, pp. 71-73.

1268. Monstrelet, vol. iv, p. 331. Wavrin du Forestel, *Anciennes chroniques*, vol. i, pp. 283 *et seq.*

1269. *Chronique de la Pucelle*, J. Chartier, Gruel, Morosini, Berry, Monstrelet, Wavrin, *loc. cit. Lettre de Jacques de Bourbon, Comte de la Marche à Guill. de Champeaux, évêque de Laon*, according to a Vienna MS. by Bougenot, in *Bull. du Com. des travaux hist. et scientif. hist. et phil., 1892*, pp. 56-65. (French translation by S. Luce, in *La revue bleue*, February 13, 1892, pp. 201-204.)

1270. *Trial*, vol. iii, p. 120. Monstrelet, vol. iv, p. 328. The clerk who wrote down Thibault de Termes' evidence, being ill-informed, described these words as having been uttered at the Battle of Patay. At Patay, Jeanne and La Hire were not near each other.

1271. Wavrin du Forestel, *Anciennes chroniques*, vol. i, p. 286.

1272. *Trial*, vol. iii, p. 11. *Chronique de la Pucelle*, p. 307. It is clear that this passage from Dunois' evidence and from *La chronique de la Pucelle* cannot refer to the battle of June 18th, as has been thought. "All the English divisions," says Dunois, "united into one army. We thought we were going to offer us battle." He is evidently referring to what happened on the 17th of June. The Duke of Alençon's evidence confuses everything. How could the Maid have said of the English: "God sends them against us," when they were fleeing?

1273. Those who would attribute this saying to the Maid have misunderstood Wavrin. *Anciennes chroniques*, vol. i, p. 287.

1274. Wavrin du Forestel, *Anciennes chroniques*, vol. i, p. 287. Monstrelet, vol. iv, pp. 326 *et seq.*

1275. *Chronique de la Pucelle, Journal du siège*, Gruel, J. Chartier, Berry, *loc. cit.*

1276. Wavrin du Forestel, *Anciennes chroniques*, vol. i, p. 289. Fauché-Prunelle, *Lettres tirées des archives de l'évêché de Grenoble*, in *Bull. acad. Delph.*, vol. ii, 1847, pp. 458 *et seq.* Letter from Charles VII to the town of Tours, in *Trial*, vol. v, pp. 262, 263.

1277. Wavrin du Forestel, *Anciennes chroniques*, vol. i, p. 289. The herald Berry, *Le livre de la description des pays*, ed. Hamy.

1278. *Trial*, vol. iii, pp. 98, 99. *Chronique de la Pucelle*, p. 306. *Chronique normande*, ch. xlviii, ed. Vallet de Viriville. Monstrelet, vol. iii, pp. 325 *et seq.* Morosini, vol. iii, pp. 72-73. Wavrin du Forestel, *Anciennes chroniques*, vol. i, pp. 289-290. These words are said to have been uttered when the English had been discovered, but then they would have been meaningless.

1279. *Trial*, vol. iii, p. 99 (the Duke of Alençon's evidence).

1280. *Ibid.*, p. 71 (evidence of Louis de Coutes). Letter from Jacques de Bourbon in *La revue bleue*, February 13, 1892, pp. 201-204. Monstrelet, vol. iv, p. 327. Wavrin du Forestel, *Anciennes chroniques*, p. 289.

1281. *Trial*, vol. iii, p. 71. *Journal du siège*, p. 140. *Chronique de la Pucelle*, p. 307. *Deux documents sur Jeanne d'Arc* in *La revue bleue*, February 13, 1892.

1282. *Trial*, vol. iii, pp. 11, 71, 98. *Chronique de la Pucelle*, pp. 306 *et seq.* *Journal du siège*, pp. 103 *et seq.* Jean Chartier, *Chronique*, vol. i, p. 85. Le Comte de Vassal, *La bataille de Patay*, Orléans, 1890.

1283. Monstrelet, vol. iv, p. 328.

1284. Wavrin du Forestel, *Anciennes chroniques*, vol. i, p. 291.

1285. *Ibid.*, pp. 291-292.

1286. Monstrelet, vol. iv, p. 329.

1287. Wavrin du Forestel, *Anciennes chroniques*, vol. i, p. 292. Monstrelet, vol. iii, pp. 329, 350.

1288. "In the neighbourhood of Lignerolles there have been found horse-shoes, a javelin-point, the iron pieces of carts, and bullets." P. Mantellier, *Histoire du siège*, Orléans, 1867, 12mo, p. 139.

1289. *Trial*, vol. iii, p. 11. Gruel, *Chronique de Richemont*, pp. 73-74. Perceval de Cagny, pp. 154 *et seq.* *Chronique normande*, in *Trial*, vol. iv, p. 340. Eberhard Windecke, p. 180. Lefèvre de Saint-Rémy, vol. ii, pp. 144, 145. Falconbridge, in *Trial*, vol. iv, p. 452. *Commentaires de Pie II*, in *Trial*, vol. iv, p. 512. Morosini, vol. iii, pp. 72-75. *Chronique de la Pucelle*, p. 306. Jean Chartier, *Chronique*, vol. i, p. 86.

Monstrelet, vol. iv, pp. 330-333. Wavrin du Forestel, *Anciennes chroniques*, vol. i, p. 293. Letter from J. de Bourbon in *La revue bleue*, February 13, 1892. Letter from Charles VII to Tours and the people of Dauphiné, in *Trial*, vol. v, pp. 345, 346.

1290. *Trial*, vol. iii, p. 120; vol. v, p. 120.

1291. "Et habuit *l'avant garde La Hire* de quo ipsa Johanna fuit multum irata, quia ipsa multum affectabat habere onus de *l'avant garde* La Hire qui conducebat *l'avant garde* percussit super Anglicos," *Trial*, vol. iii, p. 71 (evidence of Louis de Coutes).

1292. "Habebat magnam pietatem de tanta occisione," *Trial*, vol. iii, p. 71.

1293. After an examination of the documents I have concluded that Louis de Coutes' narrative refers to Patay.

1294. *Trial*, vol. iii, p. 99.

1295. Boucher de Molandon, *Janville, son donjon, son château, ses souvenirs du XVe siècle*, Orléans, 1886, 8vo.

1296. *Journal du siège*, p. 105; *Chronique de la Pucelle*, pp. 307, 308.

1297. *Chronique de la Pucelle*, pp. 307-308. *Journal du siège*, p. 105.

1298. De Beaucourt, *Histoire de Charles VII*, vol. ii, p. 222 *et seq.*; E. Cosneau, *Le connétable de Richemont*, p. 172.

1299. *Trial*, vol. iii, p. 116 (evidence of S. Charles). "*Et audivit ipse loquens ex ore regis multa bona de ea ... rex habuit pietatem de ea et de poena quam portabat.*"

1300. *Trial*, vol. iii, pp. 76, 116.

1301. Letter from Charles VII to the people of Dauphiné, published by Fauché-Prunelle, in *Bull. de l'Acad. Delphinale*, vol. ii, p. 459; to the inhabitants of Tours (Archives de Tours, *Registre des comptes XXIV*), in *Cabinet historique*, I, C. p. 109; to those of Poitiers, Redet, in *Les mémoires de la Société des Antiquaires de l'Ouest*, vol. iii, p. 406; *Relation du greffier de la Rochelle* in *Revue historique*, vol. iv, p. 459.

1302. *Journal du siège*, pp. 106, 108; Jean Chartier, *Chronique*, vol. i, p. 89; Gruel, *Chronique de Richemont*, p. 74; Monstrelet, vol. iv, pp. 344, 347; E. Cosneau, *Le connétable de Richemont*, pp. 181, 182.

1303. 1431, 8th of May. A decree condemning André de Beaumont to suffer capital punishment as being guilty of high treason. (Arch. nat. J. 366.) For a complete copy of this document I am indebted to Monsieur Pierre Champion.

1304. Monstrelet, vol. iv, p. 30; De Beaucourt, *Histoire de Charles VII*, vol. i, pp. 202 *et seq.*

1305. Dom Morice, *Histoire de Bretagne*, vol. ii, col. 1135-6; De Beaucourt, *loc. cit.*, vol. ii, chap. vii.

1306. Bellier-Dumaine, *L'administration du duché de Bretagne sous le règne de Jean V (1399-1442)* in *Les annales de Bretagne*, vol. xiv-xvi (1898-99) *passim*, and 3rd part, Jean V and commerce, industry, agriculture, public education (vol. xvi, p. 246), and 4th part, chap. iii, Jean V and towns, rural parishes (vol. xvi, p. 495).

1307. Eberhard Windecke, p. 179.

1308. Eberhard Windecke, pp. 178, 179.

1309. *Trial*, vol. v, p. 264. Eberhard Windecke, pp. 68-70, 179. Morosini, vol. iii, p. 90. Dom Lobineau, *Histoire de Bretagne*, vol. i, p. 587. Dom Morice, *Histoire de Bretagne*, vol. i, pp. 508, 580.

1310. L. Delisle, *Un nouveau témoignage relatif à la mission de Jeanne d'Arc* in *Bibliothèque de l'École des Chartes*, vol. xlvi, pp. 649, 668. Le P. Ayroles, *La Pucelle devant l'Église de son temps*, pp. 53, 60.

1311. Cathédrale du Puy. E.F. Corpet, *Portraits des arts libéraux d'après les écrivains du moyen âge*, in *Annales archéologiques*, 1857, vol. xvii, pp. 89, 103. Em. Male, *Les Arts libéraux dans la statuaire du moyen âge*, in *Revue archéologique*, 1891.

1312. Another name for Dauphiné (W.S.).

1313. *Trial*, vol. iii, pp. 411-421. Le P. Ayroles, *La Pucelle devant l'Église de son temps*, vol. i, pp. 61-68.

1314. Le P. Ayroles, vol. iv, *La vierge guerrière*, pp. 240 *et seq.*

1315. "*Sed dicta puella semper fuit opinionis quod opportebat ire Remis.*" *Trial*, vol. iii, p. 12 (evidence of Dunois).

1316. *Trial*, vol. iii, p. 20. *Journal du siège*, pp. 93, 94.

1317. See *ante*, pp. 53 *et seq.*

1318. Falconbridge, in *Trial*, vol. iv, p. 451. *Journal d'un bourgeois de Paris*, p. 239. *Chronique de la Pucelle*, p. 291. De Barante, *Histoire des ducs de Bourgogne*, vol. iii, p. 323.

1319. Le P. Denifle, *La désolation des églises*, introduction.

1320. Those of Louis XI were of a like mind: "One should fear risking a great battle if one be not constrained to it." Philippe de Comynes, ed. Mdlle. Dupont, vol. i, p. 146.

1321. *Trial*, vol. iii, pp. 12, 13. *Chronique de la Pucelle*, p. 300. Perceval de Cagny, p. 170. Jean Chartier, *Chronique*, p. 87. Morosini, vol. iii, p. 63, note 2.

1322. Wallon, *Jeanne d'Arc*, 1875, vol. i, p. 213.

1323. Rymer, *Fœdera*, 18 June, 1429. Morosini, vol. iii, pp. 132-133; vol. iv, supplement, xvii. G. Lefèvre-Pontalis, *La panique anglaise en mai 1429*, Paris, 1894, in 8vo.

1324. G. Lefèvre-Pontalis, *La guerre des partisans dans la Haute Normandie* (1424-1429), in the *Bibliothèque de l'École des Chartes* since 1893.

1325. "The King had no great sums of money with which to pay his army." Perceval de Cagny, pp. 149, 157.

1326. *Ibid.*

1327. Perceval de Cagny, p. 170.

1328. *Chronique de la Pucelle*, p. 310.

1329. E. Cosneau, *Le connétable de Richemont*, pp. 179 *et seq.*

1330. Even after the coronation Regnault de Chartres would not "suffer the Maid and the Duke of Alençon to be together nor that he should recover her." Perceval de Cagny, p. 171.

1331. Le P. Denifle, *La désolation des églises*, introduction.

1332. See *ante*, pp. 153-159.

1333. Morosini, vol. iv, supplement, xvii.

1334. *Trial*, vol. iii, pp. 20, 300. *Chronique de la Pucelle*, pp. 322, 323. *Journal du siège*, pp. 93, 114. "And although the King had not money wherewith to pay his army, all knights, squires, men-at-arms, and the commonalty refused not to serve the King in this journey in company with the Maid." Perceval de Cagny, p. 157.

1335. Le Maire, *Antiquités d'Orléans*, ch. xxv, p. 100.

1336. Pius II, *Commentarii*, in *Trial*, vol. iv, pp. 513-514. Pierre des Gros, *Jardin des nobles* in P. Paris, *Manuscrits français de la bibliothèque du roi*, vol. ii, p. 149, and *Trial*, vol. iv, pp. 533, 534.

1337. William of Worcester 1415-1482, or Botoner, chronicler and traveller, secretary to Sir John Fastolf, disputed with John Paston concerning some land near Norwich, and frequently referred to in the Paston Letters. W.S.. in *Trial*, vol. iv, p. 475. In 1430 it was the intention of the English to take their King to Reims "for which cause all the subjects of the kingdom would be more inclined to him" (advice given by Philippe le Bon to Henry VI, as cited by H. de

Lannoy, in P. Champion, *G. de Flavy*, p. 156). There was an English project for carrying off the holy Ampulla from Reims. Pius II, *Commentarii* in *Trial*, vol. iv, p. 513.

1338. *Voyages du héraut Berry*, Bibl. Nat. ms. fr. 5873, fol. 7.

1339. Jean Rogier in *Trial*, vol. iv, pp. 284-285.

1340. *Chronique de la Pucelle*, p. 312. Jean Chartier, *Chronique*, pp. 93-94. *Journal du siège*, p. 108. Cagny, p. 157. Morosini, pp. 84-85. Loiseleur, *Compte des dépenses*, pp. 90, 91.

1341. "*Gens de guerre et de commun,*" says Perceval de Cagny, p. 157.

1342. Eustache Deschamps ed. Queux de Saint-Hilaire and G. Raynaud, vol. i, p. 159, *passim*. Th. Basin, *Histoire de Charles VII et de Louis XI*, vol. i, p. 44. Letter from Nicholas de Clamanges to Gerson, LIV.

1343. *Chronique de la Pucelle*, p. 308. Perceval de Cagny, p. 157. *Journal du siège*, p. 180. Morosini, vol. iii, p. 85.

1344. S.J. Morand, *Histoire de la Sainte-Chapelle royale du Palais*, Paris, 1790, in 4to, p. 77, and *passim*.

1345. Le P. J. Doublet, *Histoire de l'abbaye de Saint-Denys en France*, Paris, 1625, in fol., ch. 1, pp. 373 *et seq.* Dom Félibien, *Histoire de l'abbaye royale de Saint-Denis*, 1706, in fol., pp. 203, 275, 543.

1346. *Journal du siège*, p. 107. *Chronique de la Pucelle*, p. 310.

1347. When the King set out in France, he had his gaiters greased; and the Queen asked him: whither will wend these damoiseaux? Quoted according to *La Chronique Messine* by Vallet de Viriville, *Histoire de Charles VII*, vol. i, p. 424, note 1.

1348. De Beaucourt, *Histoire de Charles VII*, vol. iv, p. 88.

1349. See *ante*, pp. 148-152.

1350. Perceval de Cagny, p. 157. Jean Chartier, *Chronique*, vol. i, p. 87. *Chronique de la Pucelle*, p. 313.

1351. *Trial*, vol. v, p. 125. *Registre des consaux, extraits analytiques des anciens consaux de la ville de Tournay*, ed. H. Vandenbroeck, vol. ii, p. 329. F. Hennebert, *Une lettre de Jeanne d'Arc aux Tournaisiens* in *Arch. hist. et littéraires du nord de la France*, 1837, vol. i, p. 525. De Beaucourt, *Histoire de Charles VII*, vol. iii, p. 516.

1352. Letter from Charles VII to the people of Dauphiné, published by Fauché-Prunelle, in *Bulletin de l'Académie Delphinale*, vol. ii, p. 459; to the inhabitants of Tours, in *Le Cabinet historique*, vol. i, C. p. 109; to those of Poitiers, by Redet, in *Les mémoires de la Société des*

Antiquaires de l'Ouest, vol. iii, p. 106. *Relation du greffier de la Rochelle* in *Revue historique*, vol. iv, p. 341.

1353. This is a mere form of speech. Le Tournésis has always been territory separate from the County of Flanders, the Bishops of which were the former Lords of Tournai. As early as 1187 the King of France nominally held sovereign sway there. In reality the town was divided into two factions: the rich and the merchants were for the Burgundian party, the common folk for the French (De La Grange, *Troubles à Tournai, 1422-1430*).

1354. Monstrelet, vol. iv, p. 352.

1355. *Chambre du Roi.*

1356. Morosini, vol. iii, pp. 184-185. *Chronique de Tournai*, ed. Smedt (*Recueil des chroniques de Flandre*, vol. iii, *passim*); *Troubles à Tournai* (1422-1430) in *Mémoires de la Société historique et littéraire de Tournai*, vol. xvii (1882). *Extraits des anciens registres des consaux*, ed. Vandenbroeck, vol. ii, *passim*. Monstrelet, ch. lxvii, lxix. A. Longnon, *Paris sous la domination anglaise*, pp. 143, 144.

1357. The Town Clerk of Albi in *Trial*, vol. iv, p. 301.

1358. H. Vandenbroeck, *Extraits analytiques des anciens registres des consaux de la ville de Tournai*, vol. ii, pp. 328-330.

1359. Letter from Perceval de Boulainvilliers, in *Trial*, vol. v, p. 120. Fragment of a letter concerning the marvels which have occurred in Poitou, *ibid.*, p. 122. Morosini, vol. iii, pp. 74-76.

1360. Hennebert, *Archives historiques et littéraires du nord de la France*, 1837, vol. i, p. 520. *Extraits des anciens registres des consaux*, ed. Vandenbroeck, vol. ii, *loc. cit.*

1361. *Trial*, vol. v, p. 127. These letters are now lost. Jeanne alludes to them in her letter of the 17th of July, 1429. *"Et à trois sepmaines que je vous avoye escript et envoie bonnes lettres par un héraut...."*

1362. Dom Plancher, *Histoire de Bourgogne*, vol. iv, pp. lvi, lvii. E. Cosneau, *Le connétable de Richemont*, pp. 114 *et seq.*

1363. Dom Plancher, *Histoire de Bourgogne*, vol. iv, proofs and illustrations, p. lv.

1364. De Barante, *Histoire des ducs de Bourgogne*, vol. v, p. 270. Desplanques, *Projet d'assassinat de Philippe le Bon par les Anglais* (1424-1426), in *Les mémoires couronnées par l'Académie de Bruxelles*, xxxiii (1867).

1365. *Journal du siège*, p. 70. *Chronique de la Pucelle*, p. 270. Morosini, vol. iii, pp. 20 *et seq.*

1366. Monstrelet, vol. iv, pp. 332, 333. De Beaucourt, *Histoire de Charles VII*, vol. ii, p. 36, note 7.

1367. Monstrelet, vol. iv, pp. 308-309. Quenson, *Notice sur Philippe le Bon, la Flandre et ses fêtes*, Douai, 1840, in 8vo. De Reiffenberg, *Les enfants naturels du duc Philippe le Bon*, in *Bulletin de l'Académie de Bruxelles*, vol. xiii (1846).

1368. According to Perceval de Cagny, p. 157; the 28th of June, according to Chartier, p. 90.

1369. *Trial*, vol. iv, p. 286.

1370. Jean Chartier, *Chronique*, vol. i, p. 90. *Chronique de la Pucelle*, pp. 309, 310. Perceval de Cagny, p. 157. Morosini, vol. iii, pp. 142, 143.

1371. *Chronique de la Pucelle*, p. 314. *Journal du siège*, pp. 108, 109. Monstrelet, vol. iv, p. 330. Jean Chartier, *Chronique*, vol. i, p. 92. Morosini, vol. iii, p. 142, note 2.

1372. *Trial*, vol. i, pp. 54, 222.

1373. Abbé Lebeuf, *Histoire ecclésiastique et civile d'Auxerre*, vol. ii, p. 251; vol. iii, pp. 302, 506.

1374. Chardon, *Histoire de la ville d'Auxerre*, Auxerre, 1834 (2 vols. in 8vo), vol. ii, p. 258.

1375. Dom Plancher, *Histoire de Bourgogne*, vol. iv, p. 76. Chardon, *Histoire de la ville d'Auxerre*, vol. ii, pp. 257 *et seq.* Vallet de Viriville, *Histoire de Charles VII*, vol. i, p. 383.

1376. Jean Chartier, *Chronique*, vol. i, p. 90. *Journal du siège*, p. 108. *Chronique de la Pucelle*, p. 313. Monstrelet, vol. iv, p. 436. Abbé Lebeuf, *Histoire ecclésiastique d'Auxerre*, vol. ii, p. 51. Chardon, *Histoire de la ville d'Auxerre*, vol. ii, p. 259.

1377. Jean Chartier, *Chronique*, vol. i, p. 90. *Chronique de la Pucelle*, p. 313. Morosini, vol. iii, p. 149. Monstrelet, vol. iv, p. 336. Gilles de Roye, in *Collection des chroniques belges*, pp. 206, 207. Chardon, *Histoire de la ville d'Auxerre*, vol. ii, p. 260.

1378. *"De laquelle chose furent bien mal coutans aucuns seigneurs et cappitaines d'icellui ost et en parloient bien fort."* Jean Chartier, vol. i, p. 91.

1379. In the following manner this march is described by a contemporary: "On the said day (29th of June, 1429), after much discussion, the King set out and took his way for to go straight to the city of Troye in Champaigne, and, as he passed, all the fortresses on the one hand and the other, rendered him allegiance." Perceval de Cagny, p. 157.

1380. Jean Chartier, vol. i, p. 91.

1381. J. Rogier, in *Trial*, vol. iv, p. 287. Monstrelet, vol. iv, p. 336. *Journal du siège*, p. 109. *Chronique de la Pucelle*, p. 314. Jean Chartier, *Chronique*, vol. i, p. 91. *Trial*, vol. v, pp. 264-265.

1382. Jean Chartier, vol. i, p. 91.

1383. Th. Boutiot, *Histoire de la ville de Troyes et de la Champagne méridionale*, Paris, 1872 (5 vols. in 8vo), vol. ii, p. 482. For the members of this Council see the most ancient register of its deliberations by A. Roserot, in *Collection des documents inédits relatifs à la ville de Troyes* (1886).

1384. F. Bourquelot, *Les foires de Champagne*, Paris, 1865, vol. i, p. 65. Louis Batiffol, *Jean Jouvenel, prévôt des marchands*, Paris, 1894, in 8vo.

1385. J. Rogier, in *Trial*, vol. iv, p. 292.

1386. *Gallia Christiana*, vol. xiii, cols. 514-516. Courtalon-Delaistre, *Topographie historique du diocèse de Troyes* (Troyes, 1783, 3 vols. in 8vo), vol. i, p. 384. Th. Boutiot, *Histoire de la ville de Troyes*, vol. ii, pp. 477, 478. De Pange, *Le pays de Jeanne d'Arc, le fief et l'arrière-fief*, Paris, 1902, in 8vo, p. 33.

1387. Siméon Luce, *Jeanne d'Arc à Domremy*, p. ccxxii, according to Labbe and Cossart, *Sacro-Sancta-Consilia*, vol. xii, col. 390.

1388. S. Luce, *Jeanne d'Arc à Domremy*, p. ccxx and proofs and illustrations, ccix, pp. 238-239. Robillard de Beaurepaire, *Les états de Normandie sous la domination anglaise*, Évreux, 1859, in 8vo.

1389. Labbe and Cossart, *Sacro-Sancta-Consilia*, vol. xii, col. 392.

1390. Labbe and Cossart, *Sacro-Sancta-Consilia*, vol. xii, col. 390, 399.

1391. De Pange, *Le pays de Jeanne d'Arc, le fief et l'arrière-fief*, p. 33.

1392. J. Rogier in *Trial*, vol. iv, p. 285.

1393. Th. Boutiot in *Histoire de la ville de Troyes*, vol. ii, pp. 316 *et seq.*

1394. J. Rogier, in *Trial*, vol. iv, p. 288. Th. Boutiot, *Histoire de la ville de Troyes*, vol. ii, p. 490. A. Assier, *Une cité champenoise au xve siècle*, Troyes, 1875, in 12mo.

1395. *Trial*, vol. i, pp. 99, 100. *Relation du Greffier de La Rochelle*, p. 338. *Journal du siège*, pp. 109-110. *Chronique de la Pucelle*, p. 315.

1396. Ed. Richer says his name was Roch Richard and that he was licentiate in theology. *Histoire manuscrite de la Pucelle* (Bibl. Nat. fr. 10448), book 1, folios 50 *et seq.* Siméon Luce, *Jeanne d'Arc à Domremy* (chap. x, Jeanne d'Arc et frère Richard).

1397. *Journal d'un bourgeois de Paris*, p. 235. Th. Basin, *Histoire de Charles VII et de Louis XI*, vol. i, p. 104. Vallet de Viriville, *Procès de condamnation de Jeanne d'Arc*, 1867. Introduction, *Notes sur deux médailles de plomb relatives à Jeanne d'Arc*, Paris, 1861, p. 22. S. Luce, *Jeanne d'Arc à Domremy*, p. ccxxxix.

1398. *Journal du siège*, p. 110. *Chronique de la Pucelle*, p. 315.

1399. *Journal d'un bourgeois de Paris*, p. 233. Labbe, Boutiot.

1400. *Journal d'un bourgeois de Paris*, p. 234.

1401. *Ibid.*, p. 235.

1402. Th. Basin, *Histoire des règnes de Charles VII et de Louis XI*, vol. iv, pp. 103, 104.

1403. *Journal d'un bourgeois de Paris*, p. 236.

1404. A very high head-dress, fashionable in the fifteenth century (W.S.).

1405. *Cornes*, the high-horned head-dress (W.S.).

1406. *Queues*, trains (W.S.).

1407. *Journal d'un bourgeois de Paris*, pp. 234, 235.

1408. *Journal d'un bourgeois de Paris*, p. 236.

1409. *Trial*, vol. i, pp. 89, 213. *Journal d'un bourgeois de Paris*, p. 236.

1410. *Journal d'un bourgeois de Paris*, pp. 242, 243. Vallet de Viriville, *Notes sur deux médailles de plomb relatives à Jeanne d'Arc*, in *Revue archéologique*, 1861, pp. 429, 433.

1411. *Journal d'un bourgeois de Paris*, p. 236.

1412. *Journal d'un bourgeois de Paris*, p. 237.

1413. It is yet to be explained how the author of the diary called *Journal d'un bourgeois de Paris* avoided being scandalised by them, orthodox university professor as he was; on the contrary he seems to have found the views of the good father edifying. Th. Basin, *Histoire des règnes de Charles VII et de Louis XI*, vol. iv, p. 104.

1414. J. Rogier, in *Trial*, vol. iv, p. 290.

1415. *Trial*, vol. i, p. 100, see *ante*, p. 412.

1416. *Trial*, vol. i, p. 100.

1417. *Ibid.*, vol. ii, p. 446.

1418. Gruel, *Chronique de Richemont*, p. 71. Eberhard Windecke, pp. 178, 179.

1419. *Trial*, vol. i, p. 100.

1420. *Ibid.*, pp. 99, 100.

1421. *Relation du greffier de La Rochelle*, p. 342.

1422. *Journal d'un bourgeois de Paris*, p. 235.

1423. J. Rogier, in *Trial*, vol. iv, pp. 287-288.

1424. It should be Monday, 4th July.

1425. J. Rogier, in *Trial*, vol. iv, p. 290.

1426. Th. Boutiot, *Histoire de la ville de Troyes*, vol. ii, p. 493.

1427. J. Rogier, in *Trial*, vol. iv, pp. 288, 289.

1428. *Ibid.*, p. 287. Th. Boutiot, *Histoire de la ville de Troyes*, vol. ii, p. 494.

1429. *Trial*, vol. iv, p. 289.

1430. *Ibid.*, p. 290.

1431. In the *Mystery of the siege of Orléans*, the Englishman Falconbridge likewise treats Jeanne as a boaster, lines 12689-90:

> 'Y nous fault prandre la coquarde,
> Qui veult les François gouverner.

"We must capture that braggart who desires to govern the French."

1432. J. Rogier, in *Trial*, vol. iv, p. 289.

1433. *Ibid.* Th. Boutiot, *Histoire de la ville de Troyes*, vol. ii, p. 492.

1434. L. Pigeotte, *Étude sur les travaux d'achèvement de la cathédrale de Troyes*, p. 9. A. Babeau, *Les vues d'ensemble de Troyes*, Troyes, 1892, in 8vo, p. 13. A. Assier, *Une cité champenoise au XVe siècle*, Paris, 1875, in 8vo.

1435. Ermine (W.S.).

1436. *Comptes de l'argenterie de la reine*, in Jean Chartier, *Chronique*, vol. iii, pp. 236, 237. De Barante, *Histoire des ducs de Bourgogne*, vol. iii, pp. 122, 125. Vallet de Viriville, *Histoire de Charles VII*, vol. i, p. 216. Th. Boutiot, *Histoire de la ville de Troyes*, vol. ii, pp. 418, 419.

1437. It is impossible to take seriously those protestations of loyalty to the English, addressed to the people of Reims by the townsfolk of Troyes, when the latter were on the point of surrendering to the French King, and especially after the reply they had just sent to King Charles's letters. See J. Rogier, in *Trial*, vol. iv, p. 289. "Which reply having been made each of them had gone up on to the walls, and assumed his guard with the intent and in the firm resolution that if any attack were made on them, they would resist to the death."

1438. J. Chartier, vol. i, p. 92. Th. Boutiot, *Histoire de la ville de Troyes*, vol. ii, pp. 391, 418, 419. A. Assier, *Une cité champenoise au XVe siècle*, p. 8.

1439. J. Rogier, in *Trial*, vol. iv, pp. 289, 290.

1440. *Journal du siège*, p. 109. *Chronique de la Pucelle*, pp. 314, 315. Jean Chartier, *Chronique*, vol. i, p. 91. Th. Boutiot, *Histoire de la ville de Troyes*, vol. ii, p. 497.

1441. Jean Chartier, *Chronique*, vol. i, p. 92.

1442. *Journal du siège*, pp. 109, 110. *Chronique de la Pucelle*, p. 315.

1443. Perceval de Cagny, p. 157. Nevertheless see also Morosini, vol. iii, p. 143, note.

1444. "And always desiring and discussing the submission of this city." Jean Chartier, vol. i, p. 91.

1445. *Trial*, vol. iii, p. 13. Evidence of Dunois. Jean Chartier, *Chronique*, vol. i, p. 92. *Chronique de la Pucelle*, p. 315. Chartier and the *Chronique de la Pucelle* put words into the mouths of Regnault de Chartres and Robert le Maçon which are very improbable.

1446. *Trial*, vol. iii, p. 13. Evidence of Dunois. *Chronique de la Pucelle*, p. 317. *Journal du siège*, p. 110. Jean Chartier, *Chronique*, vol. i, p. 94.

1447. Jean Chartier, vol. i, p. 95.

1448. *Trial*, vol. iii, pp. 13, 14, 117. Jean Chartier, *Chronique*, vol. i, p. 96. *Journal du siège*, p. 111. *Chronique de la Pucelle*, p. 78. De Beaucourt, *Histoire de Charles VII*, vol. ii, p. 225.

1449. Th. Boutiot, *Histoire de la ville de Troyes*, vol. ii, p. 497, note. A. Assier, *Une cité champenoise au XVe siècle*, Paris, 1875, in 8vo, p. 26.

1450. *Trial*, vol. iii, p. 117. (De Gaucourt's evidence.)

1451. *Ibid.*, p. 117. Jean Chartier, *Chronique*, vol. i, p. 96. J. Rogier, in *Trial*, vol. iv, p. 296.

1452. J. Rogier, in *Trial*, vol. iv, p. 295. *Trial*, pp. 13, 14, 17. Chartier, *Journal du siège*, *Chronique de la Pucelle*. Camusat, *Mél. hist.*, part ii, fol. 214.

1453. *Relation du greffier de La Rochelle*, in *Revue historique*, vol. iv, p. 342. *Chronique de la Pucelle*, *Journal du siège*, Chartier, *loc. cit.* Gilles de Roye in Chartier, vol. iii, p. 205.

1454. J. Rogier in *Trial*, vol. iv, p. 296.

1455. *Gabelle*, word of German origin (*gabe*), originally applied to all taxes, came to signify only the tax on salt. This tax was first rendered oppressive by Philippe de Valois (1328-1350) who created a monopoly of salt in favour of the crown. He obliged each family to pay a tax on a certain quantity whether they consumed it or not. The *Gabelle*, which led to several rebellions, was not abolished until the Revolution (1790). (W.S.) *Trial*, vol. iv, p. 296. *Ordonnances des rois de France*, vol. xiii, p. 142. Th. Boutiot, *Histoire de la ville de Troyes*, vol. ii, p. 500. A. Roserot, *Le plus ancien registre des délibérations du conseil de la ville de Troyes* in *Coll. de Doc. inédits sur la ville de Troyes*, vol. iii, p. 175.

1456. J. Rogier, in *Trial*, vol. iv, pp. 295, 296.

1457. *Relation du greffier de La Rochelle*, in *Revue historique*, vol. iv, p. 342.

1458. *Relation du greffier de La Rochelle*, in *Revue historique*, vol. iv, p. 342.

1459. J. Rogier, in *Trial*, vol. iv, pp. 296, 297.

1460. *Trial*, vol. iii, pp. 13, 117; vol. iv, pp. 296, 297. Jean Chartier, *Chronique*, vol. iii, p. 205. Th. Boutiot, *Histoire de la ville de Troyes*, vol. ii, pp. 499, 500. M. Poinsignon, *Histoire générale de la Champagne et de la Brie*, Châlons, 1885, vol. i, pp. 352 *et seq.* A. Assier, *Une cité champenoise au XVe siècle*, Paris, 1875, in 12mo, pp. 16, 17.

1461. *Trial*, vol. i, p. 102. *Chronique de la Pucelle*, p. 319.

1462. Chartier, *Journal du siège. Chronique de la Pucelle*, p. 319.

1463. Jean Chartier, *Chronique*, vol. i, pp. 95, 96. *Journal du siège*, p. 112. *Chronique de la Pucelle*, p. 319.

1464. J. Rogier, in *Trial*, vol. iv, pp. 296, 297.

1465. Lefèvre de Saint-Rémy, vol. ii, p. 168. S. Luce, *Jeanne d'Arc à Domremy*, pp. clxxiii, clxxiv. P. Champion, *Notes sur Jeanne d'Arc*, I. *Madame d'Or et Jeanne d'Arc* in *Le moyen âge*, July to August, 1907, pp. 193-199.

1466. *Chronique de la Pucelle*, p. 319. Jean Chartier, *Chronique*, vol. i, p. 96. *Journal du siège*, p. 112. *Un prince de façon*, Martial d'Auvergne, *Vigiles*, vol. i, pp. 106, 107.

1467. *Trial*, vol. i, p. 102. Letter from three noblemen of Anjou, in *Trial*, vol. v, p. 130. *Relation du greffier de La Rochelle*, p. 342. *Chronique de la Pucelle*, p. 319. Morosini, vol. iii, p. 176. Th. Boutiot, *Histoire de la ville de Troyes*, vol. ii, pp. 504 *et seq.*

411

1468. *Trial*, vol. i, p. 103.

1469. T. Babeau, *Le guet et la milice bourgeoise à Troyes*, pp. 4 *et seq.*

1470. *Relation du greffier de La Rochelle*, p. 342. *Chronique de la Pucelle*, p. 319. *Journal du siège*, p. 112. Th. Boutiot, *Histoire de la ville de Troyes*, vol. ii, p. 505. A. Roserot, *Le plus ancien registre des délibérations du conseil de Troyes* in *Coll. des documents inédits de la ville de Troyes*, vol. iii, pp. 175 *et seq.*

1471. J. Rogier, in *Trial*, vol. iv, p. 298. Morosini, vol. iii, p. 179. Edition Barthélémy of *L'histoire de la ville de Châlons-sur-Marne*, proofs and illustrations no. 25, pp. 334, 335.

1472. J. Rogier, in *Trial*, vol. iv, pp. 290, 291. Varin, *Archives législatives de la ville de Reims, Statuts*, vol. 1, pp. 596 *et seq.* (*Coll. des documents inédits sur l'histoire de France*, 1845).

1473. *Gallia Christiana*, vol. v, col. 891-895. *Chronique de la Pucelle*, pp. 319-320. Jean Chartier, *Chronique*, vol. i, p. 96. L. Barbat, *Histoire de la ville de Châlons*, 1855 (2 vols. in 4to), vol. i, p. 350. S. Luce, *Jeanne d'Arc à Domremy*, proofs and illustrations no. 33. Morosini, vol. iii, p. 182, note 2.

1474. J. Rogier, in *Trial*, vol. iv, p. 298. Letter from three noblemen of Anjou in *Trial*, vol. v, p. 130. Perceval de Cagny, p. 158. Jean Chartier, *Chronique*, vol. i, pp. 96, 97. *Chronique des Cordeliers*, fol. 85, v. E. de Barthélémy, *Châlons pendant l'invasion anglaise*, Châlons, 1851, p. 16.

1475. *Trial*, vol. ii, pp. 391, 392 (Jean Morel's evidence).

1476. French *compère*, gossip or fellow godfather, sometimes a close friend. Cf. Chaucer, Prologue to Canterbury Tales:

> "With hym ther was a gentil Pardoner
> Of Rouncivale, his freend and his compeer" (W.S.).

1477. *Commère*, fellow godmother (W.S.).

1478. *Trial*, vol. ii, p. 423 (evidence of Gérardin of Épinal).

1479. "In as much as he is the prince of the greatest discretion, understanding, and valour that has long been seen in the noble house of France." J. Rogier, in *Trial*, vol. iv, p. 296. Varin, *Archives de Reims, Statuts*, vol. i, p. 601. H. Jadart, *Jeanne d'Arc à Reims*, pp. 13 *et seq.*

1480. J. Rogier, *loc. cit.* Varin, p. 599.

1481. J. Rogier, in *Trial*, vol. iv, pp. 286 *et seq.* Varin, pp. 600 *et seq.*

1482. H. Jadart, *Jeanne d'Arc à Reims*, p. 18. Dom Marlot, *Hist. metrop. Remensis*, vol. ii, pp. 709 *et seq.*

1483. J. Rogier, in *Trial*, vol. iv, pp. 291-292.

1484. J. Rogier, in *Trial*, vol. iv, p. 291.

1485. *Ibid.*, p. 292. H. Jadart, *Jeanne d'Arc à Reims*, pp. 17 *et seq.*

1486. J. Rogier, in *Trial*, vol. iv, pp. 292, 293. Varin, *Archives de Reims*, pp. 910, 912. H. Jadart, *Jeanne d'Arc à Reims*, p. 18.

1487. J. Rogier, in *Trial*, vol. iv, p. 295. H. Jadart, *Jeanne d'Arc à Reims*, pp. 18, 19.

1488. Falconbridge, in *Trial*, vol. iv, p. 451. Jean Chartier, *Chronique*, vol. i, pp. 101, 102. *Journal du siège*, p. 118. Rymer, *Fœdera*, vol. x, p. 424. S. Bougenot, *Notices et extraits des manuscrits intéressants l'histoire de France conservés à la Bibliothèque impériale de Vienne*, p. 62. Raynaldi, *Annales ecclesiastici*, vol. ix, pp. 77, 78. Morosini, vol. iv, supplement, xvii.

1489. J. Rogier, in *Trial*, vol. iv, pp. 295, 298.

1490. *Ibid.*, p. 297. L. Paris, *Cabinet historique*, 1865, p. 77.

1491. H. Jadart, *Jeanne d'Arc à Reims*, p. 19.

1492. Perceval de Cagny, p. 159. Jean Chartier, *Chronique*, p. 97; *Chronique de la Pucelle*, p. 320. *Chronique des Cordeliers*, fol. 85, v°. *Journal du siège*, p. 112. Bergier, *Poème sur la tapisserie de Jeanne d'Arc*, p. 112. H. Jadart, *Jeanne d'Arc à Reims*, pp. 20, 21. F. Pinon, *Notice sur Sept-Saulx*, in *Travaux de l'académie de Reims*, vol. vi, p. 328.

1493. J. Rogier, in *Trial*, pp. 298 *et seq.* Dom Marlot, *Histoire de la ville de Reims*, vol. iv, Reims, 1846 (4 vol. in 4to), vol. iii, p. 174.

1494. H. Jadart, *Jeanne d'Arc à Reims*, p. 23.

1495. *Chronique de la Pucelle*, pp. 322, 323, note. "This ritual dates back certainly as far as the 13th century. It is preserved in the library at Reims in a MS. which appears to have been written about 1274." Communicated by M. H. Jadart. Varin, *Archives de Reims*, vol. i, p. 522. Dom Marlot, *Histoire de la ville de Reims*, vol. iii, p. 566, and vol. iv, proofs and illustrations no. 142. H. Jadart, *Jeanne d'Arc à Reims*, p. 7.

1496. *Chronique de la Pucelle*, p. 321. Perceval de Cagny, p. 159. Letter from three noblemen of Anjou, in *Trial*, vol. v, p. 128.

1497. *Pro evitando onus armatorum*, *Trial*, vol. i, p. 91.

413

1498. Thirion, *Les frais du sacre* in *Travaux de l'académie de Reims*, 1894. See Varin, *Archives de Reims*, table of contents under the word, *Sacre*. Dom Marlot, *Histoire de la ville de Reims*, vol. iii, pp. 461, 566, 640, 651, 819; vol. iv, pp. 25, 31, 45.

1499. *Chronique de la Pucelle*, p. 322, note 1. C. Leber, *Des cérémonies du sacre ou Recherches historiques et antiques sur les mœurs, les coutumes, les institutions et le droit public des Français dans l'ancienne monarchie*, Paris-Reims, 1825, in 8vo. A. Lenoble, *Histoire du sacre et du couronnement des rois et des reines de France*, Paris, 1825, in 8vo.

1500. "Et si ipse expectasset habuisset unam coronam millesies ditiorem," *Trial*, vol. i, p. 91. Varin, *Archives de Reims*, vol. iii, pp. 559 *et seq.*

1501. *Journal du siège*, p. 113. *Chronique de la Pucelle*, p. 321. Varin, *Archives de Reims*, vol. ii, p. 569; vol. iii, p. 555.

1502. *Trial*, vol. v, p. 129. In 1483, when Louis XI was dying, he had it brought from Reims to Plessis, "and it was upon his sideboard at the very time of his death, and his intent was to receive the same anointing he had received at his coronation, wherefore many believed that he wished to anoint his whole body, which would have been impossible, for the said Ampulla is very small and contains little. I see it at this moment." Commynes, bk. vi, ch. 9.

1503. Flodoard, *Hist. ecclesiae Remensis*, in *Coll. Guizot*, vol. v, pp. 41 *et seq.* Eustache Deschamps, Ballade 172, vol. i, p. 305; vol. ii, p. 104. Dom Marlot, *Histoire de la ville de Reims*, vol. ii, p. 48, note 1. Vertot, in *Académie des Inscriptions*, vol. ii.

1504. Froissart, book ii, ch. lxxiv.

1505. Letters from three noblemen of Anjou, in *Trial*, vol. v, pp. 127, 129. Monstrelet, vol. iv, ch. lxiv. Perceval de Cagny, p. 159. *Relation du greffier de La Rochelle*, p. 343. *Chronique de Tournai* (vol. iii of the *Recueil des chroniques de Flandre*), p. 414. *Gallia Christiana*, vol. ix, col. 551; vol. xi, col. 698.

1506. *Chronique de la Pucelle*, p. 322, note 1.

1507. Perceval de Cagny, p. 159. *Journal du siège*, p. 114. *Chronique de la Pucelle*, p. 322. Jean Chartier, *Chronique*, vol. i, p. 97.

1508. Chifletius, *De ampula Remensi nova et acurata disquisitio*, Antwerp, 1651, in 4to.

1509. The first book of Kings according to the Vulgate (W.S.).

1510. Letter from three noblemen of Anjou, in *Trial*, vol. v, p. 129. F. Boyer, *Variante inédite d'un document sur le sacre de Charles VII*, Clermont and Orléans, 1881.

1511. *Trial*, vol. i, pp. 104, 300. *Chronique de la Pucelle*, p. 322. Letter from three noblemen of Anjou, in *Trial*, vol. v, p. 129. Varin, D. Marlot, H. Jadart, *loc. cit.*

1512. *Trial*, vol. i, p. 91.

1513. See *post*, vol. i, p. 476.

1514. Letter from three noblemen of Anjou, in *Trial*, vol. v, p. 129.

1515. Morosini, vol. iii, p. 181. Letter from three noblemen, *loc. cit.*

1516. *Chronique de la Pucelle*, pp. 322, 323. *Journal du siège*, p. 114.

1517. Dom Marlot, *Histoire de la ville de Reims*, vol. iv, p. 175. H. Jadart, *Jeanne d'Arc à Reims*, p. 107.

1518. *Chronique de la Pucelle*, p. 322. *Journal du siège*, p. 114. Perceval de Cagny, p. 159. Letter of three noblemen of Anjou, in *Trial*, vol. v, p. 129. Jean Chartier, *Chronique*, vol. i, p. 97. Vallet de Viriville, *Histoire de Charles VII*, vol. ii, p. 99, note 2.

1519. Monstrelet, vol. iv, p. 339. H. Jadart, *Jeanne d'Arc à Reims*, p. 32.

1520. Thirion, *Les frais du sacre*, in *Travaux de l'Académie de Reims*, 1894. Dom Marlot, *Histoire de la ville de Reims*, vol. iv, p. 45, n. 1. Varin, *Arch. adm. de la ville de Reims*, vol. iii, p. 39.

1521. *Trial*, vol. iii, p. 198; vol. v, pp. 141, 266. H. Jadart, *Jeanne d'Arc à Reims*, pp. 47, 48. L'abbé Cerf, *Le vieux Reims*, 1875, pp. 35 and 110.

1522. *Trial*, vol. ii, p. 445.

1523. *Ibid.*, vol. iii, p. 198.

1524. S. Luce, *Jeanne d'Arc à Domremy*, pp. 1 *et seq.*; proofs and illustrations no. li, pp. 97, 100; supplement, pp. 359, 362. Boucher de Molandon, *Jacques d'Arc, père de la Pucelle, sa notabilité personnelle*, Orléans, 1885, in 8vo.

1525. *Trial*, vol. v, pp. 137, 139. In the royal records this privilege is described as having been granted at Jeanne's request; in such a request we cannot fail to discern the influence of her father.

1526. *Ibid.*, pp. 141, 266, 267.

1527. *Ibid.*, p. 103.

1528. Du Cange, *Glossarium*, under the words *Auriacum, electrum*, and *leto*. Vallet de Viriville, *Les anneaux de Jeanne d'Arc*, in *Mémoires de la Société des Antiquaires de France*, vol. xxx, January, 1867.

1529. *Trial*, vol. i, pp. 185, 238. Walter Bower, *ibid.*, vol. iv, p. 480.

1530. *Sanctissimæ virginis Coletæ vita*, Paris, in 8vo, black letter, undated, leaf 8 on the reverse side. Bollandistes, *Acta sanctorum*, March, vol. i, p. 611.

1531. *Trial*, vol. i, pp. 86, 87.

1532. *Ibid.*, p. 104. H. Jadart, *Jeanne d'Arc à Reims*, p. 37.

1533. "These figures (Goliath and David) must have been sculptured at the end of the 13th century." (L. Demaison, *Notice historique sur la cathédrale de Reims*, s.d. in 4to, p. 44.) The date of the rose window is 1280 (H. Jadart, *Jeanne d'Arc à Reims*, p. 44).

1534. According to the Vulgate. First book of Samuel according to the Authorized Version (W.S.).

1535. 1 Samuel xvii. Where the author quotes direct from the Vulgate the translator has followed the Douai version (W.S.).

1536. See the coronation of David and that of Louis XII by an unknown painter, about 1498, in the Cluny Museum. H. Bouchot, *L'exposition des primitifs français. La peinture en France sous les Valois*, book ii, figure C.

1537. *Trial*, vol. v, pp. 126-127. Hennebert, *Une lettre de Jeanne d'Arc aux Tournaisiens* in *Arch. hist. et litt. du nord de la France et du midi de la Belgique*, nouv. série, vol. i, 1837, p. 525. Facsimile in *l'Album des archives départementales*, no. 123.

1538. Morosini, vol. iii, pp. 82, 83. Eberhard Windecke, p. 61, note 9, p. 108. Christine de Pisan, in *Trial*, vol. v, p. 416. Jorga, *Notes et extraits pour servir à l'histoire des croisades au XVᵉ siècle*, Paris, 1889-1902. 3 vols. in 8vo.

1539. *Mémoires du Pape Pie II*, in *Trial*, vol. iv, pp. 514, 515. Morosini, vol. iii, p. 190.

1540. *Trial*, vol. iv, pp. 514, 515. Monstrelet, vol. iv, p. 340. *Relation du greffier de La Rochelle*, p. 37. Letter from three noblemen of Anjou, in *Trial*, vol. v, p. 130. Third account of Jean Abonnel in De Beaucourt, *Histoire de Charles VII*, vol. ii, p. 404, no. 3.

1541. Letter from three noblemen of Anjou, in *Trial*, vol. v, p. 130.

1542. The 20th or 21st. Monstrelet, vol. iv, pp. 348 *et seq.* De Beaucourt, *Histoire de Charles VII*, vol. II, pp. 404 *et seq.*

1543. Falconbridge, in *Trial*, vol. iv, p. 455. *Journal d'un bourgeois de Paris*, pp. 240, 241. Stevenson, *Letters and papers*, vol. ii, pp. 101 *et seq.* Rymer, *Fœdera*, vol. iv, part iv, p. 150.

1544. Archives de Reims, Municipal Accounts, vol. i, years 1428-29. *Trial*, vol. v, p. 141. Monstrelet, vol. iv, p. 339. H. Jadart, *Jeanne d'Arc à Reims*, p. 51.

1545. *Trial*, vol. iii, p. 199. *Chronique de la Pucelle*, p. 323. Jean Chartier, *Chronique*, vol. i, p. 97. *Journal du siège*, p. 114. Martial d'Auvergne, *Vigiles*, vol. i, p. 111.

1546. *Gallia Christ:* ix, pp, 239, 51. Le Poulle, *Notice sur Corbeny, son prieuré, et le pèlerinage de Saint-Marcoul*, Soissons, 1883, 8vo. E. de Barthélèmy, *Notice historique sur le pèlerinage de Saint-Marcoul et Corbeny*, in *Ann. Soc. Acad. de Saint-Quentin*, 1878.

1547. A. Du Laurent, *De mirabili strumas sanandi vi solis regibus Galliarum christianissimis divinitus concessa liber*, Paris, 1607, 8vo. Cerf, *Du toucher des écrouelles par le roi de France*, in *Trav. Acad. de Reims*, 1865-1867. Dom Marlot, *Histoire de la ville de Reims*, vol. iii, pp. 196 *et seq.*

1548. Perceval de Cagny, p. 160. *Chronique de la Pucelle*, pp. 323, 324. Jean Chartier, *Chronique*, vol. i, p. 98. *Journal du siège*, p. 115. *Chronique des Cordeliers*, fol. 486 r°. Morosini, iii, p. 182, note 3.

1549. Bréhal, in *Trial*, vol. iii, p. 345.

1550. *Journal du siège*, pp. 16, 88. *Chronique de l'établissement de la fête*, in *Trial*, vol. v, p. 296. Lottin, *Récits historiques sur Orléans*, vol. i, p. 279.

1551. *Trial*, vol. iv, pp. 282, 283.

1552. Tidings of the Deliverance of Orléans sent from Bruges to Venice the 10th of May (Morosini, vol. iii, pp. 23, 24).

1553. *Trial*, vol. v, pp. 123, 139, 145, 147, 156, 159, 161.

1554. Morosini, vol. iii, pp. 60, 61.

1555. Saint Vincent Ferrier; and Saint Bernardino of Siena.

1556. See *ante*, p. 64.

1557. *Trial*, vol. iii, p. 88.

1558. Eberhard Windecke, pp. 52-53. See *ante*, p. 184.

1559. L. Delisle, *Un nouveau témoignage relatif à la mission de Jeanne d'Arc*, in *Bibliothèque de l'École des Chartes*, vol. xlvi, p. 649. Le P. Ayroles, *La Pucelle devant l'Église de son temps*, pp. 57, 58.

1560. Letter written by the agents of a town or of a prince of Germany, in *Trial*, vol. v, p. 351.

1561. Morosini, vol. iii, pp. 38, 46, 61.

1562. Morosini, vol. iii, pp. 64, 65.

1563. *Ibid.*, pp. 144 *et seq.*

1564. Morosini, vol. iii, pp. 150, 153.

1565. *Ibid.*, pp. 166, 167.

1566. Fragment of a letter on the marvels in Poitou, in *Trial*, vol. v, pp. 121, 122. *Relation du greffier de La Rochelle, op. cit.*, p. 343.

1567. Morosini, vol. iii, p. 78, note 1. Eberhard Windecke, *passim.* Fauché-Prunelle, *Lettres tirées des archives de Grenoble* in *Bull. Acad. delph.*, vol. ii, 1847, 1849, pp. 459, 460. Letter written by deputies, agents of a German town, in *Trial*, vol. v, p. 347. Letter from Jean Desch, Secretary of the town of Metz, *ibid.*, pp. 352, 355.

1568. Letters from Perceval de Boulainvilliers to the Duke of Milan, in *Trial*, vol. v, pp. 114, 116.

1569. Anonymous poem on the coming of the Maid and the Deliverance of Orléans, *Trial*, vol. v, p. 27, line 70 *et seq.*

1570. "*In nocte Epiphaniarum,*" says the letter from Perceval de Boulainvilliers (*Trial*, vol. v, p. 116), that is, Jan. 6. For centuries, even after the fourth century, the birth of our Lord was celebrated on that day. In France it was the Feast of Kings and then was sung the anthem: *Magi videntes stellam.*

1571. *Trial*, vol. iii, pp. 116, 192. *Chronique de la Pucelle*, p. 273. *Journal du siège*, p. 47. Jean Chartier, *Chronique*, vol. i, p. 67. *Relation du greffier de La Rochelle*, pp. 336, 337. Martial d'Auvergne, *Vigiles*, vol. i, p. 96.

1572. *Trial*, vol. iii, pp. 103, 116, 209, *passim. Journal du siège*, p. 48. Th. Basin, *Histoire de Charles VII*, vol. i, p. 68. *Mirouer des femmes vertueuses*, in *Trial*, vol. iv, p. 271. Pierre Sala, *ibid.*, p. 280. Morosini, vol. iii, p. 104. Eberhard Windecke, p. 153.

1573. *Journal du siège*, p. 294. *Chronique de l'établissement de la fête*, in *Trial*, vol. v, p. 294.

1574. AA. SS., April 3rd. Didron, *Iconographie chrétienne*, pp. 438, 439. Alba Mignati, *Sainte Catherine de Sienne*, p. 16.

1575. Eberhard Windecke, p. 103.

1576. *Trial*, vol. iii, pp. 116, 117.

1577. *Ibid.*, vol. i, pp. 55, 84 *et seq.*, 133, 174, 232, 251, 252, 254, 331; vol. iii, pp. 99, 205, 254, 257, *passim. Journal du siège*, pp. 34, 44, 45, 48. *Chronique de la Pucelle*, pp. 212, 295. Perceval de Cagny, p. 141. Monstrelet, vol. iv, p. 320. Lefèvre de Saint-Rémy, vol. ii, p. 143. The

Clerk of the Chamber of Accounts of Brabant, in *Trial*, vol. iv, p. 426. *Chronique de Tournai* (vol. iii, *du recueil des chroniques de Flandre*), p. 411. Morosini, vol. iii, p. 121.

1578. Morosini, vol. iii, p. 57.

1579. Brother Pasquerel's evidence, in *Trial*, vol. iii, p. 102.

1580. Anonymous poem on the Maid, in *Trial*, vol. v, p. 38, lines 105 *et seq.*

1581. Evidence of J. Luillier and Brother Pasquerel, in *Trial*, vol. iii, pp. 25, 108.

1582. The *Golden Legend*. Life of Saint Ambrose.

1583. Abbé J. Th. Bizouard, *Histoire de sainte Colette et des clarisses en Franche-Comté, d'après des documents inédits et des traditions locales*, Paris, 1888, in 8vo.

1584. Morosini, vol. iii, pp. 148, 156. Eberhard Windecke, pp. 103, 105, 187. Noël Valois, *Un nouveau témoignage sur Jeanne d'Arc*, p. 17.

1585. Lanéry d'Arc, *Mémoires et consultations*, pp. 220, 222. Théodore de Leliis, in *Trial*, vol. ii, pp. 39, 42. Le P. Ayroles, *La Pucelle devant l'Église de son temps*, p. 342. Abbé Hyacinthe Chassagnon, *Les voix de Jeanne d'Arc*, Lyon 1896, in 8vo, pp. 312, 313.

1586. Eberhard Windecke, pp. 138 *et seq.* Morosini, vol. iii, pp. 62-63.

1587. The monastery of the Premonstratensians, near Laon, was founded in 1122, by St. Norbert (W.S.).

1588. *Trial*, vol. iii, pp. 422 *et seq.*, 433, 434, 465; vol. v, pp. 475, 476.

1589. *Journal du siège*, p. 44. *Chronique de la Pucelle*, p. 272.

1590. Eberhard Windecke, p. 117.

1591. *Ibid.*, p. 97.

1592. *Trial*, vol. i, p. 146.

1593. Eberhard Windecke, p. 97.

1594. *Trial*, vol. i, pp. 76, 234. *Chronique de la Pucelle*, p. 277. Jean Chartier, *Chronique*, vol. i, pp. 69, 70. *Journal du siège*, pp. 49, 50. *Relation du greffier de La Rochelle*, pp. 337, 338. Morosini, vol. iii, pp. 108, 109. Abbé Bourassé, *Les miracles de Madame Sainte Katerine*, Introduction.

1595. Morosini, vol. iii, pp. 160, 163.

1596. *Trial*, vol. i, p. 91.

1597. Dom Marlot, *Histoire de l'Église de Reims*, vol. iv, p. 175. H. Jadart, *Jeanne d'Arc à Reims*, appendix xvii.

1598. *Trial*, vol. i, p. 104.

JOAN OF ARC

VOLUME II

CHAPTER I

THE ROYAL ARMY FROM SOISSONS TO COMPIÈGNE – POEM AND PROPHECY

O N the 22nd of July, King Charles, marching with his army down the valley of the Aisne, in a place called Vailly, received the keys of the town of Soissons.[1]

This town constituted a part of the Duchy of Valois, held jointly by the Houses of Orléans and of Bar.[2] Of its dukes, one was a prisoner in the hands of the English; the other was connected with the French party through his brother-in-law, King Charles, and with the Burgundian party through his father-in-law, the Duke of Lorraine. No wonder the fealty of the townsfolk was somewhat vacillating; downtrodden by men-at-arms, forever taken and retaken, red caps and white caps alternately ran the danger of being cast into the river. The Burgundians set fire to the houses, pillaged the churches, chastised the most notable burgesses; then came the Armagnacs, who sacked everything, made great slaughter of men, women, and children, ravished nuns, worthy wives, and honest maids. The Saracens could not have done worse.[3] City dames had been seen making sacks in which Burgundians were to be sewn up and thrown into the Aisne.[4]

King Charles made his entry into the city on Saturday the 23rd, in the morning.[5] The red caps went into hiding. The bells pealed, the folk cried "Noël," and the burgesses proffered the King two barbels, six sheep and six gallons of "*bon suret*,"[6] begging the King to forgive its being so little, but the war had ruined them.[7] They, like the people of Troyes, refused to open their gates to the men-at-arms, by virtue of their privileges, and because they had not food enough for their support. The army encamped in the plain of Amblény.[8]

It would seem that at that time the leaders of the royal army had the intention of marching on Compiègne. Indeed it was important to capture this town from Duke Philip, for it was the key to l'Île-de-France and ought to be taken before the Duke had time to bring up an army. But throughout this campaign the King of France was resolved to recapture his towns rather by diplomacy and persuasion than by force. Between the 22nd and the 25th of July he three times summoned the inhabitants of Compiègne to surrender. Being desirous to gain time and to have the air of being constrained, they entered into negotiations.[9]

Having quitted Soissons, the royal army reached Château-Thierry on the 29th. All day it waited for the town to open its gates. In the evening the King entered.[10] Coulommiers, Crécy-en-Brie, and Provins submitted.[11]

On Monday, the 1st of August, the King crossed the Marne, over the Château-Thierry Bridge, and that same day took up his quarters at Montmirail. On the morrow he gained Provins and came within a short distance of the passage of the Seine and the high-roads of central France.[12] The army was sore anhungered, finding nought to eat in these ravaged fields and pillaged cities. Through lack of victuals preparations were being made for retreat into Poitou. But this design was thwarted by the English. While ungarrisoned towns were being reduced, the English Regent had been gathering an army. It was now advancing on Corbeil and Melun. On its approach the French gained La Motte-Nangis, some twelve miles from Provins, where they took up their position on ground flat and level, such as was convenient for the fighting of a battle, as battles were fought in those days. For one whole day they remained in battle array. There was no sign of the English coming to attack them.[13]

Meanwhile the people of Reims received tidings that King Charles was leaving Château-Thierry and was about to cross the Seine. Believing that they had been abandoned, they were afraid lest the English and Burgundians should make them pay dearly for the coronation of the King of the Armagnacs; and in truth they stood in great danger. On the 3rd of August, they resolved to send a message to King Charles to entreat him not to forsake those cities which had submitted to him. The city's herald set out forthwith. On the morrow they sent word to their good friends of Châlons and of Laon, how they had heard that King Charles was wending towards Orléans and Bourges, and how they had sent him a message.[14]

On the 5th of August, while the King is still at Provins[15] or in the neighbourhood, Jeanne addresses to the townsfolk of Reims a letter dated from the camp, on the road to Paris. Herein she promises not to desert her friends faithful and beloved. She appears to have no suspicion of the projected retreat on the Loire. Wherefore it is clear that the magistrates of Reims have not written to her and that she is not admitted to the royal counsels. She has been instructed, however, that the King has concluded a fifteen days' truce with the Duke of Burgundy, and thereof she informs the citizens of Reims. This truce is displeasing to her; and she doubts whether she will observe it. If she does observe it, it will be solely on account of the King's honour; and even then she must be persuaded that there is no trickery in it. She will therefore keep the royal army together and in readiness to march at the end of the fifteen days. She closes her letter with a recommendation to the townsfolk to keep good guard and to send her word if they have need of her.

Here is the letter:

"Good friends and beloved, ye good and loyal French of the city of Rains, Jehanne the Maid lets you wit of her tidings and prays and requires you not to doubt the good cause she maintains for the Blood Royal; and I promise and assure you that I will never forsake you as long as I shall live. It is true that the King has made truce with the Duke of Burgundy for the space of fifteen days, by which he is to surrender peaceably the city of Paris at the end of fifteen days. Notwithstanding, marvel ye not if I do not straightway enter into it, for truces thus made are not pleasing unto me, and I know not whether I shall keep them; but if I keep them it will be solely to maintain the King's honour; and further they shall not ensnare the Royal Blood, for I will keep and maintain together the King's army that it be ready at the end of fifteen days, if they make not peace. Wherefore my beloved and perfect friends, I pray ye to be in no disquietude as long as I shall live; but I require you to keep good watch and to defend well the good city of the King; and to make known unto me if there be any traitors who would do you hurt, and, as speedily as I may, I will take them out from among you; and send me of your tidings. To God I commend you. May he have you in his keeping."

Written this Friday, 5th day of August, near Provins,[16] a camp in the country or on the Paris road. Addressed to: the loyal French of the town of Rains.[17]

It cannot be doubted that the monk who acted as scribe wrote down faithfully what was dictated to him, and reproduced the Maid's very words, even her Lorraine dialect. She had then attained to the very highest degree of heroic saintliness. Here, in this letter, she takes to herself a supernatural power, to which the King, his Councillors and his Captains must submit. She ascribes to herself alone the right of recognising or denouncing treaties; she disposes entirely of the army. And, because she commands in the name of the King of Heaven, her commands are absolute. There is happening to her what necessarily happens to all those who believe themselves entrusted with a divine mission; they constitute themselves a spiritual and temporal power superior to the established powers and inevitably hostile to them. A dangerous illusion and productive of shocks in which the illuminated are generally the worst sufferers! Every day of her life living and holding converse with saints and angels, moving in the splendour of the Church Triumphant, this young peasant girl came to believe that in her resided all strength, all prudence, all wisdom and all counsel. This does not mean that she was lacking in intelligence; on the contrary she rightly perceived that the Duke of Burgundy, with his embassies, was but playing with the King and that Charles was being tricked by a Prince, who knew how to disguise his craft in magnificence. Not that Duke Philip was an enemy of peace; on the contrary he desired it, but he was desirous not to come to an open quarrel with the English. Jeanne knew little of the affairs of Burgundy and of France, but her judgment was none the less sound. Concerning the relative positions of the Kings of France and England, between whom there could be no agreement, since the matter in dispute was the possession of the kingdom, her ideas were very simple but very correct. Equally accurate were her views of the position of the King of France with regard to his great vassal, the Duke of Burgundy, with whom an understanding was not only possible and desirable, but necessary. She pronounced thereupon in a perfectly straightforward fashion: On the one hand there is peace with the Burgundians and on the other peace with the English; concerning the peace with the Duke of Burgundy, by letters and by ambassadors have I required him to come to terms with the King; as for the English, the only way of making peace with them is for them to go back to their country, to England.[18]

This truce that so highly displeased her we know not when it was concluded, whether at Soissons or Château-Thierry, on the 30th or 31st of July, or at Provins between the 2nd and 5th of August.[19] It would appear that it was to last fifteen days, at the end of which time the Duke was to undertake to surrender Paris to the King of France. The Maid had good reason for her mistrust.

When the Regent withdrew before him, King Charles eagerly returned to his plan of retreating into Poitou. From La Motte-Nangis he sent his quartermasters to Bray-sur-Seine, which had just submitted. Situated above Montereau and ten miles south of Provins, this town had a bridge over the river, across which the royal army was to pass on the 5th of August or in the morning of the 6th; but the English came by night, overcame the quartermasters and took possession of the bridge; with its retreat cut off, the royal army had to retrace its march.[20]

Within this army, which had not fought and which was being devoured by hunger, there existed a party of zealots, led by those whom Jeanne fondly called the Royal Blood.[21] They were the Duke of Alençon, the Duke of Bourbon, the Count of Vendôme, and likewise the Duke of Bar, who had just come from the War of the Apple Baskets.[22] Before he took to painting pictures and writing moralities in rhyme, this young son of the Lady Yolande had been a warrior. Duke of Bar and heir of Lorraine, he had been forced to join the English and Burgundians. Brother-in-law of King Charles, he must needs rejoice when the latter was victorious, because, but for that victory, he would never have been able to range himself on the side of the Queen, his sister, for which he would have been very sorry.[23] Jeanne knew him; not long before, she had asked the Duke of Lorraine to send him with her into France.[24] He was said to have been one of those who of their own free will followed her to Paris. Among the others were the two sons of the Lady of Laval, Gui, the eldest to whom she had offered wine at Selles-en-Berry, promising soon to give him to drink at Paris, and André, who afterwards became Marshal of Lohéac.[25] This was the army of the Maid: a band of youths, scarcely more than children, who ranged their banners side by side with the banner of a girl younger than they, but more innocent and better.

On learning that the retreat had been cut off, it is said that these youthful princes were well content and glad.[26] This was valour and zeal; but it was a curious position and a false when the knighthood wished for war while the royal council was desiring to treat, and when the knighthood actually rejoiced at the campaign being prolonged by the enemy and at the royal army being cornered by the *Godons*. Unhappily this war party could boast of no very able adherents; and the favourable opportunity had been lost, the Regent had been allowed time to collect his forces and to cope with the most pressing dangers.[27]

Its retreat cut off, the royal army fell back on Brie. On the morning of Sunday, the 7th, it was at Coulommiers; it recrossed the Marne at Château-Thierry.[28] King Charles received a message from the inhabitants of Reims, entreating him to draw nearer to them.[29] He was at La Ferté on the 10th, on the 11th at Crépy in Valois.[30]

At one stage of the march on La Ferté and Crépy, the Maid was riding in company with the King, between the Archbishop of Reims and my Lord the Bastard. Beholding the people hastening to come before the King and crying "Noël!" she exclaimed: "Good people! Never have I seen folk so glad at the coming of the fair King...."[31]

These peasants of Valois and of l'Île de France, who cried "Noël!" on the coming of King Charles, in like manner hailed the Regent and the Duke of Burgundy when they passed. Doubtless they were not so glad as they seemed to Jeanne, and if the little Saint had listened at the doors of their poor homes, this is about what she would have heard: "What shall we do? Let us surrender our all to the devil. It matters not what shall become of us, for, through treason and bad government, we must needs forsake our wives and children and flee into the woods, like wild beasts. And it is not one year or two but fourteen or fifteen since we have been led this unhappy dance. And most of the great nobles of France have died by the sword, or unconfessed have fallen victims to poison or to treachery, or in short have perished by some manner of violent death. Better for us would it have been to serve Saracens than Christians. Whether one lives badly or well it comes to the same thing. Let us do all the evil that lieth in our power. No worse can happen to us than to be slain or taken."[32]

It was only in the neighbourhood of towns or close to fortresses and castles, within sight of the watchman's eye as he looked from the top of tower or belfry, that land was cultivated. On the approach of men-at-arms, the watchman rang his bell or sounded his horn to warn the vine-dressers or the ploughmen to flee to a place of safety. In many districts the alarm bell was so frequent that oxen, sheep, and pigs, of their own accord went into hiding, as soon as they heard it.[33]

In the plains especially, which were easy of access, the Armagnacs and the English had destroyed everything. For some distance from Beauvais, from Senlis, from Soissons, from Laon, they had caused the fields to lie fallow, and here and there shrubs and underwood were springing up over land once cultivated. – "Noël! Noël!"

Throughout the duchy of Valois, the peasants were abandoning the open country and hiding in woods, rocks, and quarries.[34]

Many, in order to gain a livelihood, did like Jean de Bonval, the tailor of Noyant near Soissons, who, despite wife and children, joined a Burgundian band, which went up and down the country thieving, pillaging, and, when occasion offered, smoking out the folk who had taken refuge in churches. On one day Jean and his comrades took two hogsheads of corn, on another six or seven cows; on another a goat and a cow, on another a silver belt, a pair of gloves and a pair of shoes; on another a bale of eighteen ells of cloth to make cloaks withal. And Jean de Bonval said that within his knowledge many a man of worship did as much.[35] – "Noël! Noël!"

The Armagnacs and Burgundians had torn the coats off the peasants' backs and seized even their pots and pans. It was not far from Crépy to Meaux. Every one in that country had heard of the Tree of Vauru.

At one of the gates of the town of Meaux was a great elm, whereon the Bastard of Vauru, a Gascon noble of the Dauphin's party, used to hang the peasants he had taken, when they could not pay their ransom. When he had no executioner at hand he used to hang them himself. With him there lived a kinsman, my Lord Denis de Vauru, who was called his cousin, not that he was so in fact, but just to show that one was no better than the other.[36] In the month of March, in the year 1420, my Lord Denis, on one of his expeditions, came across a peasant tilling the ground. He took him prisoner, held him to ransom, and, tying him to his horse's tail, dragged him back to Meaux, where, by threats and torture, he exacted from him a promise to pay three times as much as he possessed. Dragged half dead from his dungeon, the villein sent to the wife he had married that year to ask her to bring the sum demanded by the lord. She was with child, and near the time of her delivery; notwithstanding, she came because she loved her husband and hoped to soften the heart of the Lord of Vauru. She failed; and Messire Denis told her that if by a certain day he did not receive the ransom, he would hang the man from the elm-tree. The poor woman went away in tears, fondly commending her husband to God's keeping. And her husband wept for pity of her. By a great effort, she succeeded in obtaining the sum demanded, but not by the day appointed. When she returned, her husband had been hanged from the Vauru Tree without respite or mercy. With bitter sobs she asked for him, and then fell exhausted by the side of that road, which, on the point of her delivery, she had traversed on foot. Having regained consciousness, a second time she asked for her husband. She was told that she would not see him till the ransom had been paid.

While she was before the Gascon, there in sight of her were brought forth several craftsmen, held to ransom, who, unable to pay, were straightway despatched to be hanged or drowned. At this spectacle a great fear for her husband came over her; nevertheless, her love for him gave her heart of courage and she paid the ransom. As soon as the Duke's men had counted the coins, they dismissed her saying that her husband had died like the other villeins.

At those cruel words, wild with sorrow and despair, she broke forth into curses and railing. When she refused to be silent, the Bastard of Vauru had her beaten and taken to the Elm-tree.

There she was stripped to the waist and tied to the Tree, whence hung forty to fifty men, some from the higher, some from the lower branches, so that, when the wind blew, their bodies touched her head. At nightfall she uttered shrieks so piercing that they were heard in the town. But whosoever had dared to go and unloose her would have been a dead man. Fright, fatigue, and exertion brought on her delivery. The wolves, attracted by her cries, came and consumed the fruit of her womb, and then devoured alive the body of the wretched creature.

In 1422, the town of Meaux was taken by the Burgundians. Then were the Bastard of Vauru and his cousin hanged from that Tree on which they had caused so many innocent folk to die so shameful a death.[37]

For the poor peasants of these unhappy lands, whether Armagnac or Burgundian, it was all of a piece; they had nothing to gain by changing masters. Nevertheless, it is possible that, on beholding the King, the descendant of Saint Louis and Charles the Wise, they may have taken heart of courage and of hope, so great was the fame for justice and for mercy of the illustrious house of France.

Thus, riding by the side of the Archbishop of Reims, the Maid looked with a friendly eye on the peasants crying "Noël!" After saying that she had nowhere seen folk so joyful at the coming of the fair King, she sighed: "Would to God I were so fortunate as, when I die, to find burial in this land."[38]

Peradventure the Lord Archbishop was curious to know whether from her Voices she had received any revelation concerning her approaching death. She often said that she would not last long. Doubtless he was acquainted with a prophecy widely known at that time, that the maid would die in the Holy Land, after having reconquered with King Charles the sepulchre of our Lord. There were those who attributed this prophecy to the Maid herself; for she had told her Confessor that she would die in battle with the Infidel, and that after her God would send a Maid of Rome who would take her place.[39] And it is obvious that Messire Regnault knew what store to set on such things. At any rate, for that reason or for another, he asked: "Jeanne, in what place look you for to die?"

To which she made answer: "Where it shall please God. For I am sure neither of the time nor of the place, and I know no more thereof than you."

No answer could have been more devout. My Lord the Bastard, who was present at this conversation, many years later thought he remembered that Jeanne had added: "But I would it were now God's pleasure for me to retire, leaving my arms, and to go and serve my father and mother, keeping sheep with my brethren and sister."[40]

If she really spoke thus, it was doubtless because she was haunted by dark forebodings. For some time she had believed herself betrayed.[41] Possibly she suspected the Lord Archbishop of Reims of wishing her ill. But it is hard to believe that he can have thought of getting rid of her now when he had employed her with such signal success; rather his intention was to make further use of her. Nevertheless he did not like her, and she felt it. He never consulted her and never told her what had been decided in council. And she suffered cruelly from the small account made of the revelations she was always receiving so abundantly. May we not interpret as a subtle and delicate reproach the utterance in his presence of this wish, this complaint? Doubtless she longed for her absent mother. And yet she was mistaken when she thought that henceforth she could endure the tranquil life of a village maiden. In her childhood at Domremy she seldom went to tend the flocks in the field; she preferred to occupy herself in household affairs;[42] but if, after having waged war beside the King and the nobles, she had had to return to her country and keep sheep, she would not have stayed there six months. Henceforth it was impossible for her to live save with that knighthood, to whose company she believed God had called her. All her heart was there, and she had finished with the distaff.

During the march on La Ferté and Crépy, King Charles received a challenge from the Regent, then at Montereau with his baronage, calling upon him to fix a meeting at whatsoever place he should appoint.[43] "We, who with all our hearts," said the Duke of Bedford, "desire the end of the war, summon and require you, if you have pity and compassion on the poor folk, who in your cause have so long time been cruelly treated, downtrodden, and oppressed, to appoint a place suitable either in this land of Brie, where we both are, or in l'Île-de-France. There will we meet. And if you have any proposal of peace to make unto us, we will listen to it and as beseemeth a good Catholic prince we will take counsel thereon."[44]

This arrogant and insulting letter had not been penned by the Regent in any desire or hope of peace, but rather, against all reason, to throw on King Charles's shoulders the responsibility for the miseries and suffering the war was causing the commonalty.

Writing to the King crowned in Reims Cathedral, from the beginning he addresses him in this disdainful manner: "You who were accustomed to call yourself Dauphin of Viennois and who now without reason take unto yourself the title of King." He declares that he wants peace and then adds forthwith: "Not a peace hollow, corrupt, feigned, violated, perjured, like that of Montereau, on which, by your fault and your consent, there followed that terrible and detestable murder, committed contrary to all law and honour of knighthood, on the person of our late dear and greatly loved Father, Jean, Duke of Burgundy."[45]

My Lord of Bedford had married one of the daughters of that Duke Jean, who had been treacherously murdered in revenge for the assassination of the Duke of Orléans. But indeed it was not wisely to prepare the way of peace to cast the crime of Montereau in the face of Charles of Valois, who had been dragged there as a child and with whom there had remained ever after a physical trembling and a haunting fear of crossing bridges.[46]

For the moment the Duke of Bedford's most serious grievance against Charles was that he was accompanied by the Maid and Friar

Richard. "You cause the ignorant folk to be seduced and deceived," he said, "for you are supported by superstitious and reprobate persons, such as this woman of ill fame and disorderly life, wearing man's attire and dissolute in manners, and likewise by that apostate and seditious mendicant friar, they both alike being, according to Holy Scripture, abominable in the sight of God."

To strike still greater shame into the heart of the enemy, the Duke of Bedford proceeds to a second attack on the maiden and the monk. And in the most eloquent passage of the letter, when he is citing Charles of Valois to appear before him, he says ironically that he expects to see him come led by this woman of ill fame and this apostate monk.[47]

Thus wrote the Regent of England; albeit he had a mind, subtle, moderate, and graceful, he was moreover a good Catholic and a believer in all manner of devilry and witchcraft.

His horror at the army of Charles of Valois being commanded by a witch and a heretic monk was certainly sincere, and he deemed it wise to publish the scandal. There were doubtless only too many, who, like him, were ready to believe that the Maid of the Armagnacs was a heretic, a worshipper of idols and given to the practice of magic. In the opinion of many worthy and wise Burgundians a prince must forfeit his honour by keeping such company. And if Jeanne were in very deed a witch, what a disgrace! What an abomination! The Flowers de Luce reinstated by the devil! The Dauphin's whole camp was tainted by it. And yet when my Lord of Bedford spread abroad those ideas he was not so adroit as he thought.

Jeanne, as we know, was good-hearted and in energy untiring. By inspiring the men of her party with the idea that she brought them good luck, she gave them courage.[48] Nevertheless King Charles's counsellors knew what she could do for them and avoided consulting her. She herself felt that she would not last long.[49] Then who represented her as a great war leader? Who exalted her as a supernatural power? The enemy.

This letter shows how the English had transformed an innocent child into a being unnatural, terrible, redoubtable, into a spectre of hell causing the bravest to grow pale. In a voice of lamentation the Regent cries: The devil! the witch! And then he marvels that his fighting men tremble before the Maid, and desert rather than face her.[50]

From Montereau, the English army had fallen back on Paris. Now it once again came forth to meet the French. On Saturday, the 13th of August, King Charles held the country between Crépy and Paris. Now the Maid from the heights of Dammartin could espy the summit of Montmartre with its windmills, and the light mists from the Seine veiling that great city of Paris, promised to her by those Voices which alas! she had heeded too well.[51] On the morrow, Sunday, the King and his army encamped in a village, by name Barron, on the River Nonnette on which, five miles lower down, stands Senlis.[52]

Senlis was subject to the English.[53] It was said that the Regent was approaching with a great company of men-at-arms, commanded by the Earl of Suffolk, the Lord Talbot and the Bastard Saint Pol. With him were the crusaders of the Cardinal of Winchester, the late King's uncle, between three thousand five hundred and four thousand men, paid with the Pope's money to go and fight against the Hussites in Bohemia. The Cardinal judged it well to use them against the King of France, a very Christian King forsooth, but one whose hosts were commanded by a witch and an apostate.[54] It was reported that, in the English camp, was a captain with fifteen hundred men-at-arms, clothed in white, bearing a white standard, on which was embroidered a distaff whence was suspended a spindle; and on the streamer of the banner was worked in fine letters of gold: *"Ores, vienne la Belle!"*[55] By these words the men-at-arms wished to proclaim that if they were to meet the Maid of the Armagnacs she would find her work cut out.

Captain Jean de Saintrailles, the Brother of Poton, observed the English first when, marching towards Senlis, they were crossing La Nonnette by a ford so narrow that two horses could barely pass abreast. But King Charles's army, which was coming down the Nonnette valley, did not arrive in time to surprise them.[56] It passed the night opposite them, near Montepilloy.

On the morrow, Monday, the 15th of August, at daybreak, the men-at-arms heard mass in camp and, as far as might be, cleared their consciences; for great plunderers and whoremongers as they were, they had not given up hope of winning Paradise when this life should be over. That day was a solemn feast, when the Church, on the authority of St. Grégoire de Tours, commemorates the physical and spiritual exaltation to heaven of the Virgin Mary. Churchmen taught that it behoves men to keep the feasts of Our Lord and the Holy Virgin, and that to wage battle on days consecrated to them is to sin grievously against the glorious Mother of God. No one in King Charles's camp could maintain a contrary opinion, since all were Christians as they were in the camp of the Regent. And yet, immediately after the *Deo Gratias*, every man took up his post ready for battle.[57]

According to the established rule, the army was in several divisions: the van-guard, the archers, the main body, the rear-guard and the three wings.[58] Further, and according to the same rule, there had been formed a skirmishing company, destined if need were to succour and reinforce the other divisions. It was commanded by Captain La Hire, my Lord the Bastard, and the Sire d'Albret, La Trémouille's half-brother. With this company was the Maid. At the Battle of Patay, despite her entreaties, she had been forced to keep with the rear-guard; now she rode with the bravest and ablest, with those skirmishers or scouts, whose duty it was, says Jean de Bueil,[59] to repulse the scouts of the opposite party and to observe the number and the ordering of the enemy.[60] At length justice was done her; at length she was assigned the place which her skill in horsemanship and her courage in battle merited; and yet she hesitated to follow her comrades. According to the report of a Burgundian knight chronicler, there she was, "swayed to and fro, at one moment wishing to fight, at another not."[61]

Her perplexity is easily comprehensible. The little Saint could not bring herself to decide whether to ride forth to battle on the day of our Lady's Feast or to fold her arms while fighting was going on around her. Her Voices intensified her indecision. They never instructed her what to do save when she knew herself. In the end she went with the men-at-arms, not one of whom appears to have shared her scruples. The two armies were but the space of a culverin shot apart.[62] She, with certain of her company, went right up to the dykes and to the carts, behind which the English were entrenched. Sundry *Godons* and men of Picardy came forth from their camp and fought, some on foot, others on horseback against an equal number of French. On both sides there were wounded, and prisoners were taken. This hand to hand fighting continued the whole day; at sunset the most serious skirmish happened, and so much dust was raised that it was impossible to see anything.[63] On that day there befell what had happened on the 17th of June, between Beaugency and Meung. With the armaments and the customs of warfare of those days, it was very difficult to force an army to come out of its entrenched camp. Generally, if a battle was to be fought, it was necessary for the two sides to be in accord, and, after the pledge of battle had been sent and accepted, for each to level his own half of the field where the engagement was to take place.

At nightfall the skirmishing ceased, and the two armies slept at a crossbow-shot from each other. Then King Charles went off to Crépy, leaving the English free to go and relieve the town of Évreux, which had agreed to surrender on the 27th of August. With this town the Regent made sure of Normandy.[64]

Their loss of the opportunity of conquering Normandy was the price the French had to pay for the royal coronation procession, for that march to Reims, which was at once military, civil and religious. If, after the victory of Patay, they had hastened at once to Rouen, Normandy would have been reconquered and the English cast into the sea; if, from Patay they had pushed on to Paris they would have entered the city without resistance. Yet we must not too hastily condemn that ceremonious promenading of the Lilies through Champagne. By the march to Reims the French party, those Armagnacs reviled for their cruelty and felony, that little King of Bourges compromised in an infamous ambuscade, may have won advantages greater and more solid than the conquest of the county of Maine and the duchy of Normandy and than a victorious assault on the first city of the realm. By retaking his towns of Champagne and of France without bloodshed, King Charles appeared to advantage as a good and pacific lord, as a prince wise and debonair, as the friend of the townsfolk, as the true king of cities. In short, by concluding that campaign of honest and successful negotiations and by the august ceremonial of the coronation, he came forth at once as the lawful and very holy King of France.

An illustrious lady, a descendant of Bolognese nobles and the widow of a knight of Picardy, well versed in the liberal arts, was the author of a number of lays, virelays,[65] and ballads. Christine de Pisan, noble and high-minded, wrote with distinction in prose and verse. Loyal to France and a champion of her sex, there was nothing she more fervently desired than to see the French prosperous and their ladies honoured. In her old age she was cloistered in the Abbey of Poissy, where her daughter was a nun. There, on the 31st of July, 1429, she completed a poem of sixty-one stanzas, each containing eight lines of eight syllables, in praise of the Maid. In halting measures and affected language, these verses expressed the thoughts of the finest, the most cultured and the most pious souls touching the angel of war sent of God to the Dauphin Charles.[66]

In this work she begins by saying that for eleven years she has spent her cloistered life in weeping. And in very truth, this noble-hearted woman wept over the misfortunes of the realm, into which she had been born, wherein she had grown up, where kings and princes had received her and learned poets had done her honour, and the language of which she spoke with the precision of a purist. After eleven years of mourning, the victories of the Dauphin were her first joy.

"At length," she says, "the sun begins to shine once more and the fine days to bloom again. That royal child so long despised and offended, behold him coming, wearing on his head a crown and accoutred with spurs of gold. Let us cry: 'Noël! Charles, the seventh of that great name, King of the French, thou hast recovered thy kingdom, with the help of a Maid.'"

Christine recalls a prophecy concerning a King, Charles, son of Charles, surnamed The Flying Hart,[67] who was to be emperor. Of this prophecy we know nothing save that the escutcheon of King Charles VII was borne by two winged stags and that a letter to an Italian merchant, written in 1429, contains an obscure announcement of the coronation of the Dauphin at Rome.[68]

"I pray God," continued Christine, "that thou mayest be that one, that God will grant thee life to see thy children grow up, that through thee and through them, France may have joy, that serving God, thou wage not war to the utterance. My hope is that thou shalt be good, upright, a friend of justice, greater than any other, that pride sully not thy prowess, that thou be gentle, favourable to thy people and fearing God who hath chosen thee to serve him.

"And thou, Maid most happy, most honoured of God, thou hast loosened the cord with which France was bound. Canst thou be praised enough, thou who hast brought peace to this land laid low by war?

"Jeanne, born in a propitious hour, blessed be thy creator! Maid, sent of God, in whom the Holy Ghost shed abroad a ray of his grace, who hast from him received and dost keep gifts in abundance; never did he refuse thy request. Who can ever be thankful enough unto thee?"

The Maid, saviour of the realm, Dame Christine compares to Moses who delivered Israel out of the Land of Egypt.

"That a Maid should proffer her breast, whence France may suck the sweet milk of peace, behold a matter which is above nature!

"Joshua was a mighty conqueror. What is there strange in that, since he was a strong man? But now behold, a woman, a shepherdess doth appear, of greater worship than any man. But with God all things are easy.

"By Esther, Judith and Deborah, women of high esteem, he delivered his oppressed people. And well I know there have been women of great worship. But Jeanne is above all. Through her God hath worked many miracles.

"By a miracle was she sent; the angel of the Lord led her to the King."

"Before she could be believed, to clerks and to scholars was she taken and thoroughly examined. She said she was come from God, and history proved her saying to be true, for Merlin, the Sibyl and Bede had seen her in the spirit. In their books they point to her as the saviour of France, and in their prophecies they let wit of her, saying: 'In the French wars she shall bear the banner.' And indeed they relate all the manner of her history."

We are not astonished that Dame Christine should have been acquainted with the Sibylline poems; for it is known that she was well versed in the writings of the ancients. But we perceive that the obviously mutilated prophecy of Merlin the Magician and the apocryphal chronogram of the Venerable Bede had come under her notice. The predictions and verses of the Armagnac ecclesiastics were spread abroad everywhere with amazing rapidity.[69]

Dame Christine's views concerning the Maid accord with those of the doctors of the French party; and the poem she wrote in her convent in many passages bears resemblance to the treatise of the Archbishop of Embrun.

There it is said:

"The goodness of her life proves that Jeanne possesses the grace of God.

"It was made manifest, when at the siege of Orléans her might revealed itself. Never was miracle plainer. God did so succour his own people, that the strength of the enemy was but as that of a dead dog. They were taken or slain.

"Honour to the feminine sex, God loves it. A damsel of sixteen, who is not weighed down by armour and weapons, even though she be bred to endure hardness, is not that a matter beyond nature? The enemy flees before her. Many eyes behold it.

"She goeth forth capturing towns and castles. She is the first captain of our host. Such power had not Hector or Achilles. But God, who leads her, does all.

"And you, ye men-at-arms, who suffer durance vile and risk your lives for the right, be ye faithful: in heaven shall ye have reward and glory, for whosoever fighteth for the just cause, winneth Paradise.

"Know ye that by her the English shall be cast down, for it is the will of God, who inclineth his ear to the voice of the good folk, whom they desired to overthrow. The blood of the slain crieth against them."

In the shadow of her convent Dame Christine shares the hope common to every noble soul; from the Maid she expects all the good things she longs for. She believes that Jeanne will restore concord to the Christian Church. The gentlest spirits of those days looked to fire and sword for the bringing in of unity and obedience; they never dreamed that Christian charity could mean charity towards the whole human race. Wherefore, on the strength of prophecy, the poetess expects the Maid to destroy the infidel and the heretic, or in other words the Turk and the Hussite.

"In her conquest of the Holy Land, she will tear up the Saracens like weeds. Thither will she lead King Charles, whom God defend! Before he dies he shall make that journey. He it is who shall conquer the land. There shall she end her life. There shall the thing come to pass."

The good Christine would appear to have brought her poem to this conclusion when she received tidings of the King's coronation. She then added thirteen stanzas to celebrate the mystery of Reims and to foretell the taking of Paris.[70]

Thus in the gloom and silence of one of those convents where even the hushed noises of the world penetrated but seldom, this virtuous lady collected and expressed in rhyme all those dreams of church and state which centred round a child.

In a fairly good ballad written at the time of the coronation, in love and honour "of the beautiful garden of the noble flowers de luce,"[71] and for the elevation of the white cross, King Charles VII is described by that mysterious name "the noble stag," which we have first discovered in Christine's poem. The unknown author of the ballad says that the Sibyl, daughter of King Priam, prophesied the misfortunes of this royal stag; but such a prediction need not surprise us, when we remember that Charles of Valois was of Priam's royal line, wherefore Cassandra, when she revealed the destiny of the Flying Hart, did but prolong down the centuries the vicissitudes of her own family.[72]

Rhymers on the French side celebrated the unexpected victories of Charles and the Maid as best they knew how, in a commonplace fashion, by some stiff poem but scantily clothing a thin and meagre muse.

Nevertheless there is a ballad,[73] by a Dauphinois poet, beginning with this line; "Back, English *coués*, back!"[74] which is powerful through the genuine religious spirit which prevails throughout. The author, some poor ecclesiastic, points piously to the English banner cast down, "by the will of King Jesus and of Jeanne the sweet Maid."[75]

The Maid had derived her influence over the common folk from the prophecies of Merlin the Magician and the Venerable Bede.[76] As Jeanne's deeds became known, predictions foretelling them came to be discovered. For example it was found that Engélide, daughter of an old King of Hungary,[77] had known long before of the coronation at Reims. Indeed to this royal virgin was attributed a prophecy recorded in Latin, of which the following is a literal translation:

"O Lily illustrious, watered by princes, by the sower planted in the open, in an orchard delectable, by flowers and sweet-smelling roses surrounded. But, alas! dismay of the Lily, terror of the orchard! Sundry beasts, some coming from without, others nourished within the orchard, hurtling horns against horns, have well nigh crushed the Lily, which fades for lack of water. Long do they trample upon it, destroying nearly all its roots and assaying to wither it with their poisoned breath.

"But the beasts shall be driven forth in shame from the orchard, by a virgin coming from the land whence flows the cruel venom. Behind her right ear the Virgin bears a little scarlet sign; she speaks softly, and her neck is short. To the Lily shall she give fountains of living water, and shall drive out the serpent, to all men revealing its venom. With a laurel wreath woven by no mortal hand shall she at Reims engarland happily the gardener of the Lily, named Charles, son of Charles. All around the turbulent neighbours shall submit, the waters shall surge, the folk shall cry: 'Long live the Lily! Away with the beast! Let the orchard flower!' He shall approach the fields of the Island, adding fleet to fleet, and there a multitude of beasts shall perish in the rout. Peace for many shall be established. The keys of a great number shall recognise the hand that had forged them. The citizens of a noble city shall be punished for perjury by defeat, groaning with many groans, and at the entrance [of Charles?] high walls shall fall low. Then the orchard of the Lily shall be ... (?) and long shall it flower."[78]

This prophecy attributed to the unknown daughter of a distant king would seem to us to proceed from a French ecclesiastic and an Armagnac. French royalty is portrayed in the figure of the delectable orchard, around which contend beasts nourished in the orchard as well as foreign beasts, that is Burgundians and English. King Charles of Valois is mentioned by his own name and that of his father, and the name of the coronation town occurs in full.

The reduction of certain towns by their liege lord is stated most clearly. Doubtless the prediction was made at the very time of the coronation. It explicitly mentions deeds already accomplished and dimly hints at events looked for, fulfilment of which was delayed, or happened in a manner other than what was expected, or never happened at all, such as the taking of Paris after a terrible assault, the invasion of England by the French, the conclusion of peace.

It is highly probable that when announcing that the deliverer of the orchard might be recognised by her short neck, her sweet voice and a little scarlet mark, the pseudo Engélide was carefully depicting characteristics noticeable in Jeanne herself. Moreover we know that Isabelle Romée's daughter had a sweet woman's voice.[79] That her neck was broad and firmly set on her shoulders accords with what is known concerning her robust appearance.[80] And doubtless the so-called daughter of the King of Hungary did not imagine the birth-mark behind her right ear.[81]

CHAPTER II

THE MAID'S FIRST VISIT TO COMPIÈGNE – THE
THREE POPES – SAINT DENYS – TRUCES

AFTER the English army had departed for Normandy, King Charles sent from Crépy to Senlis the Count of Vendôme, the Maréchal de Rais and the Maréchal de Boussac with their men-at-arms. The inhabitants gave them to wit that they inclined to favour the Flowers de Luce.[82] Henceforth the submission of Compiègne was sure. The King summoned the citizens to receive him; on Wednesday the 18th, the keys of the town were brought to him; on the next day he entered.[83] The Attorneys[84] (for by that name the aldermen of the town were called) presented to him Messire Guillaume de Flavy, whom they had elected governor of their town, as being their most experienced and most faithful citizen. On his being presented they asked the King, according to their privilege, to confirm and ratify his appointment. But the sire de la Trémouille took for himself the governorship of Compiègne and appointed as his lieutenant Messire Guillaume de Flavy, whom, notwithstanding, the inhabitants regarded as their captain.[85]

One by one, the King was recovering his good towns. He charged the folk of Beauvais to acknowledge him as their lord. When they saw the flowers-de-luce borne by the heralds, the citizens cried: "Long live Charles of France!" The clergy chanted a *Te Deum* and there was great rejoicing. Those who refused fealty to King Charles were put out of the town with permission to take away their possessions.[86] The Bishop and Vidame of Beauvais, Messire Pierre Cauchon, who was Grand Almoner of France to King Henry, and a negotiator of important ecclesiastical business, grieved to see his city returning to the French;[87] it was to the city's hurt, but he could not help it. He failed not to realise that part of this disgrace he owed to the Maid of the Armagnacs, who was influential with her party and had the reputation of being all powerful. As he was a good theologian he must have suspected that the devil was leading her and he wished her all possible harm.

At this time Artois, Picardy, all the Burgundian territory in the north, was slipping away from Burgundy. Had King Charles gone there the majority of the dwellers in the strong towers and castles of Picardy would have received him as their sovereign.[88] But meanwhile his enemies would have recaptured what he had just won in Valois and the Île de France.

Having entered Compiègne with the King, Jeanne lodged at the Hôtel du Bœuf, the house of the King's proctor. She slept with the proctor's wife, Marie Le Boucher, who was a kinswoman of Jacques Boucher, Treasurer of Orléans.[89]

She longed to march on Paris, which she was sure of taking since her Voices had promised it to her. It is related that at the end of two or three days she grew impatient, and, calling the Duke of Alençon, said to him: "My fair Duke, command your men and likewise those of the other captains to equip themselves," then she is said to have cried: "By my staff! I must to Paris."[90] But this could not have happened: the Maid never gave orders to the men-at-arms. The truth of the matter is that the Duke of Alençon, with a goodly company of fighting men, took his leave of the King and that Jeanne was to accompany him. She was ready to mount her horse when on Monday the 22nd of August, a messenger from the Count of Armagnac brought her a letter which she caused to be read to her.[91] The following are the contents of the missive:

"My very dear Lady, I commend myself humbly to you, and I entreat you, for God's sake, that seeing the divisions which are at present in the holy Church Universal, concerning the question of the popes (for there are three contending for the papacy: one dwells at Rome and calls himself Martin V, whom all Christian kings obey: the other dwells at Peñiscola, in the kingdom of Valentia, and calls himself Clement VIII; the third dwells no man knows where, unless it be the Cardinal de Saint-Estienne and a few folk with him, and calls himself Pope Benedict XIV; the first, who is called Pope Martin, was elected at Constance by consent of all Christian nations; he who is called Clement was elected at Peñiscola, after the death of Pope

Benedict XIII, by three of his cardinals; the third who is called Pope Benedict XIV was elected secretly at Peñiscola, by that same Cardinal Saint-Estienne himself): I pray you beseech Our Lord Jesus Christ that in his infinite mercy, he declare unto us through you, which of the three aforesaid is the true pope and whom it shall be his pleasure that henceforth we obey, him who is called Martin, or him who is called Clement or him who is called Benedict; and in whom we should believe, either in secret or under reservation or by public pronouncement: for we shall all be ready to work the will and the pleasure of Our Lord Jesus Christ.

Yours in all things,

Count d'Armagnac."[92]

He who wrote thus, calling Jeanne his very dear lady, recommending himself humbly to her, not in self-abasement, but merely, as we should say to-day, out of courtesy, was one of the greater vassals of the crown.

She had never seen this baron, and doubtless she had never heard of him. Jean IV, son of that Constable of France who had been killed in 1418, was the cruellest man in the kingdom. At that time he was between thirty-three and thirty-four years of age. He held both Armagnacs, the Black and the White, the country of the Four Valleys, the counties of Pardiac, of Fesenzac, Astarac, La Lomagne, and l'Île-Jourdain. After the Count of Foix he was the most powerful noble of Gascony.[93]

While his name was among those of the adherents of the King and while it was used to designate those who were hostile to the English and Burgundians, Jean IV himself was neither French nor English, but simply Gascon. He called himself count by the grace of God, but he was ever ready to acknowledge himself the King's vassal when it was a question of receiving gifts from that suzerain, who might not always be able to afford himself new gaiters, but who must perforce spend large sums on his great vassals. Meanwhile Jean IV showed consideration to the English, protected an adventurer in the Regent's pay, and gave appointments in his household to men wearing the red cross. He was as violent and treacherous as any of his retainers. Having unlawfully seized the Marshal de Séverac, he exacted from him the cession of all his goods and then had him strangled.[94]

This murder was quite recent. And now we have the docile son of Holy Church appearing eager to discover who is his true spiritual father. It would seem, however, that his mind was already made up on the subject and that he already knew the answer to his question. In verity the long schism, which had rent Christendom asunder, had terminated twelve years earlier. It had ended when the Conclave, which had assembled at Constance in the House of the Merchants on the 8th of November, 1417, on the 11th of that month, Saint Martin's Day, proclaimed Pope, the Cardinal Deacon Otto Colonna, who assumed the title of Martin V. In the Eternal City Martin V wore that tiara which Lorenzo Ghiberti had adorned with eight figures in gold;[95] and the wily Roman had contrived to obtain his recognition by England and even by France, who thenceforward renounced all hope of a French pontiff. While Charles VII's advisers may not have agreed with Martin V on the question of a General Council, all the rights of the Pope of Rome in the Kingdom of France had been restored to him by an edict, in 1425. Martin V was the one and only pope. Nevertheless, Alphonso of Aragon, highly incensed because Martin V supported against him the rights of Louis d'Anjou to the Kingdom of Naples, determined to oppose to the Pope of Rome a pontiff of his own making. And just ready to hand he had a canon who called himself pope, and on the following grounds: the Anti-pope, Benedict XIII, having fled to Peñiscola, had on his death-bed nominated four cardinals, three of whom appointed to succeed him a canon of Barcelona, one Gil Muñoz, who assumed the title of Clement VIII. Imprisoned in the château of Peñiscola on a barren neck of land on three sides washed by the sea, this was the Clement whom the King of Aragon had chosen to be the rival of Martin V.[96]

The Pope excommunicated the King of Aragon and then opened negotiations with him. The Count of Armagnac joined the King's party. For the baptism of his children the Count had holy water blessed by Benedict XIII brought from Peñiscola. He likewise was excommunicated. The blow had fallen upon him in this very year, 1429. Thus for some months he had been deprived of the sacraments and excluded from public worship. Hence arose all manner of secular difficulties, in addition to which he was probably afraid of the devil.

Moreover his position was becoming impossible. His powerful ally, King Alfonso, gave in, and himself called upon Clement VIII to resign. When he addressed his inquiry to the Maid of France, the Armagnac was evidently meditating the withdrawal of his allegiance from an unfortunate anti-pope, who was himself renouncing or about to renounce the tiara; for Clement VIII abdicated at Peñiscola on the

26th of July. The dictation of the Count's letter cannot have occurred long before that date and may have been after. At any rate whenever he dictated it he must have been aware of the position of the Sovereign Pontiff Clement VIII.

As for the third Pope mentioned in his missive, Benedict XIV, he had no tidings of him, and indeed he was keeping very quiet. His election to the Holy See had been singular in that it had been made by one cardinal alone. Benedict XIV's right to the papacy had been communicated to him by a cardinal created by the Anti-pope, Benedict XIII, at the time of his promotion in 1409. That Cardinal was Jean Barrère, a Frenchman, Bachelor of laws, priest and Cardinal of Saint-Étienne *in Cœlio monte*. It was not to Benedict XIV that the Armagnac was thinking of giving his allegiance; obviously he was eager to submit to Martin V.

It is not easy therefore to discover why he should have asked Jeanne to indicate the true pope. Doubtless it was customary in those days to consult on all manner of questions those holy maids to whom God vouchsafed illumination. Such an one the Maid appeared, and her fame as a prophetess had been spread abroad in a very short time. She revealed hidden things, she drew the curtain from the future. We are reminded of that *capitoul*[97] of Toulouse, who about three weeks after the deliverance of Orléans, advised her being consulted as to a remedy for the corruption of the coinage. Bona of Milan, married to a poor gentleman in the train of her cousin, Queen Ysabeau, besought the Maid's help in her endeavour to regain the duchy which she claimed through her descent from the Visconti.[98] It was just as appropriate to question the Maid concerning the Pope and the Anti-pope. But the most difficult point in this question is to discover what were the Count of Armagnac's reasons for consulting the Holy Maid on a matter concerning which he appears to have been sufficiently informed. The following seems the most probable.

Jean IV was prepared to recognise Martin V as Pope; but he desired his submission to appear honourable and reasonable. Wherefore he conceived the idea of ascribing his conduct to the command of Jesus Christ, speaking through the Holy Maid. But it was necessary for the command to be in accordance with his wishes. The letter provides for that. He is careful to indicate to Jeanne, and consequently to God, what reply would be suitable. He lays stress on the fact that Martin V, who had recently excommunicated him, was elected at Constance by the consent of all Christian nations, that he dwells at Rome and that he is obeyed by all Christian kings. He points out on the other hand the circumstances which invalidate the election of Clement VIII by only three cardinals, and the still more ridiculous election of that Benedict, who was chosen by a conclave consisting of only one cardinal.[99]

After such a setting forth could there possibly remain a single doubt as to whether Pope Martin was the true pope? But such guile was lost on Jeanne; it escaped her entirely. The Count of Armagnac's letter, which she had read to her as she was mounting her horse, must have struck her as very obscure.[100] The names of Benedict, of Clement and of Martin she had never heard. The Saints, Catherine and Margaret, with whom she was constantly holding converse, revealed to her nothing concerning the Pope. They spoke to her of nought save of the realm of France; and Jeanne's prudence generally led her to confine her prophecies to the subject of the war. This circumstance was pointed out by a German clerk as a matter extraordinary and worthy of note.[101] But for this once she consented to reply to Jean IV, in order to maintain her reputation as a prophet and because the title of Armagnac strongly appealed to her. She told him that at that moment she was unable to instruct him concerning the true pope, but that later she would inform him in which of the three he must believe, according as God should reveal it unto her. In short, she in a measure followed the example of such soothsayers as postpone the announcement of the oracle to a future day.

Jhesus † Maria

Count of Armagnac, my good friend and beloved, Jehanne the Maid lets you to wit that your message hath come before me, the which hath told me that you have sent from where you are to know from me in which of the three popes, whom you mention in your memorial, you ought to believe. This thing in sooth I cannot tell you truly for the present, until I be in Paris or at rest elsewhere, because for the present I am too much hindered by affairs of war; but when you hear that I am in Paris send a message to me, and I will give you to understand what you shall rightfully believe, and what I shall know by the counsel of my Righteous and Sovereign Lord, the King of all the world, and what you should do, as far as I may. To God I commend you; God keep you. Written at Compiengne, the 22nd day of August.[102]

Jeanne before she made this reply can have consulted neither the good Brother Pasquerel nor the good Friar Richard nor indeed any of the churchmen of her company. They would have told her that the true pope was the Pope of Rome, Martin V. They might also have represented to her that she was belittling the authority of the Church by appealing to a revelation from God concerning popes and anti-popes. Sometimes, they would have told her, God confides the secrets of his Church to holy persons. But it would be rash to count upon so rare a privilege.

Jeanne exchanged a few words with the messenger who had brought her the missive; but the interview was brief. The messenger was not safe in the town, not that the soldiers would have made him pay for his master's crimes and treasons; but the Sire de la Trémouille was at Compiègne; and he knew that Count Jean, who for the nonce was in alliance with the Constable De Richemont, was meditating something against him. La Trémouille was not so malevolent as the Count of Armagnac: and yet the poor messenger only narrowly escaped being thrown into the Oise.[103]

On the morrow, Tuesday the 23rd of August, the Maid and the Duke of Alençon took leave of the King and set out from Compiègne with a goodly company of fighting men. Before marching on Saint-Denys in France, they went to Senlis to collect a company of men-at-arms whom the King had sent there.[104] As was her custom, the Maid rode surrounded by monks. Friar Richard, who predicted the approaching end of the world, had joined the procession. It would seem that he had superseded the others, even Brother Pasquerel, the chaplain. It was to him that the Maid confessed beneath the walls of Senlis. In that same spot, with the Dukes of Clermont and Alençon,[105] she took the communion on two consecutive days. She must have been in the hands of monks who were in the habit of making a very frequent use of the Eucharist.

The Lord Bishop of Senlis was Jean Fouquerel. Hitherto, he had been on the side of the English and entirely devoted to the Lord Bishop of Beauvais. On the approach of the royal army, Jean Fouquerel, who was a cautious person, had gone off to Paris to hide a large sum of money. He was careful of his possessions. Some one in the army took his nag and gave it to the Maid. By means of a draft on the receiver of taxes and the *gabelle* officer of the town, two hundred golden *saluts*[106] were paid for it. The Lord Bishop did not approve of this transaction and demanded his hackney. Hearing of his displeasure, the Maid caused a letter to be written to him, saying that he might have back his nag if he liked; she did not want it for she found it not sufficiently hardy for men-at-arms. The horse was sent to the Sire de La Trémouille with a request that he would deliver it to the Lord Bishop, who never received it.[107]

As for the bill on the tax receiver and *gabelle* officer, it may have been worthless; and probably the Reverend Father in God, Jean Fouquerel, never had either horse or money. Jeanne was not at fault, and yet the Lord Bishop of Beauvais and the clerks of the university were shortly to bring home to her the gravity of the sacrilege of laying hands on an ecclesiastical hackney.[108]

To the north of Paris, about five miles distant from the great city, there rose the towers of Saint-Denys. On the 26th of August, the army of the Duke of Alençon arrived there, and entered without resistance, albeit the town was strongly fortified.[109] The place was famous for its illustrious abbey very rich and very ancient. The following is the story of its foundation.

Dagobert, King of the French, had from childhood been a devout worshipper of Saint Denys. And whenever he trembled before the ire of King Clotaire his father, he would take refuge in the church of the holy martyr. When he died, a pious man dreamed that he saw Dagobert summoned before the tribunal of God; a great number of saints accused him of having despoiled their churches; and the demons were about to drag him into hell when Saint Denys appeared; and by his intercession, the soul of the King was delivered and escaped punishment. The story was held to be true, and it was thought that the King's soul returned to animate his body and that he did penance.[110]

When the Maid with the army occupied Saint-Denys, the three porches, the embattled parapets, the tower of the Abbey Church, erected by the Abbot Suger, were already three centuries old. There were buried the kings of France; and thither they came to take the *oriflamme*. Fourteen years earlier the late King Charles had fetched it forth, but since then none had borne it.[111]

Many were the wonders told touching this royal standard. And with some of those marvels the Maid must needs have been acquainted, since on her coming into France, she was said to have given the Dauphin Charles the surname of *oriflamme*,[112] as a pledge and promise of victory.[113] At Saint-Denys was preserved the heart of the Constable Du Guesclin.[114] Jeanne had heard of his high renown; she had proffered wine to Madame de Laval's eldest son; and to his grandmother, who had been Sire Bertrand's second wife, she had sent a little ring of gold, out of respect for the widow of so valiant a man,[115] asking her to forgive the poverty of the gift.

The monks of Saint-Denys preserved precious relics, notably a piece of the wood of the true cross, the linen in which the Child Jesus had been wrapped, a fragment of the pitcher wherein the water had been changed to wine at the Cana marriage feast, a bar of Saint Lawrence's gridiron, the chin of Saint Mary Magdalen, a cup of tamarisk wood used by Saint Louis as a charm against the spleen. There likewise was to be seen the head of Saint Denys. True, at the same time one was being shown in the Cathedral church of Paris. The Chancellor, Jean Gerson, treating of Jeanne the Maid, a few days before his death, wrote that of her it might be said as of the head of Saint Denys, that belief in her was a matter of edification and not of faith, albeit in both places alike the head ought to be worshipped in order that edification should not be turned into scandal.[116]

In this abbey everything proclaimed the dignity, the prerogatives and the high worship of the house of France. Jeanne must joyously have wondered at the insignia, the symbols and signs of the royalty of the Lilies gathered together in this spot,[117] if indeed those eyes, occupied with celestial visions, had leisure to perceive the things of earth, and if her Voices, endlessly whispering in her ear, left her one moment's respite.

Saint Denys was a great saint, since there was no doubt of his being in very deed the Areopagite himself.[118] But since he had permitted his abbey to be taken he was no longer invoked as the patron saint of the Kings of France. The Dauphin's followers had replaced him by the Blessed Archangel Michael, whose abbey, near the city of Avranches, had victoriously held out against the English. It was Saint Michael not Saint Denys who had appeared to Jeanne in the garden at Domremy; but she knew that Saint Denys was the war cry of France.[119]

The monks of that rich abbey wasted by war lived there in poverty and in disorder.[120] Armagnacs and Burgundians in turn descended upon the neighbouring fields and villages, plundering and ravaging, leaving nought that it was possible to carry off. At Saint-Denys was held the Fair of Le Lendit, one of the greatest in Christendom. But now Merchants had ceased to attend it. At the Lendit of 1418, there were but three booths, and those for the selling of shoes from Brabant, in the high street of Saint-Denys, near the Convent of Les Filles-Dieu. Since 1426, there had been no fair at all.[121]

At the tidings that the Armagnacs were approaching Troyes, the peasants had cut their corn before it was ripe and brought it into Paris. On entering Saint-Denys, the Duke of Alençon's men-at-arms found the town deserted. The chief burgesses had taken refuge in Paris.[122] Only a few of the poorer families were left. The Maid held two newly born infants over the baptismal font.[123]

Hearing of these Saint-Denys baptisms, her enemies accused her of having lit candles and held them inclined over the infant's heads, in order that she might read their destinies in the melted wax. It was not the first time, it appeared, that she indulged in such practices. When she entered a town, little children were said to offer her candles kneeling, and she received them as an agreeable sacrifice. Then upon the heads of these innocents she would let fall three drops of burning wax, proclaiming that by virtue of this ceremony they could not fail to be good. In such acts Burgundian ecclesiastics discerned idolatry and witchcraft, in which was likewise involved heresy.[124]

Here again, at Saint-Denys, she distributed banners to the men-at-arms. Churchmen on the English side strongly suspected her of charming those banners. And as everyone in those days believed in magic, such a suspicion was not without its danger.[125]

The Maid and the Duke of Alençon lost no time. Immediately after their arrival at Saint-Denys they went forth to skirmish before the gates of Paris. Two or three times a day they engaged in this desultory warfare, notably by the wind-mill at the Saint-Denys Gate and in the village of La Chapelle. "Every day there was booty taken," says Messire Jean de Bueil.[126] It seems hardly credible that in a country which had been plundered and ravaged over and over again, there should have been anything left to be taken; and yet the statement is made and attested by one of the nobles in the army.

Out of respect for the seventh commandment, the Maid forbade the men of her company to commit any theft whatsoever. And she always refused victuals offered her when she knew they had been stolen. In reality she, like the others, lived on pillage, but she did not know it. One day when a Scotsman gave her to wit that she had just partaken of some stolen veal, she flew into a fury and would have beaten him: saintly women are subject to such fits of passion.[127]

Jeanne is said to have observed the walls of Paris carefully, seeking the spot most favourable for attack.[128] The truth is that in this matter as in all others she depended on her Voices. For the rest she was far superior to all the men-at-arms in courage and in good will. From Saint-Denys she sent the King message after message, urging him to come and take Paris.[129] But at Compiègne the King and his Council were negotiating with the ambassadors of the Duke of Burgundy, to wit: Jean de Luxembourg, Lord of Beaurevoir, Hugues de Cayeux, Bishop of Arras, David de Brimeu and my Lord of Charny.[130]

The fifteen days' truce had expired. Our only information concerning it is contained in Jeanne's letter to the citizens of Reims. According to Jeanne, the Duke of Burgundy had undertaken to surrender the city to the King of France on the fifteenth day.[131] If he had so agreed it was on conditions of which we know nothing; we are not therefore in a position to say whether or no those conditions had been carried out. The Maid placed no trust in this promise, and she was quite right; but she did not know everything; and on the very day when she was complaining of the truce to the citizens of Reims, Duke Philip was receiving the command of Paris at the hands of the Regent, and was henceforth in a position to dispose of the city as he liked.[132] Duke Philip could not bear the sight of Charles of Valois, who had been present at the murder on the Bridge of Montereau, but he detested the English and wished they would go to the devil or return to their island. The vineyards and the cloth looms of his dominions were too numerous and too important for him not to wish for peace. He had no desire to be King of France; therefore he could be treated with, despite his avarice and dissimulation. Nevertheless the fifteenth day had gone by and the city of Paris remained in the hands of the English and the Burgundians, who were not friends but allies.

On the 28th of August a truce was concluded. It was to last till Christmas and was to extend over the whole country north of the Seine, from Nogent to Harfleur, with the exception of such towns as were situated where there was a passage over the river. Concerning the city of Paris it was expressly stated that "Our Cousin of Burgundy, he and his men, may engage in the defence of the town and in resisting such as shall make war upon it or do it hurt."[133] The Chancellor

Regnault de Chartres, the Sire de la Trémouille, Christophe d'Harcourt, the Bastard of Orléans, the Bishop of Séez, and likewise certain young nobles very eager for war, such as the Counts of Clermont and of Vendôme and the Duke of Bar, in short all the Counsellors of the King and the Princes of the Blood who signed this article, were apparently giving the enemy a weapon against them and renouncing any attempt upon Paris. But they were not all fools; the Bastard of Orléans was keen witted and the Lord Archbishop of Reims was anything but an Olibrius.[134] They doubtless knew what they were about when they recognised the Duke of Burgundy's rights over Paris. Duke Philip, as we know, had been governor of the great town since the 13th of August. The Regent had ceded it with the idea that Burgundy would keep the Parisians in order better than England, for the English were few in number and were disliked as foreigners. What did it profit King Charles to recognise his cousin's rights over Paris? We fail to see precisely; but after all this truce was no better and no worse than others. In sooth it did not give Paris to the King, but neither did it prevent the King from taking it. Did truces ever hinder Armagnacs and Burgundians from fighting when they had a mind to fight? Was one of those frequent truces ever kept?[135] After having signed this one, the King advanced to Senlis. The Duke of Alençon came to him there twice. Charles reached Saint-Denys on Wednesday the 7th of September.[136]

CHAPTER III

THE ATTACK ON PARIS

I N the days when King John was a prisoner in the hands of the English, the townsfolk of Paris, beholding the enemy in the heart of the land, feared lest their city should be besieged. In all haste therefore they proceeded to put it in a state of defence; they surrounded it with trenches and counter trenches. On the side of the University the suburbs were left defenceless; small and remote, they were burned down. But on the right bank the more extensive suburbs well nigh touched the city. One part of them was enclosed by the trenches. When peace was concluded, Charles, Regent of the Realm, undertook to surround the town on the north with an embattled wall, flanked with square towers, with terraces and parapets, with a road round and steps leading up to the ramparts.

In certain places the trench was single, in others double. The work was superintended by Hugues Aubriot, Provost of Paris, to whom was entrusted also the building of the Saint-Antoine bastion, completed under King Charles VI.[137] This new fortification began on the east, near the river, on the rising ground of Les Célestins. Within its circle it enclosed the district of Saint Paul, the Culture Sainte-Catherine, the Temple, Saint-Martin, Les Filles-Dieu, Saint Sauveur, Saint Honoré, Les Quinze Vingts, which hitherto had been in the suburbs and undefended; and it reached the river below the Louvre, which was thus united to the town. There were six gates in the circumvallation, to wit: beginning on the east, the Baudet Gate or Saint-Antoine Gate, the Saint-Avoye or Temple Gate, the Gate of the Painters or of Saint-Denis, the Saint-Martin or Montmartre Gate, the Saint-Honoré Gate and the Gate of the Seine.[138]

The Parisians did not like the English and were sorely grieved by their occupation of the city. The folk murmured when, after the funeral of the late King, Charles VI, the Duke of Bedford had the sword of the King of France borne before him.[139] But what cannot be helped must be endured. The Parisians may have disliked the English; they admired Duke Philip, a prince of comely countenance and the richest potentate of Christendom. As for the little King of Bourges, mean-looking and sad-faced, strongly suspected of treason at Montereau, there was nothing pleasing in him; he was despised and his followers were regarded with fear and horror. For ten years they had been ranging round the town, pillaging, taking prisoners and holding them to ransom. The English and Burgundians indeed did likewise. When, in the August of 1423, Duke Philip came to Paris, his men ravaged all the neighbouring fields, albeit they belonged to friends and allies. But they were only passing through,[140] while the Armagnacs were for ever raiding, eternally stealing all they could lay hands on, setting fire to barns and churches, killing women and children, ravishing maids and nuns, hanging men by the thumbs. In 1420, like devils let loose, they descended upon the village of Champigny and burned at once oats, wheat, sheep, cows, oxen, women and children. Likewise did they and worse still at Croissy.[141] One ecclesiastic said they had caused more Christians to suffer martyrdom than Maximian and Diocletian.[142]

And yet, in the year 1429, there might have been discovered in the city of Paris not a few followers of the Dauphin. Christine de Pisan, who was very loyal to the House of Valois, said: "In Paris there are many wicked. Good are there also and faithful to their King. But they dare not lift up their voices."[143]

It was common knowledge that in the Parlement and even in the Chapter of Notre-Dame were to be found those who had dealings with the Armagnacs.[144]

On the morrow of their victory at Patay, those terrible Armagnacs had only to march straight on the town to take it. They were expected to enter it one day or the other. In the mind of the Regent it was as if they had already taken it. He went off and shut himself in the Castle of Vincennes with the few men who remained to him.[145] Three days after the discomfiture of the English there was a panic in the town. "The Armagnacs are coming to-night," they said. Meanwhile the Armagnacs were at Orléans awaiting orders to assemble at Gien and to march on Auxerre. At these tidings the Duke of Bedford must have sighed a deep sigh of relief; and straightway he set to work to provide for the defence of Paris and the safety of Normandy.[146]

When the panic was past, the heart of the great town returned to its allegiance, not to the English cause – it had never been English – but to the Burgundian. Its Provost, Messire Simon Morhier, who had made great slaughter of the French at the Battle of the Herrings, remained loyal to the Leopard.[147] The aldermen on the contrary were suspected of inclining a favourable ear to King Charles's proposals. On the 12th of July, the Parisians elected a new town council composed of the most zealous Burgundians they could find in commerce and on change. To be provost of the merchants they appointed the treasurer, Guillaume Sanguin, to whom the Duke of Burgundy owed more then seven thousand *livres tournois*[148] and who had the Regent's jewels in his keeping.[149] Such an alteration was greatly to the detriment of King Charles, who preferred to win back his good towns by peaceful means rather than by force, and who relied more on negotiations with the citizens than on cannon balls and stones.

Just in the nick of time the Regent surrendered the town to Duke Philip, not, we may be sure, without many regrets for having recently refused him Orléans. He realised that thus, by returning to its French allegiance, the chief city of the realm would make a more energetic defence against the Dauphin's men. The Parisians' old liking for the magnificent Duke would revive, and so would their old hatred of the disinherited son of Madame Ysabeau. In the Palais de Justice the Duke read the story of his father's death, punctuated with complaints of Armagnac treason and violated treaties; he caused the blood of Montereau[150] to cry to heaven; those who were present swore to be right loyal to him and to the Regent. On the following days the same oath was taken by the regular and secular clergy.[151]

But the citizens were strengthened in their resistance more by their remembrance of Armagnac cruelty than by their affection for the fair Duke. A rumour ran and was believed by them that Messire Charles of Valois had abandoned to his mercenaries the city and the citizens of all ranks, high and low, men and women, and that he intended to plough up the very ground on which Paris stood. Such a rumour represented him very falsely; on all occasions he was pitiful and debonair; his Council had prudently converted the coronation campaign into an armed and peaceful procession. But the Parisians were incapable of judging sanely when the intentions of the King of France were concerned; and they knew only too well that once their town was taken there would be nothing to prevent the Armagnacs from laying it waste with fire and sword.[152]

One other circumstance intensified their fear and their dislike. When they heard that Friar Richard, to whose sermons they had once listened so devoutly, was riding with the Dauphin's men and with his nimble tongue winning such good towns as Troyes in Champagne, they called down upon him the malediction of God and his Saints. They tore from their caps the pewter medals engraved with the holy name of Jesus, which the good Brother had given them, and in their bitter hatred towards him they returned straightway to the dice, bowls and draughts which they had renounced at his exhortation. With no less horror did the Maid inspire them. It was said that she was acting the prophetess and uttering such words as: "In very deed this or that shall come to pass." "With the Armagnacs is a creature in woman's form. What it is God only knows," they cried. They spoke of her as a woman of ill fame.[153] Among these enemies, there were those who filled them with even greater horror than pagans and Saracens – to wit: a monk and a maid. They all took the cross of Saint Andrew.[154]

While the Dauphin had been away at his coronation an army had come from England into France. The Regent intended it to overrun Normandy. In its march on Rouen he commanded it in person. The defence and ward of Paris he left to Louis of Luxembourg, Bishop of Thérouanne, Chancellor of France for the English, to the Sire de l'Isle-Adam, Marshal of France, Captain of Paris, to two thousand men-at-arms and to the Parisian train-bands. To the last were entrusted the defence of the ramparts and the management of the artillery. They were commanded by twenty-four burgesses, called *quarteniers* because they represented the twenty-four quarters of the city. From the end of July all danger of a surprise had been guarded against.[155]

On the 10th of August, on Saint-Laurence's Eve, while the Armagnacs were encamped at La Ferté-Milon, the Saint-Martin Gate, flanked by four towers and a double drawbridge, was closed; and all men were forbidden to go to Saint-Laurent, either to the procession or to the fair, as in previous years.[156]

On the 28th of the same month, the royal army occupied Saint-Denys. Henceforth no one dared leave the city, neither for the vintage nor for the gathering of anything in the kitchen gardens, which covered the plain north of the town. Prices immediately went up.[157]

In the early days of September, the *quarteniers*, each one in his own district, had the trenches set in order and the cannons mounted on walls, gates, and towers. At the command of the aldermen, the hewers of stone for the cannon made thousands of balls.[158]

From My Lord, the Duke of Alençon, the magistrates received letters beginning thus: "To you, Provost of Paris and Provost of the Merchants and Aldermen...." He named them by name and greeted them in eloquent language. These letters were regarded as an artifice intended to render the townsfolk suspicious of the aldermen and to incite one class of the populace against the other. The only answer sent to the Duke was a request that he would not spoil any more paper with such malicious endeavours.[159]

The chapter of Notre-Dame ordered masses to be said for the salvation of the people. On the 5th of September, three canons were authorised to make arrangements for the defence of the monastery. Those in charge of the sacristy took measures to hide the relics and the treasure of the cathedral from the Armagnac soldiers. For two hundred golden *saluts*[160] they sold the body of Saint Denys; but they kept the foot, which was of silver, the head and the crown.[161]

On Wednesday, the 7th of September, the Eve of the Virgin's Nativity, there was a procession to Sainte-Geneviève-du-Mont with the object of counteracting the evil of the times and allaying the animosity of the enemy. In it walked the canons of the Palace, bearing the True Cross.[162]

That very day the army of the Duke of Alençon and of the Maid was skirmishing beneath the walls. It retreated in the evening; and on that night the townsfolk slept in peace, for on the morrow Christians celebrated the Nativity of the Blessed Virgin.[163]

It was a great festival and a very ancient one. Its origin is described in the following manner. There was a certain holy man, who passed his life in meditation. On a day he called to mind that for many years, on the 8th of September, he had heard marvellous angelic music in the air, and he prayed to God to reveal to him the reason for this concert of instruments and of celestial voices. He was vouchsafed the answer that it was the anniversary of the birth of the glorious Virgin Mary; and he received the command to instruct the faithful in order that they on that solemn day might join their voices to the angelic chorus. The matter was reported to the Sovereign Pontiff and the other heads of the Church, who, after having prayed, fasted and consulted the witnesses and traditions of the Church, decreed that henceforth that day, the 8th of September, should be universally consecrated to the celebration of the birth of the Virgin Mary.[164]

That day were read at mass the words of the prophet Isaiah: "And there shall come forth a rod out of the stem of Jesse, and a Branch shall grow out of his roots."

The people of Paris thought that even the Armagnacs would do no work on so high a festival and would keep the third commandment.

On this Thursday, the 8th of September, about eight o'clock in the morning, the Maid, the Dukes of Alençon and of Bourbon, the Marshals of Boussac and of Rais, the Count of Vendôme, the Lords of Laval, of Albret and of Gaucourt, who with their men, to the number of ten thousand and more, had encamped in the village of La Chapelle, half-way along the road from Saint-Denys to Paris, set out on the march. At the hour of high mass, between eleven and twelve o'clock, they reached the height of Les Moulins, at the foot of which the Swine Market was held.[165] Here there was a gibbet. Fifty-six years earlier, a woman of saintly life according to the people, but according to the holy inquisitors, a heretic and *a Turlupine*, had been burned alive on that very market-place.[166]

Wherefore did the King's men appear first before the northern walls, those of Charles V, which were the strongest? It is impossible to tell. A few days earlier they had thrown a bridge across the River above Paris,[167] which looks as if they intended to attack the old fortification and get into the city from the University side. Did they mean to carry out the two attacks simultaneously? It is probable. Did they renounce the project of their own accord or against their will? We cannot tell.

Beneath the walls of Charles V they assembled a quantity of artillery, cannons, culverins, mortars; and in hand-carts they brought fagots to fill up the trenches, hurdles to bridge them over and seven hundred ladders: very elaborate material for the siege, despite their having, as we shall see, forgotten what was most necessary.[168] They came not therefore to skirmish nor to do great feats of arms. They came to attempt in broad daylight the escalading and the storming of the greatest, the most illustrious, and the most populous town of the realm; an undertaking of vast importance, proposed doubtless and decided in the royal council and with the knowledge of the King, who can have been neither indifferent nor hostile to it.[169] Charles of Valois wanted to retake Paris. It remains to be seen whether for the accomplishment of his desire he depended merely on men-at-arms and ladders.

It would seem that the Maid had not been told of the resolutions taken.[170] She was never consulted and was seldom informed of what had been decided. But she was as sure of entering the town that day as of going to Paradise when she died. For more than three years her Voices had been drumming the attack on Paris in her ears.[171] But the astonishing point is that, saint as she was, she should have consented to arm and fight on the day of the Nativity. It was contrary to her action on the 5th of May, Ascension Day, and inconsistent with what she had said on the 8th of the same month: "As ye love and honour the Sacred Sabbath do not begin the battle."[172]

True it is that afterwards, at Montepilloy, she had engaged in a skirmish on the Day of the Assumption, and thus scandalized the masters of the University. She acted according to the counsel of her Voices and her decisions depended on the vaguest murmurings in her ear. Nothing is more inconstant and more contradictory than the inspirations of such visionaries, who are but the playthings of their dreams. What is certain at least is that Jeanne now as always was convinced that she was doing right and committing no sin.[173] Arrayed on the height of Les Moulins, in front of Paris with its grey fortifications, the French had immediately before them the outermost of the trenches, dry and narrow, some sixteen or seventeen feet deep, separated by a mound from the second trench, nearly one hundred feet broad, deep and filled with water which lapped the walls of the city. Quite close, on their right, the road to Roule led up to the Saint Honoré Gate, also called the Gate of the Blind because it was near the Hospital of Les Quinze Vingts.[174] It opened beneath a castlet flanked by turrets, and for an advanced defence it had a bulwark surrounded by wooden barriers, like those of Orléans.[175]

The Parisians did not expect to be attacked on a feast day.[176] And yet the ramparts were by no means deserted, and on the walls standards could be seen waving, and especially a great white banner with a Saint Andrew's cross in silver gilt.[177]

The French arrayed themselves slightly behind the Moulin hill, which was to protect them from the stream of lead and stones beginning to be discharged from the artillery on the ramparts. There they ranged their mortars, their culverins and their cannon, ready to fire on the city walls. In this position, which commanded the widest stretch of the fortifications, was the main body of the army. Led by Messire de Saint-Vallier a knight of Dauphiné, several captains and men-at-arms approached the Saint Honoré Gate and set fire to the barriers. As the garrison of the gate had withdrawn within the fortification, and as the enemy was not seen to be coming out by any other exit, the Maréchal de Rais' company advanced with fagots, bundles and ladders right up to the ramparts. The Maid rode at the head of her company. They halted between the Saint-Denys and the Saint-Honoré Gates, but nearer the latter, and went down into the first trench, which was not difficult to cross. But on the mound they found themselves exposed to bolts and arrows which rained straight down from the walls.[178] As at Orléans, and at Les Tourelles, Jeanne had given her banner to a man of valour to hold.

When she reached the top of the mound, she cried out to the folk in Paris: "Surrender the town to the King of France."[179]

The Burgundians heard her saying also: "In Jesus' name surrender to us speedily. For if ye yield not before nightfall, we shall enter by force, whether ye will or no, and ye shall all be put to death without mercy."[180]

On the mound she remained, sounding the great dyke with her lance and marvelling to find it so full and so deep. And yet for eleven days she and her men-at-arms had been reconnoitring round the walls and seeking the most favourable point of attack. That she should not have known how to plan an attack was quite natural. But what is to be thought of the men-at-arms, who were there on the mound, taken by surprise, as baffled as she, and all aghast at finding so much water close to the Seine when the River was in flood? To be able to reconnoitre the defences of a fortress was surely the *a b c* of the trade of war. Captains and soldiers of fortune never risked advancing against a fortification without knowing first whether there were water, morass or briars, and arming themselves accordingly with siege train suitable to the occasion. When the water of the moat was deep they launched leather boats carried on horses' backs.[181] The men-at-arms of the Maréchal de Rais and my Lord of Alençon were more ignorant than the meanest adventurers. What would the doughty La Hire have thought of them? Such gross ineptitude and ignorance appeared so incredible that it was supposed that those fighting men knew the depth of the moat but concealed it from the Maid, desiring her discomfiture.[182] In such a case, while entrapping the damsel they were themselves entrapped, for there they stayed moving neither backwards nor forwards.

Certain among them idly threw fagots into the moat. Meanwhile the defenders assailed by flights of arrows, disappeared one after the other.[183] But towards four o'clock in the afternoon, the citizens arrived in crowds. The cannon of the Saint-Denys Gate thundered. Arrows and abuse flew between those above and those below. The hours passed, the sun was sinking. The Maid never ceased sounding the moat with the staff of her lance and crying out to the Parisians to surrender.

"There, wanton! There, minx!" cried a Burgundian.

And planting his cross-bow in the ground with his foot, he shot an arrow which split one of her greaves and wounded her in the thigh. Another Burgundian took aim at the Maid's standard-bearer and wounded him in the foot. The wounded man raised his visor to see whence the arrow came and straightway received another between the eyes. The Maid and the Duke of Alençon sorely regretted the loss of this man-at-arms.[184]

After she had been wounded, Jeanne cried all the more loudly that the walls must be reached and the city taken. She was placed out of reach of the arrows in the shelter of a breast-work. There she urged the men-at-arms to throw fagots into the water and make a bridge. About ten or eleven o'clock in the evening, the Sire de la Trémouille charged the combatants to retreat. The Maid would not leave the place. She was doubtless listening to her Saints and beholding celestial hosts around her. The Duke of Alençon sent for her. The aged Sire de Gaucourt[185] carried her off with the aid of a captain of Picardy, one Guichard Bournel, who did not please her on that day, and who by his treachery six months later, was to please her still less.[186] Had she not been wounded she would have resisted more strongly.[187] She yielded regretfully, saying: "In God's name! the city might have been taken."[188]

They put her on horseback; and thus she was able to follow the army. The rumour ran that she had been shot in both thighs; in sooth her wound was but slight.[189]

The French returned to La Chapelle, whence they had set out in the morning. They carried their wounded on some of the carts which they had used for the transport of fagots and ladders. In the hands of the enemy they left three hundred hand-carts, six hundred and sixty ladders, four thousand hurdles and large fagots, of which they had used but a small number.[190] Their retreat must have been somewhat hurried, seeing that, when they came to the Barn of Les Mathurins, near The Swine Market, they forsook their baggage and set fire to it. With horror it was related that, like pagans of Rome, they had cast their dead into the flames.[191] Nevertheless the Parisians dared not pursue them. In those days men-at-arms who knew their trade never retreated without laying some snare for the enemy. Consequently the King's men posted a considerable company in ambush by the roadside, to lie in wait for the light troops who should come in pursuit of the retreating army.[192] It was precisely such an ambuscade that the Parisians feared; wherefore they permitted the Armagnacs to regain their camp at La Chapelle-Saint-Denys unmolested.[193]

If we regard only the military tactics of the day, there is no doubt that the French had blundered and had lacked energy. But it was not on military tactics that the greatest reliance had been placed. Those who conducted the war, the King and his council, certainly expected to enter Paris that day. But how? As they had entered Châlons, as they had entered Reims, as they had entered all the King's good towns from Troyes to Compiègne. King Charles had shown himself determined to recover his towns by means of the townsfolk; towards Paris he acted as he had acted towards his other towns.

During the coronation march, he had entered into communication with the bishops and burgesses of the cities of Champagne; and like communications he had entered into in Paris.[194] He had dealings with the monks and notably with the Carmelites of Melun, whose Prior, Brother Pierre d'Allée, was working in his interest.[195] For some time paid agents had been watching for an opportunity of throwing the city into disorder and of bringing in the enemy in a moment of panic and confusion. During the assault they were working for him in the streets. In the afternoon, on both sides of the bridges, were heard cries of "Let every man look to his own safety! The enemy has entered! All is lost!" Such of the citizens as were listening to the sermon hastened to shut themselves in their houses. And others who were out of doors sought refuge in the churches. But the tumult was quelled. Wise men, like the clerk of the Parlement, believed that it was but a feigned attack, and that Charles of Valois looked to recover the town not so much by force of arms as by a movement of the populace.[196]

Certain monks who were acting in Paris as the King's spies, went out to him at Saint-Denys and informed him that the attempt had failed. According to them it had very nearly succeeded.[197]

The Sire de la Trémouille is said to have commanded the retreat, for fear of a massacre. Indeed, once the French had entered they were quite capable of slaughtering the townsfolk and razing the city to the ground.[198]

On the morrow, Friday the 9th, the Maid, rising with the dawn, despite her wound, asked the Duke of Alençon to have the call to arms sounded; for she was strongly determined to return to the walls of Paris, swearing not to leave them until the city should be taken.[199] Meanwhile the French captains sent a herald to Paris, charged to ask for a safe conduct for the removing of the bodies of the dead left behind in great numbers.[200]

Notwithstanding that they had suffered cruel hurt, after a retreat unmolested it is true, but none the less disastrous and involving the loss of all their siege train, several of the leaders were, like the Maid, inclined to attempt a new assault. Others would not hear of it. While they were disputing, they beheld a baron coming towards them and with him fifty nobles; it was the Sire de Montmorency, the first Christian peer of France, that is the first among the ancient vassals of the bishop of Paris. He was transferring his allegiance from the Cross of St. Andrew to the Flowers-de-luce.[201] His coming filled the King's men with courage and a desire to return to the city. The army was on its way back, when the Count of Clermont and the Duke of Bar were sent to arrest the march by order of the King, and to take the Maid back to Saint-Denys.[202]

On Saturday the 10th, at daybreak, the Duke of Alençon, with a few knights, appeared on the bank above the city, where a bridge had been thrown over the Seine some days earlier. The Maid, always eager for danger, accompanied the venturesome warriors. But the night before, the King had prudently caused the bridge to be taken down, and the little band had to retrace its steps.[203] It was not that the King had renounced the idea of taking Paris. He was thinking more than ever of the recovery of his great town; but he intended to regain it without an assault, by means of the compliance of certain burgesses.

At this same place of Saint-Denys there happened to Jeanne a misadventure, which would seem to have impressed her comrades and possibly to have lessened their faith in her good luck in war. As was customary, women of ill-fame followed the army in great numbers; each man had his own; they were called *amiètes*.[204] Jeanne could not tolerate them because they caused disorder, but more especially because their sinful lives filled her with horror. At that very time, stories like the following were circulated far and wide, and spread even into Germany.

There was a certain man in the camp, who had with him his *amiète*. She rode in armour in order not to be recognised. Now the Maid said to the nobles and captains: "There is a woman with our men." They replied that they knew of none. Whereupon the Maid assembled the army, and, approaching the woman said: "This is she."

Then addressing the wench: "Thou art of Gien and thou art big with child. Were it not so I would put thee to death. Thou hast already let one child die and thou shalt not do the same for this one."

When the Maid had thus spoken, servants took the wench and conveyed her to her own home. There they kept her under watch and ward until she was delivered of her child. And she confessed that what the Maid had said was true.

After which, the Maid again said: "There are women in the camp." Whereupon two wantons, who did not belong to the army, and had already been dismissed from it, hearing these words, rode off on horseback. But the Maid hastened after them crying: "Ye foolish women, I have forbidden you to come into my company." And she drew her sword and struck one of them on the head, so sore that she died.[205]

The tale was true; Jeanne could not suffer these wenches. Every time she met one she gave chase to her. This was precisely what she did at Gien, when she saw women of ill-fame awaiting the King's men.[206] At Château-Thierry, she espied an *amiète* riding behind a man-at-arms, and, running after her, sword in hand, she came up with her, and without striking, bade her henceforth avoid the society of men-at-arms. "If thou wilt not," she added, "I shall do thee hurt."[207]

At Saint-Denys, being accompanied by the Duke of Alençon, Jeanne pursued another of these wantons. This time she was not content with remonstrances and threats. She broke her sword over her.[208] Was it Saint Catherine's sword? So it was believed, and doubtless not without reason.[209] In those days men's minds were full of the romantic stories of Joyeuse and Durandal. It would appear that Jeanne, when she lost her sword, lost her power. A slight variation of the story was told afterwards, and it was related how the King, when he was acquainted with the matter of the broken sword, was displeased and said to the Maid: "You should have taken a stick to strike withal and should not have risked the sword you received from divine hands."[210] It was told likewise how the sword had been given to an armourer for him to join the pieces together, and that he could not, wherein lay a proof that the sword was enchanted.[211]

Before his departure, the King appointed the Count of Clermont commander of the district with several lieutenants: the Lords of Culant, Boussac, Loré, and Foucault. He constituted joint lieutenants-general the Counts of Clermont and of Vendôme, the lords Regnault de Chartres, Christophe d'Harcourt and Jean Tudert. Regnault de Chartres established himself in the town of Senlis, the lieutenant's headquarters. Having thus disposed, the King quitted Saint-Denys on the 13th of September.[212] The Maid followed him against her will notwithstanding that she had the permission of her Voices to do so.[213] She offered her armour to the image of Our Lady and to the precious body of Saint Denys.[214] This armour was white, that is to say devoid of armorial bearings.[215] She was thus following the custom of men-at-arms, who, after they had received a wound, if they did not die of it, offered their armour to Our Lady and the Saints as a token of thanksgiving. Wherefore, in those warlike days, chapels, like that of Notre-Dame de Fierbois, often presented the appearance of arsenals. To her armour the Maid added a sword which she had won before Paris.[216]

CHAPTER IV

THE TAKING OF SAINT-PIERRE-LE-MOUSTIER – FRIAR RICHARD'S SPIRITUAL DAUGHTERS – THE SIEGE OF LA CHARITÉ

HE King slept at Lagny-sur-Marne on the 14th of September, then crossed the Seine at Bray, forded the Yonne near Sens and went on through Courtenay, Châteaurenard and Montargis. On the 21st of September he reached Gien. There he disbanded the army he could no longer pay, and each man went to his own home. The Duke of Alençon withdrew into his viscounty of Beaumont-sur-Oise.[217]

Learning that the Queen was coming to meet the King, Jeanne went before her and greeted her at Selles-en-Berry.[218] She was afterwards taken to Bourges, where my Lord d'Albret, half-brother of the Sire de la Trémouille, lodged her with Messire Régnier de Bouligny. Régnier was then Receiver General. He had been one of those whose dismissal the University had requested in 1408, as being worse than useless, for they held him responsible for many of the disorders in the kingdom. He had entered the Dauphin's service, passed from the administration of the royal domain to that of taxes and attained the highest rank in the control of the finances.[219] His wife, who had accompanied the Queen to Selles, beheld the Maid and wondered. Jeanne seemed to her a creature sent by God for the relief of the King and those of France who were loyal to him. She remembered the days not so very long ago when she had seen the Dauphin and her Husband not knowing where to turn for money. Her name was Marguerite La Touroulde; she was damiselle, not dame; a comfortable *bourgeoise* and that was all.[220]

Three weeks Jeanne sojourned in the Receiver General's house. She slept there, drank there, ate there. Nearly every night, Damiselle Marguerite La Touroulde slept with her; the etiquette of those days required it. No night-gowns were worn; folk slept naked in those vast beds. It would seem that Jeanne disliked sleeping with old women.[221] Damiselle La Touroulde, although not so very old, was of matronly age;[222] she had moreover a matron's experience, and further she claimed, as we shall see directly, to know more than most matrons knew. Several times she took Jeanne to the bath and to the sweating-room.[223] That also was one of the rules of etiquette; a host was not considered to be making his guests good cheer unless he took them to the bath. In this point of courtesy princes set an example; when the King and Queen supped in the house of one of their retainers or ministers, fine baths richly ornamented were prepared for them before they came to table.[224] Mistress Marguerite doubtless did not possess what was necessary in her own house; wherefore she took Jeanne out to the bath and the sweating-room. Such are her own expressions; and they probably indicate a vapour bath[225] not a bath of hot water.

At Bourges the sweating-rooms were in the Auron quarter, in the lower town, near the river.[226] Jeanne was strictly devout, but she did not observe conventual rule; she, like chaste Suzannah therefore, might permit herself to bathe and she must have had great need to do so after having slept on straw.[227] What is more remarkable is that, after having seen Jeanne in the bath, Mistress Marguerite judged her a virgin according to all appearances.[228]

In Messire Régnier de Bouligny's house and likewise wherever she lodged, she led the life of a *béguine* but did not practise excessive austerity. She confessed frequently. Many a time she asked her hostess to come with her to matins. In the cathedral and in collegiate churches there were matins every day, between four and six, at the hour of sunset. The two women often talked together; the Receiver General's wife found Jeanne very simple and very ignorant. She was amazed to discover that the maiden knew absolutely nothing.[229]

Among other matters, Jeanne told of her visit to the old Duke of Lorraine, and how she had rebuked him for his evil life; she spoke likewise of the interrogatory to which the doctors of Poitiers had subjected her.[230] She was persuaded that these clerks had questioned her with extreme severity, and she firmly believed that she had triumphed over their ill-will. Alas! she was soon to know clerks even less accommodating.

Mistress Marguerite said to her one day: "If you are not afraid when you fight, it is because you know you will not be killed." Whereupon Jeanne answered: "I am no surer of that than are the other combatants."

Oftentimes women came to the Bouligny house, bringing paternosters and other trifling objects of devotion for the Maid to touch.

Jeanne used to say laughingly to her hostess: "Touch them yourself. Your touch will do them as much good as mine."[231]

This ready repartee must have shown Mistress Marguerite that Jeanne, ignorant as she may have been, was none the less capable of displaying a good grace and common sense in her conversation.

While in many matters this good woman found the Maid but a simple creature, in military affairs she deemed her an expert. Whether, when she judged the saintly damsel's skill in wielding arms, she was giving her own opinion or merely speaking from hearsay, as would seem probable, she at any rate declared later that Jeanne rode a horse and handled a lance as well as the best of knights and so well that the army marvelled.[232] Indeed most captains in those days could do no better.

Probably there were dice and dice-boxes in the Bouligny house, otherwise Jeanne would have had no opportunity of displaying that horror of gaming which struck her hostess. On this matter Jeanne agreed with her comrade, Friar Richard, and indeed with everyone else of good life and good doctrine.[233]

What money she had Jeanne distributed in alms. "I am come to succour the poor and needy," she used to say.[234]

When the multitude heard such words they were led to believe that this Maid of God had been raised up for something more than the glorification of the Lilies, and that she was come to dispel such ills as murder, pillage and other sins grievous to God, from which the realm was suffering. Mystic souls looked to her for the reform of the Church and the reign of Jesus Christ on earth. She was invoked as a saint, and throughout the loyal provinces were to be seen carved and painted images of her which were worshipped by the faithful. Thus, even during her lifetime, she enjoyed certain of the privileges of beatification.[235]

North of the Seine meanwhile, English and Burgundians were at their old work. The Duke of Vendôme and his company fell back on Senlis, the English descended on the town of Saint-Denys and sacked it once more. In the Abbey Church they found and carried off the Maid's armour, thus, according to the French clergy, committing undeniable sacrilege and for this reason: because they gave the monks of the Abbey nothing in exchange.

The King was then at Mehun-sur-Yèvre, quite close to Bourges, in one of the finest châteaux in the world, rising on a rock and overlooking the town. The late Duke Jean of Berry, a great builder, had erected this château with the care that he never failed to exercise in matters of art. Mehun was King Charles's favourite abode.[236]

The Duke of Alençon, eager to reconquer his duchy, was waiting for troops to accompany him into Normandy, across the marches of Brittany and Maine. He sent to the King to know if it were his good pleasure to grant him the Maid. "Many there be," said the Duke, "who would willingly come with her, while without her they will not stir from their homes." Her discomfiture before Paris had not, therefore, entirely ruined her prestige. The Sire de la Trémouille opposed her being sent to the Duke of Alençon, whom he mistrusted, and not without cause. He gave her into the care of his half-brother, the Sire d'Albret, Lieutenant of the King in his own country of Berry.[237]

The Royal Council deemed it necessary to recover La Charité, left in the hands of Perrinet Gressart at the time of the coronation campaign;[238] but it was decided first to attack Saint-Pierre-le-Moustier, which commanded the approaches to Bec-d'Allier.[239] The garrison of this little town was composed of English and Burgundians, who were constantly plundering the villages and laying waste the fields of Berry and Bourbonnais. The army for this expedition assembled at Bourges. It was commanded by my Lord d'Albret,[240] but popular report attributed the command to Jeanne. The common folk, the burgesses of the towns, especially the citizens of Orléans knew no other commander.

After two or three days' siege, the King's men stormed the town. But they were repulsed. Squire Jean d'Aulon, the Maid's steward, who some time before had been wounded in the heel and consequently walked on crutches, had retreated with the rest.[241] He went back and found Jeanne who had stayed almost alone by the side of the moat. Fearing lest harm should come to her, he leapt on to his horse, spurred towards her and cried: "What are you doing, all alone? Wherefore do you not retreat like the others?"

Jeanne doffed her sallet and replied: "I am not alone. With me are fifty thousand of my folk. I will not quit this spot till I have taken the town."

Casting his eyes around, Messire Jean d'Aulon saw the Maid surrounded by but four or five men.

More loudly he cried out to her: "Depart hence and retreat like the others."

Her only reply was a request for fagots and hurdles to fill up the moat. And straightway in a loud voice she called: "To the fagots and the hurdles all of ye, and make a bridge!"

The men-at-arms rushed to the spot, the bridge was constructed forthwith and the town taken by storm with no great difficulty. At any rate that is how the good Squire, Jean d'Aulon, told the story.[242] He was almost persuaded that the Maid's fifty thousand shadows had taken Saint-Pierre-le-Moustier.

With the little army on the Loire at that time were certain holy women who like Jeanne led a singular life and held communion with the Church Triumphant. They constituted, so to speak, a kind of flying squadron of *béguines*, which followed the men-at-arms. One of these women was called Catherine de La Rochelle; two others came from Lower Brittany.[243]

They all had miraculous visions; Jeanne saw my Lord Saint Michael in arms and Saint Catherine and Saint Margaret wearing crowns;[244] Pierronne beheld God in a long white robe and a purple cloak;[245] Catherine de La Rochelle saw a white lady, clothed in cloth of gold; and, at the moment of the consecration of the host all manner of marvels of the high mystery of Our Lord were revealed unto her.[246]

Jean Pasquerel was still with Jeanne in the capacity of chaplain.[247] He hoped to take his penitent to fight in the Crusade against the Hussites, for it was against these heretics that he felt most bitterly. But he had been entirely supplanted by the Franciscan, Friar Richard, who, after Troyes, had joined the mendicants of Jeanne's earlier days. Friar Richard dominated this little band of the illuminated. He was called their good Father. He it was who instructed them.[248] His designs for these women did not greatly differ from those of Jean Pasquerel: he intended to conduct them to those wars of the Cross, which he thought were bound to precede the impending end of the world.[249]

Meanwhile, it was his endeavour to foster a good understanding between them, which, eloquent preacher though he was, he found very difficult. Within the sisterhood there were constant suspicions and disputes. Jeanne had been on friendly terms with Catherine de la Rochelle at Montfaucon in Brie and at Jargeau; but now she began to suspect her of being a rival, and immediately she assumed an attitude of mistrust.[250] Possibly she was right. At any moment either Catherine or the Breton women might be made use of as she had been.[251] In those days a prophetess was useful in so many ways: in the edification of the people, the reformation of the Church, the leading of men-at-arms, the circulation of money, in war, in peace; no sooner did one appear than each party tried to get hold of her. It seems as if, after having employed the Maid Jeanne to deliver Orléans, the King's Councillors were now thinking of employing Dame Catherine to make peace with the Duke of Burgundy. Such a task was deemed fitting for a saint less chivalrous than Jeanne. Catherine was married and the mother of a family. In this circumstance there need be no cause for astonishment; for if the gift of prophecy be more especially reserved for virgins, the example of Judith proves that the Lord may raise up strong matrons for the serving of his people.

If we believe that, as her surname indicates, she came from La Rochelle, her origin must have inspired the Armagnacs with confidence. The inhabitants of La Rochelle, all pirates more or less, were too profitably engaged in preying upon English vessels to forsake the Dauphin's party. Moreover, he rewarded their loyalty by granting them valuable commercial privileges.[252] They had sent gifts of money to the people of Orléans; and when, in the month of May, they learned the deliverance of Duke Charles's city, they instituted a public festival to commemorate so happy an event.

The first duty of a saint in the army, it would appear, was to collect money. Jeanne was always sending letters asking the good towns for money or for munitions of war; the burgesses always promised to grant her request and sometimes they kept their promise. Catherine de la Rochelle appears to have had special revelations concerning the funds of the party; her mission, therefore, was financial, while Jeanne's was martial. She announced that she was going to the Duke of Burgundy to conclude peace.[253] If one may judge from the little that is known of her, the inspirations of this holy dame were not very elevated, not very orderly, not very profound.

Meeting Jeanne at Montfaucon in Berry (or at Jargeau) she addressed her thus:

"There came unto me a white lady, attired in cloth of gold, who said to me: 'Go thou through the good towns and let the King give unto thee heralds and trumpets to cry: "Whosoever has gold, silver or hidden treasure, let him bring it forth instantly.""

Dame Catherine added: "Such as have hidden treasure and do not thus, I shall know their treasure, and I shall go and find it."

She deemed it necessary to fight against the English and seemed to believe that Jeanne's mission was to drive them out of the land, since she obligingly offered her the whole of her miraculous takings.

"Wherewithal to pay your men-at-arms," she said. But the Maid answered disdainfully:

"Go back to your husband, look after your household, and feed your children."[254]

Disputes between saints are usually bitter. In her rival's missions Jeanne refused to see anything but folly and futility. Nevertheless it was not for her to deny the possibility of the white lady's visitations; for to Jeanne herself did there not descend every day as many saints, angels and archangels as were ever painted on the pages of books or the walls of monasteries? In order to make up her mind on the subject, she adopted the most effectual measures. A learned doctor may reason concerning matter and substance, the origin and the form of ideas, the dawn of impressions in the intellect, but a shepherdess will resort to a surer method; she will appeal to her own eyesight.

Jeanne asked Catherine if the white lady came every night, and learning that she did: "I will sleep with you," she said.

When night came, she went to bed with Catherine, watched till midnight, saw nothing and fell asleep, for she was young, and she had great need of sleep. In the morning, when she awoke, she asked: "Did she come?"

"She did," replied Catherine; "you were asleep, so I did not like to wake you."

"Will she not come to-morrow?"

Catherine assured her that she would come without fail.

This time Jeanne slept in the day in order that she might keep awake at night; so she lay down at night in the bed with Catherine and kept her eyes open. Often she asked: "Will she not come?"

And Catherine replied: "Yes, directly."

But Jeanne saw nothing.[255] She held the test to be a good one. Nevertheless she could not get the white lady attired in cloth of gold out of her head. When Saint Catherine and Saint Margaret came to her, as they delayed not to do, she spoke to them concerning this white lady and asked them what she was to think of her. The reply was such as Jeanne expected:

"This Catherine," they said, "is naught but futility and folly."[256]

Then was Jeanne constrained to cry: "That is just what I thought."

The strife between these two prophetesses was brief but bitter. Jeanne always maintained the opposite of what Catherine said. When the latter was going to make peace with the Duke of Burgundy, Jeanne said to her:

"Me seemeth that you will never find peace save at the lance's point."[257]

There was one matter at any rate wherein the White Lady proved a better prophetess than the Maid's Council, to wit, the siege of La Charité. When Jeanne wished to go and deliver that town, Catherine tried to dissuade her.

"It is too cold," she said; "I would not go."[258]

Catherine's reason was not a high one; and yet it is true Jeanne would have done better not to go to the siege of La Charité.

Taken from the Duke of Burgundy by the Dauphin in 1422, La Charité had been retaken in 1424, by Perrinet Gressart,[259] a successful captain, who had risen from the rank of mason's apprentice to that of pantler to the Duke of Burgundy and had been created Lord of Laigny by the King of England.[260] On the 30th of December, 1425, Perrinet's men arrested the Sire de La Trémouille, when he was on his way to the Duke of Burgundy, having been appointed ambassador in one of those eternal negotiations, forever in process between the King and the Duke. He was for several months kept a prisoner in the fortress which his captor commanded. He must needs pay a ransom of fourteen thousand golden crowns; and, albeit he took this sum from the royal treasury,[261] he never ceased to bear Perrinet a grudge. Wherefore it may be concluded that when he sent men-at-arms to La Charité it was in good sooth to capture the town and not with any evil design against the Maid.

The army despatched against this Burgundian captain and this great plunder of pilgrims was composed of no mean folk. Its leaders were Louis of Bourbon, Count of Montpensier, and Charles II, Sire d'Albret, La Trémouille's half-brother and Jeanne's companion in arms during the coronation campaign. The army was doubtless but scantily supplied with stores and with money.[262] That was the normal condition of armies in those days. When the King wanted to attack a stronghold of the enemy, he must needs apply to his good towns for the necessary material. The Maid, at once saint and warrior, could beg for arms with a good grace; but possibly she overrated the resources of the towns which had already given so much.

On the 7th of November, she and my Lord d'Alençon signed a letter asking the folk of Clermont in Auvergne for powder, arrows and artillery. Churchmen, magistrates, and townsfolk sent two hundredweight of saltpetre, one hundredweight of sulphur, two cases of arrows; to these they added a sword, two poniards and a battle-axe for the Maid; and they charged Messire Robert Andrieu to present this contribution to Jeanne and to my Lord d'Albret.[263]

On the 9th of November, the Maid was at Moulins in Bourbonnais.[264] What was she doing there? No one knows. There was at that time in the town an abbess very holy and very greatly venerated. Her name was Colette Boilet. She had won the highest praise and incurred the grossest insults by attempting to reform the order of Saint Clare. Colette lived in the convent of the Sisters of Saint Clare, which she had recently founded in this town. It has been thought that the Maid went to Moulins on purpose to meet her.[265] But we ought first to ascertain whether these two saints had any liking for each other. They both worked miracles and miracles which were occasionally somewhat similar;[266] but that was no reason why they should take the slightest pleasure in each other's society. One was called *La Pucelle*,[267] the other *La Petite Ancelle*.[268] But these names, both equally humble, described persons widely different in fashion of attire and in manner of life. *La Petite Ancelle* wended her way on foot, clothed in rags like a beggar-woman; *La Pucelle*, wrapped in cloth of gold, rode forth with lords on horseback. That Jeanne, surrounded by Franciscans who observed no rule, felt any veneration for the reformer of the Sisters of Saint Clare, there is no reason to believe; neither is there anything to indicate that the pacific Colette, strongly attached to the Burgundian house,[269] had any desire to hold converse with one whom the English regarded as a destroying angel.[270]

From this town of Moulins, Jeanne dictated a letter by which she informed the inhabitants of Riom that Saint-Pierre-le-Moustier was taken, and asked them for materials of war as she had asked the folk of Clermont.[271]

Here is the letter:

Good friends and beloved, ye wit how that the town of Saint Père le Moustier hath been taken by storm; and with God's help it is our intention to cause to be evacuated the other places contrary to the King; but for this there hath been great expending of powder, arrows and other munition of war before the said town, and the lords who are in this town are but scantily provided for to go and lay siege to La Charité, whither we wend presently; I pray you as ye love the welfare and honour of the King and likewise of all others here, that ye will straightway help and send for the said siege powder, saltpetre, sulphur, arrows, strong cross-bows and other munition of war. And do this lest by failure of the said powder and other habiliments of war, the siege should be long and ye should be called in this matter negligent or unwilling. Good friends and beloved, may our Lord keep you. Written at Molins, the ninth day of November.

Jehanne.

Addressed to: My good friends and beloved, the churchmen, burgesses and townsfolk of the town of Rion.[272]

The magistrates of Riom, in letters sealed with their own seal, undertook to give Jeanne the Maid and my Lord d'Albret the sum of sixty crowns; but when the masters of the siege-artillery came to demand this sum, the magistrates would not give a farthing.[273]

The folk of Orléans, on the other hand, once more appeared both zealous and munificent; for they eagerly desired the reduction of a town commanding the Loire for seventy-five miles above their own city. They deserve to be considered the true deliverers of the kingdom; had it not been for them neither Jargeau nor Beaugency would have been taken in June. Quite in the beginning of July, when they thought the Loire campaign was to be continued, they had sent their great mortar, La Bougue, to Gien. With it they had despatched ammunition and victuals; and now, in the early days of December, at the request of the King addressed to the magistrates, they sent to La Charité all the artillery brought back from Gien; likewise eighty-nine soldiers of the municipal troops, wearing the cloak with the Duke of Orléans' colours, the white cross on the breast; with their trumpeter at their head and commanded by Captain Boiau; craftsmen of all conditions, master-masons and journeymen, carpenters, smiths; the cannoneers Fauveau, Gervaise Lefèvre and Brother Jacques, monk of the Gray friars monastery, at Orléans.[274] What became of all this artillery and of these brave folk?

On the 24th of November, the Sire d'Albret and the Maid, being hard put to it before the walls of La Charité, likewise solicited the town of Bourges. On receipt of their letter, the burgesses decided to contribute thirteen hundred golden crowns. To raise this sum they had recourse to a measure by no means unusual; it had been employed notably by the townsfolk of Orléans when, some time previously, to furnish forth Jeanne with munition of war, they had bought from a certain citizen a quantity of salt which they had put up to auction in the city barn. The townsfolk of Bourges sold by auction the annual revenue of a thirteenth part of the wine sold retail in the town. But the money thus raised never reached its destination.[275]

A right goodly knighthood was gathered beneath the walls of La Charité; besides Louis de Bourbon and the Sire d'Albret, there was the Maréchal de Broussac, Jean de Bouray, Seneschal of Toulouse, and Raymon de Montremur, a Baron of Dauphiné, who was slain there.[276] It was bitterly cold and the besiegers succeeded in nothing. At the end of a month Perrinet Gressart, who was full of craft, caused them to fall into an ambush. They raised the siege, abandoning the artillery furnished by the good towns, those fine cannon bought with the savings of thrifty citizens.[277] Their action was the less excusable because the town which had not been relieved and could not well expect to be, must have surrendered sooner or later. They pleaded that the King had sent them no victuals and no money;[278] but that was not considered an excuse and their action was deemed dishonourable. According to a knight well acquainted with points of honour in war: "One ought never to besiege a place without being sure of victuals and of pay beforehand. For to besiege a stronghold and then to withdraw is great disgrace for an army, especially when there is present with it a king or a king's lieutenant."[279]

477

On the 13th of December there preached to the people of Périgueux a Dominican friar, Brother Hélie Boudant, Pope Martin's Penitentiary in that town. He took as his text the great miracles worked in France by the intervention of a Maid, whom God had sent to the King. On this occasion the Mayor and the magistrates heard mass sung and presented two candles. Now for two months Brother Hélie had been under order to appear before the Parlement of Poitiers.[280] On what charge we do not know. Mendicant monks of those days were for the most part irregular in faith and in morals. The doctrine of Friar Richard himself was not altogether beyond suspicion.

At Christmas, in the year 1429, the flying squadron of *béguines* being assembled at Jargeau,[281] this good Brother said mass and administered the communion thrice to Jeanne the Maid and twice to that Pierronne of Lower Brittany, with whom our Lord conversed as friend with friend. Such an action might well be regarded, if not as a formal violation of the Church's laws, at any rate as an unjustifiable abuse of the sacrament.[282] A menacing theological tempest was then gathering and was about to break over the heads of Friar Richard's daughters in the spirit. A few days after the attack on Paris, the venerable University had had composed or rather transcribed a treatise, *De bono et maligno spiritu*, with a view probably to finding therein arguments against Friar Richard and his prophetess Jeanne, who had both appeared before the city with the Armagnacs.[283]

About the same time, a clerk of the faculty of law had published a summary reply to Chancellor Gerson's memorial concerning the Maid. "It sufficeth not," he wrote, "that one simply affirm that he is sent of God; every heretic maketh such a claim; but he must prove the truth of that mysterious mission by some miraculous work or by some special testimony in the Bible." This Paris clerk denies that the Maid has presented any such proof, and to judge her by her acts, he believes her rather to have been sent by the Devil than by God. He reproaches her with wearing a dress forbidden to women under penalty of anathema, and he refutes the excuses for her conduct in this matter urged by Gerson. He accuses her of having excited between princes and Christian people a greater war than there had ever been before. He holds her to be an idolatress using enchantments and making false prophecies. He charges her with having induced men to slay their fellows on the two high festivals of the Holy Virgin, the Assumption and the Nativity. "Sins committed by the Enemy of Mankind, through this woman, against the Creator and his most glorious Mother. And albeit there ensued certain murders, thanks be to God they were not so many as the Enemy had intended."

"All these things do manifestly prove error and heresy," adds this devout son of the University. Whence he concludes that the Maid should be taken before the Bishop and the Inquisitor; and he ends by quoting this text from Saint Jérôme: "The unhealthy flesh must be cut off; the diseased sheep must be driven from the fold."[284]

Such was the unanimous opinion of the University of Paris concerning her in whom the French clerks beheld an Angel of the Lord. At Bruges, in November, a rumour ran and was eagerly welcomed by ecclesiastics that the University of Paris had sent an embassy to the Pope at Rome to denounce the Maid as a false prophetess and a deceiver, and likewise those who believed in her. We do not know the veritable object of this mission.[285] But there is no doubt whatever that the doctors and masters of Paris were henceforward firmly resolved that if ever they obtained possession of the damsel they would not let her go out of their hands, and certainly would not send her to be tried at Rome, where she might escape with a mere penance, and even be enlisted as one of the Pope's mercenaries.[286]

In English and Burgundian lands, not only by clerks but by folk of all conditions, she was regarded as a heretic; in those countries the few who thought well of her had to conceal their opinions carefully. After the retreat from Saint-Denys, there may have remained some in Picardy, and notably at Abbeville, who were favourable to the prophetess of the French; but such persons must not be spoken of in public.

Colin Gouye, surnamed Le Sourd, and Jehannin Daix, surnamed Le Petit, a man of Abbeville, learned this to their cost. In this town about the middle of September, Le Sourd and Le Petit were near the blacksmith's forge with divers of the burgesses and other townsfolk, among whom was a herald. They fell to talking of the Maid who was making so great a stir throughout Christendom. To certain words the herald uttered concerning her, Le Petit replied eagerly:

"Well! well! Everything that woman does and says is nought but deception."

Le Sourd spoke likewise: "That woman," he said, "is not to be trusted. Those who believe in her are mad, and there is a smell of burning about them."[287]

By that he meant that their destiny was obvious, and that they were sure to be burned at the stake as heretics.

Then he had the misfortune to add: "In this town there be many with a smell of burning about them."

Such words were for the dwellers in Abbeville a slander and a cause of suspicion. When the Mayor and the aldermen heard of this speech they ordered Le Sourd to be thrown into prison. Le Petit must have said something similar, for he too was imprisoned.[288]

By saying that divers of his fellow-citizens were suspect of heresy, Le Sourd put them in danger of being sought out by the Bishop and the Inquisitor as heretics and sorcerers of notoriously evil repute. As for the Maid, she must have been suspect indeed, for a smell of burning to be caused by the mere fact of being her partisan.

While Friar Richard and his spiritual daughters were thus threatened with a bad end should they fall into the hands of the English or Burgundians, serious troubles were agitating the sisterhood. On the subject of Catherine, Jeanne entered into an open dispute with her spiritual father. Friar Richard wanted the holy dame of La Rochelle to be set to work. Fearing lest his advice should be adopted, Jeanne wrote to her King to tell him what to do with the woman, to wit that he should send her home to her husband and children.

When she came to the King the first thing she had to say to him was: "Catherine's doings are nought but folly and futility."

Friar Richard made no attempt to hide from the Maid his profound displeasure.[289] He was thought much of at court, and it was doubtless with the consent of the Royal Council that he was endeavouring to compass the employment of Dame Catherine. The Maid had succeeded. Why should not another of the illuminated succeed?

Meanwhile the Council had by no means renounced the services Jeanne was rendering to the French cause. Even after the misfortunes of Paris and of La Charité, there were many who now as before held her power to be supernatural; and there is reason to believe that there was a party at Court intending still to employ her.[290] And even if they had wished to discard her she was now too intimately associated with the royal lilies for her rejection not to involve them too in dishonour. On the 29th of December, 1429, at Mehun-sur-Yèvre, the King gave her a charter of nobility sealed with the great seal in green wax, with a double pendant, on a strip of red and green silk.[291]

The grant of nobility was to Jeanne, her father, mother, brothers even if they were not free, and to all their posterity, male and female. It was a singular grant corresponding to the singular services rendered by a woman.

In the title she is described as Johanna d'Ay, doubtless because her father's name was given to the King's scribes by Lorrainers who would speak with a soft drawl; but whether her name were Ay or Arc, she was seldom called by it, and was commonly spoken of as Jeanne the Maid.[292]

CHAPTER V
LETTER TO THE CITIZENS OF REIMS – LETTER TO THE HUSSITES – DEPARTURE FROM SULLY

HE folk of Orléans were grateful to the Maid for what she had done for them. Far from reproaching her with the unfortunate conclusion of the siege of La Charité, they welcomed her into their city with the same rejoicing and with as good cheer as before. On the 19th of January, 1430, they honoured her and likewise Maître Jean de Velly and Maître Jean Rabateau with a banquet, at which there was abundance of capons, partridges, hares, and even a pheasant.[293] Who that Jean de Velly was, who was feasted with her, we do not know. As for Jean Rabateau, he was none other than the King's Councillor, who had been Attorney-General at the Parlement of Poitiers since 1427.[294] He had been the Maid's host at Orléans. His wife had often seen Jeanne kneeling in her private oratory.[295] The citizens of Orléans offered wine to the Attorney-General, to Jean de Velly, and to the Maid. In good sooth, 'twas a fine feast and a ceremonious. The burgesses loved and honoured Jeanne, but they cannot have observed her very closely during the repast or they would not eight years later, when an adventuress gave herself out to be the Maid, have mistaken her for Jeanne, and offered her wine in the same manner and at the hands of the same city servant, Jacques Leprestre, as now presented it.[296]

The standard that Jeanne loved even more than her Saint Catherine's sword had been painted at Tours by one Hamish Power. He was now marrying his daughter Héliote; and when Jeanne heard of it, she sent a letter to the magistrates of Tours, asking them to give a sum of one hundred crowns for the bride's trousseau. The nuptials were fixed for the 9th of February, 1430. The magistrates assembled twice to deliberate on Jeanne's request. They described her honourably and yet not without a certain caution as "the Maid who hath come into this realm to the King, concerning the matter of the war, announcing that she is sent by the King of Heaven against the English." In the end they refused to pay anything, because, they said, it behoved them to expend municipal funds on municipal matters and not otherwise; but they decided that for the affection and honour they bore the Maid, the churchmen, burgesses, and other townsfolk should be present in the church at the wedding, and should offer prayers for the bride and present her with bread and wine. This cost them four *livres*, ten *sous*.[297]

At a time which it is impossible to fix exactly the Maid bought a house at Orléans. To be more precise she took it on lease.[298] A lease (*bail à vente*) was an agreement by which the proprietor of a house or other property transferred the ownership to the lessee in return for an annual payment in kind or in money. The duration of such leases was usually fifty-nine years. The house that Jeanne acquired in this manner belonged to the Chapter of the Cathedral. It was in the centre of the town, in the parish of Saint-Malo, close to the Saint-Maclou Chapel, next door to the shop of an oil-seller, one Jean Feu, in the Rue des Petits-Souliers. It was in this street that, during the siege, there had fallen into the midst of five guests seated at table a stone cannon-ball weighing one hundred and sixty-four pounds, which had done no one any harm.[299] What price did the Maid give for this house? Apparently six crowns of fine gold (at sixty crowns to the mark), due half-yearly at Midsummer and Christmas, for fifty-nine years. In addition, she must according to custom have undertaken to keep the house in good condition and to pay out of her own purse the ecclesiastical dues as well as rates for wells and paving and all other taxes. Being obliged to have some one as surety, she chose as her guarantor a certain Guillot de Guyenne, of whom we know nothing further.[300]

There is no reason to believe that the Maid did not herself negotiate this agreement. Saint as she was, she knew well what it was to possess property. Such knowledge ran in her family; her father was the best business man in his village.[301] She herself was domesticated and thrifty; for she kept her old clothes, and even in the field she knew where to find them when she wanted to make presents of them to her friends. She counted up her possessions in arms and horses, valued them at twelve thousand crowns, and, apparently made a pretty accurate reckoning.[302] But what was her idea in taking this house? Did she think of living in it? Did she intend when the war was over to return to Orléans and pass a peaceful old age in a house of her own? Or was she planning for her parents to dwell there, or some Vouthon uncle, or her brothers, one of whom was in great poverty and had got a doublet out of the citizens of Orléans?[303]

On the third of March she followed King Charles to Sully.[304] The château, in which she lodged near the King, belonged to the Sire de la Trémouille, who had inherited it from his mother, Marie de Sully, the daughter of Louis I of Bourbon. It had been recaptured from the English after the deliverance of Orléans.[305] A stronghold on the Loire, on the highroad from Paris to Autun, and commanding the plain between Orléans and Briare and the ancient bridge with twenty arches, the château of Sully linked together central France and those northern provinces which Jeanne had so regretfully quitted, and whither with all her heart she longed to return to engage in fresh expeditions and fresh sieges.

During the first fortnight of March, from the townsfolk of Reims she received a message in which they confided to her fears only too well grounded.[306] On the 8th of March the Regent had granted to the Duke of Burgundy the counties of Champagne and of Brie on condition of his reconquering them.[307] Armagnacs and English vied with each other in offering the biggest and most tempting morsels to this Gargantuan Duke. Not being able to keep their promise and deliver to him Compiègne which refused to be delivered, the French offered him in its place Pont-Sainte-Maxence.[308] But it was Compiègne that he wanted. The truces, which had been very imperfectly kept, were to have expired at Christmas, but first they had been prolonged till the 15th of March and then till Easter. In the year 1430 Easter fell on the 16th of April; and Duke Philip was only waiting for that date to put an army in the field.[309]

In a manner concise and vivacious the Maid replied to the townsfolk of Reims:

"Dear friends and beloved and mightily desired. Jehanne the Maid hath received your letters making mention that ye fear a siege. Know ye that it shall not so betide, and I may but encounter them shortly. And if I do not encounter them and they do not come to you, if you shut your gates firmly, I shall shortly be with you: and if they be there, I shall make them put on their spurs so hastily that they will not know where to take them and so quickly that it shall be very soon. Other things I will not write unto you now, save that ye be always good and loyal. I pray God to have you in his keeping. Written at Sully, the 16th day of March.

I would announce unto you other tidings at which ye would mightily rejoice; but I fear lest the letters be taken on the road, and the said tidings be seen.

Signed. Jehanne.

Addressed to my dear friends and beloved, churchmen, burgesses and other citizens of the town of Rains."[310]

There can be no doubt that the scribe wrote this letter faithfully as it was dictated by the Maid, and that he wrote her words as they fell from her lips. In her haste she now and again forgot words and sometimes whole phrases; but the sense is clear all the same. And what confidence! "You will have no siege if I encounter the enemy." How completely is this the language of chivalry! On the eve of Patay she had asked: "Have you good spurs?"[311] Here she cries: "I will make them put on their spurs." She says that soon she will be in Champagne, that she is about to start. Surely we can no longer think of her shut up in the Castle of La Trémouille as in a kind of gilded cage.[312] In conclusion, she tells her friends at Reims that she does not write unto them all that she would like for fear lest her letter should be captured on the road. She knew what it was to be cautious. Sometimes she affixed a cross to her letters to warn her followers to pay no heed to what she wrote, in the hope that the missive would be intercepted and the enemy deceived.[313]

It was from Sully that on the 23rd of March Brother Pasquerel sent the Emperor Sigismund a letter intended for the Hussites of Bohemia.[314]

The Hussites of those days were abhorred and execrated throughout Christendom. They demanded the free preaching of God's word, communion in both kinds, and the return of the Church to that evangelical life which allowed neither the wealth of priests nor the temporal power of popes. They desired the punishment of sin by the civil magistrates, a custom which could prevail only in very holy society. They were saints indeed and heretics too on every possible point. Pope Martin held the destruction of these wicked persons to be salutary, and such was the opinion of every good Catholic. But how could this armed heresy be dealt with when it routed all the forces of the Empire and the Holy See? The Hussites were too much for that worn-out ancient chivalry of Christendom, for the knighthood of

France and of Germany, which was good for nothing but to be thrown on to the refuse heaps like so much old iron. And this was precisely what the towns of the realm of France did when over these knights of chivalry they placed a peasant girl.[315]

At Tachov, in 1427, the Crusaders, blessed by the Holy Father, had fled at the mere sound of the chariot wheels of the Procops.[316] Pope Martin knew not where to turn for defenders of Holy Church, one and indivisible. He had paid for the armament of five thousand English crusaders, which the Cardinal of Winchester was to lead against these accursed Bohemians; but in this force the Holy Father was cruelly disappointed; hardly had his five thousand crusaders landed in France, than the Regent of England diverted them from their route and sent them to Brie to occupy the attention of the Maid of the Armagnacs.[317]

Since her coming into France Jeanne had spoken of the crusade as a work good and meritorious. In the letter dictated before the expedition to Orléans, she summoned the English to join the French and go together to fight against the Church's foe. And later, writing to the Duke of Burgundy, she invited the son of the Duke vanquished at Nicopolis to make war against the Turks.[318] Who but the mendicants directing her can have put these crusading ideas into Jeanne's head? Immediately after the deliverance of Orléans it was said that she would lead King Charles to the conquest of the Holy Sepulchre and that she would die in the Holy Land.[319] At the same time it was rumoured that she would make war on the Hussites. In the month of July, 1429, when the coronation campaign had barely begun, it was proclaimed in Germany, on the faith of a prophetess of Rome, that by a prophetess of France the Bohemian kingdom should be recovered.[320]

Already zealous for the Crusade against the Turks, the Maid was now equally eager for the Crusade against the Hussites. Turks or Bohemians, it was all alike to her. Of one and the other her only knowledge lay in the stories full of witchcraft related to her by the mendicants of her company. Touching the Hussites, stories were told, not all true, but which Jeanne must have believed; and they cannot have pleased her. It was said that they worshipped the devil, and that they called him "the wronged one." It was told that as works of piety they committed all manner of fornication. Every Bohemian was said to be possessed by a hundred demons. They were accused of killing thousands of churchmen. Again, and this time with truth, they were charged with burning churches and monasteries. The Maid believed in the God who commanded Israel to wipe out the Philistines from the face of the earth. But recently there had arisen Cathari who held the God of the Old Testament to be none other than Lucifer or Luciabelus, author of evil, liar and murderer. The Cathari abhorred war; they refused to shed blood; they were heretics; they had been massacred, and none remained. The Maid believed in good faith that the extirpation of the Hussites was a work pleasing to God. Men more learned than she, not like her addicted to chivalry, but of gentle life, clerks like the Chancellor Jean Gerson, believed it likewise.[321] Of these Bohemian heretics she thought what every one thought: her opinions were those of the multitude; her views were modelled on public opinion. Wherefore in all the simplicity of her heart she hated the Hussites, but she feared them not, because she feared nothing and because she believed, God helping her, that she was able to overcome all the English, all the Turks, and all the Bohemians in the world. At the first trumpet call she was ready to sally forth against them. On the 23rd of March, 1430, Brother Pasquerel sent the Emperor Sigismund a letter written in the name of the Maid and intended for the Hussites of Bohemia. This letter was indited in Latin. The following is the purport of it:

Jhesus ✝ Maria

Long ago there reached me the tidings that ye from the true Christians that ye once were have become heretics, like unto the Saracens, that ye have abolished true religion and worship and have turned to a superstition corrupt and fatal, the which in your zeal to maintain and to spread abroad there be no shame nor cruelty ye do not dare to perpetrate. You defile the sacraments of the Church, tear to pieces the articles of her faith, overthrow her temples. The images which were made for similitudes you break and throw into the fire. Finally such Christians as embrace not your faith you massacre. What fury, what folly, what rage possesses you? That religion which God the All Powerful, which the Son, which the Holy Ghost raised up, instituted, exalted and revealed in a thousand manners, by a thousand miracles, ye persecute, ye employ all arts to overturn and to exterminate.

It is you, you who are blind and not those who have not eyes nor sight. Think ye that ye will go unpunished? Do ye not know that if God prevent not your impious violence, if he suffer you to grope on in darkness and in error, it is that he is preparing for you a greater sorrow and a greater punishment? As for me, in good sooth, were I not occupied with the English wars, I would have already come against you. But in very deed if I learn not that ye have turned from your wicked ways, I will peradventure leave the English and hasten against you, in order that I may destroy by the sword your vain and violent superstition, if I can do so in no other manner, and that I may rid you either of heresy or of life. Notwithstanding, if you prefer to return to the Catholic faith and to the light of primitive days, send unto me your ambassadors and I will tell them what ye must do. If on the other hand ye will be stiff-necked and kick against the pricks, then remember all the crimes and offences ye have perpetrated and look for to see me coming unto you with all strength divine and human to render unto you again all the evil ye have done unto others.

Given at Sully, on the 23rd of March, to the Bohemian heretics.

Signed. Pasquerel.[322]

This was the letter sent to the Emperor. How had Jeanne really expressed herself in her dialect savouring alike of the speech of Champagne and of that of l'Île de France? There can be no doubt but that her letter had been sadly embellished by the good Brother. Such Ciceronian language cannot have proceeded from the Maid. It is all very well to say that a saint of those days could do everything, could prophesy on any subject and in any tongue, so fine an epistle remains far too rhetorical to have been composed by a damsel whom even the Armagnac captains considered simple. Nevertheless, a careful examination will reveal in this missive, at any rate in the second half of it, certain of those bluntly naive passages and some of that childish assurance which are noticeable in Jeanne's genuine letters, especially in her reply to the Count of Armagnac;[323] and more than once there occurs an expression characteristic of a village sibyl. The following, for example, is quite in Jeanne's own manner: "If you will return to the bosom of the Catholic Church, send me your ambassadors; I will tell you what you have to do." And her usual threat: "Expect me with all strength human and divine."[324] As for the phrase: "If I hear not shortly of your conversion, of your return to the bosom of the Church, I will peradventure leave the English and come against you," here we may suspect the mendicant friar, less interested in the affairs of Charles VII than in those of the Church, of having ascribed to the Maid greater eagerness to set forth on the Crusade than she really felt.

Good and salutary as she deemed the taking of the Cross, as far as we know her, she would never have consented to take it until she had driven the English out of the realm of France. She believed this to be her mission, and the persistence, the consistency, the strength of will she evinced in its fulfilment, are truly admirable. It is quite probable that she dictated to the good Brother some phrase like: "When I have put the English out of the kingdom, I will turn against you." This would explain and excuse Brother Pasquerel's error. It is very likely that Jeanne believed she would dispose of the English in a trice and that she already saw herself distributing good buffets and sound clouts to the renegade and infidel Bohemians. The Maid's simplicity makes itself felt through the clerk's Latin. This epistle to the Bohemians recalls, alas! that fagot placed upon the stake whereon John Huss was burning, by the pious zeal of the good wife whose saintly simplicity John Huss himself teaches us to admire.

One cannot help reflecting that Jeanne and those very men against whom she hurled menace and invective had much in common; alike they were impelled by faith, chastity, simple ignorance, pious duty, resignation to God's will, and a tendency to magnify the minor matters of devotion. Zizka[325] had established in his camp that purity of morals which the Maid was endeavouring to introduce among the Armagnacs. The peasant soldiers of Bohemia and the peasant Maid of France bearing her sword amidst mendicant monks had much in common. On the one hand and on the other, we have the religious spirit in the place of the political spirit, the fear of sin in the place of obedience to the civil law, the spiritual introduced into the temporal. Here is indeed a woeful sight and a piteous; the devout set one against the other, the innocent against the innocent, the simple against the simple, the heretic against heretics; and it is painful to think that when she is threatening with extermination the disciples of that John Huss, who had been treacherously taken and burned as a heretic, she herself is on the point of being sold to her enemies and condemned to suffer as a witch. It would have been different if this letter, at which the accomplished wits and humorists of the day looked askance, had won the approval of theologians. But they also found fault with it, an illustrious canonist, a zealous inquisitor deemed highly presumptuous this threatening of a multitude of men by a Maid.[326]

We were right in saying that she was not prepared to leave the English immediately and hasten against the Bohemians. Five days after her appeal to the Hussites she wrote to her friends at Reims and in mysterious words gave them to understand that she would come to them shortly.[327]

The partisans of Duke Philip were at that time hatching plots in the towns of Champagne, notably at Troyes and at Reims. On the 22nd of February, 1430, a canon and a chaplain were arrested and brought before the chapter for having conspired to deliver the city to the English. It was well for them that they belonged to the Church, for having been condemned to perpetual imprisonment, they obtained from the King a mitigation of their sentence, and the canon a complete remittance.[328] The aldermen and ecclesiastics of the city, fearing they would be thought badly of on the other side of the Loire, wrote to the Maid entreating her to speak well of them to the King. The following is her reply to their request:[329]

"Very good friends and beloved, may it please you to wit that I have received your letters, the which make mention how it hath been reported to the King that within the city of Reims there be many wicked persons. Therefore I give you to wit that it is indeed true that even such things have been reported to him and that he grieves much that there be folk in alliance with the Burgundians; that they would betray the town and bring the Burgundians into it. But since then the King has known the contrary by means of the assurance ye have sent him, and he is well pleased with you. And ye may believe that ye stand well in his favour; and if ye have need, he would help you with regard to the siege; and he knows well that ye have much to suffer from the hardness of those treacherous Burgundians, your adversaries: thus may God in his pleasure deliver you shortly, that is as soon as may be. So I pray and entreat you my friends dearly beloved that ye hold well the said city for the King and that ye keep good watch. Ye will soon have good tidings of me at greater length. Other things for the present I write not unto you save that the whole of Brittany is French and that the Duke is to send to the King three thousand combatants paid for two months. To God I commend you, may he keep you.

Written at Sully, the 28th of March.

Jehanne.[330]

Addressed to: My good friends and dearly beloved, the churchmen, aldermen, burgesses and inhabitants and masters of the good town of Reyms."[331]

Touching the succour to be expected from the Duke of Brittany, the Maid was labouring under a delusion. Like all other prophetesses she was ignorant of what was passing around her. Despite her failures, she believed in her good fortune; she doubted herself no more than she doubted God; and she was eager to pursue the fulfilment of her mission. "Ye shall soon have tidings of me," she said to the townsfolk of Reims. A few days after, and she left Sully to go into France and fight, on the expiration of the truces.

It has been said that she feigned an expedition of pleasure and set out without taking leave of the King, that it was a kind of innocent stratagem, an honourable flight.[332] But it was nothing of the sort.[333] The Maid gathered a company of some hundred horse, sixty-eight archers and cross-bowmen, and two trumpeters, commanded by a Lombard captain, Bartolomeo Baretta.[334] In this company were Italian men-at-arms, bearing broad shields, like some who had come to Orléans at the time of the siege; possibly they were the same.[335] She set out at the head of this company, with her brothers and her steward, the Sire Jean d'Aulon. She was in the hands of Jean d'Aulon, and Jean d'Aulon was in the hands of the Sire de la Trémouille, to whom he owed money.[336] The good squire would not have followed the Maid against the King's will.

The flying squadron of *béguines* had recently been divided by a schism. Friar Richard, who was then in high favour with Queen Marie, and who had preached the Lenten sermons of 1430[337] at Orléans, stayed behind, on the Loire, with Catherine de la Rochelle. Jeanne took with her Pierronne and the younger Breton prophetess.[338] If she went into France, it was not without the knowledge or against the will of the King and his Council. Very probably the Chancellor of the kingdom had asked La Trémouille to send her in order that he might employ her in the approaching campaign against the Burgundians, who were threatening his government of Beauvais and his city of Reims.[339] He was not very kindly disposed towards her, but already he had made use of her and he intended to do so again. Possibly his intention was to employ her in a fresh attack on Paris.

The King had not abandoned the idea of taking his great city by the peaceful methods he always preferred. Throughout Lent, between Sully and Paris, there had been a constant passing to and fro of certain Carmelite monks of Melun, disguised as artisans. These were the churchmen who, during the attack on the Porte Saint Honoré, on the Day of the Festival of Our Lady, had stirred up the popular rising which had spread from one bank of the Seine to the other. Now they were negotiating with certain influential citizens the entrance of the King's men into the rebel city. The Prior of the Melun Carmelites was directing the conspiracy.[340] There is reason to believe that Jeanne had herself seen him or one of his monks. True it is that since the 22nd or the 23rd of March it was known at Sully that the conspiracy had been discovered;[341] but perhaps the hope of success still lingered. It was to Melun that Jeanne went with her company; and it is difficult to believe that there was no connection between the conspiracy of the Carmelites and the expedition of the Maid.

Why should Charles VII's Councillors have ceased to employ her? It cannot be said that she appeared less divine to the French or less evil to the English. Her failures, either unknown, or partially known, rendered unimportant by the fame of her victories, had not dispelled the idea that within her resided invincible power. At the time when the hapless damsel with the flower of French knighthood was receiving sore treatment under the walls of La Charité at the hands of an ex-mason's apprentice, in Burgundian lands it was rumoured that she was carrying by storm a castle twelve miles from Paris.[342] She was still considered miraculous; the burgesses, the men-at-arms of her party still believed in her. And as for the *Godons*, from the Regent to the humblest swordsman of the army, they all regarded her with a terror as great as that which had possessed them at Orléans and Patay. At this time so many English soldiers and captains refused to go to France, that a special edict was issued obliging them to do so.[343] But they doubtless discovered reasons enough for not going into a country where henceforth they could hope only for hard knocks and nothing tempting; so that many declined, terrified by the enchantments of the Maid.[344]

CHAPTER VI

THE MAID IN THE TRENCHES OF MELUN – LE SEIGNEUR DE L'OURS – THE CHILD OF LAGNY

I N Easter week, Jeanne, at the head of a band of mercenaries, is before the walls of Melun.[345] She arrives just in time to fight. The truces have expired.[346] Is it possible that the town which was subject to King Charles[347] can have refused to admit the Maid with her company when she came to it so generously? Apparently it was so. Was Jeanne able to communicate with the Carmelites of Melun? Probably. What misfortune befell her at the gates of the town? Did she suffer ill treatment at the hands of a Burgundian band? We know not. But when she was in the trenches she heard Saint Catherine and Saint Margaret saying unto her: "Thou wilt be taken before Saint John's Day."

And she entreated them: "When I am taken, let me die immediately without suffering long." And the Voices repeated that she would be taken and thus it must be.

And they added gently: "Be not troubled, be resigned. God will help thee."[348]

Saint John's Day was the 24th of June, in less than ten weeks. Many a time after that, Jeanne asked her saints at what hour she would be taken; but they did not tell her; and thus doubting she ceased to follow her own ideas and consulted the captains.[349]

On her way from Melun to Lagny-sur-Marne, in the month of May, she had to pass Corbeil. It was probably then, and in her company, that the two devout women from Lower Brittany, Pierronne and her younger sister in the spirit, were taken at Corbeil by the English.[350]

For eight months the town of Lagny had been subject to King Charles and governed by Messire Ambroise de Loré, who was energetically waging war against the English of Paris and elsewhere.[351] For the nonce Messire Ambroise de Loré was absent; but his lieutenant, Messire Jean Foucault, commanded the garrison. Shortly after Jeanne's coming to this town, tidings were brought that a company of between three and four hundred men of Picardy and of Champagne, fighting for the Duke of Burgundy, after having ranged through l'Île de France, were now on their way back to Picardy with much booty. Their captain was a valiant man-at-arms, one Franquet d'Arras.[352] The French determined to cut off their retreat. Under the command of Messire Jean Foucault, Messire Geoffroy de Saint-Bellin, Lord Hugh Kennedy, a Scotchman, and Captain Baretta, they sallied forth from the town.[353]

The Maid went with them. They encountered the Burgundians near Lagny, but failed to surprise them. Messire Franquet's archers had had time to take up their position with their backs to a hedge, in the English manner. King Charles's men barely outnumbered the enemy. A certain clerk of that time, a Frenchman, writes of the engagement. His innate ingeniousness was invincible. With candid common sense he states that this very slight numerical superiority rendered the enterprise very arduous and difficult for his party.[354] And the battle was strong indeed. The Burgundians were mightily afraid of the Maid because they believed her to be a witch and in command of armies of devils; notwithstanding, they fought right valiantly. Twice the French were repulsed; but they returned to the attack, and finally the Burgundians were all slain or taken.[355]

The conquerors returned to Lagny, loaded with booty and taking with them their prisoners, among whom was Messire Franquet d'Arras. Of noble birth and the lord of a manor, he was entitled to expect that he would be held to ransom, according to custom. Both Jean de Troissy, Bailie of Senlis,[356] and the Maid demanded him from the soldier who was his captor. It was to the Maid that he was finally delivered.[357] Did she obtain him in return for money? Probably, for soldiers were not accustomed to give up noble and profitable prisoners for nothing. Nevertheless, the Maid, when questioned on this subject, replied, that being neither mistress nor steward of France, it was not for her to give out money. We must suppose, therefore, that some one paid for her. However that may be, Captain Franquet d'Arras was given up to her, and she endeavoured to exchange him for a prisoner in the hands of the English. The man whom she thus desired to deliver was a Parisian who was called Le Seigneur de l'Ours.[358]

He was not of gentle birth and his arms were the sign of his hostelry. It was the custom in those days to give the title of Seigneur to the masters of the great Paris inns. Thus Colin, who kept the inn at the Temple Gate, was known as Seigneur du Boisseau. The hôtel de l'Ours stood in the Rue Saint-Antoine, near the Gate properly called La Porte Baudoyer, but commonly known as Porte Baudet, Baudet possessing the double advantage over Baudoyer of being shorter and more comprehensible.[359] It was an ancient and famous inn, equal in renown to the most famous, to the inn of L'Arbre Sec, in the street of that name, to the Fleur de Lis near the Pont Neuf, to the Epée in the Rue Saint-Denis, and to the Chapeau Fétu of the Rue Croix-du-Tirouer. As early as King Charles V's reign the inn was much frequented. Before huge fires the spits were turning all day long, and there were hot bread, fresh herrings, and wine of Auxerre in plenty. But since then the plunderings of men-at-arms had laid waste the countryside, and travellers no longer ventured forth for fear of being robbed and slain. Knights and pilgrims had ceased coming into the town. Only wolves came by night and devoured little children in the streets. There were no fagots in the grate, no dough in the kneading-trough. Armagnacs and Burgundians had drunk all the wine, laid waste all the vineyards, and nought was left in the cellar save a poor piquette of apples and of plums.[360]

The Seigneur de l'Ours, whom the Maid demanded, was called Jaquet Guillaume.[361] Although Jeanne, like other folk, called him Seigneur, it is not certain that he personally directed his inn, nor even that the inn was open through these years of disaster and desolation. The only ascertainable fact is that he was the proprietor of the house with the sign of the Bear (*l'Ours*). He held it by right of his wife Jeannette, and had come into possession of it in the following manner.

Fourteen years before, when King Henry with his knighthood had not yet landed in France, the host of the Bear Inn had been the King's sergeant-at-arms, one Jean Roche, a man of wealth and fair fame. He was a devoted follower of the Duke of Burgundy, and that was what ruined him. Paris was then occupied by the Armagnacs. In the year 1416, in order to turn them out of the city, Jean Roche concerted with divers burgesses. The plot was to be carried out on Easter Day, which that year fell on the 29th of April. But the Armagnacs discovered it.

They threw the conspirators into prison and brought them to trial. On the first Saturday in May the Seigneur de l'Ours was carried to the market place in a tumbrel with Durand de Brie, a dyer, master of the sixty cross-bowmen of Paris, and Jean Perquin, pin-maker and brasier. All three were beheaded, and the body of the Seigneur de l'Ours was hanged at Montfaucon where it remained until the entrance of the Burgundians. Six weeks after their coming, in July, 1418, his body was taken down from gibbet and buried in consecrated ground.[362]

Now the widow of Jean Roche had a daughter by a first marriage. Her name was Jeannette; she took for her first husband a certain Bernard le Breton; for her second, Jaquet Guillaume, who was not rich. He owed money to Maître Jean Fleury, a clerk at law and the King's secretary. His wife's affairs were not more prosperous; her father's goods had been confiscated and she had been obliged to redeem a part of her maternal inheritance. In 1424, the couple were short of money, and they sold a house, concealing the fact that it was mortgaged. Being charged by the purchaser, they were thrown into prison, where they aggravated their offence by suborning two witnesses, one a priest, the other a chambermaid. Fortunately for them, they procured a pardon.[363]

The Jaquet Guillaume couple, therefore, were in a sorry plight. There remained to them, however, the inheritance of Jean Roche, the inn near the Place Baudet, at the sign of the Bear, the title of which Jaquet Guillaume bore. This second Seigneur de l'Ours was to be as strongly Armagnac as the other had been Burgundian, and was to pay the same price for his opinions.

Six years had passed since his release from prison, when, in the March of 1430, there was plotted by the Carmelites of Melun and certain burgesses of Paris that conspiracy which we mentioned on the occasion of Jeanne's departure for l'Île de France. It was not the first plot into which the Carmelites had entered; they had plotted that rising which had been on the point of breaking out on the Day of the Nativity, when the Maid was leading the attack near La Porte Saint-Honoré; but never before had so many burgesses and so many notables entered into a conspiracy. A clerk of the Treasury, Maître Jean de la Chapelle, two magistrates of the Châtelet, Maître Renaud Savin and Maître Pierre Morant, a very wealthy man, named Jean de Calais, burgesses, merchants, artisans, more than one hundred and fifty persons, held the threads of this vast web, and among them, Jaquet Guillaume, Seigneur de l'Ours.

The Carmelites of Melun directed the whole. Clad as artisans, they went from King to burgesses, from burgesses to King; they kept up the communications between those within and those without, and regulated all the details of the enterprise. One of them asked the conspirators for a written undertaking to bring the King's men into the city. Such a demand looks as if the majority of the conspirators were in the pay of the Royal Council.

In exchange for this undertaking these monks brought acts of oblivion signed by the King. For the people of Paris to be induced to receive the Prince, whom they still called Dauphin, they must needs be assured of a full and complete amnesty. For more than ten years, while the English and Burgundians had been holding the town, no one had felt altogether free from the reproach of their lawful sovereign and the men of his party. And all the more desirous were they for Charles of Valois to forget the past when they recalled the cruel vengeance taken by the Armagnacs after the suppression of the Butchers.

One of the conspirators, Jaquet Perdriel, advocated the sounding of a trumpet and the reading of the acts of oblivion on Sunday at the Porte Baudet.

"I have no doubt," he said, "but that we shall be joined by the craftsmen, who, in great numbers will flock to hear the reading."

He intended leading them to the Saint Antoine Gate and opening it to the King's men who were lying in ambush close by.

Some eighty or a hundred Scotchmen, dressed as Englishmen, wearing the Saint Andrew's cross, were then to enter the town, bringing in fish and cattle.

"They will enter boldly by the Saint-Denys Gate," said Perdriel, "and take possession of it. Whereupon the King's men will enter in force by the Porte Saint Antoine."

The plan was deemed good, except that it was considered better for the King's men to come in by the Saint-Denys Gate.

On Sunday, the 12th of March, the second Sunday in Lent, Maître Jean de la Chapelle invited the magistrate Renaud Savin to come to the tavern of *La Pomme de Pin* and meet divers other conspirators in order to arrive at an understanding touching what was best to be done. They decided that on a certain day, under pretext of going to see his vines at

Chapelle-Saint-Denys, Jean de Calais should join the King's men outside the walls, make himself known to them by unfurling a white standard and bring them into the town. It was further determined that Maître Morant and a goodly company of citizens with him, should hold themselves in readiness in the taverns of the Rue Saint-Denys to support the French when they came in. In one of the taverns of this street must have been the Seigneur de l'Ours, who, dwelling near by, had undertaken to bring together divers folk of the neighbourhood.

The conspirators were acting in perfect agreement. All they now awaited was to be informed of the day chosen by the Royal Council; and they believed the attempt was to be made on the following Sunday. But on the 21st of March Brother Pierre d'Allée, Prior of the Carmelites of Melun, was taken by the English. Put to the torture, he confessed the plot and named his accomplices. On the information he gave, more than one hundred and fifty persons were arrested and tried. On the 8th of April, the Eve of Palm Sunday, seven of the most important were taken to the market-place on a tumbrel. They were: Jean de la Chapelle, clerk of the Treasury; Renaud Savin and Pierre Morant, magistrates at the Châtelet; Guillaume Perdriau; Jean le François, called Baudrin; Jean le Rigueur, baker, and Jaquet Guillaume, Seigneur de l'Ours. All seven were beheaded by the executioner, who afterwards quartered the bodies of Jean de la Chapelle and of Baudrin.

Jaquet Perdriel was merely deprived of his possessions. Jean de Calais soon procured a pardon. Jeannette, the wife of Jaquet Guillaume, was banished from the kingdom and her goods confiscated.[364]

How can the Maid have known the Seigneur de l'Ours? Possibly the Carmelites of Melun had recommended him to her, and perhaps it was on their advice that she demanded his surrender. She may have seen him in the September of 1429, at Saint-Denys or before the walls of Paris, and he may have then undertaken to work for the Dauphin and his party. Why were attempts made at Lagny to save this man alone of the one hundred and fifty Parisians arrested on the information of Brother Pierre d'Allée? Rather than Renaud Savin and Pierre Morant, magistrates at the Châtelet, rather than Jean de la Chapelle, clerk of the Treasury, why choose the meanest of the band? And how could they look to exchange a man accused of treachery for a prisoner of war? All this seems to us mysterious and inexplicable.

In the early days of May, Jeanne did not know what had become of Jaquet Guillaume. When she heard that he had been tried and put to death she was sore grieved and vexed. None the less, she looked upon Franquet as a captive held to ransom. But the Bailie of Senlis, who for some unknown reason was determined on the captain's ruin, took advantage of the Maid's vexation at Jaquet Guillaume's execution, and persuaded her to give up her prisoner.

He represented to her that this man had committed many a murder, many a theft, that he was a traitor, and that consequently he ought to be brought to trial.

"You will be neglecting to execute justice," he said, "if you set this Franquet free."

These reasons decided her, or rather she yielded to the Bailie's entreaty.

"Since the man I wished to have is dead," she said, "do with Franquet as justice shall require you."[365]

Thus she surrendered her prisoner. Was she right or wrong? Before deciding we must ask whether it were possible for her to do otherwise than she did. She was the Maid of God, the angel of the Lord of Hosts, that is clear. But the leaders of war, the captains, paid no great heed to what she said. As for the Bailie, he was the King's man, of noble birth and passing powerful.

Assisted by the judges of Lagny, he himself conducted the trial. The accused confessed that he was a murderer, a thief, and a traitor. We must believe him; and yet we cannot forbear a doubt as to whether he really was, any more than the majority of Armagnac or Burgundian men-at-arms, any more than a Damoiseau de Commercy or a Guillaume de Flavy, for example. He was condemned to death.

Jeanne consented that he should die, if he had deserved death, and seeing that he had confessed his crimes[366] he was beheaded.

When they heard of the scandalous treatment of Messire Franquet, the Burgundians were loud in their sorrow and indignation.[367] It would seem that in this matter the Bailie of Senlis and the judges of Lagny did not act according to custom. We, however, are not sufficiently acquainted with the circumstances to form an opinion. There may have been some reason, of which we are ignorant, why the King of France should have demanded this prisoner. He had a right to do so on condition that he paid the Maid the amount of the ransom. A soldier of those days, well informed in all things touching honour in war, was the author of *Le Jouvencel*. In his chivalrous romances he writes approvingly of the wise Amydas, King of Amydoine, who, learning that one of his enemies, the Sire de Morcellet, has been taken in battle and held to ransom, cries out that he is the vilest of traitors, ransoms him with good coins of the realm, and hands him over to the provost of the town and the officers of his council that they may execute justice upon him.[368] Such was the royal prerogative.

Whether it was that camp life was hardening her, or whether, like all mystics, she was subject to violent changes of mood, Jeanne showed at Lagny none of that gentleness she had displayed on the evening of Patay. The virgin who once had no other arm in battle than her standard, now wielded a sword found there, at Lagny, a Burgundian sword and a trusty. Those who regarded her as an angel of the Lord, good Brother Pasquerel, for example, might justify her by saying that the Archangel Saint Michael, the standard-bearer of celestial hosts, bore a flaming sword. And indeed Jeanne remained a saint.

While she was at Lagny, folk came and told her that a child had died at birth, unbaptised.[369] Having entered into the mother at the time of her conception, the devil held the soul of this child, who, for lack of water, had died the enemy of its Creator. The greatest anxiety was felt concerning the fate of this soul. Some thought it was in limbo, banished forever from God's sight, but the more general and better founded opinion was that it was seething in hell; for has not Saint Augustine demonstrated that souls, little as well as great, are damned because of original sin. And how could it be otherwise, seeing that Eve's fall had effaced the divine likeness in this child? He was destined to eternal death. And to think that with a few drops of water this death might have been avoided! So terrible a disaster afflicted not only the poor creature's kinsfolk, but likewise the neighbours and all good Christians in the town of Lagny. The body was carried to the Church of Saint-Pierre and placed before the image of Our Lady, which had been highly venerated ever since the plague of 1128. It was called Notre-Dame-des-Ardents because it cured burns, and when there were no burns to be cured it was called Notre-Dame-des-Aidants, or rather Des Aidances, that is, Our Lady the Helper, because she granted succour to those in dire necessity.[370]

The maidens of the town knelt before her, the little body in their midst, beseeching her to intercede with her divine Son so that this little child might have his share in the Redemption brought by our Saviour.[371] In such cases the Holy Virgin did not always deny her powerful intervention. Here it may not be inappropriate to relate a miracle she had worked thirty-seven years before.

At Paris, in 1393, a sinful creature, finding herself with child, concealed her pregnancy, and, when her time was come, was without aid delivered. Then, having stuffed linen into the throat of the girl she had brought forth, she went and threw her on to the dust-heap outside La Porte Saint-Martin-des-Champs. But a dog scented the body, and scratching away the other refuse, discovered it. A devout woman, who happened to be passing by, took this poor little lifeless creature, and, followed by more than four hundred people, bore it to the Church of Saint-Martin-des-Champs, there placed it on the altar of Our Lady, and kneeling down with the multitude of folk and the monks of the Abbey, with all her heart prayed the Holy Virgin not to suffer this innocent babe to be condemned eternally. The child stirred a little, opened her eyes, loosened the linen, which gagged her, and cried aloud. A priest baptized her on the altar of Our Lady, and gave her the name of Marie. A nurse was found, and she was fed from the breast. She lived three hours, then died and was carried to consecrated ground.[372]

In those days resurrections of unbaptised children were frequent. That saintly Abbess, Colette of Corbie, who, when Jeanne was at Lagny, dwelt at Moulins with the reformed Sisters of Saint Clare, had brought back to life two of these poor creatures: a girl, who received the name of Colette at the font and afterwards became nun, then abbess at Pont-à-Mousson; a boy, who was said to have been two days buried and whom the servant of the poor declared to be one of the elect. He died at six months, thus fulfilling the prophecy made by the saint.[373]

With this kind of miracle Jeanne was doubtless acquainted. About twenty-five miles from Domremy, in the duchy of Lorraine, near Lunéville, was the sanctuary of Notre-Dame-des-Aviots, of which she had probably heard. Notre-Dame-des-Aviots, or Our Lady of those brought back to life, was famed for restoring life to unbaptised children. By means of her intervention they lived again long enough to be made Christians.[374]

In the duchy of Luxembourg, near Montmédy, on the hill of Avioth,[375] multitudes of pilgrims worshipped an image of Our Lady brought there by angels. On this hill a church had been built for her, with slim pillars and elaborate stonework in trefoils, roses and light foliage. This statue worked all manner of miracles. At its feet were placed children born dead; they were restored to life and straightway baptized.[376]

The folk, gathered in the Church of Saint-Pierre de Lagny, around the statue of Notre-Dame-des-Aidances, hoped for a like grace. The damsels of the town prayed round the child's lifeless body. The Maid was asked to come and join them in praying to Our Lord and Our Lady. She went to the church, and knelt down with the maidens and prayed. The child was black, "as black as my coat," said Jeanne. When the Maid and the damsels had prayed, it yawned three times and its colour came back. It was baptized and straightway it died; it was buried in consecrated ground. Throughout the town this resurrection was said to be the work of the Maid. According to the tales in circulation, during the three days since its birth the child had given no sign of life;[377] but the gossips of Lagny had doubtless extended the period of its comatose condition, like those good wives who of a single egg laid by the husband of one of them, made a hundred before the day was out.

CHAPTER VII

SOISSONS AND COMPIÈGNE – CAPTURE OF THE MAID

EAVING Lagny, the Maid presented herself before Senlis, with her own company and with the fighting men of the French nobles whom she had joined, in all some thousand horse. And for this force she demanded entrance into the town. No misfortune was more feared by burgesses than that of receiving men-at-arms, and no privilege more jealously guarded than that of keeping them outside the walls. King Charles had experienced it during the peaceful coronation campaign. The folk of Senlis made answer to the Maid that, seeing the poverty of the town in forage, corn, oats, victuals and wine, they offered her an entrance with thirty or forty of the most notable of her company and no more.[378]

It is said that from Senlis Jeanne went to the Castle of Borenglise in the parish of Elincourt, between Compiègne and Ressons; and, in ignorance as to what can have taken her there, it is supposed that she made a pilgrimage to the Church of Elincourt, which was dedicated to Saint Margaret; and it is possible that she wished to worship Saint Margaret there as she had worshipped Saint Catherine at Fierbois, in order to do honour to one of those heavenly ladies who visited her every day and every hour.[379]

In those days, in the town of Angers, was a licentiate of laws, canon of the churches of Tours and Angers and Dean of Saint-Jean d'Angers. Less than ten days before Jeanne's coming to Sainte-Marguerite d'Elincourt, on April 18, about nine o'clock in the evening, he felt a pain in the head, which lasted until four o'clock in the morning, and was so severe that he thought he must die. He prayed to Saint Catherine, for whom he professed a special devotion, and straightway was cured. In thankfulness for so great a grace, he wended on foot to the sanctuary of Saint Catherine of Fierbois; and there, on

Friday, the 5th of May, in a loud voice, said a mass for the King, for "the Maid divinely worthy," and for the peace and prosperity of the realm.[380]

Philip, Duke of Burgundy

The Council of King Charles had made over Pont-Sainte-Maxence to the Duke of Burgundy, in lieu of Compiègne, which they were unable to deliver to him since that town absolutely refused to be delivered, and remained the King's despite the King. The Duke of Burgundy kept Pont-Sainte-Maxence which had been granted him and resolved to take Compiègne.[381]

On the 17th of April, when the truce had expired, he took the field with a goodly knighthood and a powerful army, four thousand Burgundians, Picards and Flemings, and fifteen hundred English, commanded by Jean de Luxembourg, Count of Ligny.[382]

Noble pieces of artillery did the Duke bring to that siege; notably, Remeswelle, Rouge Bombarde and Houppembière, from all three of which were fired stone balls of enormous size. Mortars, which the Duke had brought and paid ready money for to Messire Jean de Luxembourg, were brought likewise; Beaurevoir and Bourgogne, also a great *"coullard"* and a movable engine of war. The vast states of Burgundy sent their archers and cross-bowmen to Compiègne. The Duke provided himself with bows from Prussia and from Caffa in Georgia,[383] and with arrows barbed and unbarbed. He engaged sappers and miners to lay powder mines round the town and to throw Greek fire into it. In short my Lord Philip, richer than a king, the most magnificent lord in Christendom and skilled in all the arts of knighthood, was resolved to make a gallant siege.[384]

The town, then one of the largest and strongest in France, was defended by a garrison of between four and five hundred men,[385] commanded by Guillaume de Flavy. Scion of a noble house of that province, forever in dispute with the nobles his neighbours, and perpetually picking quarrels with the poor folk, he was as wicked and cruel as any Armagnac baron.[386] The citizens would have no other captain, and in that office they maintained him in defiance of King Charles and his chamberlains. They did wisely, for none was better able to defend the town than my Lord Guillaume, none was more set on doing his duty. When the King of France had commanded him to deliver the place he had refused point-blank; and when later the Duke promised him a good round sum and a rich inheritance in exchange for Compiègne, he made answer that the town was not his, but the King's.[387]

The Duke of Burgundy easily took Gournay-sur-Aronde, and then laid siege to Choisy-sur-Aisne, also called Choisy-au-Bac, at the junction of the Aisne and the Oise.[388]

The Gascon squire, Poton de Saintrailles and the men of his company crossed the Aisne between Soissons and Choisy, surprised the besiegers, and retired immediately, taking with them sundry prisoners.[389]

On the 13th of May, the Maid entered Compiègne, where she lodged in the Rue de l'Etoile.[390] On the morrow, the Attorneys[391] offered her four pots of wine.[392] They thereby intended to do her great honour, for they did no more for the Lord Archbishop of Reims, Chancellor of the realm, who was then in the town with the Count of Vendôme, the King's lieutenant and divers other leaders of war. These noble lords resolved to send artillery and other munitions to the Castle of Choisy, which could not hold out much longer;[393] and now, as before, the Maid was made use of.

The army marched towards Soissons in order to cross the Aisne.[394] The captain of the town was a squire of Picardy, called by the French Guichard Bournel, by the Burgundians Guichard de Thiembronne; he had served on both sides. Jeanne knew him well; he reminded her of a painful incident. He had been one of those, who finding her wounded in the trenches before Paris, had insisted on putting her on her horse against her will. On the approach of King Charles's barons and men-at-arms, Captain Guichard made the folk of Soissons believe that the whole army was coming to encamp in their town. Wherefore they resolved not to receive them. Then happened what had already befallen at Senlis: Captain Bournel received the Lord Archbishop of Reims, the Count of Vendôme and the Maid, with a small company, and the rest of the army abode that night outside the walls.[395] On the morrow, failing to obtain command of the bridge, they endeavoured to ford the river, but without success; for it was spring and the waters were high. The army had to turn back. When it was gone, Captain Bournel sold to the Duke of Burgundy the city he was charged to hold for the King of France; and he delivered it into the hand of Messire Jean de Luxembourg for four thousand golden *saluts*.[396]

At the tidings of this treacherous and dishonourable action on the part of the Captain of Soissons, Jeanne cried out that if she had him, she would cut his body into four pieces, which was no empty imagining of her wrath. As the penalty of certain crimes it was the custom for the executioner, after he had beheaded the condemned, to cut his body in four pieces, which was called quartering. So that it was as if Jeanne had said that the traitor deserved quartering. The words sounded hard to Burgundian ears; certain even believed that they heard Jeanne in her wrath taking God's name in vain. They did not hear correctly. Never had Jeanne taken the name of God or of any of his saints in vain. Far from swearing when she was angered, she used to exclaim: "God's good will!" or "Saint John!" or "By Our Lady!"[397]

Before Soissons, Jeanne and the generals separated. The latter with their men-at-arms went to Senlis and the banks of the Marne. The country between the Aisne and the Oise was no longer capable of supporting so large a number of men or such important personages. Jeanne and her company wended their way back to Compiègne.[398] Scarcely had she entered the town when she sallied forth to ravage the neighbourhood.

For example, she took part in an expedition against Pont-l'Evêque, a stronghold, some distance from Noyon, occupied by a small English garrison, commanded by Lord Montgomery.

The Burgundians, who were besieging Compiègne, made Pont-l'Evêque their base. In the middle of May, the French numbering about a thousand, commanded by Captain Poton, by Messire Jacques de Chabannes and divers others, and accompanied by the Maid, attacked the English under Lord Montgomery, and the battle was passing fierce. But the enemy, being relieved by the Burgundians of Noyon, the French must needs beat a retreat. They had slain thirty of their adversaries and had lost as many, wherefore the combat was held to have been right sanguinary.[399] There was no longer any question of crossing the Aisne and saving Choisy.

After returning to Compiègne, Jeanne, who never rested for a moment, hastened to Crépy-en-Valois, where were gathering the troops intended for the defence of Compiègne. Then, with these troops, she marched through the Forest of Guise, to the besieged town and entered it on the 23rd, at daybreak, without having encountered any Burgundians. There were none in the neighbourhood of the Forest, on the left bank of the Oise.[400]

They were all on the other side of the river. There meadowland extends for some three-quarters of a mile, while beyond rises the slope of Picardy. Because this meadow was low, damp and frequently flooded, a causeway had been built leading from the bridge to the village of Margny, which rose on the steep slope of the hill. Some two miles up the river there towered the belfry of Clairoix, at the junction of the Aronde and the Oise. On the opposite bank rose the belfry of Venette, about a mile and a quarter lower down, towards Pont-Sainte-Maxence.[401]

A little band of Burgundians commanded by a knight, Messire Baudot de Noyelles, occupied the high ground of the village of Margny. Most renowned among the men of war of the Burgundian party was Messire Jean de Luxembourg. He with his Picards was posted at Clairoix, on the banks of the Aronde, at the foot of Mount Ganelon. The five hundred English of Lord Montgomery watched the Oise at Venette. Duke Philip occupied Coudun, a good two and a half miles from the town, towards Picardy.[402] Such dispositions were in accordance with the precepts of the most experienced captains. It was their rule that when besieging a fortified town a large number of men-at-arms should never be concentrated in one spot, in one camp, as they said. In case of a sudden attack, it was thought that a large company, if it has but one base, will be surprised and routed just as easily as a lesser number, and the disaster will be grievous. Wherefore it is better to divide the besiegers into small companies and to place them not far apart, in order that they may aid one another. In this wise, when those of one body are discomfited those of another have time to put themselves in battle array for their succour. While the assailants are sore aghast at seeing fresh troops come down upon them, those who are being attacked take heart of grace. At any rate such was the opinion of Messire Jean de Bueil.[403]

That same day, the 23rd of May, towards five o'clock in the evening[404] riding a fine dapple-grey horse, Jeanne sallied forth, across the bridge, on to the causeway over the meadow. With her were her standard-bearer and her company of Lombards, Captain Baretta and his three or four hundred men, both horse and foot, who had entered Compiègne by night. She was girt with the Burgundian sword, found at Lagny, and over her armour she wore a surcoat of cloth of gold.[405] Such attire would have better beseemed a parade than a sortie; but in the simplicity of her rustic and religious soul she loved all the pompous show of chivalry.

The enterprise had been concerted between Captain Baretta, the other leaders of the party and Messire Guillaume de Flavy. The last-named, in order to protect the line of retreat for the French, had posted archers, cross-bowmen, and cannoneers at the head of the bridge, while on the river he launched a number of small covered boats, intended if need were to bring back as many men as possible.[406] Jeanne was not consulted in the matter; her advice was never asked. Without being told anything she was taken with the army as a bringer of good luck; she was exhibited to the enemy as a powerful enchantress, and they, especially if they were in mortal sin, feared lest she should cast a spell over them. Certain there were doubtless on both sides, who perceived that she did not greatly differ from other women;[407] but they were folk who believed in nothing, and that manner of person is always outside public opinion.

This time she had not the remotest idea of what was to be done. With her head full of dreams, she imagined she was setting forth for some great and noble emprise. It is said that she had promised to discomfit the Burgundians and bring back Duke Philip prisoner. But there was no question of that; Captain Baretta and those who commanded the soldiers of fortune proposed to surprise and plunder the little Burgundian outpost, which was nearest the town and most accessible. That was Margny, and there on a steep hill, which might be reached in twenty or twenty-five minutes along the causeway, was stationed Messire Baudot de Noyelles. The attempt was worth making. The taking of outposts constituted the perquisites of men-at-arms. And, albeit the enemy's positions were very wisely chosen, the assailants if they proceeded with extreme swiftness had a chance of success. The Burgundians at Margny were very few. Having but lately arrived, they had erected neither bastion nor bulwark, and their only defences were the outbuildings of the village.

It was five o'clock in the afternoon when the French set out on the march. The days being at their longest, they did not depend on the darkness for success. In those times indeed, men-at-arms were chary of venturing much in the darkness. They deemed the night treacherous, capable of serving the fool's turn as well as the wise man's, and thus ran the saw: "Night never blushes at her deed."[408]

Having climbed up to Margny, the assailants found the Burgundians scattered and unarmed. They took them by surprise; and the French set to work to strike here and there haphazard. The Maid, for her part, overthrew everything before her.

Now just at this time Sire Jean de Luxembourg and the Sire de Créquy had ridden over from their camp at Clairoix.[409] Wearing no armour, and accompanied by eight or ten gentlemen-at-arms, they were climbing the Margny hill. They were on their way to visit Messire Baudot de Noyelles, and all unsuspecting, they were thinking to reconnoitre the defences of the town from this elevated spot, as the Earl of Salisbury had formerly done from Les Tourelles at Orléans. Having fallen into a regular skirmish, they sent to Clairoix in all haste for their arms and to summon their company, which would take a good half hour to reach the scene of battle. Meanwhile, all unarmed as they were, they joined Messire Baudot's little band, to help it to hold out against the enemy.[410] Thus to surprise my Lord of Luxembourg might be a stroke of good luck and certainly could not be bad; for in any event the Margny men would have straightway summoned their comrades of Clairoix to their aid, as they did in very deed summon the English from Venette and the Burgundians from Coudun.

Having stormed the camp and pillaged it, the assailants should in all haste have fallen back on the town with their booty; but they dallied at Margny, for what reason is not difficult to guess: that reason which so often transformed the robber into the robbed. The wearers of the white cross as well as those of the red, no matter what danger threatened them, never quitted a place as long as anything remained to be carried away.

If the mercenaries of Compiègne incurred peril by their greed, the Maid on her side by her valour and prowess ran much greater risk; never would she consent to leave a battle; she must be wounded, pierced with bolts and arrows, before she would give in.

Meanwhile, having recovered from so sudden an alarm, Messire Baudot's men armed as best they might and endeavoured to win back the village. Now they drove out the French, now they themselves were forced to retreat with great loss. The Seigneur de Créquy, among others, was sorely wounded in the face. But the hope of being reinforced gave them courage. The men of Clairoix appeared. Duke Philip himself came up with the band from Coudun. The French, outnumbered, abandoned Margny, and retreated slowly. It may be that their booty impeded their march. But suddenly espying the *Godons* from Venette advancing over the meadowland, they were seized with panic; to the cry of "*Sauve qui peut!*" they broke into one mad rush and in utter rout reached the bank of the Oise. Some threw themselves into boats, others crowded round the bulwark of the Bridge. Thus they attracted the very misfortune they feared. For the English followed so hard on the fugitives that the defenders on the ramparts dared not fire their cannon for fear of striking the French.[411]

The latter having forced the barrier of the bulwark, the English were about to enter on their heels, cross the bridge and pass into the town. The captain of Compiègne saw the danger and gave the command to close the town gate. The bridge was raised and the portcullis lowered.[412]

In the meadow, Jeanne still laboured under the heroic delusion of victory. Surrounded by a little band of kinsmen and personal retainers, she was withstanding the Burgundians, and imagining that she would overthrow everything before her.

Her comrades shouted to her: "Strive to regain the town or we are lost."

But her eyes were dazzled by the splendour of angels and archangels, and she made answer: "Hold your peace; it will be your fault if we are discomfited. Think of nought but of attacking them."

And once again she uttered those words which were forever in her mouth: "Go forward! They are ours!"[413]

Her men took her horse by the bridle and forced her to turn towards the town. It was too late; the bulwarks commanding the bridge could not be entered: the English held the head of the causeway. The Maid with her little band was penned into the corner between the side of the bulwark and the embankment of the road. Her assailants were men of Picardy, who, striking hard and driving away her protectors, succeeded in reaching her.[414] A bowman pulled her by her cloak of cloth of gold and threw her to the ground. They all surrounded her and together cried:

"Surrender!"

Urged to give her parole, she replied: "I have plighted my word to another, and I shall keep my oath."[415]

One of those who pressed her said that he was of gentle birth. She surrendered to him.

He was an archer, by name Lyonnel, in the company of the Bastard of Wandomme. Deeming that his fortune was made, he appeared more joyful than if he had taken a king.[416]

With the Maid was taken her brother, Pierre d'Arc, Jean d'Aulon, her steward, and Jean d'Aulon's brother, Poton, surnamed the Burgundian.[417] According to the Burgundians, the French in this engagement lost four hundred fighting men, killed or drowned;[418] but according to the French most of the foot soldiers were taken up by the boats which were moored near the bank of the Oise.[419]

Had it not been for the archers, cross-bowmen and cannoneers posted at the bridge end by the Sire de Flavy, the bulwark would have been captured. The Burgundians had but twenty wounded and not one slain.[420] The Maid had not been very vigorously defended.

She was disarmed and taken to Margny.[421] At the tidings that the witch of the Armagnacs had been taken, cries and rejoicings resounded throughout the Burgundian camp. Duke Philip wished to see her. When he drew near to her, there were certain of his clergy and his knighthood who praised his piety, extolled his courage, and wondered that this mighty Duke was not afraid of the spawn of Hell.[422]

In this respect, his knighthood were as valiant as he, for many knights and squires flocked to satisfy this same curiosity. Among them was Messire Enguerrand de Monstrelet, a native of the County of Boulogne, a retainer of the House of Luxembourg, the author of the Chronicles. He heard the words the Duke addressed to the prisoner, and, albeit his calling required a good memory, he forgot them. Possibly he did not consider them chivalrous enough to be written in his book.[423]

Jeanne remained in the custody of Messire Jean de Luxembourg, to whom she belonged henceforward. The bowman, her captor, had given her up to his captain, the Bastard of Wandomme, who, in his turn, had yielded her to his Master, Messire Jean.[424]

Branches of the Luxembourg tree extended from the west to the east of Christendom, as far as Bohemia and Hungary; and it had produced six queens, an empress, four kings, and four emperors. A scion of a younger branch of this illustrious house and himself a but poorly landed cadet, Jean de Luxembourg, had with great labour won his spurs in the service of the Duke of Burgundy. When he held the Maid to ransom, he was thirty-nine years of age, covered with wounds and one-eyed.[425]

That very evening from his quarters at Coudun the Duke of Burgundy caused letters to be written to the towns of his dominions telling of the capture of the Maid. "Of this capture shall the fame spread far and wide," is written in the letter to the people of Saint-Quentin; "and there shall be bruited abroad the error and misbelief of all such as have approved and favoured the deeds of this woman."[426]

In like manner did the Duke send the tidings to the Duke of Brittany by his herald Lorraine; to the Duke of Savoy and to his good town of Ghent.[427]

The survivors of the company the Maid had taken to Compiègne abandoned the siege, and on the morrow returned to their garrisons.

The Lombard Captain, Bartolomeo Baretta, Jeanne's lieutenant, remained in the town with thirty-two men-at-arms, two trumpeters, two pages, forty-eight cross bowmen, and twenty archers or targeteers.[428]

CHAPTER VIII
THE MAID AT BEAULIEU – THE SHEPHERD OF GÉVAUDAN

T HE tidings that Jeanne was in the hands of the Burgundians reached Paris on the morning of May the 25th.[429] On the morrow, the 26th, the University sent a summons to Duke Philip requiring him to give up his prisoner to the Vicar-General of the Grand Inquisitor of France. At the same time, the Vicar-General himself by letter required the redoubtable Duke to bring prisoner before him the young woman suspected of divers crimes savouring of heresy.[430]

"... We beseech you in all good affection, O powerful Prince," he said, "and we entreat your noble vassals that by them and by you Jeanne be sent unto us surely and shortly, and we hope that thus ye will do as being the true protector of the faith and the defender of God's honour...."[431]

The Vicar-General of the Grand Inquisitor of France, Brother Martin Billoray,[432] Master of theology, belonged to the order of friars preachers, the members of which exercised the principal functions of the Holy office. In the days of Innocent III, when the Inquisition was exterminating Cathari and Albigenses, the sons of Dominic figured in paintings in monasteries and chapels as great white hounds spotted with black, biting at the throats of the wolves of heresy.[433] In France in the fifteenth century the Dominicans were always the dogs of the Lord; they, jointly with the bishops, drove out the heretic. The Grand Inquisitor or his Vicar was unable of his own initiative to set on foot and prosecute any judicial action; the bishops maintained their right to judge crimes committed against the Church. In matters of faith trials were conducted by two judges, the Ordinary, who might be the bishop himself or the Official, and the Inquisitor or his Vicar. Inquisitorial forms were observed.[434]

In the Maid's case it was not the Bishop only who was prompting the Holy Inquisition, but the Daughter of Kings, the Mother of Learning, the Bright and Shining Sun of France and of Christendom, the University of Paris. She arrogated to herself a peculiar jurisdiction in cases of heresy or other matters of doctrine occurring in the city or its neighbourhood; her advice was asked on every hand and regarded as authoritative over the face of the whole world, wheresoever the Cross had been set up. For a year her masters and doctors, many in number and filled with sound learning, had been clamouring for the Maid to be delivered up to the Inquisition, as being good for the welfare of the Church and conducive to the interests of the faith; for they had a deep-rooted suspicion that the damsel came not from God, but was deceived and seduced by the machinations of the Devil; that she acted not by divine power but by the aid of demons; that she was addicted to witchcraft and practised idolatry.[435]

Such knowledge as they possessed of things divine and methods of reasoning corroborated this grave suspicion. They were Burgundians and English by necessity and by inclination; they observed faithfully the Treaty of Troyes to which they had sworn; they were devoted to the Regent who showed them great consideration; they abhorred the Armagnacs, who desolated and laid waste their city, the most beautiful in the world;[436] they held that the Dauphin Charles had forfeited his rights to the Kingdom of the Lilies. Wherefore they inclined to believe that the Maid of the Armagnacs, the woman knight of the Dauphin Charles, was inspired by a company of loathsome demons. These scholars of the University were human; they believed what it was to their interest to believe; they were priests and they beheld the Devil everywhere, but especially in a woman. Without having devoted themselves to any profound examination of the deeds and sayings of this damsel, they knew enough to cause them to demand an immediate inquiry. She called herself the emissary of God, the daughter of God; and she appeared loquacious, vain, crafty, gorgeous in her attire. She had threatened the English that if they did not quit France she would have them all slain. She commanded armies, wherefore she was a slayer of her fellow-creatures and foolhardy. She was seditious, for are not all those seditious who support the opposite party? But recently having appeared before Paris in company with Friar Richard, a heretic, and a rebel,[437] she had threatened to put the Parisians to death without mercy and committed the mortal sin of storming the city on the Anniversary of the Nativity of Our Lady. It was important to examine whether in all this she had been inspired by a good spirit or a bad.[438]

Despite his strong attachment to the interests of the Church, the Duke of Burgundy did not respond to the urgent demand of the University; and Messire Jean de Luxembourg, after having kept the Maid three or four days in his quarters before Compiègne, had her taken to the Castle of Beaulieu in Vermandois, a few leagues from the camp.[439] Like his master, he ever appeared the obedient son of Mother Church; but prudence counselled him to await the approach of English and French and to see what each of them would offer.

At Beaulieu, Jeanne was treated courteously and ceremoniously. Her steward, Messire Jean d'Aulon, waited on her in her prison; one day he said to her pitifully:

"That poor town of Compiègne, which you so dearly loved, will now be delivered into the hands of the enemies of France, whom it must needs obey."

She made answer: "No, that shall not come to pass. For not one of those places, which the King of Heaven hath conquered through me and restored to their allegiance to the fair King Charles, shall be recaptured by the enemy, so diligently will he guard them."[440]

One day she tried to escape by slipping between two planks. She had intended to shut up her guards in the tower and take to the fields, but the porter saw and stopped her. She concluded that it was not God's will that she should escape this time.[441] Notwithstanding she had far too much self-reliance to despair. Her Voices, like her enamoured of marvellous encounters and knightly adventures, told her that she must see the King of England.[442] Thus did her dreams encourage and console her in her misfortune.

Great was the mourning on the Loire when the inhabitants of the towns loyal to King Charles learnt the disaster which had befallen the Maid. The people, who venerated her as a saint, who went so far as to say that she was the greatest of all God's saints after the Blessed Virgin Mary, who erected images of her in the chapels of saints, who ordered masses to be said for her, and collects in the churches, who wore leaden medals on which she was represented as if the Church had already canonized her,[443] did not withdraw their trust, but continued to believe in her.[444] Such faithfulness scandalized the doctors and masters of the University, who reproached the hapless Maid herself with it.

"Jeanne," they said, "hath so seduced the Catholic people, that many have adored her as a saint in her presence, and now in her absence they adore her still."[445]

This was indeed true of many folk and many places. The councillors of the town of Tours ordered public prayers to be offered for the deliverance of the Maid. There was a public procession in which took part the canons of the cathedral church, the clergy of the town, secular and regular, all walking barefoot.[446]

In the towns of Dauphiné prayers for the Maid were said at mass.

"*Collect.* O God, all powerful and eternal, who, in thy holy and ineffable mercy, hast commanded the Maid to restore and deliver the realm of France, and to repulse, confound and annihilate her enemies, and who hast permitted her, in the accomplishment of this holy work, ordained by thee, to fall into the hands and into the bonds of her enemies, we beseech thee, by the intercession of the Blessed Virgin Mary and of all the saints to deliver her out of their hands, without her having suffered any hurt, in order that she may finish the work whereto thou hast sent her."

"For the sake of Jesus Christ, etc."

"*Secret.* O God all powerful, Father of virtues, let thy holy benediction descend upon this sacrifice; let thy wondrous power be made manifest, that by the intercession of the Blessed Virgin Mary and of all the saints, it may deliver the Maid from the prisons of the enemy so that she may finish the work whereto thou hast sent her. Through our Lord Jesus Christ, etc."

"*Post Communion.* O God all powerful, incline thine ear and listen unto the prayers of thy people: by the virtue of the Sacrament we have just received, by the intercession of the Blessed Virgin Mary, and of all the saints, burst the bonds of the Maid, who, in the fulfilment of thy commands, hath been and is still confined in the prisons of our enemy; through thy divine compassion and thy mercy, permit her, freed from peril, to accomplish the work whereto thou hast sent her. Through our Lord Jesus Christ, etc."[447]

Learning that the Maid, whom he had once suspected of evil intentions and then recognised to be wholly good, had just fallen into the hands of the enemy of the realm, Messire Jacques Gélu, my Lord Archbishop of Embrun, despatched to King Charles a messenger bearing a letter touching the line of conduct to be adopted in such an unhappy conjuncture.[448]

Addressing the Prince, whom in childhood he had directed, Messire Jacques begins by recalling what the Maid had wrought for him by God's help and her own great courage. He beseeches him to examine his conscience and see whether he has in any wise sinned against the grace of God. For it may be that in wrath against the King the Lord hath permitted this virgin to be taken. For his own honour he urges him to strain every effort for her deliverance.

"I commend unto you," he said, "that for the recovery of this damsel and for her ransom, ye spare neither measures nor money, nor any cost, unless ye be ready to incur the ineffaceable disgrace of an ingratitude right unworthy."

Further he advises that prayers be ordered to be said everywhere for the deliverance of the Maid, so that if this disaster should have befallen through any misdoing of the King or of his people, it might please God to pardon it.[449]

Such were the words, lacking neither in strength nor in charity, of this aged prelate, who was more of a hermit than of a bishop. He remembered having been the Dauphin's Councillor in evil days and he dearly loved the King and the kingdom.

The Sire de la Trémouille and the Lord Archbishop of Reims have been suspected of desiring to get rid of the Maid and of having promoted her discomfiture. There are those who think they have discovered the treacherous methods employed to compass her defeat at Paris, at La Charité and at Compiègne.[450] But in good sooth such methods were unnecessary. At Paris there was but little chance of her being able to cross the moat, since neither she nor her companions in arms had ascertained its depth; besides, it was not the fault of the King and his Council that the Carmelites, on whom they relied, failed to open the gates. The siege of La Charité was conducted not by the Maid, but by the Sire d'Albret and divers valiant captains. In the sortie from Compiègne, it was certain that any dallying at Margny would cause the French to be cut off by the English from Venette and by the Burgundians from Clairoix and to be promptly overcome by the Burgundians from Coudun. They forgot themselves in the delights of pillage; and the inevitable result followed.

And why should the Lord Chamberlain and the Lord Archbishop have wanted to get rid of the Maid? She did not trouble them; on the contrary they found her useful and employed her. By her prophecy that she would cause the King to be anointed at Reims, she rendered an immense service to my Lord Regnault, who more than any other profited from the Champagne expedition, more even than the King, who, while he succeeded in being crowned, failed to recover Paris and Normandy. Notwithstanding this great advantage, the Lord Archbishop felt no gratitude towards the Maid; he was a hard man and an egoist. But did he wish her harm? Had he not need of her? At Senlis he was maintaining the King's cause; and he was maintaining it well, we may be sure, since, with the towns that had returned to their liege lord, he was defending his own episcopal and ducal city, his benefices and his canonries. Did he not intend to use her against the Burgundians? We have already noted reasons for believing that towards the end of March, he had asked the Sire de la Trémouille to send her from Sully with a goodly company to wage war in l'Île-de-France. And our hypothesis is confirmed when, after they had been unhappily deprived of Jeanne's services, we find the bishop and the Chamberlain driven to replace her by someone likewise favoured with visions and claiming to be sent of God. Unable to discover a maid they had to make shift with a youth. This resolution they took a few days after Jeanne's capture and this is how it came about.

Some time before, a shepherd lad of Gévaudan, by name Guillaume, while tending his flocks at the foot of the Lozère Mountains and guarding them from wolf and lynx, had a revelation concerning the realm of France. This shepherd, like John, Our Lord's favourite disciple, was virgin. In one of the caves of the Mende Mountain, where the holy apostle Privat had prayed and fasted, his ear was struck by a heavenly voice, and thus he knew that God was sending him to the King of France. He went to Mende, just as Jeanne had gone to Vaucouleurs in order that he might be taken to the King. There he found pious folk, who, touched by his holiness and persuaded that there was power in him, provided for his equipment and for his journey, which provisions, in sooth, amounted to very little. The words he addressed to the King were much the same as those uttered by the Maid.

"Sire," he said, "I am commanded to go with your people; and without fail the English and Burgundians shall be discomfited."[451]

The King received him kindly. The clerks who had examined the Maid must have feared lest if they repulsed this shepherd lad they might be rejecting the aid of the Holy Ghost. Amos was a shepherd, and to him God granted the gift of prophecy: "I thank thee, O Father,

Lord of heaven and earth, because thou hast hid these things from the wise and prudent, and hast revealed them unto babes." Matt. xi, 25.

But before this shepherd could be believed he must give a sign. The clerks of Poitiers, who in those evil days languished in dire penury, did not appear exacting in their demand for proofs; they had counselled the King to employ the Maid merely on the promise that as a token of her mission she would deliver Orléans. The Gévaudan shepherd had more than promises to allege; he showed wondrous marks on his body. Like Saint Francis he had received the stigmata; and on his hands, his feet and in his side were bleeding wounds.[452]

The mendicant monks rejoiced that their spiritual father had thus participated in the Passion of Our Lord. A like grace had been granted to the Blessed Catherine of Sienna, of the order of Saint Dominic. But if there were miraculous stigmata imprinted by Jesus Christ himself, there were also the stigmata of enchantment, which were the work of the Devil, and very important was it to distinguish between the two.[453] It could only be done by great knowledge and great piety. It would appear that Guillaume's stigmata were not the work of the devil; for it was resolved to employ him in the same manner as Jeanne, as Catherine de la Rochelle, and as the two Breton women, the spiritual daughters of Friar Richard.

When the Maid fell into the hands of the Burgundians, the Sire de la Trémouille was with the King, on the Loire, where fighting had ceased since the disastrous siege of La Charité. He sent the shepherd youth to the banks of the Oise, to the Lord Archbishop of Reims, who was there opposing the Burgundians, commanded by Duke Philip, himself. Messire Regnault had probably asked for the boy. In any case he welcomed him willingly and kept him at Beauvais, supervising and interrogating him, ready to use him at an auspicious moment. One day, either to try him or because the rumour was really in circulation, young Guillaume was told that the English had put Jeanne to death.

"Then," said he, "it will be the worse for them."[454]

By this time, after all the rivalries and jealousies which had torn asunder this company of the King's *béguines*, there remained to Friar Richard one only of his penitents, Dame Catherine of La Rochelle, who had the gift of discovering hidden treasure.[455] The young shepherd approved of the Maid as little as Dame Catherine had done.

"God suffered Jeanne to be taken," he said, "because she was puffed up with pride and because of the rich clothes she wore and because she had not done as God commanded her but according to her own will."[456]

Were these words suggested to him by the enemies of the Maid? That may be: but it is also possible that he derived them from inspiration. Saints are not always kind to one another.

Meanwhile Messire Regnault de Chartres believed himself possessed of a marvel far surpassing the marvel he had lost. He wrote a letter to the inhabitants of his town of Reims telling them that the Maid had been taken at Compiègne.

This misfortune had befallen her through her own fault, he added. "She would not take advice, but would follow her own will." In her stead God had sent a shepherd, "who says neither more nor less than Jeanne." God has strictly commanded him to discomfit the English and the Burgundians. And the Lord Archbishop neglects not to repeat the words by which the prophet of Gévaudan had represented Jeanne as proud, gorgeous in attire, rebellious of heart.[457] The Reverend Father in God, my Lord Regnault, would never have consented to employ a heretic and a sorcerer; he believed in Guillaume as he had believed in Jeanne; he held both one and the other to have been divinely sent, in the sense that all which is not of the devil is of God. It was sufficient for him that no evil had been found in the child, and he intended to essay him, hoping that Guillaume would do what Jeanne had done. Whether the Archbishop thus acted rightly or wrongly the issue was to decide, but he might have exalted the shepherd without denying the Saint who was so near her martyrdom. Doubtless he deemed it necessary to distinguish between the fortune of the kingdom and the fortune of Jeanne. And he had the courage to do it.

CHAPTER IX

THE MAID AT BEAUREVOIR – CATHERINE DE LA ROCHELLE AT PARIS – EXECUTION OF LA PIERRONNE

HE Maid had been taken captive in the diocese of Beauvais.[458] At that time the Bishop Count of Beauvais was Pierre Cauchon of Reims, a great and pompous clerk of the University of Paris, which had elected him rector in 1403. Messire Pierre Cauchon was not a moderate man; with great ardour he had thrown himself into the Cabochien riots.[459] In 1414, the Duke of Burgundy had sent him on an embassy to the Council of Constance to defend the doctrines of Jean Petit;[460] then he had appointed him Master of Requests in 1418, and finally raised him to the episcopal see of Beauvais.[461] Standing equally high in the favour of the English, Messire Pierre was Councillor of King Henry VI, Almoner of France and Chancellor to the Queen of England. Since 1423, his usual residence had been at Rouen. By their submission to King Charles the people of Beauvais had deprived him of his episcopal revenue.[462] And, as the English said and believed that the army of the King of France was at that time commanded by Friar Richard and the Maid, Messire Pierre Cauchon, the impoverished Bishop of Beauvais, had a personal grievance against Jeanne. It would have been better for his own reputation that he should have abstained from avenging the Church's honour on a damsel who was possibly an idolatress, a soothsayer and the invoker of devils, but who had certainly incurred his personal ill-will. He was in the Regent's pay;[463] and the Regent was filled with bitter hatred of the Maid.[464] Again for his reputation's sake, my Lord Bishop of Beauvais should have reflected that in prosecuting Jeanne for a matter of faith he was serving his master's wrath and furthering the temporal interests of the great of this world. On these things he did not reflect; on the contrary, this case at once temporal and spiritual, as ambiguous as his own position, excited his worst passions. He flung himself into it with all the thoughtlessness of the violent. A maiden to be denounced, a heretic and an Armagnac to boot, what a feast for the prelate, the Councillor of King Henry! After having concerted with the doctors and masters of the University of Paris, on the 14th of July, he presented himself before the camp of Compiègne and demanded the Maid as subject to his jurisdiction.[465]

He supported his demand by letters from the *Alma Mater* to the Duke of Burgundy and the Lord Jean de Luxembourg.

The University made known to the most illustrious Prince, the Duke of Burgundy, that once before it had claimed this woman, called the Maid, and had received no reply.

"We greatly fear," continued the doctors and masters, "that by the false and seductive power of the Hellish Enemy and by the malice and subtlety of wicked persons, your enemies and adversaries who, it is said, are making every effort to deliver this woman by crooked means, will in some manner remove her out of your power.

"Wherefore, the University hopes that so great a dishonour may be spared to the most Christian name of the house of France, and again it supplicates your Highness, the Duke of Burgundy, to deliver over this woman either to the Inquisitor of the evil of heresy or to my Lord Bishop of Beauvais within whose spiritual jurisdiction she was captured."

Here follows the letter which the doctors and masters of the University entrusted to the Lord Bishop of Beauvais for the Lord Jean de Luxembourg:

Most noble, honoured and powerful lord, to your high nobility we very affectionately commend us. Your noble wisdom doth well know and recognise that all good Catholic knights should employ their strength and their power first in God's service and then for the common weal. Above all, the first oath of the order of knighthood is to defend and keep the honour of God, the Catholic Faith and holy Church. This sacred oath was present to your mind when you employed your noble power and your person in the taking of the woman who calleth herself the Maid, by whom the glory of God hath been infinitely offended, the Faith deeply wounded and the Church greatly dishonoured: for through her there have arisen in this kingdom, idolatries, errors, false doctrines and other evils and misfortunes without end. And in truth all loyal Christians must give unto you hearty thanks for having rendered so great service to our holy Faith and to all the kingdom. As for us, we thank God with all our hearts, and you we thank for your noble prowess as affectionately as we may. But such a capture alone would be but a small thing were it not followed by a worthy issue whereby this woman may answer for the offences she hath committed against our merciful Creator, his faith and his holy Church, as well as for her other evil deeds which are said to be without number. The mischief would be greater than ever, the people would be wrapped in yet grosser error than before and his Divine Majesty too insufferably offended, if matters continued in their present state, or if it befell that this woman were delivered or retaken, as we are told, is wished, plotted and endeavoured by divers of our enemies, by all secret ways and by what is even worse by bribe or by ransom. But it is our hope that God will not permit so great an evil to betide his people, and that your great and high wisdom will not suffer it so to befall but will provide against it as becometh your nobility.

For if without the retribution that behoveth she were to be delivered, irreparable would be the dishonour which should fall on your great nobility and on all those who have dealt in this matter. But your good and noble wisdom will know how to devise means whereby such scandal shall cease as soon as may be, whereof there is great need. And because all delay in this matter is very perilous and very injurious to this kingdom, very kindly and with a cordial affection do we beseech your powerful and honoured nobility to grant that for the glory of God, for the maintenance of the Holy Catholic Faith, for the good and honour of the kingdom, this woman be delivered up to justice and given over here to the Inquisitor of the Faith, who hath demanded her and doth now demand her urgently, in order that he may examine the grievous charges under which she labours, so that God may be satisfied and the folk duly edified in good and holy doctrine. Or, an it please you better, hand over this woman to the reverend Father in God, our highly honoured Lord Bishop of Beauvais, who it is said hath likewise claimed her, because she was taken within his jurisdiction. This prelate and this inquisitor are judges of this woman in matters of faith; and every Christian of whatsoever estate owes them obedience in this case under heavy penalty of the law. By so doing you will attain to the love and grace of the most High and you will be the means of exalting the holy Faith, and likewise will you glorify your own high and noble name and also that of the most high and most powerful Prince, our redoubtable Lord and yours, my Lord of

Burgundy. Every man shall be required to pray God for the prosperity of your most noble worship, whom may it please God our Saviour in his grace, to guide and keep in all his affairs and finally to grant eternal joy.

Given at Paris, the 14th day of July, 1430.[466]

At the same time that he bore these letters, the Reverend Father in God, the Bishop of Beauvais was charged to offer money.[467] To us it seems strange indeed that just at the very time when, by the mouth of the University, he was representing to the Lord of Luxembourg that he could not sell his prisoner without committing a crime, the Bishop should himself offer to purchase her. According to these ecclesiastics, Jean would incur terrible penalties in this world and in the next, if in conformity with the laws and customs of war he surrendered a prisoner held to ransom in return for money, and he would win praise and blessing if he treacherously sold his captive to those who wished to put her to death. But at least we might expect that this Lord Bishop who had come to buy this woman for the Church, would purchase her with the Church's money. Not at all! The purchase money is furnished by the English. In the end therefore she is delivered not to the Church but to the English. And it is a priest, acting in the interests of God and of his Church, by virtue of his episcopal jurisdiction, who concludes the bargain. He offers ten thousand golden francs, a sum in return for which, he says, according to the custom prevailing in France, the King has the right to claim any prisoner even were he of the blood royal.[468]

There can be no doubt whatever that the high and solemn ecclesiastic, Pierre Cauchon, suspected Jeanne of witchcraft. Wishing to bring her to trial, he exercised his ecclesiastical functions. But he knew her to be the enemy of the English as well as of himself; there is no doubt on that point. So when he wished to bring her to trial he acted as the Councillor of King Henry. Was it a witch or the enemy of the English he was buying with his ten thousand gold francs? And if it were merely a witch and an idolatress that the Holy Inquisitor, that the University, that the Ordinary demanded for the glory of God, and at the price of gold, wherefore so much ado, wherefore so great an expenditure of money? Would it not be better in this matter to act in concert with the ecclesiastics of King Charles's party? The Armagnacs were neither infidels nor heretics; they were neither Turks nor Hussites; they were Catholics; they acknowledged the Pope of Rome to be the true head of Christendom. The Dauphin Charles and his clergy had not been excommunicated. Neither those who regarded the Treaty of Troyes as invalid nor those who had sworn to it had been pronounced anathema by the Pope. This was not a question of faith. In the provinces ruled over by King Charles the Holy Inquisition prosecuted heresy in a curious manner and the secular arm saw to it that the sentences pronounced by the Church did not remain a dead letter. The Armagnacs burned witches just as much as the French and the Burgundians. For the present doubtless they did not believe the Maid to be possessed by devils; most of them on the contrary were inclined to regard her as a saint. But might they not be undeceived? Would it not be good Christian charity to present them with fine canonical arguments? If the Maid's case were really a case for the ecclesiastical court why not join with Churchmen of both parties and take her before the Pope and the Council? And just at that time a Council for the reformation of the Church and the establishment of peace in the kingdom was sitting in the town of Bâle; the University was sending its delegates, who would there meet the ecclesiastics of King Charles, also Gallicans and firmly attached to the privileges of the Church of France.[469] Why not have this Armagnac prophetess tried by the assembled Fathers? But for the sake of Henry of Lancaster and the glory of Old England matters had to take another turn. The Regent's Councillors were already accusing Jeanne of witchcraft when she summoned them in the name of the King of Heaven to depart out of France. During the siege of Orléans, they wanted to burn her heralds and said that if they had her they would burn her also at the stake. Such in good sooth was their firm intent and their unvarying intimation. This does not look as if they would be likely to hand her over to the Church as soon as she was taken. In their own kingdom they burned as many witches and wizards as possible; but they had never suffered the Holy Inquisition to be established in their land, and they were ill acquainted with that form of justice. Informed that Jeanne was in the hands of the Sire de Luxembourg, the Great Council of England were unanimously in favour of her being purchased at any price. Divers lords recommended that as soon as they obtained possession of the Maid she should be sewn in a sack and cast into the river. But one of them (it is said to have been the Earl of Warwick) represented to them that she ought first to be tried, convicted of heresy and witchcraft by an ecclesiastical tribunal, and then solemnly degraded in order that her King might be degraded with her.[470] What a disgrace for Charles of Valois, calling himself King of France, if the

University of Paris, if the French ecclesiastical dignitaries, bishops, abbots, canons, if in short the Church Universal were to declare that a witch had sat in his Council and that a witch led his host, that one possessed had conducted him to his impious, sacrilegious and void anointing! Thus would the trial of the Maid be the trial of Charles VII, the condemnation of the Maid the condemnation of Charles VII. The idea seemed good to them and was adopted.

The Lord Bishop of Beauvais was eager to put it into execution. He, a priest and Councillor of State, was consumed with a desire, under the semblance of trying an unfortunate heretic, to sit in judgment on the descendant of Clovis, of Saint Charlemagne and of Saint Louis.

Early in August, the Sire de Luxembourg had the Maid taken from Beaulieu, which was not safe enough, to Beaurevoir, near Cambrai.[471] There dwelt Dame Jeanne de Luxembourg and Dame Jeanne de Béthune. Jeanne de Luxembourg was the aunt of Lord Jean, whom she loved dearly. Among the great of this world she had lived as a saint, and she had never married. Formerly lady-in-waiting to Queen Ysabeau, King Charles VII's godmother, one of the most important events of her life had been to solicit from Pope Martin the canonisation of her Brother, the Cardinal of Luxembourg, who had died at Avignon in his ninetieth year. She was known as the Demoiselle de Luxembourg. She was sixty-seven years of age, infirm and near her end.[472]

Jeanne de Béthune, widow of Lord Robert de Bar, slain at the Battle of Azincourt, had married Lord Jean in 1418. She was reputed pitiful, because, in 1424, she had obtained from her husband the pardon of a nobleman of Picardy, who had been brought prisoner to Beaurevoir and was in great danger of being beheaded and quartered.[473]

These two ladies treated Jeanne kindly. They offered her woman's clothes or cloth with which to make them; and they urged her to abandon a dress which appeared to them unseemly. Jeanne refused, alleging that she had not received permission from Our Lord and that it was not yet time; later she admitted that had she been able to quit man's attire, she would have done so at the request of these two dames rather than for any other dame of France, the Queen excepted.[474]

A noble of the Burgundian party, one Aimond de Macy, often came to see her and was pleased to converse with her. To him she seemed modest in word and in deed. Still Sire Aimond, who was but thirty, had found her personally attractive.[475] If certain witnesses of her own party are to be believed, Jeanne, although beautiful, did not inspire men with desire.

This singular grace however applied to the Armagnacs only; it was not extended to the Burgundians, and Seigneur Aimond did not experience it, for one day he tried to thrust his hand into her bosom. She resisted and repulsed him with all her strength. Lord Aimond concluded as more than one would have done in his place that this was a damsel of rare virtue. He took warning.[476]

Confined in the castle keep, Jeanne's mind was for ever running on her return to her friends at Compiègne; her one idea was to escape. Somehow there reached her evil tidings from France. She got the idea that all the inhabitants of Compiègne over seven years of age were to be massacred, "to perish by fire and sword," she said; and indeed such a fate was bound to overtake them if the town were taken.

Confiding her distress and her unconquerable desire to Saint Catherine, she asked: "How can God abandon to destruction those good folk of Compiègne who have been so loyal to their Lord?"[477]

And in her dream, surrounded by saints, like the donors in church pictures, kneeling and in rapture, she wrestled with her heavenly counsellors for the poor folk of Compiègne.

What she had heard of their fate caused her infinite distress; she herself would rather die than continue to live after such a destruction of worthy people. For this reason she was strongly tempted to leap from the top of the keep. And because she knew all that could be said against it, she heard her Voices putting her in mind of those arguments.

Nearly every day Saint Catherine said to her: "Do not leap, God will help both you and those of Compiègne."

And Jeanne replied to her: "Since God will help those of Compiègne, I want to be there."

And once again Saint Catherine told her the marvellous story of the shepherdess and the King: "To all things must you be resigned. And you will not be delivered until you have seen the King of the English."

To which Jeanne made answer: "But in good sooth I do not desire to see him. I would rather die than fall into the hands of the English."[478]

One day she heard a rumour that the English had come to fetch her. The arrival of the Lord Bishop of Beauvais who came to offer the blood money at Beaurevoir may have given rise to the report.[479] Straightway Jeanne became frantic and beside herself. She ceased to listen to her Voices, who forbade her the fatal leap. The keep was at least seventy feet high; she commended her soul to God and leapt.

Having fallen to the ground, she heard cries: "She is dead."

The guards hurried to the spot. Finding her still alive, in their amazement they could only ask: "Did you leap?"

She felt sorely shaken; but Saint Catherine spoke to her and said: "Be of good courage. You will recover." At the same time the Saint gave her good tidings of her friends. "You will recover and the people of Compiègne will receive succour." And she added that this succour would come before Saint Martin's Day in the winter.[480]

Henceforth Jeanne believed that it was her saints who had helped her and guarded her from death. She knew well that she had been wrong in attempting such a leap, despite her Voices.

Saint Catherine said to her: "You must confess and ask God to forgive you for having leapt."

Jeanne did confess and ask pardon of Our Lord. And after her confession Saint Catherine made known unto her that God had forgiven her. For three or four days she remained without eating or drinking; then she took some food and was whole.[481]

Another story was told of the leap from Beaurevoir; it was related that she had tried to escape through a window letting herself down by a sheet or something that broke; but we must believe the Maid: she says she leapt; if she had been attached to a cord, she would not have committed sin and would not have confessed. This leap was known and the rumour spread abroad that she had escaped and joined her own party.[482]

Meanwhile the Lenten sermons at Orléans had been delivered by that good preacher, Friar Richard, who was ill content with Jeanne, and whom Jeanne disliked and had quitted. The townsfolk as a token of regard presented him with the image of Jesus sculptured in copper by a certain Philippe, a metal-worker of the city. And the bookseller, Jean Moreau, bound him a book of hours at the town's expense.[483]

He brought back Queen Marie to Jargeau and succeeded in obtaining her favour. Jeanne was spared the bitterness of learning that while she was languishing in prison her friends at Orléans, her fair Dauphin and his Queen Marie, were making good cheer for the monk who had turned from her to prefer a dame Catherine whom she considered worthless.[484] Only lately the idea of employing Dame Catherine had filled Jeanne with alarm; she wrote to her King about it, and as soon as she saw him besought him not to employ her. However the King set no store by what she had said; he agreed to Friar Richard's favourite being allowed to set forth on her mission to obtain money from the good towns and to negotiate peace with the Duke of Burgundy. But perhaps this saintly dame was not possessed of all the wisdom necessary for the performance of man's work and King's service. For immediately she became a cause of embarrassment to her friends.

Being in the town of Tours, she fell to saying: "In this town there be carpenters who work, but not at houses, and if ye have not a care, this town is in the way to a bad end and there be those in the town that know it."[485]

This was a denunciation in the form of a parable. Dame Catherine was thereby accusing the churchmen and burgesses of Tours of working against Charles of Valois, their lord. The woman must have been held to have influence with the King, his kinsmen and his Council; for the inhabitants of Tours took fright and sent an Augustinian monk, Brother Jean Bourget, to King Charles, to the Queen of Sicily, to the Bishop of Séez, and to the Lord of Trèves, to inquire whether the words of this holy woman had been believed by them. The Queen of Sicily and the Councillors of King Charles gave the monk letters wherein they announced to the townsfolk of Tours that they had never heard of such things, and King Charles declared that he had every confidence in the churchmen, the burgesses and the other citizens of his town of Tours.[486]

Dame Catherine had in like manner slandered the inhabitants of Angers.[487]

Whether, following the example of the Blessed Colette of Corbie, this devout person wished to pass from one party to the other, or whether she had chanced to be taken captive by Burgundian men-at-

530

arms, she was brought before the Official at Paris. In their interrogation of her the ecclesiastics appear to have been concerned less about her than about the Maid Jeanne, whose prosecution was then being instituted.

On the subject of the Maid, Catherine said: "Jeanne has two counsellors, whom she calls Counsellors of the Spring."[488]

Such was the confused recollection of the conversations she had had at Jargeau and at Montfaucon. The term Council was the one Jeanne usually employed when speaking of her Voices; but Dame Catherine was confusing Jeanne's heavenly visitants with what the Maid had told her of the Gooseberry Spring at Domremy.

If Jeanne felt unkindly towards Catherine, Catherine did not feel kindly towards Jeanne. She did not assert Jeanne's mission to be nought; but she let it be clearly understood that the hapless damsel, then a prisoner in the hands of the Burgundians, was addicted to invoking evil spirits.

"If Jeanne be not well guarded," Catherine told the Official, "she will escape from prison with the aid of the devil."[489]

Whether Jeanne was or was not aided by the devil was a matter to be decided between herself and the doctors of the church. But it is certain that her one thought was to burst her bonds, and that she was ceaselessly imagining means of escape. Catherine de la Rochelle knew her well and wished her ill.

Catherine was released. Her ecclesiastical judges would not have treated her so leniently had she spoken well of the Maid. The La Rochelle Dame returned to King Charles.[490]

The two religious women who had followed Jeanne on her departure from Sully and had been taken at Corbeil, Pierronne of Lower Brittany and her companion, had been confined in ecclesiastical prisons at Paris since the spring. They openly said that God had sent them to succour the Maid Jeanne. Friar Richard had been their spiritual father and they had been in the Maid's company. Wherefore they were strongly suspected of having offended against God and his Holy Religion. The Grand Inquisitor of France, Brother Jean Graverent, Prior of the Jacobins at Paris, prosecuted them according to the forms usual in that country. He proceeded in concurrence with the Ordinary, represented by the official.

531

Pierronne maintained and believed it to be true that Jeanne was good, and that what she did was well done and according to God's will. She admitted that on the Christmas night of that year, at Jargeau, Friar Richard had twice given her the body of Jesus Christ and had given it three times to Jeanne.[491] Besides, the fact had been well proved by information gathered from eye-witnesses. The judges, who were authorities on this subject, held that the monk should not thus have lavished the bread of angels on such women. However, since frequent communion was not formally forbidden by canon law, Pierronne could not be censured for having received it. The informers, who were then giving evidence against Jeanne, did not remember the three communions at Jargeau.[492]

Heavier charges weighed upon the two Breton women. They were labouring under the accusation of witchcraft and sorcery.

Pierronne stated and took her oath that God often appeared to her in human form and spoke to her as friend to friend, and that the last time she had seen him he was clothed in a purple cloak and a long white robe.[493]

The illustrious masters who were trying her, represented to her that to speak thus of such apparitions was to blaspheme. And these women were convicted of being possessed by evil spirits, who caused them to err in word and in deed.

On Sunday, the 3rd of September, 1430, they were taken to the Parvis Notre Dame to hear a sermon. Platforms had been erected as usual, and Sunday had been chosen as the day in order that folk might benefit from this edifying spectacle. A famous doctor addressed a charitable exhortation to both women. One of them, the youngest, as she listened to him and looked at the stake that had been erected, was filled with repentance. She confessed that she had been seduced by an angel of the devil and duly renounced her error.

Pierronne, on the contrary, refused to retract. She obstinately persisted in the belief that she saw God often, clothed as she had said. The Church could do nothing for her. Given over to the secular arm, she was straightway conducted to the stake which had been prepared for her, and burned alive by the executioner.[494]

Thus did the Grand Inquisitor of France and the Bishop of Paris cruelly cause to perish by an ignominious death one of those women who had followed Friar Richard, one of the saints of the Dauphin Charles. But the most famous of these women and the most abounding in works was in their hands. The death of La Pierronne was an earnest of the fate reserved for the Maid.

CHAPTER X

BEAUREVOIR – ARRAS – ROUEN – THE TRIAL FOR LAPSE

I N the month of September, 1430, two inhabitants of Tournai, the chief alderman, Bietremieu Carlier, and the chief Councillor, Henri Romain, were returning from the banks of the Loire, whither their town had despatched them on a mission to the King of France. They stopped at Beaurevoir. Albeit this place lay upon their direct route and afforded them a halt between two stages of their journey, one cannot help supposing some connection to have existed between their mission to Charles of Valois and their arrival in the domain of the Sire de Luxembourg. The existence of such a connection seems all the more probable when we remember the attachment of their fellow-citizens to the Fleurs-de-Lis, and when we know the relations already existing between the Maid and these emissaries.[495]

It has been said that the district of the provost of Tournai was loyal to the King of France, who had granted it freedom and privileges. Message after message it sent him; it organised public processions in his honour, and it was ready to grant him anything, so long as he demanded neither men nor money. The alderman, Carlier, and the Councillor, Romain, had both previously gone to Reims as representatives of their town to witness the anointing and the coronation of King Charles. There they had doubtless seen the Maid in her glory and had held her to be a very great saint. In those days, their town, attentively watching the progress of the royal army, was in regular correspondence with the warlike *béguine*, and with her confessor, Friar Richard, or more probably Friar Pasquerel. To-day they wended to the castle, wherein she was imprisoned in the hands of her cruel enemies. We know not what it was they came to say to the

Sire de Luxembourg, nor even whether he received them. He cannot have refused to hear them if he thought they came to make secret offers on the part of King Charles for the ransom of the Maid, who had fought in his battles. We know not, either, whether they were able to see the prisoner. The idea that they did enter her presence is quite tenable; for in those days it was generally easy to approach captives, and passers by when they visited them were given every facility for the performance of one of the seven works of mercy.

One thing, however, is certain; that when they left Beaurevoir, they carried with them a letter which Jeanne had given them, charging them to deliver it to the magistrates of their town. In this letter she asked the folk of Tournai, for the sake of her Lord the King and in view of the good services she had rendered him, to send unto her twenty or thirty crowns, that she might employ them for her necessities.[496]

It was the custom in those days thus to permit prisoners to beg their bread.

It is said that the Demoiselle de Luxembourg, who had just made her will, and had but a few days longer to live,[497] entreated her noble nephew not to give the Maid up to the English.[498] But what power had this good dame against the Norman gold of the King of England and against the anathemas of Holy Church? For if my Lord Jean had refused to give up this damsel suspected of enchantments, of idolatries, of invoking devils and committing other crimes against religion, he would have been excommunicated. The venerable University of Paris had not neglected to make him aware that a refusal would expose him to heavy legal penalties.[499]

The Sire de Luxembourg, meanwhile, was ill at ease; he feared that in his castle of Beaurevoir, a prisoner worth ten thousand golden livres was not sufficiently secure in case of a descent on the part of the French or of the English or of the Burgundians, or of any of those folk, who, caring nought for Burgundy or England or France, might wish to carry her off, cast her into a pit, and hold her to ransom, according to the custom of brigands in those days.[500]

Towards the end of September, he asked his lord, the Duke of Burgundy, who ruled over fine towns and strong cities, if he would undertake the safe custody of the Maid. My Lord Philip consented and, by his command, Jeanne was taken to Arras. This town was encircled by high walls; it had two castles, one of which, La Cour-le-Comte, was in the centre of the town. It was probably in the cells of Cour-le-Comte that Jeanne was confined, under the watch and ward of my Lord David de Brimeu, Lord of Ligny, Knight of the Golden Fleece, Governor of Arras.

At that time it was rare for prisoners to be kept in isolation.[501] At Arras, Jeanne received visitors; and among others, a Scotsman, who showed her her portrait, in which she was represented kneeling on one knee and presenting a letter to her King.[502] This letter might be supposed to have been from the Sire de Baudricourt, or from any other clerk or captain by whom the painter may have thought Jeanne to have been sent to the Dauphin; it might have been a letter announcing to the King the deliverance of Orléans or the victory of Patay.

This was the only portrait of herself Jeanne ever saw and, for her own part, she never had any painted; but during the brief duration of her power, the inhabitants of the French towns placed images of her, carved and painted, in the chapels of the saints, and wore leaden medals on which she was represented; thus in her case following a custom established in honour of the saints canonised by the Church.[503]

Many Burgundian lords, and among them a knight, one Jean de Pressy, Controller of the Finances of Burgundy, offered her woman's dress, as the Luxembourg dame had done, for her own good and in order to avoid scandal; but for nothing in the world would Jeanne have cast off the garb which she had assumed according to divine command.

She also received in her prison at Arras a clerk of Tournai, one Jean Naviel, charged by the magistrates of his town to deliver to her the sum of twenty-two golden crowns. This ecclesiastic enjoyed the confidence of his fellow citizens, who employed him in the town's most urgent affairs. In the May of this year, 1430, he had been sent to Messire Regnault de Chartres, Chancellor of King Charles. He had been taken by the Burgundians at the same time as Jeanne and held to ransom; but out of that predicament he soon escaped and at no great cost.

He acquitted himself well of his mission[504] to the Maid, and, it would seem, received nothing for his trouble, doubtless because he wanted the reward of this work of mercy to be placed to his account in heaven.[505]

Neither the capture of the Maid nor the retreat of the men-at-arms she had brought, put an end to the siege of Compiègne. Guillaume de

Flavy and his two brothers, Charles and Louis, and Captain Baretta with his Italians, and the five hundred of the garrison[506] displayed skill, vigour, and untiring energy. The Burgundians conducted the siege in the same manner as the English had conducted that of Orléans; mines, trenches, bulwarks, cannonades and bastions, those gigantic and absurd erections good for nothing but for burning. The suburbs of the town Guillaume de Flavy had demolished because they were in the way of his firing; boats he had sunk in order to bar the river. To the mortars and huge *couillards* of the Burgundians he replied with his artillery, and notably with those little copper culverins which did such good service.[507] If the gay cannoneer of Orléans and Jargeau, Maître Jean de Montesclère, were absent, there was a shoemaker of Valenciennes, an artilleryman, named Noirouffle, tall, dark, terrible to see, and terrible to hear.[508] The townsfolk of Compiègne, like those of Orléans, made unsuccessful sallies. One day Louis de Flavy, the governor's brother, was killed by a Burgundian bullet. But none the less on that day Guillaume did as he was wont to do and made the minstrels play to keep his men-at-arms in good cheer.[509]

In the month of June the bulwark, defending the bridge over the Oise, like les Tourelles at Orléans which defended the bridge over the Loire, was captured by the enemy without bringing about the reduction of the town. In like manner, the capture of Les Tourelles had not occasioned the fall of the town of Duke Charles.[510]

As for the bastions, they were just as little good on the Oise as they had been on the Loire; everything passed by them. The Burgundians were unable to invest Compiègne because its circumference was too great.[511] They were short of money; and their men-at-arms, for lack of food and of pay, deserted with that perfect assurance which in those days characterised alike mercenaries of the red cross and of the white.[512] To complete his misfortunes, Duke Philip was obliged to take away some of the troops engaged in the siege and send them against the inhabitants of Liège who had revolted.[513] On the 24th of October, a relieving army, commanded by the Count of Vendôme and the Marshal de Boussac, approached Compiègne. The English and the Burgundians having turned to encounter them, the garrison and all the inhabitants of the town, even the women, fell upon the rear of the besiegers and routed them.[514] The relieving army entered Compiègne. The flaring of the bastions was a fine sight. The Duke of Burgundy lost all his artillery.[515] The Sire de

Luxembourg, who had come to Beaurevoir, where he had received the Count Bishop of Beauvais, now appeared before Compiègne just in time to bear his share in the disaster.[516] The same causes which had constrained the English to depart, as they put it, from Orléans, now obliged the Burgundians to leave Compiègne. But in those days the most ordinary events must needs have a supernatural cause assigned to them, wherefore the deliverance of the town was attributed to the vow of the Count of Vendôme, who, in the cathedral of Senlis, had promised an annual mass to Notre-Dame-de-la-Pierre if the place were not taken.[517]

The Lord Treasurer of Normandy raised aids to the amount of eighty thousand *livres tournois*, ten thousand of which were to be devoted to the purchase of Jeanne. The Count Bishop of Beauvais, who was taking this matter to heart, urged the Sire de Luxembourg to come to terms, mingled threats with coaxings, and caused the Norman gold to glitter before his eyes. He seemed to fear, and his fear was shared by the masters and doctors of the University, that King Charles would likewise make an offer, that he would promise more than King Henry's ten thousand golden francs and that in the end, by dint of costly gifts, the Armagnacs would succeed in winning back their fairy-godmother.[518] The rumour ran that King Charles, hearing that the English were about to gain possession of Jeanne for a sum of money, sent an ambassador to warn the Duke of Burgundy not on any account to consent to such an agreement, adding that if he did, the Burgundians in the hands of the King of France would be made to pay for the fate of the Maid.[519] Doubtless the rumour was false; albeit the fears of the Lord Bishop and the masters of the Paris University were not entirely groundless; and it is certain that from the banks of the Loire the negotiations were being attentively followed with a view to intervention at a favourable moment.

Besides, some sudden descent of the French was always to be feared. Captain La Hire was ravaging Normandy, the knight Barbazan, la Champagne, and Marshal de Boussac, the country between the Seine, the Marne and the Somme.[520]

At length, about the middle of November, the Sire de Luxembourg consented to the bargain; Jeanne was delivered up to the English. It was decided to take her to Rouen, through Ponthieu, along the sea-shore, through the north of Normandy, where there would be less risk of falling in with the scouts of the various parties.

Henry VI
(from a portrait in the "Election Chamber" at Eton, reproduced by
permission of the Provost)

From Arras she was taken to the Château of Drugy, where the monks of Saint-Riquier were said to have visited her in prison.[521] She was afterwards taken to Crotoy, where the castle walls were washed by the ocean waves. The Duke of Alençon, whom she called her fair Duke, had been imprisoned there after the Battle of Verneuil.[522] At the time of her arrival, Maître Nicolas Gueuville, Chancellor of the Cathedral church of Notre Dame d'Amiens, was a prisoner in that castle in the hands of the English. He heard her confess and administered the Communion to her.[523] And there on that vast Bay of the Somme, grey and monotonous, with its low sky traversed by sea-birds in their long flight, Jeanne beheld coming down to her the visitant of earlier days, the Archangel Saint Michael; and she was comforted. It was said that the damsels and burgesses of Abbeville went to see her in the castle where she was imprisoned.[524] At the time of the coronation, these burgesses had thought of turning French; and they would have done so if King Charles had come to their town; he did not come; and perhaps it was through Christian charity that the folk of Abbeville visited Jeanne; but those among them who thought well of her did not say so, for fear they too should be suspected of heresy.[525]

The doctors and masters of the University pursued her with a bitterness hardly credible. In November, after they had been informed of the conclusion of the bargain between Jean de Luxembourg and the English, they wrote through their rector to the Lord Bishop of Beauvais reproaching him for his delay in the matter of this woman and exhorting him to be more diligent.

"For you it is no slight matter, holding as you do so high an office in God's Church," ran this letter, "that the scandals committed against the Christian religion be stamped out, especially when such scandals arise within your actual jurisdiction."[526]

Filled with faith and zeal for the avenging of God's honour, these clerks were, as they said, always ready to burn witches. They feared the devil; but, perchance, though they may not have admitted it even to themselves, they feared him twenty times more when he was Armagnac.

Jeanne was taken out of Crotoy at high tide and conveyed by boat to Saint-Valery, then to Dieppe, as is supposed, and certainly in the end to Rouen.[527]

She was conducted to the old castle, built in the time of Philippe-Auguste on the slope of the Bouvreuil hill.[528] King Henry VI, who had come to France for his coronation, had been there since the end of August. He was a sad, serious child, harshly treated by the Earl of Warwick, who was governor of the castle.[529] The castle was strongly fortified;[530] it had seven towers, including the keep. Jeanne was placed in a tower looking on to the open country.[531] Her room was on the middle storey, between the dungeon and the state apartment. Eight steps led up to it.[532] It extended over the whole of that floor, which was forty-three feet across, including the walls.[533] A stone staircase approached it at an angle. There was but a dim light, for some of the window slits had been filled in.[534] From a locksmith of Rouen, one Étienne Castille, the English had ordered an iron cage, in which it was said to be impossible to stand upright. If the reports of the ecclesiastical registrars are to be believed, Jeanne was placed in it and chained by the neck, feet, and hands,[535] and left there till the opening of the trial. At Jean Salvart's, at *l'Écu de France*, in front of the Official's courtyard,[536] a mason's apprentice saw the cage weighed. But no one ever found Jeanne in it. If this treatment were inflicted on Jeanne, it was not invented for her; when Captain La Hire, in the February of this same year, 1430, took Château Gaillard, near Rouen, he found the good knight Barbazan in an iron cage, from which he would not come out, alleging that he was a prisoner on parole.[537] Jeanne, on the contrary, had been careful to promise nothing, or rather she had promised to escape as soon as she could.[538] Therefore the English, who believed that she had magical powers, mistrusted her greatly.[539] As she was being prosecuted by the Church, she ought to have been detained in an ecclesiastical prison,[540] but the *Godons* were resolved to keep her in their custody. One among them said she was dear to them because they had paid dearly for her. On her feet they put shackles and round her waist a chain padlocked to a beam five or six feet long. At night this chain was carried over the foot of her bed and attached to the principal beam.[541] In like manner, John Huss, in 1415, when he was delivered up to the Bishop of Constance and transferred to the fortress of Gottlieben, was chained night and day until he was taken to the stake.

Five English men-at-arms,[542] common soldiers (*houspilleurs*), guarded the prisoner;[543] they were not the flower of chivalry. They mocked her and she rebuked them, a circumstance they must have found consolatory. At night two of them stayed behind the door; three remained with her, and constantly troubled her by saying first that she would die, then that she would be delivered. No one could speak to her without their consent.[544]

Nevertheless folk entered the prison as if it were a fair (*comme au moulin*); people of all ranks came to see Jeanne as they pleased. Thus Maître Laurent Guesdon, Lieutenant of the Bailie of Rouen, came,[545] and Maître Pierre Manuel, Advocate of the King of England, who was accompanied by Maître Pierre Daron, magistrate of the city of Rouen. They found her with her feet in shackles, guarded by soldiers.[546]

Maître Pierre Manuel felt called upon to tell her that for certain she would never have come there if she had not been brought. Sensible persons were always surprised when they saw witches and soothsayers falling into a trap like any ordinary Christian. The King's Advocate must have been a sensible person, since his surprise appeared in the questions he put to Jeanne.

"Did you know you were to be taken?" he asked her.

"I thought it likely," she replied.

"Then why," asked Maître Pierre again, "if you thought it likely, did you not take better care on the day you were captured?"

"I knew neither the day nor the hour when I should be taken, nor when it should happen."[547]

A young fellow, one Pierre Cusquel, who worked for Jean Salvart, also called Jeanson, the master-mason of the castle, through the influence of his employer, was permitted to enter the tower. He also found Jeanne bound with a long chain attached to a beam, and with her feet in shackles. Much later, he claimed to have warned her to be careful of what she said, because her life was involved in it. It is true that she talked volubly to her guards and that all she said was reported to her judges. And it may have happened that the young Pierre, whose master was on the English side, wished to advise her and even did so. There is a suspicion, however, that like so many others he was merely boasting.[548]

The Sire Jean de Luxembourg came to Rouen. He went to the Maid's tower accompanied by his brother, the Lord Bishop of Thérouanne, Chancellor of England; and also by Humphrey, Earl of Stafford, Constable of France for King Henry; and the Earl of Warwick, Governor of the Castle of Rouen. At this interview there was also present the young Seigneur de Macy, who held Jeanne to be of very modest bearing, since she had repulsed his attempted familiarity.

"Jeanne," said the Sire de Luxembourg, "I have come to ransom you if you will promise never again to bear arms against us."

These words do not accord with our knowledge of the negotiation for the purchase of the Maid. They seem to indicate that even then the contract was not complete, or at any rate that the vendor thought he could break it if he chose. But the most remarkable point about the Sire de Luxembourg's speech is the condition on which he says he will ransom the Maid. He asks her to promise never again to fight against England and Burgundy. From these words it would seem to have been his intention to sell her to the King of France or to his representative.[549]

There is no evidence, however, of this speech having made any impression on the English. Jeanne set no store by it.

"In God's name, you do but jest," she replied; "for I know well that it lieth neither within your will nor within your power."

It is related that when he persisted in his statement, she replied:

"I know that these English will put me to death, believing that afterwards they will conquer France."

Since she certainly did not believe it, it seems highly improbable that she should have said that the English would have put her to death. Throughout the trial she was expecting, on the faith of her Voices, to be delivered. She knew not how or when that deliverance would come to pass, but she was as certain of it as of the presence of Our Lord in the Holy Sacrament. She may have said to the Sire de Luxembourg: "I know that the English want to put me to death." Then she repeated courageously what she had already said a thousand times:

"But were there one hundred thousand *Godons* more than at present, they would not conquer the kingdom."

On hearing these words, the Earl of Stafford unsheathed his sword and the Earl of Warwick had to restrain his hand.[550] That the English Constable of France should have raised his sword against a woman in chains would be incredible, did we not know that about this time this Earl of Stafford, hearing some one speak well of Jeanne, straightway wished to transfix him.[551]

In order that the Bishop and Vidame of Beauvais might exercise jurisdiction at Rouen it was necessary that a concession of territory should be granted him. The archiepiscopal see of Rouen was vacant.[552] For this concession, therefore, the Bishop of Beauvais applied to the chapter, with whom he had had misunderstandings.[553] The canons of Rouen lacked neither firmness nor independence; more of them were honest than dishonest; some were highly educated, well-lettered and even kind-hearted. None of them nourished any ill will toward the

English. The Regent Bedford himself was a canon of Rouen, as Charles VII was a canon of Puy.[554] On the 20th of October, in that same year 1430, the Regent, donning surplice and amice, had distributed the dole of bread and wine for the chapter.[555] The canons of Rouen were not prejudiced in favour of the Maid of the Armagnacs; they agreed to the demand of the Bishop of Beauvais and granted him the formal concession of territory.[556]

On the 3rd of January, 1431, by royal decree, King Henry ordered the Maid to be given up to the Bishop and Count of Beauvais, reserving to himself the right to bring her before him, if she should be acquitted by the ecclesiastical tribunal.[557]

Nevertheless she was not placed in the Church prison, in one of those dungeons near the Booksellers' Porch, where in the shadow of the gigantic cathedral there rotted unhappy wretches who had erred in matters of faith.[558] There she would have endured sufferings far more terrible than even the horrors of her military tower. The wrong the Great Council of England inflicted on Jeanne by not handing her over to the ecclesiastical powers of Rouen was far less than the indignity they thereby inflicted on her judges.

With the way thus opened before him, the Bishop of Beauvais proceeded with all the violence one might expect from a Cabochien, albeit that violence was qualified by worldly arts and canonical knowledge.[559] As promoter in the case, that is, as the magistrate who was to conduct the prosecution, he selected one Jean d'Estivet, called Bénédicité, canon of Bayeux and of Beauvais, Promoter-General of the diocese of Beauvais. Jean d'Estivet was a friend of the Lord Bishop, and had been driven out of the diocese by the French at the same time. He was suspected of hostility to the Maid.[560] The Lord Bishop appointed Jean de la Fontaine, master of arts, licentiate of canon law, to be "councillor commissary" of the trial.[561] One of the clerks of the ecclesiastical court of Rouen, Guillaume Manchon, priest, he appointed first registrar.

In the course of instructing this official as to what would be expected of him, the Lord Bishop said to Messire Guillaume:

"You must do the King good service. It is our intention to institute an elaborate prosecution (*un beau procès*) against this Jeanne."[562]

As to the King's service, the Lord Bishop did not mean that it should be rendered at the expense of justice; he was a man of some priestly pride and was not likely to reveal his own evil designs. If he spoke thus, it was because in France, for a century at least, the jurisdiction of the Inquisition had been regarded as the jurisdiction of the King.[563] And as for the expression "an elaborate prosecution" (*un beau procès*), that meant a trial in which legal forms were observed and irregularities avoided, for it was a case in which were interested the doctors and masters of the realm of France and indeed the whole of Christendom. Messire Guillaume Manchon, well skilled in legal procedure, was not likely to err in a matter of legal language. An elaborate trial was a strictly regular trial. It was said, for example, that "N— and N— had by elaborate judicial procedure found such an one to be guilty."[564]

Charged by the Bishop to choose another registrar to assist him, Guillaume Manchon selected as his colleague Guillaume Colles, surnamed Boisguillaume, who like him was a notary of the Church.[565]

Jean Massieu, priest, ecclesiastical dean of Rouen, was appointed usher of the court.[566]

In that kind of trial, which was very common in those days, there were strictly only two judges, the Ordinary and the Inquisitor. But it was the custom for the Bishop to summon as councillors and assessors persons learned in both canon and civil law. The number and the rank of those councillors varied according to the case. And it is clear that the obstinate upholder of a very pestilent heresy must needs be more particularly and more ceremoniously tried than an old wife, who had sold herself to some insignificant demon, and whose spells could harm nothing more important than cabbages. For the common wizard, for the multitude of those females, or *mulierculæ*, as they were described by one inquisitor who boasted of having burnt many, the judges were content with three or four ecclesiastical advocates and as many canons.[567] When it was a question of a very notable personage who had set a highly pernicious example, of a king's advocate, for instance like Master Jean Segueut, who that very year, in Normandy, had spoken against the temporal power of the Church, a large assembly of doctors and prelates, English and French, were convoked, and the doctors and masters of the University of Paris were consulted in writing.[568] Now it was fitting that the Maid of the Armagnacs should be yet more elaborately and more solemnly tried, with a yet greater concourse of doctors and of prelates; and thus it was ordained by the Lord Bishop of Beauvais. As councillors and assessors he summoned the canons of Rouen in as great a number as possible. Among those who answered his summons we may mention Raoul Roussel, treasurer of the chapter; Gilles Deschamps, who had been chaplain to the late King, Charles VI, in 1415; Pierre Maurice, doctor in theology, rector of the University of Paris in 1428; Jean Alespée, one of the sixteen who during the siege of 1418 had gone robed in black and with cheerful countenance to place at the feet of King Henry V the life and honour of the city; Pasquier de Vaux, apostolic notary at the Council of Constance, President of the Norman *Chambre des Comptes*; Nicolas de Vendères, whose candidature for the vacant see of Rouen was being advocated by a powerful party; and, lastly, Nicolas Loiseleur. For the same purpose, the Lord Bishop summoned the abbots of the great Norman abbeys, Mont Saint-Michel-au-Péril-de-la-Mer, Fécamp, Jumièges, Préaux, Mortemer, Saint-Georges de Boscherville, la Trinité-du-mont-Sainte-Catherine, Saint-Ouen, Bec, Cormeilles, the priors of Saint-Lô, of Rouen, of Sigy, of Longueville, and the abbot of Saint Corneille of Compiègne. He summoned twelve ecclesiastical advocates; likewise famous doctors and masters of the University of Paris, Jean Beaupère, rector in 1412; Thomas Fiefvé, rector in 1427; Guillaume Erart, Nicolas Midi,[569] and that young doctor, abounding in knowledge and in modesty, the brightest star in the Christian firmament of the day, Thomas de Courcelles.[570] The Lord Bishop is bent upon turning the tribunal, which is to try Jeanne, into a veritable synod; it is indeed a provincial council, before which she is cited. Moreover, in effect, it is not only Jeanne the Maid, but Charles of Valois, calling himself King of France, and lawful successor of Charles VI who is to be brought to justice. Wherefore are assembled so many croziered and mitred abbots, so many renowned doctors and masters.

Nevertheless, there were other bright and shining lights of the Church, whom the Bishop of Beauvais neglected to summon. He consulted the two bishops of Coutances and Lisieux; he did not consult the senior bishop of Normandy, the Bishop of Avranches, Messire Jean de Saint-Avit, whom the chapter of the cathedral had charged with the duty of ordination throughout the diocese during the vacancy of the see of Rouen. But Messire Jean de Saint-Avit was considered and rightly considered to favour King Charles.[571] On the other hand those English doctors and masters, residing at Rouen, who had been consulted in Segueut's trial, were not consulted in that of Jeanne.[572] The doctors and masters of the University of Paris, the abbots of Normandy, the chapter of Rouen, held firmly to the Treaty of Troyes;

they were as prejudiced as the English clerks against the Maid and the Dauphin Charles, and they were less suspected; it was all to the good.[573]

On Tuesday, the 9th of January, my Lord of Beauvais summoned eight councillors to his house: the abbots of Fécamp and of Jumièges, the prior of Longueville, the canons Roussel, Venderès, Barbier, Coppequesne and Loiseleur.

"Before entering upon the prosecution of this woman," he said to them, "we have judged it good, maturely and fully to confer with men learned and skilled in law, human and divine, of whom, thank God, there be great number in this city of Rouen."

The opinion of the doctors and masters was that information should be collected concerning the deeds and sayings publicly imputed to this woman.

The Lord Bishop informed them that already certain information had been obtained by his command, and that he had decided to order more to be collected, which would be ultimately presented to the Council.[574]

It is certain that a tabellion[575] of Andelot in Champagne, Nicolas Bailly, requisitioned by Messire Jean de Torcenay, Bailie of Chaumont for King Henry, went to Domremy, and with Gérard Petit, provost of Andelot, and divers mendicant monks, made inquiry touching Jeanne's life and reputation. The interrogators heard twelve or fifteen witnesses and among others Jean Hannequin[576] of Greux and Jean Bégot, with whom they lodged.[577] We know from Nicolas Bailly himself that they gathered not a single fact derogatory to Jeanne. And if we may believe Jean Moreau, a citizen of Rouen, Maître Nicolas, having brought my Lord of Beauvais the result of his researches, was treated as a wicked man and a traitor; and obtained no reward for his expenditure or his labour.[578] This is possible, but it seems strange. It can in no wise be true, however, that neither at Vaucouleurs nor at Domremy, nor in the neighbouring villages was anything discovered against Jeanne. Quite on the contrary, numbers of accusations were collected against the inhabitants in general, who were addicted to evil practices, and in particular against Jeanne, who held intercourse with fairies,[579] carried a mandrake in her bosom, and disobeyed her father and mother.[580]

Abundant information was forthcoming, not only from Lorraine and from Paris, but from the districts loyal to King Charles, from Lagny, Beauvais, Reims, and even from so far as Touraine and

Berry;[581] which was information enough to burn ten heretics and twenty witches. Devilries were discovered which filled the priests with horror: the finding of a lost cup and gloves, the exposure of an immoral priest, the sword of Saint Catherine, the restoration of a child to life. There was also a report of a rash letter concerning the Pope and there were many other indications of witchcraft, heresy, and religious error.[582] Such information was not to be included among the documents of the trial.[583] It was the custom of the Holy Inquisition to keep secret the evidence and even the names of the witnesses.[584] In this case the Bishop of Beauvais might have pleaded as an excuse for so doing the safety of the deponents, who might have suffered had he published information gathered in provinces subject to the Dauphin Charles. Even if their names were concealed, they would be identified by their evidence. For the purposes of the trial, Jeanne's own conversation in prison was the best source of information: she spoke much and without any of the reserve which prudence might have dictated.

A painter, whose name is unknown, came to see her in her tower. He asked her aloud and before her guards what arms she bore, as if he wished to represent her with her escutcheon. In those days portraits were very seldom painted from life, except of persons of very high rank, and they were generally represented kneeling and with clasped hands in an attitude of prayer. Though in Flanders and in Burgundy there may have been a few portraits bearing no signs of devotion, they were very rare. A portrait naturally suggested a person praying to God, to the Holy Virgin, or to some saint. Wherefore the idea of painting the Maid's picture doubtless must have met with the stern disapproval of her ecclesiastical judges. All the more so because they must have feared that the painter would represent this excommunicated woman in the guise of a saint, canonised by the Church, as the Armagnacs were wont to do.

A careful consideration of this incident inclines us to think that this man was no painter but a spy. Jeanne told him of the arms which the King had granted to her brothers: an azure shield bearing a sword between two golden *fleurs de lis*. And our suspicion is confirmed when at the trial she is reproached with pomp and vanity for having caused her arms to be painted.[585]

Sundry clerks introduced into her prison gave her to believe that they were men-at-arms of the party of Charles of Valois.[586] In order to deceive her, the Promoter himself, Maître Jean d'Estivet, disguised himself as a poor prisoner.[587] One of the canons of Rouen, who was summoned to the trial, by name Maître Nicolas Loiseleur, would seem to have been especially inventive of devices for the discovery of Jeanne's heresies. A native of Chartres, he was not only a master of arts, but was greatly renowned for astuteness. In 1427 and 1428 he carried through difficult negotiations, which detained him long months in Paris. In 1430 he was one of those deputed by the chapter to go to the Cardinal of Winchester in order to obtain an audience of King Henry and commend to him the church of Rouen. Maître Nicolas Loiseleur was therefore a *persona grata* with the Great Council.[588]

Having concerted with the Bishop of Beauvais and the Earl of Warwick, he entered Jeanne's prison, wearing a short jacket like a layman. The guards had been instructed to withdraw; and Maître Nicolas, left alone with his prisoner, confided to her that he, like herself, was a native of the Lorraine Marches, a shoemaker by trade, one who held to the French party and had been taken prisoner by the English. From King Charles he brought her tidings which were the fruit of his own imagination. No one was dearer to Jeanne than her King. Thus having won her confidence, the pseudo-shoemaker asked her sundry questions concerning the angels and saints who visited her. She answered him confidingly, speaking as friend to friend, as countryman to countryman. He gave her counsel, advising her not to believe all these churchmen and not to do all that they asked her; "For," he said, "if thou believest in them thou shalt be destroyed."

Many a time, we are told, did Maître Nicolas Loiseleur act the part of the Lorraine shoemaker. Afterwards he dictated to the registrars all that Jeanne had said, providing thus a valuable source of information of which a memorandum was made to be used during the examination. It would even appear that during certain of these visits the registrars were stationed at a peep-hole in an adjoining room.[589] If we may believe the rumours current in the town, Maître Nicolas also disguised himself as Saint Catherine, and by this means brought Jeanne to say all that he wanted.

He may not have been proud of such deceptions, but at any rate he made no secret of them.[590] Many famous masters approved him; others censured him.[591]

The angel of the schools, Thomas de Courcelles, when Nicolas told him of his disguises, counselled him to abandon them.

Afterwards the registrars pretended that it had been extremely repugnant to them thus to overhear in hiding a conversation so craftily contrived. The golden age of inquisitorial justice must have been well over when so strict a doctor as Maître Thomas was willing thus to criticise the most solemn forms of that justice. Inquisitorial proceedings must indeed have fallen into decay when two notaries of the Church dream of eluding its most common prescriptions. The clerks who disguised themselves as soldiers, the Promoter who took on the semblance of a poor prisoner, were exercising the most regular functions of the judicial system instituted by Innocent III.

In acting the shoemaker and Saint Catherine, if he were seeking the salvation and not the destruction of the sinner, if, contrary to public report, far from inciting her to rebellion, he was reducing her to obedience, if, in short, he were but deceiving her for her own temporal and spiritual good, Maître Nicolas Loiseleur was proceeding in conformity with established rules. In the *Tractatus de Hæresi* it is written: "Let no man approach the heretic, save from time to time two persons of faith and tact, who may warn him with precaution and as having compassion upon him, to eschew death by confessing his errors, and who may promise him that by so doing he shall escape death by fire; for the fear of death, and the hope of life may peradventure soften a heart which could be touched in no other wise."[592]

The duty of registrars was laid down in the following manner:

"Matters shall be ordained thus, that certain persons shall be stationed in a suitable place so as to surprise the confidences of heretics and to overhear their words."[593]

As for the Bishop of Beauvais, who had ordained and permitted such procedure, he found his justification and approbation in the words of the Apostle Saint Paul to the Corinthians: "I did not burden you: nevertheless, being crafty, I caught you with guile." "*Ego vos non gravavi; sed cum essem astutus, dolo vos cepi*" (II Corinthians xii, 16).[594]

Meanwhile, when Jeanne saw the Promoter, Jean d'Estivet, in his churchman's habit she did not recognise him. And Maître Nicolas Loiseleur also often came to her in monkish dress. In this guise he inspired her with great confidence; she confessed to him devoutly and had no other confessor.[595] She saw him sometimes as a shoemaker and sometimes as a canon and never perceived that he was the same person. Wherefore we must indeed believe her to have been incredibly simple in certain respects; and these great theologians must have realised that it was not difficult to deceive her.

It was well known to all men versed in science, divine and human, that the Enemy never entered into dealings with a maid without depriving her of her virginity.[596] At Poitiers the French clerks had thought of it, and when Queen Yolande assured them that Jeanne was a virgin, they ceased to fear that she was sent by the devil.[597] The Lord Bishop of Beauvais in a different hope awaited a similar examination. The Duchess of Bedford herself went to the prison. She was assisted by Lady Anna Bavon and another matron. It has been said that the Regent was hidden meanwhile in an adjoining room and looking through a hole in the wall.[598] This is by no means certain, but it is not impossible; he was at Rouen a fortnight after Jeanne had been brought there.[599] Whether the charge were groundless or well founded he was seriously reproached for this curiosity. If there were many who in his place would have been equally curious, every one must judge for himself; but we must bear in mind that my Lord of Bedford believed Jeanne a witch, and that it was not the custom in those days to treat witches with the respect due to ladies. We must remember also that this was a matter in which Old England was greatly concerned, and the Regent loved his country with all his heart and all his strength.

Upon the examination of the Duchess of Bedford as upon that of the Queen of Sicily Jeanne appeared a virgin. The matrons knew various signs of virginity; but for us a more certain sign is Jeanne's own word. When she was asked wherefore she called herself the Maid, whether she were one in reality, she replied: "I may tell you that such I am."[600] The judges, as far as we know, set no store by this favourable result of the examination. Did they believe with the wise King Solomon that in such matters all inquiry is vain, and did they reject the matrons' verdict by virtue of the saying: *Virginitatis probatio non minus difficilis quam custodia*? No, they knew well that she was indeed a virgin. They allowed it to be understood when they did not assert the contrary.[601] And since they persisted in believing her a witch, it must have been because they imagined her to have given herself to devils who had left her as they found her. The morals of devils abounded in such inconsistencies, which were the despair of the most learned doctors; every day new inconsistencies were being discovered.

On Saturday, the 13th of January, the Lord Abbot of Fécamp, the doctors and masters, Nicolas de Venderès, Guillaume Haiton, Nicolas Coppequesne, Jean de la Fontaine, and Nicolas Loiseleur, met in the house of the Lord Bishop. There was read to them the information concerning the Maid gathered in Lorraine and elsewhere. And it was decided that according to this information a certain number of articles should be drawn up in due form; which was done.[602]

On Tuesday, the 23rd of January, the doctors and masters above named considered the terms of these articles, and, finding them sufficient, they decided that they might be used for the examination. Then they resolved that the Bishop of Beauvais should order a preliminary inquiry as to the deeds and sayings of Jeanne.[603]

On Tuesday, the 13th of February, Jean d'Estivet, called Bénédicité, Promoter, Jean de la Fontaine, Commissioner, Boisguillaume and Manchon, Registrars, and Jean Massieu, Usher, took the oath faithfully to discharge their various offices. Then straightway Maître Jean de la Fontaine, assisted by two registrars, proceeded to the preliminary inquiry.[604]

On Monday, the 19th of February, at eight o'clock in the morning, the doctors and masters assembled, to the number of eleven, in the house of the Bishop of Beauvais; there they heard the reading of the articles and the preliminary information. Whereupon they gave it as their opinion, and, in conformity with this opinion, the Bishop decided that there was matter sufficient to justify the woman called the Maid being cited and charged touching a question of faith.[605]

But now a fresh difficulty arose. In such a trial it was necessary for the accused to appear at once before the Ordinary and before the Inquisitor. The two judges were equally necessary for the validity of the trial. Now the Grand Inquisitor for the realm of France, Brother Jean Graverent, was then at Saint-Lô, prosecuting on a religious charge a citizen of the town, one Jean Le Couvreur.[606] In the absence of Brother Jean Graverent, the Bishop of Beauvais had invited the Vice-Inquisitor for the diocese of Rouen to proceed against Jeanne conjointly with himself. Meanwhile the Vice-Inquisitor seemed not to understand; he made no response; and the Bishop was left in embarrassment with his lawsuit on his hands.

This Vice-Inquisitor was Brother Jean Lemaistre, Prior of the Dominicans of Rouen, bachelor of theology, a monk right prudent and scrupulous.[607] At length in answer to a summons from the Usher, at four o'clock on the 19th of February, 1413, he appeared in the house of the Bishop of Beauvais. He declared himself ready to intervene provided that he had the right to do so, which he doubted. As the reason for his uncertainty he alleged that he was the Inquisitor of Rouen; now the Bishop of Beauvais was exercising his jurisdiction as bishop of the diocese of Beauvais, but on borrowed territory; wherefore was it not rather for the Inquisitor of Beauvais not for the Inquisitor of Rouen, to sit on the judgment seat side by side with the Bishop?[608] He declared that he would ask the Grand Inquisitor of France for an authorisation which should hold good for the diocese of Beauvais. Meanwhile he consented to act in order to satisfy his own conscience and to prevent the proceedings from lapsing, which, in the opinion of all, must have ensued had the trial been instituted without the concurrence of the Holy Inquisition.[609] All preliminary difficulties were now removed. The Maid was cited to appear on Wednesday, the 21st of February,[610] 1431.

On that day, at eight o'clock in the morning, the Bishop of Beauvais, the Vicar of the Inquisitor, and forty-one Councillors and Assessors assembled in the castle chapel. Fifteen of them were doctors in theology, five doctors in civil and canon law, six bachelors in theology, eleven bachelors in canon law, four licentiates in civil law. The Bishop sat as judge. At his side were the Councillors and Assessors, clothed either in the fine camlet of canons or in the coarse cloth of mendicants, expressive, the one of sacerdotal solemnity, the other of evangelical meekness. Some glared fiercely, others cast down their eyes. Brother Jean Lemaistre, Vice-Inquisitor of the faith, was among them, silent, in the black and white livery of poverty and obedience.[611]

Before bringing in the accused, the usher informed the Bishop that Jeanne, to whom the citation had been delivered, had replied that she would be willing to appear, but she demanded that an equal number of ecclesiastics of the French party should be added to those of the English party. She requested also the permission to hear mass.[612] The Bishop refused both demands;[613] and Jeanne was brought in, dressed as a man, with her feet in shackles. She was made to sit down at the table of the registrars.

And now from the very outset these theologians and this damsel regarded each other with mutual horror and hatred. Contrary to the custom of her sex, a custom which even loose women did not dare to infringe, she displayed her hair, which was brown and cut short over the ears. It was possibly the first time that some of those young monks seated behind their elders had ever seen a woman's hair. She wore hose like a youth. To them her dress appeared immodest and abominable.[614] She exasperated and irritated them. Had the Bishop of Beauvais insisted on her appearing in hood and gown their anger against her would have been less violent. This man's attire brought before their minds the works performed by the Maid in the camp of the Dauphin Charles, calling himself king. By the stroke of a magic wand she had deprived the English men-at-arms of all their strength, and thereby she had inflicted sore hurt on the majority of the churchmen who were to judge her. Some among them were thinking of the benefices of which she had despoiled them; others, doctors and masters of the University, recalled how she had been about to lay Paris waste with fire and sword;[615] others again, canons and abbots, could not forgive her perchance for having struck fear into their hearts even in remote Normandy. Was it possible for them to pardon the havoc she had thus wrought in a great part of the Church of France, when they knew she had done it by sorcery, by divination and by invoking devils? "A man must be very ignorant if he will deny the reality of magic," said Sprenger. As they were very learned, they saw magicians and wizards where others would never have suspected them; they held that to doubt the power of demons over men and things was not only heretical and impious, but tending to subvert the whole natural and social order. These doctors, seated in the castle chapel, had burned each one of them ten, twenty, fifty witches, all of whom had confessed their crimes. Would it not have been madness after that to doubt the existence of witches?

To us it seems curious that beings capable of causing hail-storms and casting spells over men and animals should allow themselves to be taken, judged, tortured, and burned without making any defence; but it was constantly occurring; every ecclesiastical judge must have observed it. Very learned men were able to account for it: they explained that wizards and witches lost their power as soon as they fell into the hands of churchmen. This explanation was deemed sufficient. The hapless Maid had lost her power like the others; they feared her no longer.

At least Jeanne hated them as bitterly as they hated her. It was natural for unlettered saints, for the fair inspired, frank of mind, capricious, and enthusiastic to feel an antipathy towards doctors all inflated with knowledge and stiffened with scholasticism. Such an antipathy Jeanne had recently felt towards clerks, even when as at Poitiers they had been on the French side, and had not wished her evil and had not greatly troubled her. Wherefore we may easily imagine how intense was the repulsion with which the clerks of Rouen now inspired her. She knew that they sought to compass her death. But she feared them not; confidently she awaited from her saints and angels the fulfilment of their promise, their coming for her deliverance. She knew not when nor how her deliverance should come; but that come it would she never once doubted. To doubt it would indeed have been to doubt Saint Michael, Saint Catherine, and even Our Lord; it would have been to believe evil of her Voices. They had told her to fear nothing, and of nothing was she afeard.[616] Fearless simplicity; whence came her confidence in her Voices if not from her own heart?

The Bishop required her to swear, according to the prescribed form with both hands on the holy Gospels, that she would reply truly to all that should be asked her.

She could not. Her Voices forbade her telling any one of the revelations they had so abundantly vouchsafed to her.

She answered: "I do not know on what you wish to question me. You might ask me things that I would not tell you."

And when the Bishop insisted on her swearing to tell the whole truth:

"Touching my father and mother and what I did after my coming into France I will willingly swear," she said; "but touching God's revelations to me, those I have neither told nor communicated to any man, save to Charles my King. And nought of them will I reveal, were I to lose my head for it."

Then, either because she wished to gain time or because she counted on receiving some new directions from her *Council*, she added that in a week she would know whether she might so reveal those things.

At length she took the oath, according to the prescribed form, on her knees, with both hands on the missal.[617] Then she answered concerning her name, her country, her parents, her baptism, her godfathers and godmothers. She said that to the best of her knowledge she was about nineteen years of age.[618]

Questioned concerning her education, she replied: "From my mother I learnt my Paternoster, my Ave Maria and my Credo."

But, asked to repeat her Paternoster, she refused, for, she said, she would only say it in confession. This was because she wanted the Bishop to hear her confess.[619]

The assembly was profoundly agitated; all spoke at once. Jeanne with her soft voice had scandalised the doctors.

The Bishop forbade her to leave her prison, under pain of being convicted of the crime of heresy.

She refused to submit to this prohibition. "If I did escape," she said, "none could reproach me with having broken faith, for I never gave my word to any one."

Afterwards she complained of her chains.

The Bishop told her they were on account of her attempt to escape.

She agreed: "It is true that I wanted to escape, and I still want to, just like every other prisoner."[620]

Such a confession was very bold, if she had rightly understood the judge when he said that by flight from prison she would incur the punishment of a heretic. To escape from an ecclesiastical prison was to commit a crime against the Church, but it was folly as well as crime; for the prisons of the Church are penitentiaries, and the prisoner who refuses salutary penance is as foolish as he is guilty; for he is like a sick man who refuses to be cured. But Jeanne was not, strictly speaking, in an ecclesiastical prison; she was in the castle of Rouen, a prisoner of war in the hands of the English. Could it be said that if she escaped she would incur excommunication and the spiritual and temporal penalties inflicted on the enemies of religion? There lay the difficulty. The Lord Bishop removed it forthwith by an elaborate legal fiction. Three English men-at-arms, John Grey, John Berwoist, and William Talbot, were appointed by the King to be Jeanne's custodians. The Bishop, acting as an ecclesiastical judge, himself delivered to them their charge, and made them swear on the holy Gospels to bind the damsel and confine her.[621] In this wise the Maid became the prisoner of our holy Mother, the Church; and she could not burst her bonds without falling into heresy. The second sitting was appointed for the next day, the 22nd of February.[622]

CHAPTER XI
THE TRIAL FOR LAPSE (CONTINUED)

HEN a record of the proceedings came to be written down after the first sitting, a dispute arose between the ecclesiastical notaries and the two or three royal registrars who had likewise taken down the replies of the accused. As might be expected, the two records differed in several places. It was decided that on the contested points Jeanne should be further examined.[623] The notaries of the Church complained also that they experienced great difficulty in seizing Jeanne's words on account of the constant interruptions of the bystanders.

In a trial by the Inquisition there was no place fixed for the examination any more than for the other acts of the procedure. The judges might examine the accused in a chapel, in a chapter-house, or even in a prison or a torture-chamber. According to Messire Guillaume Manchon it was in order to escape from the tumult of the first sitting,[624] and because there was no longer any reason for proceeding with such solemn ceremony as at the opening of the trial, that the judge and his councillors met in the Robing Room, a little chamber at one end of the castle hall;[625] and two English guards were stationed at the door. According to the rules of inquisitorial procedure, the assessors were not bound to be present at all the deliberations.[626] This time forty-two were present, twenty-six of the original ones and six newly appointed. Among these high clerics was Brother Jean Lemaistre, Vice Inquisitor of the Faith, a humble preaching friar. No longer as in the days of Saint Dominic was the Vice Inquisitor the hunting hound of the Lord, now he was but the dog of the Bishop, a poor monk, who dared neither to do nor to abstain from doing. Such was the result of the assertion of Gallican independence against papal supremacy. Dumb and timid, Brother Jean Lemaistre was the last and the least of all the brethren in that assembly, but he was ever looking for the day when he should be sovereign judge and without appeal.[627]

Jeanne was brought in by the Usher, Messire Jean Massieu. Again she endeavoured to avoid taking the oath to tell everything; but she had to swear on the Gospel.[628]

She was examined by Maître Jean Beaupère, doctor in theology. In his University of Paris he was regarded as a scholar of light and leading; it had twice appointed him rector. It had charged him with the functions of chancellor in the absence of Gerson, and, in 1419, had sent him with Messire Pierre Cauchon to the town of Troyes, to give aid and counsel to King Charles VI. Three years later it had despatched him to the Queen of England and the Duke of Gloucester to enlist their support in its endeavour to obtain the confirmation of its privileges. King Henry VI had just appointed him canon of Rouen.[629]

Maître Jean's first question to Jeanne was what was her age when she left her father's house. She was unable to say, although on the previous day she had stated her present age to be about nineteen.[630]

Interrogated as to the occupations of her childhood, she replied that she was busy with household duties and seldom went into the fields with the cattle.

"For spinning and sewing," she said, "I am as good as any woman in Rouen."[631]

Thus even in things domestic she displayed her ardour and her chivalrous zeal; at the spinning-wheel and with the needle she challenged all the women in a town, without knowing one of them.

Questioned as to her confessions and her communions, she answered that she confessed to her parish priest or to another priest when the former was not able to hear her. But she refused to say whether she had received the communion on other feast-days than Easter.[632]

In order to take her unawares, Maître Jean Beaupère proceeded without method, passing abruptly from one subject to another. Suddenly he spoke of her Voices. She gave him the following reply:

"Being thirteen years of age, I heard the Voice of God, bidding me lead a good life. And the first time I was sore afeard. And the Voice came almost at the hour of noon, in summer, in my father's garden...."

She heard the Voice on the right towards the church. Rarely did she hear it without seeing a light. This light was in the direction whence the Voice came.[633]

When Jeanne said that her Voice spoke to her from the right, a doctor more learned and more kindly disposed than Maître Jean would have interpreted this circumstance favourably; for do we not read in Ezekiel that the angels were upon the right hand of the dwelling; do we not find in the last chapter of Saint Mark, that the women beheld the Angel seated on the right, and finally does not Saint Luke expressly state that the Angel appeared unto Zacharias on the right of the altar burning with incense; whereupon the Venerable Bede observes: "he appeared on the right as a sign that he was the bringer of divine mercy."[634] But such things never occurred to the examiner. Thinking to embarrass Jeanne, he asked how she came to see the light if it appeared at her side.[635] Jeanne made no reply, and as if distraught, she said:

"If I were in a wood I should easily hear the Voices coming towards me.... It seems to me to be a Voice right worthy. I believe that this Voice was sent to me by God. After having heard it three times I knew it to be the voice of an angel."

"What instruction did this Voice give you for the salvation of your soul?"

"It taught me to live well, to go to church, and it told me to fare forth into France."[636]

Then Jeanne related how, by the command of her Voice, she had gone to Vaucouleurs, to Sire Robert de Baudricourt, whom she had recognised without ever having seen him before, how the Duke of Lorraine had summoned her to cure him, and how she had come into France.[637]

Thereafter she was brought to say that she knew well that God loved the Duke of Orléans and that concerning him she had had more revelations than concerning any man living, save the King; that she had been obliged to change her woman's dress for man's attire and that her *Council* had advised her well.[638]

The letter to the English was read before her. She admitted having dictated it in those terms, with the exception of three passages. She had not said *body for body* nor *chieftain of war*; and she had said *surrender to the King* in the place *of surrender to the Maid*. That the judges had not tampered with the text of the letter we may assure ourselves by comparing it with other texts, which did not pass through their hands, and which contain the expressions challenged by Jeanne.[639]

In the beginning of her career, she believed that Our Lord, the true King of France, had ordained her to deliver the government of the realm to Charles of Valois, as His deputy. The words in which she gave utterance to this idea are reported by too many persons strangers one to another for us to doubt her having spoken them. "The King shall hold the kingdom as a fief (*en commande*); the King of France is the lieutenant of the King of Heaven." These are her own words and she did actually say to the Dauphin: "Make a gift of your realm to the King of Heaven."[640] But we are bound to admit that at Rouen not one of these mystic ideas persists, indeed there they seem altogether beyond her. In all her replies to her examiners, she seems incapable of any abstract reasoning whatsoever and of any speculation however simple, so that it is hard to understand how she should ever have conceived the idea of the temporal rule of Jesus Christ over the Land of the Lilies. There is nothing in her speech or in her thoughts to suggest such meditations, wherefore we are led to believe that this politico-theology had been taught her in her tender, teachable years by ecclesiastics desiring to remove the woes of Church and kingdom, but that she had failed to seize its spirit or grasp its inner meaning. Now, in the midst of a hard life lived with men-at-arms, whose simple souls accorded better with her own than the more cultivated minds of the early directors of her meditations, she had forgotten even the phraseology in which those suggested meditations were expressed. Interrogated concerning her coming to Chinon, she replied:

"Without let or hindrance I went to my King. When I reached the town of Sainte-Catherine de Fierbois, I sent first to the town of Château-Chinon, where my King was. I arrived there about the hour of noon and lodged in an inn, and, after dinner, I went to my King who was in his castle."

If we may believe the registrars, they never ceased wondering at her memory. They were amazed that she should recollect exactly what she had said a week before.[641] Nevertheless her memory was sometimes curiously uncertain, and we have reason for thinking with the Bastard that she waited two days at the inn before being received by the King.[642]

With regard to this audience in the castle of Chinon, she told her judges she had recognised the King as she had recognised the Sire de Baudricourt, by revelation.[643]

The interrogator asked her: "When the Voice revealed your King to you, was there any light?"[644]

This question bore upon matters which were of great moment to her judges; for they suspected the Maid of having committed a sacrilegious fraud, or rather witchcraft, with the complicity of the King of France. Indeed, they had learnt from their informers that Jeanne boasted of having given the King a sign in the form of a precious crown.[645] The following is the actual truth of the matter:

The legend of Saint Catherine relates that on a day she received from the hand of an angel a resplendent crown and placed it on the head of the Empress of the Romans. This crown was the symbol of eternal blessedness.[646] Jeanne, who had been brought up on this legend, said that the same thing had happened to her. In France she had told sundry marvellous stories of crowns, and in one of these stories she imagined herself to be in the great hall of the castle at Chinon, in the midst of the barons, receiving a crown from the hand of an angel to give it to her King.[647] This was true in a spiritual sense, for she had taken Charles to his anointing and to his coronation. Jeanne was not quick to grasp the distinction between two kinds of truth. She may, nevertheless, have doubted the material reality of this vision. She may even have held it to be true in a spiritual sense only. In any case, she had of her own accord promised Saint Catherine and Saint Margaret not to speak of it to her judges.[648]

"Saw you any angel above the King?"

She refused to reply.[649]

This time nothing more was said of the crown. Maître Jean Beaupère asked Jeanne if she often heard the Voice.

"Not a day passes without my hearing it. And it is my stay in great need."[650]

She never spoke of her Voices without describing them as her refuge and relief, her consolation and her joy. Now all theologians agreed in believing that good spirits when they depart leave the soul filled with joy, with peace, and with comfort, and as proof they cited the angel's words to Zacharias and Mary: "Be not afraid."[651] This reason, however, was not strong enough to persuade clerks of the English party that Voices hostile to the English were of God.

And the Maid added: "Never have I required of them any other final reward than the salvation of my soul."[652]

The examination ended with a capital charge: the attack on Paris on a feast day. It was in this connection possibly that Brother Jacques of Touraine, a friar of the Franciscan order, who from time to time put a question, asked Jeanne whether she had ever been in a place where Englishmen were being slain.

"In God's name, was I ever in such a place?" Jeanne responded vehemently. "How glibly you speak. Why did they not depart from France and go into their own country?"

A nobleman of England, who was in the chamber, on hearing these words, said to his neighbours: "By my troth she is a good woman. Why is she not English?"[653]

The third public sitting was appointed for two days thence, Saturday, the 24th of February.[654]

It was Lent. Jeanne observed the fast very strictly.[655]

On Friday, the 23rd, in the morning, she was awakened by her Voices themselves. She arose from her bed and remained seated, her hands clasped, giving thanks. Then she asked what she should reply to her judges, beseeching the Voices thereupon to take counsel of Our Lord. First the Voices uttered words she could not understand. That happened sometimes, in difficult circumstances especially. Then they said:[656] "Reply boldly, God will aid thee."

That day she heard them a second time at the hour of vespers and a third time when the bells were ringing the *Ave Maria* in the evening. In the night of Friday and Saturday they came and revealed to her many secrets for the weal of the King of France. Thereupon she received great consolation.[657] Very probably they repeated the assurance that she would be delivered from the hands of her enemies, and that on the other hand her judges stood in great danger.

She depended absolutely on her Voices for direction. When she was in difficulty as to what to say to her judges, she prayed to Our Lord; she addressed him devoutly, saying: "Good God, for the sake of thy holy Passion, I beseech thee if thou lovest me to reveal unto me what I should reply to these churchmen. Touching my dress I know well how I was commanded to put it on; but as to leaving it I know nothing. In this may it please thee to teach me."

Then straightway the Voices came.[658]

At the third sitting, held in the Robing Chamber, there were present sixty-two assessors, of whom twenty were new.[659]

Jeanne showed a greater repugnance than before to swearing on the holy Gospels to reply to all that should be asked her. In charity the Bishop warned her that this obstinate refusal caused her to be suspected, and he required her to swear, under pain of being convicted upon all the charges.[660] Such was indeed the rule in a trial by the Inquisition. In 1310 a *béguine*, one La Porète, refused to take the oath as required by the Holy Inquisitor of the Faith, Brother Guillaume of Paris. She was excommunicated forthwith, and without being further examined, after lengthy proceedings, she was handed over to the Provost of Paris, who caused her to be burned alive. Her piety at the stake drew tears from all the bystanders.[661]

Still the Bishop failed to force an unconditional oath from the Maid; she swore to tell the truth on all she knew concerning the trial, reserving to herself the right to be silent on everything which in her opinion did not concern it. She spoke freely of the Voices she had heard the previous day, but not of the revelations touching the King. When, however, Maître Jean Beaupère appeared desirous to know them, she asked for a fortnight's delay before replying, sure that before then she would be delivered; and straightway she fell to boasting of the secrets her Voices had confided to her for the King's weal.

"I would wish him to know them at this moment," she said; "even if as the result I were to drink no wine from now till Easter."[662]

"Drink no wine from now till Easter!" Did she thus casually use an expression common in that land of the rose-tinted wine (*vin gris*), a drop or two of which with a slice of bread sufficed the Domremy women for a meal?[663] Or had she caught this manner of speech with the habit of dealing hard clouts and good blows from the men-at-arms of her company? Alas! what hypocras was she to drink during the five weeks before Easter! She was merely making use of a current phrase, as was frequently her custom, and attributing no precise meaning to it, unless it were that wine vaguely suggested to her mind the idea of cordiality and the hope that after her deliverance she would see the Lords of France filling a cup in her honour.

Maître Jean Beaupère asked her whether she saw anything when she heard her Voices.

She replied: "I cannot tell you everything. I am not permitted. The Voice is good and worthy.... To this question I am not bound to reply."

And she asked them to give her in writing the points concerning which she had not given an immediate reply.[664]

What use did she intend to make of this writing? She did not know how to read; she had no counsel. Did she want to show the document to some false friend, like Loiseleur, who was deceiving her? Or was it her intent to present it to her saints?

Maître Beaupère asked whether her Voice had a face and eyes.

She refused to answer and quoted a saying frequently on the lips of children: "One is often hanged for having spoken the truth."[665]

Maître Beaupère asked: "Do you know whether you stand in God's grace?"

This was an extremely insidious question; it placed Jeanne in the dilemma of having to avow herself sinful or of appearing unpardonably bold. One of the assessors, Maître Jean Lefèvre of the Order of the Hermit Friars, observed that she was not bound to reply. There was murmuring throughout the chamber.

But Jeanne said: "If I be not, then may God bring me into it; if I be, then may God keep me in it."[666]

The assessors were astonished at so ready an answer. And yet no improvement ensued in their disposition towards her. They admitted that touching her King she spoke well, but for the rest she was too subtle, and with a subtlety peculiar to women.[667]

Thereafter, Maître Jean Beaupère examined Jeanne concerning her childhood in her village. He essayed to show that she had been cruel, had displayed a homicidal tendency from her earliest years, and had been addicted to those idolatrous practices which had given the folk of Domremy a bad name.[668]

Then he touched on a point of prime importance in elucidating the obscure origin of Jeanne's mission:

"Were you not regarded as the one who was sent from the Oak Wood?"

In this direction he might have succeeded in obtaining important revelations. False prophecies had indeed established Jeanne's reputation in France; but these clerks were incapable of discriminating amongst all these pseudo-Bedes and pseudo-Merlins.[669]

Jeanne replied: "When I came to the King, certain asked me whether there were in my country a wood called the Oak Wood; because of prophecies saying that from the neighbourhood of this wood should come a damsel who would work wonders. But to such things I paid no heed."

This statement we must needs believe; but if she denied credence to the prophecy of Merlin touching the Virgin of the Oak Wood, she paid good heed to the prophecy foretelling the appearance of a Deliverer in the person of a Maid coming from the Lorraine Marches, since she repeated that prophecy to the two Leroyers and to her Uncle Lassois, with an emphasis which filled them with astonishment. Now we must admit that the two prophecies are as alike as two peas.[670]

Passing abruptly from Merlin the Magician, Maître Jean Beaupère asked: "Jeanne, will you have a woman's dress?"

She answered: "Give me one; and I will accept it and depart. Otherwise I will not have it. I will be content with this one, since God is pleased for me to wear it."

On this reply, which contained two errors tending to heresy, the Lord Bishop adjourned the court.[671]

The morrow, the 25th of February, was the first Sunday in Lent. On that day or another, but probably on that day, my Lord Bishop sent Jeanne a shad. Having partaken of this fish she had fever and was seized with vomiting.[672] Two masters of arts of the Paris University, both doctors of medicine, Jean Tiphaine and Guillaume Delachambre, assessors in the trial, were summoned by the Earl of Warwick, who said to them:

"According to what has been told me, Jeanne is sick. I have summoned you to devise measures for her recovery. The King would not for the world have her die a natural death. She is dear to him, for he has bought her dearly; his intent is that she die not, save by the hand of justice, and that she should be burned. Do all that may be necessary, therefore, visit her attentively, and endeavour to restore her."[673]

Conducted to Jeanne by Maître Jean d'Estivet, the doctors inquired of her the cause of her suffering.

She answered that she had eaten a carp sent her by the Lord Bishop of Beauvais, and that she believed it to be the cause of her sickness.

Did Jeanne suspect the Bishop of designing to poison her? That is what Maître Jean d'Estivet thought, for he flew into a violent rage:

"Whore!" he cried, "it is thine own doing; thou hast eaten herrings and other things which have made thee ill."

"I have not," she answered.

They exchanged insults, and Jeanne's sickness thereupon grew worse.[674]

The doctors examined her and found that she had fever. Wherefore they decided to bleed her.

They informed the Earl of Warwick, who became anxious:

"A bleeding!" he cried; "take heed! She is artful and might kill herself."

Nevertheless Jeanne was bled and recovered.[675]

On Monday, the 26th, there was no examination.[676] On the opening of the fourth sitting, Tuesday, the 27th, Maître Jean Beaupère asked her how she had been, which inquiry touched her but little. She replied drily:

"You can see for yourself. I am as well as it is possible for me to be."[677]

This sitting was held in the Robing Chamber in the presence of fifty-four assessors.[678] Five of them had not been present before, and among them was Maître Nicolas Loiseleur, canon of Rouen, whose share in the proceedings had been to act the Lorraine shoemaker and Saint Catherine of Alexandria.[679]

Maître Jean Beaupère, as on the previous Saturday, was curious to know whether Jeanne had heard her Voices. She heard them every day.[680]

He asked her: "Is it an angel's voice that speaketh unto you, or the voice of a woman saint or of a man saint? Or is it God speaking without an interpreter?"

Said Jeanne: "This voice is the voice of Saint Catherine and of Saint Margaret; and on their heads are beautiful crowns, right rich and right precious. I am permitted to tell you so by Messire. If you doubt it send to Poitiers, where I was examined."[681]

She was right in appealing to the clerks of France. The Armagnac doctors had no less authority in matters of faith than the English and Burgundian doctors. Were they not all to meet at the Council?

The examiner asked: "How know ye that they are these two saints? Know ye them one from another?"

Said Jeanne: "Well do I know who they are; and I do know one from the other."

"How?"

"By the greeting they give me."[682]

Let not Jeanne be hastily taxed with error or untruth. Did not the Angel salute Gideon (Judges vi), and Raphaël salute Tobias (Tobit xii)?[683]

Thereafter Jeanne gave another reason: "I know them because they call themselves by name."[684]

When she was asked whether her saints were both clothed alike, whether they were of the same age, whether they spoke at once, whether one of them appeared before the other, she refused to reply, saying she had not permission to do so.[685]

Maître Jean Beaupère inquired which of the apparitions came to her the first when she was about thirteen.

Jeanne said: "It was Saint Michael. I beheld him with my eyes. And he was not alone, but with him were angels from heaven. It was by Messire's command alone that I came into France."

"Did you actually behold Saint Michael and these angels in the body?"

"I saw them with the eyes of my head as plainly as I see you; and when they went away I wept and should have liked them to take me with them."

"In what semblance was Saint Michael?"[686]

She was not permitted to say.

She was asked whether she had received permission from God to go into France and whether God had commanded her to put on man's dress.

By keeping silence on this point she became liable to be suspected of heresy, and however she replied she laid herself open to serious charges, – she either took upon herself homicide and abomination, or she attributed it to God, which manifestly was to blaspheme.

Concerning her coming into France, she said: "I would rather have been dragged by the hair of my head than have come into France without permission from Messire." Concerning her dress she added: "Dress is but a little thing, less than nothing. It was not according to the counsel of any man of this world that I put on man's clothing. I neither wore this attire nor did anything save by the command of Messire and his angels."[687]

Maître Jean Beaupère asked: "When you behold this Voice coming towards you, is there any light?"

Then she replied with a jest, as at Poitiers: "Every light cometh not to you, my fair lord."[688]

After all it was virtually against the King of France that these doctors of Rouen were proceeding with craft and with cunning.

Maître Jean Beaupère threw out the question: "How did your King come to have faith in your sayings?"

"Because they were proved good to him by signs and also because of his clerks."

"What revelations were made unto your King?"

"That you will not hear from me this year."

As he listened to the damsel's words, must not my Lord of Beauvais, who was in the counsels of King Henry, have reflected on that verse in the Book of Tobias (xii, 7): "It is good to keep close the secret of a king"?

Thereafter Jeanne was called upon to reply at length concerning the sword of Saint Catherine. The clerks suspected her of having found it by the art of divination, and by invoking the aid of demons, and of having cast a spell over it. All that she was able to say did not remove their suspicions.[689]

Then they passed on to the sword she had captured from a Burgundian.

"I wore it at Compiègne," she said, "because it was good for dealing sound clouts and good buffets."[690] The buffet was a flat blow, the clout was a side stroke. Some moments later, on the subject of her banner, she said that, in order to avoid killing any one, she bore it herself when they charged the enemy. And she added: "I have never slain any one."[691]

The doctors found that her replies varied.[692] Of course they varied. But if like her every hour of the day and night the doctors had been seeing the heavens descending, if all their thoughts, all their instincts, good and bad, all their desires barely formulated, had been undergoing instant transformation into divine commands, their replies would likewise have varied, and they would have doubtless been in such a state of illusion that in their words and in their actions they would have displayed less good sense, less gentleness and less courage.

The examinations were long; they lasted between three and four hours.[693] Before closing this one, Maître Jean Beaupère wished to know whether Jeanne had been wounded at Orléans. This was an interesting point. It was generally admitted that witches lost their power when they shed blood. Finally, the doctors quibbled over the capitulation of Jargeau, and the court adjourned.[694]

A famous Norman clerk, Maître Jean Lohier, having come to Rouen, the Count Bishop of Beauvais commanded that he should be informed concerning the trial. On the first Saturday in Lent, the 24th of February, the Bishop summoned him to his house near Saint-Nicolas-le-Painteur, and invited him to give his opinion of the proceedings. The views of Maître Jean Lohier greatly disturbed the Bishop. Off he rushed to the doctors and masters, Jean Beaupère, Jacques de Touraine, Nicolas Midi, Pierre Maurice, Thomas de Courcelles, Nicolas Loiseleur, and said to them:

"Here's Lohier, who holds fine views concerning our trial! He wants to object to everything, and says that our proceedings are invalid. If we were to take his advice we should begin everything over again, and all we have done would be worthless! It is easy to see what he is aiming at. By Saint John, we will do nothing of the kind; we will go on with our trial now it is begun."

The next day, in the Church of Notre Dame, Guillaume Manchon met Maître Jean Lohier and asked him:

"Have you seen anything of the records of the trial?"

"I have," replied Maître Jean. "This trial is void. It is impossible to support it on many grounds: firstly, it is not in regular form."[695]

By that he meant that proceedings should not have been taken against Jeanne without preliminary inquiries concerning the probability of her guilt; either he did not know of the inquiries instituted by my Lord of Beauvais, or he deemed them insufficient.[696]

"Secondly," continued Maître Jean Lohier, "the judges and assessors when they are trying this case are shut up in the castle, where they are not free to utter their opinions frankly. Thirdly, the trial involves divers persons who are not called, notably it touches the reputation of the King of France, to whose party Jeanne belonged, yet neither he nor his representative is cited. Fourthly, neither documents nor definite written charges have been produced, wherefore this woman, this simple girl, is left to reply without guidance to so many masters, to such great doctors and on such grave matters, especially those concerning her revelations. For all these reasons the trial appears to me to be invalid." Then he added: "You see how they proceed. They will catch her if they can in her words. They take advantage of the statements in which she says, 'I know for certain,' concerning her apparitions. But if she were to say, 'It seems to me,' instead of 'I know for certain,' it is my opinion that no man could convict her. I perceive that the dominant sentiment which actuates them is one of hatred. Their intention is to bring her to her death. Wherefore I shall stay here no longer. I cannot witness it. What I say gives offence."[697]

That same day Maître Jean left Rouen.[698]

A somewhat similar incident occurred with regard to Maître Nicolas de Houppeville, a famous cleric. In conference with certain churchmen, he expressed the opinion that to appoint as Jeanne's judges members of the party hostile to her was not a correct method of procedure; and he added that Jeanne had already been examined by the clerks of Poitiers and by the Archbishop of Reims, the metropolitan of this very Bishop of Beauvais. Hearing of this expression of opinion, my Lord of Beauvais flew into a violent rage, and summoned Maître Nicolas to appear before him. The latter replied that the Official of Rouen was his superior, and that the Bishop of Beauvais was not his judge. If it be true, as is related, that Maître Nicolas was thereafter cast into the King's prison, it was doubtless for a reason more strictly judicial than that of having offended the Lord Bishop of Beauvais. It is more probable, however, that this famous cleric did not wish to act as assessor, and that he left Rouen in order to avoid being summoned to take part in the trial.[699]

Certain ecclesiastics, among others Maître Jean Pigache, Maître Pierre Minier, and Maître Richard de Grouchet, discovered long afterwards that being threatened they had given their opinions under the influence of fear. "We were present at that trial," they said, "but throughout the proceedings we were always contemplating flight."[700] As a matter of fact, no violence was done to any man's opinions, and such as refused to attend the trial were in no way molested. Threats! But why should there be any? Was it difficult to convict a witch in those days? Jeanne was no witch. But, then, neither were the others. Still, between Jeanne and the other alleged witches there was this difference, that Jeanne had cast her spells in favour of the Armagnacs, and to convict her was to render a service to the English, who were the masters. This was a point to be taken into consideration; but there was something else which ought also to be borne in mind by thoughtful folk: such a conviction would at the same time offend the French, who were in a fair way to become the masters once more in the place of the English. These matters were very perplexing to the doctors; but the second consideration had less weight with them than the first; they had no idea that the French were so near reconquering Normandy.

The fifth session of the court took place in the usual chamber on the 1st of March, in the presence of fifty-eight assessors, of whom nine had not sat previously.[701]

The first question the examiner put Jeanne was:

"What say you of our Lord the Pope, and whom think you to be the true pope?"

She adroitly made answer by asking another question: "Are there two?"[702]

No, there were not two; Clement VIII's abdication had put an end to the schism; the great rift in the Church had been closed for thirteen years and all Christian nations recognized the Pope of Rome; even France who had become resigned to the disappearance of her Avignon popes. There was something, however, which neither the accused nor her judges knew; on that 1st of March, 1431, far from there being two popes, there was not even one; the Holy See had fallen vacant by the death of Martin V on the 20th of February, and the vacancy was only to be filled on the 3rd of March, by the election of Eugenius IV.[703]

The examiner in questioning Jeanne concerning the Holy See was not without a motive. That motive became obvious when he asked her whether she had not received a letter from the Count of Armagnac. She admitted having received the letter and having replied to it.

Copies of these two letters were included in the evidence to be used at the trial. They were read to Jeanne.

It appeared that the Count of Armagnac had asked the Maid by letter which of the three popes was the true one, and that Jeanne had replied to him, likewise by letter, that for the moment she had not time to answer, but that she would do so at her leisure when she should come to Paris.

Having heard these two letters read, Jeanne declared that the one attributed to her was only partially hers. And since she always dictated and could never read what had been taken down, it is conceivable that hasty words, uttered with her foot in the stirrup, may not have been accurately transcribed; but in a series of involved and contradictory replies she was unable to demonstrate how that which she had dictated differed from the written text;[704] and in itself the letter appears much more likely to have proceeded from an ignorant visionary than from a clerk who would have some knowledge, however little, of church affairs.

It contains certain words and turns of expression which are to be found in Jeanne's other letters. There can hardly be any doubt that this letter is by her; she had forgotten it. There is nothing surprising in that; her memory, as we have seen, was curiously liable to fail her.[705]

On this document the judges based the most serious of charges; they regarded it as furnishing proof of a most blamable temerity. What arrogance on the part of this woman, so it seemed to them, to claim to have been told by God himself that which the Church alone is entitled to teach! And to undertake by means of an inner illumination to point out the true pope, was that not to commit grave sin against the Bride of Christ, and with sacrilegious hand to rend the seamless robe of our Lord?

For once Jeanne saw clearly how her judges were endeavouring to entrap her, wherefore she twice declared her belief in the Sovereign Pontiff of Rome.[706] How bitterly she would have smiled had she known that the lights of the University of Paris, these famous doctors who held it mortal sin to believe in the wrong pope, themselves believed in his Holiness about as much as they disbelieved in him; that at that very time certain of their number, Maître Thomas de Courcelles, so great a doctor, Maître Jean Beaupère, the examiner, Maître Nicolas Loiseleur, who acted the part of Saint Catherine, were hastening to despatch her, in order that they might bestride their mules and amble away to Bâle, there in the Synagogue of Satan to hurl thunderbolts against the Holy Apostolic See, and diabolically to decree the subjection of the Pope to the Council, the confiscation of his annates, dearer to him than the apple of his eye, and finally his own deposition.[707] Now would have been the time for her to have cried, with the voice of a simple soul, to the priests so keen to avenge upon her the Church's honour: "I am more of a Catholic than you!" And the words in her mouth would have been even more appropriate than on the lips of the Limousin clerk of old. Yet we must not reproach these clerics for having been good Gallicans at Bâle, but rather for having been cruel and hypocritical at Rouen.

In her prison the Maid prophesied before her guard, John Grey. Informed of these prophecies, the judges wished to hear them from Jeanne's own mouth.

"Before seven years have passed," she said to them, "the English shall lose a greater wager than any they lost at Orléans. They shall lose everything in France. They shall suffer greater loss than ever they have suffered in France, and that shall come to pass because God shall vouchsafe unto the French great victory."

"How do you know this?"

"I know it by revelation made unto me and that this shall befall within seven years. And greatly should I sorrow were it further delayed. I know it by revelation as surely as I know that you are before my eyes at this moment."

"When shall this come to pass?"

"I know neither the day nor the hour."

"But the year?"

"That ye shall not know for the present. But I should wish it to be before Saint John's Day."

"Did you not say that it should come to pass before Saint Martin in the winter?"

"I said that before Saint Martin in the winter many things should befall and it might be that the English would be discomfited."

Whereupon the examiner asked Jeanne whether when Saint Michael came to her he was accompanied by Saint Gabriel.

Jeanne replied: "I do not remember."[708]

She did not remember whether, in the multitude of angels who visited her, was the Angel Gabriel who had saluted Our Lady and announced unto her the salvation of mankind. So many angels and archangels had she seen that this one had not particularly impressed her.

After an answer of such perfect simplicity how could these priests proceed to question her on her visions? Were they not sufficiently edified? But no! These innocent answers whetted the examiner's zeal. With intense ardour and copious amplification, passing from angels to saints, he multiplied petty and insidious questions. Did you see the hair on their heads? Had they rings in their ears? Was there anything between their crowns and their hair? Was their hair long and hanging? Had they arms? How did they speak? What kind of voices had they?[709]

This last question touched on an important theological point. Demons, whose voices are as rasping as a cart wheel or a winepress screw, cannot imitate the sweet tones of saints.[710]

Jeanne replied that the Voice was beautiful, sweet, and soft, and spoke in French.

Whereupon she was asked craftily wherefore Saint Margaret did not speak English.

She replied: "How should she speak English, since she is not on the side of the English?"[711]

Two hundred years before, a poet of Champagne had said that the French language, which Our Lord created beautiful and graceful, was the language of Paradise.

She was afterwards asked concerning her rings. This was a hard matter; in those days there were many magic rings or rings bearing amulets. They were fashioned by magicians under the influence of planets; and, by means of wonder-working herbs and stones, these rings had spells cast upon them and received miraculous virtues. Constellation rings worked miracles. Jeanne, alas! had possessed but two poor rings, one of brass, inscribed with the names Jésus and Marie, which she received from her father and mother, the other her brother had given her. The Bishop kept the latter; the other had been taken from her by the Burgundians.[712]

An attempt was made to incriminate her in a pact made with the Devil near the Fairy Tree. She was not to be caught thus, but retorted by prophesying her deliverance and the destruction of her enemies. "Those who wish to banish me from this world may very likely leave it before me.... I know that my King will win the realm of France."

She was asked what she had done with her mandrake. She said she had never had one.[713]

Then the examiner appeared to be seized with curiosity concerning Saint Michael. "Was he clothed?"

She replied: "Doubt ye that Messire lacks wherewithal to clothe himself?"

"Had he hair?"

"Wherefore should he have cut it off?"

"Did he hold scales?"

"I don't know."[714]

Their object was to ascertain whether she saw Saint Michael as he was represented in the churches, with scales for weighing souls.[715]

When she said that at the sight of the Archangel it seemed to her she was not in a state of mortal sin, the examiner fell to arguing on the subject of her conscience. She replied like a true Christian.[716] Then he returned to the miracle of the sign, which had not been referred to since the first sitting, to the mystery of Chinon, to that wondrous crown, which Jeanne, following Saint Catherine of Alexandria, believed she had received from the hand of an angel. But she had promised Saint Catherine and Saint Margaret to say nothing about it.

"When you showed the King the sign was there any one with him?"

"I think there was no other person, albeit there were many folk not far off."

"Did you see a crown on the King's head when you gave him this sign?"

"I cannot say without committing perjury."

"Had your King a crown at Reims?"

"My King, methinketh, took with pleasure the crown he found at Reims. But afterwards a very rich crown was brought him. He did not wait for it, because he wished to hurry on the ceremony according to the request of the inhabitants of Reims who desired to rid their town of the burden of men-at-arms. If he had waited he would have had a crown a thousand times more rich."

"Have you seen that richer crown?"

"I cannot tell you without committing perjury. If I have not seen it I have heard tell how rich and how magnificent it is."[717]

Jeanne suffered intensely from being deprived of the sacraments. One day when Messire Jean Massieu, performing the office of ecclesiastical usher, was taking her before her judges, she asked him whether there were not on the way some church or chapel in which was the body of Our Lord Jesus Christ.[718]

Messire Jean Massieu, dean of Rouen, was a cleric of manners dissolute; his inveterate lewdness had involved him in difficulties with the Chapter and with the Official.[719] He may have been neither as brave nor as frank as he wished to make out, but he was not hard or pitiless.

He told his prisoner that there was a chapel on the way. And he pointed out to her the chapel of the castle.

Then she besought him urgently to take her into the chapel in order that she might worship Messire and pray.

Readily did Messire Jean Massieu consent; and he permitted her to kneel before the sanctuary. Devoutly bending, Jeanne offered her prayer.

The Lord Bishop, being informed of this incident, was highly displeased. He instructed the Usher that in the future such devotions must not be tolerated.

And the Promoter, Maître Jean d'Estivet, on his part, addressed many a reprimand to Messire Jean Massieu.

"Rascal," he said, "what possesses thee to allow an excommunicated whore to approach a church without permission? If ever thou doest the like again I will imprison thee in that tower, where for a month thou wilt see neither sun nor moon."

Messire Jean Massieu heeded not this threat. And the Promoter, perceiving this, himself took up his post at the chapel door when Jeanne went that way. Thus he prevented the hapless damsel from engaging in her devotions.[720]

The sixth sitting was held in the same court as before, in the presence of forty-one assessors, of whom six or seven were new, and among them was Maître Guillaume Erart, doctor in theology.[721]

In the beginning, the examiner asked Jeanne whether she had seen Saint Michael and the saints, and whether she had seen anything but their faces. He insisted: "You must say what you know."

"Rather than say all that I know, I would have my head cut off."[722]

They puzzled her with questions touching the nature of angelic bodies. She was simple; with her own eyes she had seen Saint Michael; she said so and could not say otherwise.

The examiner, now as always, informed of the words she had let fall in prison, asked her whether she had heard her Voices.

"Yes, in good sooth. They told me that I should be delivered. But I know neither the day nor the hour. And they told me to have good courage, and to be of good cheer."[723]

Of all this the judges believed nothing, because demonologists teach that witches lose their power when an officer of Holy Church lays hands upon them.

The examiner recurred to her man's dress. Then he endeavoured to find out whether she had cast spells over the banners of her companions in arms.

He sought out by what secret power she led the soldiers.

This power she was willing to reveal: "I said to them: 'Go on boldly against the English;' and at the same time I went myself."[724]

In this examination, which was the most diffuse and the most captious of all, the following curious question was put to the accused: "When you were before Jargeau, what was it you were wearing behind your helmet? Was there not something round?"[725]

At the siege of Jargeau she had been struck on the head by a huge stone which had not hurt her; and this her own party deemed miraculous.[726] Did the judges of Rouen imagine that she wore a golden halo, like the saints, and that this halo had protected her?

Later she was examined on a more ordinary subject, concerning a picture in the house of her host at Orléans, representing three women: Justice, Peace, Union.

Jeanne knew nothing about it;[727] she was no connoisseur in tapestry and in paintings, like the Duke of Bar and the Duke of Orléans; neither were her judges, not on this occasion at any rate. And if they were concerned about a picture in the house of Maître Boucher, it was not so much on account of the painting as of the doctrine. These three women that the wealthy Maître Boucher kept in his house were doubtless nude. The painters of those days depicted on small panels allegories and bathing scenes, and they painted nude women. Full foreheads, round heads, golden hair, short figures of small build but with embonpoint, their nudity minutely represented and but thinly veiled; many such were produced in Flanders and in Italy. The illustrious masters, to whom those pictures appeared corrupt and indecent, doubtless wished to reproach Jeanne with having looked at them in the house of the treasurer of the Duke of Orléans. It is not difficult to divine what were the doctors' suspicions when they are found asking Jeanne whether Saint Michael wore clothes, in what manner she greeted her saints, and how she gave them her rings to touch.[728]

They also wanted to make her admit that she had caused herself to be honoured as a saint. She disconcerted them by the following reply: "The poor folk came to me readily, because I did them no hurt, but aided them to the best of my power."[729]

Then the examination ranged over many and various subjects: Friar Richard; the children Jeanne had held over the baptismal fonts; the good wives of the town of Reims who touched rings with her; the butterflies caught in a standard at Château Thierry.[730]

In this town, certain of the Maid's followers were said to have caught butterflies in her standard. Now doctors in theology knew for a certainty that necromancers sacrificed butterflies to the devil. A century before, at Pamiers, the tribunal of the Holy Inquisition had condemned the Carmelite Pierre Recordi, who was accused of having celebrated such a sacrifice. He had killed a butterfly and the devil had revealed his presence by a breath of wind.[731] Jeanne's judges may have wished to involve her in similar fashion, or their design may have been quite different. In war a butterfly in the cap was a sign either of unconditional surrender or of the possession of a safe conduct.[732] Were the judges accusing her or her followers of having feigned to surrender in order treacherously to attack the enemy? They were quite capable of making such a charge. However that may be, the examiner passed on to inquire concerning a lost glove found by Jeanne in the town of Reims.[733] It was important to know whether it had been discovered by magic art. Then the magistrate returned to several of the capital charges of the trial: communion received in man's dress; the hackney of the Bishop of Senlis, which Jeanne had taken, thus committing a kind of sacrilege; the discoloured child she had brought back to life at Lagny; Catherine de La Rochelle, who had recently borne witness against her before the Official at Paris; the siege of La Charité which she had been obliged to raise; the leap which she had made in her despair from the keep of Beaurevoir, and, finally, certain blasphemy she was falsely accused of having uttered at Soissons concerning Captain Bournel.[734]

Then the Lord Bishop declared the examination concluded. He added, however, that should it appear expedient to interrogate Jeanne more fully, certain doctors and masters would be appointed for that purpose.[735]

Accordingly, on Saturday, March the 10th, Maître Jean de la Fontaine, the Bishop's commissioner, went to the prison. He was accompanied by Nicolas Midi, Gérard Feuillet, Jean Fécard, and Jean Massieu.[736] The first point touched upon at this inquiry was the sortie from Compiègne. The priests took great pains to prove to Jeanne that her Voices must be bad or that she must have failed to understand them since her obedience to them had brought about her destruction. Jacques Gélu[737] and Jean Gerson had foreseen this dilemma and had met it in anticipation with elaborate theological arguments.[738] She was examined concerning the paintings on her standard, and she replied:

"Saint Catherine and Saint Margaret bade me take the standard and bear it boldly, and have painted upon it the King of Heaven. And this, much against my will, I told to my King. Touching its meaning I know nought else."[739]

They tried to make her out avaricious, proud, and ostentatious because she possessed a shield and arms, a stable, chargers, demi-chargers, and hackneys, and because she had money with which to pay her household, some ten to twelve thousand livres.[740] But the point on which they questioned her most closely was the sign which had already been twice discussed in the public examinations. On this subject the doctors displayed an insatiable curiosity. For the sign was the exact reverse of the coronation at Reims; it was an anointing, not with divine unction but with magic charm, the crowning of the King of France by a witch. Maître Jean de la Fontaine had this advantage over Jeanne, he knew what she was going to say and what she wished to conceal. "What is the sign that was given to your King?"

"It is beautiful and honourable and very credible; it is the best and the richest in the world...."

"Does it still last?"

"It is well to know that it lasts and will last for a thousand years. My sign is in the King's treasury."

"Is it of gold or silver, or of precious stones, or is it a crown?"

"Nothing more will I tell unto you and no man can devise anything so rich as is this sign. Nevertheless, the sign that you need is that God should deliver me out of your hands and no surer sign can he send you...."

"When the sign came to your King what reverence did you make to it?"

"I thanked Our Lord for having delivered me from the troubles caused me by the clerks of our party, who were arguing against me. And I knelt down several times. An angel from God and from none other gave the sign to my King. And many times did I give thanks to Our Lord. The clerks ceased to attack me when they had seen the said sign."[741]

"Did the churchmen of your party behold the sign?"

"When my King and such as were with him had seen the sign and also the angel who gave it, I asked my King whether he were pleased, and he replied that he was. Then I departed and went into a little chapel near by. I have since heard that after my departure more than three hundred persons saw the sign. For love of me and in order that I should be questioned no further, God was pleased to permit this sign to be seen by all those of my party who did see it."

"Did your King and you make any reverence to the angel when he brought the sign?"

"Yes, for my part, I did. I knelt and took off my hood."[742]

CHAPTER XII
THE TRIAL FOR LAPSE (CONTINUED)

N Monday, the 12th of March, Brother Jean Lemaistre received from Brother Jean Graverent, Inquisitor of France, an order to proceed against and to pronounce the final sentence on a certain woman, named Jeanne, commonly called the Maid.[743] On that same day, in the morning, Maître Jean de la Fontaine, in presence of the Bishop, for the second time examined Jeanne in her prison.[744]

He first returned to the sign. "Did not the angel who brought the sign speak?"

"Yes, he told my King that he must set me to work in order that the country might soon be relieved."

"Was the angel, who brought the sign, the angel who first appeared unto you or another?"

"It was always the same and never did he fail me."

"But inasmuch as you have been taken hath not the angel failed you with regard to the good things of this life?"

"Since it is Our Lord's good pleasure, I believe it was best for me to be taken."

"In the good things of grace hath not your angel failed you?"

"How can he have failed me when he comforteth me every day?"[745]

Maître Jean de la Fontaine then put her a subtle question and one as nearly approaching humour as was permissible in an ecclesiastical trial.

"Did Saint Denys ever appear to you?"[746]

Saint Denys, patron of the most Christian kings, Saint Denys, the war cry of France, had allowed the English to take his abbey, that rich church, to which queens came to receive their crowns, and wherein kings had their burying. He had turned English and Burgundian, and it was not likely he would come to hold converse with the Maid of the Armagnacs.

To the question: "Were you addressing God himself when you promised to remain a virgin?" she replied:

"It sufficed to give the promise to the messengers of God, to wit, Saint Catherine and Saint Margaret."[747]

They had sought to entrap her, for a vow must be made directly to God. However, it might be argued, that it is lawful to promise a good thing to an angel or to a man; and that this good thing, thus promised, may form the substance of a vow. One vows to God what one has promised to the saints. Pierre of Tarentaise (iv, dist: xxviii, a. 1) teaches that all vows should be made to God: either to himself directly or through the mediation of his saints.[748]

According to a statement made during the inquiry, Jeanne had given a promise of marriage to a young peasant. Now the examiner endeavoured to prove that she had been at liberty to break her vow of virginity made in an irregular form; but Jeanne maintained that she had not promised marriage, and she added:

"The first time I heard my Voices, I vowed to remain a virgin as long as it should please God."

But this time it was Saint Michael and not the saints who had appeared to her.[749] She herself found it difficult to unravel the tangled web of her dreams and her ecstasies. And from these vague visions of a child the doctors were laboriously essaying to elaborate a capital charge.

Then a very grave and serious question was asked her by the examiner: "Did you speak to your priest or to any other churchman of those visions which you say were vouchsafed to you?"

"No, I spoke of them only to Robert de Baudricourt and to my King."[750]

The vavasour of Champagne, a man of mature years and sound sense, when in the days of King John, he, like the Maid, had heard a Voice in the fields bidding him go to his King, went straightway and told his priest. The latter commanded him to fast for three days, to do penance, and then to return to the field where the Voice had spoken to him.

The vavasour obeyed. Again the Voice was heard repeating the command it had previously given. The peasant again told his priest, who said to him: "My brother, thou and I will abstain and fast for three days, and I will pray for thee to Our Lord Jesus Christ." This they did, and on the fourth day the good man returned to the field. After the Voice had spoken for the third time, the priest enjoined his parishioner to go forthwith and fulfil his mission, since such was the will of God.[751]

There is no doubt that, according to all appearances, this vavasour had acted with greater wisdom than La Romée's daughter. By concealing her visions from the priest the latter had slighted the authority of the Church Militant. Still there might be urged in her defence the words of the Apostle Paul, that where the spirit of God is there is liberty.[752] If ye be led of the Spirit ye are not under the law.[753] Was she a heretic or was she a saint? Therein lay the whole trial.

Then came this remarkable question: "Have you received letters from Saint Michael or from your Voices?"

She replied: "I have not permission to tell you; but in a week I will willingly say all I know."[754]

Such was her manner of speaking when there was something she wanted to conceal but not to deny. The question must have been embarrassing therefore. Moreover, these interrogatories were based on a good store of facts either true or false; and in the questions addressed to the Maid we may generally discern a certain anticipation of her replies. What were those letters from Saint Michael and her other saints, the existence of which she did not deny, but which were never produced by her judges? Did certain of her party send them in the hope that she would carry out their intentions, while under the impression that she was obeying divine commands?

Without insisting further for the present, the examiner passed on to another grievance:

"Have not your Voices called you daughter of God, daughter of the Church, great-hearted damsel?"

"Before the siege of Orléans and since, every day when they speak to me, many times have they called me *Jeanne the Maid, daughter of God*."[755]

The examination was suspended and resumed in the afternoon.

Maître Jean de la Fontaine questioned Jeanne concerning a dream of her father, of which the judges had been informed in the preliminary inquiry.[756]

Sad it is to reflect that when Jeanne was accused of the sin of having broken God's commandment, "Thou shalt honour thy father and thy mother," neither her mother nor any of her kin asked to be heard as witnesses. And yet there were churchmen in her family;[757] but a trial on a question of faith struck terror into all hearts.

Again her man's dress was reverted to, and not for the last time.[758] We marvel at the profound meditations into which the Maid's doublet and hose plunged these clerics. They contemplated them with gloomy terror and in the light of the precepts of Deuteronomy.

Thereafter they questioned her touching the Duke of Orléans. Their object was to show from her own replies that her Voices had deceived her when they promised the prisoner's deliverance. Here they easily succeeded. Then she pleaded that she had not had sufficient time.

"Had I continued for three years without let or hindrance I should have delivered him."

In her revelations there had been mentioned a term shorter than three years and longer than one.[759]

Questioned again touching the sign vouchsafed to her King, she replied that she would take counsel with Saint Catherine.

On the morrow, Tuesday, the 13th of March, the Bishop and the Vice-Inquisitor went to her prison. For the first time the Vice-Inquisitor opened his mouth:[760] "Have you promised and sworn to Saint Catherine that you will not tell this sign?"

He spoke of the sign given to the King. Jeanne replied:

"I have sworn and I have promised that I will not myself reveal this sign, because I was too urgently pressed to tell it. I vow that never again will I speak of it to living man."[761]

Then she continued forthwith: "The sign was that the Angel assured my King, when bringing him the crown, that he should have the whole realm of France, with God's help and my labours, and that he should set me to work. That is to say, he should grant me men-at-arms. Otherwise he would not be so soon crowned and anointed."

"In what manner did the Angel bring the crown? Did he place it on your King's head?"

"It was given to an archbishop, to the Archbishop of Reims, meseemeth in the King's presence. The said Archbishop received it and gave it to the King; and I myself was present; and it is put in the King's treasury."

"To what place was the crown brought?"

"To the King's chamber in the castle of Chinon."

"On what day and at what hour?"

"The day I know not, the hour was full day. No further recollection have I of the hour or of the month. But meeemeth it was the month of April or March; it will be two years this month or next April. It was after Easter."[762]

"On the first day that you saw the sign did your King see it?"

"Yes. He had it the same day."

"Of what was the crown made?"

"It is well to know that it was of fine gold, and so rich that I cannot count its riches; and the crown meant that he would hold the realm of France."

"Were there jewels in it?"

"I have told you that I do not know."

"Did you touch it or kiss it?"

"No."

"Did the Angel who bore it come from above, or did he come from the earth?"

"He came from above. I understand that he came by Our Lord's command, and he came in by the door of the chamber."

"Did the Angel come along the ground, walking from the door of the room?"

"When he was come before the King he did him reverence, bowing low before him and uttering the words concerning the sign which I have already repeated; and thereupon the Angel recalled to the King's mind the great patience he had had in the midst of the long tribulation that had befallen him; and as he came towards the King the Angel walked and touched the ground."

"How far was it from the door to the King?"

"Methinketh it was a full lance's length;[763] and as he had come so he returned. When the Angel came, I accompanied him and went with him up the steps into the King's chamber; and the Angel went in first. And I said to the King: 'Sire, behold your sign; take it.'"[764]

In a spiritual sense we may say that this fable is true. This crown, which "flowers sweetly and will flower sweetly if it be well guarded,"[765] is the crown of victory. When the Maid beholds the Angel who brought it, it is her own image that appears before her. Had not a theologian of her own party said that she might be called an angel? Not that she had the nature of an angel, but she did the work of one.[766]

She began to describe the angels who had come with her to the King:

"So far as I saw, certain among them were very like, the others different. Some had wings. Some wore crowns, others did not. And they were with Saint Catherine and Saint Margaret, and they accompanied the Angel of whom I have spoken and the other angels also into the chamber of the King."[767]

And thus for a long time, as she was pressed by her interrogator, she continued to tell these marvellous stories one after another.

When she was asked for the second time whether the Angel had written her letters, she denied it.[768] But now it was the Angel who bore the crown and not Saint Michael who was in question. And despite her having said they were one and the same, she may have distinguished between them. Therefore we shall never know whether she did receive letters from Saint Michael the Archangel, or from Saint Catherine and from Saint Margaret.

Thereafter the examiner inquired touching a cup lost at Reims and found by Jeanne as well as the gloves.[769] Saints sometimes condescended to find things that had been lost, as is proved by the example of Saint Antony of Padua. It was always with the help of God. Necromancers imitated their powers by invoking the aid of demons and by profaning sacred things.

She was also questioned concerning the priest who had a concubine. Here again she was reproached with being possessed of a magic gift of clairvoyance. It was by magic she had known that this priest had a concubine. Many other such things were reported of her. For example, it was said that at the sight of a certain loose woman she knew that this woman had killed her child.[770]

Then recurred the same old questions: "When you went to the attack on Paris did you receive a revelation from your Voices? Was it revealed to you that you should go against La Charité? Was it a revelation that caused you to go to Pont-l'Evêque?"

She denied that she had then received any revelation from her Voices.

The last question was: "Did you not say before Paris, 'Surrender the town in the name of Jesus'?"

She answered that she had not spoken those words, but had said, "Surrender the town to the King of France."[771]

The Parisians who were engaged in repelling the attack had heard her saying, "Surrender to us speedily in the name of Jesus." These words are consistent with all we know of Jeanne in the early years of her career. She believed it to be the will of Messire that the towns of the realm should surrender to her, whom he had sent to reconquer them. We have noticed already that at the time of her trial Jeanne had completely lost touch with her early illuminations and that she spoke in quite another language.

On the morrow, Wednesday, the 14th of March, there were two more examinations in the prison. The morning interrogatory turned on the leap from Beaurevoir. She confessed to having leapt without permission from her Voices, preferring to die rather than to fall into the hands of the English.[772]

She was accused of blasphemy against God; but that was false.[773]

The Bishop intervened: "You have said that we, the Lord Bishop, run great danger by bringing you to trial. Of what danger were you speaking? In what peril do we stand, we, your judges, and others?"

"I said to my Lord of Beauvais: 'You declare that you are my judge, I know not if you be. But take heed that ye judge not wrongly, for thus would ye run great danger; and I warn you, so that if Our Lord chastise you for it, I have done my duty by warning you.'"

"What is this peril or this danger?"

"Saint Catherine has told me that I shall have succour. I know not whether it will be my deliverance from prison, or whether, during the trial, some tumult shall arise whereby I shall be delivered. I think it will be either one or the other. My Voices most often tell me I shall be delivered by a great victory. And afterwards they say to me: 'Be thou resigned, grieve not at thy martyrdom; thou shalt come in the end to the kingdom of Paradise.' This do my Voices say unto me simply and absolutely. I mean to say without fail. And I call my martyrdom the trouble and anguish I suffer in prison. I know not whether still greater sufferings are before me, but I wait on the Lord."[774]

It would seem that thus her Voices promised the Maid at once a spiritual and a material deliverance, but the two could hardly occur together. This reply, expressive alike of fear and of illusion, was one to call forth pity from the hardest; and yet her judges regarded it merely as a means whereby they might entrap her. Feigning to understand that from her revelations she derived a heretical confidence in her eternal salvation, the examiner put to her an old question in a new form. She had already given it a saintly answer. He inquired whether her Voices had told her that she would finally come to the kingdom of Paradise if she continued in the assurance that she would be saved and not condemned in Hell. To this she replied with that perfect faith with which her Voices inspired her: "I believe what my Voices have told me touching my salvation as strongly as if I were already in Paradise."

Such a reply was heretical. The examiner, albeit he was not accustomed to discuss the Maid's replies, could not forbear remarking that this one was of great importance.[775]

Accordingly in the afternoon of that same day, she was shown a consequence of her error; to wit, that if she received from her Voices the assurance of eternal salvation she needed not to confess.[776]

On this occasion Jeanne was questioned touching the affair of Franquet d'Arras. The Bailie of Senlis had done wrong in asking the Maid for her prisoner,[777] the Lord Franquet,[778] in order to put him to death, and Jeanne's judges now incriminated her.

The examiner pointed out the mortal sins with which the accused might be charged: first, having attacked Paris on a feast-day; second, having stolen the hackney of the Lord Bishop of Senlis; third, having leapt from Beaurevoir; fourth, having worn man's dress; fifth, having consented to the death of a prisoner of war. Touching all these matters, Jeanne did not believe that she had committed mortal sin; but with regard to the leap from Beaurevoir she acknowledged that she was wrong, and that she had asked God to forgive her.[779]

It was sufficiently established that the accused had fallen into religious error. The tribunal of the Inquisition, out of its abounding mercy, desired the salvation of the sinner. Wherefore on the morning of the very next day, Thursday, the 15th of March, my Lord of

Beauvais exhorted Jeanne to submit to the Church, and essayed to make her understand that she ought to obey the Church Militant, for the Church Militant was one thing and the Church Triumphant another. Jeanne listened to him dubiously.[780] On that day she was again questioned touching her flight from the château of Beaulieu and her intention to leave the tower without the permission of my Lord of Beauvais. As to the latter she was firmly resolute.

"Were I to see the door open, I would go, and it would be with the permission of Our Lord. I firmly believe that if I were to see the door open and if my guards and the other English were beyond power of resistance, I should regard it as my permission and as succour sent unto me by Our Lord. But without permission I would not go, save that I might essay to go, in order to know whether it were Our Lord's will. The proverb says: 'Help thyself and God will help thee.'[781] This I say so that, if I were to go, it should not be said I went without permission."[782]

Then they reverted to the question of her wearing man's dress.

"Which would you prefer, to wear a woman's dress and hear mass, or to continue in man's dress and not to hear mass?"

"Promise me that I shall hear mass if I am in woman's dress, and then I will answer you."

"I promise you that you shall hear mass when you are in woman's dress."

"And what do you say if I have promised and sworn to our King not to put off these clothes? Nevertheless, I say unto you: 'Have me a robe made, long enough to touch the ground, but without a train. I will go to mass in it; then, when I come back, I will return to my present clothes.'"

"You must wear woman's dress altogether and without conditions."

"Send me a dress like that worn by your burgess's daughters, to wit, a long *houppelande*; and I will take it and even a woman's hood to go and hear mass. But with all my heart I entreat you to leave me these clothes I am now wearing, and let me hear mass without changing anything."[783]

Her aversion to putting off man's dress is not to be explained solely by the fact that this dress preserved her best against the violence of the men-at-arms; it is possible that no such objection existed. She was averse to wearing woman's dress because she had not received permission from her Voices; and we may easily divine why not. Was she not a chieftain of war? How humiliating for such an one to wear petticoats like a townsman's wife! And above all things just now, when at any moment the French might come and deliver her by some great feat of arms. Ought they not to find their Maid in man's attire, ready to put on her armour and fight with them?

Thereafter the examiner asked her whether she would submit to the Church, whether she made a reverence to her Voices, whether she believed the saints, whether she offered them lighted candles, whether she obeyed them, whether in war she had ever done anything without their permission or contrary to their command.[784]

Then they came to the question which they held to be the most difficult of all:

"If the devil were to take upon himself the form of an angel, how would you know whether he were a good angel or a bad?"

She replied with a simplicity which appeared presumptuous: "I should easily discern whether it were Saint Michael or an imitation of him."[785]

Two days later, on Saturday, the 17th of March, Jeanne was examined in her prison both morning and evening.[786]

Hitherto she had been very loath to describe the countenance and the dress of the angel and the saints who had visited her in the village. Maître Jean de la Fontaine endeavoured to obtain some light on this subject.

"In what form and semblance did Saint Michael come to you? Was he tall and how was he clothed?"

"He came in the form of a true *prud'homme*."[787]

Jeanne was not one to believe she saw the Archangel in a long doctor's robe or wearing a cope of gold. Moreover it was not thus that he figured in the churches. There he was represented in painting and in sculpture, clothed in glittering armour, with a golden crown on his helmet.[788] In such guise did he appear to her "in the form of a right true *prud'homme*," to take a word from the *Chanson de Roland*, where a great sword thrust is called the thrust of a *prud'homme*. He came to her in the garb of a great knight, like Arthur and Charlemagne, wearing full armour.

Once again the examiner put to Jeanne that question on which her life or death depended:

"Will you submit all your deeds and sayings, good or bad, to the judgment of our mother, Holy Church?"

"As for the Church, I love her and would maintain her with all my power, for religion's sake," the Maid replied; "and I am not one to be kept from church and from hearing mass. But as for the good works which I have wrought, and touching my coming, for them I must give an account to the King of Heaven, who has sent me to Charles, son of Charles, King of France. And you will see that the French will shortly accomplish a great work, to which God will appoint them, in which they will shake nearly all France. I say it in order that when it shall come to pass, it may be remembered that I have said it."[789]

But she was unable to name the time when this great work should be accomplished; and Maître Jean de la Fontaine returned to the point on which Jeanne's fate depended.

"Will you submit to the judgment of the Church?"

"I appeal to Our Lord, who hath sent me, to Our Lady and to all the blessed saints in Paradise. To my mind Our Lord and his Church are one, and no distinction should be made. Wherefore do you essay to make out that they are not one?"

In justice to Maître Jean de la Fontaine we are bound to admit the lucidity of his reply. "There is the Church Triumphant, in which are God, his saints, the angels and the souls that are saved," he said. "There is also the Church Militant, which is our Holy Father, the Pope, the Vicar of God on earth; the cardinals, the prelates of the Church and the clergy, with all good Christians and Catholics; and this Church in its assembly cannot err, for it is moved by the Holy Ghost. Will you appeal to the Church Militant?"

"I am come to the King of France from God, from the Virgin Mary and all the blessed saints in Paradise and from the Church Victorious above and by their command. To this Church I submit all the good deeds I have done and shall do. As to replying whether I will submit to the Church Militant, for the present, I will make no further answer."[790]

Again she was offered a woman's dress in which to hear mass; she refused it.

"As for a woman's dress, I will not take it yet, not until it be Our Lord's will. And if it should come to pass that I be taken to judgment and there divested of my clothes, I beg my lords of the Church the favour of a woman's smock and covering for my head. I would rather die than deny what Our Lord hath caused me to do. I believe firmly that Our Lord will not let it come to pass that I should be cast so low, and that soon I shall have help from God, and that by a miracle."

Thereafter the following questions were put to her: "Do you not believe to-day that fairies are evil spirits?"

"I do not know."

"Do you know whether Saint Catherine and Saint Margaret hate the English?"

"They love what Our Lord loves and hate what God hates."

"Does God hate the English?"

"Touching the love or hatred of God for the English and what he will do for their souls I know nothing. But I do know that they will all be driven out of France, save those who die there, and that God will send victory to the French and defeat to the English."

"Was God on the side of the English when they prospered in France?"

"I know not whether God hated the French. But I believe that he permitted them to be beaten for their sins, if they were in sin."[791]

Jeanne was asked certain questions touching the banner on which she had caused angels to be painted.

She replied that she had had angels painted as she had seen them represented in churches.[792]

At this point the examination was adjourned. The last interrogation in the prison[793] took place after dinner. She had now endured fifteen in twenty-five days, but her courage never flagged. This last time the subjects were more than usually diverse and confused. First, the examiner essayed to discover by what charms and evil practices good fortune and victory had attended the standard painted with angelic figures. Then he wanted to know wherefore the clerks put on Jeanne's letters the sacred names of Jésus and Marie.[794]

Then came the following subtle question: "Do you believe that if you were married your Voices would come to you?"

It was well known that she dearly cherished her virginity. Certain of her words might be interpreted to mean that she considered this virginity to be the cause of her good fortune; wherefore her examiners were curious to know whether if she were adroitly approached she might not be brought to cast scorn on the married state and to condemn intercourse between husbands and wives. Such a condemnation would have been a grievous error, savouring of the heresy of the Cathari.[795]

She replied: "I know not and I appeal to Our Lord."[796] Then there followed another question much more dangerous for one who like Jeanne loved her King with all her heart.

"Do you think and firmly believe that your King did right to kill or cause to be killed my Lord of Burgundy?"

"It was sore pity for the realm of France."[797]

Then did the examiner put to her this grave question: "Do you hold yourself bound to answer the whole truth to the Pope, God's Vicar, on all that may be asked you touching religion and your conscience?"

"I demand to be taken before him. Then will I make unto him such answer as behoveth."[798]

These words involved an appeal to the Pope, and such an appeal was lawful. "In doubtful matters touching on religion," said St. Thomas, "there ought always to be an appeal to the Pope or to the General Council." If Jeanne's appeal were not in regular judicial form, it was not her fault. She was ignorant of legal matters and neither guide nor counsel had been granted to her. To the best of her knowledge, and according to wont and justice, she appealed to the common father of the faithful.

The doctors and masters were silent. And thus was closed against the accused the one way of deliverance remaining to her. She was now hopelessly lost. It is not surprising that Jeanne's judges, who were partisans of England, ignored her right of appeal; but it is surprising that the doctors and masters of the French party, the clerks of the provinces loyal to King Charles, did not all and with one voice sign an appeal and demand that the Maid, who had been judged worthy by her examiners at Poitiers, should be taken before the Pope and the Council.

Instead of replying to Jeanne's request, the examiners inquired further concerning those much discussed magic rings and apparitions of demons.[799]

"Did you ever kiss and embrace the Saints, Catherine and Margaret?"

"I embraced them both."

"Were they of a sweet savour?"

"It is well to know. Yea, their savour was sweet."

"When embracing them did you feel heat or anything else?"

"I could not have embraced them without feeling and touching them."

"What part did you kiss, face or feet?"

"It is more fitting to kiss their feet than their faces."

"Did you not give them chaplets of flowers?"

"I have often done them honour by crowning with flowers their images in churches. But to those who appeared to me never have I given flowers as far as I can remember."

"Know you aught of those who consort with fairies?"

"I have never done so nor have I known anything about them. Yet I have heard of them and that they were seen on Thursdays; but I do not believe it, and to me it seems sorcery."[800]

Then came a question touching her standard, deemed enchanted by her judges. It elicited one of those epigrammatic replies she loved.

"Wherefore was your standard rather than those of the other captains carried into the church of Reims?"

"It had been in the contest, wherefore should it not share the prize?"[801]

Now that the inquiries and examinations were concluded, it was announced that the preliminary trial was at an end. The so-called trial in ordinary opened on the Tuesday after Palm Sunday, the 27th of March, in a room near the great hall of the castle.[802]

Before ordering the deed of accusation to be read, my Lord of Beauvais offered Jeanne the aid of an advocate.[803] If this offer had been postponed till then, it was doubtless because in his opinion Jeanne had not previously needed such aid. It is well known that a heretic's advocate, if he would himself escape falling into heresy, must strictly limit his methods of defence. During the preliminary inquiry he must confine himself to discovering the names of the witnesses for the prosecution and to making them known to the accused. If the heretic pleaded guilty then it was useless to grant him an advocate.[804] Now my Lord maintained that the accusation was founded not on the evidence of witnesses but on the avowals of the accused. And this was doubtless his reason for not offering Jeanne an advocate before the opening of the trial in ordinary, which bore upon matters of doctrine.

The Lord Bishop thus addressed the Maid: "Jeanne," said he, "all persons here present are churchmen of consummate knowledge, whose will and intention it is to proceed against you in all piety and kindness, seeking neither vengeance nor corporal chastisement, but your instruction and your return into the way of truth and salvation. As you are neither learned nor sufficiently instructed in letters or in the difficult matters which are to be discussed, to take counsel of yourself, touching what you should do or reply, we offer you to choose as your advocate one or more of those present, as you will. If you will not choose, then one shall be appointed for you by us, in order that he may advise you touching what you may do or say...."[805]

Considering what the method of procedure was, this was a gracious offer. And even though my Lord of Beauvais obliged the accused to choose from among the counsellors and assessors, whom he had himself summoned to the trial, he did more than he was bound to do. The choice of a counsel did not belong to the accused; it belonged to the judge, whose duty it was to appoint an honest, upright person. Moreover, it was permissible for an ecclesiastical judge to refuse to the end to grant the accused any counsel whatsoever. Nicolas Eymeric, in his *Directorium*, decides that the Bishop and the Inquisitor, acting conjointly, may constitute authority sufficient for the interpretation of the law and may proceed informally, *de plano*, dispensing with the ceremony of appointing counsel and all the paraphernalia of a trial.[806]

We may notice that my Lord of Beauvais offered the accused an advocate on the ground of her ignorance of things divine and human, but without taking her youthfulness into account. In other courts of law proceedings against a minor – that is, a person under twenty-five – who was not assisted by an advocate, were legally void.[807] If this rule had been binding in Inquisitorial procedure the Bishop, by his offer of legal aid, would have avoided any breach of this rule; and as the choice of an advocate lay with him, he might well have done so without running any risk. "Our justice is not like theirs," Bernard Gui rightly said, when he was comparing inquisitorial procedure with that of the other ecclesiastical courts which conformed to the Roman law.

Jeanne did not accept the judge's offer: "First," she said, "touching what you admonish me for my good and in matters of religion, I thank you and the company here assembled. As for the advocate you offer me, I also thank you, but it is not my intent to depart from the counsel of Our Lord. As for the oath you wish me to take, I am ready to swear to speak the truth in all that concerns your suit."[808]

Thereupon Maître Thomas de Courcelles began to read in French the indictment which the Promoter had drawn up in seventy articles.[809] This text set forth in order the deeds with which Jeanne had already been reproached and which were groundlessly held to have been confessed by her and duly proved. There were no less than seventy distinct charges of horrible crimes committed against religion and Holy Mother Church. Questioned on each article, Jeanne with heroic candour repeated her previous replies. The tedious reading of this long accusation was continued and completed on the 28th of March, the Wednesday after Palm Sunday.[810] As was her wont, she asked for delay in order to reply on certain points. On Easter Eve, the 31st of March, the time granted having expired, my Lord of Beauvais went to the prison, and, in the presence of the doctors and masters of the University, demanded the promised replies. They nearly all touched on the one accusation which included all the rest, the heresy in which all heresies were comprehended, – the refusal to obey the Church Militant. Jeanne finally declared her resolve to appeal to Our Lord rather than to any man; this was to set at naught the authority of the Pope and the Council.[811]

The doctors and masters of the University of Paris advised that an epitome should be made of the Promoter's voluminous indictment, its chief points selected, and the seventy charges considerably reduced.[812] Maître Nicolas Midi, doctor in theology, performed this task and submitted it when done to the judges and assessors.[813] One of them proposed emendations. Brother Jacques of Touraine, a friar of the Franciscan order, who was charged to draw up the document in its final stage, admitted most of the corrections requested.[814] In this wise the incriminating propositions,[815] which the judges claimed, but claimed falsely, to have derived from the replies of the accused, were resolved into twelve articles.[816]

These twelve articles were not communicated to Jeanne. On Thursday, the 12th of April, twenty-one masters and doctors met in the chapel of the Bishop's Palace, and, after having examined the articles, engaged in a conference, the result of which was unfavourable to the accused.[817]

According to them, the apparitions and revelations of which she boasted came not from God. They were human inventions, or the work of an evil spirit. She had not received signs sufficient to warrant her believing in them. In the case of this woman these doctors and masters discovered lies; a lack of verisimilitude; faith lightly given; superstitious divinings; deeds scandalous and irreligious; sayings rash, presumptuous, full of boasting; blasphemies against God and his saints. They found her to have lacked piety in her behaviour towards father and mother; to have come short in love towards her neighbour; to have been addicted to idolatry, or at any rate to the invention of lying tales and to schismatic conversation destructive of the unity, the authority and the power of the Church; and, finally, to have been skilled in the black art and to have strongly inclined to heresy.[818]

Had she not been sustained and comforted by her heavenly Voices, the Voices of her own heart, Jeanne would never have endured to the end of this terrible trial. Not only was she being tortured at once by the princes of the Church and the rascals of the army, but her sufferings of body and mind were such as could never have been borne by any ordinary human being. Yet she suffered them without her constancy, her faith, her divine hope, one might almost say her cheerfulness, ever being diminished. Finally she gave way; her physical strength, but not her courage, was exhausted; she fell a victim to an illness which was expected to be fatal. She seemed near her end, or rather, alas! near her release.[819]

On Wednesday, the 18th of April, my Lord of Beauvais and the Vice-Inquisitor of the Faith went to her with divers doctors and masters to exhort her in all charity; she was still very seriously sick.[820] My Lord of Beauvais represented to her that when on certain difficult matters she had been examined before persons of great wisdom, many things she had said had been noted as contrary to religion. Wherefore, considering that she was but an unlettered woman, he offered to provide her with men learned and upright who would instruct her. He requested the doctors present to give her salutary counsel, and he invited her herself, if any other such persons were known to her, to indicate them, promising to summon them without fail.

"The Church," he added, "never closes her heart against those who will return to her."

Jeanne answered that she thanked him for what he had said for her salvation, and she added: "Meseemeth, that seeing the sickness in which I lie, I am in great danger of death. If it be thus, then may God do with me according to his good pleasure. I demand that ye permit me to confess, that ye also give me the body of my Saviour and bury me in holy ground."

My Lord of Beauvais represented to her that if she would receive the sacraments she must submit to the Church.

"If my body die in prison," she replied, "I depend on you to have it put in holy ground; if you do not, then I appeal to Our Lord."[821]

Then she vehemently maintained the truth of the revelations she had received from God, Saint Michael, Saint Catherine, and Saint Margaret.

And when she was asked yet again whether she would submit herself and her acts to Holy Mother Church, she replied: "Whatever happens to me, I will never do or say aught save what I have already said at the trial."[822]

The doctors and masters one after the other exhorted her to submit to Holy Mother Church. They quoted numerous passages from Holy Writ. They promised her the body of Our Lord if she would obey; but she remained resolute.

"Touching this submission," she said, "I will reply naught save what I have said already. I love God, I serve him, I am a good Christian, and I wish with all my power to aid and support Holy Church."[823]

In times of great need recourse was had to processions. "Do you not wish," she was asked, "that a fine and famous procession be ordained to restore you to a good estate if you be not therein?"

She replied, "I desire the Church and all Catholics to pray for me."[824]

Among the doctors consulted there were many who recommended that she should be again instructed and charitably admonished. On Wednesday, the 2nd of May, sixty-three reverend doctors and masters met in the Robing Room of the castle.[825] She was brought in, and Maître Jean de Castillon, doctor in theology, Archdeacon of Évreux,[826] read a document in French, in which the deeds and sayings with which Jeanne was reproached were summed up in six articles. Then many doctors and masters addressed to her in turn admonitions and charitable counsels. They exhorted her to submit to the Church Militant Universal, to the Holy Father the Pope and to the General

Council. They warned her that if the Church abandoned her, her soul would stand in great peril of the penalty of eternal fire, whilst her body might be burned in an earthly fire, and that by the sentence of other judges.

Jeanne replied as before.[827] On the morrow, Thursday, the 3rd of May, the day of the Invention of the Holy Cross, the Archangel Gabriel appeared to her. She was not sure whether she had seen him before. But this time she had no doubt. Her Voices told her that it was he, and she was greatly comforted.

That same day she asked her Voices whether she should submit to the Church and obey the exhortation of the clerics.

Her Voices replied: "If thou desirest help from Our Lord, then submit to him all thy doings."

Jeanne wanted to know from her Voices whether she would be burned.

Her Voices told her to wait upon the Lord and he would help her.[828] This mystic aid strengthened Jeanne's heart.

Among heretics and those possessed, such obstinacy as hers was not unparalleled. Ecclesiastical judges were well acquainted with the stiff-neckedness of women who had been deceived by the Devil. In order to force them to tell the truth, when admonitions and exhortations failed, recourse was had to torture. And even such a measure did not always succeed. Many of these wicked females (*mulierculæ*) endured the cruellest suffering with a constancy passing the ordinary strength of human nature. The doctors would not believe such constancy to be natural; they attributed it to the machinations of the Evil One. The devil was capable of protecting his servants even when they had fallen into the hands of judges of the Church; he granted them strength to bear the torture in silence. This strength was called the gift of taciturnity.[829]

On Wednesday, the 9th of May, Jeanne was taken to the great tower of the castle, into the torture-chamber. There my Lord of Beauvais, in the presence of the Vice Inquisitor and nine doctors and masters, read her the articles, to which she had hitherto refused to reply; and he threatened her that if she did not confess the whole truth she would be put to the torture.[830]

The instruments were prepared; the two executioners, Mauger Leparmentier, a married clerk, and his companion, were in readiness close by her, awaiting the Bishop's orders.

Six days before Jeanne had received great comfort from her Voices. Now she replied resolutely: "Verily, if you were to tear my limbs asunder and drive my soul out of my body, naught else would I tell you, and if I did say anything unto you, I would always maintain afterwards that you had dragged it from me by force."[831]

My Lord of Beauvais decided to defer the torture, fearing that it would do no good to so hardened a subject.[832] On the following Saturday, he deliberated in his house, with the Vice-Inquisitor and thirteen doctors and masters; opinion was divided. Maître Raoul Roussel advised that Jeanne should not be tortured lest ground for complaint should be given against a trial so carefully conducted. It would seem that he anticipated the Devil's granting Jeanne the gift of taciturnity, whereby in diabolical silence she would be able to brave the tortures of the Holy Inquisition. On the other hand Maître Aubert Morel, licentiate in canon law, counsellor to the Official of Rouen, Canon of the Cathedral, and Maître Thomas de Courcelles, deemed it expedient to apply torture. Maître Nicolas Loiseleur, master of arts, Canon of Rouen, whose share in the proceedings had been to act Saint Catherine and the Lorraine shoemaker, had no very decided opinion on the subject, still it seemed to him by no means unprofitable that Jeanne for her soul's welfare should be tortured. The majority of doctors and masters agreed that for the present there was no need to subject her to this trial. Some gave no reasons, others alleged that it behoved them yet once again to warn her charitably. Maître Guillaume Erard, doctor in theology, held that sufficient material for the pronouncing of a sentence existed already.[833] Thus among those, who spared Jeanne the torture, were to be found the least merciful; for the spirit of ecclesiastical tribunals was such that to refuse to torture an accused was in certain cases to refuse him mercy.

To the trial of Marguerite la Porète, the judges summoned no experts.[834] Touching the charges held as proven, they submitted a written report to the University of Paris. The University gave its opinion on everything but the truth of the charges. This reservation was merely formal, and the decision of the University had the force of a sentence. In Jeanne's trial this precedent was cited. On the 21st of April, Maître Jean Beaupère, Maître Jacques de Touraine and Maître

Nicolas Midi left Rouen, and, at the risk of being attacked on the road by men-at-arms, journeyed to Paris in order to present the twelve articles to their colleagues of the University.

On the 28th of April, the University, meeting in its general assembly at Saint-Bernard, charged the Holy Faculty of Theology and the Venerable Faculty of Decrees with the examination of the twelve articles.[835]

On the 14th of May, the deliberations of the two Faculties were submitted to all the Faculties in solemn assembly, who ratified them and made them their own. The University then sent them to King Henry, beseeching his Royal Majesty to execute justice promptly, in order that the people, so greatly scandalised by this woman, be brought back to good doctrine and holy faith.[836] It is worthy of notice that in a trial, in which the Pope, represented by the Vice-Inquisitor, was one judge, and the King, represented by the Bishop, another, the Eldest Daughter of Kings[837] should have communicated directly with the King of France, the guardian of her privileges.

According to the Sacred Faculty of Theology, Jeanne's apparitions were fictitious, lying, deceptive, inspired by devils. The sign given to the King was a presumptuous and pernicious lie, derogatory to the dignity of angels. Jeanne's belief in the visitations of Saint Michael, Saint Catherine and Saint Margaret was an error rash and injurious because Jeanne placed it on the same plane as the truths of religion. Jeanne's predictions were but superstitions, idle divinations and vain boasting. Her statement that she wore man's dress by the command of God was blasphemy, a violation of divine law and ecclesiastical sanction, a contemning of the sacraments and tainted with idolatry. In the letters she had dictated, Jeanne appeared treacherous, perfidious, cruel, sanguinary, seditious, blasphemous and in favour of tyranny. In setting out for France she had broken the commandment to honour father and mother, she had given an occasion for scandal, she had committed blasphemy and had fallen from the faith. In the leap from Beaurevoir, she had displayed a pusillanimity bordering on despair and homicide; and, moreover, it had caused her to utter rash statements touching the remission of her sin and erroneous pronouncements concerning free will. By proclaiming her confidence in her salvation, she uttered presumptuous and pernicious lies; by saying that Saint Catherine and Saint Margaret did not speak English, she blasphemed these saints and violated the precept: "Thou shalt love thy neighbour."

The honours she rendered these saints were nought but idolatry and the worship of devils. Her refusal to submit her doings to the Church tended to schism, to the denial of the unity and authority of the Church and to apostasy.[838]

The doctors of the Faculty of Theology were very learned. They knew who the three evil spirits were whom Jeanne in her delusion took for Saint Michael, Saint Catherine, and Saint Margaret. They were Belial, Satan, and Behemoth. Belial, worshipped by the people of Sidon, was sometimes represented as an angel of great beauty; he is the demon of disobedience. Satan is the Lord of Hell; and Behemoth is a dull, heavy creature, who feeds on hay like an ox.[839]

The venerable Faculty of Decrees decided that this schismatic, this erring woman, this apostate, this liar, this soothsayer, be charitably exhorted and duly warned by competent judges, and that if notwithstanding she persisted in refusing to abjure her error, she must be given up to the secular arm to receive due chastisement.[840] Such were the deliberations and decisions which the Venerable University of Paris submitted to the examination and to the verdict of the Holy Apostolic See and of the sacrosanct General Council.

Meanwhile, where were the clerks of France? Had they nothing to say in this matter? Had they no decision to submit to the Pope and to the Council? Why did they not urge their opinions in opposition to those of the Faculties of Paris? Why did they keep silence? Jeanne demanded the record of the Poitiers trial. Wherefore did those Poitiers doctors, who had recommended the King to employ the Maid lest, by rejecting her, he should refuse the gift of the Holy Spirit, fail to send the record to Rouen?[841] Before the Maid espoused their waning cause, these Poitiers doctors, these magistrates, these University professors banished from Paris, advocates and counsellors of an exiled Parlement, had not a robe to their backs nor shoes for their children. Now, thanks to the Maid, they were every day regaining new hope and vigour. And yet they left her, who had so nobly served their King, to be treated as a heretic and a reprobate. Where were Brother Pasquerel, Friar Richard, and all those churchmen who but lately surrounded her in France and who looked to go with her to the Crusade against the Bohemians and the Turks? Why did they not demand a safe-conduct and come and give evidence at the trial? Or at least why did they not send their evidence? Why did not the Archbishop of Embrun, who but recently gave such noble counsels to the King, send some written statement in favour of the Maid to the judges at Rouen? My Lord of Reims, Chancellor of the Kingdom, had said that she was proud but not heretical. Wherefore now, acting contrary to his own interests and honour, did he refrain from testifying in favour of her through whom he had recovered his episcopal city? Wherefore did he not assert his right and do his duty as metropolitan and censure and suspend his suffragan, the Bishop of Beauvais, who was guilty of prevarication in the administration of justice? Why did not the illustrious clerics, whom King Charles had appointed deputies at the Council of Bâle, undertake to bring the cause of the Maid before the Council? And finally, why did not the priests, the ecclesiastics of the realm, with one voice demand an appeal to the Holy Father?

They all with one accord, as if struck dumb with astonishment, remained passive and silent. Can they have feared that too searching a light would be cast on Jeanne's cause by that illustrious University, that Sun of the Church, which was consulted on religious matters by all Christian states? Can they have suspected that this woman, who in France had been considered a saint, might after all have been inspired by the devil? But if what they had once believed they still held to be true, if they believed that the Maid had come from God to lead their King to his glorious coronation, then what are we to think of those clerks, those ecclesiastics who denied the Daughter of God, on the eve of her passion?

CHAPTER XIII
THE ABJURATION – THE FIRST SENTENCE

O N Saturday, the 19th of May, the doctors and masters, to the number of fifty, assembled in the archiepiscopal chapel of Rouen. There they unanimously declared their agreement with the decision of the University of Paris; and my Lord of Beauvais ordained that a new charitable admonition be addressed to Jeanne.[842] Accordingly, on Wednesday the 23rd, the Bishop, the Vice-Inquisitor, and the Promoter went to a room in the castle, near Jeanne's cell. They were accompanied by seven doctors and masters, by the Lord Bishop of Noyon and by the Lord Bishop of Thérouanne.[843] The latter, brother to Messire Jean de Luxembourg who had sold the Maid, was held one of the most notable personages of the Great Council of England; he was Chancellor of France for King Henry, as Messire Regnault de Chartres was for King Charles.[844]

The accused was brought in, and Maître Pierre Maurice, doctor in theology, read to her the twelve articles as they had been abridged and commented upon, in conformity with the deliberations of the University; the whole was drawn up as a discourse addressed to Jeanne directly:[845]

Article I

First, Jeanne, thou saidst that at about the age of thirteen, thou didst receive revelations and behold apparitions of angels and of the Saints, Catherine and Margaret, that thou didst behold them frequently with thy bodily eyes, that they spoke unto thee and do still oftentimes speak unto thee, and that they have said unto thee many things that thou hast fully declared in thy trial.

The clerks of the University of Paris and others have considered the manner of these revelations and apparitions, their object, the substance of the things revealed, the person to whom they were revealed; all points touching them have they considered. And now they pronounce these revelations and apparitions to be either lying fictions, deceptive and dangerous, or superstitions, proceeding from spirits evil and devilish.

Article II

Item, thou hast said that thy King received a sign, by which he knew that thou wast sent of God: to wit that Saint Michael, accompanied by a multitude of angels, certain of whom had wings, others crowns, and with whom were Saint Catherine and Saint Margaret, came to thee in the town of Château-Chinon; and that they all entered with thee and went up the staircase of the castle, into the chamber of thy King, before whom the angel who wore the crown made obeisance. And once didst thou say that this crown which thou callest a sign, was delivered to the Archbishop of Reims who gave it to thy King, in the presence of a multitude of princes and lords whom thou didst call by name.

Now concerning this sign, the aforesaid clerks declare it to lack verisimilitude, to be a presumptuous lie, deceptive, pernicious, a thing counterfeited and attacking the dignity of angels.

Article III

Item, thou hast said that thou knewest the angels and the saints by the good counsel, the comfort and the instruction they gave thee, because they told thee their names and because the saints saluted thee. Thou didst believe also that it was Saint Michael who appeared unto thee; and that the deeds and sayings of this angel and these saints are good thou didst believe as firmly as thou believest in Christ.

Now the clerks declare such signs to be insufficient for the recognition of the said saints and angels. The clerks maintain that thou hast lightly believed and rashly affirmed, and further that when thou sayst thou dost believe as firmly etc., thou dost err from the faith.

Article IV

Item, thou hast said thou art assured of certain things which are to come, that thou hast known hidden things, that thou hast also recognized men whom thou hadst never seen before, and this by the Voices of Saint Catherine and Saint Margaret.

Thereupon the clerks declare that in these sayings are superstition, divination, presumptuous assertion and vain boasting.

Article V

Item, thou hast said that by God's command and according to his will, thou hast worn and dost still wear man's apparel. Because thou hast God's commandment to wear this dress thou hast donned a short tunic, jerkin, and hose with many points. Thou dost even wear thy hair cut short above the ears, without keeping about thee anything to denote the feminine sex, save what nature hath given thee. And oftentimes hast thou in this garb received the Sacrament of the Eucharist. And albeit thou hast been many times admonished to leave it, thou wouldest not, saying that thou wouldst liefer die than quit this apparel, unless it were by God's command; and that if thou wert still in this dress and with those of thine own party it would be for the great weal of France. Thou sayest also that for nothing wouldst thou take an oath not to wear this dress and bear these arms; and for all this that thou doest thou dost plead divine command.

In such matters the clerks declare that thou blasphemest against God, despising him and his Sacraments, that thou dost transgress divine law, Holy Scripture and the canons of the Church, that thou thinkest evil and dost err from the faith, that thou art full of vain boasting, that thou art addicted to idolatry and worship of thyself and thy clothes, according to the customs of the heathen.

Article VI

Item, thou hast often said, that in thy letters thou hast put these names, *Jhesus Maria*, and the sign of the cross, to warn those to whom thou didst write not to do what was indicated in the letter. In other letters thou hast boasted that thou wouldst slay all those who did not obey thee, and that by thy blows thou wouldst prove who had God on his side. Also hast thou oftentimes said that all thy deeds were by revelation and according to divine command.

Touching such affirmations the clerks declare thee to be a traitor, perfidious, cruel, desiring human bloodshed, seditious, an instigator of tyranny, a blasphemer of God's commandments and revelations.

Article VII

Item, thou sayest that according to revelations vouchsafed unto thee at the age of seventeen, thou didst leave thy parents' house against their will, driving them almost mad. Thou didst go to Robert de Baudricourt, who, at thy request, gave thee man's apparel and a sword, also men-at-arms to take thee to thy King. And being come to the King, thou didst say unto him that his enemies should be driven away, thou didst promise to bring him into a great kingdom, to make him victorious over his foes, and that for this God had sent thee. These things thou sayest thou didst accomplish in obedience to God and according to revelation.

In such things the clerks declare thee to have been irreverent to thy father and mother, thus disobeying God's command; to have given occasion for scandal, to have blasphemed, to have erred from the faith and to have made a rash and presumptuous promise.

Article VIII

Item, thou hast said, that voluntarily thou didst leap from the Tower of Beaurevoir, preferring rather to die than to be delivered into the hands of the English and to live after the destruction of Compiègne. And albeit Saint Catherine and Saint Margaret forbade thee to leap, thou couldst not restrain thyself. And despite the great sin thou hast committed in offending these saints, thou didst know by thy Voices, that after thy confession, thy sin was forgiven thee.

This deed the clerks declare thee to have committed through cowardice turning to despair and probably to suicide. In this matter likewise thou didst utter a rash and presumptuous statement in asserting that thy sin is forgiven, and thou dost err from the faith touching the doctrine of free will.

Article IX

Item, thou hast said that Saint Catherine and Saint Margaret promised to lead thee to Paradise provided thou didst remain a virgin; and that thou hadst vowed and promised them to cherish thy virginity, and of that thou art as well assured as if already thou hadst entered into the glory of the Blessed. Thou believest that thou hast not committed mortal sin. And it seemeth to thee that if thou wert in mortal sin the saints would not visit thee daily as they do.

Such an assertion the clerks pronounce to be a pernicious lie, presumptuous and rash, that therein lieth a contradiction of what thou hadst previously said, and that finally thy beliefs do err from the true Christian faith.

Article X

Item, thou hast declared it to be within thy knowledge that God loveth certain living persons better than thee, and that this thou hast learnt by revelation from Saint Catherine and Saint Margaret: also that those saints speak French, not English, since they are not on the side of the English. And when thou knewest that thy Voices were for thy King, you didst fall to disliking the Burgundians.

Such matters the clerks pronounce to be a rash and presumptuous assertion, a superstitious divination, a blasphemy uttered against Saint Catherine and Saint Margaret, and a transgression of the commandment to love our neighbours.

Article XI

Item, thou hast said that to those whom thou callest Saint Michael, Saint Catherine and Saint Margaret, thou didst do reverence, bending the knee, taking off thy cap, kissing the ground on which they trod, vowing to them thy virginity: that in the instruction of these saints, whom thou didst invoke and kiss and embrace, thou didst believe as soon as they appeared unto thee, and without seeking counsel from thy priest or from any other ecclesiastic. And, notwithstanding, thou believest that these Voices came from God as firmly as thou believest in the Christian religion and the Passion of Our Lord Jesus Christ. Moreover thou hast said that did any evil spirit appear to thee in the form of Saint Michael thou wouldest know such a spirit and distinguish him from the saint. And again hast thou said, that of thine own accord, thou hast sworn not to reveal the sign thou gavest to thy King. And finally thou didst add: "Save at God's command."

Now touching these matters, the clerks affirm that supposing thou hast had the revelations and beheld the apparitions of which thou boastest and in such a manner as thou dost say, then art thou an idolatress, an invoker of demons, an apostate from the faith, a maker of rash statements, a swearer of an unlawful oath.

Article XII

Item, thou hast said that if the Church wished thee to disobey the orders thou sayest God gave thee, nothing would induce thee to do it; that thou knowest that all the deeds of which thou hast been accused in thy trial were wrought according to the command of God and that it was impossible for thee to do otherwise. Touching these deeds, thou dost refuse to submit to the judgment of the Church on earth or of any living man, and will submit therein to God alone. And moreover thou didst declare this reply itself not to be made of thine own accord but by God's command; despite the article of faith: *Unam sanctam Ecclesiam catholicam*, having been many times declared unto thee, and notwithstanding that it behoveth all Christians to submit their deeds and sayings to the Church militant especially concerning revelations and such like matters.

Wherefore the clerks declare thee to be schismatic, disbelieving in the unity and authority of the Church, apostate and obstinately erring from the faith.[846]

Having completed the reading of the articles, Maître Pierre Maurice, on the invitation of the Bishop, proceeded to exhort Jeanne. He had been rector of the University of Paris in 1428.[847] He was esteemed an orator. He it was who, on the 5th of June, had discoursed in the name of the chapter, before King Henry VI on the occasion of his entering Rouen. He would seem to have been distinguished by some knowledge of and taste for ancient letters, and to have been possessed of precious manuscripts, amongst which were the comedies of Terence and the *Æneid* of Virgil.[848]

In terms of calculated simplicity did this illustrious doctor call upon Jeanne to reflect on the effects of her words and sayings, and tenderly did he exhort her to submit to the Church. After the wormwood he offered her the honey; he spoke to her in words kind and familiar. With remarkable adroitness he entered into the feelings and inclinations of the maiden's heart. Seeing her filled with knightly enthusiasm and loyalty to King Charles, whose coronation was her doing, he drew his comparisons from chivalry, thereby essaying to prove to her that she ought rather to believe in the Church Militant than in her Voices and apparitions.

"If your King," he said to her, "had appointed you to defend a fortress, forbidding you to let any one enter it, would you not refuse to admit whomsoever claiming to come from him did not present letters and some other token. Likewise, when Our Lord Jesus Christ, on his ascension into heaven, committed to the Blessed Apostle Peter and to his successors the government of his Church, he forbade them to receive such as claimed to come in his name but brought no credentials."

And, to bring home to her how grievous a sin it was to disobey the Church, he recalled the time when she waged war, and put the case of a knight who should disobey his king:

"When you were in your King's dominion," he said to her, "if a knight or some other owing fealty to him had arisen, saying, 'I will not obey the King; I will not submit either to him or to his officers,' would you not have said, 'He is a man to be censured'? What say you then of yourself, you who, engendered in Christ's religion, having become by baptism the daughter of the Church and the bride of Christ, dost now refuse obedience to the officers of Christ, that is, to the prelates of the Church?"[849]

Thus did Maître Pierre Maurice endeavour to make Jeanne understand him. He did not succeed. Against the courage of this child all the reasons and all the eloquence of the world would have availed nothing. When Maître Pierre had finished speaking, Jeanne, being asked whether she did not hold herself bound to submit her deeds and sayings to the Church, replied:

"What I have always held and said in the trial that will I maintain.... If I were condemned and saw the fagots lighted, and the executioner ready to stir the fire, and I in the fire, I would say and maintain till I died nought other than what I said during the trial."

At these words the Bishop declared the discussion at an end, and deferred the pronouncing of the sentence till the morrow.[850]

The next day, the Thursday after Whitsuntide and the 24th day of May, early in the morning, Maître Jean Beaupère visited Jeanne in her prison and warned her that she would be shortly taken to the scaffold to hear a sermon.

"If you are a good Christian," he said, "you will agree to submit all your deeds and sayings to Holy Mother Church, and especially to the ecclesiastical judges."

Maître Jean Beaupère thought he heard her reply, "So I will."[851]

If such were her answer, then it must have been because, worn out by a flight of agony, her physical courage quailed at the thought of death by burning.

Just when he was leaving her, as she stood near a door, Maître Nicolas Loiseleur gave her the same advice, and in order to induce her to follow it, he made her a false promise:

"Jeanne, believe me," he said. "You have your deliverance in your own hands. Wear the apparel of your sex, and do what shall be required of you. Otherwise you stand in danger of death. If you do as I tell you, good will come to you and no harm. You will be delivered into the hands of the Church."[852]

She was taken in a cart and with an armed guard to that part of the town called Bourg-l'Abbé, lying beneath the castle walls. And but a short distance away the cart was stopped, in the cemetery of Saint-Ouen, also called *les aitres*[853] *Saint-Ouen*. Here a highly popular fair was held every year on the feast day of the patron saint of the Abbey.[854] Here it was that Jeanne was to hear the sermon, as so many other unhappy creatures had done before her. Places like this, to which the folk could flock in crowds, were generally chosen for these edifying spectacles. On the border of this vast charnel-house for a hundred years there had towered a parish church, and on the south there rose the nave of the abbey. Against the magnificent edifice of the church two scaffolds had been erected,[855] one large, the other smaller. They were west of the porch which was called *portail des Marmousets*, because of the multitudes of tiny figures carved upon it.[856]

On the great scaffold the two judges, the Lord Bishop and the Vice-Inquisitor, took their places. They were assisted by the most reverend Cardinal of Winchester, the Lord Bishops of Thérouanne, of Noyon, and of Norwich, the Lord Abbots of Fécamp, of Jumièges, of Bec, of Corneilles, of Mont-Saint-Michel-au-Péril-de-la-Mer, of Mortemart, of Préaux, and of Saint-Ouen of Rouen, where the assembly was held, the Priors of Longueville and of Saint-Lô, also many doctors and bachelors in theology, doctors and licentiates in canon and civil law.[857] Likewise were there many high personages of the English party. The other scaffold was a kind of pulpit. To it ascended the doctor who, according to the use and custom of the Holy Inquisition was to preach the sermon against Jeanne. He was Maître Guillaume Erard, doctor in theology, canon of the churches of Langres and of Beauvais.[858] At this time he was very eager to go to Flanders, where he was urgently needed; and he confided to his young servitor, Brother Jean de Lenisoles, that the preaching of this sermon caused him great inconvenience. "I want to be in Flanders," he said. "This affair is very annoying for me."[859]

From one point of view, however, he must have been pleased to perform this duty, since it afforded him the opportunity of attacking the King of France, Charles VII, and of thereby showing his devotion to the English cause, to which he was strongly attached.

Jeanne, dressed as a man, was brought up and placed at his side, before all the people.[860]

Maître Guillaume Erard began his sermon in the following manner:

"I take as my text the words of God in the Gospel of Saint John, chapter xv: 'The branch cannot bear fruit of itself, except it abide in the vine.'[861] Thus it behoveth all Catholics to remain abiding in Holy Mother Church, the true vine, which the hand of Our Lord Jesus Christ hath planted. Now this Jeanne, whom you see before you, falling from error into error, and from crime into crime, hath become separate from the unity of Holy Mother Church and in a thousand manners hath scandalised Christian people."

Then he reproached her with having failed, with having sinned against royal Majesty and against God and the Catholic Faith; and all these things must she henceforth eschew under pain of death by burning.

He declaimed vehemently against the pride of this woman. He said that never had there appeared in France a monster so great as that which was manifest in Jeanne; that she was a witch, a heretic, a schismatic, and that the King, who protected her, risked the same reproach from the moment that he became willing to recover his throne with the help of such a heretic.[862]

Towards the middle of his sermon, he cried out with a loud voice:

"Ah! right terribly hast thou been deceived, noble house of France, once the most Christian of houses! Charles, who calls himself thy head and assumes the title of King hath, like a heretic and schismatic, received the words of an infamous woman, abounding in evil works and in all dishonour. And not he alone, but all the clergy in his lordship and dominion, by whom this woman, so she sayeth, hath been examined and not rejected. Full sore is the pity of it."[863]

Two or three times did Maître Guillaume repeat these words concerning King Charles. Then pointing at Jeanne with his finger he said:

"It is to you, Jeanne, that I speak; and I say unto you that your King is a heretic and a schismatic."

At these words Jeanne was deeply wounded in her love for the Lilies of France and for King Charles. She was moved with great feeling, and she heard her Voices saying unto her:

"Reply boldly to the preacher who is preaching to you."[864]

Then obeying them heartily, she interrupted Maître Jean:

"By my troth, Messire," she said to him, "saving your reverence, I dare say unto you and swear at the risk of my life, that he is the noblest Christian of all Christians, that none loveth better religion and the Church, and that he is not at all what you say."[865]

Maître Guillaume ordered the Usher, Jean Massieu, to silence her.[866] Then he went on with his sermon, and concluded with these words: "Jeanne, behold my Lords the Judges, who oftentimes have summoned you and required you to submit all your acts and sayings to Mother Church. In these acts and sayings were many things which, so it seemed to these clerics, were good neither to say nor to maintain."[867]

"I will answer you," said Jeanne. Touching the article of submission to the Church, she recalled how she had asked for all the deeds she had wrought and the words she had uttered to be reported to Rome, to Our Holy Father the Pope, to whom, after God, she appealed. Then she added: "And as for the sayings I have uttered and the deeds I have done, they have all been by God's command."[868]

She declared that she had not understood that the record of her trial was being sent to Rome to be judged by the Pope.

"I will not have it thus," she said. "I know not what you will insert in the record of these proceedings. I demand to be taken to the Pope and questioned by him."[869]

They urged her to incriminate her King. But they wasted their breath.

"For my deeds and sayings I hold no man responsible, neither my King nor another."[870]

"Will you abjure all your deeds and sayings? Will you abjure such of your deeds and sayings as have been condemned by the clerks?"

"I appeal to God and to Our Holy Father, the Pope."

"But that is not sufficient. We cannot go so far to seek the Pope. Each Ordinary is judge in his own diocese. Wherefore it is needful for you to appeal to Our Holy Mother Church, and to hold as true all that clerks and folks well learned in the matter say and determine touching your actions and your sayings."[871]

Admonished with yet a third admonition, Jeanne refused to recant.[872] With confidence she awaited the deliverance promised by her Voices, certain that of a sudden there would come men-at-arms from France and that in one great tumult of fighting-men and angels she would be liberated. That was why she had insisted on retaining man's attire.

Two sentences had been prepared: one for the case in which the accused should abjure her error, the other for the case in which she should persevere. By the first there was removed from Jeanne the ban of excommunication. By the second, the tribunal, declaring that it could do nothing more for her, abandoned her to the secular arm. The Lord Bishop had them both with him.[873]

He took the second and began to read: "In the name of the Lord, Amen. All the pastors of the Church who have it in their hearts faithfully to tend their flocks...."[874]

Meanwhile, as he read, the clerks who were round Jeanne urged her to recant, while there was yet time. Maître Nicolas Loiseleur exhorted her to do as he had recommended, and to put on woman's dress.[875]

Maître Guillaume Erard was saying: "Do as you are advised and you will be delivered from prison."[876]

Then straightway came the Voices unto her and said: "Jeanne, passing sore is our pity for you! You must recant what you have said, or we abandon you to secular justice.... Jeanne, do as you are advised. Jeanne, will you bring death upon yourself!"[877]

The sentence was long and the Lord Bishop read slowly:

"We judges, having Christ before our eyes and also the honour of the true faith, in order that our judgment may proceed from the Lord himself, do say and decree that thou hast been a liar, an inventor of revelations and apparitions said to be divine; a deceiver, pernicious, presumptuous, light of faith, rash, superstitious, a soothsayer, a blasphemer against God and his saints. We declare thee to be a contemner of God even in his sacraments, a prevaricator of divine law, of sacred doctrine and of ecclesiastical sanction, seditious, cruel, apostate, schismatic, having committed a thousand errors against religion, and by all these tokens rashly guilty towards God and Holy Church.[878]"

Time was passing. Already the Lord Bishop had uttered the greater part of the sentence.[879] The executioner was there, ready to take off the condemned in his cart.[880]

Then suddenly, with hands clasped, Jeanne cried that she was willing to obey the Church.[881]

The judge paused in the reading of the sentence.

An uproar arose in the crowd, consisting largely of English men-at-arms and officers of King Henry. Ignorant of the customs of the Inquisition, which had not been introduced into their country, these *Godons* could not understand what was going on; all they knew was that the witch was saved. Now they held Jeanne's death to be necessary for the welfare of England; wherefore the unaccountable actions of these doctors and the Lord Bishop threw them into a fury. In their Island witches were not treated thus; no mercy was shown them, and they were burned speedily. Angry murmurs arose; stones were thrown at the registrars of the trial.[882] Maître Pierre Maurice, who was doing his best to strengthen Jeanne in the resolution she had taken, was threatened and the *coués* very nearly made short work with him.[883] Neither did Maître Jean Beaupère and the delegates from the University of Paris escape their share of the insults. They were accused of favouring Jeanne's errors.[884] Who better than they knew the injustice of these reproaches?

Certain of the high personages sitting on the platform at the side of the judge complained to the Lord Bishop that he had not gone on to the end of the sentence but had admitted Jeanne to repentance.

He was even reproached with insults, for one was heard to cry: "You shall pay for this."

He threatened to suspend the trial.

"I have been insulted," he said. "I will proceed no further until honourable amends have been done me."[885]

In the tumult, Maître Guillaume Erard unfolded a double sheet of paper, and read Jeanne the form of abjuration, written down according to the opinion of the masters. It was no longer than the Lord's Prayer and consisted of six or seven lines of writing. It was in French and began with these words: "I, Jeanne...." The Maid submitted therein to the sentence, the judgment, and the commandment of the Church; she acknowledged having committed the crime of high treason and having deceived the people. She undertook never again to bear arms or to wear man's dress or her hair cut round her ears.[886]

When Maître Guillaume had read the document, Jeanne declared she did not understand it, and wished to be advised thereupon.[887] She was heard to ask counsel of Saint Michael.[888] She still believed firmly in her Voices, albeit they had not aided her in her dire necessity, neither had spared her the shame of denying them. For, simple as she was, at the bottom of her heart she knew well what the clerks were asking of her; she realised that they would not let her go until she had pronounced a great recantation. All that she said was merely in order to gain time and because she was afraid of death; yet she could not bring herself to lie.

Without losing a moment Maître Guillaume said to Messire Jean Massieu, the Usher: "Advise her touching this abjuration."

And he passed him the document.[889]

Messire Jean Massieu at first made excuse, but afterwards he complied and warned Jeanne of the danger she was running by her refusal to recant.

"You must know," he said, "that if you oppose any of these articles you will be burned. I counsel you to appeal to the Church Universal as to whether you should abjure these articles or not."

Maître Guillaume Erard asked Jean Massieu: "Well, what are you saying to her?"

Jean Massieu replied: "I make known unto Jeanne the text of the deed of abjuration and I urge her to sign it. But she declares that she knoweth not whether she will."

At this juncture, Jeanne, who was still being pressed to sign, said aloud: "I wish the Church to deliberate on the articles. I appeal to the Church Universal as to whether I should abjure them. Let the document be read by the Church and the clerks into whose hands I am to be delivered. If it be their counsel that I ought to sign it and do what I am told, then willingly will I do it."[890]

Maître Guillaume Erard replied: "Do it now, or you will be burned this very day."

And he forbade Jean Massieu to confer with her any longer.

Whereupon Jeanne said that she would liefer sign than be burned.[891]

Then straightway Messire Jean Massieu gave her a second reading of the deed of abjuration. And she repeated the words after the Usher. As she spoke her countenance seemed to express a kind of sneer. It may have been that her features were contracted by the violent emotions which swayed her and that the horrors and tortures of an ecclesiastical trial may have overclouded her reason, subject at all times to strange vagaries, and that after such bitter suffering there may have come upon her the actual paroxysm of madness. On the other hand it may have been that with sound sense and calm mind she was mocking at the clerks of Rouen; she was quite capable of it, for she had mocked at the clerks of Poitiers. At any rate she had a jesting air, and the bystanders noticed that she pronounced the words of her abjuration with a smile.[892] And her gaiety, whether real or apparent, roused the wrath of those burgesses, priests, artisans, and men-at-arms who desired her death.

"'Tis all a mockery. Jeanne doth but jest,"[893] they cried.

Among the most irate was Master Lawrence Calot, Secretary to the King of England. He was seen to be in a violent rage and to approach first the judge and then the accused. A noble of Picardy who was present, the very same who had essayed familiarities with Jeanne in the Castle of Beaurevoir, thought he saw this Englishman forcing Jeanne to sign a paper.[894] He was mistaken. In every crowd there are those who see things that never happen. The Bishop would not have permitted such a thing; he was devoted to the Regent, but on a question of form he would never have given way. Meanwhile, under this storm of insults, amidst the throwing of stones and the clashing of swords, these illustrious masters, these worthy doctors grew pale. The Prior of Longueville was awaiting an opportunity to make an apology to the Cardinal of Winchester.[895]

On the platform a chaplain of the Cardinal violently accused the Lord Bishop. "You do wrong to accept such an abjuration. 'Tis a mere mockery," he said.

"You lie," retorted my Lord Pierre. "I, the judge of a religious suit, ought to seek the salvation of this woman rather than her death."

The Cardinal silenced his chaplain.[896]

It is said that the Earl of Warwick came up to the judges and complained of what they had done, adding: "The King is not well served, since Jeanne escapes."

And it is stated that one of them replied: "Have no fear, my Lord. She will not escape us long."[897]

It is hardly credible that any one should have actually said so, but doubtless there were many at that time who thought it.

With what scorn must the Bishop of Beauvais have regarded those dull minds, incapable of understanding the service he was rendering to Old England by forcing this damsel to acknowledge that all she had declared and maintained in honour of her King was but lying and illusion.

With a pen that Massieu gave her Jeanne made a cross at the bottom of the deed.[898]

In the midst of howls and oaths from the English, my Lord of Beauvais read the more merciful of the sentences. It relieved Jeanne from excommunication and reconciled her to Holy Mother Church.[899] Further the sentence ran:

"... Because thou hast rashly sinned against God and Holy Church, we, thy judges, that thou mayest do salutary penance, out of our Grace and moderation, do condemn thee finally and definitely to perpetual prison, with the bread of sorrow and the water of affliction, so that there thou mayest weep over thy offences and commit no other that may be an occasion of weeping."[900]

This penalty, like all other penalties, save death and mutilation, lay within the power of ecclesiastical judges. They inflicted it so frequently that in the early days of the Holy Inquisition, the Fathers of the Council of Narbonne said that stones and mortar would become as scarce as money.[901] It was a penalty doubtless, but one which in character and significance differed from the penalties inflicted by secular courts; it was a penance. According to the mercy of ecclesiastical law, prison was a place suitable for repentance, where, in one perpetual penance, the condemned might eat the bread of sorrow and drink the waters of affliction.

How foolish was he, who by refusing to enter that prison or by escaping from it, should reject the salutary healing of his soul! By so doing he was fleeing from the gentle tribunal of penance, and the Church in sadness cut him off from the communion of the faithful. By inflicting this penalty, which a good Catholic must needs regard rather as a favour than a punishment, my Lord the Bishop and my Lord the Holy Vicar of the Inquisition were conforming to the custom, whereby our Holy Mother Church became reconciled to heretics. But had they power to execute their sentence? The prison to which they condemned Jeanne, the expiatory prison, the salutary confinement, must be in a dungeon of the Church. Could they send her there?

Jeanne, turning towards them, said: "Now, you Churchmen, take me to your prison. Let me be no longer in the hands of the English."[902]

Many of those clerics had promised it to her.[903] They had deceived her. They knew it was not possible; for it had been stipulated that the King of England's men should resume possession of Jeanne after the trial.[904]

The Lord Bishop gave the order: "Take her back to the place whence you brought her."[905]

He, a judge of the Church, committed the crime of surrendering the Church's daughter reconciled and penitent, to laymen. Among them she could not mourn over her sins; and they, hating her body and caring nought for her soul, were to tempt her and cause her to fall back into error.

While Jeanne was being taken back in the cart to her tower in the fields, the soldiers insulted her and their captains did not rebuke them.[906]

Thereafter, the Vice-Inquisitor and with him divers doctors and masters, went to her prison and charitably exhorted her. She promised to wear woman's apparel, and to let her head be shaved.[907]

The Duchess of Bedford, knowing that she was a virgin, saw to it that she was treated with respect.[908] As the ladies of Luxembourg had done formerly, she essayed to persuade her to wear the clothing of her sex. By a certain tailor, one Jeannotin Simon, she had had made for Jeanne a gown which she had hitherto refused to wear. Jeannotin brought the garment to the prisoner, who this time did not refuse it. In putting it on, Jeannotin touched her bosom, which she resented. She boxed his ears;[909] but she consented to wear the gown provided by the Duchess.

CHAPTER XIV
THE TRIAL FOR RELAPSE – SECOND SENTENCE – DEATH OF THE MAID

N the following Sunday, which was Trinity Sunday, there arose a rumour that Jeanne had resumed man's apparel. The report spread rapidly from the castle down the narrow streets where lived the clerks in the shadow of the cathedral. Straightway notaries and assessors hastened to the tower which looked on the fields.

In the outer court of the castle they found some hundred men-at-arms, who welcomed them with threats and curses.[910] These fellows did not yet understand that the judges had conducted the trial so as to bring honour to old England and dishonour to the French. They did not realise what it meant when the Maid of the Armagnacs, who hitherto had obstinately persisted in her utterances, was at length brought to confess her impostures. They did not see how great was the advantage to their country when it was published abroad throughout the world that Charles of Valois had been conducted to his coronation by a heretic. But no, the only idea these brutes were capable of grasping was the burning of the girl prisoner who had struck terror into their hearts. The doctors and masters they treated as traitors, false counsellors and Armagnacs.[911]

In the castle yard is Maître André Marguerie, bachelor in decrees, archdeacon of Petit-Caux, King's Counsellor,[912] who is inquiring what has happened. He had displayed great assiduity in the trial. The Maid he held to be a crafty damsel.[913] Now again he desired to give an expert's judgment touching what had just occurred.

"That Jeanne is to be seen dressed as a man is not everything," he said. "We must know what motives induced her to resume masculine attire."

Maître André Marguerie was an eloquent orator, one of the shining lights of the Council of Constance. But, when a man-at-arms raised his axe against him and called out "Traitor! Armagnac!" Maître Marguerie asked no further questions, but speedily departed, and went to bed very sick.[914]

The next day, Monday the 25th, there came to the castle the Vice-Inquisitor, accompanied by divers doctors and masters. The Registrar, Messire Guillaume Manchon, was summoned. He was such a coward that he dared not come save under the escort of one of the Earl of Warwick's men-at-arms.[915] They found Jeanne wearing man's apparel, jerkin and short tunic, with a hood covering her shaved head. Her face was in tears and disfigured by terrible suffering.[916]

She was asked when and why she had assumed this attire.

She replied: "'Tis but now that I have donned man's dress and put off woman's."

"Wherefore did you put it on and who made you?"

"I put it on of my own will and without constraint. I had liefer wear man's dress than woman's."

"You promised and swore not to wear man's dress."

"I never meant to take an oath not to wear it."

"Wherefore did you return to it?"

"Because it is more seemly to take it and wear man's dress, being amongst men, than to wear woman's dress.... I returned to it because the promise made me was not kept, to wit, that I should go to mass and should receive my Saviour and be loosed from my bonds."

"Did you not abjure, and promise not to return to this dress?"

"I had liefer die than be in bonds. But if I be allowed to go to mass and taken out of my bonds and put in a prison of grace, and given a woman to be with me, I will be good and do as the Church shall command."

"Have you heard your Voices since Thursday?"

"Yes."

"What did they say unto you?"

"They told me that through Saint Catherine and Saint Margaret God gave me to wit his sore pity for the treachery, to which I consented in abjuring and recanting to save my life, and that in saving my life I was losing my soul. Before Thursday my Voices had told me what I should do and what I did do on that day. On the scaffold my Voices told me to reply boldly to the preacher. He is a false preacher.... Many things did he say that I have never done. If I were to say that God has not sent me I should be damned. It is true that God has sent me. My Voices have since told me that by confessing I committed a great wickedness which I ought never to have done. All that I said I uttered through fear of the fire."[917]

Thus spake Jeanne in sore sorrow. And now what becomes of those monkish tales of attempted violence related long afterwards by a registrar and two churchmen?[918] And how can Messire Massieu make us believe that Jeanne, unable to find her petticoats, put on her hose in order not to appear before her guards unclothed?[919] The truth is very different. It is Jeanne herself who confesses bravely and simply. She repented of her abjuration, as of the greatest sin she had ever committed. She could not forgive herself for having lied through fear of death. Her Voices, who, before the sermon at Saint-Ouen had foretold that she would deny them, now came to her and spoke of "the sore pity of her treachery." Could they say otherwise since they were the voices of her own heart? And could Jeanne fail to listen to them since she had always listened to them whenever they had counselled her to sacrifice and self-abnegation?

It was out of obedience to her heavenly *Council* that Jeanne had returned to man's apparel, because she would not purchase her life at the price of denying the Angel and the Saints, and because with her whole heart and soul she rebelled against her recantation.

Still the English were seriously to blame for having left her man's clothes. It would have been more humane to have taken them from her, since if she wore them she must needs die. They had been put in a bag.[920] Her guards may even be suspected of having tempted her by placing under her very eyes those garments which recalled to her days of happiness. They had taken away all her few possessions, even her poor brass ring, everything save that suit which meant death to her.

To blame also were her ecclesiastical judges who should not have sentenced her to imprisonment if they foresaw that they could not place her in an ecclesiastical prison, nor have commanded her a penance which they knew they were unable to enforce. Likewise to blame were the Bishop of Beauvais and the Vice-Inquisitor; because after having, for the good of her sinful soul, prescribed the bread of bitterness and the water of affliction, they gave her not this bread and this water, but delivered her in disgrace into the hands of her cruel enemies.

When she uttered the words, "God by Saint Catherine and Saint Margaret hath given me to wit the sore pity of the treason to which I consented," Jeanne consummated the sacrifice of her life.[921]

The Bishop and the Inquisitor had now to proceed in conformity with the law. The interrogatory however lasted a few moments longer.

"Do you believe that your Voices are Saint Margaret and Saint Catherine?"

"Yes, and they come from God."

"Tell us the truth touching the crown."

"To the best of my knowledge I told you the truth of everything at the trial."

"On the scaffold, at the time of your abjuration, you did acknowledge before us your judges and before many others, and in the presence of the people, that you had falsely boasted your Voices to be those of Saint Catherine and Saint Margaret."

"I did not mean thus to do or to say. I did not deny, neither did I intend to deny, my apparitions and to say that they were not Saint Margaret and Saint Catherine. All that I have said was through fear of the fire, and I recanted nothing that was not contrary to the truth. I had liefer do my penance once and for all, to wit by dying, than endure further anguish in prison. Whatsoever abjuration I have been forced to make, I never did anything against God and religion. I did not understand what was in the deed of abjuration, wherefore I did not mean to abjure anything unless it were Our Lord's will. If the judges wish I will resume my woman's dress. But nothing else will I do."[922]

Coming out of the prison, my Lord of Beauvais met the Earl of Warwick accompanied by many persons. He said to him: "Farewell. *Faites bonne chère.*" It is said that he added, laughing: "It is done! We have caught her."[923] The words are his, doubtless, but we are not certain that he laughed.

On the morrow, Tuesday the 29th, he assembled the tribunal in the chapel of the Archbishop's house. The forty-two assessors present were informed of what had happened on the previous day and invited to state their opinions, the nature of which might easily be anticipated.[924] Every heretic who retracted his confession was held a perjurer, not only impenitent but relapsed. And the relapsed were given up to the secular arm.[925]

Maître Nicholas de Venderès, canon, archdeacon, was the first to state his opinion.

"Jeanne is and must be held a heretic. She must be delivered to the secular authority."[926]

The Lord Abbot of Fécamp expressed his opinion in the following terms: "Jeanne has relapsed. Nevertheless it is well that the terms of her abjuration once read to her, be read a second time and explained, and that at the same time she be reminded of God's word. This done, it is for us, her judges, to declare her a heretic and to abandon her to the secular authority, entreating it to deal leniently with her."[927]

This plea for leniency was a mere matter of form. If the Provost of Rouen had taken it into consideration he also would have been excommunicated, with a further possibility of temporal punishment.[928] And yet there were certain counsellors who even wished to dispense with this empty show of pity, urging that there was no need for such a supplication.

Maître Guillaume Erard and sundry other assessors, among whom were Maîtres Marguerie, Loiseleur, Pierre Maurice, and Brother Martin Ladvenu, were of the opinion of my Lord Abbot of Fécamp.[929]

Maître Thomas de Courcelles advised the woman being again charitably admonished touching the salvation of her soul.

Such likewise was the opinion of Brother Isambart de la Pierre.[930]

The Lord Bishop, having listened to these opinions, concluded that Jeanne must be proceeded against as one having relapsed. Accordingly he summoned her to appear on the morrow, the 30th of May, in the old Market Square.[931]

On the morning of that Wednesday, the 30th of May, by the command of my Lord of Beauvais, the two young friars preachers, bachelors in theology, Brother Martin Ladvenu and Brother Isambart de la Pierre, went to Jeanne in her prison. Brother Martin told her that she was to die that day.

At the approach of this cruel death, amidst the silence of her Voices, she understood at length that she would not be delivered.

Cruelly awakened from her dream, she felt heaven and earth failing her, and fell into a deep despair.

"Alas!" she cried, "shall so terrible a fate betide me as that my body ever pure and intact shall to-day be burned and reduced to ashes? Ah me! Ah me! Liefer would I be seven times beheaded than thus be burned. Alas! had I been in the prison of the Church, to which I submitted, and guarded by ecclesiastics and not by my foes and adversaries, so woeful a misfortune as this would not have befallen me. Oh! I appeal to God, the great judge, against this violence and these sore wrongs with which I am afflicted."[932]

While she was lamenting, the doctors and masters, Nicolas de Venderès, Pierre Maurice and Nicolas Loiseleur, entered the prison; they came by order of my Lord of Beauvais.[933] On the previous day thirty-nine counsellors out of forty-two, declaring that Jeanne had relapsed, had added that they deemed it well she should be reminded of the terms of her abjuration.[934] Wherefore, according to the counsel of these clerics, the Lord Bishop had sent certain learned doctors to the relapsed heretic and had resolved to come to her himself.

She must needs submit to one last examination.

"Do you believe that your Voices and apparitions come from good or from evil spirits?"

"I know not; but I appeal to my Mother the Church."[935]

Maître Pierre Maurice, a reader of Terence and Virgil, was filled with pity for this hapless Maid.[936] On the previous day he had declared her to have relapsed because his knowledge of theology forced him to it; and now he was concerned for the salvation of this soul in peril, which could not be saved except by recognising the falseness of its Voices.

"Are they indeed real?" he asked her.

She replied, "Whether they be good or bad, they appeared to me."

She affirmed that with her eyes she had seen, with her ears heard, the Voices and apparitions which had been spoken of at the trial.

She heard them most frequently, she said, at the hour of compline and of matins, when the bells were ringing.[937]

Maître Pierre Maurice, being the Pope's secretary, was debarred from openly professing the Pyrrhonic philosophy. He inclined, however, to a rational interpretation of natural phenomena, if we may judge from his remarking to Jeanne that the ringing of bells often sounded like voices.

Without describing the exact form of her apparitions, Jeanne said they came to her in a great multitude and were very tiny. She believed in them no longer, being fully persuaded that they had deceived her.

Maître Pierre Maurice asked about the Angel who had brought the crown.

She replied that there had never been a crown save that promised by her to her King, and that the Angel was herself.[938]

At that moment the Lord Bishop of Beauvais and the Vice-Inquisitor entered the prison, accompanied by Maître Thomas de Courcelles and Maître Jacques Lecamus.[939]

At the sight of the Judge who had brought her to such a pass she cried, "Bishop, I die through you."

He replied by piously admonishing her. "Ah! Jeanne, bear all in patience. You die because you have not kept your promise and have returned to evil-doing.[940] Now, Jeanne," he asked her, "you have always said that your Voices promised you deliverance; you behold how they have deceived you, wherefore tell us the truth."

She replied, "Verily, I see that they have deceived me."[941]

The Bishop and the Vice-Inquisitor withdrew. They had triumphed over a poor girl of twenty.

"If after their condemnation heretics repent, and if the signs of their repentance are manifest, the sacraments of confession and the Eucharist may not be denied them, provided they demand them with humility."[942] Thus ran the sacred decretals. But no recantation, no assurance of conformity, could save the relapsed heretic. He was permitted confession, absolution, and communion; which means that at the bar of the Sacrament the sincerity of his repentance and conversion was believed in. But at the same time it was declared judicially that his repentance was not believed in and that consequently he must die.[943]

Brother Martin Ladvenu heard Jeanne's confession. Then he sent Messire Massieu, the Usher, to my Lord of Beauvais, to inform him that she asked to be given the body of Jesus Christ.

The Bishop assembled certain doctors to confer on this subject; and after they had deliberated, he replied to the Usher: "Tell Brother Martin to give her the communion and all that she shall ask."[944]

Messire Massieu returned to the castle to bear this reply to Brother Martin. For a second time Brother Martin heard Jeanne in confession and gave her absolution.[945]

A cleric, one Pierre, brought the body of Our Lord in an unceremonious fashion, on a paten covered with the cloth used to put over the chalice, without lights or procession, without surplice or stole.[946]

This did not please Brother Martin, who sent to fetch a stole and candles.

Then, taking the consecrated host in his fingers and presenting it to Jeanne, he said: "Do you believe this to be the body of Christ?"

"Yes, and it alone is able to deliver me."

And she entreated that it should be given to her.

"Do you still believe in your Voices?" asked the officiating priest.

"I believe in God alone, and will place no trust in the Voices who have thus deceived me."[947]

And shedding many tears she received the body of Our Lord very devoutly. Then to God, to the Virgin Mary and to the saints she offered prayers beautiful and reverent and gave such signs of repentance that those present were moved to tears.[948]

Contrite and sorrowful she said to Maître Pierre Maurice:[949] "Maître Pierre, where shall I be this evening?"

"Do you not trust in the Lord?" asked the canon.

"Yea, God helping me, I shall be in Paradise."[950]

Maître Nicolas Loiseleur exhorted her to correct the error she had caused to grow up among the people.

"To this end you must openly declare that you have been deceived and have deceived the folk and that you humbly ask pardon."

Then, fearing lest she might forget when the time came for her to be publicly judged, she asked Brother Martin to put her in mind of this matter and of others touching her salvation.[951]

Maître Loiseleur went away giving signs of violent grief. Walking through the streets like a madman, he was howled at by the *Godons*.[952]

It was about nine o'clock in the morning when Brother Martin and Messire Massieu took Jeanne out of the prison, wherein she had been in bonds one hundred and seventy-eight days. She was placed in a cart, and, escorted by eighty men-at-arms, was driven along the narrow streets to the Old Market Square, close to the River.[953] This square was bordered on the east by a wooden market-house, the butcher's market, on the west by the cemetery of Saint-Sauveur, on the edge of which, towards the square, stood the church of Saint-Sauveur.[954] In this place three scaffolds had been raised, one against the northern gable of the market-house; and in its erection several tiles of the roof had been broken.[955] On this scaffold Jeanne was to be stationed, there to listen to the sermon. Another and a larger scaffold had been erected adjoining the cemetery. There the judges and the prelates were to sit.[956] The pronouncing of sentence in a religious trial was an act of ecclesiastical jurisdiction. For the place of its pronouncement the Inquisitor and the Ordinary preferred consecrated territory, holy ground. True it is that a bull of Pope Lucius forbade such sentences to be given in churches and cemeteries; but the judges eluded this rule by recommending the secular arm to modify its sentence. The third scaffold, opposite the second, was of plaster, and stood in the middle of the square, on the spot whereon executions usually took place. On it was piled the wood for the burning. On the stake which surmounted it was a scroll bearing the words:

"Jehanne, who hath caused herself to be called the Maid, a liar, pernicious, deceiver of the people, soothsayer, superstitious, a blasphemer against God, presumptuous, miscreant, boaster, idolatress, cruel, dissolute, an invoker of devils, apostate, schismatic, and heretic."[957]

The square was guarded by one hundred and sixty men-at-arms. A crowd of curious folk pressed behind the guards, the windows were filled and the roofs covered with onlookers. Jeanne was brought on to the scaffold which had its back to the market-house gable. She wore a long gown and hood.[958] Maître Nicolas Midi, doctor in theology, came up on to the same platform and began to preach to her.[959] As the text of his sermon he took the words of the Apostle in the first Epistle to the Corinthians:[960] "And whether one member suffer, all the members suffer with it." Jeanne patiently listened to the sermon.[961]

Then my Lord of Beauvais, in his own name and that of the Vice-Inquisitor, pronounced the sentence.

He declared Jeanne to be a relapsed heretic.

"We declare that thou, Jeanne, art a corrupt member, and in order that thou mayest not infect the other members, we are resolved to sever thee from the unity of the Church, to tear thee from its body, and to deliver thee to the secular power. And we reject thee, we tear thee out, we abandon thee, beseeching this same secular power, that touching death and the mutilation of the limbs, it may be pleased to moderate its sentence...."[962]

By this formula, the ecclesiastical judge withdrew from any share in the violent death of a fellow creature: *Ecclesia abhorret a sanguine.*[963] But every one knew how much such an entreaty was worth; and all were aware that if the impossible had happened and the magistrate had granted it, he would have been subject to the same penalties as the heretic. Things had now come to such a pass that had the city of Rouen belonged to King Charles, he himself could not have saved the Maid from the stake.

When the sentence was announced Jeanne breathed heart-rending sighs. Weeping bitterly, she fell on her knees, commended her soul to God, to Our Lady, to the blessed saints of Paradise, many of whom she mentioned by name. Very humbly did she ask for mercy from all manner of folk, of whatsoever rank or condition, of her own party and of the enemy's, entreating them to forgive the wrong. she had done them and to pray for her. She asked pardon of her judges, of the English, of King Henry, of the English princes of the realm. Addressing all the priests there present she besought each one to say a mass for the salvation of her soul.[964]

Thus for one half hour did she continue with sighs and tears to give expression to the sentiments of humiliation and contrition with which the clerics had inspired her.[965]

And even now she did not neglect to defend the honour of the fair Dauphin, whom she had so greatly loved.

She was heard to say: "It was never my King who induced me to do anything I have done, either good or evil."[966]

Many of the bystanders wept. A few English laughed. Certain of the captains, who could make nothing of the edifying ceremonial of ecclesiastical justice, grew impatient. Seeing Messire Massieu in the pulpit and hearing him exhort Jeanne to make a good end, they cried:

"What now, priest! Art thou going to keep us here to dinner?"[967]

At Rouen, when a heretic was given up to the secular arm, it was customary to take him to the town hall, where the town council made known unto him his sentence.[968] In Jeanne's case these forms were not observed. The Bailie, Messire le Bouteiller, who was present, waved his hand and said: "Take her, take her."[969] Straightway, two of the King's sergeants dragged her to the base of the scaffold and placed her in a cart which was waiting. On her head was set a great fool's cap made of paper, on which were written the words: "*Hérétique, relapse, apostate, idolâtre*"; and she was handed over to the executioner.[970]

A bystander heard her saying: "Ah! Rouen, sorely do I fear that thou mayest have to suffer for my death."[971]

She evidently still regarded herself as the messenger from Heaven, the angel of the realm of France. Possibly the illusion, so cruelly reft from her, returned at last to enfold her in its beneficent veil. At any rate, she appears to have been crushed; all that remained to her was an infinite horror of death and a childlike piety.

The ecclesiastical judges had barely time to descend and flee from a spectacle which they could not have witnessed without violating the laws of clerical procedure. They were all weeping: the Lord Bishop of Thérouanne, Chancellor of England, had his eyes full of tears. The Cardinal of Winchester, who was said never to enter a church save to pray for the death of an enemy,[972] had pity on this damsel so woeful and so contrite. Brother Pierre Maurice, the canon who was a reader of the Æneid, could not keep back his tears. All the priests who had delivered her to the executioner were edified to see her make so holy an end. That is what Maître Jean Alespée meant when he sighed: "I would that my soul were where I believe the soul of that woman to be."[973] To himself and the hapless sufferer he applied the following lines from the *Dies iræ*:

> *Qui Mariam absolvisti,*
> *Mihi quoque spem dedisti.*[974]

But none the less he must have believed that by her heresies and her obstinacy she had brought death on herself.

The two young friars preachers and the Usher Massieu accompanied Jeanne to the stake.

She asked for a cross. An Englishman made a tiny one out of two pieces of wood, and gave it to her. She took it devoutly and put it in her bosom, on her breast. Then she besought Brother Isambart to go to the neighbouring church to fetch a cross, to bring it to her and hold it before her, so that as long as she lived, the cross on which God was crucified should be ever in her sight.

Massieu asked a priest of Saint-Sauveur for one, and it was brought. Jeanne weeping kissed it long and tenderly, and her hands held it while they were free.[975]

As she was being bound to the stake she invoked the aid of Saint Michael; and now at length no examiner was present to ask her whether it were really he she saw in her father's garden. She prayed also to Saint Catherine.[976]

When she saw a light put to the stake, she cried loudly, "Jesus!" This name she repeated six times.[977] She was also heard asking for holy water.[978]

It was usual for the executioner, in order to cut short the sufferings of the victim, to stifle him in dense smoke before the flames had had time to ascend; but the Rouen executioner was too terrified of the prodigies worked by the Maid to do thus; and besides he would have found it difficult to reach her, because the Bailie had had the plaster scaffold made unusually high. Wherefore the executioner himself, hardened man that he was, judged her death to have been a terribly cruel one.[979]

Once again Jeanne uttered the name of Jesus; then she bowed her head and gave up her spirit.[980]

As soon as she was dead the Bailie commanded the executioner to scatter the flames in order to see that the prophetess of the Armagnacs had not escaped with the aid of the devil or in some other manner.[981] Then, after the poor blackened body had been shown to the people, the executioner, in order to reduce it to ashes, threw on to the fire coal, oil and sulphur.

In such an execution the combustion of the corpse was rarely complete.[982] Among the ashes, when the fire was extinguished, the heart and entrails were found intact. For fear lest Jeanne's remains should be taken and used for witchcraft or other evil practices,[983] the Bailie had them thrown into the Seine.[984]

CHAPTER XV

AFTER THE DEATH OF THE MAID – THE END OF THE SHEPHERD – LA DAME DES ARMOISES

N the evening, after the burning, the executioner, as was his wont, went whining and begging to the monastery of the preaching friars. The creature complained that he had found it very difficult to make an end of Jeanne. According to a legend invented afterwards, he told the monks that he feared damnation for having burned a saint.[985] Had he actually spoken thus in the house of the Vice-Inquisitor he would have been straightway cast into the lowest dungeon, there to await a trial for heresy, which would have probably resulted in his being sentenced to suffer the death he had inflicted on her whom he had called a saint. And what could have led him to suppose that the woman condemned by good Father Lemaistre and my Lord of Beauvais was not a bad woman? The truth is that in the presence of these friars he arrogated to himself merit for having executed a witch and taken pains therein, wherefore he came to ask for his pot of wine. One of the monks, who happened to be a friar preacher, Brother Pierre Bosquier, forgot himself so far as to say that it was wrong to have condemned the Maid. These words, albeit they were heard by only a few persons, were carried to the Inquisitor General. When he was summoned to answer for them, Brother Pierre Bosquier declared very humbly that his words were altogether wrong and tainted with heresy, and that indeed he had only uttered them when he was full of wine. On his knees and with clasped hands he entreated Holy Mother Church, his judges and the most redoubtable lords to pardon him. Having regard to his repentance and in consideration of his cloth and of his having spoken in a state of intoxication, my Lord of Beauvais and the Vice-Inquisitor showed indulgence to Brother Pierre Bosquier. By a sentence pronounced on the 8th of August, 1431, they condemned him to be imprisoned in the house of the friars preachers and fed on bread and water until Easter.[986]

On the 12th of June the judges and counsellors, who had sat in judgment on Jeanne, received letters of indemnity from the Great Council. What was the object of these letters? Was it in case the holders of them should be proceeded against by the French? But in that event the letters would have done them more harm than good.[987]

The Lord Chancellor of England sent to the Emperor, to the Kings and to the princes of Christendom, letters in Latin; to the prelates, dukes, counts, lords, and all the towns of France, letters in French.[988] Herein he made known unto them that King Henry and his Counsellors had had sore pity on the Maid, and that if they had caused her death it was through their zeal for the faith and their solicitude Christian folk.[989]

In like tenor did the University of Paris write to the Holy Father, the Emperor and the College of Cardinals.[990]

On the 4th of July, the day of Saint-Martin-le-Bouillant, Master Jean Graverent, Prior of the Jacobins, Inquisitor of the Faith, preached at Saint-Martin-des-Champs. In his sermon he related the deeds of Jeanne, and told how for her errors and shortcomings she had been delivered to the secular judges and burned alive.

Then he added: "There were four, three of whom have been taken, to wit, this Maid, Pierronne, and her companion. One, Catherine de la Rochelle, still remaineth with the Armagnacs. Friar Richard, the Franciscan, who attracted so great a multitude of folk when he preached in Paris at the Innocents and elsewhere, directed these women; he was their spiritual father."[991]

With Pierronne burned in Paris, her companion eating the bread of bitterness and drinking the water of affliction in the prison of the Church, and Jeanne burned at Rouen, the royal company of *béguines* was now almost entirely annihilated. There only remained to the King the holy dame of La Rochelle, who had escaped from the hands of the Paris Official; but her indiscreet talk had rendered her troublesome.[992] While his penitents were being discredited, good Friar Richard himself had fallen on evil days. The Vicars in the diocese of Poitiers and the Inquisitor of the Faith had forbidden him to preach. The great orator, who had converted so many Christian folk, could no longer thunder against gaming-tables and dice, against women's finery, and mandrakes arrayed in magnificent attire. No longer could he declare the coming of Antichrist nor prepare souls for the terrible trials which were to herald the imminent end of the world. He was ordered to lie under arrest in the Franciscan monastery at Poitiers. And doubtless it was with no great docility that he submitted to the sentence of his superiors; for on Friday, the 23rd of March, 1431, we find the Ordinary and the Inquisitor, asking aid in the execution of the sentence from the Parliament of Poitiers, which did not refuse it. Why did Holy Church exercise such severity towards a preacher endowed with so wondrous a power of moving sinful souls? We may at any rate suspect the reason. For some time the English and Burgundian clergy had been accusing him of apostasy and magic. Now, owing to the unity of the Church in general and to that of the Gallican Church in particular, owing also to the authority of that bright sun of Christendom, the University of Paris, when a clerk was suspected of error and heresy by the doctors of the English and Burgundian party he came to be looked at askance by the clergy who were loyal to King Charles. Especially was this so when in a matter touching the Catholic faith, the University had pronounced against him and in favour of the English. It is quite likely that the clerks of Poitiers had been prejudiced against Friar Richard by Pierronne's conviction and even by the Maid's trial. The good brother, who persisted in preaching the end of the world, was strongly suspected of dealing in the black art. Wherefore, realising the fate which was threatening him, he fled, and was never heard of again.[993]

None the less, however, did the counsellors of King Charles continue to employ the devout in the army. At the time of the disappearance of Friar Richard and his penitents, they were making use of a young shepherd whom my Lord the Archbishop, Duke of Reims and Chancellor of the kingdom, had proclaimed to be Jeanne's miraculous successor. And it was in the following circumstance that the shepherd was permitted to display his power.

The war continued. Twenty days after Jeanne's death the English in great force marched to recapture the town of Louviers. They had delayed till then, not, as some have stated, because they despaired of succeeding in anything as long as the Maid lived, but because they needed time to collect money and engines for the siege.[994] In the July and August of this same year, at Senlis and at Beauvais, my Lord of Reims, Chancellor of France and the Maréchal de Boussac, were upholding the French cause. And we may be sure that my Lord of

Reims was upholding it with no little vigour since at the same time he was defending the benefices which were so dear to him.[995] A Maid had reconquered them, now he intended a lad to hold them. With this object he employed the little shepherd, Guillaume, from the Lozère Mountains, who, like Saint Francis of Assisi and Saint Catherine of Sienna, had received stigmata. A party of French surprised the Regent at Mantes and were on the point of taking him prisoner. The alarm was given to the army besieging Louviers; and two or three companies of men-at-arms were despatched. They hastened to Mantes, where they learnt that the Regent had succeeded in reaching Paris. Thereupon, having been reinforced by troops from Gournay and certain other English garrisons, being some two thousand strong and commanded by the Earls of Warwick, Arundel, Salisbury, and Suffolk, and by Lord Talbot and Sir Thomas Kiriel, the English made bold to march upon Beauvais. The French, informed of their approach, left the town at daybreak, and marched out to meet them in the direction of Savignies. King Charles's men, numbering between eight hundred and one thousand combatants, were commanded by the Maréchal de Boussac, the Captains La Hire, Poton, and others.[996]

The shepherd Guillaume, whom they believed to be sent of God, was at their head, riding side-saddle and displaying the miraculous wounds in his hands, his feet, and his left side.[997]

When they were about two and a half miles from the town, just when they least expected it, a shower of arrows came down upon them. The English, informed by their scouts of the French approach, had lain in wait for them in a hollow of the road. Now they attacked them closely both in the van and in the rear. Each side fought valiantly. A considerable number were slain, which was not the case in most of the battles of those days, when few but the fugitives were killed. But the French, feeling themselves surrounded, were seized with panic, and thus brought about their own destruction. Most of them, with the Maréchal de Boussac and Captain La Hire, fled to the town of Beauvais. Captain Poton and the shepherd, Guillaume, remained in the hands of the English, who returned to Rouen in triumph.[998]

Poton made sure of being ransomed in the usual manner. But the little shepherd could not hope for such a fate; he was suspected of heresy and magic; he had deceived Christian folk and accepted from them idolatrous veneration. The signs of our Saviour's passion that he bore upon him helped him not a whit; on the contrary the wounds, by the French held to have been divinely imprinted, to the English seemed the marks of the devil.

Guillaume, like the Maid, had been taken in the diocese of Beauvais. The Lord Bishop of this town, Messire Pierre Cauchon, who had claimed the right to try Jeanne, made a similar claim for Guillaume; and the shepherd was granted what the Maid had been refused, he was cast into an ecclesiastical prison.[999] He would seem to have been less difficult to guard than Jeanne and also less important. But the English had recently learnt what was involved in a trial by the Inquisition; they now knew how lengthy and how punctilious it was. Moreover, they did not see how it would profit them if this shepherd were convicted of heresy. If the French had set their hope of success in war[1000] in Guillaume as they had done in Jeanne, then that hope was but short-lived. To put the Armagnacs to shame by proving that their shepherd lad came from the devil, that game was not worth the candle. The youth was taken to Rouen and thence to Paris.[1001]

He had been a prisoner for four months when King Henry VI, who was nine years old, came to Paris to be crowned in the church of Notre Dame with the two crowns of France and England. With high pomp and great rejoicing he made his entrance into the city on Sunday, the 16th of December. Along the route of the procession, in the Rue du Ponceau-Saint-Denys, had been constructed a fountain adorned with three sirens; and from their midst rose a tall lily stalk, from the buds and blossoms of which flowed streams of wine and milk. Folk flocked to drink of the fountain; and around its basin men disguised as savages entertained them with games and sham fights.

From the Porte Saint-Denys to the Hôtel Saint-Paul in the Marais, the child King rode beneath a great azure canopy, embroidered with flowers-de-luce in gold, borne first by the four aldermen hooded and clothed in purple, then by the corporations, drapers, grocers, money-changers, goldsmiths and hosiers. Before him went twenty-five heralds and twenty-five trumpeters; followed by nine handsome men and nine beautiful ladies, wearing magnificent armour and bearing great shields, representing the nine *preux* and the nine *preuses*, also by a number of knights and squires. In this brilliant procession appeared the little shepherd Guillaume; he no longer stretched out his arms to show the wounds of the passion, for he was strongly bound.[1002]

After the ceremony he was conducted back to prison, whence he was taken later to be sewn in a sack and thrown into the Seine.[1003] Even the French admitted that Guillaume was but a simpleton and that his mission was not of God.[1004]

In 1433, the Constable, with the assistance of the Queen of Sicily, caused the capture and planned the assassination of La Trémouille. It was the custom of the nobles of that day to appoint counsellors for King Charles and afterwards to kill them. However, the sword which was to have caused the death of La Trémouille, owing to his corpulence, failed to inflict a mortal wound. His life was saved, but his influence was dead. King Charles tolerated the Constable as he had tolerated the Sire de la Trémouille.[1005]

The latter left behind him the reputation of having been grasping and indifferent to the welfare of the kingdom. Perhaps his greatest fault was that he governed in a time of war and pillage, when friends and foes alike were devouring the realm. He was charged with the destruction of the Maid, of whom he was said to have been jealous. This accusation proceeds from the House of Alençon, with whom the Lord Chamberlain was not popular.[1006] On the contrary, it must be admitted, that after the Lord Chancellor, La Trémouille was the boldest in employing the Maid, and if later she did thwart his plans there is nothing to prove that it was his intention to have her destroyed by the English. She destroyed herself and was consumed by her own zeal.

Rightly or wrongly, the Lord Chamberlain was held to be a bad man; and, although his successor in the King's favour, the Duc de Richemont, was avaricious, hard, violent, incredibly stupid, surly, malicious, always beaten and always discontented, the exchange appeared to be no loss. The Constable came in a fortunate hour, when the Duke of Burgundy was making peace with the King of France.

In the words of a Carthusian friar, the English who had entered the kingdom by the hole made in Duke John's head on the Bridge of Montereau, only retained their hold on the kingdom by the hand of Duke Philip. They were but few in number, and if the giant were to withdraw his hand a breath of wind would suffice to blow them away. The Regent died of sorrow and wrath, beholding the fulfilment of the horoscope of King Henry VI: "Exeter shall lose what Monmouth hath won."[1007]

On the 13th of April, 1436, the Count of Richemont entered Paris. The nursing mother of Burgundian clerks and *Cabochien* doctors, the University herself, had helped to mediate peace.[1008]

Now, one month after Paris had returned to her allegiance to King Charles, there appeared in Lorraine a certain damsel. She was about twenty-five years old. Hitherto she had been called Claude; but she now made herself known to divers lords of the town of Metz as being Jeanne the Maid.[1009]

At this time, Jeanne's father and eldest brother were dead.[1010] Isabelle Romée was alive. Her two youngest sons were in the service of the King of France, who had raised them to the rank of nobility and given them the name of Du Lys. Jean, the eldest, called Petit-Jean,[1011] had been appointed Bailie of Vermandois, then Captain of Chartres. About this year, 1436, he was provost and captain of Vaucouleurs.[1012]

The youngest, Pierre, or Pierrelot, who had fallen into the hands of the Burgundians before Compiègne at the same time as Jeanne, had just been liberated from the prison of the Bastard of Vergy.[1013]

Both brothers believed that their sister had been burned at Rouen. But when they were told that she was living and wished to see them, they appointed a meeting at La-Grange-aux-Ormes, a village in the meadows of the Sablon, between the Seille and the Moselle, about two and a half miles south of Metz. They reached this place on the 20th of May. There they saw her and recognised her immediately to be their sister; and she recognised them to be her brothers.[1014]

She was accompanied by certain lords of Metz, among whom was a man right noble, Messire Nicole Lowe, who was chamberlain to Charles VII.[1015] By divers tokens these nobles recognised her to be the Maid Jeanne who had taken King Charles to be crowned at Reims. These tokens were certain signs on the skin.[1016] Now there was a prophecy concerning Jeanne which stated her to have a little red mark beneath the ear.[1017] But this prophecy was invented after the events to which it referred. Consequently we may believe the Maid to have been thus marked. Was this the token by which the nobles of Metz recognised her?

We do not know by what means she claimed to have escaped death; but there is reason to think[1018] that she attributed her deliverance to her holiness. Did she say that an angel had saved her from the fire? It might be read in books how in the ancient amphitheatres lions licked the bare feet of virgins, how boiling oil was as soothing as balm to the bodies of holy martyrs; and how according to many of the old stories nothing short of the sword could take the life of God's maidens. These ancient histories rested on a sure foundation. But if such tales had been related of the fifteenth century they might have appeared less credible. And this damsel does not seem to have employed them to adorn her adventure. She was probably content to say that another woman had been burned in her place.

According to a confession she made afterwards, she came from Rome, where, accoutred in harness of war, she had fought valiantly in the service of Pope Eugenius. She may even have told the Lorrainers of the feats of prowess she had there accomplished.

Now Jeanne had prophesied (at least so it was believed) that she would die in battle against the infidel and that her mantle would fall upon a maid of Rome. But such a saying, if it were known to these nobles of Metz, would be more likely to denounce this so-called Jeanne as an imposture than witness to the truth of her mission.[1019] However this might be, they believed what this woman told them.

Perhaps, like many a noble of the republic,[1020] they were more inclined to King Charles than to the Duke of Burgundy. And we may be sure that, chivalrous knights as they were, they esteemed chivalry wherever they found it; wherefore, because of her valour they admired the Maid; and they made her good cheer.

Messire Nicole Lowe gave her a charger and a pair of hose. The charger was worth thirty francs – a sum well-nigh royal – for of the two horses which at Soissons and at Senlis the King gave the Maid Jeanne, one was worth thirty-eight livres ten sous, and the other thirty-seven livres ten sous.[1021] Not more than sixteen francs had been paid for the horse with which she had been provided at Vaucouleurs.[1022]

Nicole Grognot, governor of the town,[1023] offered a sword to the sister of the Du Lys brothers; Aubert Boullay presented her with a hood.[1024]

She rode her horse with the same skill which seven years earlier, if we may believe some rather mythical stories, had filled with wonder the old Duke of Lorraine.[1025] And she spoke certain words to Messire Nicole Lowe which confirmed him in his belief that she was indeed that same Maid Jeanne who had fared forth into France. She had the ready tongue of a prophetess, and spoke in symbols and parables, revealing nought of her intent.

Her power would not come to her before Saint John the Baptist's Day, she said. Now this was the very time which the Maid, after the Battle of Patay, in 1429, had fixed for the extermination of the English in France.[1026]

This prophecy had not been fulfilled and consequently had not been mentioned again. Jeanne, if she ever uttered it, and it is quite possible that she did, must have been the first to forget it. Moreover, Saint John's Day was a term commonly cited in leases, fairs, contracts, hirings, etc., and it is quite conceivable that the calendar of a prophetess may have been the same as that of a labourer.

The day after their arrival at La Grange-aux-Ormes, Monday, the 21st of May, the Du Lys brothers took her, whom they held to be their sister, to that town of Vaucouleurs[1027] whither Isabelle Romée's daughter had gone to see Sire Robert de Baudricourt. In this town, in the year 1436, there were still living many persons of different conditions, such as the Leroyer couple and the Seigneur Aubert d'Ourches,[1028] who had seen Jeanne in February, 1429.

After a week at Vaucouleurs she went to Marville, a small town between Corny and Pont-á-Mousson. There she spent Whitsuntide and abode for three weeks in the house of one Jean Quenat.[1029] On her departure she was visited by sundry inhabitants of Metz, who gave her jewels, recognising her to be the Maid of France.[1030] Jeanne, it will be remembered, had been seen by divers knights of Metz at the time of King Charles's coronation at Reims. At Marville, Geoffroy Desch, following the example of Nicole Lowe, presented the so-called Jeanne with a horse. Geoffroy Desch belonged to one of the most influential families of the Republic of Metz. He was related to Jean Desch, municipal secretary in 1429.[1031]

From Marville, she went on a pilgrimage to Notre Dame de Liance, called Lienche by the Picards and known later as Notre Dame de Liesse. At Liance was worshipped a black image of the Virgin, which, according to tradition, had been brought by the crusaders from the Holy Land. The chapel containing this image was situated between Laon and Reims. It was said, by the priests who officiated there, to be one of the halting places on the route of the coronation procession, where the kings and their retinues were accustomed to stop on their return from Reims; but this is very likely not to be true. Whether it were such a halting place or no, there is no doubt that the folk of Metz displayed a particular devotion to Our Lady of Liance; and it seemed fitting that Jeanne, who had escaped from an English prison, should go and give thanks for her marvellous deliverance to the Black Virgin of Picardy.[1032]

Thence she went on her way to Arlon, to Elisabeth of Gorlitz, Duchess of Luxembourg, an aunt by marriage of the Duke of Burgundy.[1033] She was an old woman, who had been twice a widow. By extortion and oppression she had made herself detested by her vassals. By this princess Jeanne was well received. There was nothing strange in that. Persons living holy lives and working miracles were much sought after by princes and nobles who desired to discover secrets or to obtain the fulfilment of some wish. And the Duchess of Luxembourg might well believe this damsel to be the Maid Jeanne herself, since the brothers Du Lys, the nobles of Metz and the folk of Vaucouleurs were of that opinion.

For the generality of men, Jeanne's life and death were surrounded by marvels and mysteries. Many had from the first doubted her having perished by the hand of the executioner. Certain were curiously reticent on this point; they said: "the English had her publicly burnt at Rouen, or some other woman like her."[1034] Others confessed that they did not know what had become of her.[1035]

Thus, when throughout Germany and France the rumour spread that the Maid was alive and had been seen near Metz, the tidings were variously received. Some believed them, others did not. An ardent dispute, which arose between two citizens of Arles, gives some idea of the emotion aroused by such tidings. One maintained that the Maid was still alive; the other asserted that she was dead; each one wagered that what he said was true. This was no light wager, for it was made and registered in the presence of a notary, on the 27th of June, 1436, only five weeks after the interview at La Grange-aux-Ormes.[1036]

Meanwhile, in the beginning of August, the Maid's eldest brother, Jean du Lys, called Petit-Jean, had gone to Orléans to announce that his sister was alive. As a reward for these good tidings, he received for himself and his followers ten pints of wine, twelve hens, two goslings, and two leverets.[1037]

The birds had been purchased by two magistrates; the name of one, Pierre Baratin, is to be found in the account books of the fortress, in 1429,[1038] at the time of the expedition to Jargeau; the other was an old man of sixty-six, a burgess passing rich, Aignan de Saint-Mesmin.[1039]

641

Messengers were passing to and fro between the town of Duke Charles and the town of the Duchess of Luxembourg. On the 9th of August a letter from Arlon reached Orléans. About the middle of the month a pursuivant arrived at Arlon. He was called Cœur-de-Lis, in honour of the heraldic symbol of the city of Orléans, which was a lily-bud, a kind of trefoil. The magistrates of Orléans had sent him to Jeanne with a letter, the contents of which are unknown. Jeanne gave him a letter for the King, in which she probably requested an audience. He took it straight to Loches, where King Charles was negotiating the betrothal of his daughter Yolande to Prince Amedée of Savoie.[1040]

After forty-one days' journey the pursuivant returned to the magistrates, who had despatched him on the 2nd of September. The messenger complained of a great thirst, wherefore the magistrates, according to their wont, had him served in the chamber of the town-hall with bread, wine, pears, and green walnuts. This repast cost the town two *sous* four *deniers* of Paris, while the pursuivant's travelling expenses amounted to six *livres* which were paid in the following month. The town varlet who provided the walnuts was that same Jacquet Leprestre who had served during the siege. Another letter from the Maid had been received by the magistrates on the 25th of August.[1041]

Jean du Lys proceeded just as if his miracle-working sister had in very deed been restored to him. He went to the King, to whom he announced the wonderful tidings. Charles cannot have entirely disbelieved them since he ordered Jean du Lys to be given a gratuity of one hundred francs. Whereupon Jean promptly demanded these hundred francs from the King's treasurer, who gave him twenty. The coffers of the victorious King were not full even then.

Having returned to Orléans, Jean appeared before the town-council. He gave the magistrates to wit that he had only eight francs, a sum by no means sufficient to enable him and four retainers to return to Lorraine. The magistrates gave him twelve francs.[1042]

Every year until then the anniversary of the Maid had been celebrated in the church of Saint-Sanxon[1043] on the eve of Corpus Christi and on the previous day. In 1435, eight ecclesiastics of the four mendicant orders sang a mass for the repose of Jeanne's soul. In this year, 1436, the magistrates had four candles burnt, weighing together nine and a half pounds, and pendent therefrom the Maid's escutcheon, a silver shield bearing the crown of France. But when they heard the

Maid was alive they cancelled the arrangements for a funeral service in her memory.[1044]

While these things were occurring in France, Jeanne was still with the Duchess of Luxembourg. There she met the young Count Ulrich of Wurtemberg, who refused to leave her. He had a handsome cuirasse made for her and took her to Cologne. She still called herself the Maid of France sent by God.[1045]

Since the 24th of June, Saint John the Baptist's Day, her power had returned to her. Count Ulrich, recognising her supernatural gifts, entreated her to employ them on behalf of himself and his friends. Being very contentious, he had become seriously involved in the schism which was then rending asunder the diocese of Trèves. Two prelates were contending for the see; one, Udalric of Manderscheit, appointed by the chapter, the other Raban of Helmstat, Bishop of Speyer, appointed by the Pope.[1046] Udalric took the field with a small force and twice besieged and bombarded the town of which he called himself the true shepherd. These proceedings brought the greater part of the diocese on to his side.[1047] But although aged and infirm, Raban too had weapons; they were spiritual but powerful: he pronounced an interdict against all such as should espouse the cause of his rival.

Count Ulrich of Wurtemberg, who was among the most zealous of Udalric's supporters, questioned the Maid of God concerning him.[1048] Similar cases had been submitted to the first Jeanne when she was in France. She had been asked, for example, which of the three popes, Benedict, Martin, or Clement, was the true father of the faithful, and without immediately pronouncing on the subject she had promised to designate the Pope to whom obedience was due, after she had reached Paris and rested there.[1049] The second Jeanne replied with even more assurance; she declared that she knew who was the true archbishop and boasted that she would enthrone him.

According to her, it was Udalric of Manderscheit, he whom the Chapter had appointed. But when Udalric was summoned before the Council of Bâle, he was declared an usurper; and the fathers did what it was by no means their unvarying rule to do, – they confirmed the nomination of the Pope.

Unfortunately the Maid's intervention in this dispute attracted the attention of the Inquisitor General of the city of Cologne, Heinrich Kalt Eysen, an illustrious professor of theology. He inquired into the rumours which were being circulated in the city touching the young prince's protégée; and he learnt that she wore unseemly apparel, danced with men, ate and drank more than she ought, and practised magic. He was informed notably that in a certain assembly the Maid tore a table-cloth and straightway restored it to its original condition, and that having broken a glass against the wall she with marvellous skill put all its pieces together again. Such deeds caused Kalt Eysen to suspect her strongly of heresy and witchcraft. He summoned her before his tribunal; she refused to appear. This disobedience displeased the Inquisitor General, and he sent to fetch the defaulter. But the young Count of Wurtemberg hid his Maid in his house, and afterwards contrived to get her secretly out of the town. Thus she escaped the fate of her whom she was willing only partially to imitate. As he could do nothing else, the Inquisitor excommunicated her.[1050] She took refuge at Arlon with her protectress, the Duchess of Luxembourg. There she met Robert des Armoises, Lord of Tichemont. She may have seen him before, in the spring, at Marville, where he usually resided. This nobleman was probably the son of Lord Richard, Governor of the Duchy of Bar in 1416. Nothing is known of him, save that he surrendered this territory to the foreigner without the Duke of Bar's consent, and then beheld it confiscated and granted to the Lord of Apremont on condition that he should conquer it.

It was not extraordinary that Lord Robert should be at Arlon, seeing that his château of Tichemont was near this town. He was poor, albeit of noble birth.[1051]

The so-called Maid married him,[1052] apparently with the approval of the Duchess of Luxembourg. According to the opinion of the Holy Inquisitor of Cologne, this marriage was contracted merely to protect the woman against the interdict and to save her from the sword of the Church.[1053]

Soon after her marriage she went to live at Metz in her husband's house, opposite the church of Sainte-Ségolène, over the Sainte-Barbe Gate. Henceforth she was Jeanne du Lys, the Maid of France, the Lady of Tichemont. By these names she is described in a contract dated the 7th of November, 1436, by which Robert des Armoises and his wife, authorised by him, sell to Collard de Failly, squire, dwelling at Marville, and to Poinsette, his wife, one quarter of the lordship of Haraucourt. At the request of their dear friends, Messire Robert and Dame Jeanne, Jean de Thoneletil, Lord of Villette, and Saubelet de

Dun, Provost of Marville, as well as the vendors, put their seals to the contract to testify to its validity.[1054]

In her dwelling, opposite the Sainte-Ségolène Church, la Dame des Armoises gave birth to two children.[1055] Somewhere in Languedoc[1056] there was an honest squire who, when he heard of these births, seriously doubted whether Jeanne the Maid and la Dame des Armoises could be one and the same person. This was Jean d'Aulon, who had once been Jeanne's steward. From information he had received from women who knew, he did not believe her to be the kind of woman likely to have children.[1057]

According to Brother Jean Nider, doctor in theology of the University of Vienne, this fruitful union turned out badly. A priest, and, as he says, a priest who might more appropriately be called a pander, seduced this witch with words of love and carried her off. But Brother Jean Nider adds that the priest secretly took la Dame des Armoises to Metz and there lived with her as his concubine.[1058] Now it is proved that her own home was in that very town; hence we may conclude that this friar preacher does not know what he is talking about.[1059]

The fact of the matter is that she did not remain longer than two years in the shadow of Sainte-Ségolène.

Although she had married, it was by no means her intention to forswear prophesying and chivalry. During her trial Jeanne had been asked by the examiner: "Jeanne, was it not revealed to you that if you lost your virginity your good fortune would cease and your Voices desert you?" She denied that such things had been revealed to her. And when he insisted, asking her whether she believed that if she were married her Voices would still come to her, she answered like a good Christian: "I know not, and I appeal to God."[1060] Jeanne des Armoises likewise held that good fortune had not forsaken her on account of her marriage. Moreover, in those days of prophecy there were both widows and married women who, like Judith of Bethulia, acted by divine inspiration. Such had been Dame Catherine de la Rochelle, although perhaps after all she had not done anything so very great.[1061]

In the summer of 1439, la Dame des Armoises went to Orléans. The magistrates offered her wine and meat as a token of gladness and devotion. On the first of August they gave her a dinner and presented her with two hundred and ten livres of Paris as an acknowledgment of the service she had rendered to the town during the siege. These are the very terms in which this expenditure is entered in the account books of that city.[1062]

If the folk of Orléans did actually take her for the real Maid, Jeanne, then it must have been more on account of the evidence of the Du Lys brothers, than on that of their own eyes. For, when one comes to think of it, they had seen her but very seldom. During that week in May, she had only appeared before them armed and on horseback. Afterwards in June, 1429, and January, 1430, she had merely passed through the town. True it was she had been offered wine and the magistrates had sat at table with her;[1063] but that was nine years ago. And the lapse of nine years works many a change in a woman's face. They had seen her last as a young girl, now they found her a woman and the mother of two children. Moreover they were guided by the opinion of her kinsfolk. Their attitude provokes some astonishment, however, when one thinks of the conversation at the banquet, and of the awkward and inconsistent remarks the dame must have uttered. If they were not then undeceived, these burgesses must have been passing simple and strongly prejudiced in favour of their guest.

And who can say that they were not? Who can say that, after having given credence to the tidings brought by Jean du Lys, the townsfolk did not begin to discover the imposture? That the belief in the survival of Jeanne was by no means general in the city, during the visit of la Dame des Armoises, is proved by the entries in the municipal accounts of sums expended on the funeral services, which we have already mentioned. Supposing we abstract the years 1437 and 1438, the anniversary service had at any rate been held in 1439, two days before Corpus-Christi, and only about three months before the banquet on the 1st of August.[1064] Thus these grateful burgesses of Orléans were at one and the same time entertaining their benefactress at banquets and saying masses in memory of her death.

La Dame des Armoises only spent a fortnight with them. She left the city towards the end of July. Her departure would seem to have been hasty and sudden. She was invited to a supper, at which she was to have been presented with eight pints of wine, but when the wine was served she had gone, and the banquet had to be held without her.[1065] Jean Quillier and Thévanon of Bourges were present. This Thévanon may have been that Thévenin Villedart, with whom Jeanne's brothers dwelt during the siege.[1066] In Jean Quillier we recognise the young draper who, in June, 1429, had furnished fine Brussels cloth of purple, wherewith to make a gown for the Maid.[1067]

La Dame des Armoises had gone to Tours, where she gave herself out to be the true Jeanne. She gave the Bailie of Touraine a letter for the King; and the Bailie undertook to see that it was delivered to the Prince, who was then at Orléans, having arrived there but shortly after Jeanne's departure. The Bailie of Touraine in 1439 was none other than that Guillaume Bellier who ten years before as lieutenant of Chinon had received the Maid into his house and committed her to the care of his devout wife.[1068]

To the messenger, who bore this letter, Guillaume Bellier also gave a note for the King written by himself, and "touching the deeds of la Dame des Armoises."[1069] We know nothing of its purport.[1070]

Shortly afterwards the Dame went off into Poitou. There she placed herself at the service of Seigneur Gille de Rais, Marshal of France.[1071] He it was who in his early youth had conducted the Maid to Orléans, had been with her throughout the coronation campaign, had fought at her side before the walls of Paris. During Jeanne's captivity he had occupied Louviers and pushed on boldly to Rouen. Now throughout the length and breadth of his vast domains he was kidnapping children, mingling magic with debauchery, and offering to demons the blood and the limbs of his countless victims. His monstrous doings spread terror round his castles of Tiffauges and Machecoul, and already the hand of the Church was upon him.

According to the Holy Inquisitor of Cologne, la Dame des Armoises practised magic; but it was not as an invoker of demons that the Maréchal de Rais employed her; he placed her in authority over the men-at-arms,[1072] in somewhat the same position as Jeanne had occupied at Lagny and Compiègne. Did she do great prowess? We do not know. At any rate she did not hold her office long; and after her it was bestowed on a Gascon squire, one Jean de Siquemville.[1073] In the spring of 1440 she was near Paris.[1074]

For nearly two years and a half the great town had been loyal to King Charles. He had entered the city, but had failed to restore it to prosperity. Deserted houses were everywhere falling into ruins; wolves penetrated into the suburbs and devoured little children.[1075] The townsfolk, who had so recently been Burgundian, could not all forget how the Maid in company with Friar Richard and the Armagnacs had attacked the city on the day of the Nativity of Our Lady. There were many, doubtless, who bore her ill will and believed she had been burned for her sins; but her name no longer excited universal reprobation as in 1429. Certain even among her former enemies regarded her as a martyr to the cause of her liege lord.[1076] Even in Rouen such an opinion was not unknown, and it was much more likely to be held in the city of Paris which had lately turned French. At the rumour that Jeanne was not dead, that she had been recognised by the people of Orléans and was coming to Paris, the lower orders in the city grew excited and disturbances were threatening.

Under Charles of Valois in 1440, the spirit of the University was just the same as it had been under Henry of Lancaster in 1431. It honoured and respected the King of France, the guardian of its privileges and the defender of the liberties of the Gallican Church. The illustrious masters felt no remorse at having demanded and obtained the chastisement of the rebel and heretic, Jeanne the Maid. Whosoever persists in error is a heretic; whosoever essays and fails to overthrow the powers that be is a rebel. It was God's will that in 1440 Charles of Valois should possess the city of Paris; it had not been God's will in 1429; wherefore the Maid had striven against God. With equal bitterness would the University, in 1440, have proceeded against a Maid of the English.

The magistrates who had returned to their Paris homes from their long dreary exile at Poitiers sat in the Parlement side by side with the converted Burgundians.[1077] In the days of adversity these faithful servants of King Charles had set the Maid to work, but now in 1440 it was none of their business to maintain publicly the truth of her mission and the purity of her faith. Burned by the English, that was all very well. But a trial conducted by a bishop and a vice-inquisitor with the concurrence of the University is not an English trial; it is a trial at once essentially Gallican and essentially Catholic. Jeanne's name was forever branded throughout Christendom. That ecclesiastical sentence could be reversed by the Pope alone. But the Pope had no intention of doing this. He was too much afraid of displeasing the King of Catholic England; and moreover were he once to admit that an inquisitor of the faith had pronounced a wrong sentence he would undermine all human authority. The French clerks submit and are silent. In the assemblies of the clergy no one dares to utter Jeanne's name.

Fortunately for them neither the doctors and masters of the University nor the sometime members of the Parlement of Poitiers share the popular delusion touching la Dame des Armoises. They have no doubt that the Maid was burned at Rouen. And they fear lest this woman, who gives herself out to be the deliverer of Orléans, may arouse a tumult by her entrance into the city. Wherefore the Parlement and the University send out men-at-arms to meet her. She is arrested and brought to the Palais.[1078]

She was examined, tried and sentenced to be publicly exhibited. In the Palais de Justice, leading up from the court called the Cour-de-Mai, there was a marble slab on which malefactors were exhibited. La Dame des Armoises was put up there and shown to the people whom she had deceived. The usual sermon was preached at her and she was forced to confess publicly.[1079]

She declared that she was not the Maid, that she was married to a knight and had two sons. She told how one day, in her mother's presence, she heard a woman speak slightingly of her; whereupon she proceeded to attack the slanderer, and, when her mother restrained her, she turned her blows against her parent. Had she not been in a passion she would never have struck her mother. Notwithstanding this provocation, here was a special case and one reserved for the papal jurisdiction. Whosoever had raised his hand against his father or his mother, as likewise against a priest or a clerk, must go and ask forgiveness of the Holy Father, to whom alone belonged the power of convicting or acquitting the sinner. This was what she had done. "I went to Rome," she said, "attired in man's apparel. I engaged as a soldier in the war of the Holy Father Eugenius, and in this war I twice committed homicide."

When had she journeyed to Rome? Probably before the exile of Pope Eugenius to Florence, about the year 1433, when the condottieri of the Duke of Milan were advancing to the gates of the Eternal City.[1080]

We do not find either the University, or the Ordinary, or the Grand Inquisitor demanding the trial of this woman, who was suspected of witchcraft and of homicide, and who was attired in unseemly garments. She was not prosecuted as a heretic, doubtless because she was not obstinate, and obstinacy alone constitutes heresy.

Henceforth she attracted no further attention. It is believed, but on no very trustworthy evidence, that she ended by returning to Metz, to her husband, le Chevalier des Armoises, and that she lived quietly and respectably to a good old age, dwelling in the house over the door of

649

which were her armorial bearings, or rather those of Jeanne the Maid, the sword, the crown and the Lilies.[1081]

The success of this fraud had endured four years. After all it is not so very surprising. In every age people have been loath to believe in the final end of existences which have touched their imagination; they will not admit that great personalities can be struck down by death like ordinary folk; such an end to a noble career is repugnant to them. Impostors, like la Dame des Armoises, never fail to find some who will believe in them. And the Dame appeared at a time which was singularly favourable to such a delusion; intellects had been dulled by long suffering; communication between one district and another was rendered impossible or difficult, and what was happening in one place was unknown quite near at hand; in the minds of men there reigned dimness, ignorance, confusion.

But even then folk would not have been imposed upon so long by this pseudo-Jeanne had it not been for the support given her by the Du Lys brothers. Were they her dupes or her accomplices? Dull-witted as they may have been, it seems hardly credible that the adventuress could have imposed upon them. Admitting that she very closely resembled La Romée's daughter, the woman from La Grange-aux-Ormes cannot possibly for any length of time have deceived two men who knew Jeanne intimately, having been brought up with her and come with her into France.

If they were not imposed upon, then how can we account for their conduct? They had lost much when they lost their sister. When he arrived at La Grange-aux-Ormes, Pierre du Lys had just quitted a Burgundian prison; his ransom had been paid with his wife's dowry, and he was then absolutely destitute.[1082] Jean, Bailie of Vermandois, afterwards Governor of Chartres and about 1436 Bailie of Vaucouleurs, was hardly more prosperous.[1083] Such circumstances explained much. And yet it is unlikely that they of themselves alone and unsupported would have played a game so difficult, so risky, and so dangerous. From the little we know of their lives we should conclude that they were both too simple, too naïf, too placid, to carry on such an intrigue.

We are tempted to believe that they were urged on by some higher and greater power. Who knows? Perhaps by certain indiscreet persons in the service of the King of France. The condemnation and death of Jeanne was a serious attack upon the prestige of Charles VII. May he not have had in his household or among his counsellors certain subjects who were rashly jealous enough to invent this appearance, in order to spread abroad the belief that Jeanne the Maid had not died the death of a witch, but that by virtue of her innocence and her holiness she had escaped the flames? If this were so, then we may regard the imposture of the pseudo-Jeanne, invented at a time when it seemed impossible ever to obtain a papal revision of the trial of 1431, as an attempt, surreptitious and fraudulent and speedily abandoned, to bring about her rehabilitation.

Such a hypothesis would explain why the Du Lys brothers were not punished or even disgraced, when they had put themselves in the wrong, had deceived King and people and committed the crime of high treason. Jean continued provost of Vaucouleurs for many a long year, and then, when relieved of his office, received a sum of money in lieu of it. Pierre, as well as his mother, La Romée, was living at Orléans. In 1443 he received from Duke Charles, who had returned to France three years before, the grant of an island in the Loire, l'Île-aux-Bœufs,[1084] which was fair grazing land. Nevertheless, he remained poor, and was constantly receiving help from the Duke and the townsfolk of Orléans.[1085]

CHAPTER XVI

AFTER THE DEATH OF THE MAID (CONTINUED) – THE ROUEN JUDGES AT THE COUNCIL OF BÂLE AND THE PRAGMATIC SANCTION – THE REHABILITATION TRIAL – THE MAID OF SARMAIZE – THE MAID OF LE MANS

ROM year to year the Council of Bâle drew out its deliberations in a series of sessions well nigh as lengthy as the tail of the dragon in the Apocalypse. Its manner of reforming at once the Church, its members, and its head struck terror into the hearts of the sovereign Pontiff and the Sacred College. Sorrowfully did Æneus Sylvius exclaim, "There is assembled at Bâle, not the Church of God indeed, but the synagogue of Satan."[1086] But though uttered by a Roman cardinal, even such an expression can hardly be termed violent when applied to the synod which established free elections to bishoprics, suppressed the right of bestowing the pallium, of exacting annates and payments to the papal chancery, and which was endeavouring to restore the papacy to evangelical poverty. The King of France and the Emperor, on the other hand, looked favourably on the Council when it essayed to bridle the ambition and greed of the Bishop of Rome.

Now among the Fathers who displayed the greatest zeal in the reformation of the Church were the masters and doctors of the University of Paris, those who had sat in judgment on Jeanne the Maid, and notably Maître Nicolas Loiseleur and Maître Thomas de Courcelles. Charles VII convoked an assembly of the clergy of the realm in order to examine the canons of Bâle. The assembly met in the Sainte-Chapelle at Bourges, on the 1st of May, 1438. Master Thomas de Courcelles, appointed delegate by the Council, there conferred with the Lord Bishop of Castres. Now in 1438 the Bishop of Castres was that elegant humanist, that zealous counsellor of the crown, who, in style truly Ciceronian, complained in his letters that so closely was he bound to his glebe, the court, that no time remained to him to visit his spouse.[1087] He was none other than that Gérard Machet, the King's confessor, who had, in 1429, along with the clerks at Poitiers, pleaded the authority of prophecy in favour of the Maid, in whom he found nought but sincerity and goodness.[1088] Maître Thomas de Courcelles at Rouen had urged the Maid's being tortured and delivered to the secular arm.[1089] At the Bourges assembly the two churchmen agreed touching the supremacy of General Councils, the freedom of episcopal elections, the suppression of annates and the rights of the Gallican Church. At that moment it was not likely that either one or the other remembered the poor Maid. From the deliberations of this assembly, in which Maître Thomas played an important part, there issued the solemn edict promulgated by the King on the 7th of July, 1438; the Pragmatic Sanction. By this edict the canons of Bâle became the constitution of the Church of France.[1090]

The Emperor also agreed to the reforms of Bâle. So audacious did the Fathers become that they summoned Pope Eugenius to appear before their tribunal. When he refused to obey their summons, they deposed him, declaring him to be disobedient, obstinate, rebellious, a breaker of rules, a perturber of ecclesiastical unity, a perjurer, a schismatic, a hardened heretic, a squanderer of the treasures of the Church, scandalous, simoniacal, pernicious and damnable.[1091] Such was the condemnation of the Holy Fathers pronounced among other doctors by Maître Jean Beaupère, Maître Thomas de Courcelles and Maître Nicolas Loiseleur, who had all three so sternly reproached Jeanne with having refused to submit to the Pope.[1092] Maître Nicolas had been extremely energetic throughout the Maid's trial, playing alternately the parts of the Lorraine prisoner and Saint Catherine; when she was led to the stake he had run after her like a madman.[1093] This same Maître Nicolas now displayed great activity in the Council wherein he attained to some eminence. He upheld the view that the General Council canonically convoked, was superior to the Pope and in a position to depose him. And albeit this canon was a mere master of arts, he made such an impression on the Fathers at Bâle that in 1439, they despatched him to act as juris-consult at the Diet of Mainz. Meanwhile his attitude was strongly displeasing to the chapter which had sent him as deputy to the Council. The canons of Rouen sided with the Sovereign Pontiff and against the Fathers, on this point joining issue with the University of Paris. They disowned their delegate and sent to recall him on the 28th of July, 1438.[1094]

Maître Thomas de Courcelles, one of those who had declared the Pope disobedient, obstinate, rebellious and the rest, was nominated one of the commissioners to preside over the election of a new pope, and, like Loiseleur, a delegate to the Diet of Mainz. But, unlike Loiseleur, he was not disowned by those who had appointed him, for he was the deputy of the University of Paris who recognised the Pope of the Council, Felix, to be the true Father of the Faithful.[1095] In the assembly of the French clergy held at Bourges in the August of 1440, Maître Thomas spoke in the name of the Fathers of Bâle. He discoursed for two hours to the complete satisfaction of the King.[1096] Charles VII, while remaining loyal to Pope Eugenius, maintained the Pragmatic Sanction. Maître Thomas de Courcelles was henceforth one of the pillars of the French Church.

Meanwhile the English government had declared for the Pope and against the Council.[1097] My Lord Pierre Cauchon, who had become Bishop of Lisieux, was Henry VI's ambassador at the Council. And at Bâle a somewhat unpleasant experience befell him. By reason of his translation to the see of Lisieux he owed Rome annates to the amount of 400 golden florins. In Germany he was informed by the Pope's Treasurer that by his failure to pay this sum, despite the long delays granted to him, he had incurred excommunication, and that being excommunicate, by presuming to celebrate divine service he had committed irregularity.[1098] Such accusations must have caused him considerable annoyance. But after all, such occurrences were frequent and of no great consequence. On churchmen these thunderbolts fell but lightly, doing them no great hurt.

From 1444, the realm of France, disembarrassed alike of adversaries and of defenders, was free to labour, to work at various trades, to engage in commerce and to grow rich. In the intervals between wars and during truces, King Charles's government, by the interchange of natural products and of merchandise, also, we may add, by the abolition of tolls and dues on the Rivers Seine, Oise, and Loire, effected the actual conquest of Normandy. Thus, when the time for nominal conquest came, the French had only to take possession of the province. So easy had this become, that in the rapid campaign of 1449,[1099] even the Constable was not beaten, neither was the Duke of Alençon. In his royal and peaceful manner Charles VII resumed possession of his town of Rouen, just as twenty years before he had taken Troyes and Reims, as the result of an understanding with the townsfolk and in return for an amnesty and the grant of rights and privileges to the burghers. He entered the city on Monday, the 10th of November, 1449.

The French government felt itself strong enough even to attempt the reconquest of that essentially English province, Aquitaine. In 1451, my Lord the Bastard, now Count of Dunois, took possession of the fortress of Blaye. Bordeaux and Bayonne surrendered in the same year. In the following manner did the Lord Bishop of Le Mans celebrate these conquests, worthy of the majesty of the most Christian King.

"Maine, Normandy, Aquitaine, these goodly provinces have returned to their allegiance to the King. Almost without the shedding of French blood hath this been accomplished. It hath not been necessary to overthrow the ramparts of many strongly walled towns, or to demolish their fortifications or for the inhabitants to suffer either pillage or murder."[1100]

Indeed Normandy and Maine were quite content at being French once more. The town of Bordeaux was alone in regretting the English, whose departure spelt its ruin. It revolted in 1452; and then after considerable difficulty was reconquered once and for all.

King Charles, henceforth rich and victorious, now desired to efface the stain inflicted on his reputation by the sentence of 1431. He wanted to prove to the whole world that it was no witch who had conducted him to his coronation. He was now eager to appeal against the condemnation of the Maid. But this condemnation had been pronounced by the church, and the Pope alone could order it to be cancelled. The King hoped to bring the Pope to do this, although he knew it would not be easy. In the March of 1450, he proceeded to a preliminary inquiry;[1101] and matters remained in that position until the arrival in France of Cardinal d'Estouteville, the legate of the Holy See. Pope Nicolas had sent him to negotiate with the King of France a peace with England and a crusade against the Turks. Cardinal d'Estouteville, who belonged to a Norman family, was just the man to discover the weak points in Jeanne's trial. In order to curry favour with Charles, he, as legate, set on foot a new inquiry at Rouen, with the assistance of Jean Bréhal, of the order of preaching friars, the Inquisitor of the Faith in the kingdom of France. But the Pope did not approve of the legate's intervention;[1102] and for three years the revision was not proceeded with. Nicolas V would not allow it to be thought that the sacred tribunal of the most holy Inquisition was fallible and had even once pronounced an unjust sentence. And there existed at Rome a stronger reason for not interfering with the trial of 1431: the French demanded revision; the English were opposed to it; and the Pope did not wish to annoy the English, for they were then just as good and even better Catholics than the French.[1103]

In order to relieve the Pope from embarrassment and set him at his ease, the government of Charles VII invented an expedient: the King was not to appear in the suit; his place was to be taken by the family of the Maid. Jeanne's mother, Isabelle Romée de Vouthon, who lived in retirement at Orléans,[1104] and her two sons, Pierre and Jean du Lys, demanded the revision.[1105] By this legal artifice the case was converted from a political into a private suit. At this juncture Nicolas V died, on the 24th of March, 1455. His successor, Calixtus III, a Borgia, an old man of seventy-eight, by a rescript dated the 11th of June, 1455, authorised the institution of proceedings. To this end he appointed Jean Jouvenel des Ursins, Archbishop of Reims, Guillaume Chartier, Bishop of Paris, and Richard Olivier, Bishop of Coutances, who were to act conjointly with the Grand Inquisitor of France.[1106]

From the first it was agreed that certain of those concerned in the original trial were not now to be involved, "for they had been deceived." Notably it was admitted that the Daughter of Kings, the Mother of Learning, the University of Paris, had been led into error by a fraudulent indictment consisting of twelve articles. It was agreed that the whole responsibility should be thrown on to the Bishop of Beauvais and the Promoter, Guillaume d'Estivet, who were both deceased. The precaution was necessary. Had it not been taken, certain doctors very influential with the King and very dear to the Church of France would have been greatly embarrassed.

On the 7th of November, 1455, Isabelle Romée and her two sons, followed by a long procession of innumerable ecclesiastics, laymen, and worthy women, approached the church of Notre Dame in Paris to demand justice from the prelates and papal commissioners.[1107]

Informers and accusers in the trial of the late Jeanne were summoned to appear at Rouen on the 12th of December. Not one came.[1108] The heirs of the late Messire Pierre Cauchon declined all liability for the deeds of their deceased kinsman, and touching the civil responsibility, they pleaded the amnesty granted by the King on the reconquest of Normandy.[1109] As had been expected, the proceedings went forward without any obstacle or even any discussion.

Inquiries were instituted at Domremy, at Orléans, at Paris, at Rouen.[1110] The friends of Jeannette's childhood, Hauviette, Mengette, either married or grown old; Jeannette, the wife of Thévenin; Jeannette, the widow of Estellin; Jean Morel of Greux; Gérardin of Épinal, the Burgundian, and his wife Isabellette, who had been godmother to Jacques d'Arc's daughter; Perrin, the bell-ringer; Jeanne's uncle Lassois; the Leroyer couple and a score of peasants from Domremy all appeared. Bertrand de Poulengy, then sixty-three and gentleman of the horse to the King of France, was heard; likewise Jean de Novelompont, called Jean de Metz, who had been raised to noble rank and was now living at Vaucouleurs, where he held some military office. Gentlemen and ecclesiastics of Lorraine and Champagne were examined.[1111] Burgesses of Orléans were also called, and notably Jean Luillier, the draper, who in June, 1429, had furnished fine Brussels cloth of purple for Jeanne's gown and ten years later had been present at the banquet given by the magistrates of Orléans in honour of the Maid who, as it was believed, had escaped burning.[1112] Jean Luillier was the most intelligent of the witnesses; as for the others, of whom there were about two dozen townsmen and townswomen, of between fifty and sixty years of age, they did little but repeat his evidence.[1113] He spoke well; but the fear of the English dazzled him and he saw many more of them than there had ever been.

Touching the examination at Poitiers there were called an advocate, a squire, a man of business, François Garivel, who was fifteen at the time of Jeanne's interrogation.[1114] The only cleric summoned was Brother Seguin of Limousin.[1115] The clerics of Poitiers were first as disinclined to risk themselves in this matter as were those of Rouen; a burnt child dreads the fire. La Hire and Poton of Saintrailles were dead. The survivors of Orléans and of Patay were called; the Bastard Jean, now Count of Dunois and Longueville, who gave his evidence like a clerk;[1116] the old Sire de Gaucourt, who in his eighty-fifth year made some effort of memory, and for the rest gave the same evidence as the Count of Dunois;[1117] the Duke of Alençon, on the point of making an alliance with the English and of procuring a powder with which to dry up the King,[1118] but who was none the less talkative and vain-glorious;[1119] Jeanne's steward, Messire Jean d'Aulon, who had become a knight, a King's Counsellor and

Seneschal of Beaucaire,[1120] and the little page Louis de Coutes, now a noble of forty-two.[1121] Brother Pasquerel too was called; even in his old-age he remained superficial and credulous.[1122] And there was heard also the widow of Maître René de Bouligny, Demoiselle Marguerite la Toroulde, who delicately and with a good grace related what she remembered.[1123]

Care was taken not to summon the Lord Archbishop of Rouen, Messire Raoul Roussel, as a witness of the actual incidents of the trial, albeit he had sat in judgment on the Maid, side by side with my Lord of Beauvais. As for the Vice Inquisitor of Religion, Brother Jean Lemaistre, he might have been dead, so completely was he ignored. Nevertheless, certain of the assessors were called: Jean Beaupère, canon of Paris, of Besançon and of Rouen; Jean de Mailly, Lord Bishop of Noyon; Jean Lefèvre, Bishop of Démétriade; divers canons of Rouen, sundry ecclesiastics who appeared some unctuous, others stern and frowning;[1124] and, finally, the most illustrious Thomas de Courcelles, who, after having been the most laborious and assiduous collaborator of the Bishop of Beauvais, recalled nothing when he came before the commissioners for the revision.[1125]

Among those who had been most zealous to procure Jeanne's condemnation were those who were now most eagerly labouring for her rehabilitation. The registrars of the Lord Bishop of Beauvais, the Boisguillaumes, the Manchons, the Taquels, all those ink-pots of the Church who had been used for her death sentence, worked wonders when that sentence had to be annulled; all the zeal they had displayed in the institution of the trial they now displayed in its revision; they were prepared to discover in it every possible flaw.[1126]

And in what a poor and paltry tone did these benign fabricators of legal artifices denounce the cruel iniquity which they had themselves perpetrated in due form! Among them was the Usher, Jean Massieu, a dissolute priest,[1127] of scandalous morals, but a kindly fellow for all that, albeit somewhat crafty and the inventor of a thousand ridiculous stories against Cauchon, as if the old Bishop were not black enough already.[1128] The revision commissioners produced a couple of sorry monks, Friar Martin Ladvenu and Friar Isambart de la Pierre, from the monastery of the preaching friars at Rouen. They wept in a heart-rending manner as they told of the pious end of that poor Maid, whom they had declared a heretic, then a relapsed heretic, and had finally burned alive. There was not one of the clerks charged with the examination of Jeanne but was touched to the heart at the memory of so saintly a damsel.[1129]

Huge piles of memoranda drawn up by doctors of high repute, canonists, theologians and jurists, both French and foreign, were furnished for the trial. Their chief object was to establish by scholastic reasoning that Jeanne had submitted her deeds and sayings to the judgment of the Church and of the Holy Father. These doctors proved that the judges of 1431 had been very subtle and Jeanne very simple. Doubtless, it was the best way to make out that she had submitted to the Church; but they over-reached themselves and made her too simple. According to them she was absolutely ignorant, almost an idiot, understanding nothing, imagining that the clerics who examined her in themselves alone constituted the Church Militant. This had been the impression of the doctors on the French side in 1429. *La Pucelle,* *"une puce,"* said the Lord Archbishop of Embrun.[1130]

Declarations confirming this view of the Maid were obtained by the commissioners from most of the witnesses. She was simple, she was very simple, she was absolutely simple, they repeated one after the other. And they all in the same words added: "Yes, she was simple, save in deeds of war, wherein she was well skilled."[1131] Then the captains said how clever she was in placing cannon, albeit they knew well to the contrary. But how could she have failed to be well versed in deeds of war, since God himself led her against the English? And in this possession of the art of war by an unskilled girl lay the miracle.

The Grand Inquisitor of France, Jean Bréhal, in his reminiscence enumerates the reasons for believing that Jeanne came from God. One of the proofs which seems to have struck him most forcibly is that her coming is foretold in the prophecies of Merlin, the Magician.[1132]

But there was another reason for making her appear as weak and imbecile as possible. Such a representation exalted the power of God, who through her had restored the King of France to his inheritance.

Believing that he could prove from one of Jeanne's answers that her first apparitions were in her thirteenth year, Brother Jean Bréhal argues that the fact is all the more credible seeing that this number 13, composed of 3, which indicates the Blessed Trinity, and of 10, which expresses the perfect observation of the Decalogue, is marvellously favourable to divine visitations.[1133]

On the 16th of June, 1455, the sentence of 1431 was declared unjust, unfounded, iniquitous. It was nullified and pronounced invalid.

The Bastard of Orleans
(from an old engraving)

Thus was honour restored to the messenger of the coronation, thus was her memory reconciled with the Church. But that abundant source whence on the appearance of this child there had flowed so many pious legends and heroic fables was henceforth dried up. The rehabilitation trial added little to the popular legend. It rendered it possible to connect with Jeanne's death the usual incidents narrated of the martyrdom of virgins, such as the dove taking flight from the stake, the name of Jesus written in letters of flame, the heart intact in the ashes.[1134] The miserable deaths of the wicked judges were insisted upon. True it is that Jean d'Estivet, the Promoter, was found dead in a dove-cot,[1135] that Nicolas Midi was attacked by leprosy, that Pierre Cauchon died when he was being shaved.[1136] But, among those who aided and accompanied the Maid, more than one came to a bad end. Sire Robert de Baudricourt, who had sent Jeanne to the King, died in prison, excommunicated for having laid waste the lands of the chapter of Toul.[1137] The Maréchal de Rais was sentenced to death.[1138] The Duke of Alençon, convicted of high treason, was pardoned only to fall under a new condemnation and to die in captivity.[1139]

Two years after Charles VII had ordered the preliminary inquiry into the trial of 1431, a woman, following the example of la Dame des Armoises, passed herself off as the Maid Jeanne.

At this time there lived in the little town of Sarmaize, between the Marne and the Meuse, two cousins german of the Maid, Poiresson and Périnet, both sons of the late Jean de Vouthon, Isabelle Romée's brother, who in his lifetime had been a thatcher by trade. Now, on a day in 1452, it befell that the curé of Notre Dame de Sarmaize, Simon Fauchard, being in the market-house of the town, there came to him a woman dressed as a youth who asked him to play at tennis with her.

He consented, and when they had begun their game the woman said to him, "Say boldly that you have played tennis with the Maid." And at these words Simon Fauchard was right joyful.

The woman afterwards went to the house of Périnet, the carpenter, and said, "I am the Maid; I come to visit my Cousin Henri."

Périnet, Poiresson, and Henri de Vouthon made her good cheer and kept her in their house, where she ate and drank as she pleased.[1140]

Then, when she had had enough, she went away.

Whence came she? No one knows. Whither did she go? She may probably be recognised in an adventuress, who not long afterwards, with her hair cut short and a hood on her head, wearing doublet and hose, wandered through Anjou, calling herself Jeanne the Maid. While the doctors and masters, engaged in the revision of the trial, were gathering evidence of Jeanne's life and death from all parts of the kingdom, this false Jeanne was finding credence with many folk. But she became involved in difficulties with a certain Dame of

Saumoussay,[1141] and was cast into the prison of Saumur, where she lay for three months. At the end of this time, having been banished from the dominions of the good King René, she married one Jean Douillet; and, by a document dated the 3rd day of February, 1456, she received permission to return to Saumur, on condition of living there respectably and ceasing to wear man's apparel.[1142]

About this time there came to Laval in the diocese of Le Mans, a damsel between eighteen and twenty-two, who was a native of a neighbouring place called Chassé-les-Usson. Her father's name was Jean Féron and she was commonly called Jeanne la Férone.

She was inspired from heaven, and the names Jesus and Mary were for ever on her lips; yet the devil cruelly tormented her. The Dame de Laval, mother of the Lords André and Guy, being now very aged, marvelled at the piety and the sufferings of the holy damsel; and she sent her to Le Mans, to the Bishop.

Since 1449, the see of Le Mans had been held by Messire Martin Berruyer of Touraine. In his youth he had been professor of philosophy and rhetoric at the University of Paris. Later he had devoted himself to theology and had become one of the directors of the College of Navarre. Although he was infirm with age, his learning was such that he was consulted by the commissioners for the rehabilitation trial,[1143] whereupon he drew up a memorandum touching the Maid. Herein he believes her to have been verily sent of God because she was abject and very poor and appeared well nigh imbecile in everything that did not concern her mission. Messire Martin argues that it was by reason of the King's virtues that God had vouchsafed to him the help of the Maid.[1144] Such an idea found favour with the theologians of the French party.

The Lord Bishop, Martin Berruyer, heard Jeanne la Férone in confession, renewed her baptism, confirmed her in the faith and gave her the name of Marie, in gratitude for the abounding grace which the most Holy Virgin, Mother of God, had granted to his servant.

This maid was subject to the violent attacks of evil spirits. Many a time did my Lord of Mans behold her covered with bleeding wounds, struggling in the grasp of the enemy, and on several occasions he delivered her by means of exorcisms. Greatly was he edified by this holy damsel, who made known unto him marvellous secrets, who abounded in pious revelations and noble Christian utterances.

Wherefore in praise of La Férone he wrote many letters[1145] to princes and communities of the realm.

The Queen of France, who was then very old and whose husband had long ago deserted her, heard tell of the Maid of Le Mans, and wrote to Messire Martin Berruyer, requesting him to make the damsel known unto her.

Thus there befel, what we have seen happening over and over again in this history, that when a devout person, leading a contemplative life uttered prophecies, those in places of authority grew curious concerning her and desired to submit her to the judgment of the Church that they might know whether the goodness that appeared in her were true or false. Certain officers of the King visited La Férone at Le Mans.

As revelations touching the realm of France had been vouchsafed to her, she spoke to them the following words:

"Commend me very humbly to the King and bid him recognise the grace which God granteth unto him, and lighten the burdens of his people."

In the December of 1460, she was summoned before the Royal Council, which was then sitting at Tours, while the King, who was sick of an ulcer in the leg, was residing in the Château of Les Montils.[1146] The Maid of Le Mans was examined in like manner as the Maid Jeanne had been, but the result was unfavourable; she was found wanting in everything. Brought before the ecclesiastical court she was convicted of imposture. It appeared that she was no maid, but was living in concubinage with a cleric, that certain persons in the service of my Lord of Le Mans instructed her in what she was to say, and that such was the origin of the revelations she made to the Reverend Father in God, Messire Martin Berruyer, under the seal of the confession. Convicted of being a hypocrite, an idolatress, an invoker of demons, a witch, a magician, lascivious, dissolute, an enchantress, a mine of falsehood, she was condemned to have a fool's cap put on her head and to be preached at in public, in the towns of Le Mans, Tours and Laval. On the 2nd of May, 1461, she was exhibited to the folk at Tours, wearing a paper cap and over her head a scroll on which her deeds were set forth in lines of Latin and of French. Maître Guillaume de Châteaufort, Grand Master of the Royal College of Navarre, preached to her. Then she was cast into close confinement in a prison, there to weep over her sins for the space of seven years, eating the bread of sorrow and drinking the water of affliction;[1147] at the end of which time she rented a house of ill fame.[1148]

On Wednesday, the 22nd of July, 1461, covered with ulcers internal and external, believing himself poisoned and perhaps not without reason, Charles VII died, in the fifty-ninth year of his age, in his Château of Mehun-sur-Yèvre.[1149]

On Thursday, the 6th of August, his body was borne to the Church of Saint-Denys in France and placed in a chapel hung with velvet; the nave was draped with black satin, the vault was covered with blue cloth embroidered with flowers-de-luce.[1150] During the ceremony, which took place on the following day, a funeral oration was delivered on Charles VII. The preacher was no less a personage than the most highly renowned professor at the University of Paris, the doctor, who according to the Princes of the Roman Church was ever aimable and modest, he who had been the stoutest defender of the liberties of the Gallican Church, the ecclesiastic who, having declined a Cardinal's hat, bore to the threshold of an illustrious old age none other title than that of Dean of the Canons of Notre Dame de Paris, Maître Thomas de Courcelles.[1151] Thus it befell that the assessor of Rouen, who had been the most bitterly bent on procuring Jeanne's cruel condemnation, celebrated the memory of the victorious King whom the Maid had conducted to his solemn coronation.

Appendices

APPENDIX I
LETTER FROM DOCTOR G. DUMAS

MY DEAR MASTER, – You ask for my medical opinion in the case of Jeanne d'Arc. Had I been able to examine it at my leisure with the Doctors Tiphaine and Delachambre, who were summoned before the tribunal at Rouen, I might have found it difficult to come to any definite conclusion. And even more difficult do I find it now, when my diagnosis must necessarily be retrospective and based upon examinations conducted by persons who never dreamed of attempting to discover the existence of any nervous disease. However since they ascribed what we now call disease to the influence of the devil, their questions are not without significance for us. Therefore with many reservations I will endeavour to answer your question.

Of Jeanne's inherited constitution we know nothing; and of her personal antecedents we are almost entirely ignorant. Our only information concerning such matters comes from Jean d'Aulon, who, on the evidence of several women, states[1152] that she was never fully developed, a condition which frequently occurs in neurotic subjects.

We should, however, be unable to arrive at any conclusion concerning Jeanne's nervous constitution had not her judges, and in particular Maître Jean Beaupère, in the numerous examinations to which they subjected her, elicited certain significant details on the subject of her hallucinations.

Maître Beaupère begins by inquiring very judiciously whether Jeanne had fasted the day before she first heard her voices. Whence we infer that the interdependence of inanition and hallucinations was recognised by this illustrious professor of theology. Before condemning Jeanne as a witch he wanted to make sure that she was not merely suffering from weakness. Some time later we find Saint Theresa suspecting that the visions said to have been seen by a certain nun were merely the result of long fasting. Saint Theresa insisted on the nun's partaking of food, and the visions ceased.

Jeanne replies that she had only fasted since the morning, and Maître Beaupère proceeds to ask:

Q. "In what direction did you hear the voice?"

A. "I heard it on the right, towards the church."

Q. "Was the voice accompanied by any light?"

A. "I seldom heard it without there being a light. This light appeared in the direction whence the voice came."[1153]

We might wonder whether by the expression "*à droite*" (*a latere dextro*) Jeanne meant her own right side or the position of the church in relation to her; and in the latter case, the information would have no clinical significance; but the context leaves no doubt as to the veritable meaning of her words.

"How can you," urges Jean Beaupère, "see this light which you say appears to you, if it is on your right?"

If it had been merely a question of the situation of the church and not of Jeanne's own right side, she would only have had to turn her face to see the light in front of her, and Jean Beaupère's objection would have been pointless.

Consequently at about the age of thirteen, at the period of puberty, which for her never came, Jeanne would appear to have been subject on her right side to unilateral hallucinations of sight and hearing. Now Charcot[1154] considered unilateral hallucinations of sight to be common in cases of hysteria.[1155] He even thought that in hysterical subjects they are allied to a hemianæsthesia situated on the same side of the body, and which in Jeanne would be on the right side. Jeanne's trial might have proved the existence of this hemianæsthesia, an extremely significant symptom in the diagnosis of hysteria, if the judges had applied torture or merely had examined the skin of the subject in order to discover anæsthesia patches which were called marks of the devil.[1156] But from the merely oral examination which took place we can only draw inferences concerning Jeanne's general physical condition. In case excessive importance should be attached to such inferences I should add that in the diagnosis of hysteria contemporary neurologists pay less attention than did Charcot to unilateral hallucinations of sight.

The other characteristics of Jeanne's hallucinations revealed by her examinations during the trial are no less interesting than these, although they do not lead to any more certain conclusions.

Those visions and voices, which the subject refers to an external source and which are so characteristic of hysterical hallucinations, proceed suddenly from the subconscious self. Jeanne's conscious self was so far from being prepared for her voices that she declares she was very much afraid when she first heard them: "I was thirteen when I heard a voice coming from God telling me to lead a good life. And the first time I was very much afraid. This voice came to me about noon; it was in the summer, in my father's garden."[1157]

And then straightway the voice becomes imperative. It demands an obedience which is not refused: "It said to me: 'Go forth into France,' and I could no longer stay where I was."[1158]

Her visions all occur in the same manner. They appeal to the senses in exactly the same way and are received by the Maid with equal credulity.

Finally, these hallucinations of hearing and of sight are soon associated with similar hallucinations of smell and touch, which serve to confirm Jeanne's belief in their reality.

Q. "Which part of Saint Catherine did you touch?"

A. "You will hear nothing more."

Q. "Did you kiss or embrace Saint Catherine or Saint Margaret?"

A. "I embraced them both."

Q. "In embracing them did you feel heat or anything?"

A. "I could not embrace them without feeling and touching them."[1159]

Because they thus appeal to the senses and seem to possess a certain material reality, hysterical hallucinations make a profound and ineffaceable impression on those who experience them. The subjects speak of them as being actual and very striking facts. When they become accusers, as so many women do who claim to have been the victims of imaginary assaults, they support their assertions in the most energetic fashion.

Not only does Jeanne see, hear, smell and touch her saints, she joins the procession of angels they bring in their train. With them she performs actual deeds, as if there were perfect unity between her life and her hallucinations.

"I was in my lodging, in the house of a good woman, near the *château* of Chinon, when the angel came. And then he and I went together to the King."

Q. "Was this angel alone?"

A. "This angel was with a goodly company of other angels.[1160] They were with him, but not every one saw them.... Some were very much alike; others were not, or at any rate not as I saw them. Some had wings. Certain even wore crowns, and in their company were Saint Catherine and Saint Margaret. With the angel aforesaid and with the other angels they went right into the King's chamber."

Q. "Tell us how the angel left you."

A. "He left me in a little chapel, and at his departure I was very sorrowful, and I even wept. Willingly would I have gone away with him; I mean my soul would have gone."[1161]

In all these hallucinations there is the same objective clearness, the same subjective certitude as in toxic hallucinations; and this clearness, this certitude, may in Jeanne's case suggest hysteria.

But if in certain respects Jeanne resembles hysterical subjects, in others she differs from them. She seems early to have acquired an independence of her visions and an authority over them.

Without ever doubting their reality, she resists them and sometimes disobeys them, when, for example, in defiance of Saint Catherine, she leaps from her prison of Beaurevoir: "Well nigh every day Saint Catherine told me not to leap and that God would come to my aid, and also would succour those of Compiègne. And I said to Saint Catherine: 'Since God is to help those of Compiègne, I want to be with them.'"[1162]

On another occasion she assumes such authority over her visions that she can make the two saints come at her bidding when they do not come of themselves.

Q. "Do you call these saints, or do they come without being called?"

A. "They often come without being called, and sometimes when they did not come I asked God to send them speedily."[1163]

All this is not in the accepted manner of the hysterical, who are usually somewhat passive with regard to their nervous fits and hallucinations. But Jeanne's dominance over her visions is a characteristic I have noted in many of the higher mystics and in those who have attained notoriety. This kind of subject, after having at first passively submitted to his hysteria, afterwards uses it rather than submits to it, and finally by means of it attains in his ecstasy to that divine union after which he strives.

If Jeanne were hysterical, such a characteristic would help us to determine the part played by the neurotic side of her nature in the development of her character and in her life.

If there were any hysterical strain in her nature, then it was by means of this hysterical strain that the most secret sentiments of her heart took shape in the form of visions and celestial voices. Her hysteria became the open door by which the divine – or what Jeanne deemed the divine – entered into her life. It strengthened her faith and consecrated her mission; but in her intellect and in her will Jeanne remains healthy and normal. Nervous pathology can therefore cast but a feeble light on Jeanne's nature. It can reveal only one part of that spirit which your book resuscitates in its entirety. With the expression of my respectful admiration, believe me, my dear master,

Doctor G. Dumas.

APPENDIX II
THE FARRIER OF SALON

OWARDS the end of the seventeenth century, there lived at Salon-en-Crau, near Aix, a farrier, one François Michel. He came of a respectable family. He himself had served in the cavalry regiment of the Chevalier de Grignan. He was held to be a sensible man, honest and devout. He was close on forty when, in February, 1697, he had a vision.

Returning to his home one evening, he beheld a spectre, holding a torch in its hand. This spectre said to him:

"Fear nothing. Go to Paris and speak to the King. If thou dost not obey this command thou shalt die. When thou shalt approach to within a league of Versailles, I will not fail to make known unto thee what things thou shalt say to his Majesty. Go to the Governor of thy province, who will order all that is necessary for thy journey."

The figure which thus addressed him was in the form of a woman. She wore a royal crown and a mantle embroidered with flowers-de-luce of gold, like the late Queen, Marie-Thérèse, who had died a holy death full fourteen years before.

The poor farrier was greatly afraid. He fell down at the foot of a tree, knowing not whether he dreamed or was awake. Then he went back to his house, and told no man of what he had seen.

Two days afterwards he passed the same spot. There again he beheld the same spectre, who repeated the same orders and the same threats. The farrier could no longer doubt the reality of what he saw; but as yet he could not make up his mind what to do.

A third apparition, more imperious and more importunate than the first, reduced him to obedience. He went to Aix, to the Governor of the province; he saw him and told him how he had been given a mission to speak to the King. The Governor at first paid no great heed to him. But the visionary's patient persistence could not fail to impress him. Moreover, since the King was personally concerned in the matter, it ought not to be entirely neglected. These considerations led the Governor to inquire from the magistrates of Salon touching the farrier's family and manner of life. The result of these inquiries was very favourable. Accordingly the Governor deemed it fitting to proceed forthwith to action. In those days no one was quite sure whether advice, very useful to the most Christian of Kings, might not be sent by some member of the Church Triumphant through the medium of a common artisan. Still less were they sure that some plot in which the welfare of the State was concerned might not be hatched under colour of an apparition. In both contingencies, the second of which was quite probable, it would be advisable to send François Michel to Versailles. And this was the decision arrived at by the Governor.

For the transport of François Michel he adopted measures at once sure and inexpensive. He confided him to an officer who was taking recruits in that direction. After having received the communion in the church of the Franciscans, who were edified by his pious bearing, the farrier set out on February 25 with his Majesty's young soldiers, with whom he travelled as far as La Ferté-sous-Jouarre. On his arrival at Versailles, he asked to see the King or at least one of his Ministers of State. He was directed to M. de Barbezieux, who, when he was still very young, had succeeded his father, M. de Louvois, and in that position had displayed some talent. But the good farrier declined to tell him anything, because he was not a Minister of State.

And it was true that Barbezieux, although a Minister, was not a Minister of State. But that a farrier from Provence should be capable of drawing such a distinction occasioned considerable surprise.

M. de Barbezieux doubtless did not evince such scorn for this compatriot of Nostradamus as would have been shown in his place by a man of broader mind. For he, like his father, was addicted to the practice of astrology, and he was always inquiring concerning his horoscope of a certain Franciscan friar who had predicted the hour of his death.

We do not know whether he gave the King a favourable report of the farrier, or whether the latter was admitted to the presence of M. de

Pomponne, who was then at the head of the administration of Provence. But we do know that Louis XIV consented to see the man. He had him brought up the steps leading to the marble courtyard, and then granted him a lengthy audience in his private apartments.

On the morrow, as the King was coming down his private staircase on his way out hunting, he met Marshal de Duras, who was Captain of the King's bodyguard for the day. With his usual freedom of speech the Marshal spoke to the King of the farrier, using a common saying:

"Either the man is mad, or the King is not noble."

At these words the King, contrary to his usual habit, paused and turned to the Marshal de Duras:

"Then I am not noble," he said, "for I talked to him for a long time, and he spoke very sensibly; I assure you he is far from being mad."

The last words he uttered with so solemn a gravity that those who were present were astonished.

Persons who claim to be inspired are expected to show some sign of their mission. In a second interview, François Michel showed the King a sign in fulfilment of a promise he had given. He reminded him of an extraordinary circumstance which the son of Anne of Austria believed known to himself alone. Louis XIV himself admitted it, but for the rest preserved a profound silence touching this interview.

Saint Simon, always eager to collect every court rumour, believed it was a question of some phantom, which more than twenty years before had appeared to Louis XIV in the Forest of Saint-Germain.

For the third and last time the King received the farrier of Salon.

The courtiers displayed so much curiosity in this visionary that he had to be shut up in the monastery of Des Rècollets. There the little Princess of Savoy, who was shortly to marry the Duke of Burgundy, came to see him with several lords and ladies of the court.

He appeared slow to speak, good, simple, and humble. The King ordered him to be furnished with a fine horse, clothes, and money; then he sent him back to Provence.

Public opinion was divided on the subject of the apparition which had appeared to the farrier and the mission he had received from it. Most people believed that he had seen the spirit of Marie-Thérèse; but some said it was Nostradamus.[1164]

It was only at Salon, where he slept in the church of the Franciscans, that this astrologer was absolutely believed in. His "Centuries," which appeared at Paris and at Lyon in no less than ten editions in the course of one century, entertained the credulous throughout the kingdom. In 1693, there had just been published a book of the prophecies of Nostradamus showing how they had been fulfilled in history from the reign of Henry II down to that of Louis the Great.

It came to be believed that in the following mysterious quatrain the farrier's coming had been prophesied:

> *"Le penultiesme du surnom du Prophète,*
> *Prendra Diane pour son iour et repos:*
> *Loing vaguera par frénétique teste,*
> *En délivrant un grand peuple d'impos."*[1165]

An attempt was made to apply these obscure lines to the poor prophet of Salon. In the first line he is said to figure as one of the twelve minor prophets, Micah, which name is closely allied to Michel. In the second line Diane was said to be the mother of the farrier, who was certainly called by that name. But if the line means anything at all, it is more likely to refer to the day of the moon, Monday. It was carefully pointed out that in the third line *frénétique* means not *mad* but *inspired*. The fourth and only intelligible line would suggest that the spectre bade Michel ask the King to lessen the taxes and dues which then weighed so heavily on the good folk of town and country:

En délivrant un grand peuple d'impos. This was enough to make the farrier popular and to cause those unhappy sufferers to centre in this poor windbag their hopes for a better future. His portrait was engraved in copper-plate, and below it was written the quatrain of Nostradamus. M. d'Argenson,[1166] who was at the head of the police department, had these portraits seized. They were suppressed, so says the *Gazette d'Amsterdam*, on account of the last line of the quatrain written beneath the portrait, the line which runs: *En délivrant un grand peuple d'impos.* Such an expression was hardly likely to please the court.

No one ever knew exactly what was the mission the farrier received from his spectre. Subtle folk suspected one of Madame de Maintenon's intrigues. She had a friend at Marseille, a Madame Arnoul, who was as ugly as sin, it was said, and yet who managed to make men fall in love with her. They thought that this Madame Arnoul had shown Marie-Thérèse to the good man of Salon in order to induce the King to live honourably with widow Scarron. But in 1697 widow Scarron had been married to Louis for twelve years at least; and one cannot see why ghostly aid should have been necessary to attach the old King to her.

On his return to his native town, François Michel shoed horses as before.

He died at Lançon, near Salon, on December 10, 1726.[1167]

APPENDIX III
MARTIN DE GALLARDON

GNACE THOMAS MARTIN was by calling a husbandman. A native of Gallardon in Eure-et-Loir, he dwelt there with his wife and four children in the beginning of the nineteenth century. Those who knew him tell us that he was of average height, with brown straight hair, a calm glance, a thin countenance and an air of quiet and assurance. A pencil portrait, which his son, M. le Docteur Martin, has kindly sent me, gives a more exact idea of the visionary. The portrait, which is in profile, presents a forehead curiously high and straight, a long narrow head, round eyes, broad nostrils, a compressed mouth, a protruding chin, hollow cheeks and an air of austerity. He is dressed as a *bourgeois*, with a collar and white cravat.

According to the evidence of his brother, a man both physically and mentally sound, his was the gentlest of natures; he never sought to attract attention; in his regular piety there was nothing ecstatic. Both the mayor and the priest of Gallardon confirmed this description. They agreed in representing him to have been a good simple creature, with an intellect well-balanced although not very active.

In 1816 he was thirty-three. On January 15 in this year he was alone in his field, over which he was spreading manure, when in his ear he heard a voice which had not been preceded by footsteps. Then he turned his head in the direction of the voice and saw a figure which alarmed him. In comparison with human size it was but slight; its countenance, which was very thin, dazzled by its unnatural whiteness. It was wearing a high hat and a frock-coat of a light colour, with laced shoes.

It said in a kindly tone: "You must go to the King; you must warn him that his person is in danger, that wicked people are seeking to overthrow his Government."

It added further recommendations to Louis XVIII touching the necessity of having an efficient police, of keeping holy the Sabbath, of ordering public prayers and of suppressing the disorders of the Carnival. If such measures be neglected, it said, "France will fall into yet greater misfortunes." All this was doubtless nothing more or less than what M. La Perruque, Priest of Gallardon, had a hundred times repeated from the pulpit on Sunday.

Martin replied:

"Since you know so much about it, why don't you perform your errand yourself? Why do you appeal to a poor man like me who knows not how to express himself?"

Then the unknown replied to Martin:

"It is not I who will go, but you; do as I command you."

As soon as he had uttered these words, his feet rose from the ground, his body bent, and with this double movement he vanished.

From this time onwards, Martin was haunted by the mysterious being. One day, having gone down into his cellar, he found him there. On another occasion, during vespers, he saw him in church, near the holy water stoup, in a devout attitude. When the service was over, the unknown accompanied Martin on his way home and again commanded him to go and see the King. The farmer told his relatives who were with him, but neither of them had seen or heard anything.

Tormented by these apparitions, Martin communicated them to his priest, M. La Perruque. He, being certain of the good faith of his parishioner and deeming that the case ought to be submitted to the diocesan authority, sent the visionary to the Bishop of Versailles. The Bishop was then M. Louis Charrier de la Roche, a priest who in the days of the Revolution had taken the oath to the Republic. He resolved to subject Martin to a thorough examination; and from the first he told him to ask the unknown what was his name, and who it was who sent him.

But when the messenger in the light-coloured frock-coat appeared again, he declared that his name must remain unknown.

"I come," he added, "from him who has sent me, and he who has sent me is above me."

676

He may have wished to conceal his name; but at least he did not conceal his views; the vexation he displayed on the escape of La Valette[1168] proved that in politics he was an ultra Royalist of the most violent type.

Meanwhile the Comte de Bréteuil, Prefect of Eure-et-Loir, had been told of the visionary at the same time as the Bishop. He also questioned Martin. He expected to find him a nervous, agitated person; but when he found him tranquil, speaking simply, but with logical sequence and precision, he was very astonished.

Like M. l'Abbé La Perruque he deemed the matter sufficiently important to bring before the higher authorities. Accordingly he sent Martin, under the escort of a lieutenant of *gendarmerie*, to the Ministre de la Police Générale.

Having reached Paris on March 8, Martin lodged with the *gendarme* at the Hôtel de Calais, in the Rue Montmartre. They occupied a double-bedded room. One morning, when Martin was in bed, he beheld an apparition and told Lieutenant André, who could see nothing, although it was broad daylight. Indeed, Martin's visitations became so frequent that they ceased to cause him either surprise or concern. It was only to the abrupt disappearance of the unknown that he could never grow accustomed. The voice continued to give the same command. One day it told him that if it were not obeyed France would not know peace until 1840.

In 1816 the Ministre de la Police Générale was the Comte Decazes who was afterwards created a duke. He was in the King's confidence. But he knew that the extreme Royalists were hatching plots against his royal master. Decazes wished to see the good man from Gallardon, suspecting doubtless, that he was but a tool in the hands of the Extremists. Martin was brought to the Minister, who questioned him and at once perceived that the poor creature was in no way dangerous. He spoke to him as he would to a madman, endeavouring to regard the subject of his mania as if it were real, and so he said:

"Don't be agitated; the man who has been troubling you is arrested; you will have nothing more to fear from him."

But these words did not produce the desired effect. Three or four hours after this interview, Martin again beheld the unknown, who, after speaking to him in his usual manner, said: "When you were told that I had been arrested, you were told a lie; he who said so has no power over me."

On Sunday, March 10, the unknown returned; and on that day he disclosed the matter concerning which the Bishop of Versailles had inquired, and which he had said at first he would never reveal.

"I am," he declared, "the Archangel Raphaël, an angel of great renown in the presence of God, and I have received power to afflict France with all manner of suffering."

Three days later, Martin was shut up in Charenton on the certificate of Doctor Pinel, who stated him to be suffering from intermittent mania with alienation of mind.

He was treated in the kindest manner and was even permitted to enjoy some appearance of liberty. Pinel himself originated the humane treatment of the insane. Martin in the asylum was not forsaken by the blessed Raphaël. On Friday, the 15th, as the peasant was tying his shoe laces, the Archangel in his frock-coat of a light colour, spoke to him these words:

"Have faith in God. If France persists in her incredulity, the misfortunes I have predicted will happen. Moreover, if they doubt the truth of your visions, they have but to cause you to be examined by doctors in theology."

These words Martin repeated to M. Legros; Director of the Royal Institution of Charenton, and asked him what a doctor in theology was. He did not know the meaning of the term. In the same manner, when he was at Gallardon he had asked the priest, M. La Perruque, the meaning of certain expressions the voice had used. For example, he did not understand the wild frenzy of France [*le délvie de la France*] nor the evils to which she would fall a victim [*elle serait en proie*]. But there is nothing that need puzzle us in such ignorance, if it really existed. Martin may well have remembered the words he did not understand and which he afterwards attributed to his Archangel still without understanding them.

The visions recurred at brief intervals. On Sunday, March 31, the Archangel appeared to him in the garden, took his hand, which he pressed affectionately, opened his coat and displayed a bosom of so dazzling a whiteness that Martin could not bear to gaze on it. Then he took off his hat.

"Behold my forehead," he said, "and give heed that it beareth not the mark of the beast whereby the fallen angels were sealed."

Louis XVIII expressed a desire to see Martin and to question him. The King, like his favourite Minister, believed the visionary to be a tool in the hands of the extreme party.

On Tuesday, April 2, Martin was taken to the Tuileries and brought into the King's closet, where was also M. Decazes. As soon as the King saw the farmer, he said to him: "Martin, I salute you."

Then he signed to his Minister to withdraw. Thereupon Martin, according to his own telling, repeated to the King all that the Archangel had revealed to him, and disclosed to Louis XVIII sundry secret matters concerning the years he had spent in exile; finally he made known to him certain plots which had been formed against his person. Then the King, profoundly agitated and in tears, raised his hands and his eyes to heaven and said to Martin:

"Martin, these are things which must never be known save to you and to me."

The visionary promised him absolute secrecy.

Such was the interview of April 2, according to the account given of it by Martin, who then, under the influence of M. La Perruque's sermons, was an infatuated Royalist. It would be interesting to know more of this priest whose inspiration is obvious throughout the whole story. Louis XVIII agreed with M. Decazes that the man was quite harmless; and he was sent back to his plough.

Later, the agents of one of those false dauphins so numerous under the Restoration, got hold of Martin and made use of him in their own interest. After Louis XVIII's death, under the influence of these adventurers, the poor man, reconstituting the story of his interview with the late King, introduced into it other revelations he claimed to have received and completely changed the whole character of the incident. In this second version the passionate Royalist of 1816 was transformed into an accusing prophet, who came to the King's own palace to denounce him as a usurper and a regicide, forbidding him in God's name to be crowned at Reims.

Such ramblings I cannot relate at length. They are to be found fully detailed in the book of M. Paul Marin. The author of this work would have done well to indicate that these follies were suggested to the unhappy man by the partisans of Naundorf, who was passing himself off as the Duke of Normandy, who had escaped from the Temple.

Thomas Ignace Martin died at Chartres in 1834. It is alleged, but it has never been proved, that he was poisoned.[1169]

APPENDIX IV
ICONOGRAPHICAL NOTE

HERE is no authentic picture of Jeanne. From her we know that at Arras she saw in the hands of a Scotsman a picture in which she was represented on her knees presenting a letter to her King. From her we know also that she never caused to be made either image or painting of herself, and that she was not aware of the existence of any such image or painting. The portrait painted by the Scotsman, which was doubtless very small, is unfortunately lost and no copy of it is known.[1170] The slight pen-and-ink figure, drawn on a register of May 10, 1429, by a clerk of the Parlement of Paris, who had never seen the Maid, must be regarded as the mere scribbling of a scribe who was incapable of even designing a good initial letter.[1171] I shall not attempt to reconstruct the iconography of the Maid.[1172] The bronze equestrian statue in the Cluny Museum produces a grotesque effect that one is tempted to believe deliberate, if one may ascribe such an intention to an old sculptor. It dates from the reign of Charles VIII. It is a Saint George or a Saint Maurice, which, at a time doubtless quite recent, was taken to represent the Maid. Between the legs of the miserable jade, on which the figure is mounted, was engraved the inscription: *La pucelle dorlians*, a description which would not have been employed in the fifteenth century.[1173] About 1875, the Cluny Museum exhibited another statuette, slightly larger, in painted wood, which was also believed to be fifteenth century, and to represent Jeanne d'Arc. It was relegated to the store-room, when it turned out to be a bad seventeenth-century Saint Maurice from a church at Montargis.[1174] Any saint in armour is frequently described as a Jeanne d'Arc. This is what happened to a small fifteenth-century head wearing a helmet, found buried in the ground at Orléans, broken off from a statue and still bearing traces of painting: a work in good style and with a charming expression.[1175] I have not patience to relate how many initial letters of antiphonaries and sixteenth-, seventeenth- and even eighteenth-century miniatures have been touched up or repainted and passed off as true and ancient representations of Jeanne. Many of them I have had the opportunity of seeing.[1176] On the other hand, if they were not so well known, it would give me pleasure to recall certain manuscripts of the fifteenth century, which, like *Le Champion des Dames* and *Les Vigiles de Charles VII*, contain miniatures in which the Maid is portrayed according to the fancy of the illuminator. Such pictures are interesting because they reveal her as she was imagined by those who lived during her lifetime or shortly afterwards. It is not their merit that appeals to us; they possess none; and in no way do they suggest Jean Foucquet.[1177]

While the Maid lived, and especially while she was in captivity, the French hung her picture in churches.[1178] In the Museum of Versailles there is a little painting on wood which is said to be one of those votive pictures. It represents the Virgin with the Child Jesus, having Saint Michael on her right and Jeanne d'Arc on her left.[1179] It is of Italian workmanship and very roughly executed. Jeanne's head, which has disappeared beneath the blows of some hard-pointed instrument, must have been execrably drawn, if we may judge from the others remaining on this panel. All four figures are represented with a scrolled and beaded nimbus, which would have certainly been condemned by the clerics of Paris and Rouen. And indeed others less strict might accuse the painter of idolatry when he exalted to the left hand of the Virgin, to be equal with the Prince of Heavenly Hosts, a mere creature of the Church Militant.

Standing, her head, neck, and shoulders covered with a kind of furred hood and tippet fringed with black, her gauntlets and shoes of mail, girt above her red tunic with a belt of gold, Jeanne may be recognised by her name inscribed over her head, and also by the white banner, embroidered with *fleurs-de-lis*, which she raises in her right hand, and by her silver shield, embossed in the German style; on the shield is a sword bearing on its point a crown. A three-lined inscription in French is on the steps of the throne, whereon sits the Virgin Mary. Although the inscription is three parts effaced and almost unintelligible, with the aid of my learned friend, M. Pierre de Nolhac, Director of the Museum of Versailles, I have succeeded in deciphering a few words. These would convey the idea that the inscription consisted of prayers and wishes for the salvation of Jeanne, who had fallen into the hands of the enemy. It would appear therefore that we have here one of those *ex voto* hung in the churches of France during the captivity of the Maid. In such a case the nimbus round the head of a living person and the isolated position of Jeanne would be easily explained; it is possible that certain excellent Frenchmen, thinking no evil, adapted to their own use some picture which originally represented the Virgin between two personages of the Church Triumphant. By a few touches they transformed one of these personages into the Maid of God. In so small a panel they could find no place more suitable to her mortal state, none like those generally occupied at the feet of the Virgin and saints by the kneeling donors of pictures. This too might explain perhaps why Saint Michael, the Virgin and the Maid have their names inscribed above them. Over the head of the Maid we read *ane darc*. This form *Darc* may have been used in 1430.[1180] In the inscription on the steps of the throne I discern *Jehane dArc*, with a small *d* and a capital *A* for *dArc*, which is very curious. This causes me to doubt the genuineness of the inscription.

The *bestion* tapestry[1181] in the Orléans Museum,[1182] which represents Jeanne's arrival before the King at Chinon, is of German fifteenth-century workmanship. Coarse of tissue, barbarous in design, and monotonous in colour, it evinces a certain taste for sumptuous adornment but also an absolute disregard for literal truth.

Another German work was exhibited at Ratisbonne in 1429. It represented the Maid fighting in France. But this painting is lost.[1183]

† END OF VOLUME II †

REFERENCES TO VOLUME II

1. *Chronique de la Pucelle*, pp. 323, 324. Perceval de Cagny, pp. 160, 161. *Journal du siège*, p. 115. Jean Chartier, *Chronique*, vol. i, p. 98. Morosini, vol. iii, p. 196.

2. *Ordonnances des rois de France*, vol. ix, p. 71. H. Martin and Lacroix, *Histoire de la ville de Soissons*, Soissons, 1837, in 8vo, ii, pp. 283 *et seq.*

3. *Journal d'un bourgeois de Paris*, p. 53, *passim*.

4. *Ibid.*, p. 103.

5. *Chronique de la Pucelle*, pp. 323, 324. Perceval de Cagny, p. 160. Monstrelet, vol. iv, p. 339.

6. *Suret* is sour wine (W.S.).

7. C. Dormay, *Histoire de la ville de Soissons*, Soissons, 1664, vol. ii, pp. 382 *et seq.* H. Martin and Lacroix, *Histoire de Soissons*, vol. ii, p. 319. Pécheur, *Annales du diocèse de Soissons*, vol. iv, p. 513. Félix Brun, *Jeanne d'Arc et le capitaine de Soissons en 1430*, Soissons, 1904, p. 34.

8. Berry, in *Trial*, vol. iv, pp. 49, 50. Le P. Daniel, *Histoire de la milice française*, vol. i, p. 356. Félix Brun, *Jeanne d'Arc et le capitaine de Soissons*, pp. 26, 39.

9. De l'Epinois, *Notes extraites des archives communales de Compiègne*, in *Bibliothèque de l'École des Chartes*, vol. xxix, p. 483. Sorel, *Prise de Jeanne d'Arc*, pp. 101, 102.

10. Perceval de Cagny, p. 160. Monstrelet, vol. iv, p. 340.

11. Monstrelet, vol. iv, p. 340. *Chronique de la Pucelle*, p. 323. Félix Bourquelot, *Histoire de Provins*, Provins, vol. iv, pp. 79 *et seq.* Th. Robillard, *Histoire pittoresque topographique et archéologique de Crécy-en-Brie*, 1852, p. 42. L'Abbé C. Poquet, *Histoire de Château-Thierry*, 1839, vol. i, pp. 290 *et seq.*

12. Perceval de Cagny, pp. 160, 161.

13. *Chronique de la Pucelle*, pp. 324, 325. *Journal du siège*, p. 115. Jean Chartier, *Chronique*, vol. i, pp. 98, 99. Perceval de Cagny, p. 161. Rymer, *Fœdera*, June to July, 1429. *Proceedings*, vol. iii, pp. 322 *et seq.* Morosini, vol. iv, appendix xvii.

14. Jean Chartier, *Chronique*, vol. i, p. 98. Varin, *Archives législatives de la ville de Reims*, Statuts, vol. i (annot. according to doc. no. xxi), p. 741. H. Jadart, *Jeanne d'Arc à Reims*, original doc. no. 19, p. 118.

15. Perceval de Cagny, p. 160.

16. This place name is not to be found in Rogier's copy.

17. *Trial*, vol. v, pp. 139, 140, and Varin, *loc. cit. Statuts*, vol. i, p. 603, according to Rogier's copy. H. Jadart, *Jeanne d'Arc à Reims*, proofs and illustrations, vol. xiv, pp. 104, 105, and facsimile of the original copy formerly in the Reims municipal archives, now in the possession of M. le Comte de Maleissye.

18. *Trial*, vol. i, pp. 233, 234.

19. Morosini, vol. iii, pp. 202, 203, note 2.

20. *Chronique de la Pucelle*, p. 325. Jean Chartier, *Chronique*, vol. i, pp. 99, 100. *Journal du siège*, pp. 119, 120. Gilles de Roye, p. 207.

21. *Trial*, vol. iii, p. 91.

22. *Guerre de la Hottée de Pommes*, cf. vol. i, p. 92. (W.S.)

23. *Chronique du doyen de Saint-Thibaut de Metz* in D. Calmet. *Histoire de Lorraine*, vol. v, orig. docs., cols, xli-xlvii. Villeneuve-Bargemont, *Précis historique de la vie du roi René*, Aix, 1820, in 8vo. Lecoy de la Marche, *Le roi René*, Paris, 1875, 2 vols. in 8vo. Vallet de Viriville, in *Nouvelle biographie générale*, 1866, xli, pp. 1009-1015.

24. *Trial*, vol. ii, p. 444. S. Luce, *Jeanne d'Arc à Domremy*, p. cxcix. Morosini, vol. iii, p. 156, note 3.

25. *Trial*, vol. v, pp. 105-111.

26. *Chronique de la Pucelle*, Jean Chartier. *Journal du siège*, *loc. cit.*

27. Monstrelet, vol. iv, pp. 340, 344.

28. Perceval de Cagny, p. 161. Jean Chartier, *Chronique*, vol. i, p. 100. *Chronique de la Pucelle*, p. 325.

29. Varin, *Archives législatives de la ville de Reims*, Statuts, vol. i, p. 742.

30. Perceval de Cagny, p. 161.

31. *Trial*, vol. iii, pp. 14, 15. *Chronique de la Pucelle*, p. 326.

32. *Journal d'un bourgeois de Paris*, p. 164.

33. Thomas Basin, *Histoire de Charles VII*, chap. vi. A. Tuetey, *Les écorcheurs sous Charles VII*, Montbéliard, 1874, 2 vols. in 8vo, *passim*. H. Lepage, *Épisodes de l'histoire des routiers en Lorraine* (1362-1446), in *Journal d'archéologie lorraine*, vol. xv, pp. 161 *et seq.* Le P. Denifle, *La désolation des églises*, *passim*. H. Martin et Lacroix, *Histoire de Soissons*, p. 318, *passim*. G. Lefèvre-Pontalis, *Épisodes de l'invasion anglaise. La guerre de partisans dans la Haute Normandie* (1424-1429), in *Bibliothèque de l'École des Chartes*, vol. liv, pp. 475-521; vol. lv, pp. 258-305; vol. lvi, pp. 432-508.

34. Pardon issued by King Henry VI to an inhabitant of Noyant, in Stevenson, *Letters and Papers*, vol. i, pp. 23, 31. F. Brun, *Jeanne d'Arc et le capitaine de Soissons*, note iii, p. 41.

35. Stevenson, *Letters and Papers*, vol. i, pp. 23, 31.

36. *Journal d'un bourgeois de Paris*, pp. 170, 171. Monstrelet, vol. iv, p. 96. *Livre des trahisons*, pp. 167, 168.

37. *Journal d'un bourgeois de Paris*, p. 170. According to Monstrelet (vol. iv, p. 96), Denis de Vauru, the Bastard's cousin, was beheaded in the Market of Paris.

38. *Trial*, vol. iii, pp. 14, 15. *Chronique de la Pucelle*, p. 326.

39. Eberhard Windecke, pp. 108, 109, 188, 189.

40. *Trial*, vol. iii, pp. 14, 15. It is Dunois who is giving evidence, and the text runs: *In custodiendo oves ipsorum, cum sorore et fratribus meis, qui multum gauderent videre me.* But there is reason to believe she had only one sister, whom she had lost before coming into France. As for her brothers, two of them were with her. Dunois' evidence appears to have been written down by a clerk unacquainted with events. The hagiographical character of the passage is obvious.

41. *Trial*, vol. ii, p. 423.

42. *Ibid.*, vol. i, pp. 51, 66.

43. Monstrelet, vol. iv, pp. 340, 344.

44. Monstrelet, vol. iv, p. 342.

45. *Ibid.*, pp. 342, 343.

46. Georges Chastellain, fragments published by J. Quicherat in *La Bibliothèque de l'École des Chartes*, 1st series, vol. iv, p. 78.

47. Monstrelet, vol. iv, pp. 341, 342.

48. *Trial*, vol. ii, p. 324; vol. iii, p. 130. Monstrelet, vol. iv, p. 388.

49. *Trial*, vol. iii, p. 99.

50. *Ibid.*, vol. iv, pp. 206, 406, 444, 470, 472. Rymer, *Fœdera*, vol. iv, p. 141. G. Lefèvre-Pontalis, *La panique anglaise*.

51. *Trial*, vol. i, pp. 246, 298. Letter from Alain Chartier in *Trial*, vol. v, pp. 131 *et seq.*

52. Monstrelet, vol. iv, pp. 344, 345. Perceval de Cagny, pp. 161, 162.

53. Flammermont, *Histoire de Senlis pendant la seconds partie de la guerre de cent ans* (1405-1441), in *Mémoires de la Société de l'Histoire de Paris.*

54. Jean Chartier, *Chronique*, vol. i, pp. 101, 102. *Chronique de la Pucelle*, p. 328. *Journal du siège*, p. 118. Falconbridge, in *Trial*, vol. iv, p. 453. Morosini, vol. iii, pp. 188, 189; vol. iv, appendix xvii. Rymer, *Fœdera*, July, 1429. Raynaldi, *Annales ecclesiastici*, pp. 77, 88. S. Bougenot, *Notices et extraits de manuscrits intéressant l'histoire de France conservés a la Bibliothèque impérial de Vienne*, p. 62.

55. Now, come forth Beauty (W.S.). *Le Livre des trahisons de France*, ed. Kervyn de Lettenhove, in *La collection des chroniques belges*, 1873, p. 198.

56. Perceval de Cagny, p. 162. Jean Chartier, *Chronique*, vol. i, p. 102. *Chronique de la Pucelle*, p. 329. *Journal du siège*, pp. 119, 120.

57. Perceval de Cagny, p. 161.

58. *Le Jouvencel, passim.*

59. *Chronique de la Pucelle*, p. 329. *Journal du siège*, p. 121.

60. *Le Jouvencel*, vol. ii, p. 35.

61. Monstrelet, vol. iv, p. 346.

62. Perceval de Cagny, p. 162.

63. Jean Chartier, *Chronique de la Pucelle. Journal du siège*. Monstrelet, *loc. cit.*

64. *Chronique de la Pucelle*, p. 332. Perceval de Cagny, p. 165. Jean Chartier, *Chronique*, vol. i, p. 106. Cochon, p. 457. G. Lefèvre-Pontalis, *La panique anglaise*, Paris, 1894, in 8vo, pp. 10, 11. Morosini, vol. iii, p. 215, note 3. Ch. de Beaurepaire, *De l'administration de la Normandie sous la domination anglaise aux années 1424, 1425, 1429*, p. 62 (*Mémoires de la Société des Antiquaires de Normandie*, vol. xxiv).

65. A virelay was a later variation of the lay, differing from it chiefly in the arrangement of the rhymes (W.S.).

66. Le Roux de Lincy and Tisserand, *Paris et ses historiens*, pp. 426 *et seq.*

67. A winged stag (*le cerf-volant*) is the symbol of a king. Froissart thus explains its origin. Before setting out for Flanders, in 1382, Charles VI dreamed that his falcon had flown away. "Thē apered sodenly before hym a great hart with wynges whereof he had great joye." And the hart bore him to his lost bird. Froissart, Bk. II, ch. clxiv. The Chronycle of Syr John Froissart translated by Lord Berners, vol. iii, p. 339, Tudor Translation, 1901.. (W.S.) According to Juvénal des Ursins, Charles VI, in 1380, met in the Forest of Senlis a stag with a golden collar bearing this inscription: *Hoc me Cæsar donavit* (Paillot, *Parfaite science des armoiries*, Paris, 1660, in fo., p. 595). In the works of Eustache Deschamps this same allegory is frequently employed to designate the king. (Eustache Deschamps, *œuvres*, ed. G. Raynaud, vol. ii, p. 57.)

68. Morosini, vol. iii, pp. 66, 67.

69. *Trial*, vol. iii, pp. 133, 338, 340 *et seq.*; vol. iv, pp. 305, 480; vol. v, p. 12.

70. *Trial*, vol. v, pp. 3 *et seq.* R. Thomassy, *Essai sur les écrits politiques de Christine de Pisan, suivi d'une notice littéraire et de pièces inédites*, Paris, 1838, in 8vo.

71. *Du beau jardin des nobles fleurs de lis.*

72. M. Pierre Champion has kindly communicated to me the text of this unpublished ballad, which he discovered in a French MS. at Stockholm, LIII, fol. 238. This is the title which the copyist affixed to it about 1472: *Ballade faicte quant le Roy Charles VIIeme fut couronne a Rains du temps de Jehanne daiz dicte la Pucelle.*

73. P. Meyer, *Ballade contre les Anglais* (1429), in *Romania*, xxi (1892), pp. 50, 52.

74. *Arrière, Englois coués, arrière!* For Coués see vol. i, p. 22, note 2.

75.

> *Par le vouloir dou roy Jésus*
> *Et Jeanne la douce Pucelle.*

76. For the legend cf. *Merlin, roman en prose du XIIIe siècle*, ed. G. Paris and J. Ulrich, 1886, 2 vols. in 8vo, introduction. *Premier volume de Merlin*, Paris, Vérard, 1498, in fol. Hersart de la Villemarqué, *Myrdhin ou l'enchanteur Merlin, son histoire, ses œuvres, son influence*, Paris, 1862, in 12mo. La Borderie, *Les véritables prophéties de Merlin; examen des poèmes bretons attribués à ce barde*, in *Revue de Bretagne*, vol. liii (1883). D'Arbois de Jubainville, *Merlin est il un*

personnage réel ou les origines de la légende de Merlin, in *Revue des questions historiques*, vol. v (1868), pp. 559, 568.

77. *Trial*, vol. iii, p. 340. Lanéry d'Arc, *Mémoires et consultations*, p. 402.

78. *Trial*, vol. iii, pp. 344, 345.

79. Philippe de Bergame, in *Trial*, vol. iv, p. 523; vol. v, pp. 108, 120.

80. *Trial*, vol. iii, p. 100. Philippe de Bergame, *De claris mulieribus*, in *Trial*, vol. iv, p. 323. *Chronique de la Pucelle*, p. 271. Perceval de Boulainvilliers, *Lettre au duc de Milan*, in *Trial*, vol. v, pp. 119, 120.

81. J. Bréhal, in *Trial*, vol. iii, p. 345.

82. *Chronique de la Pucelle*, p. 328. *Journal du siège*, p. 18. Jean Chartier, *Chronique*, vol. i, p. 106. Perceval de Cagny, pp. 163, 164. Morosini, pp. 212, 213. Flammermont, *Senlis pendant la seconde période de la guerre cent ans*, in *Mémoires de la Société de l'Histoire de Paris*, vol. v, 1878, p. 241.

83. Perceval de Cagny, p. 164. Monstrelet, p. 352. De l'Epinois, *Notes extraites des archives communales de Compiègne*, pp. 483, 484. A. Sorel, *Séjours de Jeanne d'Arc à Compiègne, maisons ou elle a logé en 1429 et 1430*, Paris, 1889, in 8vo, 20 pages.

84. French *attournés*, cf. La Curne, *attournés*, Godefroi, *atornés*, magistrates at Compiègne, elected on St. John the Baptist's Day for three years (W.S.). *Procès*, vol. v, p. 174.

85. *Chronique de la Pucelle*, p. 331. Jean Chartier, *Chronique*, vol. i, p. 106. A. Sorel, *La prise de Jeanne d'Arc devant Compiègne*, Paris, 1889, in 8vo, pp. 117, 118. Duc de la Trémoïlle, *Les La Trémoïlle pendant cinq siècles*, Nantes, 1890, in 4to, vol. i, pp. 185, 212. P. Champion, *Guillaume de Flavy, capitaine de Compiègne*, Paris, 1906, in 8vo, proofs and illustrations, vol. xiii, p. 137.

86. *Chronique de la Pucelle*, p. 327. *Journal du siège*, p. 118. Jean Chartier, *Chronique*, vol. i, p. 106. Monstrelet, vol. iv, pp. 353, 354. Morosini, vol. iii, pp. 214, 215.

87. A. Sarrazin, *Pierre Cauchon, juge de Jeanne d'Arc*, Paris, 1901, in 8vo, pp. 49 *et seq.*

88. Monstrelet, vol. iv, p. 354.

89. A. Sorel, *Séjours de Jeanne d'Arc à Compiègne*, p. 6.

90. Perceval de Cagny, pp. 164, 165. *Chronique de Tournai*, vol. iii, in the *Recueil des chroniques de Flandre*, ed. Smedt, p. 414.

91. *Trial*, vol. i, pp. 82, 83.

92. *Ibid.*, pp. 245, 246.

93. A. Longnon, *Les limites de la France et l'étendue de la domination anglaise à l'époque de la mission de Jeanne d'Arc*, Paris, 1875, in 8vo. Vallet de Viriville, in *Nouvelle biographie générale*, iii, col. 255, 257.

94. *Chronique de Mathieu d'Escouchy*, vol. i, p. 68, and proofs and illustrations, pp. 126, 128, 139, 140. Dom Vaissette, *Histoire générale du Languedoc*, vol. iv, pp. 469, 470. De Beaucourt, *Histoire de Charles VII*, vol. ii, p. 151. Vallet de Viriville, in *Nouvelle biographie générale*, 1861, vol. iii, pp. 255-257. Le P. Ayroles, *La vierge guerrière*, p. 66.

95. *Annales juris pontificis* (1872-1875), vii, 385. E. Muntz, *La tiare pontificale du VIIIe au XVIe siècle* in *Mem. Acad. Inscript. et Belles Lettres*, vol. xxvi, I, pp. 235-324, fig. *Les arts à la cour des papes pendant les XVe et XVIe siècles*, in *Bibl. des Écoles françaises d'Athènes et Rome*, vol. iv.

96. Baluze, *Vitæ paparum Avenionensium*, 1693, I, pp. 1182 *et seq.* Fabricius, *Bibliotheca medii ævi*, 1734, I, p. 1109.

97. Cf. vol. i, p. 337 (W.S.).

98. According to Le Maire, *Histoire et antiquités de la ville et duché d'Orléans*, p. 197, this request is addressed to "Jeanne the Maid, greatly to be honoured and most devout, sent by the King of Heaven for the restoration, and for the extirpation of the English who tyrannize over France." *Trial*, vol. v, p. 253. Vallet de Viriville, *Histoire de Charles VII*, vol. ii, p. 131.

99. Noël Valois, *La France et le grand schisme d'Occident*, vol. iv (1902), in 8vo, *passim*.

100. *Trial*, vol. i, p. 82.

101. *Trial*, vol. iii, pp. 466, 467.

102. *Ibid.*, vol. i, pp. 245, 246.

103. *Trial*, vol. i, p. 83.

104. Perceval de Cagny, p. 165. *Chronique de la Pucelle*, p. 331. Jean Chartier, *Chronique*, vol. i, p. 106. Morosini, vol. iii, pp. 212, 213. The accounts of Hémon Raguier, in the *Trial*, vol. iv, p. 24.

105. *Trial*, vol. ii, p. 450.

106. So called because stamped with the picture of the Annunciation and bearing the inscription: *Salus populi suprema lex est*; the coin was worth about £1 of our money (W.S.).

107. *Trial*, vol. i, p. 104. Extracts from the 13th account of Hémon Raguier, in *Trial*, vol. v, p. 267. E. Dupuis, *Jean Fouquerel, évêque de*

Senlis, in *Mémoires du comité archéologique de Senlis*, 1875, vol. i, p. 93. Vatin, *Combat sous Senlis entre Charles VII et les Anglais*, in *Comité archéologique de Senlis, Comptes rendus et mémoires*, 1866, pp. 41, 54.

108. *Trial*, vol. i, p. 264.

109. Perceval de Cagny, p. 165. The 25th according to *Le journal d'un bourgeois de Paris*, p. 243.

110. J. Doublet, *Histoire de l'abbaye de Saint-Denys en France, contenant les antiquités d'icelle, les fondations, prérogatives et privileges*, Paris, 1625, 2 vol. in 4to, vol. i, ch. xx and xxiv. Des Rues, *Les antiquités, fondations et singularités des plus célèbres villes*, pp. 84, 85.

111. J. Doublet, *Histoire de l'abbaye de Saint-Denys*, vol. i, ch. xxxi, xxxiv.

112. Cf. vol. i, p. 182 (W.S.).

113. Thomassin, *Registre Delphinal*, in *Trial*, vol. iv, p. 304. See Du Cange, *Glossaire* under the word *Auriflamme*.

114. J. Doublet, *Histoire de l'abbaye de Saint-Denys*, vol. i, ch. xxii. D. Michel Félibien, *Histoire de l'abbaye royale de Saint-Denys en France*, Paris, in folio, 1706, pp. 229, 320. Vallet de Viriville, *Notice du manuscrit de P. Cochon*, at the end of *La chronique de la Pucelle*, p. 360. *Chronique de Du Guesclin*, ed. Francisque-Michel, pp. 452 *et seq.*

115. *Trial*, vol. v, pp. 107, 109.

116. D. M. Félibien, *op. cit.*, ch. ii, pp. 528 *et seq.* Illustrations. J. Doublet, *op. cit.*, vol. i, ch. xliii, xlvi. *Trial*, vol. iii, p. 301. *Gallia Christiana*, vol. vii, col. 142.

117. *Religieux de Saint-Denis*, pp. 154, 156, 226.

118. Estienne Binet, *La vie apostolique de saint Denys l'Aréopagite, patron et apostre de la France*, Paris, 1624, in 12mo. J. Doublet, *Histoire chronologique pour la vérité de Saint Denys l'Aréopagite, apôtre de France et premier évêque de Paris*, Paris, 1646, in 4to, and *Histoire de l'abbaye de Saint-Denys en France*, p. 95. J. Havet, *Les origines de Saint-Denis*, in *Les Questions mérovingiennes*.

119. *Trial*, vol. i, p. 179.

120. *Journal d'un bourgeois de Paris*, p. 179, note 5.

121. *Ibid.*, pp. 101, 209, note 1.

122. *Ibid.*, pp. 241, 242. Monstrelet, vol. iv, p. 354.

123. *Trial*, vol. i, p. 103.

124. *Ibid.*, p. 304. Noël Valois, *Un nouveau témoignage sur Jeanne d'Arc,* in *Annuaire-bulletin de la Société de l'Histoire de France,* Paris, 1907, in 8vo, separate issue, pp. 17, 18.

125. *Trial,* vol. i, p. 236.

126. *Le Jouvencel,* vol. ii, p. 281.

127. *Trial,* vol. iii, p. 81.

128. Perceval de Cagny, p. 166.

129. *Ibid.*, p. 166.

130. Vallet de Viriville, *Histoire de Charles VII,* vol. ii, p. 112. De Beaucourt, *Histoire de Charles VII,* vol. ii, pp. 404, 408. Morosini, vol. iii, p. 192; vol. iv, appendix xviii.

131. *Trial,* vol. v, p. 140.

132. *Chronique de la Pucelle,* p. 332. Jean Chartier, *Chronique,* vol. i, p. 106. P. Cochon, p. 457. Perceval de Cagny, p. 165.

133. Monstrelet, vol. iv, pp. 352, 353. *Journal d'un bourgeois de Paris,* pp. 247, 248. D. Félibien, *Histoire de Paris,* vol. ii, p. 813, and proofs and illustrations, vol. iv, p. 591. Morosini, vol. iii, pp. 208, 209, 224, note 2; vol. iv, appendix xviii, pp. 343, 344.

134. Cf. vol. i, p. 34, note 3 (W.S.).

135. De Beaucourt, *Histoire de Charles VII,* vol. ii, ch. vii. *La diplomatie de Charles VII jusqu'au traité d'Arras.*

136. Perceval de Cagny, p. 166.

137. Le Roux de Lincy, *Hugues Aubriot, prévôt de Paris sous Charles V,* Paris, 1862, in 8vo, *passim. Paris et ses historiens au XIVe et XVe siècle* by Le Roux de Lincy and Tisserand, Paris, in fol. *Histoire générale de Paris.*.

138. Delamare, *Traité de la police,* Paris, 1710, in folio, vol. i, p. 79. A. Bonnardot, *Dissertation archéologique sur les enceintes de Paris, suivie de recherches sur les portes fortifiées qui dépendaient des enceintes de Paris,* 1851, in 4to, with plan. *Études archéologiques sur les anciens plans de Paris,* 1853, in 4to. *Appendice aux études archéologiques sur les anciens plans de Paris et aux dissertations sur les enceintes de Paris,* Paris, 1877, in 4to. *Étude sur Gilles Corrozet, suivie d'une notice sur un manuscrit de la Bibliothèque des ducs de Bourgogne, contenant une description de Paris, en 1432,* par Guillebert de Metz, Paris, 1846, in 8vo, 56 pages. Kausler, *Atlas des plus mémorables batailles,* Carlsruhe, 1831, pl. 34. H. Legrand, *Paris en 1380,* with plan conjecturally reconstructed, Paris in fol. 1868, p.

58. A. Guilaumot, *Les Portes de l'enceinte de Paris sous Charles V*, Paris, 1879. Rigaud, *Chronique de la Pucelle, campagne de Paris, cartes et plans*, Bergerac, 1886, in 8vo.

139. *Journal d'un bourgeois de Paris*, p. 180.

140. *Journal d'un bourgeois de Paris*, p. 189.

141. *Ibid.*, pp. 136, 137.

142. *Ibid.*, p. 107. *Document inédit relatif à l'état de Paris en 1430*, in *Revue des sociétés savantes*, 1863, p. 203.

143. Christine de Pisan, in *Trial*, vol. v, stanza 56, p. 20. Le Roux de Lincy and Tisserand, *Paris et ses historiens*, p. 426.

144. *Journal d'un bourgeois de Paris*, p. 251. A. Longnon, *Paris pendant la domination anglaise (1420-1436), documents extraits des registres de la chancellerie de France*, Paris, 1877, in 8vo, introduction, p. xiij. Vallet de Viriville, *Histoire de Charles VII*, vol. ii, p. 116, note 1.

145. *Journal d'un bourgeois de Paris*, p. 248. *Chronique de la Pucelle*, p. 297. Morosini, vol. iii, p. 79, note.

146. *Journal d'un bourgeois de Paris*, p. 257. Falconbridge, in *Trial*, vol. iv, p. 453. Morosini, vol. iii, p. 198.

147. *Journal du siège*, p. 38. Jean Chartier, *Chronique*, vol. i, pp. 106, 107. Falconbridge, in *Trial*, vol. iv, p. 454.

148. See vol. i, p. 222, note 2 (W.S.).

149. *Journal d'un bourgeois de Paris*, p. 239, note 2. Le Roux de Lincy and Tisserand, *Paris et ses historiens*, pp. 340 *et seq.*

150. 14th July, 1429, *Journal d'un bourgeois de Paris*, pp. 240, 241. Falconbridge, in *Trial*, vol. iv, p. 240. Morosini, vol. iii, p. 186.

151. *Journal d'un bourgeois de Paris*, p. 241.

152. Falconbridge, in *Trial*, vol. iv, p. 356.

153. *Journal d'un bourgeois de Paris*, p. 242.

154. *Ibid.*, p. 243.

155. Rymer, *Fœdera*, May. *Chronique de la Pucelle*, p. 332. Monstrelet, vol. iv, p. 355. Jean Chartier, *Chronique*, vol. i, pp. 106, 107. Wallon, *Jeanne d'Arc*, vol. i, p. 290, note 1. G. Lefèvre-Pontalis, *La panique anglaise*, p. 9. Morosini, vol. iii, p. 216, note 5; vol. iv, appendix xviii.

156. *Journal d'un bourgeois de Paris*, p. 243.

157. *Journal d'un bourgeois de Paris*, p. 243. Perceval de Cagny, p. 166. *Chronique des cordeliers*, folio, 486 verso.

158. *Journal d'un bourgeois de Paris*, p. 243.

159. *Ibid.*, pp. 243, 244.

160. Cf. *ante*, p. 45, note 2 (W.S.).

161. Register of the Deliberations of the Chapter of Notre Dame (Arch. Nat., LL, 716, pp. 173, 174), in *Le journal d'un bourgeois de Paris, loc. cit.* Le P. Ayroles, *La vraie Jeanne d'Arc*, vol. iii, pp. 530, 531, proofs and illustrations, J, p. 639. Le P. Denifle and Chatelain, *Le procès de Jeanne d'Arc et l'université de Paris*, Nogent-le-Rotrou, 1898, in 8vo.

162. Register of the Deliberations of the Chapter of Notre Dame, in Tuetey, notes to *Le Journal d'un bourgeois de Paris*, p. 241, note 1. Falconbridge, in *Trial*, vol. iv, p. 456. Le P. Ayroles, *La vraie Jeanne d'Arc*, vol. iii, proofs and illustrations, p. 640.

163. Register of the Deliberations of the Chapter of Notre Dame, *loc. cit. Chronique de la Pucelle*, p. 332. *Journal d'un bourgeois de Paris*, p. 244. Monstrelet, vol. iv, p. 354. Martial d'Auvergne, *Vigiles*, ed. Coustelier, vol. i, p. 113. Perceval de Cagny, p. 166. *Chronique des cordeliers*, folio, 486 verso. Le P. Ayroles, *La vrai Jeanne d'Arc*, vol. iii, p. 531.

164. Voragine, *Legenda Aurea*. Anquetil, *La nativité, miracle extrait de la légende dorée*, in *Mem. Soc. Agr. de Bayeux*, 1883, vol. x, p. 286. Douhet, *Dictionnaire des mystères*, 1854, p. 545.

165. Perceval de Cagny, pp. 166, 168. *Chronique de la Pucelle*, pp. 333, 334. Jean Chartier, *Chronique*, vol. i, pp. 107, 109. Falconbridge, in *Trial*, vol. iv, pp. 456, 458. *Journal d'un bourgeois de Paris*, pp. 244, 245. *Chronique des cordeliers*, fol. 486 verso. P. Cochon, ed. Beaurepaire, p. 307. Morosini, vol. iii, p. 210.

166. Gaguin, *Hist. Francorum*, Frankfort, 1577, book viii, chap. ii, p. 158. Tanon, *Histoire des tribunaux de l'inquisition en France*, p. 121. Lea, History of the Inquisition in the Middle Age, vol. ii, p. 126. (The Turlupins were a German sect who called themselves "the Brethren of the Free Spirit." W.S.)

167. Perceval de Cagny, p. 161. Vallet de Viriville, *Histoire de Charles VII*, vol. ii, p. 120, note 1. G. Lefèvre-Pontalis, *Un détail du siège de Paris, par Jeanne d'Arc*, in *Bibliothèque de l'École des Chartes*, vol. xlvi, 1885, pp. 5 *et seq.*

168. Deliberation of the Chapter of Notre Dame, *loc. cit. Journal d'un bourgeois de Paris*, p. 245. Falconbridge, in *Trial*, vol. iv, p. 457.

169. *Trial*, vol. i, pp. 240, 246, 298; vol. iii, pp. 425, 427; vol. v, pp. 97, 107, 130, 140.

170. *Ibid.*, pp. 57, 146, 168, 250.

171. *Ibid.*, vol. v, p. 130 (letter of the 17th of July, 1429), vol. i, p. 298. "Et hoc sciebar per revelationem." Cf. vol. i, pp. 57, 260, 288 in contradiction.

172. *Journal du siège*, p. 89.

173. *Trial*, vol. i, pp. 147, 148.

174. In 1254 Saint Louis founded this hospital for three hundred blind knights whose eyes had been put out by the Saracens. (W.S.)

175. Le Roux de Lincy and Tisserand, *Paris et ses historiens*, pp. 205 and 231, note 4. Adolphe Berty, *Topographie historique du vieux Paris, région du Louvre et des Tuileries*, p. 180, and app. vi, p. ix. E. Eude, *L'attaque de Jeanne d'Arc contre Paris, 1429*, in *Cosmos*, nouv. série, xxix (1894), pp. 241, 244.

176. *Journal d'un bourgeois de Paris*, p. 246.

177. *Chronique de la Pucelle*, pp. 332, 333. Jean Chartier, *Chronique*, vol. i, p. 108.

178. Perceval de Cagny, p. 167.

179. *Trial*, vol. i, p. 148.

180. *Journal d'un bourgeois de Paris*, p. 245.

181. *Le Jouvencel*, vol. i, p. 67.

182. *Chronique de la Pucelle*, p. 333. Jean Chartier, *Chronique*, vol. i, p. 109. *Journal du siège*, p. 127. Martial d'Auvergne, *Vigiles*, ed. Coustelier, 1724, vol. i, p. 113.

183. Perceval de Cagny, p. 167. Monstrelet, vol. iv, pp. 355, 356. Morosini, vol. iii, note 3. E. Eude, *L'attaque de Jeanne d'Arc contre Paris*, in *Cosmos*, 22 Sept., 1894, vol. xxix. P. Marin, *Le génie militaire de Jeanne d'Arc*, in *Grande revue de Paris et de Saint-Pétersbourg*, 2nd year, vol. i, 1889, p. 142.

184. *Trial*, vol. i, pp. 57, 246. *Journal d'un bourgeois de Paris*, p. 245. Deliberations of the Chapter of Notre Dame, *loc. cit.* Falconbridge, in *Trial*, vol. iv, p. 457. Perceval de Cagny, Jean Chartier, *Journal du siège*, Monstrelet, Morosini, *loc. cit.*

185. *Trial*, vol. i, p. 298.

186. *Trial*, vol. i, p. 111, 273. Berry, in *Trial*, vol. iv, p. 50. F. Brun, *Jeanne d Arc et le capitaine de Soissons*, pp. 31 *et seq.*

187. *Trial*, vol. i, p. 57.

188. The oath *"Par mon martin"* (by my staff) is an invention of the scribe who wrote the *Chronicle* which is attributed to Perceval de Cagny, p. 168.

189. *Chronique de la Pucelle*, p. 334. *Journal du siège*, p. 128. Jean Chartier, *Chronique*, vol. i, p. 109. Monstrelet, vol. iv, pp. 355, 356.

190. Deliberation of the Chapter of Notre Dame, *loc. cit.*

191. *Journal d'un bourgeois de Paris*, p. 245.

192. *Le Jouvencel*, vol. i, p. 142.

193. *Journal d'un bourgeois de Paris*, pp. 245, 246.

194. For the opinions of the townsfolk of Paris, see various acts of Henry VI of the 18th and 25th of Sept., 1429 (MS. Fontanieu, 115). Sauval, *Antiquités de Paris*, vol. iii, p. 586 and *circ.*

195. A. Longnon, *Paris pendant la domination anglaise*, p. 302.

196. Falconbridge, in *Trial*, vol. iv, pp. 456, 458.

197. *Relation du greffier de La Rochelle*, p. 344.

198. *Chronique de Normandie*, in *Trial*, vol. iv, pp. 342, 343.

199. Perceval de Cagny, p. 168.

200. *Ibid. Chronique normande*, in *La chronique de la Pucelle*, p. 465. Vallet de Viriville, *Histoire de Charles VII*, vol. ii, p. 120, note 1.

201. Duchesne, *Histoire de la maison de Montmorency*, p. 232. Perceval de Cagny, p. 168. Vallet de Viriville, *Histoire de Charles VII*, vol. ii, pp. 118, 119.

202. G. Lefèvre-Pontalis, *Un détail du siège de Paris*, in *Bibliothèque de l'École des Chartes*, vol. xlvi, 1885, p. 12.

203. Perceval de Cagny, pp. 168, 169. Morosini, vol. iii, p. 219, note 4. Vallet de Viriville, *Histoire de Charles VII*, vol. ii, p. 120, note 1. G. Lefèvre-Pontalis, *Un détail du siège de Paris*, *loc. cit.*

204. Diminutive of *amie* (W.S.).

205. Eberhard Windecke, pp. 184, 186.

206. Jean Chartier, *Chronique*, vol. i, p. 90.

207. *Trial*, vol. iii, p. 73.

208. *Ibid.*, p. 99.

209. *Ibid.*, vol. i, p. 76.

210. Jean Chartier, *Chronique*, vol. i, p. 90.

211. Jean Chartier, *Chronique*, vol. i, pp. 122, 123.

212. Perceval de Cagny, p. 169. *Chronique de la Pucelle*, pp. 335 *et seq.* Jean Chartier, *Chronique*, vol. i, pp. 112 *et seq.* Monstrelet, vol. iv, p. 356. *Journal d'un bourgeois de Paris*, p. 246. Berry in *Trial*, vol. iv, p. 48. Gilles de Roye, p. 208.

213. *Trial*, vol. i, p. 260.

214. Jean Chartier, *Chronique*, vol. i, p. 109. Perceval de Cagny, p. 170. Martial d'Auvergne, *Vigiles*, vol. i, p. 114. Jacques Doublet, *Histoire de l'abbaye de Saint-Denys*, pp. 13, 14.

215. La Curne, at the word *Blanc*: white armour was worn by squires, gilded armour by knights. Bouteiller, in his *Somme Rurale*, refers to the *"harnais doré"* (gilded armour) of the knights. Cf. Du Tillet, *Recueil des rois de France*, ch. *Des chevaliers*, p. 431. Du Cange, *Observations sur les établissements de la France*, p. 373.

216. *Trial*, vol. i, p. 179.

217. *Journal du siège*, p. 130. Perceval de Cagny, pp. 170, 171. *Journal d'un bourgeois de Paris*, pp. 246, 247. Berry, in *Trial*, vol. iv, p. 79. Morosini, vol. iii, p. 219.

218. *Trial*, vol. iii, p. 86. De Beaucourt, *Histoire de Charles VII*, vol. ii, p. 265. P. Lanéry d'Arc and L. Jeny, *Jeanne d'Arc en Berry, avec des documents et des éclaircissements inédits*, Paris, 1892, in 12mo, chap. vi.

219. *Trial*, vol. iii, p. 85, note 1. De Beaucourt, *Histoire de Charles VII*, vol. i, p. 418, note 7.

220. *Trial*, vol. iii, p. 85.

221. *Ibid.*, pp. 81, 86.

222. Lanéry d'Arc and L. Jeny, *Jeanne d'Arc en Berry*, pp. 72, 73.

223. *"In balneo et stuphis."* *Trial*, vol. iii, p. 88.

224. *L'amant rendu cordelier à l'observance d'amour*; poem attributed to Martial d'Auvergne, A. de Montaiglon, Paris, 1881, in 8vo, lines 1761-1776 and note p. 184. A. Franklin, *La vie privée d'autrefois*, vol. ii, *Les soins de la toilette*, Paris, 1887, in 18mo, pp. 20 *et seq.* A. Lecoy de la Marche, *Le bain au moyen âge*, in *Revue du monde catholique*, vol. xiv, pp. 870-881.

225. *Livre des métiers*, by Étienne Boileau, edited by De Lespinasse and F. Bonnardot, Paris, 1879, pp. 154, 155, and note. G. Bayle, *Notes pour servir à l'histoire de la prostitution au moyen âge*, in *Mémoires de l'Académie de Vauctuse*, 1887, pp. 241, 242. Dr. P. Pansier, *Histoire des prétendus statuts de la reine Jeanne*, in *Le Janus*, 1902, p. 14.

226. Lanéry d'Arc and L. Jeny, *Jeanne d'Arc en Berry*, pp. 76, 77.

227. *Trial*, vol. iii, p. 100.

228. *Ibid.*, p. 88.

229. *Trial*, vol. iii, p. 87. Lanéry d'Arc and L. Jeny, *Jeanne d'Arc en Berry*, pp. 73, 74.

230. *Trial*, vol. iii, pp. 86, 87.

231. *Ibid.*, pp. 86, 88.

232. *Trial*, vol. iii, p. 88.

233. *Ibid.*, p. 87.

234. *Ibid.*, pp. 87, 88.

235. Noël Valois, *Un nouveau témoignage sur Jeanne d'Arc*, in *Annuaire bulletin de la Société de l'Histoire de France*, Paris, 1907, in 8vo, pp. 8 and 18 (separate issue).

236. *Trial*, vol. iii, p. 217. De Beaucourt, *Histoire de Charles VII*, vol. ii, p. 265. A. Buhot de Kersers, *Histoire et statistique du département du Cher, canton de Mehun*, Bourges, 1891, in 4to, pp. 261 *et seq.* A. de Champeaux and P. Gauchery, *Les travaux d'art exécutés pour Jean de France, duc de Berry*, Paris, 1894, in 4to, pp. 7, 9, and the miniature in *Les grandes heures* of Duke Jean of Berry at Chantilly.

237. Perceval de Cagny, pp. 170, 171. Berry, in *Trial*, vol. iv, p. 48. Letter from the Sire d'Albret to the people of Riom, in *Trial*, vol. v, pp. 148, 149. Martin Le Franc, *Champion des dames*, in *Trial*, vol. v, p. 71.

238. *Chronique de la Pucelle*, p. 310. *Journal du siège*, p. 107. Morosini, vol. ii, p. 229, note 4. Perceval de Cagny, p. 172.

239. *Trial*, vol. iii, p. 217. Jaladon de la Barre, *Jeanne d'Arc à Saint-Pierre-le-Moustier et deux juges nivernais à Rouen*, Nevers, 1868, in 8vo, chaps. ix *et seq.*

240. *Trial*, vol. v, p. 356. Lanéry d'Arc and L. Jeny, *Jeanne d'Arc en Berry*, p. 89.

241. *Trial*, vol. iii, p. 217.

242. *Ibid.*, p. 218.

243. *Ibid.*, vol. i, p. 106. *Journal d'un bourgeois de Paris*, pp. 259, 260, 271, 272. Nider, *Formicarium*, in *Trial*, vol. iv, pp. 503, 504. J. Quicherat, *Aperçus nouveaux*, pp. 74 *et seq.* N. Quellien, *Perrinaïc, une compagne de Jeanne d'Arc*, Paris, 1891, in 8vo. Mme. Pascal-Estienne, *Perrinaïk*, Paris, 1893, in 8vo. J. Trévedy, *Histoire du roman de Perrinaïc*, Saint-Brieuc, 1894, in 8vo. *Le roman de Perrinaïc*, Vannes, 1894, in 8vo. A. de la Borderie, *Pierronne et Perrinaïc*, Paris, 1894, in 8vo.

244. *Trial*, vol. v, index at the words *Catherine, Michel, Marguerite*.

245. *Ibid.*, vol. i, p. 106.

246. *Journal d'un bourgeois de Paris*, pp. 271, 272.

247. *Trial*, vol. iii, pp. 104 *et seq.*

248. *Ibid.*, vol. ii, p. 450. *Journal d'un bourgeois de Paris*, pp. 271, 272.

249. *Journal d'un bourgeois de Paris*, p. 235.

250. *Trial*, vol. i, p. 106.

251. *Ibid.*, p. 107.

252. Arcère, *Histoire de La Rochelle*, 1756, in 4to, vol. i, p. 271. *Trial*, vol. v, p. 104, note. Vallet de Viriville, *Histoire de Charles VII*, vol. ii, pp. 24, 75 *et seq.*, 219, 279.

253. *Trial*, vol. i, pp. 107, 108.

254. *Trial*, vol. i, p. 107.

255. *Trial*, vol. i, pp. 108, 109.

256. *Ibid.*, p. 107.

257. *Ibid.*, p. 108.

258. *Ibid.*

259. "Perrinet Crasset, mason and captain of men-at-arms." *Chronique des cordeliers*, fol. 446 verso. Jean Chartier, *Chronique*, vol. i, p. 117. Monstrelet, vol. iv, p. 174. Vallet de Viriville, *Histoire de Charles VII*, vol. i, p. 328.

260. S. Luce, *Jeanne d'Arc à Domremy*, p. cclxxviii. A. de Villaret, *Campagne des Anglais*, p. 109. Le P. Ayroles, *La vraie Jeanne d'Arc*, vol. iii, pp. 20, 21, 373 *et seq.* J. de Fréminville, *Les écorcheurs en Bourgogne* (1435-1445); *Étude sur les compagnies franches au XVe siècle*, Dijon, 1888, in 8vo. P. Champion, *Guillaume de Flavy*. Proofs and illustrations, xxx.

261. Sainte-Marthe, *Histoire généalogique de la maison de la Trémoïlle*, 1668, in 12mo, pp. 149 *et seq.* L. de La Trémoïlle, *Les La Trémoïlle pendant cinq siècles*, Nantes, 1890, vol. i, p. 165.

262. *Trial*, vol. v, p. 149. Jean Chartier, *Chronique*, vol. iii. *Journal du siège*, p. 129. Monstrelet, vol. v, chap, lxxii. A. de Villaret, *Campagne des Anglais*, p. 108.

263. *Trial*, vol. v, p. 146. F. Perot, *Un document inédit sur Jeanne d'Arc*, in *Bulletin de la Société archéologique de l'Orléanais*, vol. xii, 1898-1901, p. 231.

264. *Trial*, vol. v, pp. 147-150. Lanéry d'Arc and L. Jeny, *Jeanne d'Arc en Berry*, ch. viii.

265. S. Luce, *Jeanne d'Arc à Domremy*, p. cclxxix.

266. Acta Sanctorum, March, i, 554, col. 2, no. 61. Abbé Bizouard, *Histoire de sainte Colette*, pp. 35, 37. Silvere., *Histoire chronologique de la bienheureuse Colette*, Paris, 1628, in 8vo.

267. *The Maid* (W.S.).

268. *Servant*. Cf. Godefroy, *Lexique de l'ancien Français* (W.S.).

269. *Histoire chronologique de la bienheureuse Colette*, pp. 168-200.

270. S. Luce, *Jeanne d'Arc et les ordres mendiants*, in *Revue des deux mondes*, 1881, vol. xlv, p. 90. L. de Kerval, *Jeanne d'Arc et les Franciscains*, Vanves, 1893, pp. 49, 51. S. Luce, *Jeanne d'Arc à Domremy*, pp. cclxxviii *et seq*. F. Perot, *Jeanne d'Arc en Bourbonnais*, Orléans, in 8vo, 26 pp., 1889. F. André, *La vérité sur Jeanne d'Arc*, in 8vo, 1895, pp. 308 *et seq*.

271. *Trial*, vol. v, pp. 146-148.

272. *Ibid.*, pp. 146, 148. Facsimile in *Le Musée des archives départementales*, p. 124.

273. F. Perot (*Bulletin de la Société archéologique de l'Orléanais*, vol. xii, p. 231).

274. A. de Villaret, *Campagne des Anglais*, p. 107, proofs and illustrations, xvii, pp. 159, 168. *Trial*, vol. v, pp. 268, 270, according to the original documents in the Orléans Library.

275. La Thaumassière, *Histoire du Berry*, p. 161. *Trial*, vol. v, pp. 356, 357. Lanéry d'Arc and L. Jeny, *Jeanne d'Arc en Berry*, pp. 105 *et seq*. A. de Villaret, *Campagne des Anglais*, pp. 111, 112.

276. *Mémoires de la Société des Antiquaires du Centre*, vol. iv, 1870-1872, pp. 211, 239.

277. Vallet de Viriville, *Histoire de Charles VII*, vol. ii, p. 126. Lanéry d'Arc and L. Jeny, *Jeanne d'Arc en Berry*, p. 89.

278. Perceval de Cagny, p. 172.

279. *Le Jouvencel*, vol. ii, pp. 216, 217.

280. Extract from the Book of Accounts of the town of Périgueux, in *Bulletin de la Société historique et archéologique du Périgord*, vol. xiv, January to February, 1887. S. Luce, *Jeanne d'Arc à Domremy*, proofs and illustrations, ccxvii, p. 252. Le P. Chapotin, *La guerre de cent ans et les dominicains*, pp. 74 *et seq*.

281. *Trial*, vol. i, p. 106.

282. *Journal d'un bourgeois de Paris*, p. 271.

283. Morosini, vol. iii, pp. 232, 233. Le P. Denifle and Chatelain, *Cartularium Univ. Paris*, vol. iv, p. 515.

284. Noël Valois, *Un nouveau témoignage sur Jeanne d'Arc*, Paris, 1907, in 8vo, 19 pages.

285. Morosini, vol. iii, p. 232.

286. *Journal d'un bourgeois de Paris*, pp. 354, 355.

287. *Sentent la persinée*: literally, smell of roast parsley. Cf. Godefroy, *Lexique de l'ancien français* at the word *persinée*. *Sentir la persinée*: to be suspected of heresy (W.S.).

288. Pardon granted to Le Sourd and Jehannin Daix, in *Trial*, vol. v, pp. 142-145.

289. *Trial*, vol. i, p. 107.

290. *Ibid.*, vol. iii, p. 84; vol. iv, pp. 312 *et passim*. A. de Villaret, *loc. cit.* Proofs and illustrations.

291. *Trial*, vol. v, pp. 150-153. J. Hordal, *Heroinae nobilissimae Joannae Darc, lotharingæ, vulgo aurelianensis puellae historia....* Ponti-Mussi, 1612, small 4to. C. du Lys, *Traité sommaire tant du nom et des armes que de la naissance et parenté de la Pucelle, justifié par plusieurs patentes et arrêts, enquêtes et informations....* Paris, 1633, in 4to. De la Roque, *Traité de la noblesse*, Paris, 1678, in 4to, ch. xliii. Lanéry d'Arc, *Jeanne d'Arc en Berry*, ch. x.

292. See analytical index, in *Trial*, vol. v, at the word *Pucelle*.

293. *Trial*, vol. v, p. 270.

294. *Ibid.*, vol. iii, pp. 19, 74, 203. H. Daniel Lacombe, *L'hôte de Jeanne d'Arc à Poitiers, Maître Jean Rabateau, président du parlement de Paris*, in *Revue du Bas-Poitou*, 1891, pp. 48, 66.

295. *Trial*, vol. iii, pp. 88 *et seq.*

296. Extract from the Accounts of the town of Orléans, in *Trial*, vol. v, p. 331.

297. Vallet de Viriville, *Un épisode de la vie de Jeanne d'Arc*, in *Bibliothèque de l'École des Chartes*, vol. iv (1st series), p. 488. *Trial*, vol. v, pp. 154-156.

298. Jules Doinel, *Note sur une maison de Jeanne d'Arc*, in *Mémoires de la Société archéologique et historique de l'Orléanais*, vol. xv, pp. 491-500.

299. *Journal du siège*, pp. 15, 16.

300. Jules Doinel, *Note sur une maison de Jeanne d'Arc*, *loc. cit.*

301. S. Luce, *Jeanne d'Arc à Domremy*, p. 360.

302. *Trial*, vol. i, p. 295.

303. Accounts of the fortress, in *Trial*, vol. v, pp. 259, 260.

304. *Trial*, vol. v, p. 159.

305. Perceval de Cagny, p. 173. *Chronique de la Pucelle*, p. 258. *Berry*, in Godefroy, p. 376. Morosini, vol. iii, p. 294, notes 4, 5. Vallet de Viriville, *Histoire de Charles VII*, vol. i, pp. 139, 163. De Beaucourt, *Histoire de Charles VII*, vol. ii, p. 144.

306. Monstrelet, vol. iv, p. 378. D. Plancher, *Histoire de Bourgogne*, vol. iv, p. 137. Morosini, vol. iii, p. 268.

307. Du Tillet, *Recueil des rois de France*, vol. ii, p. 39 (ed. 1601-1602). Rymer, *Fœdera*, March, 1430.

308. P. Champion, *Guillaume de Flavy*, pp. 35, 152.

309. De Beaucourt, *Histoire de Charles VII*, vol. ii, pp. 351, 389.

310. *Trial*, vol. v, p. 160, according to Rogier's copy. H. Jadart, *Jeanne d'Arc à Reims*, proofs and illustrations xv. Facsimile in Wallon, 1876 edition, p. 200. The original of this letter exists, likewise the original of the letter addressed on the 9th of November, 1429, to the citizens of Riom. These two letters, about one hundred and twenty-six days apart, are not written by the same scribe. The signature of neither one nor the other can be attributed to the hand which indited the rest of the letter. The seven letters of the name *Jehanne* seem to have been written by some one whose hand was being held, which is not surprising, seeing that the Maid did not know how to write. But a comparison of the two signatures reveals their close similarity. In both the stem of the J slopes in the same direction and is of identical length; the first *n* through one letter being written on the top of another has three pothooks instead of two; the second pothook of the second *n* obviously written in two strokes is too long, in short the two signatures correspond exactly. We must conclude therefore that having once obtained the Maid's signature by guiding her hand, an impression was taken to serve as a model for all her other letters. To judge from the two missives of the 9th of November, 1429 and the 16th of March, 1430, this impression was most faithfully reproduced. Cf. *post*, p. 117, note 2.

311. *Trial*, vol. iii, p. 11.

312. Perceval de Cagny, p. 172.

313. *Trial*, vol. i, p. 83.

314. *Ibid.*, vol. v, p. 156.

315. Monstrelet, vol. iv, pp. 24, 86, 87. J. Zeller, *Histoire d'Allemagne*, vol. vii, *La réforme*, Paris, 1891, pp. 78 *et seq.* E. Denis, *Jean Hus et la*

guerre des Hussites (1879); *Les origines de l'Unité des Frères Bohêmes*, Angers, 1885, in 8vo, pp. 5 *et seq.*

316. Two of the great leaders of the Hussites who held large parts of central Germany in terror from 1419-1434 (W.S.).

317. L. Paris, *Cabinet historique*, vol. i, 1855, pp. 74, 76. Rogier, in *Trial*, vol. iv, p. 294. Morosini, vol. iii, pp. 132, 133, 136, 137, 168, 169, 188, 189; vol. iv, supplement, xvii.

318. *Trial*, vol. i, p. 240; vol. v, p. 126.

319. Morosini, vol. iii, pp. 82-85. Christine de Pisan, in *Trial*, vol. v, p. 416. Eberhard Windecke, pp. 60-63.

320. Eberhard Windecke, pp. 108, 115, 188.

321. Lea, *A History of the Inquisition in the Middle Ages*, vol. ii, p. 481 (1906).

322. Th. de Sickel, *Lettre de Jeanne d'Arc aux Hussites*, in *Bibliothèque de l'École des Chartes*, 3rd series, vol. ii, p. 81. A wrong date is given in the German translation used by Quicherat, *Trial*, vol. v, pp. 156-159.

323. *Trial*, vol. i, p. 246.

324. *Ibid.*, vol. v, p. 95.

325. Another of the Hussite leaders (W.S.).

326. J. Nider, *Formicarium* in *Trial*, vol. iv, pp. 502-504.

327. *Trial*, vol. v, pp. 161, 162.

328. *Ibid.*, vol. iv, p. 299, and H. Jadart, *Jeanne d'Arc à Reims*, pp. 60 *et seq.* Mémoires de Pierre Coquault, *ibid.*, pp. 109 *et seq.*

329. This letter was published by J. Quicherat, in *Trial*, vol. v, pp. 161, 162, and by M. H. Jadart, *Jeanne d'Arc à Reims*, pp. 106, 107 and document XVI, according to Rogier's inaccurate copy. The original which had disappeared from the municipal archives at Reims was considered to be lost; but it has been found in the possession of the Count de Maleissye. Cf. the reproduction by A. Marty and M. Lepet, *L'histoire de Jeanne d'Arc.... Cent facsimilés de manuscrits, de miniatures*, Paris, 1907, in large 4to. Here for the first time is to be found a text correct according to the original document.

330. The signature appears to be autograph. It differs from the two identical signatures of the letters from Riom and Reims (see *ante*, p. 108, note 1); and it bears trace of the resistance of a hand which was being guided.

331. *Trial*, vol. v, pp. 161, 162. Varin, *Archives législatives de la ville de Reims*, vol. i, p. 596. H. Jadart, *Jeanne d'Arc à Reims*, pp. 106, 107.

332. Perceval de Cagny, who was in the pay of the Duke of Alençon, is the only chronicler to suggest it, p. 173.

333. "In the year 1430, Jeanne the Maid started from the country of Berry accompanied by divers fighting men...." Jean Chartier, *Chronique*, vol. i, p. 120.

334. Jean Chartier, *Chronique*, vol. i, p. 120. Martial d'Auvergne, *Vigiles*, ed. Coustellier, vol. i, p. 117. Note concerning G. de Flavy, in *Trial*, vol. v, p. 177. P. Champion, *Guillaume de Flavy*, p. 36, note 2.

335. *Journal du siège*, p. 12.

336. De Beaucourt, *Histoire de Charles VII*, vol. ii, p. 293, note 3. True, the loan was made later; none the less the dependence of Jean d'Aulon on the Sire de la Trémouille existed at this time.

337. *Trial*, vol. i, p. 99, note. *Journal du siège*, pp. 235, 238.

338. This comes from the *Journal d'un bourgeois de Paris*, p. 271.

339. *Trial*, vol. v, pp. 159, 160.

340. The Pardon of Jean de Calais in A. Longnon, *Paris sous la domination anglaise*, pp. 301-309. Stevenson, *Letters and Papers*, vol. i, pp. 34-50.

341. So it appears from Morosini, vol. iii, pp. 274-275.

342. Morosini, vol. iii, pp. 228-231. Concerning Perrinet Gressart see vol. i, p. 389.

343. May 3, 1430.

344. G. Lefèvre-Pontalis, *La panique anglaise*. Le P. Ayroles, *La vraie Jeanne d'Arc*, vol. iii, pp. 572-574.

345. *Trial*, vol. i, pp. 115, 253, April 17-23. Perceval de Cagny, p. 173. *Chronique des cordeliers*, fol. 502 recto. P. Champion, *Guillaume de Flavy*, p. 158, note 2.

346. Monstrelet, vol. iv, p. 363 (April 16).

347. Jean Chartier, *Chronique*, vol. i, p. 125. Monstrelet, vol. iv, p. 378. Chastellain, vol. ii, p. 28. Melun certainly belonged to the French on the 23rd of April, 1430.

348. *Trial*, vol. i, pp. 114-116. G. Leroy, *Histoire de Melun*, Melun, 1887, in 8vo, ch. xvi ... x ... *Jeanne d'Arc à Melun, mi-avril, 1430*, Melun, 1896, 32 pp.

349. *Trial*, vol. i, p. 147.

350. *Journal d'un bourgeois de Paris*, p. 259.

351. *Chronique de la Pucelle*, pp. 334, 335. Jean Chartier, *Chronique*, vol. i, pp. 110, 111. F.A. Denis, *Le séjour de Jeanne d'Arc à Lagny*, Lagny, 1894, in 8vo, pp. 3 *et seq.*

352. Monstrelet, vol. iv, p. 384. Jean Chartier, *Chronique*, vol. i, pp. 120, 121. Perceval de Cagny, p. 173.

353. Jean Chartier, *loc. cit.* Martial d'Auvergne, *Vigiles*, vol. i, p. 117. P. Champion, *Guillaume de Flavy*, p. 38, note.

354. Jean Chartier, *Chronique*, vol. i, p. 121.

355. Monstrelet, vol. iv, p. 384.

356. H. Jadart, *Jeanne d'Arc à Reims*, p. 61.

357. *Trial*, vol. i, p. 158.

358. *Ibid.*, pp. 158, 159.

359. *Journal d'un bourgeois de Paris*, pp. 71, 72. Sauval, *Antiquités de Paris*, vol. i, p. 104. A. Longnon, *Paris pendant la domination anglaise*, p. 118. H. Legrand, *Paris en 1380*, Paris, 1868, in 4to, p. 65.

360. *Piquette*, a sour wine or cider, made from the residue of grapes or apples. A kind of second brewing (W.S.). *Journal d'un bourgeois de Paris*, pp. 150, 154, 156, 187. Francisque-Michel and Edouard Fournier, *Histoire des hôtelleries, cabarets, hôtels garnis*, Paris, 1851 (2 vols. in 8vo), vol. ii, p. 5.

361. A. Longnon, *Paris pendant la domination anglaise*, p. 117.

362. *Journal d'un bourgeois de Paris*, pp. 71, 72. A. Longnon, *Paris pendant la domination anglaise*, p. 118, note 1.

363. A. Longnon, *Paris pendant la domination anglaise*, pp. 119-123.

364. *Journal d'un bourgeois de Paris*, pp. 251, 253. Falconbridge, in A. Longnon, *Paris pendant la domination anglaise*, p. 302, note 1. Sauval, *Antiquités de Paris*, vol. iii, p. 536. Vallet de Viriville, *Histoire de Charles VII*, vol. ii, p. 140. Morosini, vol. iii, pp. 274 *et seq.*

365. *Trial*, vol. i, pp. 158, 159.

366. *Ibid.*, p. 159.

367. *Ibid.*, p. 254. Monstrelet, vol. iv, p. 385. E. Richer, *Histoire manuscrite de la Pucelle*, book i, folio 82.

368. *Le Jouvencel*, vol. ii, pp. 210, 211.

369. *Trial*, vol. i, p. 105.

370. A. Denis, *Jeanne d'Arc à Lagny*, Lagny, 1896, in 8vo, pp. 4 *et seq.* J.A. Lepaire, *Jeanne d'Arc à Lagny*, Lagny, 1880, in 8vo, 38 pages.

371. *Trial*, vol. i, p. 105.

372. *Religieux de Saint-Denis*, vol. ii, p. 82. Jean Juvénal des Ursins, in *Coll. Michaud et Poujoulat*, p. 395, col. 2.

373. *Acta Sanctorum*, 6th of March, pp. 381 and 617. Abbé Bizouard, *Histoire de Sainte Colette*, pp. 35, 37. Abbé Douillet, *Sainte Colette, sa vie, ses œuvres*, 1884, pp. 150-154.

374. Le Curé de Saint-Sulpice, *Notre-Dame de France*, Paris, in 8vo, vol. vi, 1860, p. 57.

375. For the etymology of Avioth see C. Bonnabelle, *Petite étude sur Avioth et son église*, in *Annuaire de la Meuse*, 1883, in 18mo, p. 14.

376. Le Curé de Saint-Sulpice, *loc. cit.*, vol. v, pp. 107 *et seq.* Bonnabelle, *loc. cit.*, pp. 13 *et seq.* Jacquemain, *Notre-Dame d'Avioth et son église monumentale*, Sedan, 1876, in 8vo.

377. *Trial*, vol. i, pp. 105, 106.

378. Arch. mun. of Senlis in *Musé des archives départementales*, pp. 304, 305. J. Flammermont, *Histoire de Senlis pendant la seconds partie de la guerre de cent ans*, p. 245. Perceval de Cagny, p. 173. Morosini, vol. iii, p. 294, note 5.

379. Manuscript History of Beauvais by Hermant, in *Trial*, vol. v, p. 165. G. Lecocq, *Étude historique sur le séjour de Jeanne d'Arc à Elincourt-Sainte-Marguerite*, ,Amiens, 1879, in 8vo, 13 pages. A. Peyrecave, *Notes sur le séjour de Jeanne d'Arc à Elincourt-Sainte-Marguerite*, Paris, 1875, in 8vo. *Elincourt-Sainte-Marguerite, notice historique et archéologique*, Compiègne, 1888. Ch. vii, pp. 113, 123.

380. *Trial*, vol. v, pp. 164, 165. *Les miracles de Madame Sainte Katerine de Fierboys*, pp. 16, 62, 63.

381. P. Champion, *Guillaume de Flavy*. Proofs and illustrations, pp. 150, 154. Morosini, vol. iii, p. 276, note 3. Note concerning G. de Flavy, in *Trial*, vol. v, p. 176.

382. Monstrelet, ch. xxx. Note concerning G. de Flavy, in *Trial*, vol. v, p. 175. P. Champion, *Guillaume de Flavy*. Proofs and illustrations, xliv, xlv.

383. "In this country the Emperor of Constantinople. has a city called Capha, which is a seaport belonging to the Genoese and whence is obtained wood for the making of bows and cross-bows, likewise wine called Rommenie." *Le Livre de description des pays de Gilles le Bouvier*. Ed. E.T. Hamy, Paris, 1908, p. 90.

384. De La Fons-Mélicocq, *Documents inédits sur le siège de Compiègne de 1430* in *La Picardie*, vol. iii, 1857, pp. 22, 23. P. Champion, *Guillaume de Flavy*. Proofs and illustrations, p. 176.

385. Lefèvre de Saint-Rémy, vol. ii, p. 178. H. de Lépinois, *Notes extraites des archives communales de Compiègne*, in *Bibliothèque de l'École des Chartes*, 1863, vol. xxiv, p. 486. A. Sorel, *La prise de Jeanne d'Arc devant Compiègne et l'histoire des sièges de la même ville sous Charles VI et Charles VII, d'après des documents inédits avec vues et plans*, Paris, 1889, in 8vo, p. 268.

386. Jacques Duclercq, *Mémoires*, ed. Reiffenberg, vol. i, p. 419. *Le Temple de Bocace* in *Les œuvres de Georges Chastellain*, ed. Kervyn de Lettenhove, vol. vii, p. 95. P. Champion, *Guillaume de Flavy, capitaine de Compiègne, contribution à l'histoire de Jeanne d'Arc et à l'étude de la vie militaire et privée au XVième siècle*, Paris, 1906, in 8vo, *passim*.

387. Jean Chartier, *Chronique*, vol. i, p. 125. *Chronique des cordeliers*, fol. 495 recto. Rogier, in Varin, *Arch. de la ville de Reims*, 11th part, Statuts, vol. i, p. 604. A. Sorel, *loc. cit.*, p. 167. P. Champion, *loc. cit.*, p. 33.

388. Monstrelet, vol. iv, pp. 379, 381. *Chronique des cordeliers*, fol. 495 recto. *Livre des trahisons*, p. 202.

389. Monstrelet, vol. iv, pp. 382, 383. Berry, in *Trial*, vol. iv, p. 49.

390. According to a note by Dom Bertheau, in A. Sorel, *Séjours de Jeanne d'Arc à Compiègne, maisons où elle a logé en 1429 et 1430*, with view and plans, Paris, 1888, in 8vo, pp. 11, 12.

391. Magistrates of the town. Cf. *ante*, p. 34, note 3.

392. *Accounts of the town of Compiègne*, CC 13, folio 291. Dom Gillesson, *Antiquités de Compiègne*, vol. v, p. 95. A. Sorel, *La prise de Jeanne d'Arc*, p. 145, note 3.

393. Choisy surrendered on the 16th of May. *Chronique des cordeliers*, fol. 497, verso. *Livre des trahisons*, p. 201. Monstrelet, vol. iv, p. 382. Berry, in *Trial*, vol. iv, p. 49. A. Sorel, *La prise de Jeanne d'Arc*, pp. 145, 146. P. Champion, *Guillaume de Flavy*, pp. 40-41, 162-163.

394. Berry, in *Trial*, vol. iv, pp. 49, 50.

395. F. Brun, *Jeanne d'Arc et le capitaine de Soissons en 1430*, Soissons, 1904, p. 5 (extract from *l'Argus Soissonnais*). P. Champion, *loc. cit.*, p. 41.

396. Berry, in *Trial*, vol. iv, p. 50. P. Champion, *loc. cit.*, p. 168. Proofs and illustrations, xxxv, p. 168. F. Brun, *Nouvelles recherches sur le*

fait de Soissons (Jeanne d'Arc et Bournel en 1430) à propos d'un livre récent, Meulan, 1907, in 8vo.

397. *Trial*, vol. i, p. 273.

398. I have rejected the story told by Alain Bouchard of Jeanne's meeting with the little children in the Church of Saint Jacques. (*Les grandes croniques de Bretaigne*, Paris, Galliot Du Pré, 1514, fol. cclxxxi.) M. Pierre Champion (*Guillaume de Flavy*, p. 283) has irrefutably demonstrated its unauthenticity.

399. Monstrelet, vol. iv, p. 382. Lefèvre de Saint-Rémy, vol. ii, p. 178. *Chronique des cordeliers*, fol. 498 verso.

400. *Trial*, vol. i, p. 114. Perceval de Cagny, p. 174. Extract from a note concerning G. de Flavy, in *Trial*, vol. v, p. 176. Morosini, vol. iii, p. 296, note 1.

401. Manuscript map of Compiègne in 1509, in Debout, *Jeanne d'Arc*, vol. ii, p. 293. Plan of the town of Compiègne, engraved by Aveline in the 17th century, reduction published by *La Société historique de Compiègne*, May, 1877. Lambert de Ballyhier, *Compiègne historique et monumental*, 1842, 2 vols. in 8vo, engravings. Plan of the restitution of the town of Compiègne in 1430, in A. Sorel, *La prise de Jeanne d'Arc*. P. Champion, *Guillaume de Flavy*, p. 43.

402. Monstrelet, vol. iv, pp. 383, 384.

403. *Le Jouvencel*, vol. ii, p. 196.

404. *Trial*, vol. i, p. 116. Letter from Philippe le Bon to the inhabitants of Saint-Quentin, *Trial*, vol. v, p. 166. Letter from Philippe le Bon to Amédée, Duke of Savoy in P. Champion, *loc. cit.* Proofs and illustrations, xxxvii. Falconbridge, in *Trial*, vol. iv, p. 458. William Worcester, in *Trial*, vol. iv, p. 475, and *Le Journal d'un bourgeois de Paris*, p. 255.

405. *Trial*, vol. i, pp. 78, 223, 224. Chastellain, vol. ii, p. 49. The Clerk of the Brabant *Chambre des Comptes*, in *Trial*, vol. iv, p. 428.

406. Notes concerning G. de Flavy, in *Trial*, vol. v, p. 177. *Chronique de Tournai*, in *Recueil des Chroniques de Flandre*, 1856, vol. iii, pp. 415, 416.

407. Chastellain, vol. ii, p. 49.

408. *Le Jouvencel*, vol. i, p. 91.

409. Monstrelet, vol. iv, p. 387. Lefèvre de Saint-Rémy, vol. ii, p. 179. Chastellain, vol. ii, p. 48. Note concerning G. de Flavy, in *Trial*, vol. v, p. 176.

410. Letter from the Duke of Burgundy to the inhabitants of Saint-Quentin, in *Trial*, vol. v, p. 166. Monstrelet, Lefèvre de Saint-Rémy, Chastellain. Notes concerning G. de Flavy, *loc. cit.*

411. Perceval de Cagny, p. 176. Falconbridge, in *Trial*, vol. iv, p. 458. Monstrelet. Note concerning G. de Flavy; Lefèvre de Saint-Rémy, Chastellain, *loc. cit.*

412. Note concerning G. de Flavy, *loc. cit.* Du Fresne de Beaucourt, *Jeanne d'Arc et Guillaume de Flavy* in *Bulletin de la Société de l'Histoire de France*, vol. iii, 1861, pp. 173 *et seq.* Z. Rendu, *Jeanne d'Arc et G. de Flavy*, Compiègne, 1865, in 8vo, 32 pp. A. Sorel, *La prise de Jeanne d'Arc*, p. 209. P. Champion, *Guillaume de Flavy*, appendix i, pp. 282, 286.

413. Perceval de Cagny, p. 175.

414. Perceval de Cagny, p. 175. Chastellain, vol. ii, p. 49. Jean Chartier, *Chronique*, vol. i, p. 122; vol. iii, p. 207. Quicherat, *Aperçus nouveaux*, p. 87.

415. Perceval de Cagny, p. 176.

416. Letter from the Duke of Burgundy in *Trial*, vol. v, p. 166. Perceval de Cagny, p. 175. Monstrelet, vol. iv, p. 400. Lefèvre de Saint-Rémy, p. 175. Chastellain, vol. ii, p. 49. Note concerning G. de Flavy, in *Trial*, vol. v, p. 174. Martial d'Auvergne, *Vigiles*, vol. i, p. 118. P. Champion, *loc. cit.*, pp. 46, 49. Lanéry d'Arc, *Livre d'Or*, pp. 513-518.

417. Richer, *Histoire manuscrite de la Pucelle*, book iv, fol. 188 *et seq.* P. Champion, *loc. cit.* Proofs and illustrations, xxxiii. Monstrelet, vol. iv, p. 388. Note concerning G. de Flavy, *loc. cit.* Letter from the Duke of Burgundy to the inhabitants of Saint-Quentin, *loc. cit. Journal d'un bourgeois de Paris*, p. 255. Falconbridge, in *Trial*, vol. iv, p. 459.

418. According to *Le Journal d'un bourgeois de Paris*, p. 255, four hundred French were killed or drowned.

419. Note concerning G. de Flavy, in *Trial*, vol. v, p. 176. Perceval de Cagny, p. 175.

420. Letter from the Duke of Burgundy to the inhabitants of Saint-Quentin, in *Trial*, vol. v, p. 166.

421. Monstrelet, vol. iv, p. 388. Chastellain, vol. ii, p. 50. A. Sorel, *La prise de Jeanne d'Arc*, pp. 253 *et seq.*

422. Jean Jouffroy, in d'Achery, *Spicilegium*, iii, pp. 823 *et seq.*

423. Monstrelet, vol. iv, p. 388.

424. *Ibid.*, p. 389. P. Champion, *loc. cit.*, p. 168.

425. *La Chronique des cordeliers*, and Monstrelet, *passim*. Vallet de Viriville, *Histoire de Charles VII*, vol. ii, pp. 165, 166.

426. *Trial*, vol. v, p. 167. J. Quicherat, *Aperçus nouveaux*, p. 95.

427. *Trial*, vol. v, p. 358. Le P. Ayroles, *La vraie Jeanne d'Arc*, vol. iii, p. 534. P. Champion, *Guillaume de Flavy*, pp. 169-171.

428. Note concerning Guillaume de Flavy in *Trial*, vol. v, p. 177. A. Sorel, *La prise de Jeanne d'Arc*, p. 333.

429. Falconbridge, in *Trial*, vol. iv, p. 458. *Journal d'un bourgeois de Paris*, p. 255. J. Quicherat, *Aperçus nouveaux*, p. 96. U. Chevalier, *L'abjuration de Jeanne d'Arc au cimetière de Saint-Ouen et l'authenticité de sa formule*, Paris, 1902, in 8vo, p. 18.

430. *Trial*, vol. i, pp. 8-10. E. O'Reilly, *Les deux procès*, vol. ii, pp. 13, 14. P. Denifle and Chatelain, *Chartularium Universitatis Parisiensis*, vol. iv, p. 516, no. 2372.

431. *Trial*, vol. i, p. 12. E. O'Reilly, *Les deux procès*.

432. *Trial*, vol. i, pp. 3, 12; vol. iii, p. 378; vol. v, p. 392.

433. *Domini canes*. Thus they are represented in the frescoes of the Capella degli Spagnuoli in Santa-Maria-Novella at Florence.

434. Tanon, *Histoire des tribuneaux de l'inquisition en France*, ch. ii.

435. Le P. Denifle and Chatelain, *Chartularium universitatis Parisiensis*, vol. iv, p. 510; *Le procès de Jeanne d'Arc et l'université de Paris*, Paris, 1897, in 8vo, 32 pp.

436. *Journal d'un bourgeois de Paris*, *passim*. Falconbridge, in *Trial*, vol. iv, p. 450.

437. *Journal d'un bourgeois de Paris*, p. 237. T. Basin, *Histoire de Charles VII et de Louis XI*, vol. iv, pp. 103, 104. Monstrelet, vol. iv, ch. lxiii. Bougenot, *Deux documents inédits relatifs à Jeanne d'Arc*, in *Revue bleue*, 13 Feb., 1892, pp. 203, 204.

438. Le P. Denifle and Chatelain, *Chartularium Universitatis Parisiensis*, vol. iv, p. 515, no. 2370; *Le procès de Jeanne d'Arc et l'université de Paris*.

439. Monstrelet, vol. iv, p. 389. Perceval de Cagny, p. 176. Morosini, vol. iii, pp. 300-302; vol. iv, pp. 254-355. De La Fons-Mélicocq, *Une cité picarde au moyen âge ou Noyon et les Noyonnais aux XIVe et XVe siècles*, Noyon, 1841, vol. ii, pp. 100-105. In 1441 Lyonnel de Wandomme, who was governor of this town, was driven out by the

inhabitants on the death of Jean de Luxembourg (Monstrelet, vol. v, p. 456).

440. Perceval de Cagny, p. 177, very doubtful.

441. *Trial*, vol. i, pp. 163-164, 249.

442. *Ibid.*, p. 151.

443. Vallet de Viriville, *Note sur deux médailles de plomb relatives à Jeanne d'Arc*, Paris, 1861, in 8vo, 30 pages. Forgeais, *Notice sur les plombs historiés trouvés dans la Seine*, Paris, 1860, in 8vo. J. Quicherat, *Médaille frappée en l'honneur de la Pucelle, Six dessins sur Jeanne d'Arc tirés d'un manuscrit du XVe siècle*, in *L'autographe*, No. 24, 15 Nov., 1864.

444. P. Lanéry d'Arc, *Le culte de Jeanne d'Arc au XVe siècle*, Paris, 1887, in 8vo, 29 pages.

445. *Trial*, vol. i, p. 290.

446. Carreau, *Histoire manuscrite de Touraine*, in *Procès*, vol. v, pp. 253, 254.

447. *Trial*, vol. v, p. 104. E. Maignien, *Oraisons latines pour la délivrance de Jeanne d'Arc*. Grenoble, 1867, in 8vo (*Revue des Sociétés savantes*, vol. iv, pp. 412-414). G. de Braux, *Trois oraisons pour la délivrance de Jeanne d'Arc*, in *Journal de la Société d'Archéologie Lorraine*, June, 1887, pp. 125, 127.

448. *Vita Jacobi Gelu ab ipso conscripta*, in *Bulletin de la Société archéologique de Touraine*, iii, 1867, pp. 266 *et seq.* The Rev. Father Marcellin Fornier, *Histoire des Alpes Maritimes ou Cottiennes*, vol. ii, pp. 313 *et seq.*

449. *Ibid.*, pp. 319, 320.

450. Thomassin, in *Trial*, vol. iv, p. 312. *Chronique du doyen de Saint-Thibaud*, in *Trial*, vol. iv, p. 323. *Chronique de Tournai*, in *Recueil des chroniques de Flandre*, vol. iii, p. 415. *Chronique de Normandie*, ed. A. Hellot, Rouen, 1881, in 8vo, pp. 77, 78. *Chronique de Lorraine*, ed. Abbé Marchal (*Recueil de documents sur l'histoire de Lorraine*, vol. v).

451. Summary of a letter from Regnault de Chartres to the inhabitants of Reims, *Trial*, vol. v, p. 168.

452. *Journal d'un bourgeois de Paris*, p. 272. Lefèvre de Saint-Rémy, vol. ii, p. 263. Martial d'Auvergne, *Vigiles*, vol. i, p. 124.

453. A. Maury, *La stigmatisation et les stigmates*, in *Revue des Deux Mondes*, 1854, ch. viii, pp. 454-482. Dr. Subled, *Les stigmates selon*

la science, in *Science catholique*, 1894, vol. viii, pp. 1073 *et seq.*; vol. ix, pp. 2 *et seq.*

454. Letter from Regnault de Chartres, in *Trial*, vol. v, p. 168.

455. *Trial*, vol. i, pp. 295 *et seq.*

456. Letter from Regnault de Chartres, in *Ibid.*, vol. v, p. 168.

457. *Ibid.*, p. 168.

458. This point was not called in question at the time; but what might be discussed is whether the Bishop of Beauvais could exercise ordinary jurisdiction over the Maid. On this subject see: Abbé Ph. H. Dunand, *Histoire complète de Jeanne d'Arc*, Paris, 1899, vol. ii, pp. 412, 413.

459. Robillard de Beaurepaire, *Notes sur les juges et assesseurs du procès de Jeanne d'Arc*, Rouen, 1890, p. 12. Douet d'Arcq, *Choix de pièces inédites relatives au règne de Charles VI*, vol. i, pp. 356, 357. Chanoine Cerf, *Pierre Cauchon de Sommièvre, chanoine de Reims et de Beauvais, évêque de Beauvais et de Lisieux; son origine, ses dignités, sa mort et ses sépultures*, in *Travaux de l'Académie de Reims*, CI (1898), pp. 363 *et seq.*, A. Sarrazin, *Pierre Cauchon, juge de Jeanne d'Arc*, Paris, 1901, in 8vo, pp. 26 *et seq.*

460. Le P. Ayroles, *La vraie Jeanne d'Arc*, vol. i, p. 116. A. Sarrazin, *P. Cauchon*, pp. 36, 37.

461. Du Boulay, *Historia Universitatis Parisiensis*, 1670, vol. v, p. 912. The Abbé Delettre, *Histoire du diocèse de Beauvais*, Beauvais, 1842, vol. ii, p. 348.

462. Robillard de Beaurepaire, *Notes sur les juges*, p. 13.

463. A. Sarrazin, *P. Cauchon*, pp. 58 *et seq.*

464. Rymer, *Fœdera*, vol. x, p. 408, *passim*.

465. *Trial*, vol. i, p. 13. Vallet de Viriville, *Procès de condamnation*, pp. 10 *et seq.* A. Sarrazin, *P. Cauchon*, pp. 108 *et seq.*

466. *Trial*, vol. i, pp. 10, 11. M. Fournier, *La faculté de décret*, vol. i, p. 353, note.

467. *Trial*, vol. i, pp. 13, 14.

468. *Trial*, vol. i, p. 14.

469. Du Boulay, *Historia Universitatis Parisiensis*, vol. v, pp. 393-408. *Monumenta conciliorum generalium seculi decimi quinti*, vol. i, pp. 70 *et seq.* Le P. Denifle and Chatelain, *Le procès de Jeanne d'Arc et l'Université de Paris*.

470. Valeran Varanius, ed. Prarond, Paris, 1889, book iv, p. 100.

471. *Trial*, vol. i, pp. 109, 110; vol. ii, p. 298; vol. iii, p. 121. Monstrelet, vol. iv, p. 389. E. Gomart, *Jeanne d'Arc au château de Beaurevoir*, Cambrai, 1865, in 8vo, 47 pages (*Mem. de la Société d'émulation de Cambrai*, xxxviii, 2, pp. 305-348). L. Sambier, *Jeanne d'Arc et la région du Nord*, Lille, 1901, in 8vo, 63 pages. Cf. Morosini, vol. iii, p. 300, notes 3 and 4, vol. iv, supplement xxi.

472. *Trial*, vol. i, pp. 95, 231. Monstrelet, vol. iv, p. 402. Vallet de Viriville, *Histoire de Charles VII*, vol. i, p. 2; vol. ii, pp. 72, 73.

473. A. Duchêne, *Histoire de la maison de Béthune*, ch. iii, and proofs and illustrations, p. 33. Vallet de Viriville, *loc. cit.*, and Morosini, vol. iv, pp. 352, 354.

474. *Trial*, vol. i, pp. 95, 231.

475. *Ibid.*, vol. ii, pp. 438, 457; vol. iii, p. 121.

476. *Trial*, vol. iii, pp. 120, 121.

477. *Ibid.*, vol. i, p. 150.

478. *Trial*, vol. i, pp. 150, 151.

479. *Ibid.*, p. 13; vol. v, p. 194.

480. *Ibid.*, vol. i, pp. 110, 151, 152.

481. *Trial*, vol. i, p. 166. *Journal d'un bourgeois de Paris*, p. 268. J. Quicherat, *Aperçus nouveaux*, pp. 53, 58.

482. *Chronique des cordeliers*, fol. 507, recto. Morosini, vol. iii, pp. 301-303. *Chronique de Tournai*, ed. Smedt, in *Recueil des Chroniques de Flandre*, vol. iii, pp. 416, 417.

483. Lottin, *Recherches sur la ville d'Orléans*, vol. i, p. 252. *Trial*, vol. i, p. 99, note 1. *Journal du siège*, pp. 235-238. S. Luce, *Jeanne d'Arc à Domremy*, p. cclxiii, note 2.

484. *Trial*, vol. i, pp. 296, 297.

485. Register of the Accounts of the town of Tours for the year 1430, in *Trial*, vol. iv, p. 473, note 1.

486. *Trial*, vol. iv, p. 473.

487. *Ibid.*, p. 473.

488. *Ibid.*, vol. i, p. 295.

489. *Trial*, vol. i, p. 106, note. *Journal d'un bourgeois de Paris*, p. 271. Vallet de Viriville, *Procès de condamnation de Jeanne d'Arc*, pp. lxi-lxv.

490. *Journal d'un bourgeois de Paris*, p. 271.

491. *Journal d'un bourgeois de Paris*, pp. 271, 272.

492. Voltaire, *Dictionnaire philosophique*, article, Arc.

493. *Journal d'un bourgeois de Paris*, pp. 259, 260.

494. *Journal d'un bourgeois de Paris*, pp. 259-260, 271-272. Jean Nider, *Formicarium*, in *Trial*, vol. iv, p. 504. A. de la Borderie, *Pierronne et Perrinaïc*, pp. 7 *et seq.*

495. H. Vandenbroeck, *Extraits des anciens registres des consaux de la ville de Tournai*, vol. ii (1422-1430), and Morosini, vol. iii, pp. 185, 186.

496. H. Vandenbroeck, *Extraits analytiques des anciens registres des consaux de la ville de Tournai*, vol. ii, pp. 338, 371-373. Canon H. Debout, *Jeanne d'Arc et les villes d'Arras et de Tournai*, Paris, n.d., p. 24.

497. Le P. Anselme, *Histoire généalogique de la maison de France*, vol. iii, pp. 723, 724. Vallet de Viriville, *Histoire de Charles VII*, vol. ii, pp. 175, 176. Morosini, vol. iv, supplement xix.

498. *Trial*, vol. i, pp. 95, 231.

499. *Ibid.*, pp. 13, 14.

500. *Les miracles de madame Sainte Katerine*, Bourassé, *passim*.

501. "Was waited on in prison like a lady," says *Le Journal d'un bourgeois de Paris*, p. 271, concerning the Rouen prison.

502. *Trial*, vol. i, p. 100.

503. *Ibid.*, pp. 101, 206, 291; vol. iii, p. 87; vol. v, pp. 104, 305. Chastellain, ed. Kervyn de Lettenhove, vol. ii, p. 46. P. Lanéry d'Arc, *Le culte de Jeanne d'Arc au XVe siècle*, Orléans, 1887, in 8vo. Noël Valois, *Un nouveau témoignage sur Jeanne d'Arc*, pp. 8, 13, 18.

504. *Trial*, vol. i, pp. 95, 96, 231. Canon Henri Debout, *Jeanne d'Arc prisonnière à Arras*, Arras, 1894, in 16mo; *Jeanne d'Arc et les villes d'Arras et de Tournai*, Paris, 1904, in 8vo; *Jeanne d'Arc*, vol. ii, pp. 394 *et seq.*

505. On the 7th of November, 1430, a messenger from the town of Arras received forty shillings for having taken two sealed letters to the Duke of Burgundy, one from Jean de Luxembourg, the other from David de Brimeu, Governor of the Bailiwick of Arras; we know nothing of the tenor of these letters written concerning "the case of the Maid." P. Champion, *Notes sur Jeanne d'Arc, II; Jeanne d'Arc à Arras*, in *Le Moyen Âge*, July-August, 1907, pp. 200, 201.

506. H. de Lépinois, *Notes extraites des archives communales de Compiègne*, in *Bibliothèque de l'École des Chartes*, 1863, vol. xxiv, p.

486. A. Sorel, *Prise de Jeanne d'Arc*, p. 268. P. Champion, *Guillaume de Flavy*, pp. 38, 48 *et seq.*

507. *Chronique des cordeliers*, fol. 500 verso.

508. Chastellain, vol. ii, p. 53.

509. Monstrelet, vol. iv, p. 390.

510. Monstrelet, vol. iv, pp. 390, 391. Lefèvre de Saint-Rémy, vol. ii, p. 180. Morosini, vol. iii, pp. 306, 307. Chastellain, vol. ii, pp. 51, 54. A. Sorel, *La prise de Jeanne d'Arc*, pp. 233 *et seq.* P. Champion. *Guillaume de Flavy*, p. 50.

511. *Le Jouvencel*, vol. i, pp. 49 *et seq.*

512. *Chronique des cordeliers*, fol. 502 verso. P. Champion, *Guillaume de Flavy*, proofs and illustrations, xli, xlii, xliii.

513. *Livre des trahisons*, p. 202.

514. Monstrelet, vol. iii, pp. 410-415. Lefèvre de Saint-Rémy, vol. ii, p. 185. *Livre des trahisons*, p. 202. A. Sorel, *La prise de Jeanne d'Arc*, proofs and illustrations, xiii, p. 341. P. Champion, *loc. cit.*, p. 176.

515. Monstrelet, vol. iv, p. 418. De La Fons-Mélicocq, *Documents inédits sur le siège de Compiègne*, in *La Picardie*, vol. iii, 1857, pp. 22, 23. Stevenson, *Letters and Papers*, vol. ii, part i, p. 156.

516. Monstrelet, vol. iv, p. 419. P. Champion, *Guillaume de Flavy*, p. 57.

517. Sorel, *La prise de Jeanne d'Arc*, proofs and illustrations, p. 343.

518. *Trial*, vol. i, p. 9. Vallet de Viriville, *Histoire de Charles VII*, vol. ii, p. 175.

519. Morosini, vol. iii, p. 236. U. Chevalier, *L'abjuration de Jeanne d'Arc*, p. 18, note.

520. Morosini, vol. iii, p. 276, note.

521. Chronicle of Jean de la Chapelle, in *Trial*, vol. v, pp. 358-360. Lefils, *Histoire de la ville du Crotoy et de son château*, pp. 111-118. G. Lefèvre-Pontalis, *La panique anglaise*, p. 8, note 5. L'Abbé Bouthors, *Histoire de Saint-Riquier*, Abbeville, 1902, pp. 185, 215, 220.

522. Perceval de Cagny, pp. 22, 137.

523. *Trial*, vol. iii, p. 121. A. Sarrazin, *Jeanne d'Arc et la Normandie*, pp. 63 *et seq.*; Lanéry d'Arc, *Livre d'or*, p. 521.

524. *Trial*, vol. i, p. 89; vol. iii, p. 121. Le P. Ignace de Jésus Maria, *Histoire généalogique des comtes de Ponthieu et maïeurs d'Abbeville*, Paris, 1657, p. 490. *Trial*, vol. v, p. 361.

525. Monstrelet, vol. iv, pp. 353, 354. *Trial*, vol. v, p. 143.

526. *Trial*, vol. i, pp. 15, 16. M. Fournier, *La Faculté de décret et l'Université de Paris*, vol. i, p. 353.

527. *Trial*, vol. i, p. 21. Le P. Ignace de Jésus Maria, in *Trial*, vol. v, p. 363. F. Poulaine, *Jeanne d'Arc à Rouen*, Paris, 1899, in 16mo. Ch. Lemire, *Jeanne d'Arc en Picardie et en Normandie*, Paris, 1903, p. 10, *passim*. Lanéry d'Arc, *Livre d'or*, pp. 524, 549.

528. A. Sarrazin, *Jeanne d'Arc et la Normandie au XVe siècle*, Rouen, 1896, in 4to, ch. v.

529. *Trial*, vol. iii, pp. 136-137. Vallet de Viriville, *Histoire de Charles VII*, vol. ii, p. 198.

530. L. de Duranville, *Le château de Bouvreuil*, in *La Revue de Rouen*, 1852, p. 387. A. Deville, *La tour de la Pucelle du château de Rouen*, in *Précis des travaux de l'Académie de Rouen*, 1865-1866, pp. 236-268. Bouquet, *Notice sur le donjon du château de Philippe-Auguste*, Rouen, 1877, pp. 7 *et seq.*

531. *Trial*, vol. ii, pp. 317, 345; vol. iii, p. 121.

532. *Ibid.*, p. 154. A. Sarrazin, *Jeanne d'Arc et la Normandie*, p. 190, note 1. L. Delisle, *Revue des Sociétés savantes*, 1867, 4th series, vol. v, p. 440. F. Bouquet, *Jeanne d'Arc au donjon de Rouen*, in *Revue de Normandie*, 1867, vol. vi, pp. 873-883. L. Delisle, *Revue des Sociétés savantes*, vol. v (1867). Lanéry d'Arc, pp. 528-533.

533. Ballin, *Renseignements sur le Vieux-Château de Rouen*, in *Revue de Rouen*, 1842, p. 35. A. Sarrazin, *Jeanne d'Arc et la Normandie*, p. 188.

534. *Trial*, vol. ii, p. 7.

535. *Ibid.*, vol. iii, p. 155.

536. *Ibid.*, vol. iii, p. 180. A. Sarrazin, pp. 191, 192.

537. Vallet de Viriville, *Histoire de Charles VII*, vol. ii, pp. 240, 241.

538. *Trial*, vol. i, p. 47.

539. *Ibid.*, vol. ii, p. 322.

540. *Ibid.*, vol. ii, pp. 216, 217. J. Quicherat, *Aperçus nouveaux*, p. 112.

541. *Trial*, vol. ii, p. 18.

542. Lea, *A History of the Inquisition in the Middle Ages* (1906), vol. iii, p. 359.

543. *Trial*, vol. iii, p. 154.

544. *Ibid.*, vol. ii, pp. 318, 319; vol. iii, pp. 131, 140, 148, 161. A. Sarrazin, *P. Cauchon*, p. 200.

545. *Trial*, vol. iii, pp. 186, 187.

546. *Ibid.*, pp. 199, 200.

547. *Ibid.*, p. 200.

548. *Trial*, vol. iii, p. 179.

549. Morosini, vol. iii, p. 236.

550. *Trial*, vol. iii, pp. 121, 123.

551. *Ibid.*, p. 140.

552. C. de Beaurepaire, *Recherches sur le procès de condamnation de Jeanne d'Arc*, in *Précis des travaux de l'Académie de Rouen*, 1867-1868, pp. 470-479. U. Chevalier, *L'abjuration de Jeanne d'Arc*, p. 29.

553. De Beaurepaire, *Notes sur les juges*, p. 17.

554. *Gallia Christiana*, vol. ii, p. 732. Vallet de Viriville, *Histoire de Charles VII*, vol. ii, pp. 213, 214. S. Luce, *Jeanne d'Arc à Domremy*, p. ccxcv.

555. C. de Beaurepaire, *Recherches sur le procès de condamnation de Jeanne d'Arc*, loc. cit. A. Sarrazin, *Jeanne d'Arc et la Normandie*, pp. 168, 171.

556. 28 December, 1430. *Trial*, vol. i, pp. 20, 23. De Beaurepaire, *Notes sur les juges*, p. 46.

557. *Trial*, vol. i, pp. 18, 19.

558. A. Sarrazin, *Jeanne d'Arc et la Normandie*, pp. 1771, 1778.

559. J. Quicherat, *Aperçus nouveaux*, p. 147. De Beaurepaire, *Notes sur les juges*, p. 9.

560. *Trial*, vol. i, p. 24; vol. iii, p. 162. De Beaurepaire, *Notes sur les juges*, p. 26. A. Sarrazin, *Jeanne d'Arc et la Normandie*, p. 220.

561. *Trial*, vol. i, p. 25.

562. *Trial*, vol. i, p. 25; vol. iii, p. 137. A. Sarrazin, *loc. cit.*, pp. 221, 222.

563. L. Tanon, *Histoire des tribunaux de l'inquisition en France*, pp. 550, 551.

564. De Beaurepaire, *Recherches sur le procès de condamnation*, p. 320.

565. *Trial*, vol. i, p. 25; vol. iii, p. 137. De Beaurepaire, *Recherches....* p. 103. A. Sarrazin, *loc. cit.*, pp. 222, 223.

566. *Trial*, vol. i, p. 26. De Beaurepaire, *Recherches....* p. 115. A. Sarrazin, *loc. cit.*, pp. 223, 224.

567. Eymeric, *Directorium Inquisitorium*, quest. 85. J. Quicherat, *Aperçus nouveaux*, p. 109. De Beaurepaire, *Notes sur les juges*, p. 9.

568. De Beaurepaire, *Recherches....* pp. 321 *et seq.*

569. De Beaurepaire, *Notes sur les juges*, pp. 27-114. J. Quicherat, *Aperçus nouveaux*, pp. 103, 104. Boucher de Molandon, *Guillaume Erard l'un des juges de la Pucelle*, in *Bulletin du comité hist. and phil.*, 1892, pp. 3-10.

570. *Trial*, vol. i, p. 30, note. Du Boulay, *Historia Universitatis, Paris*, vol. v, pp. 912, 920. J. Quicherat, *Aperçus nouveaux*, p. 105. De Beaurepaire, *Notes*, pp. 30, 31. A. Sarrazin, *loc. cit.*, pp. 226, 227.

571. *Trial*, vol. ii, pp. 5, 6. De Beaurepaire, *Notes*, pp. 121-125. A. Sarrazin, *loc. cit.*, pp. 308-310.

572. De Beaurepaire, *Recherches*, pp. 321 *et seq.*

573. J. Quicherat, *Aperçus nouveaux*, p. 101.

574. *Trial*, vol. i, pp. 5-8.

575. A notary or secretary in France under the old monarchy (W.S.).

576. *Trial*, vol. ii, p. 463.

577. *Ibid.*, p. 453.

578. *Trial*, vol. iii, pp. 192, 193.

579. *Ibid.*, vol. i, pp. 105, 146, 234.

580. *Ibid.*, pp. 208, 209, 213.

581. J. Quicherat, *Aperçus nouveaux*, p. 117.

582. *Trial*, vol. i, pp. 245, 246.

583. *Ibid.*, vol. ii, p. 200.

584. De Beaurepaire, *Recherches*, *loc. cit.* J. Quicherat, *Aperçus nouveaux*, pp. 122-124. L. Tanon, *Histoire des tribunaux de l'inquisition*, pp. 389-395.

585. *Trial*, vol. i, pp. 117, 300.

586. *Trial*, vol. ii, p. 362.

587. *Ibid.*, vol. iii, p. 63.

588. De Beaurepaire, *Notes sur les juges*, pp. 72-82. A. Sorel, *loc. cit.*, pp. 243, 247.

589. *Trial*, vol. ii, pp. 10, 342; vol. iii, pp. 140, 141, 156, 160 *et seq.*

590. *Ibid.*, vol. iii, p. 181.

591. *Ibid.*, p. 141.

592. *Tractatus de hæresi pauperum de Lugduno*, apud Martene, *Thesaurus anecd.*, vol. v, col. 1787. J. Quicherat, *Aperçus nouveaux*, pp. 131, 132.

593. Eymeric, *Directorium*, part iii, *Cautelæ inquisitorum contra hæreticorum cavilationes et fraudes*.

594. L. Tanon, *Histoire des tribunaux de l'inquisition en France*, p. 394.

595. *Trial*, vol. ii, pp. 10, 342.

596. Vallet de Viriville, *Nouvelles recherches sur Agnès Sorel*, pp. 33 *et seq*. Du Cange, *Glossaire*, at the word *Matrimonium*.

597. *Trial*, vol. iii, pp. 102, 209.

598. *Trial*, vol. iii, pp. 155, 163.

599. A. Sarrazin, *Jeanne d'Arc et la Normandie*, p. 40.

600. *Trial*, vol. iii, p. 175.

601. *Ibid.*, vol. i, pp. 217, 218.

602. *Trial*, vol. i, pp. 27, 28.

603. *Ibid.*, pp. 28, 29.

604. *Ibid.*, pp. 29, 31.

605. *Trial*, vol. i, pp. 31-33.

606. *Ibid.*, p. 32. J. Quicherat, *Aperçus nouveaux*, p. 102. De Beaurepaire, *Notes sur les juges*, pp. 24-27. Le P. Chapotin, *La guerre de cent ans, Jeanne d'Arc et les dominicains*, pp. 141-143. A. Sarrazin, *P. Cauchon*, p. 124.

607. *Trial*, vol. i, p. 33.

608. *Trial*, vol. i, p. 35. De Beaurepaire, *Notes sur les juges*, p. 394. Doinel, *Mémoire de la Société archéologique-historique de l'Orléanais*, 1892, vol. xxiv, p. 403. Le P. Chapotin, *La guerre de cent ans, Jeanne d'Arc et les dominicains*, p. 141. U. Chevalier, *L'abjuration de Jeanne d'Arc*, p. 32.

609. *Trial*, vol. i, p. 35.

610. *Ibid.*, pp. 40-42.

611. *Trial*, vol. i, pp. 38, 39.

612. *Ibid.*, pp. 42-43.

613. *Ibid.*, p. 43.

614. *Ibid.*, p. 43.

615. Le P. Denifle and Chatelain, *Le procès de Jeanne d'Arc et l'Université de Paris*.

616. *Trial*, vol. i, pp. 88, 94, 151, 155, *passim*.

617. *Trial*, vol. i, p. 45.

618. *Ibid.*, p. 46.

619. *Ibid.*, pp. 46-47.

620. *Trial*, vol. i, p. 47.

621. *Ibid.*, pp. 47, 48.

622. *Trial*, vol. i, p. 48.

623. *Trial*, vol. iii, pp. 131-136.

624. *Ibid.*, p. 135.

625. *Trial*, vol. i, p. 48. A. Sarrazin, *Jeanne d'Arc et la Normandie*, pp. 323, 324.

626. L. Tanon, *Histoire des tribunaux de l'inquisition*, p. 420.

627. *Trial*, vol. i, pp. 48-50.

628. *Ibid.*, p. 50.

629. Du Boulay, *Historia Universitatis Paris.*, vol. v, p. 919. De Beaurepaire, *Notes sur les juges*, pp. 27-30.

630. *Trial*, vol. i, p. 51.

631. *Ibid.*

632. *Ibid.*, pp. 51, 52.

633. *Trial*, vol. i, p. 52.

634. Bréhal, *Mémoires et consultations en faveur de Jeanne d'Arc*, ed. Lanéry d'Arc, p. 409.

635. See Appendix I, Letter from Doctor G. Dumas.

636. *Trial*, vol. i, p. 52.

637. *Ibid.*, pp. 53, 54.

638. *Ibid.*, p. 54.

639. *Ibid.*, pp. 55, 56; vol. v, p. 95.

640. *Trial*, vol. ii, p. 456; vol. iii, pp. 91, 92. Morosini, vol. iii, p. 104. Eberhard Windecke, pp. 152, 153. J. Quicherat, *Aperçus nouveaux*, pp. 131-133. Le P. Ayroles, *La vraie Jeanne d'Arc*, vol. iv, p. 440, ch. i, *La royauté de Jésus Christ*.

641. *Trial*, vol. iii, pp. 89, 142, 161, 176, 178, 201.

642. *Ibid.*, p. 4.

643. *Ibid.*, vol. i, p. 56.

644. *Ibid.*, p. 56.

645. We find it impossible to agree with Quicherat (*Aperçus nouveaux*) and admit that Jeanne gradually invented the fable of the crown during her examination and while her judges were questioning her

as to "the sign." The manner in which the judges conducted this part of their examination proves that they were acquainted with the whole of the extraordinary story.

646. *Legenda Aurea*, ed. 1846, pp. 789 *et seq.*

647. *Trial*, vol. i, pp. 120-122.

648. *Ibid.*, p. 90.

649. *Ibid.*, p. 56.

650. *Ibid.*, vol. iii, p. 57.

651. Jean Bréhal, *Mémoires et consultations en faveur de Jeanne d'Arc*, ed. Lanéry d'Arc, p. 409.

652. *Trial*, vol. iii, p. 57.

653. *Ibid.*, p. 48.

654. *Ibid.*, vol. i, p. 57.

655. *Ibid.*, pp. 61, 70.

656. *Trial*, vol. i, p. 62.

657. *Ibid.*, pp. 61-64.

658. *Ibid.*, p. 279.

659. *Ibid.*, pp. 58-60.

660. *Ibid.*, pp. 60, 61.

661. *Grandes chroniques*, ed. P. Paris, vol. v, p. 188.

662. *Trial*, vol. i, p. 64.

663. E. Hinzelin, *Chez Jeanne d'Arc*, pp. 37, 177.

664. *Trial*, vol. i, pp. 64, 65.

665. *Ibid.*, p. 65. "*Souvent on est blâmé de trop parler*," a proverb common in the 15th century. Cf. Le Roux de Lincy, *Les proverbes français*, vol. ii, p. 417.

666. *Trial*, vol. i, p. 65.

667. *Ibid.*, vol. ii, pp. 21, 358.

668. *Ibid.*, vol. i, pp. 65-68.

669. *Ibid.*, p. 68.

670. The French expression runs, "*se resemblent comme deux sœurs.*"

671. *Trial*, vol. i, p. 68.

672. *Ibid.*, vol. iii, pp. 48, 49.

673. *Trial*, vol. iii, p. 51.

674. *Ibid.*, p. 49.

675. *Ibid.*, pp. 51, 52.

676. What induces me to fix this illness on the 25th of February is Jean Beaupère's question at the sitting of the 27th, "How have you been?" and Jeanne's ironical reply. This indisposition must not be confused, as it generally has been, with Jeanne's serious illness, which occurred after Easter. The shad and the herrings belong naturally to Lent; and Maître Delachambre says explicitly that Jeanne recovered after the bleeding.

677. *Trial*, vol. i, p. 70.

678. *Ibid.*, pp. 68, 69.

679. *Ibid.*, vol. ii, pp. 332, 362; vol. iii, pp. 60, 133, 141, 156, 162, 173, 181.

680. *Ibid.*, vol. i, p. 70.

681. *Ibid.*, p. 71.

682. *Trial*, vol. i, p. 72.

683. Lanéry d'Arc, *Mémoires et consultations en faveur de Jeanne d'Arc*, p. 406.

684. *Trial*, vol. i, p. 72.

685. *Ibid.*, pp. 72, 73.

686. *Trial*, vol. i, p. 73.

687. *Ibid.*, pp. 74, 75.

688. *Ibid.*, p. 75. I have re-inserted "my fine lord" according to *Trial*, vol. iii, p. 80.

689. *Trial*, vol. i, pp. 75-77.

690. *Ibid.*, pp. 77, 78.

691. *Ibid.*, p. 78.

692. *Ibid.*, p. 34; vol. ii, p. 318.

693. *Trial*, vol. ii, pp. 350, 365.

694. *Ibid.*, vol. i, pp. 79, 80.

695. *Trial*, vol. ii, pp. 11, 341.

696. See the evidence of Thomas de Courcelles in *Trial*, vol. iii, p. 38.

697. *Trial*, vol. ii, pp. 12, 300, 341; vol. iii, p. 138.

698. *Ibid.*, vol. ii, pp. 12, 203, 252, 300; vol. iii, pp. 50, 138.

699. *Ibid.*, vol. i, pp. 252, 326, 354, 356; vol. iii, pp. 171, 172.

700. *Trial*, vol. ii, pp. 356, 359.

701. *Ibid.*, vol. i, pp. 80, 81.

702. *Ibid.*, p. 82.

703. *Analecta juris Pontif.*, vol. xiv, p. 117.

704. *Trial*, vol. i, pp. 82, 84.

705. The expression, "*À Dieu vous recommande, Dieu soit garde de vous,*" occurs in the letters to the people of Tournai, to those of Troyes and of Reims, and in the letter to the Duke of Burgundy. And what is still more significant, in two of these letters, one to the people of Troyes, the other to the Duke of Burgundy, are the words: "*Le Roi du ciel, mon droiturier et souverain seigneur.*" *Trial*, vol. i, p. 246.

706. *Ibid.*, pp. 82, 83.

707. De Beaurepaire, *Notes sur les juges*, pp. 27, 32, 75, 82.

708. *Trial*, vol. i, pp. 84, 85.

709. *Trial*, vol. i, p. 86.

710. Le Loyer, iv, *Livres des Spectres*, Angers, 1605, in 4to.

711. *Trial*, vol. i, p. 86.

712. *Ibid.*, pp. 86, 87. Vallet de Viriville, *Les anneaux de Jeanne d'Arc*, in *Mémoires de la Société des Antiquaires de France*, vol. xxx, 1868, pp. 82, 97.

713. *Trial*, vol. i, p. 86.

714. *Ibid.*, p. 89.

715. A. Maury, *Croyances et légendes du moyen âge*, pp. 171 *et seq.*

716. *Trial*, vol. i, p. 90.

717. *Trial*, vol. i, pp. 90, 91.

718. *Ibid.*, vol. ii, p. 16.

719. De Beaurepaire, *Recherches sur le procès de condamnation*, p. 115.

720. *Trial*, vol. ii, p. 16.

721. *Ibid.*, vol. i, pp. 91, 92.

722. *Trial*, vol. i, p. 93.

723. *Ibid.*, p. 94.

724. *Ibid.*, pp. 95-97.

725. *Ibid.*, p. 99.

726. *Chronique de la Pucelle*, p. 301. *Journal du siège*, pp. 98, 99.

727. *Trial*, vol. i, p. 101.

728. *Ibid.*, p. 89.

729. *Trial*, vol. i, p. 102.

730. *Ibid.*, p. 103.

731. Lea (1906), vol. iii, p. 456.

732. *Le Jouvencel*, vol. ii, p. 237.

733. *Trial*, vol. i, p. 104.

734. *Trial*, vol. i, p. 111.

735. *Ibid.*, pp. 111, 112.

736. *Ibid.*, p. 113.

737. Gélu, *Questio quinta*, in *Mémoires et consultations en faveur de Jeanne d'Arc*, ed. Lanéry d'Arc, pp. 593 *et seq.*

738. *Trial*, vol. iii, pp. 299 *et seq.*

739. *Ibid.*, vol. i, p. 117.

740. *Ibid.*, pp. 117, 119.

741. On the contrary it was then that they began to argue against her or that they began to argue most effectively. She seems to forget that the interview at Chinon preceded the examination at Poitiers. It is interesting to notice that Brother Pasquerel, who was informed of these matters by her, makes the same error in his evidence.

742. *Trial*, vol. i, pp. 120, 122.

743. *Trial*, vol. i, pp. 122-124.

744. *Ibid.*, p. 125.

745. *Trial*, vol. i, p. 126.

746. *Ibid.*

747. *Ibid.*

748. Lanéry d'Arc, *Mémoires et consultations*, pp. 224, 434, 435. Le P. Ayroles, *La vraie Jeanne d'Arc*, vol. i, pp. 351 *et seq.*, 481 *et seq.*

749. *Trial*, vol. i, p. 128.

750. *Ibid.*

751. *Chronique des quatre premiers Valois*, p. 47.

752. II Corinthians, iv.

753. Galatians v, 18. Lanéry d'Arc, *Mémoires et consultations*, p. 275.

754. *Trial*, vol. i, p. 130.

755. *Trial*, vol. i, pp. 130, 131.

756. *Ibid.*, pp. 131, 132.

757. *Ibid.*, vol. v, p. 252. E. de Bouteiller and G. de Braux, *Nouvelles recherches sur la famille de Jeanne d'Arc*, pp. 14, 15. S. Luce, *Jeanne d'Arc à Domremy*, pp. xlvi *et seq.*

758. *Trial*, vol. i, p. 133.

759. *Trial*, vol. i, p. 134.

760. *Ibid.*, pp. 134, 138.

761. *Ibid.*, p. 139.

762. *Trial*, vol. i, pp. 140, 141.

763. About ten feet (W.S.).

764. *Trial*, vol. i, pp. 141-142.

765. "*Fleure bon et fleurera bon, pourvu qu'elle soit bien gardée.*"

766. Lanéry d'Arc, *Mémoires et consultations*, p. 212. Le P. Ayroles, *La vraie Jeanne d'Arc*, vol. i, p. 346.

767. *Trial*, vol. i, p. 144.

768. *Trial*, vol. i, p. 145.

769. *Ibid.*, p. 146.

770. Eberhard Windecke, pp. 184, 186.

771. *Trial*, vol. i, pp. 147, 148.

772. *Ibid.*, pp. 150, 152.

773. *Ibid.*, p. 157.

774. *Trial*, vol. i, pp. 154, 156.

775. *Trial*, vol. i, p. 156.

776. *Ibid.*, p. 157.

777. See *ante*, pp. 124 *et seq.* (W.S.).

778. *Trial*, vol. i, pp. 158, 159.

779. *Ibid.*, pp. 159, 161.

780. *Trial*, vol. i, p. 162.

781. *Ayde-toy, Dieu te aidera. Le Jouvencel*, vol. ii, p. 33.

782. *Trial*, vol. i, pp. 163, 164.

783. *Trial*, vol. i, pp. 165, 166.

784. *Ibid.*, pp. 166-169.

785. *Trial*, vol. i, pp. 170, 171.

786. *Ibid.*, p. 173.

787. *Ibid.*

788. S. Luce, *Jeanne d'Arc à Domremy*. Proofs and illustrations, pp. 74, 75.

789. *Trial*, vol. i, p. 174.

790. *Trial*, vol. i, pp. 174, 176.

791. *Trial*, vol. i, p. 178.

792. *Ibid.*, p. 180.

793. *Ibid.*, p. 181.

794. *Ibid.*, pp. 182-183.

795. Martène and Durand, *Thesaurus novus anecdotorum*, vol. v, col. 1760 *et seq.*

796. *Trial*, vol. i, p. 183.

797. *Ibid.*, p. 184.

798. *Ibid.*, pp. 184, 185.

799. *Trial*, vol. i, p. 185.

800. *Trial*, vol. i, p. 187.

801. *Ibid.*

802. *Ibid.*, p. 194.

803. *Ibid.*, p. 195.

804. J. Quicherat, *Aperçus nouveaux*, pp. 130, 131. E. Méru, *Directorium Inquisitorium*, Romæ, 1578, p. 295.

805. *Trial*, vol. i, pp. 200, 201. J. Quicherat, *Aperçus nouveaux*, pp. 129, 130.

806. L. Tanon, *Histoire des tribunaux de l'inquisition*, pp. 400 *et seq.* U. Chevalier, *L'abjuration de Jeanne d'Arc*, p. 34.

807. Méru, *Directorium Inquisitorium*, p. 147.

808. *Trial*, vol. i, p. 201.

809. *Trial*, vol. i, pp. 202-323.

810. *Ibid.*, p. 202.

811. *Ibid.*, pp. 324, 325.

812. *Ibid.*, p. 327; vol. iii, p. 143.

813. *Ibid.*, vol. iii, p. 60. U. Chevalier, *L'abjuration de Jeanne d'Arc*, p. 38.

814. *Trial*, vol. iii, p. 232. J. Quicherat, *Aperçus nouveaux*, pp. 124, 129.

815. *Trial*, vol. ii, pp. 22, 212; vol. iii, p. 306; vol. v, p. 461.

816. *Ibid.*, vol. i, pp. 328, 336.

817. *Ibid.*, p. 337.

818. *Trial*, vol. i, pp. 337, 374.

819. *Ibid.*, vol. iii, p. 51.

820. *Ibid.*, vol. i, pp. 374-375.

821. *Trial*, vol. i, pp. 376, 378.

822. *Ibid.*, p. 379.

823. *Ibid.*, pp. 380, 381.

824. *Trial*, vol. i, p. 381.

825. *Ibid.*, pp. 381, 382.

826. De Beaurepaire, *Notes sur les juges*, pp. 114, 117.

827. *Trial*, vol. i, pp. 383, 399.

828. *Trial*, vol. i, pp. 400, 401.

829. Nicolas Eymeric, *Directorium inquisitorium....* Rome, 1586, in fol. p. 24, col. 1. Ludovicus a Paramo, *De origine et progressu officii sanctæ inquisitionis*, MDXCIIX, in fol., lib. III, questio 5, p. 709.

830. *Trial*, vol. i, p. 399.

831. *Ibid.*, pp. 399, 400.

832. *Ibid.*, pp. 401, 402.

833. *Trial*, vol. i, pp. 402, 404.

834. *Recueil des historiens de la France*, vol. xx, p. 601; vol. xxi, p. 34. *Histoire littéraire de la France*, vol. xxvii, p. 70.

835. *Trial*, vol. i, pp. 407, 413, 420. M. Fournier, *La faculté de décret de l'Université de Paris*, p. 353. Le P. Denifle and Chatelain, *Chartularium Universitatis Parisiensis*, vol. iv, pp. 510 *et seq.*

836. *Trial*, vol. i, pp. 407, 408. U. Chevalier, *L'abjuration de Jeanne d'Arc*, p. 42.

837. The University of Paris (W.S.).

838. *Trial*, vol. i, pp. 414, 419.

839. *Ibid.*, p. 414. Migne, *Dictionnaire des sciences occultes*.

840. *Trial*, vol. i, pp. 417, 420.

841. From a theological point of view the record of the Poitiers trial may have been insignificant; but at any rate it contained the arguments presented to the King and the memoranda of Gélu and of Gerson.

842. *Trial*, vol. i, pp. 404, 429.

843. *Ibid.*, vol. i, pp. 429, 430.

844. De Beaurepaire, *Notes sur les juges*, pp. 126-127.

845. *Trial*, vol. i, p. 430.

846. *Trial*, vol. i, pp. 430, 437.

847. Du Boulay, *Historia Universitatis Parisiensis*, vol. v, p. 929.

848. De Beaurepaire, *Notes sur les juges*, p. 88.

849. *Trial*, vol. i, pp. 437, 441.

850. *Ibid.*, pp. 441, 442.

851. *Trial*, vol. ii, p. 21.

852. *Ibid.*, vol. iii, p. 146. De Beaurepaire, *Notes sur les juges*, pp. 445 *et seq.*

853. Old name for a cemetery close to a church. Godefroy, *Lexique de l'ancien français* (W.S.).

854. *Trial*, vol. ii, p. 351.

855. *Trial*, vol. iii, p. 54.

856. De Beaurepaire, *Notes sur le cimetière de Saint-Ouen de Rouen*, in *Précis analytique des travaux de l'Académie de Rouen 1875-1876*, pp. 211, 230, plan. U. Chevalier, *L'abjuration de Jeanne d'Arc et l'authenticité de sa formule*, p. 44. A. Sarrazin, *Jeanne d'Arc et la Normandie*, p. 351.

857. *Trial*, vol. i, pp. 442, 444. O'Reilly, *Les deux procès*, vol. i, pp. 70-93.

858. De Beaurepaire, *Notes sur les juges*, pp. 402, 408.

859. *Trial*, vol. iii, p. 113.

860. *Ibid.*, vol. i, pp. 469, 470.

861. *Ibid.*, p. 444. E. Richer, *Histoire manuscrite de la Pucelle d'Orléans*, bk. i, fol. 8; bk. ii, fol. 198, v°.

862. *Trial*, vol. iii, p. 61.

863. *Ibid.*, vol. ii, pp. 15, 17.

864. *Ibid.*, vol. i, pp. 456, 457. U. Chevalier, *L'abjuration de Jeanne d'Arc*, pp. 46, 47.

865. *Trial*, vol. ii, pp. 15, 17, 335, 345, 353, 367.

866. *Ibid.*, p. 17.

867. *Ibid.*, vol. i, pp. 444, 445.

868. *Ibid.*, p. 445.

869. *Ibid.*, vol. ii, p. 358.

870. *Ibid.*, vol. i, p. 445.

871. *Trial*, vol. i, pp. 445, 446.

872. *Ibid.*, p. 446.

873. *Ibid.*, vol. iii, p. 146.

874. *Ibid.*, vol. i, p. 473.

875. *Trial*, vol. iii, p. 146.

876. *Ibid.*, vol. ii, pp. 17, 331; vol. iii, pp. 52, 156.

877. *Ibid.*, p. 123.

878. *Ibid.*, vol. i, pp. 474, 475.

879. *Ibid.*, p. 473 note.

880. *Ibid.*, vol. iii, pp. 65, 147, 149, 273. De Beaurepaire, *Recherches sur le procès*, p. 358.

881. *Trial*, vol. ii, p. 323.

882. *Ibid.*, pp. 137, 376.

883. *Ibid.*, p. 356; vol. iii, pp. 157, 178.

884. *Ibid.*, p. 55.

885. *Trial*, vol. iii, pp. 90, 147, 156.

886. *Ibid.*, pp. 52, 65, 132, 156, 197. U. Chevalier, *L'Abjuration de Jeanne d'Arc.*

887. *Trial*, vol. iii, pp. 156, 157 (evidence of Jean Massieu, Usher of the court).

888. *Ibid.*, vol. ii, p. 323.

889. *Trial*, vol. iii, p. 157.

890. *Ibid.*, vol. ii, p. 331; vol. iii, p. 157. This deed, written in a large hand and containing but a few lines, appears to be an abridgment of that contained in the *Trial*, vol. i, pp. 447, 448 (cf. vol. iii, pp. 156, 197).

891. *Trial*, vol. iii, pp. 156, 197.

892. *Trial*, vol. ii, p. 338; vol. iii, p. 147.

893. *Ibid.*, pp. 55, 143.

894. *Ibid.*, p. 123.

895. *Trial*, vol. ii, p. 361. J. Quicherat, *Aperçus nouveaux*, p. 135.

896. *Trial*, vol. iii, pp. 147, 156.

897. *Ibid.*, vol. ii, p. 376.

898. *Ibid.*, p. 17; vol. iii, p. 164.

899. *Trial*, vol. i, pp. 450, 452.

900. *Ibid.*, p. 452.

901. L. Tanon, *Tribunaux de l'inquisition*, p. 454.

902. *Trial*, vol. ii, p. 14.

903. *Ibid.*, vol. iii, pp. 52, 149.

904. *Ibid.*, vol. i, p. 19.

905. *Ibid.*, vol. ii, p. 14.

906. *Ibid.*, p. 376.

907. *Ibid.*, vol. i, pp. 452-453.

908. *Trial*, vol. iii, p. 155.

909. *Ibid.*, p. 89.

910. *Trial*, vol. iii, p. 148.

911. *Trial*, vol. ii, p. 14; vol. iii, p. 148.

912. De Beaurepaire, *Notes sur les juges*, pp. 82 *et seq.*

913. *Trial*, vol. ii, p. 354.

914. *Ibid.*, vol. iii, pp. 158, 180.

915. *Ibid.*, vol. i, p. 454; vol. iii, p. 148.

916. *Ibid.*, vol. ii, p. 5. Isambart's evidence refers to this day, the 28th.

917. *Trial*, vol. i, pp. 455-457.

918. *Ibid.*, vol. ii, pp. 5, 8, 365; vol. iii, pp. 148, 149.

919. *Ibid.*, vol. ii, p. 18.

920. *Trial*, vol. ii, p. 18.

921. "*Responsio mortifera*," wrote the notary Boisguillaume in the margin of his minutes. *Trial*, vol. i, pp. 456, 457.

922. *Trial*, vol. i, pp. 456-458.

923. *Ibid.*, vol. ii, pp. 5, 8, 305.

924. *Ibid.*, vol. i, pp. 459, 467.

925. Bernard Gui, *Pratique*, part iii, p. 144. L. Tanon, *Tribunaux de l'inquisition*, pp. 464 *et seq.*

926. *Trial*, vol. i, pp. 462, 463.

927. *Ibid.*, p. 463.

928. L. Tanon, *Tribunaux de l'inquisition*, pp. 472, 473.

929. *Trial*, vol. i, pp. 463, 467.

930. *Trial*, vol. i, p. 466.

931. *Ibid.*, pp. 467, 469.

932. *Ibid.*, vol. ii, pp. 3, 4 (evidence of Brother Isambart de la Pierre). *Ibid.*, p. 8 (evidence of Brother Martin Ladvenu).

933. *Trial*, vol. i, p. 481. (In the Introduction I have given my reasons for regarding the information given after the death of the Maid as possessing great historical significance.)

934. *Trial*, vol. i, pp. 462-467.

935. *Ibid.*, p. 479. Or "to such of you as are churchmen." *Ibid.*, p. 482 (information furnished after her death).

936. Robillard de Beaurepaire, *Notes sur les juges*.

937. *Trial*, vol. i, p. 480.

938. *Ibid.*, pp. 480, 481 (information furnished after her death).

939. *Ibid.*, pp. 482, 483.

940. *Ibid.*, vol. ii, p. 114 (evidence of Brother Jehan Toutmouillé).

941. *Trial*, vol. i, pp. 481, 482 (information given after Jeanne's death).

942. *Textus decretalium*, lib. v, ch. iv.

943. Ignace de Doellinger, *La Papauté*, traduit par A. Giraud-Teulon, Paris, 1904, in 8vo, p. 105.

944. *Trial*, vol. iii, p. 158.

945. *Trial*, vol. ii, p. 334.

946. *Ibid.*, vol. ii, pp. 19, 334. De Beaurepaire, *Recherches sur le procès*, pp. 116, 117.

947. *Trial*, vol. i, pp. 482, 483 (information procured after Jeanne's death).

948. *Ibid.*, vol. ii, pp. 19, 308, 320; vol. iii, pp. 114, 158, 183, 197.

949. For Jeanne's communion see also De Beaurepaire, *Recherches sur le procès*, pp. 116-117.

950. *Trial*, vol. iii, p. 191.

951. *Ibid.*, vol. i, p. 485. Maître N. Taquel would lead us to believe that the interrogatories took place after Jeanne's communion, but this can hardly be admitted.

952. *Trial*, vol. ii, p. 320; vol. iii, p. 162.

953. A. Sarrazin, *Jeanne d'Arc et la Normandie*, p. 369.

954. Bouquet, *Rouen aux différentes époques de son histoire*, pp. 25 et seq. A. Sarrazin, *Jeanne d'Arc et la Normandie*, pp. 374, 375. De Beaurepaire, *Mémoires sur le lieu du supplice de Jeanne d'Arc*, with plan of the Old Market Square of Rouen according to the *Livre de fontaine de 1525*, Rouen, 1867, in 8vo.

955. De Beaurepaire, *Note sur la prise du château de Rouen, par Ricarville*, Rouen, 1857, in 8vo, p. 5.

956. Bouquet, *Jeanne d'Arc au château de Rouen*, p. 25. De Beaurepaire, *Mémoire sur le lieu du supplice de Jeanne d'Arc*, p. 32. A. Sarrazin, *Jeanne d'Arc et la Normandie*, pp. 376 et seq.

957. *Trial*, vol. iv, p. 459.

958. *Trial*, vol. i, pp. 470; vol. ii, pp. 14, 303, 328; vol. iii, pp. 159, 173.

959. *Ibid.*, vol. i, p. 470; vol. ii, p. 334; vol. iii, pp. 53, 114, 159.

960. Chapter xii, 26 (W.S.).

961. *Trial*, vol. iii, p. 194.

962. *Ibid.*, p. 159.

963. L. Tanon, *Histoire des tribunaux de l'inquisition*, p. 374.

964. *Trial*, vol. ii, p. 19; vol. iii, p. 177.

965. *Ibid.*, vol. ii, pp. 19, 351.

966. *Ibid.*, vol. iii, p. 56.

967. *Trial*, vol. ii, pp. 6, 20; vol. iii, pp. 53, 177, 186.

968. *Ibid.*, vol. iii, p. 188. A. Sarrazin, *Jeanne d'Arc et la Normandie*, p. 386. Guedon and Ladvenu added to their evidence that not long afterwards a certain Georges Folenfant was also given up to the secular arm. But the Archbishop and the Inquisitor sent Ladvenu to the Bailie "in order to warn him that the said Georges was not to be treated like the Maid who was burned without the pronouncement of any definite and final sentence." *Trial*, vol. ii, p. 9.

969. *Ibid.*, p. 344.

970. Falconbridge, in *Trial*, vol. iv, p. 459. Yet Martin Ladvenu says "until the last hour," etc., which is obviously false.

971. *Trial*, vol. iii, p. 53.

972. Shakespeare, Henry VI, part 1, act i, scene 1.

973. *Trial*, vol. ii, p. 6; vol. iii, pp. 53, 191, 375.

974. *Missel Romain, Office des morts.* Cf. Le P. C. Clair, *Le Dies iræ, histoire, traduction et commentaire*, Paris, in 8vo, 1881, pp. 38-142.

975. *Trial*, vol. ii, pp. 6, 20.

976. *Ibid.*, vol. iii, p. 170.

977. *Ibid.*, p. 186.

978. *Ibid.*, vol. ii, p. 8; vol. iii, pp. 169, 194.

979. *Ibid.*, vol. ii, p. 7.

980. *Ibid.*, vol. iii, p. 186.

981. *Trial*, vol. iii, p. 191. *Journal d'un bourgeois de Paris*, pp. 269, 270.

982. L. Tanon, *Histoire des tribunaux de l'inquisition*, p. 478.

983. *Chronique des cordeliers*, fol. 507 verso. *Journal d'un bourgeois de Paris*, p. 269.

984. *Trial*, vol. iii, pp. 159, 160, 185; vol. iv, p. 518. Th. Basin, *Histoire de Charles VII et de Louis XI*, vol. i, p. 83. Th. Cochard, *Existe-t-il des reliques de Jeanne d'Arc?* Orléans, 1891, in 8vo.

985. *Trial*, vol. ii, pp. 7, 352, 366.

986. *Trial*, vol. i, pp. 493, 495.

987. Le P. Denifle and Chatelain, *Cartularium Universitatis Parisiensis*, vol. iv, p. 527.

988. *Trial*, vol. iii, pp. 240, 243.

989. *Trial*, vol. i, pp. 485, 496; vol. iv, p. 403. Monstrelet, vol. iv, ch. cv.

990. *Trial*, vol. i, pp. 496, 500.

991. *Journal d'un bourgeois de Paris*, pp. 270, 272. This sermon contains curious inaccuracies. Are they the fault of the Inquisitor or of the author of *Le Journal*?

992. *Trial*, vol. iv, p. 473.

993. Th. Basin, *Histoire de Charles VII et de Louis XI*, vol. iv, pp. 103, 104. Monstrelet, ch. lxiii. Bougenot, *Deux documents inédits relatifs à Jeanne d'Arc*, in *Revue bleue*, 13 Feb., 1892, pp. 203, 204.

994. *Trial*, vol. ii, pp. 3, 344, 348, 373; vol. iii, p. 189; vol. v, pp. 169, 179, 181. Dibon, *Essai sur Louviers*, Rouen, 1836, in 8vo, pp. 33 *et seq.* Vallet de Viriville, *Histoire de Charles VII*, vol. ii, pp. 246 *et seq.*

995. Le P. Denifle, *La désolation des églises de France vers le milieu du XVe siècle*, vol. i, p. xvi.

996. Jean Chartier, *Chronique*, vol. i, p. 132. Monstrelet, vol. iv, p. 433. Lefèvre de Saint-Rémy, vol. ii, p. 265.

997. *Journal d'un bourgeois de Paris*, p. 272.

998. *Journal d'un bourgeois de Paris*, p. 272.

999. Vallet de Viriville, *Histoire de Charles VII*, vol. ii, p. 248. De Beaurepaire, *Recherches sur les juges*, p. 43.

1000. Lea, *History of the Inquisition*, vol. iii, 377 (ed. 1905).

1001. Lefèvre de Saint-Rémy, vol. ii, pp. 263, 264.

1002. *Journal d'un bourgeois de Paris*, p. 274.

1003. Lefèvre de Saint-Rémy, vol. ii, p. 264.

1004. Martial d'Auvergne, *Vigiles*, ed. Coustelier, vol. i.

1005. Gruel, *Chronique d'Arthur de Richemont*, p. 81. Vallet de Viriville, in *Nouvelle biographie générale*. De Beaucourt, *Histoire de Charles VII*, vol. ii, p. 297. E. Cosneau, *Le connétable de Richemont*, pp. 200, 201.

1006. Perceval de Cagny, pp. 170, 173, *passim*.

1007. Carlier, *Histoire des Valois*, 1764, in 4to, vol. ii, p. 442. Vallet de Viriville, *Histoire de Charles VII*, vol. i, p. 307. The Regent also believed in astrology (B.N. MS. 1352).

1008. Gruel, *Chronique d'Arthur de Richemont*, pp. 120, 121. Dom Félibien, *Histoire de Paris*, vol. iv, p. 597.

1009. *Chronique du doyen de Saint-Thibaud de Metz*, in *Trial*, vol. v, pp. 321, 324. Jacomin Husson, *Chronique de Metz*, ed. Michelant, Metz, 1870, pp. 64, 65. Cf. Lecoy de la Marche, *Une fausse Jeanne d'Arc*, in *Revue des questions historiques*, October, 1871, pp. 562 *et seq.* Vergniaud-Romagnési, *Des portraits de Jeanne d'Arc et de la fausse Jeanne d'Arc*, in *Mémoires de la Société d'Agriculture d'Orléans*, vol. i (1853), pp. 250, 253. De Puymaigre, *La fausse Jeanne d'Arc*, in *Revue nouvelle d'Alsace-Lorraine*, vol. v (1885), pp. 533 *et seq.* A. France, *Une fausse Jeanne d'Arc*, in *Revue des familles*, 15 February, 1891.

1010. Varanius alone says that Jacques d'Arc died of sorrow at the loss of his daughter. *Trial*, vol. v, p. 85.

1011. *Ibid.*, p. 280.

1012. *Ibid.*, pp. 279, 280. G. Lefèvre-Pontalis, *La fausse Jeanne d'Arc*, p. 6, note 1.

1013. *Trial*, vol. v, p. 210. Lefèvre de Saint-Rémy, vol. ii, p. 176.

1014. *Trial*, vol. v, pp. 321, 324.

1015. *Le Metz ancien* (Metz, 1856, 2 vol. in folio) by the Baron d'Hannoncelles, which contains the genealogy of Nicole Lowe.

1016. "And was recognised by divers tokens" (*enseignes*) (*Trial*, vol. v, p. 322). M. Lecoy de la Marche (*Une fausse Jeanne d'Arc*, in *Revue des questions historiques*, October, 1871, p. 565), and M. Gaston Save (*Jehanne des Armoises, Pucelle d'Orléans*, Nancy, 1893, p. 11) understand that she was recognised by several officers or ensigns (*enseignes*). I have interpreted *enseignes* in the ordinary sense of marks on the skin, birth-marks. (Cf. La Curne.)

1017. *Chronique du doyen de Saint-Thibaud*, in *Trial*, vol. v, p. 322.

1018. *Journal d'un bourgeois de Paris*, p. 354.

1019. Nevertheless see on this subject M. Germain Lefèvre-Pontalis, who is our authority for this prophecy (Eberhard Windecke, pp. 108-111).

1020. The republic of Metz (W.S.)

1021. *Chronique du doyen de Saint-Thibaud*, in *Trial*, vol. v, p. 322. Chronique de Philippe de Vigneulles, in *Les chroniques Messines* of Huguenin, p. 198.

1022. *Trial*, vol. ii, p. 457. L. Champion, *Jeanne d'Arc écuyère*, ch. ii, ch. vi.

1023. Variant of *La chronique du doyen de Saint-Thibaud* sent from Metz to Pierre du Puy, in *Trial*, vol. v, pp. 322, 324.

1024. *Ibid.*, pp. 322, 324.

1025. D. Calmet, *Histoire de Lorraine*, vol. vii. Proofs and illustrations, col. vi.

1026. *Trial*, vol. v, pp. 322, 324. Eberhard Windecke, p. 108. Morosini, vol. iii, p. 62, note.

1027. M. le Baron de Braux was kind enough to write to me from Boucq near Foug, Meurthe-et-Moselle, on the 28th of June, 1896, explaining that Bacquillon (*Trial*, vol. v, p. 322) is an erroneous reading of one of the manuscripts of the Doyen of Saint-Thibaud. "By comparing," he added, "the various versions (V. Quicherat and *Les chroniques Messines*) we may ascertain that it is really Vaucouleurs, Valquelou," mistaken for Bacquillon.

1028. *Trial*, vol. ii, pp. 406, 408, 445, 449.

1029. The *Chronique de Tournai* says of the true Jeanne that she came from Mareville, a small town between Metz and Pont-à-Mousson. "This Jeanne had long dwelt and served in a *métairie* a kind of farm. of this place."

1030. *Chronique du doyen Saint-Thibaud*, in *Trial*, vol. v, pp. 322, 324. Lecoy de la Marche, *Jeanne des Armoises*, p. 566. G. Save, *Jehanne des Armoises, pucelle d'Orléans*, p. 14.

1031. *Trial*, vol. v, pp. 352 *et seq.*

1032. *Chronique du doyen de Saint-Thibaud*, in *Trial*, vol. v, pp. 322, 324. Dom Lelong, *Histoire du diocèse de Laon*, 1783, p. 371. Abbé Ledouble, *Les origines de Liesse et du pèlerinage de Notre-Dame*, Soissons, 1885, pp. 6 *et seq.*

1033. *Trial*, vol. v, p. 322, note 2. G. Lefèvre-Pontalis, *La fausse Jeanne d'Arc*, p. 21, note 1.

1034. *Chronique normande* (MS. in the British Museum), in *Trial*, vol. iv, p. 344. Symphorien Champier, *Nef des Dames*, Lyon, 1503, *ibid.*

1035. *Journal d'un bourgeois de Paris*, p. 272. *Chronique normande*, in *Bibliothèque de l'École des Chartes*, second series, vol. iii, p. 116. D. Calmet, *Histoire de Lorraine*, p. vi, proofs and illustrations. G. Save, *Jehanne des Armoises*, pp. 6, 7. It is well known that Gabriel Naudé maintained the paradox that Jeanne was only burned in effigy. *Considérations politiques sur les coups d'état*, Rome, 1639, in 4to. G. Lefèvre-Pontalis, *La fausse Jeanne d'Arc*, p. 8.

1036. Lanéry d'Arc, *Le culte de Jeanne d'Arc*, Orléans, 1887, in 8vo. *Revue du Midi.*

1037. *Trial*, vol. v, p. 275. Lottin, *Recherches*, vol. ii, p. 286.

1038. *Trial*, vol. v, p. 262. Lecoy de la Marche, *Jeanne des Armoises*, p. 568.

1039. He died at the age of one hundred and eighteen. *Trial*, iii, p. 29.

1040. *Trial*, vol. v, p. 326. Vallet de Viriville, *Histoire de Charles VII*, vol. ii, p. 376, note. G. Lefèvre-Pontalis, *La fausse Jeanne d'Arc*, p. 23, note 5.

1041. *Trial*, vol. v, p. 327.

1042. *Trial*, vol. v, p. 326. Lottin, *Recherches*, vol. i, pp. 284-285.

1043. Since 1432. But there is no evidence of any anniversary service having been held in 1433 and 1434. It was reinstituted in 1439.

1044. *Trial*, vol. v, pp. 274, 275. Lottin, *Recherches*, vol. i, p. 286.

1045. *Chronique du doyen de Saint-Thibaud*, in *Trial*, vol. v, p. 323. Jean Nider, *Formicarium*, in *Trial*, vol. iv, p. 325. Lecoy de la Marche, *loc. cit.*, p. 566.

1046. *Art de vérifier les dates*, vol. xv, pp. 236 *et seq.* *Gallia Christiana*, vol. xiii, pp. 970 *et seq.*; Gams, *Series Episcoporum* (1873), pp. 317, 319.

1047. Quicherat, in *Trial*, vol. iv, p. 502, note, erroneously states that the contest for the Archbishopric of Trèves was between Raban of Helmstat and Jacques of Syrck. Concerning Jacques of Syrck or Sierck, see de Beaucourt, *Histoire de Charles VII*, vol. iv, p. 264.

1048. Jean Nider, *Formicarium*, book v, ch. viii. D. Calmet, *Histoire de Lorraine*, vol. ii, p. 906.

1049. *Trial*, vol. i, pp. 245-246.

1050. Jean Nider, *Formicarium*, in *Trial*, vol. iv, p. 502; vol. v, p. 324.

1051. H. Vincent, *La maison des Armoises, originaire de Champagne*, in *Mémoires de la Société d'Archéologie Lorraine*, 3rd series, vol. v (1877), p. 324. G. Lefèvre-Pontalis, *La fausse Jeanne d'Arc*, p. 2, note 4.

1052. In his *Histoire de Lorraine* (vol. v, pp. clxiv *et seq.*), Dom Calmet says that the contract of marriage between Robert des Armoises and the Maid of France, which had long been preserved in the family, was lost in his day. There is no need to regret it, for it is now known that this contract was forged by Father Jérôme Vignier. Le Comte de Marsy (*La fausse Jeanne d'Arc, Claude des Armoises; du degré de confiance à accorder aux découvertes de Jérôme Vignier*, Compiègne, 1890) and M. Tamizey de Larroque (*Revue critique*, the 20th October, 1890). For Vignier's other forgeries cf. Julien Havet, *Questions Mérovingiennes*, ii.

1053. Jean Nider, *Formicarium*, bk. v, ch. viii. *Trial*, vol. iv, pp. 503, 504.

1054. The preceding deed, by which "*Robert des Harmoises et la Pucelle Jehanne d'Arc, sa femme*," acquired the estate of Fléville, is very doubtful (D. Calmet, 2nd edition, vol. v, p. clxiv, note).

1055. *Chronique du doyen de Saint-Thibaud*, in *Trial*, vol. v, p. 323. *Journal d'un bourgeois de Paris*, pp. 354-355.

1056. *Trial*, vol. iii, p. 206, note 2.

1057. *Ibid.*, p. 219.

1058. Jean Nider, *Formicarium*, in *Trial*, vol. v, p. 325.

1059. *Chronique du doyen de Saint-Thibaud*, in *Trial*, vol. v, pp. 323-324.

1060. *Trial*, vol. i, p. 183.

1061. *Ibid.*, vol. i, pp. 106, 108, 119, 296. *Journal d'un bourgeois de Paris*.

1062. Extracts from the accounts of the town of Orléans, in *Trial*, vol. v, pp. 331-332. Lecoy de la Marche, *Une fausse Jeanne d'Arc*, pp. 570-571.

1063. Original documents of Orléans, in *Trial*, vol. v, p. 270.

1064. *Trial*, vol. v, p. 274. Lottin, *Recherches*, vol. i, p. 286.

1065. Extracts from the accounts of the town of Orléans, in *Trial*, vol. v, pp. 331-332. Lottin, *Recherches*, vol. i, p. 287.

1066. *Trial*, vol. v, p. 260.

1067. *Ibid.*, pp. 112-113.

1068. *Trial*, vol. iii, p. 17; vol. v, p. 327.

1069. *Ibid.*, vol. v, p. 332. G. Lefèvre-Pontalis, *La fausse Jeanne d'Arc*, pp. 23-24.

1070. *Trial*, vol. v, p. 332.

1071. Vallet de Viriville, *Notices et extraits de chartes et de manuscrits appartenant au British Museum*, in *Bibliothèque de l'École des Chartes*, vol. viii, 1846, p. 116.

1072. Abbé Bossard, *Gille de Rais*, p. 174.

1073. Pardon, in *Trial*, vol. v, pp. 332-334.

1074. *Journal d'un bourgeois de Paris*, p. 335. Lecoy de la Marche, *Une fausse Jeanne d'Arc*, p. 574.

1075. *Journal d'un bourgeois de Paris*, pp. 338 *et seq.* De Beaucourt, *Histoire de Charles VII*, vol. iii, pp. 384 *et seq.*

1076. *Journal d'un bourgeois de Paris*, p. 270.

1077. De Beaucourt, *Histoire de Charles VII*, vol. iii, ch. xvi.

1078. *Journal d'un bourgeois de Paris*, pp. 354, 355. Lecoy de la Marche, *Une fausse Jeanne d'Arc*, p. 574.

1079. *Journal d'un bourgeois de Paris*, *loc. cit.*

1080. *Journal d'un bourgeois de Paris*, pp. 354, 355. Lecoy de la Marche, *Une fausse Jeanne d'Arc*, p. 574. G. Lefèvre-Pontalis, *La fausse Jeanne d'Arc*, p. 27.

1081. Vergnaud-Romagnési, *Des portraits de Jeanne d'Arc et de la fausse Jeanne d'Arc* and *Mémoire sur les fausses Jeanne d'Arc*, in *Les Mémoires de la Société d'Agriculture d'Orléans*, 1854, in 8vo.

1082. *Trial*, vol. v, pp. 210, 213.

1083. *Trial*, vol. v, p. 279.

1084. *Trial*, vol. v, pp. 212, 214. Lottin, *Recherches*, vol. i, p. 287. Duleau, *Vidimus d'une charte de Charles VII, concédant à Pierre du Lys la possession de l'Isle-aux-Bœufs*, Orléans, 1860, in 8vo. 6. G. Lefèvre-Pontalis, *La fausse Jeanne d'Arc*, p. 28, note 1.

1085. I have not made use of the very late evidence given by Pierre Sala (*Trial*, vol. iv, p. 281). It is vague and somewhat legendary, and cannot possibly be introduced into the Life of La Dame des Armoises. For the bibliography of this interesting subject, see Lanéry d'Arc, *Le livre d'or de Jeanne d'Arc*, pp. 573, 580, and G. Lefèvre-Pontalis, *La fausse Jeanne d'Arc*, Paris, 1895, in 8vo, concerning the account given by M. Gaston Save.

There are those who have supposed, without adducing any proof, that this pseudo-Jeanne was a sister of the Maid (Lebrun de Charmettes,

Histoire de Jeanne d'Arc, vol. iv, pp. 291 *et seq.*). Francis André, *La vérité sur Jeanne d'Arc*, Paris, 1895, in 18mo, pp. 75 *et seq.*

1086. De Beaucourt, *Histoire de Charles VII*, vol. iii, p. 335.

1087. Le P. Ayroles, *La Pucelle devant l'église de son temps*, p. 10.

1088. *Trial*, vol. iii, p. 565.

1089. *Ibid.*, vol. i, p. 403.

1090. *Ordonnances*, vol. xiii, pp. 267, 291. *Preuves des libertés de l'église gallicane*, edited by Lenglet-Dufresnoy, second part, p. 6. De Beaucourt, *Histoire de Charles VII*, vol. iii, pp. 353, 361. N. Arlos, *Histoire de la pragmatique sanction, etc.*

1091. Hefelé, *Histoire de l'Église gallicane*, vol. xx, p. 357. De Beaucourt, *Histoire de Charles VII*, vol. iii, p. 363. De Beaurepaire, *Les états de Normandie sous la domination anglaise*, pp. 66, 67, 185, 188.

1092. Du Boulay, *Hist. Universitatis*, vol. v, p. 431. De Beaurepaire, *Notes sur les juges*, p. 28.

1093. *Trial*, vol. ii, pp. 10, 12, 332, 362; vol. iii, pp. 60, 133, 141, 145, 156, 162, 173, 181.

1094. De Beaurepaire, *Notes sur les juges et assesseurs du procès de condamnation*, pp. 78, 82.

1095. J. Quicherat, *Aperçus nouveaux*, p. 106.

1096. De Beaucourt, *Histoire de Charles VII*, vol. iii, p. 372.

1097. De Beaurepaire, *Les états de Normandie sous la domination anglaise*, pp. 66, 67, 185, 188. De Beaucourt, *loc. cit.* p. 362.

1098. De Beaurepaire, *loc. cit.*, p. 17. *Notes sur les juges et assesseurs du procès de condamnation*, p. 117. *Recherches sur le procès*, p. 124.

1099. De Beaucourt, *Histoire de Charles VII*, vol. v, ch. i.

1100. Lanéry d'Arc, *Mémoires et consultations en faveur de Jeanne d'Arc*, p. 249.

1101. *Trial*, vol. ii, pp. 1, 22.

1102. *Gallia Christiana*, vol. iii, col. 1129 and vol. xi, col. 90. De Beaucourt, *Histoire de Charles VII*, vol. v, p. 219. Le P. Ayroles, *La Pucelle devant l'église de son temps*, ch. vi.

1103. De Beaurepaire, *Les états de Normandie sous la domination anglaise*, pp. 185, 188.

1104. *Trial*, vol. v, p. 276.

1105. *Ibid.*, vol. ii, pp. 108, 112.

1106. *Ibid.*, p. 95. Le P. Ayroles, *La Pucelle devant l'église de son temps*, p. 607. J. Belon and F. Balme, *Jean Bréhal, grand inquisiteur de France et la réhabilitation de Jeanne d'Arc*, Paris, 1893, in 4to.

1107. *Trial*, vol. ii, pp. 82, 92.

1108. *Ibid.*, pp. 92, 112.

1109. *Ibid.*, pp. 193, 196.

1110. *Ibid.*, pp. 291, 463; vol. iii, pp. 1, 202.

1111. *Trial*, vol. ii, pp. 378, 463.

1112. *Ibid.*, vol. v, pp. 112, 113, 331.

1113. *Ibid.*, vol. ii, pp. 23, 35.

1114. *Ibid.*, pp. 1, 19.

1115. *Ibid.*, vol. iii, p. 202.

1116. *Ibid.*, pp. 2 *et seq.*

1117. *Ibid.*, p. 16.

1118. De Beaucourt, *Histoire de Charles VII*, vol. vi, p. 43. P. Dupuy, *Histoire des Templiers*, 1658, in 4to. Cimber and Danjou, *Archives curieuses de l'histoire de France*, vol. i, pp. 137-157. (See also, Michelet, History of France, translated by G.H. Smith, vol. ii, p. 206.) Note – Alençon says to his English valet: "If I could have a powder that I wot of and put it in the vessel in which the King's sheets are washed, he should sleep sound enough *dormir tout sec..*" *Trial of Alençon* (W.S.).

1119. *Trial*, vol. iii, p. 90.

1120. *Ibid.*, p. 209.

1121. *Ibid.*, p. 65.

1122. *Ibid.*, p. 100.

1123. *Ibid.*, p. 85.

1124. *Ibid.*, vol. ii, pp. 20, 21, 161; vol. iii, pp. 43, 53, *passim*.

1125. *Trial*, vol. iii, pp. 44, 56. J. Quicherat, *Aperçus nouveaux*, p. 106.

1126. *Ibid.*, vol. ii, pp. 161; vol. iii, pp. 41, 42, 195.

1127. De Beaurepaire, *Notes sur les juges*.

1128. *Trial*, vol. ii, pp. 329 *et seq.*

1129. *Trial*, vol. ii, pp. 363 *et seq.*, 434 *et seq.*

1130. Lanéry d'Arc, *Mémoires et consultations en faveur de Jeanne d'Arc*, p. 576.

1131. *Trial*, vol. iii, pp. 32, 87, 100, 116, 119, 120, 126, 128 *et passim*.

1132. Lanéry d'Arc, *Mémoires et consultations*, p. 402.

1133. *Trial*, vol. iii, p. 398.

1134. *Trial*, vol. iii, p. 355.

1135. *Ibid.*, p. 162.

1136. *Gallia Christiana*, vol. xi, col. 793.

1137. *Histoire ecclésiastique et politique de la ville et du diocèse de Toul*, 1707, p. 529.

1138. Abbé Bossard, *Gilles de Rais*, pp. 333 *et seq.*

1139. De Beaucourt, *Histoire de Charles VII*, vol. vi, p. 197.

1140. Inquiry of 1476, in G. de Braux and E. de Bouteiller, *Nouvelles recherches*, p. 10.

1141. Or Chaumussay. Lecoy de la Marche, *Une fausse Jeanne d'Arc*, Paris, 1871, in 8vo, p. 19.

1142. Lecoy de la Marche, *Une fausse Jeanne d'Arc*, in *Revue des questions historiques*, October, 1871, p. 576. *Le roi René*, Paris, 1875, vol. i, pp. 308-327; vol. ii, pp. 281-283.

1143. *Trial*, vol. iii, p. 314, note 1. *Gallia Christiana*, vol. ii, fol. 518. Du Boulay, *Hist. Univ. Paris*, vol. v, p. 905. Le P. Ayroles, *La Pucelle devant l'église de son temps*, pp. 403, 404.

1144. Lanéry d'Arc, *Mémoires et consultations*, p. 247.

1145. Du Clercq, *Mémoires*, ed. Reiffenberg, Brussels, 1823, vol. iii, pp. 98 *et seq.* Jean de Roye, *Chronique scandaleuse*, ed. Bernard de Mandrot, 1894, vol. i, pp. 13, 14. *Chronique de Bourdigné*, ed. Quatrebarbes, vol. ii, p. 212. Dom Piolin, *Histoire de l'église du Mans*, vol. v, p. 163.

1146. Chastellain, ed. Kervyn de Lettenhove, vol. iii, p. 444.

1147. Jacques du Clercq, *Mémoires*, vol. iii, pp. 107 *et seq.*

1148. Antoine du Faur, *Livre des femmes célèbres*, in *Trial*, vol. v, p. 336.

1149. De Beaucourt, *Histoire de Charles VII*, vol. vi, pp. 442, 451. *Chronique Martiniane*, ed. P. Champion, p. 110.

1150. Mathieu d'Escouchy, vol. ii, p. 422. Jean Chartier, *Chronique*, vol. iii, pp. 114-121.

1151. *Gallia Christiana*, vol. vii, col. 151 and 214. Hardouin, *Acta Conciliorum*, vol. ix, col. 1423. De Beaucourt, *Histoire de Charles VII*, vol. vi, p. 444.

1152. *Trial*, vol. iii. p. 219.

1153. *Trial*, vol. i, p. 52 and *passim*.

1154. A famous French alienist (1825-1893). – W.S.

1155. *Progrès medical*, January 19, 1878.

1156. The existence of patches devoid of feeling was considered in the Middle Ages to prove that the subject was a witch. Hence needles were run into the supposed witch. And if she felt them in every part of her body she was acquitted. – W.S.

1157. *Trial*, vol. i, p. 52.

1158. *Trial*, vol. i, p. 53.

1159. *Trial*, vol. i, p. 186.

1160. According to the evidence of Maître Pierre Maurice, at the condemnation trial (vol. i. p. 480), Jeanne must have seen the angels "in the form of certain infinitesimal things" (*sub specie quarumdam rerum minimarum*). This was also the character of the hallucinations experienced by Saint Rose of Lima ("Vie de Sainte Rose de Lima," by P. Léonard Hansen, p. 179).

1161. *Trial*, vol. i, p. 144.

1162. *Trial*, vol. i, p. 110.

1163. *Trial*, vol. i, p. 279 and *passim*.

1164. Michel de Nostre-Dame, called Nostradamus (1503-1566), a Provençal astrologer, whose prophecies were published under the title of "Centuries." He was invited to the French court by Catherine de' Medici, and became the doctor of Charles IX. – W.S.

1165. The last syllable but one of the surname of the Prophet will Diane take for her day and her rest. Far shall wander that inspired one delivering a great nation from the burden of taxes.

1166. Marc René Marquis d'Argenson (1652-1721), after being Lieutenant Général de la Police at Paris, became, from 1718-1720, Président du Conseil des Finances and Garde des Sceaux. – W.S.

1167. *Gazette d'Amsterdam*, March-May, 1697; *Annales de la cour et de Paris* (vol. ii. pp. 204, 219); *Theatrum Europæum* (vol. xv. pp. 359-360); *Mémoires de Sourches* (vol. v. pp. 260, 263); *Lettres de Madame Dunoyer* (Letter xxvi); *Saint Simon, Mémoires*, ed. Régnier (*Collection des Grands Ecrivains de la France*), vol. vi. pp. 222, 228, 231; Appendix X, p. 545; *Mémoires du duc de Luynes*, vol. x. pp. 410, 412 – Abbé Proyart, *Vie du duc de Bourgogne* (ed. 1782), vol. i. pp. 978, 981.

1168. Antoine Marie Chamans, Comte de La Valette (1769-1830), was a French general during the first empire. Having been arrested in 1815 and condemned to death, he was saved by his wife. – W.S.

1169. *Rapport adressé à S. Ex. le Ministre de la Police Générale sur l'état du nommé Martin, envoyé par son ordre à la maison royale de Charenton, le 13 Mars, 1816, par MM. Pinel, médecin en chef de l'hôpital de la Salpêtriere, et Royer-Collard, médecin en chef de la maison royale de Charenton, et l'un et l'autre professeurs à la faculté de médecine de Paris.* Inscribed at the end with the date – Paris, 6 May, 1816 – 39 pages in 4° MS. in the library of the author. Le Capitaine Paul Marin, *Thomas Martin de Gallardon Les Médecins et les thaumaturges du XIXe siècle*, Paris, s.d. in 18°. *Mémoires de la Comtesse de Boignes*, edited by Charles Nicoullaud, Paris, 1907, vol. iii. pp. 355 and *passim*.

1170. *Trial*, vol. i, pp. 100, 292.

1171. There is a wood engraving of this figure in Wallon, *Jeanne d'Arc*, p. 95.

1172. E. de Bouteiller and G. de Braux, *Notes iconographiques sur Jeanne d'Arc*, Paris and Orléans, 1879, in 18° royal paper.

1173. Reproduced in many works, notably opposite p. 17 in the book of E. de Bouteiller and G. de Braux, referred to above.

1174. *Ibid.*, see woodcut opposite p. 8.

1175. In the Orléans Museum. A copper-plate engraving by M. Georges Lavalley, in the *Jeanne d'Arc*, of M. Raoul Bergot, Tours, s.d. large 8°.

1176. Of this class of so-called portrait, I will merely mention the miniature which serves as frontispiece to vol. iv. of *La Vrai Jeanne d'Arc*, of P. Ayroles, Paris, 1898, in large 8°, and the miniature of the Spetz Collection, reproduced in the *Jeanne d'Arc* of Canon Henri Debout, vol. ii. p. 103 (also in *The Maid of France* by Andrew Lang, 1908. W.S.).

1177. *Le champion des dames*, MS. of the fifteenth century; *Bibl. nat.*, fonds français, No. 841; Martial d'Auvergne, MS. of the end of the fifteenth century, fonds français, No. 5054. An initial of a fifteenth-century Latin MS., *Bibl. nat.*, No. 14665.

1178. *Trial*, vol. i, p. 100. N. Valois, *Un nouveau témoignage sur Jeanne d'Arc*, pp. 8, 13.

1179. Reproduced in chromo in Wallon's *Jeanne d'Arc*.

1180. The form *Darc* occurs in the condemnation trial (*Trial*, vol. i, p. 191, vol. ii, p. 82). But side by side we find also *Dars* (document dated March 31, 1427), *Day* (patent of nobility), *Daiz* (communicated to me by M. Pierre Champion) and *Daix* (*Chronique de la Pucelle*).

1181. Tapestry representing small animals. – W.S.

1182. Reproduced in chromo in Wallon's *Jeanne d'Arc*, cf. J. Quicherat, *Histoire du costume en France depuis les temps les plus reculés, jusqu' la fin du XVIIIe siècle*, Paris, 1875, large octavo, p. 271.

1183. *Trial*, vol. v, p. 270.

Also from Benediction Books ...
Wandering Between Two Worlds: Essays on Faith and Art
Anita Mathias
Benediction Books, 2007
152 pages
ISBN: 0955373700

Available from www.amazon.com, www.amazon.co.uk

In these wide-ranging lyrical essays, Anita Mathias writes, in lush, lovely prose, of her naughty Catholic childhood in Jamshedpur, India; her large, eccentric family in Mangalore, a seacoast town converted by the Portuguese in the sixteenth century; her rebellion and atheism as a teenager in her Himalayan boarding school, run by German missionary nuns, St. Mary's Convent, Nainital; and her abrupt religious conversion after which she entered Mother Teresa's convent in Calcutta as a novice. Later rich, elegant essays explore the dualities of her life as a writer, mother, and Christian in the United States-- Domesticity and Art, Writing and Prayer, and the experience of being "an alien and stranger" as an immigrant in America, sensing the need for roots.

About the Author

Anita Mathias is the author of *Wandering Between Two Worlds: Essays on Faith and Art.* She has a B.A. and M.A. in English from Somerville College, Oxford University, and an M.A. in Creative Writing from the Ohio State University, USA. Anita won a National Endowment of the Arts fellowship in Creative Nonfiction in 1997. She lives in Oxford, England with her husband, Roy, and her daughters, Zoe and Irene.

Visit Anita's website
    http://www.anitamathias.com,
and Anita's blog
    http://dreamingbeneaththespires.blogspot.com.

The Church That Had Too Much
Anita Mathias
Benediction Books, 2010
52 pages
ISBN: 9781849026567

Available from www.amazon.com, www.amazon.co.uk

The Church That Had Too Much was very well-intentioned. She wanted to love God, she wanted to love people, but she was both hampered by her muchness and the abundance of her possessions, and beset by ambition, power struggles and snobbery. Read about the surprising way The Church That Had Too Much began to resolve her problems in this deceptively simple and enchanting fable.

About the Author

Anita Mathias is the author of *Wandering Between Two Worlds: Essays on Faith and Art*. She has a B.A. and M.A. in English from Somerville College, Oxford University, and an M.A. in Creative Writing from the Ohio State University, USA. Anita won a National Endowment of the Arts fellowship in Creative Nonfiction in 1997. She lives in Oxford, England with her husband, Roy, and her daughters, Zoe and Irene.

Visit Anita's website
    http://www.anitamathias.com,
and Anita's blog
    http://dreamingbeneaththespires.blogspot..